RETHINKING SOCIETY IN THE 21ST CENTURY

RETHINKING SOCIETY IN THE 21ST CENTURY

CRITICAL READINGS IN SOCIOLOGY

Fourth Edition

EDITED BY
MICHELLE WEBBER AND KATE BEZANSON

Canadian Scholars' Press Inc.
Toronto

Rethinking Society in the 21st Century: Critical Readings in Sociology, Fourth Edition
Edited by Michelle Webber and Kate Bezanson

First published in 2016 by
Canadian Scholars' Press Inc.
425 Adelaide Street West, Suite 200
Toronto, Ontario
M5V 3C1
www.cspi.org

Library and Archives Canada Cataloguing in Publication

Rethinking society in the 21st century : critical readings in sociology / edited by Michelle Webber and Kate Bezanson. -- Fourth edition.

Includes bibliographical references.
Issued in print and electronic formats.
ISBN 978-1-55130-936-1 (paperback).--ISBN 978-1-55130-937-8 (pdf).--ISBN 978-1-55130-938-5 (epub)

1. Sociology--Textbooks. 2. Canada--Social conditions--1991- --Textbooks. I. Webber, Michelle, editor II. Bezanson, Kate, editor

HM586.R48 2016 301 C2016-903779-7 C2016-903780-0

Text and cover design by Jennifer Stimson Design
Cover image by Lauren Corman

Printed and bound in Canada by Webcom.

MIX
Paper from responsible sources
FSC® C004071

CONTENTS

SECTION 5: SOCIAL MOVEMENTS, SOCIAL CHANGE, AND EMERGING FIELDS 505

PREFACE

Originally faced with the double cohort, as instructors in introduction to sociology, we struggled to pull together readings for the first edition that were at once accessible, critical, and engaging. We decided to prepare a reader that we would want to use in our classes. We sought to weave feminist, class-conscious, and anti-racist approaches to the study of sociology. This reader reflects our various interests and strengths, but also aims to broaden the traditional theoretical and political approaches found in many sociology readers. It incorporates considerable Canadian material, drawing on the contributions of scholars from a range of disciplines. The reader balances classical theoretical approaches to sociology with contemporary approaches to theory and social issues.

We are pleased to present this fourth edition of *Rethinking Society in the 21st Century.* We have responded to our reviewers' helpful comments and included emerging topics and more Canadian content. We hope that the readings in this book provoke substantive debate and discussion.

Acknowledgements

We would like to thank Sarah Bezanson, who assisted us in putting this edition together. Thanks to Canadian Scholars' Press Inc. for their continued support of our project.

SECTION 1
INTRODUCTION TO SOCIOLOGY

The Readings

The opening sections of this book introduce students to key classical pieces in the discipline of sociology, namely C. Wright Mills, Anthony Giddens, Emile Durkheim, Karl Marx, Friedrich Engels, and Max Weber. All of these pieces appear in their original form; the editors of this anthology have not changed the author's language so as to preserve the historical authenticity of these pieces. Students should note that these classics (and some of the other older selections) utilize male pronouns instead of non-sexist alternatives. We encourage faculty and students, while reading and discussing these classic pieces, to consider the importance of shifts in language over time.

Introduction: The Sociological Perspective

The first piece is C. Wright Mills's "The Promise." Mills was writing in postwar North American society (1950s and 1960s). Mills was critical of the tendencies of sociologists, especially those working in the functionalist tradition, to develop concepts devoid of political meaning. He was critical of broad and abstract concepts (such as "functional imperatives") that were completely removed from public and political concerns, historical change, and people's lives. This selection is from Mills's book, *The Sociological Imagination*. Here Mills captures the meaning of the sociological perspective with his term the "sociological imagination" as a way of thinking that enables people to understand how problems they experience in their own lives can be linked to public issues. These public issues are the result of broad historical and social forces. If one can understand these broad forces, then, Mills argues, one can act to alter these forces.

Next is Anthony Giddens with an excerpt from "In Defence of Sociology." In this selection Giddens carries on some of the same themes that Mills raises about sociology—how it has the ability to unnerve people as it can challenge common assumptions we have about ourselves and our social worlds.

Classical Theory

In our classical theory section we begin with Emile Durkheim's "What Is a Social Fact?" Durkheim is considered the founder of modern sociology and an influential thinker in the functionalist paradigm in sociology. Durkheim argues that sociology is a science of society. In order to explain human actions we must look at the level of society, not at the level of individuals' behaviours and motivations. He describes a "category of facts" that exerts control over individuals in aspects such as ways of acting, being, and thinking. These facts are seen as external to individuals, yet affect people's behaviours. Durkheim understands these facts as being distinct from biological and psychological phenomena.

The second selection is from Karl Marx and Friedrich Engels's classic piece, the *Communist Manifesto*. Their writing on capitalism as a global economic, social, and cultural system, although written in the mid-1800s, remains incisive. Their piece asserts that all societies in history are divided on a class basis and that all human relationships are understood as being organized along capitalist lines, including the structure of families. Countries enter markets to become successful capitalist societies. If this success is not realized, these countries risk humiliation and colonization. Marx and Engels assert that the working class—those whose labour creates the wealth of capitalism—will organize to draw an end to their exploitation and an end to the domination of the bourgeoisie, those who own the means of production. The ideas of Marx and Engels have been central in the development of the social-conflict paradigm in sociology.

Our last classical piece is a selection from "The Spirit of Capitalism" by Max Weber. In this selection Weber discusses capitalism's development as an economic system built upon particular religious ideas—for example, he writes, "Waste of time is thus the first and in principle the deadliest of sins." However, modern capitalism no longer requires a connection to religious principles to survive and flourish.

Contemporary Theory

Our first contemporary theory piece is a pioneering feminist consideration of epistemology (theory of knowledge). Dorothy Smith exposes gender-biased assumptions within sociology itself. Smith argues that women have been excluded from the production of sociological knowledge. Even though there are attempts to present knowledge as universal and objective, knowledge cannot be separated from the context in which that knowledge is generated. Members of dominant groups have the power to describe and define the world around them. Smith argues that members of dominant groups have historically been unable to see how their view of the world has depended on the often invisible yet essential work of women and members of the working class. Smith explores how sociology might be transformed by women's perspectives.

The next contemporary theory piece represents poststructuralism and is from a French scholar who transformed modern social theory, Michel Foucault. In this excerpt from *Power/Knowledge*, Foucault outlines his concepts of genealogy and disciplinary power. Foucault explains how this modern mechanism of power is different from sovereign forms of power.

Antonio Gramsci, a neo-Marxist scholar, forms the content for the next contemporary theoretical piece. His work is explored here by Diana Coben. Following a brief biography, Coben outlines one of Gramsci's main contributions to theoretical debate, his concept of hegemony. Unlike traditional Marxists, Gramsci argues that the state cannot rule by coercion alone, but there must be some form of consent to domination by the oppressed class. Hegemony accounts for the subtle, negotiated consent that the dominant class is able to secure over the oppressed class. It is important to understand that this hegemony is never fully reached; it is constantly in motion, always in negotiation.

Our last piece for the theory section is by Michael Omi and Howard Winant. The excerpt is from their book *Racial Formation in the United States.* Omi and Winant argue against understanding race as biological or as simply a subjective classification. Rather, Omi and Winant outline the importance of understanding race as a social process that changes over time and by context.

Research Methods

We include two pieces in our Research Methods section. First is Alan Bryman, James Teevan, and Edward Bell's general introductory chapter on social research. They explore the relationship between theory and research, epistemological considerations (asking the question: How can we know what we know?), ontological considerations, and the influences on how we carry out social research.

Karen Potts and Leslie Brown introduce us to anti-oppressive research. They discuss what it means to engage in anti-oppressive research and how this political engagement permeates all aspects of the research process. They recognize that all knowledge is socially constructed and is implicated in relations of power, and discuss ways to highlight these relations and still work productively for change.

SECTION 1A

INTRODUCTION:

THE SOCIOLOGICAL PERSPECTIVE

CHAPTER 1

The Promise

C. Wright Mills

Nowadays men often feel that their private lives are a series of traps. They sense that within their everyday worlds, they cannot overcome their troubles, and in this feeling, they are often quite correct: What ordinary men are directly aware of and what they try to do are bounded by the private orbits in which they live; their visions and their powers are limited to the close-up scenes of job, family, neighborhood; in other milieux, they move vicariously and remain spectators. And the more aware they become, however vaguely, of ambitions and of threats which transcend their immediate locales, the more trapped they seem to feel.

Underlying this sense of being trapped are seemingly impersonal changes in the very structure of continent-wide societies. The facts of contemporary history are also facts about the success and the failure of individual men and women. When a society is industrialized, a peasant becomes a worker; a feudal lord is liquidated or becomes a businessman. When classes rise or fall, a man is employed or unemployed; when the rate of investment goes up or down, a man takes new heart or goes broke. When wars happen, an insurance salesman becomes a rocket launcher; a store clerk, a radar man; a wife lives alone; a child grows up without a father. Neither the life of an individual nor the history of a society can be understood without understanding both.

Yet men do not usually define the troubles they endure in terms of historical change and institutional contradiction. The well-being they enjoy, they do not usually impute to the big ups and downs of the societies in which they live. Seldom aware of the intricate connection between the patterns of their own lives and the course of world history, ordinary men do not usually know what this connection means for the kinds of men they are becoming and for the kinds of history-making in which they might take part. They do not possess the quality of mind essential to grasp the interplay of man and society, of biography and history, of self and world. They cannot cope with their personal troubles in such ways as to control the structural transformations that usually lie behind them.

Surely it is no wonder. In what period have so many men been so totally exposed at so fast a pace to such earthquakes of change? That Americans have not known such catastrophic changes as have the men and women of other societies is due to historical facts that are now quickly becoming "merely history." The history that now affects every man is world history. Within this scene and this period, in the course of a single generation, one sixth of mankind is transformed from all that is feudal and backward into all that is modern, advanced, and fearful. Political colonies are freed; new and less visible forms of imperialism installed. Revolutions occur; men feel the intimate grip of new kinds of authority. Totalitarian societies rise, and are smashed to bits—or succeed fabulously. After two centuries of ascendancy, capitalism is shown up as only one way to make society into an industrial apparatus. After two centuries of hope, even formal democracy is restricted to a quite small portion of mankind. Everywhere in the underdeveloped world, ancient ways of life are broken up and vague expectations become urgent demands. Everywhere in the overdeveloped world, the means of authority and of violence become total in scope and bureaucratic in form. Humanity itself now lies before us, the super-nation at either pole concentrating its most co-ordinated and massive efforts upon the preparation of World War Three.

The very shaping of history now outpaces the ability of men to orient themselves in accordance with cherished values. And which values? Even when they do not panic, men often sense that older ways of feeling and thinking have collapsed and that newer beginnings are ambiguous to the point of moral stasis. Is it any wonder that ordinary men feel they cannot cope with the larger worlds with which they are so suddenly confronted? That they cannot understand the meaning of their epoch for their own lives? That—in defense of selfhood—they become morally insensible, trying to remain altogether private men? Is it any wonder that they come to be possessed by a sense of the trap?

It is not only information that they need—in this Age of Fact, information often dominates their attention and overwhelms their capacities to assimilate it. It is not only the skills of reason that they need—although their struggles to acquire these often exhaust their limited moral energy.

What they need, and what they feel they need, is a quality of mind that will help them to use information and to develop reason in order to achieve lucid summations of what is going on in the world and of what may be happening within themselves. It is this quality, I am going to contend, that journalists and scholars, artists and publics, scientists and editors are coming to expect of what may be called the sociological imagination.

The sociological imagination enables its possessor to understand the larger historical scene in terms of its meaning for the inner life and the external career of a variety of individuals.

It enables him to take into account how individuals, in the welter of their daily experience, often become falsely conscious of their social positions. Within that welter, the framework of modern society is sought, and within that framework the psychologies of a variety of men and women are formulated. By such means the personal uneasiness of individuals is focused upon explicit troubles and the indifference of publics is transformed into involvement with public issues.

The first fruit of this imagination—and the first lesson of the social science that embodies it—is the idea that the individual can understand his own experience and gauge his own fate only by locating himself within his period, that he can know his own chances in life only by becoming aware of those of all individuals in his circumstances. In many ways it is a terrible lesson; in many ways a magnificent one. We do not know the limits of man's capacities for supreme effort or willing degradation, for agony or glee, for pleasurable brutality or the sweetness of reason. But in our time we have come to know that the limits of "human nature" are frighteningly broad. We have come to know that every individual lives, from one generation to the next, in some society; that he lives out a biography, and that he lives it out within some historical sequence. By the fact of his living he contributes, however minutely, to the shaping of this society and to the course of its history, even as he is made by society and by its historical push and shove.

The sociological imagination enables us to grasp history and biography and the relations between the two within society. That is its task and its promise. To recognize this task and this promise is the mark of the classic social analyst. It is characteristic of Herbert Spencer—turgid, polysyllabic, comprehensive; of E.A. Ross—graceful, muckraking, upright; of Auguste Comte and Emile Durkheim; of the intricate and subtle Karl Mannheim. It is the quality of all that is intellectually excellent in Karl Marx; it is the clue to Thorstein Veblen's brilliant and ironic insight, to Joseph Schumpeter's many-sided constructions of reality; it is the basis of the psychological sweep of W.E.H. Lecky no less than of the profundity and clarity of Max Weber. And it is the signal of what is best in contemporary studies of man and society.

No social study that does not come back to the problems of biography, of history and of their intersections within a society has completed its intellectual journey. Whatever the specific problems of the classic social analysts, however limited or however broad the features of social reality they have examined, those who have been imaginatively aware of the promise of their work have consistently asked three sorts of questions:

1. What is the structure of this particular society as a whole? What are its essential components, and how are they related to one another? How does it differ from other varieties of social order? Within it, what is the meaning of any particular feature for its continuance and for its change?
2. Where does this society stand in human history? What are the mechanics by which it is changing? What is its place within and its meaning for the development of humanity as a whole? How does any particular feature we are examining affect, and how is it affected by, the historical period in which it moves? And this period—what are its essential features?

How does it differ from other periods? What are its characteristic ways of history-making?

3. What varieties of men and women now prevail in this society and in this period? And what varieties are coming to prevail? In what ways are they selected and formed, liberated and repressed, made sensitive and blunted? What kinds of "human nature" are revealed in the conduct and character we observe in this society in this period? And what is the meaning for "human nature" of each and every feature of the society we are examining?

Whether the point of interest is a great power state or a minor literary mood, a family, a prison, a creed—these are the kinds of questions the best social analysts have asked. They are the intellectual pivots of classic studies of man in society—and they are the questions inevitably raised by any mind possessing the sociological imagination. For that imagination is the capacity to shift from one perspective to another—from the political to the psychological; from examination of a single family to comparative assessment of the national budgets of the world, from the theological school to the military establishment; from considerations of an oil industry to studies of contemporary poetry. It is the capacity to range from the most impersonal and remote transformations to the most intimate features of the human self—and to see the relations between the two. Back of its use there is always the urge to know the social and historical meaning of the individual in the society and in the period in which he has his quality and his being.

That, in brief, is why it is by means of the sociological imagination that men now hope to grasp what is going on in the world, and to understand what is happening in themselves as minute points of the intersections of biography and history within society. In large part, contemporary man's self-conscious view of himself as at least an outsider, if not a permanent stranger, rests upon an absorbed realization of social relativity and of the transformative power of history. The sociological imagination is the most fruitful form of this self-consciousness. By its use men whose mentalities have swept only a series of limited orbits often come to feel as if suddenly awakened in a house with which they had only supposed themselves to be familiar. Correctly or incorrectly, they often come to feel that they can now provide themselves with adequate summations, cohesive assessments, comprehensive orientations. Older decisions that once appeared sound now seem to them products of a mind unaccountably dense. Their capacity for astonishment is made lively again. They acquire a new way of thinking, they experience a transvaluation of values: in a word, by their reflection and by their sensibility, they realize the cultural meaning of the social sciences.

Perhaps the most fruitful distinction with which the sociological imagination works is between "the personal troubles of milieu" and "the public issues of social structure." This distinction is an essential tool of the sociological imagination and a feature of all classic work in social science.

Troubles occur within the character of the individual and within the range of his immediate relations with others; they have to do with his self and with those limited areas of social life of which he is directly and personally aware. Accordingly, the statement and the resolution of troubles properly lie within the individual as a biographical entity and within the scope of his immediate milieu—the social setting that is directly open to his personal experience and to some extent his willful activity. A trouble is a private matter: values cherished by an individual are felt by him to be threatened.

Issues have to do with matters that transcend these local environments of the individual and the range of his inner life. They have to do with the organization of many such milieux into the institutions of an historical society as a whole, with the ways in which various milieux overlap and interpenetrate to form the larger structure of social and historical life. An issue is a public matter: some value cherished by publics is felt to be threatened. Often there is a debate about what that value really is and about what it is that really threatens it. This debate is often without focus if only because it is the very nature of an issue, unlike even widespread trouble, that it cannot very well be defined in terms of the immediate and everyday environments of ordinary men. An issue, in fact, often involves a crisis in institutional arrangements, and often too it involves what Marxists call "contradictions" or "antagonisms."

In these terms, consider unemployment. When, in a city of 100,000, only one man is unemployed, that is his personal trouble, and for its relief we properly look to the character of the man, his skills, and his immediate opportunities. But when in a nation of 50 million employees, 15 million men are unemployed, that is an issue, and we may not hope to find its solution within the range of opportunities open to any one individual. The very structure of opportunities has collapsed. Both the correct statement of the problem and the range of possible solutions require us to consider the economic and political institutions of the society, and not merely the personal situation and character of a scatter of individuals.

Consider war. The personal problem of war, when it occurs, may be how to survive it or how to die in it with honor; how to make money out of it; how to climb into the higher safety of the military apparatus; or how to contribute to the war's termination. In short, according to one's values, to find a set of milieux and within it to survive the war or make one's death in it meaningful. But the structural issues of war have to do with its causes; with what types of men it throws up into command; with its effects upon economic and political, family and religious institutions, with the unorganized irresponsibility of a world of nation-states.

Consider marriage. Inside a marriage a man and a woman may experience personal troubles, but when the divorce rate during the first four years of marriage is 250 out of every 1,000 attempts, this is an indication of a structural issue having to do with the institutions of marriage and the family and other institutions that bear upon them.

Or consider the metropolis—the horrible, beautiful, ugly, magnificent sprawl of the great city. For many upper-class people, the personal solution to "the problem of the city" is to have an apartment with private garage under it in the heart of the city, and forty miles out, a house by Henry Hill, garden by Garrett Eckbo, on a hundred acres of private land. In these two controlled environments—with a small staff at each end and a private helicopter connection—most people could solve many of the problems of personal milieux caused by the facts of the city. But all this, however splendid, does not solve the public issues that the structural fact of the city poses. What should be done with this wonderful monstrosity? Break it all up into scattered units, combining residence and work? Refurbish it as it stands? Or, after evacuation, dynamite it and build new cities according to new plans in new places? What should those plans be? And who is to decide and to accomplish whatever choice is made? These are structural issues; to confront them and to solve them requires us to consider political and economic issues that affect innumerable milieux.

In so far as an economy is so arranged that slumps occur, the problem of unemployment becomes incapable of personal solution. In so far as war is inherent in the nation-state system and in the uneven industrialization of the world, the ordinary individual in his restricted milieu will be powerless—with or without psychiatric aid—to solve the troubles this system or lack of system imposes upon him. In so far as the family as an institution turns women into darling little slaves and men into their chief providers and unweaned dependents, the problem of a satisfactory marriage remains incapable of purely private solution. In so far as the overdeveloped megalopolis and the overdeveloped automobile are built-in features of the overdeveloped society, the issues of urban living will not be solved by personal ingenuity and private wealth.

What we experience in various and specific milieux, I have noted, is often caused by structural changes. Accordingly, to understand the changes of many personal milieux we are required to look beyond them. And the number and variety of such structural changes increase as the institutions within which we live become more embracing and more intricately connected with one another. To be aware of the idea of social structure and to use it with sensibility is to be capable of tracing such linkages among a great variety of milieux. To be able to do that is to possess the sociological imagination.

CHAPTER 2

In Defence of Sociology

Anthony Giddens

There's something about sociology that raises hackles other academic subjects fail to reach. Economics may be the dismal science, full of obscure terms few can understand and seemingly irrelevant to the practical tasks of day-to-day life. Yet sociology is often indicted on all counts—diffuse and lacking a coherent subject-matter, as well as being jargon-ridden. What do you get when you cross a sociologist with a member of the Mafia? An offer you can't understand.

What is it with sociology? Why is it so irritating to so many? Some sociologists might answer: ignorance; others: fear. Why fear? Well, because they like to think of their subject as a dangerous and discomfiting one. Sociology, they are prone to say, tends to subvert: it challenges our assumptions about ourselves as individuals and about the wider social contexts in which we live. It has a direct connection with political radicalism. In the 1960s, the discipline seemed to many to live up to this firebrand reputation.

In truth, however, even in the 1960s and early 1970s sociology wasn't intrinsically associated with the left, let alone with revolutionaries. It came in for a great deal of criticism from Marxists of various persuasions who, far from regarding the subject as subversive, saw it as the very epitome of the bourgeois order they found so distasteful.

In some aspects and situations of its development sociology has in fact a long history of being bound up with the political right. Max Weber, commonly regarded as one of its classical founders, inclined more to the right than to the left and was savagely critical of the self-proclaimed revolutionaries of his time. Vilfredo Pareto and Robert Michels both flirted with Italian fascism towards the end of their lives. Most sociologists have probably been liberals by temperament and political inclination: this was true of Emile Durkheim and in later generations of R.K. Merton, Talcott Parsons, Erving Goffman, and Ralf Dahrendorf, among many other prominent sociological thinkers.

Sociology has currently been going through a hard time in the very country where it has long been most well developed, the US. A prominent American sociologist, Irving Louis Horowitz, [...] published a book entitled *The Decomposition of Sociology*, a work which he reports was "more a matter of pain rather than pride to have felt the need to write." The discipline, he argues, has gone sour. [...]

Undergraduate student numbers in sociology in the US have fallen substantially over the [...] decades since the 1970s. [...] According to Horowitz, however, the travails of sociology aren't just expressed in declining student appeal. [...] There has been an outflow of respectable, empirically-oriented social scientists into other, more narrowly defined areas—such as urban planning, demography, criminology, or jurisprudence. The deterioration of sociology doesn't imply the disintegration of social research, which is still flourishing in many domains; but much of such research has degenerated into pure empiricism, no longer guided by worthwhile theoretical perspectives. What has disappeared is the capacity of sociology to provide a unifying centre for the diverse branches of social research.

Is sociology in the doldrums? And, if so, is this in some sense a peculiarly American phenomenon or something that applies worldwide? Or was sociology perhaps always the rag-tail affair its critics have long proclaimed it to be?

Let's deal first of all with the old chestnut that sociology doesn't have a proper field of investigation. The truth of the matter is that the field of study of sociology, as understood by the bulk of its practitioners, is no more, but no less, clearly defined than that of any other academic area. Consider, for example, history. That discipline has an obvious subject-matter, it would seem—the past. But the past embraces everything! No clear or bounded field of study here, and history is every bit as riven by methodological disputes about its true nature as sociology has ever been.

Sociology is a generalizing discipline that concerns itself above all with modernity—with the character and dynamics of modern or industrialized societies. It shares many of its methodological strategies—and problems—not only with history but with the whole gamut of the social sciences. The more empirical issues it deals with are very real. Of all the social sciences, sociology bears most directly on the issues that concern us in our everyday lives—the development of modern urbanism, crime and punishment, gender, the family, religion, social and economic power.

Given that sociological research and thinking are more or less indispensable in contemporary society, it is difficult to make sense of the criticism that it is unenlightening—that it is common sense wrapped up in somewhat unattractive jargon. Although specific pieces of research could always be questioned, no one could argue that there is no point in carrying out, say, comparative studies of the incidence of divorce in different countries. Sociologists engage in all sorts of research which, once one has some awareness of them, would prove interesting, and be thought important, by most reasonably neutral observers.

There is, however, another, more subtle reason why sociology may appear quite often to proclaim what is obvious to common sense. This is that social research doesn't, and can't, remain separate from the social world it describes. Social research forms so much a part of our consciousness today that we take it for granted. All of us depend upon such research for what we regard *as* common sense—as "what everyone knows." Everyone knows, for example, that divorce rates are high in today's society; yet such "obvious knowledge," of course, depends upon regular social research, whether it happens to be carried out by government researchers or academic sociologists.

It is therefore to some degree the fate of sociology to be taken as less original and less central to our social existence than actually it is. Not only empirical research but sociological theorizing and sociological concepts can become so much part of our everyday repertoire as to appear as "just common sense." Many people, for instance, now ask whether a leader has charisma, discuss moral panics, or talk of someone's social status—all notions that originated in sociological discourse.

These considerations, obviously, don't help with the issue of whether sociology as an academic discipline is in a state of sorry decline or even dissolution since its heyday in the 1960s, if that period was indeed its apogee. Things *have* changed in sociology, [...] but not all for the worse. For one thing, the centre of power has shifted. American sociology used to dominate world sociology, but it does so no longer. Especially so far as sociological theorizing is concerned, the centre of gravity has shifted elsewhere, particularly to Europe. The major sociological thinkers now are over here rather than over there, authors like Pierre Bourdieu, Niklas Luhmann, or Ulrich Beck.

There's a good deal of justification for [the] advice to sociologists to engage in research immediately relevant to public policy issues and to participate forcefully in the wide debates their work may arouse. After all, many questions raised in the political arena are sociological—questions to do, for instance, with welfare, crime, or the family. Sociological work is relevant, not just to their formulation as particular types of policy question, but to grasping the likely consequences of whatever policies might be initiated in relation to them.

If one compares sociology to economics, it has to be conceded that sociology is much more internally diverse. In economics there exists a variety of different schools of thought and theoretical approaches, but the neo-classical view tends to dominate almost everywhere and forms the basic stuff of virtually all introductory texts. Sociology isn't to the same degree in the thrall of a single conceptual system. However, this surely should be seen more as a strength than a weakness. I don't believe such diversity has produced complete disarray, but instead gives voice to the pluralism that must exist when one studies something as complex and controversial as human social behaviour and institutions.

Is there any evidence that talented scholars who might once have been attracted to working in sociology have now migrated elsewhere? There's no doubt that in the 1960s some were drawn into sociology because they saw it, if not offering a route to revolution, as trendy and new; and it doesn't have that reputation any longer. But most such individuals probably weren't interested in a career within the confines of the academy. More relevant are factors that have affected the academic world as a whole, not sociology in particular. Many talented people who might once have gone into academic life probably won't do so today, because academic salaries have fallen sharply in relative terms over the last two decades and working conditions have deteriorated.

Yet a good case could actually be made for saying that British sociology is doing better than in previous generations. Compare, for instance, the fortunes of sociology in Britain over recent years with those of anthropology. In the early postwar period, this country boasted anthropologists of worldwide reputation; no crop of comparably distinguished sociological authors was to be found at that time.

Now things are more or less reversed. There are few, if any, anthropologists of the current generation who can match the achievements of the preceding one. British sociology, however, can offer a clutch of individuals with a worldwide reputation, such as John Goldthorpe, Steven Lukes, Stuart Hall, Michèle Barrett, Ray Pahl, Janet Wolff, and Michael Mann.

Moreover, in sheer statistical terms, sociology is not in decline in [the UK] in the way it has been in the US. A-level sociology is extremely popular and flourishing rather than shrinking. University admissions in sociology are, at worst, stable in relation to other subjects.

Everything in the sociological garden isn't rosy—although was it ever? Funding for social research has dropped off sharply since the early 1970s; there isn't the scale of empirical work there once was. But it would be difficult to argue that sociology is off the pace intellectually, especially if one broadens the angle again and moves back to a more international perspective. Most of the debates that grab the intellectual headlines today, across the social sciences, and even the humanities, carry a strong sociological input. Sociological authors have pioneered discussions of postmodernism, the post-industrial or information society, globalization, the transformation of everyday life, gender and sexuality, the changing nature of work and the family, the "underclass," and ethnicity.

You might still ask: what do all these changes add up to? Here there is a lot of sociological work to be done. Some of that work has to be investigatory or empirical, but some must be theoretical. More than any other intellectual endeavour, sociological reflection is central to grasping the social forces remaking our lives today. Social life has become episodic, fragmentary, and dogged with new uncertainties, which it must be the business of creative sociological thought to help us understand. [...] Sociologists should focus their attention on the practical and policy-making implications of the changes currently transforming social life. Yet sociology would indeed become dreary, and quite possibly disaggregated, if it didn't also concern itself with the big issues.

Sociology should rehone its cutting edge, as neo-liberalism disappears into the distance along with orthodox socialism. Some questions to which we need new answers have a perennial quality, while others are dramatically new. Tackling both of these, as in previous times, calls for a healthy dose of what C. Wright Mills famously called the sociological imagination. Sociologists, don't despair! You still have a world to win, or at least interpret.

SECTION 1B

CLASSICAL THEORY

CHAPTER 3

What Is a Social Fact?

Emile Durkheim

Before beginning the search for the method appropriate to the study of social facts it is important to know what are the facts termed "social."

The question is all the more necessary because the term is used without much precision. It is commonly used to designate almost all the phenomena that occur within society, however little social interest of some generality they present. Yet under this heading there is, so to speak, no human occurrence that cannot be called social. Every individual drinks, sleeps, eats, or employs his reason, and society has every interest in seeing that these functions are regularly exercised. If therefore these facts were social ones, sociology would possess no subject matter peculiarly its own, and its domain would be confused with that of biology and psychology.

However, in reality there is in every society a clearly determined group of phenomena separable, because of their distinct characteristics, from those that form the subject matter of other sciences of nature.

When I perform my duties as a brother, a husband or a citizen and carry out the commitments I have entered into, I fulfil obligations which are defined in law and custom and which are external to myself and my actions. Even when they conform to my own sentiments and when I feel their reality within me, that reality does not cease to be objective, for it is not I who have prescribed these duties; I have received them through education. Moreover, how often does it happen that we are ignorant of the details of the obligations that we must assume, and that, to know them, we must consult the legal code and its authorised interpreters! Similarly the believer has discovered from birth, ready fashioned, the beliefs and practices of his religious life; if they existed before he did, it follows that they exist outside him. The system of signs that I employ to express my thoughts, the monetary system I use to pay my debts, the credit instruments I utilise in my commercial relationships, the practices I follow in my profession, etc., all function independently of the use I make of them. Considering in turn each member of society, the foregoing remarks can be repeated for each single one of them. Thus there are ways of acting, thinking and feeling which possess the remarkable property of existing outside the consciousness of the individual.

Not only are these types of behaviour and thinking external to the individual, but they are endued with a compelling and coercive power by virtue of which, whether he wishes it or not, they impose themselves upon him. Undoubtedly when I conform to them of my own free will, this coercion is not felt or felt hardly at all, since it is unnecessary. None the less it is intrinsically a characteristic of these facts; the proof of this is that it asserts itself as soon as I try to resist. If I attempt to violate the rules of law they react against me so as to forestall my action, if there is still time. Alternatively, they annul it or make my action conform to the norm if it is already accomplished but capable of being reversed; or they cause me to pay the penalty for it if it is irreparable. If purely moral rules are at stake, the public conscience restricts any act which infringes them by the surveillance it exercises over the conduct of citizens and by the special punishments it has at its disposal. In other cases the constraint is less violent; nevertheless, it does not cease to exist. If I do not conform to ordinary conventions, if in my mode of dress I pay no heed to what is customary in my country and in my social class, the laughter I provoke, the social distance at which I am kept, produce, although in a more mitigated form, the same results as any real penalty. In other cases, although it may be indirect, constraint is no less effective. I am not forced to speak French with my compatriots, nor to use the legal currency, but it is impossible for me to do otherwise. If I tried to escape the necessity, my attempt would fail miserably. As an industrialist nothing prevents me from working with the processes and methods of the previous century, but if I do I will most certainly ruin myself. Even when in fact I can struggle free from these rules and successfully break them, it is never without being forced to fight against them. Even if in the end they are overcome, they make their constraining power sufficiently felt in the resistance that they afford. There is no innovator, even a fortunate one, whose ventures do not encounter opposition of this kind.

Here, then, is a category of facts which present very special characteristics: they consist of manners of acting, thinking and feeling external to the individual, which are invested with a coercive power by virtue of which they exercise control over him. Consequently, since they consist of representations and actions, they cannot be confused with organic phenomena, nor with psychical phenomena, which have no existence save in and through the individual consciousness. Thus they constitute a new species and to them must be exclusively assigned the term social. It is appropriate, since it is clear that, not having the individual as their substratum, they can have none other than society, either political society in its entirety or one of the partial groups that it includes - religious denominations, political and literary schools, occupational corporations, etc. Moreover, it is for such as these alone that the term is fitting, for the word 'social' has the sole meaning of designating those phenomena which fall into none of the categories of facts already constituted and labelled. They are consequently the proper field of sociology. It is true that this word 'constraint', in terms of which we define them, is in danger of infuriating those who zealously uphold out-and-out individualism. Since they maintain that the individual is completely autonomous, it seems to them that he is diminished every time he is made aware that he is not dependent on himself alone. Yet since it is indisputable today that most of our ideas and tendencies are not developed by ourselves, but come to us from outside, they can only penetrate us by imposing themselves upon us. This is all that our definition implies. Moreover, we know that all social constraints do not necessarily exclude the individual personality.[1]

Yet since the examples just cited (legal and moral rules, religious dogmas, financial systems, etc.) consist wholly of beliefs and practices already well established, in view of what has been said it might be maintained that no social fact can exist except where there is a well defined social organisation. But there are other facts which do not present themselves in this already crystallised form but which also possess the same objectivity and ascendancy over the individual. These are what are called social 'currents'. Thus in a public gathering the great waves of enthusiasm, indignation and pity that are produced have their seat in no one individual consciousness. They come to each one of us from outside and can sweep us along in spite of ourselves. If perhaps I abandon myself to them I may not be conscious of the pressure that they are exerting upon me, but that pressure makes its presence felt immediately I attempt to struggle against them. If an individual tries to pit himself against one of these collective manifestations, the sentiments that he is rejecting will be turned against him. Now if this external coercive power asserts itself so acutely in cases of resistance, it must be because it exists in the other instances cited above without our being conscious of it. Hence we are the victims of an illusion which leads us to believe we have ourselves produced what has been imposed upon us externally. But if the willingness with which we let ourselves be carried along disguises the pressure we have undergone, it does not eradicate it. Thus air does not cease to have weight, although we no longer feel that weight. Even when we have individually and spontaneously shared in the common emotion, the impression we have experienced is utterly different from what we would have felt if we had been alone. Once the assembly has broken up and these social influences have ceased to act upon us, and we are once more on our own, the emotions we have felt seem an alien phenomenon, one in which we no longer recognise ourselves. It is then we perceive that we have undergone the emotions much more than generated them. These emotions may even perhaps fill us with horror, so much do they go against the grain. Thus individuals who are normally perfectly harmless may, when gathered together in a crowd, let themselves be drawn into acts of atrocity. And what we assert about these transitory outbreaks likewise applies to those more lasting movements of opinion which relate to religious, political, literary and artistic matters, etc., and which are constantly being produced around us, whether throughout society or in a more limited sphere.

Moreover, this definition of a social fact can be verified by examining an experience that is characteristic. It is sufficient to observe how children are brought up. If one views the facts as they are and indeed as they have always been, it is patently obvious that all education consists of a continual effort to impose upon the child ways of seeing, thinking and acting which he himself would not have arrived at spontaneously. From his earliest years we oblige him to eat, drink and sleep at regular hours, and to observe cleanliness, calm and obedience; later we force him to learn how to be mindful of others, to respect customs and conventions, and to work, etc. If this constraint in time ceases to be felt it is because it gradually gives rise to habits, to inner tendencies which render it superfluous; but they supplant the constraint only because they are derived from it. It is true that, in Spencer's view, a rational education should shun such means and allow the child complete freedom to do what he will. Yet as this educational theory has never been put into practice among any known people, it can only be the personal expression of a desideratum and not a fact which can be established in contradiction to the other facts given above. What renders these latter facts particularly illuminating is that education sets out precisely with the object of creating a social being. Thus there can be seen, as in an abbreviated form, how the social being has been fashioned historically. The pressure to which the child is subjected unremittingly is the same pressure of the social environment which seeks to shape him in its own image, and in which parents and teachers are only the representatives and intermediaries.

Thus it is not the fact that they are general which can serve to characterise sociological phenomena. Thoughts to be found in the consciousness of each individual and movements which are repeated by all individuals are not for this reason social facts. If some have been content with using this characteristic in order to define them it is because they have been confused, wrongly, with what might be termed their individual incarnations. What constitutes social facts are the beliefs, tendencies and practices of the group taken collectively. But the forms that these collective states may assume when they are 'refracted' through individuals are things of a different kind. What irrefutably demonstrates this duality of kind is that these two categories of facts frequently are manifested dissociated from each other. Indeed some of these ways of acting or thinking acquire, by dint of repetition, a sort of consistency which, so to speak, separates them out, isolating them from the particular events which reflect them. Thus they assume a shape, a tangible form peculiar to them and constitute a reality sui generis vastly distinct from the individual facts which manifest that reality. Collective custom does not exist only in a state of immanence in the successive actions which it determines, but, by a privilege without example in the biological kingdom, expresses itself once and for all in a formula repeated by word of mouth, transmitted by education and even enshrined in the written word. Such are the origins and nature of legal and moral rules, aphorisms and popular sayings, articles of faith in which religious or political sects epitomise their beliefs, and standards of taste drawn up by literary schools, etc. None of these modes of acting and thinking are to be found wholly in the application made of them by individuals, since they can even exist without being applied at the time.

Undoubtedly this state of dissociation does not always present itself with equal distinctiveness. It is sufficient for dissociation to exist unquestionably in the numerous important instances cited, for us to prove that the social fact exists separately from its individual effects. Moreover, even when the dissociation is not immediately observable, it can often be made so with the help of certain methodological devices. Indeed it is essential to embark on such procedures if one wishes to refine out the social fact from any amalgam and so observe it in its pure state. Thus certain currents of opinion, whose intensity varies according to the time and country in which they occur, impel us, for example, towards marriage or suicide, towards higher or lower birth-rates, etc. Such currents are plainly social facts. At first sight they seem inseparable from the forms they assume in individual cases. But statistics afford us a means of isolating them. They are indeed not inaccurately represented by rates of births, marriages and suicides, that is, by the result obtained after dividing the average annual total of marriages, births, and voluntary homicides by the number of persons of an age to marry, produce children, or commit suicide. [2] Since each one of these statistics includes without distinction all individual cases, the individual circumstances which may have played some part in producing the phenomenon cancel each other out and consequently do not contribute to determining the nature of the phenomenon. What it expresses is a certain state of the collective mind.

That is what social phenomena are when stripped of all extraneous elements. As regards their private manifestations, these do indeed have something social about them, since in part they reproduce the collective model. But to a large extent each one depends also upon the psychical and organic constitution of the individual, and on the particular circumstances in which he is placed. Therefore they are not phenomena which are in the strict sense sociological. They depend on both domains at the same time, and could be termed socio-psychical. They are of interest to the sociologist without constituting the immediate content of sociology. The same characteristic is to be found in the organisms of those mixed phenomena of nature studied in the combined sciences such as biochemistry.

It may be objected that a phenomenon can only be collective if it is common to all the members of society, or at the very least to a majority, and consequently, if it is general. This is doubtless the case, but if it is general it is because it is collective (that is, more or less obligatory); but it is very far from being collective because it is general. It is a condition of the group repeated in individuals because it imposes itself upon them. It is in each part because it is in the whole, but far from being in the whole because it is in the parts. This is supremely evident in those beliefs and practices which are handed down to us ready fashioned by previous generations. We accept and adopt them because, since they are the work of the collectivity and one that is centuries old, they are invested with a special authority that our education has taught us to recognise and respect. It is worthy of note that the vast majority of social phenomena come to us in this way. But even when the social fact is partly due to our direct co-operation, it is no different in nature. An outburst of collective emotion in a gathering does not merely express the sum total of what individual feelings share in common, but is something of a very different order, as we have demonstrated. It is a product of shared existence, of actions and reactions called into play between the consciousnesses of individuals. If it is echoed in each one of them it is precisely by virtue of the special energy derived from its collective origins. If all hearts beat in unison, this is not as a consequence of a spontaneous, preestablished harmony; it is because one and the same force is propelling them in the same direction. Each one is borne along by the rest.

We have therefore succeeded in delineating for ourselves the exact field of sociology. It embraces one single, well defined group of phenomena. A social fact is identifiable through the power of external coercion which it exerts or is capable of exerting upon individuals. The presence of this power is in turn recognisable because of the existence of some pre-determined sanction, or through the resistance that the fact opposes to any individual action that may threaten it. However, it can also be defined by ascertaining how widespread it is within the group, provided that, as noted above, one is careful to add a second essential characteristic; this is, that it exists independently of the particular forms that it may assume in the process of spreading itself within the group. In certain cases this latter criterion can even be more easily applied than the former one. The presence of constraint is easily ascertainable when it is manifested externally through some direct reaction of society, as in the case of law, morality, beliefs, customs and even fashions. But when constraint is merely indirect, as with that exerted by an economic organization, it is not always so clearly discernible. Generality combined with objectivity may then be easier to establish. Moreover, this second definition is simply another formulation of the first one: if a mode of behaviour existing outside the consciousnesses of individuals becomes general, it can only do so by exerting pressure upon them. [3]

However, one may well ask whether this definition is complete. Indeed the facts which have provided us with its basis are all ways of functioning: they are 'physiological' in nature. But there are also collective ways of being, namely, social facts of an 'anatomical' or morphological nature. Sociology cannot dissociate itself from what concerns the substratum of collective life. Yet the number and nature of the elementary parts which constitute society, the way in which they are articulated, the degree of coalescence they have attained, the distribution of population over the earth's surface, the extent and nature of the network of communications, the design of dwellings, etc., do not at first sight seem relatable to ways of acting, feeling or thinking.

Yet, first and foremost, these various phenomena present the same characteristic which has served us in defining the others. These ways of being impose themselves upon the individual just as do the ways of acting we have dealt with. In fact, when we wish to learn how a society is divided up politically, in what its divisions consist and the degree of solidarity that exists between them, it is not through physical inspection and geographical observation that we may come to find this out: such divisions are social, although they may have some physical basis. It is only through public law that we can study such political organisation, because this law is what determines its nature, just as it determines our domestic and civic relationships. The organisation is no less a form of compulsion. If the population clusters together in our cities instead of being scattered over the rural areas, it is because there exists a trend of opinion, a collective drive which imposes this concentration upon individuals. We can no more choose the design of our houses than the cut of our clothes—at least, the one is as much obligatory as the other. The communication network forcibly prescribes the direction of internal migrations or commercial exchanges, etc., and even their intensity. Consequently, at the most there are grounds for adding one further category to the list of phenomena already enumerated as bearing the distinctive stamp of a social fact. But as that enumeration was in no wise strictly exhaustive, this addition would not be indispensable.

Moreover, it does not even serve a purpose, for these ways of being are only ways of acting that have been consolidated. A society's political structure is only the way in which its various component segments have become accustomed to living with each other. If relationships between them are traditionally close, the segments tend to merge together; if the contrary, they tend to remain distinct. The type of dwelling imposed upon us is merely the way in which everyone around us and, in part, previous generations, have customarily built their houses. The communication network is only the channel which has been cut by the regular current of commerce and migrations, etc., flowing in the same direction. Doubtless if phenomena of a morphological kind were the only ones that displayed this rigidity, it might be thought that they constituted a separate species. But a legal rule is no less permanent an arrangement than an architectural style, and yet it is a 'physiological' fact. A simple moral maxim is certainly more malleable, yet it is cast in forms much more rigid than a mere professional custom or fashion. Thus there exists a whole range of gradations which, without any break in continuity, join the most clearly delineated structural facts to those free currents of social life which are not yet caught in any definite mould. This therefore signifies that the differences between them concern only the degree to which they have become consolidated. Both are forms of life at varying stages of crystallisation. It would undoubtedly be advantageous to reserve the term 'morphological' for those social facts which relate to the social substratum, but only on condition that one is aware that they are of the same nature as the others.

Our definition will therefore subsume all that has to be defined it if states:

A social fact is any way of acting, whether fixed or not, capable of exerting over the individual an external constraint;

or:

which is general over the whole of a given society whilst having an existence of its own, independent of its individual manifestations.[4]

Notes

1. Moreover, this is not to say that all constraint is normal. We shall return to this point later.
2. Suicides do not occur at any age, nor do they occur at all ages of life with the same frequency.
3. It can be seen how far removed this definition of the social fact is from that which serves as the basis for the ingenious system of Tarde. We must first state that our research has nowhere led us to corroboration of the preponderant influence that Tarde attributes to imitation in the genesis of collective facts. Moreover, from this definition, which is not a theory but a mere resume of the immediate data observed, it seems clearly to follow that imitation does not always express, indeed never expresses, what is essential and characteristic in the social fact. Doubtless every social fact is imitated and has, as we have just shown, a tendency to become generalised, but this is because it is social, i.e. obligatory. Its capacity for expansion is not the cause but the consequence of its sociological character. If social facts were unique in bringing about this effect, imitation might serve, if not to

explain them, at least to define them. But an individual state which impacts on others none the less remains individual. Moreover, one may speculate whether the term 'imitation' is indeed appropriate to designate a proliferation which occurs through some coercive influence. In such a single term very different phenomena, which need to be distinguished, are confused.

4. This close affinity of life and structure, organ and function, can be readily established in sociology because there exists between these two extremes a whole series of intermediate stages, immediately observable, which reveal the link between them. Biology lacks this methodological resource. But one may believe legitimately that sociological inductions on this subject are applicable to biology and that, in organisms as in societies, between these two categories of facts only differences in degree exist.

CHAPTER 4

Manifesto of the Communist Party

Karl Marx and Friedrich Engels

Bourgeois and Proletarians[1]

The history of all hitherto existing society[2] is the history of class struggles.

Freeman and slave, patrician and plebian, lord and serf, guild-master[3] and journeyman, in a word, oppressor and oppressed, stood in constant opposition to one another, carried on an uninterrupted, now hidden, now open fight, a fight that each time ended either in a revolutionary re-constitution of society at large, or in the common ruin of the contending classes.

In the earlier epochs of history we find almost everywhere a complicated arrangement of society into various orders, a manifold gradation of social rank. In ancient Rome we have patricians, knights, plebians, slaves; in the middle ages, feudal lords, vassals, guild-masters, journeymen, apprentices, serfs; in almost all of these classes, again, subordinate gradations.

The modern bourgeois society that has sprouted from the ruins of feudal society has not done away with class antagonisms. It has only established new classes, new conditions of oppression, new forms of struggle in place of the old ones.

Our epoch, the epoch of the bourgeoisie, possesses, however, this distinctive feature: it has simplified the class antagonism. Society as a whole is more and more splitting up into two great hostile camps, into two great classes directly facing each other: bourgeoisie and proletariat.

From the serfs of the middle ages sprang the chartered burghers[4] of the earliest towns. From these burgesses the first elements of the bourgeoisie were developed.

The discovery of America, the rounding of the Cape, opened up fresh ground for the rising bourgeoisie. The East-Indian and Chinese markets, the colonization of America, trade with the colonies, the increase in the means of exchange and in commodities generally, gave to commerce, to navigation, to industry, an impulse never before known, and thereby gave rapid development to the revolutionary element in the tottering feudal society.

The feudal system of industry, under which industrial production was monopolized by closed guilds, now no longer sufficed for the growing wants of the new markets. The manufacturing system took its place. The guildmasters were pushed on one side by the manufacturing middle class[5]; division of labour between the different corporate guilds vanished in the face of the division of labour in each single workshop.

Meantime the markets kept ever growing, the demand ever rising. Even manufacture[6] no longer sufficed. Thereupon steam and machinery revolutionized industrial production. The place of manufacture was taken by the giant, modern industry, the place of the industrial middle class, by industrial millionaires, the leaders of whole industrial armies, the modern bourgeois.

Modern industry has established the world market, for which the discovery of America paved the way. This market has given an immense development to commerce, to navigation, to communication by land. This development has, in its turn, reacted on the extension of industry; and in proportion as industry, commerce, navigation, railways extended, in the same proportion the bourgeoisie developed, increased its capital, and pushed into the background every class handed down from the Middle Ages.

We see, therefore, how the modern bourgeoisie is itself the product of a long course of development, of a series of revolutions in the modes of production and of exchange.

Each step in the development of the bourgeoisie was accompanied by a corresponding political advance of that class. An oppressed class under the sway of the feudal nobility, an armed and self-governing association in the medieval commune[7]; here independent urban republic (as in Italy and Germany), there taxable "third estate"[8] of the monarchy (as in France), afterwards, in the period of manufacture proper, serving either the semi-feudal or the absolutist monarchy as a counterpoise against the nobility, and, in fact, corner-stone of the great monarchies in general, the bourgeoisie has at last, since the establishment of modern industry and of the world market, conquered for itself, in a modern representative state, exclusive political sway. The executive of the modern state is but a committee for managing the common affairs of the whole bourgeoisie.

The bourgeoisie, historically, has played a most revolutionary part.

The bourgeoisie, wherever it has got the upper hand, has put an end to all feudal, patriarchal, idyllic relations. It has pitilessly torn asunder the motley feudal ties that bound man to his "natural superiors," and has left remaining no other nexus between man and man than naked self-interest, than callous "cash payment." It has drowned the most heavenly ecstasies of religious fervour, of chivalrous enthusiasm, of philistine sentimentalism, in the icy water of egotistical calculation. It has resolved personal worth into exchange value, and in place of the numberless indefeasible chartered freedoms, has set up that single, unconscionable freedom—free trade. In one word, for exploitation veiled by religious and political illusions it has substituted naked, shameless, direct, brutal exploitation.

The bourgeoisie has stripped of its halo every occupation hitherto honoured and looked up to with reverent awe. It has converted the physician, the lawyer, the priest, the poet, the man of science, into its paid wage labourers.

The bourgeoisie has torn away from the family its sentimental veil, and has reduced the family relation to a mere money relation.

The bourgeoisie has disclosed how it came to pass that the brutal display of vigour in the Middle Ages, which reactionists so much admire, found its fitting complement in the most slothful indolence. It has been the first to show what man's activity can bring about. It has accomplished wonders far surpassing Egyptian pyramids, Roman aqueducts, and Gothic cathedrals; it has conducted expeditions that put in the shade all former exoduses of nations and crusades.

The bourgeoisie cannot exist without constantly revolutionizing the instruments of production, and thereby the relations of production, and with them the whole relations of society. Conservation of the old modes of production in unaltered form, was, on the contrary, the first condition of existence for all earlier industrial classes. All fixed, fast-frozen relations, with their train of ancient and venerable prejudices and opinions are swept away, all new-formed ones become antiquated before they can ossify. All that is solid melts into air, all that is holy is profaned, and man is at last compelled to face with sober senses his real conditions of life, and his relations with his kind.

The need for a constantly expanding market for its products chases the bourgeoisie over the whole surface of the globe. It must nestle everywhere, settle everywhere, establish connections everywhere.

The bourgeoisie has through its exploitation of the world-market given a cosmopolitan character to production and consumption in every country. To the great chagrin of reactionists, it has drawn from under the feet of industry the national ground on which it stood. All old-established national industries have been destroyed or are daily being destroyed. They are dislodged by new industries, whose introduction becomes a life and death question for all civilized nations, by industries that no longer work up indigenous raw material, but raw material drawn from the remotest zones; industries whose products are consumed, not only at home, but in every quarter of the globe. In place of the old wants, satisfied by the productions of the country, we find new wants, requiring for their satisfaction the products of distant lands and climes. In place of the old local and national seclusion and self-sufficiency, we have intercourse in every direction, universal interdependence of nations. And as in material, so also in intellectual production. The intellectual creations of individual nations become common property. National one-sidedness and narrow-mindedness become more and more impossible, and from the numerous national and local literatures there arises a world literature.

The bourgeoisie, by the rapid improvement of all instruments of production, by the immensely facilitated means of communication, draws all, even the most barbarian, nations into civilization. The cheap prices of commodities are the heavy artillery with which it batters down all Chinese walls, with which it forces the barbarians' intensely obstinate hatred of foreigners to capitulate. It compels all nations, on pain of extinction, to adopt the bourgeois mode of production; it compels them to introduce what it calls civilization into their midst, *i.e.*, to become bourgeois themselves. In one word, it creates a world after its own image.

The bourgeoisie has subjected the country to the rule of the towns. It has created enormous cities, has greatly increased the urban population as compared with the rural, and has thus rescued a considerable part of the population from the idiocy of rural life. Just as it has made the country dependent on the towns, so it has made the barbarian and semi-barbarian countries dependent on the civilized ones, nations of peasants on nations of bourgeois, the East on the West.

The bourgeoisie keeps more and more doing away with the scattered state of the population, of the means of production, and of property. It has agglomerated population, centralized means of production, and has concentrated property in a few hands. The necessary consequence of this was political centralization. Independent, or but loosely connected provinces, with separate interests, laws, governments, and systems of taxation became lumped together into one nation, with one government, one code of laws, one national class-interest, one frontier, and one customs-tariff.

The bourgeoisie, during its rule of scarce one hundred years, has created more massive and more colossal productive forces than have all preceding generations together. Subjection of Nature's forces to man, machinery, application of chemistry to industry and agriculture, steam-navigation, railways, electric telegraphs, clearing of whole continents for cultivation, canalization of rivers, whole populations conjured out of the ground—what earlier century had even a presentiment that such productive forces slumbered in the lap of social labour?

We see then: the means of production and exchange, on whose foundation the bourgeoisie built itself up, were generated in feudal society. At a certain stage in the development of these means of production and exchange, the conditions under which feudal society produced and exchanged, the feudal organization of agriculture and manufacturing industry, in one word, the feudal relations of property became no longer compatible with the already developed productive forces; they became so many fetters. They had to be burst asunder; they were burst asunder.

Into their place stepped free competition, accompanied by a social and political constitution adapted to it, and by the economic and political sway of the bourgeois class.

A similar movement is going on before our own eyes. Modern bourgeois society with its relations of production, of exchange, and of property, a society that has conjured up such gigantic means of production and exchange, is like the sorcerer, who is no longer able to control the powers of the nether world whom he has called up by his spells. For many a decade past the history of industry and commerce is but the history of revolt of modern productive forces against modern conditions of production, against property relations that are the conditions for the existence of the bourgeoisie and of its rule. It is enough to mention that the commercial crises by their periodical return put on its trial, each time more threateningly, the existence of the entire bourgeois society. (In these crises a great part not only of the existing products, but also of the previously created productive forces, are periodically destroyed. In these crises there breaks out an epidemic that, in all earlier epochs, would have seemed an absurdity—the epidemic of over-production. Society suddenly finds itself put back into a state of momentary barbarism; it appears as if famine, a universal war of devastation had cut off the supply of every means of subsistence; industry and commerce seem to be destroyed; and why? Because there is too much civilization, too much means of subsistence, too much industry, too much commerce. The productive forces at the disposal of society no longer tend to further the development of the conditions of bourgeois property; on the contrary, they have become too powerful for these conditions, by which they are fettered, and so soon as they overcome these fetters, they bring disorder into the whole of bourgeois society, endanger the existence of bourgeois property. The conditions of bourgeois society are too narrow to comprise the wealth created by them. And how does the bourgeoisie get over these crises? On the one hand by enforced destruction of a mass of productive forces; on the other, by the conquest of new markets, and by the more through exploitation of the old ones. That is to say, by paving the way for more extensive and more destructive crises, and by diminishing the means whereby crises are prevented.

The weapons with which the bourgeoisie felled feudalism to the ground are now turned against the bourgeoisie itself.

But not only has the bourgeoisie forged the weapons that bring death to itself; it has also called into existence the men who are to wield those weapons—the modern working class—the proletarians.

In proportion as the bourgeoisie, *i.e.*, capital, is developed, in the same proportion is the proletariat, the modern working class, developed—a class of labourers, who live only so long as they find work, and who find work only so long as their labour increases capital. These labourers, who must sell themselves piecemeal, are a commodity,[9] like every other article of commerce, and are consequently exposed to all the vicissitudes of competition, to all the fluctuations of the market.

Owing to the extensive use of machinery and to division of labour, the work of the proletarians has lost all individual character, and, consequently, all charm for the workman. He becomes an appendage of the machine, and it is only the most simple, most monotonous, and most easily acquired knack, that is required of him. Hence, the cost of production of a workman is restricted, almost entirely, to the means of subsistence that he requires for his maintenance, and for the propagation of his race. But the price of a commodity, and therefore also of labour, is equal to its cost of production. In proportion, therefore, as the repulsiveness of the work increases, the wage decreases. Nay more, in the same proportion the burden of toil also increases, whether by prolongation of the working hours, by increase of the work exacted in a given time or by increased speed of the machinery, etc.

Modern industry has converted the little workshop of the patriarchal master into the great factory of the industrial capitalist. Masses of labourers, crowded into the factory, are organized like soldiers. As privates of the industrial army they are placed under the command of a perfect hierarchy of officers and sergeants. Not only are they slaves of the bourgeois class, and of the bourgeois state; they are daily and hourly enslaved by the machine, by the over-looker, and, above all, by the individual bourgeois manufacturer himself. The more openly this despotism proclaims gain to be its end and aim, the more petty, the more hateful and the more embittering it is.

The less the skill and the exertion of strength implied in manual labour, in other words, the more modern industry becomes developed, the more is the labour of men superseded by that of women. Differences of age and sex no longer have any distinctive social validity for the working class. All are instruments of labour, more or less expensive to use, according to their age and sex.

No sooner is the exploitation of the labour by the manufacturer, so far, at an end, than he receives his wages in cash, than he is set upon by the other portions of the bourgeoisie, the landlord, the shopkeeper, the pawnbroker, etc.

The lower strata of the middle class—the small tradespeople, shopkeepers, and retired tradesmen generally, the handicraftsmen and peasants—all these sink gradually into the proletariat, partly because their diminutive capital does not suffice for the scale on which modern industry is carried on, and is swamped in the competition with the large capitalists, partly because their specialized skill is rendered worthless by new methods of production. Thus the proletariat is recruited from all classes of the population.

The proletariat goes through various stages of development. With its birth begins its struggle with the bourgeoisie. At first the contest is carried on by individual labourers, then by the workpeople of a factory, then by the operatives of one trade, in one locality, against the individual bourgeois who directly exploits them. They direct their attacks not against the bourgeois conditions of production, but against the instruments of production themselves; they destroy imported wares that compete with their labour, they smash pieces of machinery, they set factories ablaze, they seek to restore by force the vanished status of the workman of the Middle Ages.

At this stage the labourers still form an incoherent mass scattered over the whole country, and broken up by their mutual competition. If anywhere they unite to form more compact bodies, this is not yet the consequence of their own active union, but of the union of the bourgeoisie, which class, in order to attain its own political ends, is compelled to set the whole proletariat in motion, and is moreover yet, for a time, able to do so. At this stage, therefore, the proletarians do not fight their enemies, but the enemies of their enemies, the remnants of the absolute monarchy, the landowners, the non-industrial bourgeois, the petty bourgeoisie. Thus the whole historical movement is concentrated in the hands of the bourgeoisie; every victory so attained is a victory for the bourgeoisie.

But with the development of industry the proletariat not only increases in number, it becomes concentrated in greater masses, its strength grows, and it feels that strength more. The various interests and conditions of life within the ranks of the proletariat are more and more equalized, in proportion as machinery obliterates all distinctions of labour, and nearly everywhere reduces wages to the same low level. The growing competition of the bourgeois, and the resulting commercial crises, make the wages of the workers ever more fluctuating. The unceasing improvement of machinery, ever more rapidly developing, makes their livelihood more and more precarious; the collisions between individual workmen and individual bourgeois take more and more of the character of collisions between two classes. Thereupon the workers begin to form combinations (trades' unions) against the bourgeois; they club together in order to keep up the rate of wages; they found permanent associations in order to make provision beforehand for these occasional revolts. Here and there the contest breaks out into riots.

Now and then the workers are victorious, but only for a time. The real fruit of their battle lies, not in the immediate result, but in the ever-expanding union of the workers. This union is helped on by the improved means of communication that are created by modern industry and that place workers of different localities in contact with one another. It was just this contact that was needed to centralize the numerous local struggles, all of the same character, into one national struggle between classes. But every class struggle is a political struggle. And that union, to attain which the burghers of the Middle Ages, with their miserable highways, required centuries, the modern proletarians, thanks to railways, achieve in a few years.

This organization of the proletarians into a class, and consequently into a political party, is continually being upset again by the competition between the workers themselves. But it ever rises up again, stronger, firmer, mightier. It compels legislative recognition of particular interests of the workers, by taking advantage of the divisions among the bourgeoisie itself. Thus the ten-hour[10] bill in England was carried.

Altogether, collisions between the classes of the old society further, in many ways, the course of development of the proletariat. The bourgeoisie finds itself involved in a constant battle. At first with the aristocracy; later on, with those portions of the bourgeoisie itself, whose interests have become antagonistic to the progress of industry; at all times, with the bourgeoisie of foreign countries. In all these battles it sees itself compelled to appeal to the proletariat, to ask for its help, and thus, to drag it into the political arena. The bourgeoisie itself, therefore, supplies the proletariat with its own elements of political and general education; in other words, it furnishes the proletariat with weapons for fighting the bourgeoisie.

Further, as we have already seen, entire sections of the ruling classes are, by the advance of industry, precipitated into the proletariat, or are at least threatened in their conditions of existence. These also supply the proletariat with fresh elements of enlightenment and progress.

Finally, in times when the class struggle nears the decisive hour, the process of dissolution going on within the ruling class, in fact within the whole range of old society, assumes such a violent, glaring character, that a small section of the ruling class cuts itself adrift, and joins the revolutionary class, the class that holds the future in its hands. Just as, therefore, at an earlier period, a section of the nobility went over to the bourgeoisie, so now a portion of the bourgeoisie goes over to the proletariat, and in particular, a portion of the bourgeois ideologists, who have raised themselves to a level of comprehending theoretically the historical movement as a whole.

Of all the classes that stand face to face with the bourgeoisie today, the proletariat alone is a really revolutionary class. The other classes decay and finally disappear in the face of modern industry; the proletariat is its special and essential product.

The lower middle class, the small manufacturer, the shopkeeper, the artisan, the peasant, all these fight against the bourgeoisie, to save from extinction their existence as fractions of the middle class. They are therefore not revolutionary, but conservative. Nay more, they are reactionary, for they try to roll back the wheel of history. If by chance they are revolutionary, they are so only in view of their impending transfer into the proletariat, they thus defend not their present, but their future interests, they desert their own standpoint to place themselves at that of the proletariat.

The "dangerous class," the social scum, that passively rotting mass thrown off by the lowest layers of old society, may, here and there, be swept into the movement by a proletarian revolution; its conditions of life, however, prepare it far more for the part of a bribed tool of reactionary intrigue.

In the conditions of the proletariat, those of old society at large are already virtually swamped. The proletarian is without property; his relation to his wife and children has no longer anything in common with the bourgeois family relations; modern industrial labour, modern subjection to capital, the same in England as in France, in America as in Germany, has stripped him of every trace of national character. Law, morality, religion, are to him so many bourgeois prejudices, behind which lurk in ambush just as many bourgeois interests.

All the preceding classes that got the upper hand, sought to fortify their already acquired status by subjecting society at large to their conditions of appropriation. The proletarians cannot become masters of the productive forces of society, except by abolishing their own previous mode of appropriation, and thereby every other previous mode of appropriation. They have nothing of their own to secure and to fortify; their mission is to destroy all previous securities for, and insurances of, individual property.

All previous historical movements were movements of minorities, or in the interests of minorities. The proletarian movement is the self-conscious, independent movement of the immense majority, in the interests of the immense majority. The proletariat, the lowest stratum of our present society, cannot stir, cannot raise itself up, without the whole superincumbent strata of official society being sprung into the air.

Though not in substance, yet in form, the struggle of the proletariat with the bourgeoisie is at first a national struggle. The proletariat of each country must, of course, first of all settle matters with its own bourgeoisie.

In depicting the most general phases of the development of the proletariat, we traced the more or less veiled civil war, raging within existing society, up to the point where that war breaks out into open revolution, and where the violent overthrow of the bourgeoisie lays the foundation for the sway of the proletariat.

Hitherto every form of society has been based, as we have already seen, on the antagonism of oppressing and oppressed classes. But in order to oppress a class, certain conditions must be assured to it under which it can, at least, continue its slavish existence. The serf, in the period of serfdom, raised himself to membership in the commune, just as the petty bourgeois, under the yoke of feudal absolutism, managed to develop into a bourgeois. The modern labourer, on the contrary, instead of rising with the progress of industry, sinks deeper and deeper below the conditions of existence of his own class. He becomes a pauper, and pauperism develops more rapidly than population and wealth. And here it becomes evident that the bourgeoisie is unfit any longer to be the ruling class in society, and to impose its conditions of existence upon society as an over-riding law. It is unfit to rule because it is incompetent to assure an existence to its slave within his slavery, because it cannot help letting him sink into such a state, that it has to feed him, instead of being fed by him. Society can no longer live under this bourgeoisie; in other words, its existence is no longer compatible with society.

The essential condition for the existence, and for the sway of the bourgeois class, is the formation and augmentation of capital; the condition for capital is wage labour. Wage labour rests exclusively on the competition between the labourers. The advance of industry, whose involuntary promoter is the bourgeoisie, replaces the isolation of the labourers, due to competition, by their revolutionary combination, due to association. The development of modern industry, therefore, cuts from under its feet the very foundation on which the bourgeoisie produces and appropriates products. What the bourgeoisie, therefore, produces, above all, is its own grave-diggers. Its fall and the victory of the proletariat are equally inevitable.

Notes

1. By bourgeoisie is meant the class of modern capitalists, owners of the means of social production and employers of wage-labour. By proletariat, the class of modern wage-labourers who, having no means of production of their own, are reduced to selling their labour-power in order to live. [Engels]
2. That is, all written history. In 1847, the pre-history of society, the social organization existing previous to recorded history, was all but unknown .... With the dissolution of these primaeval communities society begins to be differentiated into separate and finally antagonistic classes. I have attempted to retrace this process of dissolution in The Origin of the Family, Private Property and the State. [Engels] Engels's *The Origin of the Family, Private Property and the State* was first published in 1884. [JW]
3. Guild-master, that is, a full member of a guild, a master within, not a head of a guild. [Engels]
4. A burgher was a citizen of a town. In the Middle Ages serfs sometimes attempted to escape bondage by fleeing to the towns. In late feudalism, in the epoch of the great absolutist states, the monarch gave charters to the towns, making them legal corporations. The term "burgess" in the following sentence is used interchangeably with the term "burgher" by Marx and Engels. [JW]
5. In *The Condition of the Working Class in England*, first published in 1845, Engels amplified his use of the term "middle class." "The English word middle class ... [l]ike the French word *bourgeoisie* ... means the possessing class, specifically that possessing class which is differentiated from the so-called aristocracy ...." (p. 15) [JW]
6. In *Capital*, Volume 1, Part III, Chapter XIV, Marx distinguishes between the period of manufacture, which extends from about 1550 to about 1780, and the period of modern industry, which follows it. During the period of manufacture capitalists employed wage labourers in their workshops to produce commodities by hand, using a division of labour among the workers to operate more economically than the craftsman and his apprentices. In the period of modern industry the tools of manual production were replaced by machines. "Manufacture" is thus understood literally, as the process of making by hand. [JW]
7. "Commune" was the name taken, in France, by the nascent towns even before they had conquered local self-government and political rights as the "third estate" from their feudal lords and masters. Generally speaking, for the economic development of the bourgeoisie, England is here taken as the typical country; for its political development, France. [Engels]
8. The clergy and the nobility were the first two estates. [JW]

9. Marx was later to argue that it was labour-power, the capacity to labour, and not labour itself which the worker sold to the capitalist. This enabled Marx to distinguish between the slave mode of production, in which the slave was a commodity and could be bought and sold, and capitalism, in which the labourer remained free, but was forced to sell his or her labour-power in order to live. [JW]
10. The British Factory Act of 1847 specified that on May 1st, 1848, the working day would be reduced to ten hours from the twelve hours that had become common in the preceding decade. For a more elaborate analysis by Marx on the struggle of the workers for a shorter working day see *Capital*, Vol. 1, Part III, Section 6. [JW]

CHAPTER 5

The Protestant Ethic and the Spirit of Capitalism

Max Weber

Religious Affiliation and Social Stratification

A glance at the occupational statistics of any country of mixed religious composition brings to light with remarkable frequency a situation which has several times provoked discussion in the Catholic press and literature, and in Catholic congresses in Germany, namely, the fact that business leaders and owners of capital, as well as the higher grades of skilled labour, and even more the higher technically and commercially trained personnel of modern enterprises, are overwhelmingly Protestant. This is true not only in cases where the difference in religion coincides with one of nationality, and thus of cultural development, as in Eastern Germany between Germans and Poles. The same thing is shown in the figures of religious affiliation almost wherever capitalism, at the time of its great expansion, has had a free hand to alter the social distribution of the population in accordance with its needs, and to determine its occupational structure. The more freedom it has had, the more clearly is the effect shown. It is true that the greater relative participation of Protestants in the ownership of capital, in management, and the upper ranks of labour in great modern industrial and commercial enterprises, may in part be explained in terms of historical circumstances which extend far back into the past, and in which religious affiliation is not a cause of the economic conditions, but to a certain extent appears to be a result of them. Participation in the above economic functions usually involves some previous ownership of capital, and generally an expensive education; often both. These are today largely dependent on the possession of inherited wealth, or at least on a certain degree of material wellbeing. A number of those sections of the old Empire which were most highly developed economically and most favoured by natural resources and situation, in particular a majority of the wealthy towns, went over to Protestantism in the sixteenth century. The results of that circumstance favour the Protestants even today in their struggle for economic existence. There arises thus the historical question: why were the districts of highest economic development at the same time particularly favourable to a revolution in the Church? The answer is by no means so simple as one might think.

The emancipation from economic traditionalism appears, no doubt, to be a factor which would greatly strengthen the tendency to doubt the sanctity of the religious tradition, as of all traditional authorities. But it is necessary to note, what has often been forgotten, that the Reformation meant not the elimination of the Church's control over everyday life, but rather the substitution of a new form of control for the previous one. It meant the repudiation of a control which was very lax, at that time scarcely perceptible in practice, and hardly more than formal, in favour of a regulation of the whole of conduct which, penetrating to all departments of private and public life, was infinitely burdensome and earnestly enforced. The rule of the Catholic Church, "punishing the heretic, but indulgent to the sinner," as it was in the past even more than to-day, is now tolerated by peoples of thoroughly modern economic character, and was borne by the richest and economically most advanced peoples on earth at about the turn of the fifteenth century. The rule of Calvinism, on the other hand, as it was enforced in the sixteenth century in Geneva and in Scotland, at the turn of the sixteenth and seventeenth centuries in large parts of the Netherlands, in the seventeenth in New England, and for a time in England itself, would be for us the most absolutely unbearable form of ecclesiastical control of the individual which could possibly exist. That was exactly what large numbers of the old commercial aristocracy of those times, in Geneva as well as in Holland and England, felt about it. And what the reformers complained of in those areas of high economic development was not too much supervision of life on the part of the Church, but too little. Now how does it happen that at that time those countries which were most advanced economically, and within them the rising bourgeois middle classes, not only failed to resist this unexampled tyranny of Puritanism, but even developed a heroism in its defence? For bourgeois classes as such have seldom before and never since displayed heroism. It was "the last of our heroisms," as Carlyle, not without reason, has said.

But further, and especially important: it may be, as has been claimed, that the greater participation of Protestants in the positions of ownership and management in modern economic life may to-day be understood, in part at least, simply as a result of the greater material wealth they have inherited. But there are certain other phenomena which cannot be explained in the same way. Thus, to mention only a few facts: there is a great difference discoverable in Baden, in Bavaria, in Hungary, in the type of higher education which Catholic parents, as opposed to Protestant, give their children. That the percentage of Catholics among the students and graduates of higher educational institutions in general lags behind their proportion of the total population, may, to be sure, be largely explicable in terms of inherited differences of wealth. But among the Catholic graduates themselves the percentage of those graduating from the institutions preparing, in particular, for technical studies and industrial and commercial occupations, but in general from those preparing for middle-class business life, lags still farther behind the percentage of Protestants. On the other hand, Catholics prefer the sort of training which the humanistic Gymnasium affords. That is a circumstance to which the above explanation does not apply, but which, on the contrary, is one reason why so few Catholics are engaged in capitalistic enterprise.

Even more striking is a fact which partly explains the smaller proportion of Catholics among the skilled labourers of modern industry. It is well known that the factory has taken its skilled labour to a large extent from young men in the handicrafts; but this is much more true of Protestant than of Catholic journeymen. Among journeymen, in other words, the Catholics show a stronger propensity to remain in their crafts, that is they more often become master craftsmen, whereas the Protestants are attracted to a larger extent into the factories in order to fill the upper ranks of skilled labour and administrative positions. The explanation of these cases is undoubtedly that the mental and spiritual peculiarities acquired from the environment, here the type of education favoured by the religious atmosphere of the home community and the parental home, have determined the choice of occupation, and through it the professional career.

The smaller participation of Catholics in the modern business life of Germany is all the more striking because it runs counter to a tendency which has been observed at all times including the present. National or religious minorities which are in a position of subordination to a group of rulers are likely, through their voluntary or involuntary exclusion from positions of political influence, to be driven with peculiar force into economic activity. Their ablest members seek to satisfy the desire for recognition of their abilities in this field, since there is no opportunity in the service of the State. This has undoubtedly been true of the Poles in Russia and Eastern Prussia, who have without question been undergoing a more rapid economic advance than in Galicia, where they have been in the ascendant. It has in earlier times been true of the Huguenots in France under Louis XIV, the Nonconformists and Quakers in England, and, last but not least, the Jew for two thousand years. But the Catholics in Germany have shown no striking evidence of such a result of their position. In the past they have, unlike the Protestants, undergone no particularly prominent economic development in the times when they were persecuted or only tolerated, either in Holland or in England. On the other hand, it is a fact that the Protestants (especially certain branches of the movement to be fully discussed later) both as ruling classes and as ruled, both as majority and as minority, have shown a special tendency to develop economic rationalism which cannot be observed to the same extent among Catholics either in the one situation or in the other. Thus the principal explanation of this difference must be sought in the permanent intrinsic character of their religious beliefs, and not only in their temporary external historico-political situations.

It will be our task to investigate these religions with a view to finding out what peculiarities they have or have had which might have resulted in the behaviour we have described. On superficial analysis, and on the basis of certain current impressions, one might be tempted to express the difference by saying that the greater other-worldliness of Catholicism, the ascetic character of its highest ideals, must have brought up its adherents to a greater indifference toward the good things of this world. Such an explanation fits the popular tendency in the judgment of both religions. On the Protestant side it is used as a basis of criticism of those (real or imagined) ascetic ideals of the Catholic way of life, while the Catholics answer with the accusation that materialism results from the secularization of all ideals through Protestantism. One recent writer has attempted to formulate the difference of their attitudes toward economic life in the following manner: "The Catholic is quieter, having less of the acquisitive impulse; he prefers a life of the greatest possible security, even with a smaller income, to a life of risk and excitement, even though it may bring the chance of gaining honour and riches. The proverb says jokingly, 'either eat well or sleep well'. In the present case the Protestant prefers to eat well, the Catholic to sleep undisturbed."

In fact, this desire to eat well may be a correct though incomplete characterization of the motives of many nominal Protestants in Germany at the present time. But things were very different in the past: the English, Dutch, and American Puritans were characterized by the exact opposite of the joy of living, a fact which is indeed, as we shall see, most important for our present study. Moreover, the French Protestants, among others, long retained, and retain to a certain extent up to the present, the characteristics which were impressed upon the Calvinistic Churches everywhere, especially under the cross in the time of the religious struggles. Nevertheless (or was it, perhaps, as we shall ask later, precisely on that account?) it is well known that these characteristics were one of the most important factors in the industrial and capitalistic development of France, and on the small scale permitted them by their persecution remained so. If we may call this seriousness and the strong predominance of religious interests in the whole conduct of life otherworldliness, then the French Calvinists were and still are at least as otherworldly as, for instance, the North German Catholics, to whom their Catholicism is undoubtedly as vital a matter as religion is to any other people in the world. Both differ from the predominant religious trends in their respective countries in much the same way. The Catholics of France are, in their lower ranks, greatly interested in the enjoyment of life, in the upper directly hostile to religion. Similarly, the Protestants of Germany are to-day absorbed in worldly economic life, and their upper ranks are most indifferent to religion. Hardly anything shows so clearly as this parallel that, with such vague ideas as that of the alleged otherworldliness of Catholicism, and the alleged materialistic joy of living of Protestantism, and others like them, nothing can be accomplished for our purpose. In such general terms the distinction does not even adequately fit the facts of to-day, and certainly not of the past. If, however, one wishes to make use of it at all, several other observations present themselves at once which, combined with the above remarks, suggest that the supposed conflict between otherworldliness, asceticism, and ecclesiastical piety on the one side, and participation in capitalistic acquisition on the other, might actually turn out to be an intimate relationship.

As a matter of fact it is surely remarkable, to begin with quite a superficial observation, how large is the number of representatives of the most spiritual forms of Christian piety who have sprung from commercial circles. In particular, very many of the most zealous adherents of Pietism are of this origin. It might be explained as a sort of reaction against mammonism on the part of sensitive natures not adapted to commercial life, and, as in the case of Francis of Assisi, many Pietists have themselves interpreted the process of their conversion in these terms. Similarly, the remarkable circumstance that so many of the greatest capitalistic entrepreneurs—down to Cecil Rhodes—have come from clergymen's families might be explained as a reaction against their ascetic upbringing. But this form of explanation fails where an extraordinary capitalistic business sense is combined in the same persons and groups with the most intensive forms of a piety which penetrates and dominates their whole lives. Such cases are not isolated, but these traits are characteristic of many of the most important Churches and sects in the history of Protestantism. Especially Calvinism, wherever it has appeared, has shown this combination. However little, in the time of the expansion of the Reformation, it (or any other Protestant belief) was bound up with any particular social class, it is characteristic and in a certain sense typical that in French Huguenot Churches monks and business men (merchants, craftsmen) were particularly numerous among the proselytes, especially at the time of the persecution. Even the Spaniards knew that heresy (i.e., the Calvinism of the Dutch) promoted trade, and this coincides with the opinions which Sir William Petty expressed in his discussion of the reasons for the capitalistic development of the Netherlands. Gothein rightly calls the Calvinistic diaspora the seed-bed of capitalistic economy. Even in this case one might consider the decisive factor to be the superiority of the French and Dutch economic cultures from which these communities sprang, or perhaps the immense influence of exile in the breakdown of traditional relationships. But in France the situation was, as we know from Colbert's struggles, the same even in the seventeenth century. Even Austria, not to speak of other countries, directly imported Protestant craftsmen.

But not all the Protestant denominations seem to have had an equally strong influence in this direction. That of Calvinism, even in Germany, was among the strongest, it seems, and the reformed faith more than the others seems to have promoted the development of the spirit of capitalism, in the Wupperthal as well as elsewhere. Much more so than Lutheranism, as comparison both in general and in particular instances, especially in the Wupperthal, seems to prove. For Scotland, Buckle, and among English poets, Keats, have emphasized these same relationships. Even more striking, as it is only necessary to mention, is the connection of a religious way of life with the most intensive development of business acumen among those sects whose otherworldliness is as proverbial as their wealth, especially the Quakers and the Mennonites. The part which the former have played in England and North America fell to the latter in Germany and the Netherlands. That in East Prussia Frederick William I tolerated the Mennonites as indispensable to industry, in spite of their absolute refusal to perform military service, is only one of the numerous well-known cases which illustrates the fact, though, considering the character of that monarch, it is one of the most striking. Finally, that this combination of intense piety with just as strong a development of business acumen, was also characteristic of the Pietists, is common knowledge.

It is only necessary to think of the Rhine country and of Calw. In this purely introductory discussion it is unnecessary to pile up more examples. For these few already all show one thing: that the spirit of hard work, of progress, or whatever else it may be called, the awakening of which one is inclined to ascribe to Protestantism, must not be understood, as there is a tendency to do, as joy of living nor in any other sense as connected with the Enlightenment. The old Protestantism of Luther, Calvin, Knox, Voet, had precious little to do with what to-day is called progress. To whole aspects of modern life which the most extreme religionist would not wish to suppress to-day, it was directly hostile. If any inner relationship between certain expressions of the old Protestant spirit and modern capitalistic culture is to be found, we must attempt to find it, for better or worse not in its alleged more or less materialistic or at least anti-ascetic joy of living, but in its purely religious characteristics. Montesquieu says (*Esprit des Lois*, Book XX, chap. 7) of the English that they "had progressed the farthest of all peoples of the world in three important things: in piety, in commerce, and in freedom." Is it not possible that their commercial superiority and their adaptation to free political institutions are connected in some way with that record of piety which Montesquieu ascribes to them? [...]

Luther's Conception of the Calling

Now it is unmistakable that even in the German word *Beruf*, and perhaps still more clearly in the English *calling*, a religious conception, that of a task set by God, is at least suggested. The more emphasis is put upon the word in a concrete case, the more evident is the connotation. And if we trace the history of the word through the civilized languages, it appears that neither the predominantly Catholic peoples nor those of classical antiquity have possessed any expression of similar connotation for what we know as a calling (in the sense of a life-task, a definite field in which to work), while one has existed for all predominantly Protestant peoples. It may be further shown that this is not due to any ethnical peculiarity of the languages concerned. It is not, for instance, the product of a Germanic spirit, but in its modern meaning the word comes from the Bible translations, through the spirit of the translator, not that of the original. In Luther's translation of the Bible it appears to have first been used at a point in Jesus Sirach (xi. 20 and 21) precisely in our modern sense. After that it speedily took on its present meaning in the everyday speech of all Protestant peoples, while earlier not even a suggestion of such a meaning could be found in the secular literature of any of them, and even, in religious writings, so far as I can ascertain, it is only found in one of the German mystics whose influence on Luther is well known.

Like the meaning of the word, the idea is new, a product of the Reformation. This may be assumed as generally known. It is true that certain suggestions of the positive valuation of routine activity in the world, which is contained in this conception of the calling, had already existed in the Middle Ages, and even in late Hellenistic antiquity. We shall speak of that later. But at least one thing was unquestionably new: the valuation of the fulfilment of duty in worldly affairs as the highest form which the moral activity of the individual could assume. This it was which inevitably gave every-day worldly activity a religious significance, and which first created the conception of a calling in this sense. The conception of the calling thus brings out that central dogma of all Protestant denominations which the Catholic division of ethical precepts into *præcepta* and *consilia* discards. The only way of living acceptably to God was not to surpass worldly morality in monastic asceticism, but solely through the fulfilment of the obligations imposed upon the individual by his position in the world. That was his calling.

Luther developed the conception in the course of the first decade of his activity as a reformer. At first, quite in harmony with the prevailing tradition of the Middle Ages, as represented, for example, by Thomas Aquinas, he thought of activity in the world as a thing of the flesh, even though willed by God. It is the indispensable natural condition of a life of faith, but in itself, like eating and drinking, morally neutral. But with the development of the conception of *sola fide* in all its consequences, and its logical result, the increasingly sharp emphasis against the Catholic *consilia evangelica* of the monks as dictates of the devil, the calling grew in importance. The monastic life is not only quite devoid of value as a means of justification before God, but he also looks upon its renunciation of the duties of this world as the product of selfishness, withdrawing from temporal obligations. In contrast, labour in a calling appears to him as the outward expression of brotherly love. This he proves by the observation that the division of labour forces every individual to work for others, but his view-point is highly naïve, forming an almost grotesque contrast to Adam Smith's well-known statements on the same subject. However, this justification, which is evidently essentially scholastic, soon disappears again, and there remains, more and more strongly emphasized, the statement that the fulfilment of worldly duties is under all circumstances the only way to live acceptably to God. It and it alone is the will of God, and hence every legitimate calling has exactly the same worth in the sight of God.

That this moral justification of worldly activity was one of the most important results of the Reformation, especially of Luther's part in it, is beyond doubt, and may even be considered a platitude. This attitude is worlds removed from the deep hatred of Pascal, in his contemplative moods, for all worldly activity, which he was deeply convinced could only be understood in terms of vanity or low cunning. And it differs even more from the liberal utilitarian compromise with the world at which the Jesuits arrived. But just what the practical significance of this achievement of Protestantism was in detail is dimly felt rather than clearly perceived.[...]

Asceticism and the Spirit of Capitalism

In order to understand the connection between the fundamental religious ideas of ascetic Protestantism and its maxims for everyday economic conduct, it is necessary to examine with especial care such writings as have evidently been derived from ministerial practice. For in a time in which the beyond meant everything, when the social position of the Christian depended upon his admission to the Communion, the clergyman, through his ministry, Church discipline, and preaching, exercised an influence (as a glance at collections of *consilia*, *casus conscientæ*, etc., shows) which we modern men are entirely unable to picture. In such a time the religious forces which express themselves through such channels are the decisive influences in the formation of national character.

For the purposes of this chapter, though by no means for all purposes, we can treat ascetic Protestantism as a single whole. But since that side of English Puritanism which was derived from Calvinism gives the most consistent religious basis for the idea of the calling, we shall, following our previous method, place one of its representatives at the centre of the discussion. Richard Baxter stands out above many other writers on Puritan ethics, both because of his eminently practical and realistic attitude, and, at the same time, because of the universal recognition accorded to his works, which have gone through many new editions and translations. He was a Presbyterian and an apologist of the Westminster Synod, but at the same time, like so many of the best spirits of his time, gradually grew away from the dogmas of pure Calvinism. At heart he opposed Cromwell's usurpation as he would any revolution. He was unfavourable to the sects and the fanatical enthusiasm of the saints, but was very broad-minded about external peculiarities and objective towards his opponents. He sought his field of labour most especially in the practical promotion of the moral life through the Church. In the pursuit of this end, as one of the most successful ministers known to history, he placed his services at the disposal of the Parliamentary Government, of Cromwell, and of the Restoration, until he retired from office under the last, before St. Bartholomew's day. His *Christian Directory* is the most complete compendium of Puritan ethics, and is continually adjusted to the practical experiences of his own ministerial activity. In comparison we shall make use of Spener's *Theologische Bedenken*, as representative of German Pietism, Barclay's *Apology* for the Quakers, and some other representatives of ascetic ethics, which, however, in the interest of space, will be limited as far as possible.

Now, in glancing at Baxter's *Saints' Everlasting Rest*, or his *Christian Directory*, or similar works of others, one is struck at first glance by the emphasis placed, in the discussion of wealth and its acquisition, on the ebionitic elements of the New Testament. Wealth as such is a great danger; its temptations never end, and its pursuit is not only senseless as compared with the dominating importance of the Kingdom of God, but it is morally suspect. Here asceticism seems to have turned much more sharply against the acquisition of earthly goods than it did in Calvin, who saw no hindrance to the effectiveness of the clergy in their wealth, but rather a thoroughly desirable enhancement of their prestige. Hence he permitted them to employ their means profitably. Examples of the condemnation of the pursuit of money and goods may be gathered without end from Puritan writings, and may be contrasted with the late mediæval ethical literature, which was much more open-minded on this point.

Moreover, these doubts were meant with perfect seriousness; only it is necessary to examine them somewhat more closely in order to understand their true ethical significance and implications. The real moral objection is to relaxation in the security of possession, the enjoyment of wealth with the consequence of idleness and the temptations of the flesh, above all of distraction from the pursuit of a righteous life. In fact, it is only because possession involves this danger of relaxation that it is objectionable at all. For the saints' everlasting rest is in the next world; on earth man must, to be certain of his state of grace, "do the works of him who sent him, as long as it is yet day." Not leisure and enjoyment, but only activity serves to increase the glory of God, according to the definite manifestations of His will.

Waste of time is thus the first and in principle the deadliest of sins. The span of human life is infinitely short and precious to make sure of one's own election. Loss of time through sociability, idle talk, luxury, even more sleep than is necessary for health, six to at most eight hours, is worthy of absolute moral condemnation. It does not yet hold, with Franklin, that time is money, but the proposition is true in a certain spiritual sense. It is infinitely valuable because every hour lost is lost to labour for the glory of God. Thus inactive contemplation is also valueless, or even directly reprehensible if it is at the expense of one's daily work. For it is less pleasing to God than the active performance of His will in a calling. Besides, Sunday is provided for that, and, according to Baxter, it is always those who are not diligent in their callings who have no time for God when the occasion demands it.

Accordingly, Baxter's principal work is dominated by the continually repeated, often almost passionate preaching of hard, continuous bodily or mental labour. It is due to a combination of two different motives. Labour is, on the one hand, an approved ascetic technique, as it always has been in the Western Church, in sharp contrast not only to the Orient but to almost all monastic rules the world over. It is in particular the specific defence against all those temptations which Puritanism united under the name of the unclean life, whose rôle for it was by no means small. The sexual asceticism of Puritanism differs only in degree, not in fundamental principle, from that of monasticism; and on account of the Puritan conception of marriage, its practical influence is more far-reaching than that of the latter. For sexual intercourse is permitted, even within marriage, only as the means willed by God for the increase of His glory according to the commandment, "Be fruitful and multiply." Along with a moderate vegetable diet and cold baths, the same prescription is given for all sexual temptations as is used against religious doubts and a sense of moral unworthiness: "Work hard in your calling." But the most important thing was that even beyond that labour came to be considered in itself the end of life, ordained as such by God. St. Paul's "He who will not work shall not eat" holds unconditionally for everyone. Unwillingness to work is symptomatic of the lack of grace.

Here the difference from the mediæval viewpoint becomes quite evident. Thomas Aquinas also gave an interpretation of that statement of St. Paul. But for him labour is only necessary *naturali ratione* for the maintenance of individual and community. Where this end is achieved, the precept ceases to have any meaning. Moreover, it holds only for the race, not for every individual. It does not apply to anyone who can live without labour on his possessions, and of course contemplation, as a spiritual form of action in the Kingdom of God, takes precedence over the commandment in its literal sense. Moreover, for the popular theology of the time, the highest form of monastic productivity lay in the increase of the *Thesaurus ecclesiæ* through prayer and chant.

Now only do these exceptions to the duty to labour naturally no longer hold for Baxter, but he holds most emphatically that wealth does not exempt anyone from the unconditional command. Even the wealthy shall not eat without working, for even though they do not need to labour to support their own needs, there is God's commandment which they, like the poor, must obey. For everyone without exception God's Providence has prepared a calling, which he should profess and in which he should labour. And this calling is not, as it was for the Lutheran, a fate to which he must submit and which he must make the best of, but God's commandment to the individual to work for the divine glory. This seemingly subtle difference had far-reaching psychological consequences, and became connected with a further development of the providential interpretation of the economic order which had begun in scholasticism.

The phenomenon of the division of labour and occupations in society had, among others, been interpreted by Thomas Aquinas, to whom we may most conveniently refer, as a direct consequence of the divine scheme of things. But the places assigned to each man in this cosmos follow *ex causis naturalibus* and are fortuitous (contingent in the Scholastic terminology). The differentiation of men into the classes and occupations established through historical development became for Luther, as we have seen, a direct result of the divine will.

The perseverance of the individual in the place and within the limits which God had assigned to him was a religious duty. This was the more certainly the consequence since the relations of Lutheranism to the world were in general uncertain from the beginning and remained so. Ethical principles for the reform of the world could not be found in Luther's realm of ideas; in fact it never quite freed itself from Pauline indifference. Hence the world had to be accepted as it was, and this alone could be made a religious duty.

But in the Puritan view, the providential character of the play of private economic interests takes on a somewhat different emphasis. True to the Puritan tendency to pragmatic interpretations, the providential purpose of the division of labour is to be known by its fruits. On this point Baxter expresses himself in terms which more than once directly recall Adam Smith's well-known apotheosis of the division of labour. The specialization of occupations leads, since it makes the development of skill possible, to a quantitative and qualitative improvement in production, and thus serves the common good, which is identical with the good of the greatest possible number. So far, the motivation is purely utilitarian, and is closely related to the customary viewpoint of much of the secular literature of the time.

But the characteristic Puritan element appears when Baxter sets at the head of his discussion the statement that "outside of a well-marked calling the accomplishments of a man are only casual and irregular, and he spends more time in idleness than at work," and when he concludes it as follows: "and he [the specialized worker] will carry out his work in order while another remains in constant confusion, and his business knows neither time nor place … therefore is a certain calling the best for everyone." Irregular work, which the ordinary labourer is often forced to accept, is often unavoidable, but always an unwelcome state of transition. A man without a calling thus lacks the systematic, methodical character which is, as we have seen, demanded by worldly asceticism.

The Quaker ethic also holds that a man's life in his calling is an exercise in ascetic virtue, a proof of his state of grace through his conscientiousness, which is expressed in the care and method with which he pursues his calling. What God demands is not labour in itself, but rational labour in a calling. In the Puritan concept of the calling the emphasis is always placed on this methodical character of worldly asceticism, not, as with Luther, on the acceptance of the lot which God has irretrievably assigned to man.

Hence the question whether anyone may combine several callings is answered in the affirmative, if it is useful for the common good or one's own, and not injurious to anyone, and if it does not lead to unfaithfulness in one of the callings. Even a change of calling is by no means regarded as objectionable, if it is not thoughtless and is made for the purpose of pursuing a calling more pleasing to God, which means, on general principles, one more useful.

It is true that the usefulness of a calling, and thus its favour in the sight of God, is measured primarily in moral terms, and thus in terms of the importance of the goods produced in it for the community. But a further, and, above all, in practice the most important, criterion is found in private profitableness. For if that God, whose hand the Puritan sees in all the occurrences of life, shows one of His elect a chance of profit, he must do it with a purpose. Hence the faithful Christian must follow the call by taking advantage of the opportunity. "If God show you a way in which you may lawfully get more than in another way (without wrong to your soul or to any other), if you refuse this, and choose the less gainful way, you cross one of the ends of your calling, and you refuse to be God's steward, and to accept His gifts and use them for Him when He requireth it: you may labour to be rich for God, though not for the flesh and sin."

Wealth is thus bad ethically only in so far as it is a temptation to idleness and sinful enjoyment of life, and its acquisition is bad only when it is with the purpose of later living merrily and without care. But as a performance of duty in a calling it is not only morally permissible, but actually enjoined. The parable of the servant who was rejected because he did not increase the talent which was entrusted to him seemed to say so directly. To wish to be poor was, it was often argued, the same as wishing to be unhealthy; it is objectionable as a glorification of works and derogatory to the glory of God. Especially begging, on the part of one able to work, is not only the sin of slothfulness, but a violation of the duty of brotherly love according to the Apostle's own word.

The emphasis on the ascetic importance of a fixed calling provided an ethical justification of the modern specialized division of labour. In a similar way the providential interpretation of profit-making justified the activities of the business man. The superior indulgence of the *seigneur* and the parvenu ostentation of the *nouveau riche* are equally detestable to asceticism. But, on the other hand, it has the highest ethical appreciation of the sober, middle-class, self-made man. "God blesseth His trade" is a stock remark about those good men who had successfully followed the divine hints. The whole power of the God of the Old Testament, who rewards His people for their obedience in this life, necessarily exercised a similar influence on the Puritan who, following Baxter's advice, compared his own state of grace with that of the heroes of the Bible, and in the process interpreted the statements of the Scriptures as the articles of a book of statutes.

This worldly Protestant asceticism, as we may recapitulate up to this point, acted powerfully against the spontaneous enjoyment of possessions; it restricted consumption, especially of luxuries. On the other hand, it had the psychological effect of freeing the acquisition of goods from the inhibitions of traditionalistic ethics. It broke the bonds of the impulse of acquisition in that it not only legalized it, but (in the sense discussed) looked upon it as directly willed by God. The campaign against the temptations of the flesh, and the dependence on external things, was, as besides the Puritans the great Quaker apologist Barclay expressly says, not a struggle against the rational acquisition, but against the irrational use of wealth.

But this irrational use was exemplified in the outward forms of luxury which their code condemned as idolatry of the flesh, however natural they had appeared to the feudal mind. On the other hand, they approved the rational and utilitarian uses of wealth which were willed by God for the needs of the individual and the community. They did not wish to impose mortification on the man of wealth, but the use of his means for necessary and practical things. The idea of comfort characteristically limits the extent of ethically permissible expenditures. It is naturally no accident that the development of a manner of living consistent with that idea may be observed earliest and most clearly among the most consistent representatives of this whole attitude toward life. Over against the glitter and ostentation of feudal magnificence which, resting on an unsound economic basis, prefers a sordid elegance to a sober simplicity, they set the clean and solid comfort of the middle-class home as an ideal.

On the side of the production of private wealth, asceticism condemned both dishonesty and impulsive avarice. What was condemned as covetousness, Mammonism, etc., was the pursuit of riches for their own sake. For wealth in itself was a temptation. But here asceticism was the power "which ever seeks the good but ever creates evil"; what was evil in its sense was possession and its temptations. For, in conformity with the Old Testament and in analogy to the ethical valuation of good works, asceticism looked upon the pursuit of wealth as an end in itself as highly reprehensible; but the attainment of it as a fruit of labour in a calling was a sign of God's blessing. And even more important: the religious valuation of restless, continuous, systematic work in a worldly calling, as the highest means to asceticism, and at the same time the surest and most evident proof of rebirth and genuine faith, must have been the most powerful conceivable lever for the expansion of that attitude toward life which we have here called the spirit of capitalism.

Now naturally the whole ascetic literature of almost all denominations is saturated with the idea that faithful labour, even at low wages, on the part of those whom life offers no other opportunities, is highly pleasing to God. In this respect Protestant Asceticism added in itself nothing new. But it not only deepened this idea most powerfully, it also created the force which was alone decisive for its effectiveness: the psychological sanction of it through the conception of this labour as a calling, as the best, often in the last analysis the only means of attaining certainty of grace. And on the other hand it legalized the exploitation of this specific willingness to work, in that it also interpreted the employer's business activity as a calling. It is obvious how powerfully the exclusive search for the Kingdom of God only through the fulfilment of duty in the calling, and the strict asceticism which Church discipline naturally imposed, especially on the propertyless classes, was bound to affect the productivity of labour in the capitalistic sense of the word. The treatment of labour as a calling became as characteristic of the modern worker as the corresponding attitude toward acquisition of the business man. [...]

The idea that modern labour has an ascetic character is of course not new. Limitation to specialized work, with a renunciation of the Faustian universality of man which it involves, is a condition of any valuable work in the modern world; hence deeds and renunciation inevitably condition each other to-day. This fundamentally ascetic trait of middle-class life, if it attempts to be a way of life at all, and not simply the absence of any, was what Goethe wanted to teach. [...] For him the realization meant a renunciation, a departure from an age of full and beautiful humanity, which can no more be repeated in the course of our cultural development than can the flower of the Athenian culture of antiquity.

The Puritan wanted to work in a calling; we are forced to do so. For when asceticism was carried out of monastic cells into everyday life, and began to dominate worldly morality, it did its part in building the tremendous cosmos of the modern economic order. This order is now bound to the technical and economic conditions of machine production which to-day determine the lives of all the individuals who are born into this mechanism, not only those directly concerned with economic acquisition, with irresistible force. Perhaps it will so determine them until the last ton of fossilized coal is burnt. In Baxter's view the care for external goods should only lie on the shoulders of the "saint like a light cloak, which can be thrown aside at any moment." But fate decreed that the cloak should become an iron cage.

Since asceticism undertook to remodel the world and to work out its ideals in the world, material goods have gained an increasing and finally an inexorable power over the lives of men as at no previous period in history. To-day the spirit of religious asceticism—whether finally, who knows?—has escaped from the cage. But victorious capitalism, since it rests on mechanical foundations, needs its support no longer. The rosy blush of its laughing heir, the Enlightenment, seems also to be irretrievably fading, and the idea of duty in one's calling prowls about in our lives like the ghost of dead religious beliefs. Where the fulfilment of the calling cannot directly be related to the highest spiritual and cultural values, or when, on the other hand, it need not be felt simply as economic compulsion, the individual generally abandons the attempt to justify it at all. In the field of its highest development, in the United States, the pursuit of wealth, stripped of its religious and ethical meaning, tends to become associated with purely mundane passions, which often actually give it the character of sport.

SECTION 1C

CONTEMPORARY THEORY

CHAPTER 6

Women's Perspective as a Radical Critique of Sociology[1]

Dorothy E. Smith

The women's movement has given us a sense of our right to have women's interests represented in sociology, rather than just receiving as authoritative the interests traditionally represented in a sociology put together by men. What can we make of this access to a social reality that was previously unavailable, was indeed repressed? What happens as we begin to relate to it in the terms of our discipline? We can of course think as many do merely of the addition of courses to the existing repertoire—courses on sex roles, on the women's movement, on women at work, on the social psychology of women and perhaps somewhat different versions of the sociology of the family. But thinking more boldly or perhaps just thinking the whole thing through a little further might bring us to ask first how a sociology might look if it began from the point of view of women's traditional place in it and what happens to a sociology which attempts to deal seriously with that. Following this line of thought, I have found, has consequences larger than they seem at first.

From this point of view of "women's place" the values assigned to different aspects of the world are changed. Some come into prominence while other standard sociological enterprises diminish. [...]

But it is not enough to supplement an established sociology by addressing ourselves to what has been left out, overlooked, or by making sociological issues of the relevances of the world of women. That merely extends the authority of the existing sociological procedures and makes of a women's sociology an addendum. We cannot rest at that because it does not account for the separation between the two worlds and it does not account for or analyze for us the relation between them. [...]

The sociologist enters the conceptually ordered society when he goes to work. He enters it as a member and he enters it also as a mode in which he investigates it. He observes, analyzes, explains and examines as if there were no problem in how that world becomes observable to him. He moves among the doings of organizations, governmental processes, bureaucracies, etc., as a person who is at home in that medium. The nature of that world itself, how it is known to him and the conditions of existence or his relation to it are not called into question. His methods of observation and inquiry extend into it as procedures which are essentially of the same order as those which bring about the phenomena with which he is concerned, or which he is concerned to bring under the jurisdiction of that order. His perspectives and interests may differ, but the substance is the same. He works with facts and information which have been worked up from actualities and appear in the form of documents which are themselves the product of organizational processes, whether his own or administered by him, or of some other agency. He fits that information back into a framework of entities and organizational processes which he takes for granted as known, without asking how it is that he knows them or what are the social processes by which the phenomena which correspond to or provide the empirical events, acts, decisions, etc., of that world, may be recognized. He passes beyond the particular and immediate setting in which he is always located in the body (the office he writes in, the libraries he consults, the streets he travels, the home he returns to) without any sense of having made a transition. He works in the same medium as he studies.

But like everyone else he also exists in the body in the place in which it is. This is also then the place of his sensory organization of immediate experience, then place where his coordinates of here and now before and after are organized around himself as centre; the place where he confronts people face to face in the physical mode in which he expresses himself to them and they to him as more and other than either can speak. It is in this place that things smell. The irrelevant birds fly away in front of the window. Here he has indigestion. It is a place he dies in. Into this space must come as actual material events, whether as the sounds of speech, the scratchings on the surface of paper which he constitutes as document, or directly anything he knows of the world. It has to happen here somehow if he is to experience it at all.

Entering the governing mode of our kind of society lifts the actor out of the immediate local and particular place in which he is in the body. He uses what becomes present to him in this place as a means to pass beyond it to the conceptual order. This mode of action creates then a bifurcation of consciousness, a bifurcation of course which is there for all those who participate in this mode of action. It establishes two modes of knowing and experiencing and doing, one located in the body and in the space which it occupies and moves into, the other which passes beyond it. Sociology is written in and aims at this second mode. Vide Bierstedt

> Sociology can liberate the mind from time and space themselves and remove it to a new and transcendental realm where it no longer depends upon these Aristotelian categories. (1966)

Women are outside and subservient to this structure. They have a very specific relation to it which anchors them into the local and particular phase of the bifurcated world. For both traditionally and as a matter of occupational practices in our society, the governing conceptual mode is appropriated by men and the world organized in the natural attitude, the home, is appropriated by (or assigned to) women (Smith, 1973).

It is a condition of a man's being able to enter and become absorbed in the conceptual mode that he does not have to focus his activities and interests upon his bodily existence. If he is to participate fully in the abstract mode of action, then he must be liberated also from having to attend to his needs, etc., in the concrete and particular. The organization of work and expectations in managerial and professional circles both constitutes and depends upon the alienation of man from his bodily and local existence. The structure of work and the structure of career take for granted that these matters are provided for in such a way that they will not interfere with his action and participation in that world. Providing for the liberation from the Aristotelian categories of which Bierstedt speaks, is a woman who keeps house for him, bears and cares for his children, washes his clothes, looks after him when his is sick and generally provides for the logistics of his bodily existence.

The place of women then in relation to this mode of action is that where the work is done to create conditions which facilitate his occupation of the conceptual mode of consciousness. The meeting of a man's physical needs, the organization of his daily life, even the consistency of expressive background, are made maximally congruent with his commitment. A similar relation exists for women who work in and around the professional and managerial scene. They do those things which give concrete form to the conceptual activities. They do the clerical work, the computer programming, the interviewing for the survey, the nursing, the secretarial work. At almost every point women mediate for men the relation between the conceptual mode of action and the actual concrete forms in which it is and must be realized, and the actual material conditions upon which it depends.

Marx's concept of alienation is applicable here in a modified form. The simplest formulation of alienation posits a relation between the work an individual does and an external order which oppresses her, such that the harder she works the more she strengthens the order which oppresses her. This is the situation of women in this relation. The more successful women are in mediating the world of concrete particulars so that men do not have to become engaged with (and therefore conscious of) that world as a condition to their abstract activities, the more complete man's absorption in it, the more effective the authority of that world and the more total women's subservience to it. And also the more complete the dichotomy between the two worlds, and the estrangement between them.

Women sociologists stand at the centre of a contradiction in the relation of our discipline to our experience of the world. Transcending that contradiction means setting up a different kind of relation than that which we discover in the routine practice of our worlds.

The theories, concepts and methods of our discipline claim to account for, or to be capable of accounting for and analyzing the same world as that which we experience directly. But these theories, concepts and methods have been organizing around and built up out of a way of knowing the world which takes for granted the boundaries of an experience in the same medium which it is constituted. It therefore takes for granted and subsumes without examining the conditions of its existence. It is not capable of analyzing its own relation to its conditions because the sociologist as actual person in an actual concrete setting has been cancelled in the procedures which objectify and separate him from his knowledge. Thus the linkage which points back to its conditions is lacking.

For women those conditions are central as a direct practical matter, to be somehow solved in the decision to take up a sociological career. The relation between ourselves as practicing sociologists and ourselves as working women is continually visible to us, a central feature of experience of the world, so that the bifurcation of consciousness becomes for us a daily chasm which is to be crossed, on the one side of which is this special conceptual activity of thought, research, teaching, administration and on the other the world of concrete practical activities in keeping things clean, managing somehow the house and household and the children a world in which the particularities of persons in their full organic immediacy (cleaning up the vomit, changing the diapers, as well as feeding) are inescapable. Even if we don't have that as a direct contingency in our lives, we are aware of that as something that our becoming may be inserted into as a possible predicate.

It is also present for us to discover that the discipline is not one which we enter and occupy on the same terms as men enter and occupy it. We do not fully appropriate its authority, i.e., the right to author and authorize the acts and knowing and thinking which are the acts and knowing and thinking of the discipline as it is thought. We cannot therefore command the inner principles of our action. That remains lodged outside us. The frames of reference which order the terms upon which inquiry and discussion are conducted originate with men. The subjects of sociological sentences (if they have a subject) are male. The sociologist is "he." And even before we become conscious of our sex as the basis of an exclusion (*they* are not talking about *us*), we nonetheless do not fully enter ourselves as the subjects of its statements, since we must suspend our sex, and suspend our knowledge of who we are as well as who it is that in fact is speaking and of whom. Therefore we do not fully participate in the declarations and formulations of its mode of consciousness. The externalization of sociology as a profession which I have described above becomes for women a double estrangement.

There is then for women a basic organization of their experience which displays for them the structure of the bifurcated consciousness. At the same time it attenuates their commitment to a sociology which aims at an externalized body of knowledge based on an organization of experience which excludes their and excludes them expect in a subordinate relation.

Women's perspective, as I have analyzed it here, discredits sociology's claim to constitute an objective knowledge independent of the sociologist's situation. Its conceptual procedures, methods and relevances are seen to organize its subject matter from a determinate position in society. This critical disclosure becomes then the basis for an alternative way of thinking sociology. If sociology cannot avoid being situated, then sociology should take that as its beginning and build it into its methodological and theoretical strategies. As it is now, these separate a sociologically constructed world from that which is known in direct experience and it is precisely that separation which must be undone.

I am not proposing an immediate and radical transformation of the subject matter and methods of the discipline nor the junking of everything that has gone before. What I am suggesting is more in the nature of a re-organization which changes the relation of the sociologist to the object of her knowledge and changes also her problematic. This re-organization involves first placing the sociologist where she is actually situated, namely at the beginning of those acts by which she knows or will come to know; and second, making her direct experience of the everyday world the primary ground of her knowledge.

The only way of knowing a socially constructed world is knowing it from within. We can never stand outside it. A relation in which sociological phenomena are objectified and presented as external to and independent of the observer is itself a special social practice also known from within. The relation of observer and object of observation, of sociologist to "subject," is a specialized social relationship. Even to be a stranger is to enter a world constituted from within as strange. The strangeness itself is the mode in which it is experienced. [...]

An alternative sociology must be reflexive (Gouldner, 1971), i.e., one that preserves in it the presence, concerns and experience of the sociologist as knower and discoverer.

To begin from direct experience and to return to it as a constraint or "test" of the adequacy of a systematic knowledge is to begin from where we are located bodily. The actualities of our everyday world are already socially organized. Settings, equipment, "environment," schedules, occasions, etc., as well as the enterprises and routines of actors are socially produced and concretely and symbolically organized prior to our practice. By beginning from her original and immediate knowledge of her world, sociology offers a way of making its socially organized properties first observable and then problematic.

Let me make it clear that when I speak of "experience" I do not use the term as a synonym for "perspective." Nor in proposing a sociology grounded in the sociologist's actual experience, am I recommending the self-indulgence of inner exploration or any other enterprise with self as sole focus and object. Such subjectivist interpretations of "experience" are themselves an aspect of that organization of consciousness which bifurcates it and transports us into mind country while stashing away the concrete conditions and practices upon which it depends. We can never escape the circles of our own heads if we accept that as our territory. Rather the sociologist's investigation of our directly experienced world as a problem is a mode of discovering or rediscovering the society from within. She begins from her own original but tacit knowledge and from within the acts by which she brings it into her grasp in making it observable and in understanding how it works. She aims not at a reiteration of what she already (tacitly) knows, but at an exploration through that of what passes beyond it and is deeply implicated in how it is.

Women's situation in sociology discloses to her a typical bifurcate structure with the abstracted conceptual practices on the one hand and the concrete realizations, the maintenance routines, etc., on the other. Taking each for granted depends upon being fully situated in one or the other so that the other does not appear in contradiction to it. Women's direct experience places her a step back where we can recognize the uneasiness that comes in sociology from its claim to be about the world we live in and its failure to account for or even describe its actual features as we find them in living them. The aim of an alternative sociology would be to develop precisely that capacity from that beginning so that it might be a means to anyone of understanding how the world comes about for her and how it is organized so that it happens to her as it does in her experience.

Though such a sociology would not be exclusively for or done by women it does begin from the analysis and critique originating in their situation. Its elaboration therefore depends upon a grasp of that which is prior to and fuller than its formulation. It is a little like the problem of making a formal description of the grammar of a language. The linguist depends and always refers back to the competent speakers' sense of what is correct usage, what makes sense, etc. In her own language she depends to a large extent upon her own competence. Women are native speakers of this situation and in explicating it or its implications and realizing them conceptually, they have that relation to it of knowing it before it has been said.

The incomprehensibility of the determinations of our immediate local world is for women a particularly striking metaphor. It recovers an inner organization in common with their typical relation to the world. For women's activities and existence are determined outside them and beyond the world which is their "place." They are oriented by their training and by the daily practices which confirm it, towards the demands and initiations and authority of others. But more than that, the very organization of the world which has been assigned to them as the primary locus of their being is determined by and subordinate to the corporate organization of society (Smith, 1973). Thus as I have expressed her relation to sociology, its logic lies elsewhere. She lacks the inner principle of her own activity. She does not grasp how it is put together because it is determined elsewhere than where she is. As a sociologist then the grasp and exploration of her own experience as a method of discovering society restores to her a centre which in this enterprise at least is wholly hers.

Note

1. This paper was originally prepared for the meetings of the American Academy for the Advancement of Science (Pacific Division) Eugene, Oregon, June, 1972. The original draft of this paper was typed by Jane Lemke and the final version by Mildred Brown. I am indebted to both of them.

References

Bierstedt, Robert. 1966. "Sociology and General Education." In Charles H. Page (ed.), *Sociology and Contemporary Education*. New York: Random House.

Briggs, Jean L. 1970. *Never in Anger*. Cambridge, Mass.: Harvard University Press.

Gouldner, Alvin. 1971. *The Coming Crisis in Western Sociology*. London: Heinemann Educational Books.

Smith, Dorothy E. 1973. "Women, the Family and Corporate Capitalism." In M.L. Stephenson (ed.), *Women in Canada*. Toronto: Newpress.

CHAPTER 7

Power/Knowledge

Michel Foucault

I would say, then, that what has emerged in the course of the last ten or fifteen years is a sense of the increasing vulnerability to criticism of things, institutions, practices, discourses. A certain fragility has been discovered in the very bedrock of existence—even, and perhaps above all, in those aspects of it that are most familiar, most solid and most intimately related to our bodies and to our everyday behaviour. But together with this sense of instability and this amazing efficacy of discontinuous, particular and local criticism, one in fact also discovers something that perhaps was not initially foreseen, something one might describe as precisely the inhibiting effect of global, *totalitarian theories*. It is not that these global theories have not provided nor continue to provide in a fairly consistent fashion useful tools for local research: Marxism and psychoanalysis are proofs of this. But I believe these tools have only been provided on the condition that the theoretical unity of these discourses was in some sense put in abeyance, or at least curtailed, divided, overthrown, caricatured, theatricalised, or what you will. In each case, the attempt to think in terms of a totality has in fact proved a hindrance to research.

So, the main point to be gleaned from these events of the last fifteen years, their predominant feature, is the *local* character of criticism. That should not, I believe, be taken to mean that its qualities are those of an obtuse, naive or primitive empiricism; nor is it a soggy eclecticism, an opportunism that laps up any and every kind of theoretical approach; nor does it mean a self-imposed ascetism which taken by itself would reduce to the worst kind of theoretical impoverishment. I believe that what this essentially local character of criticism indicates in reality is an autonomous, non-centralised kind of theoretical production, one that is to say whose validity is not dependent on the approval of the established regimes of thought.

It is here that we touch upon another feature of these events that has been manifest for some time now: it seems to me that this local criticism has proceeded by means of what one might term "a return of knowledge." What I mean by that phrase is this: it is a fact that we have repeatedly encountered, at least at a superficial level, in the course of most recent times, an entire thematic to the effect that it is not theory but life that matters, not knowledge but reality, not books but money etc.; but it also seems to me that over and above, and arising out of this thematic, there is something else to which we are witness, and which we might describe as an *insurrection of subjugated knowledges*.

By subjugated knowledges I mean two things: on the one hand, I am referring to the historical contents that have been buried and disguised in a functionalist coherence or formal systemisation. Concretely, it is not a semiology of the life of the asylum, it is not even a sociology of delinquency, that has made it possible to produce an effective criticism of the asylum and likewise of the prison, but rather the immediate emergence of historical contents. And this is simply because only the historical contents allow us to rediscover the ruptural effects of conflict and struggle that the order imposed by functionalist or systematising thought is designed to mask. Subjugated knowledges are thus those blocs of historical knowledge which were present but disguised within the body of functionalist and systematising theory and which criticism—which obviously draws upon scholarship—has been able to reveal.

On the other hand, I believe that by subjugated knowledges one should understand something else, something which in a sense is altogether different, namely, a whole set of knowledges that have been disqualified as inadequate to their task or insufficiently elaborated: naive knowledges, located low down on the hierarchy, beneath the required level of cognition or scientificity. I also believe that it is through the reemergence of these low-ranking knowledges, these unqualified, even directly disqualified knowledges (such as that of the psychiatric patient, of the ill person, of the nurse, of the doctor—parallel and marginal as they are to the knowledge of medicine—that of the delinquent, etc.), and which involve what I would call a popular knowledge (*le savoir des gens*) though it is far from being a general commonsense knowledge, but is on the contrary a particular, local, regional knowledge, a differential knowledge incapable of unanimity and which owes its force only to the harshness with which it is opposed by everything surrounding it—that it is through the reappearance of this knowledge, of these local popular knowledges, these disqualified knowledges, that criticism performs its work.

However, there is a strange kind of paradox in the desire to assign to this same category of subjugated knowledges what are on the one hand the products of meticulous, erudite, exact historical knowledge, and on the other hand local and specific knowledges which have no common meaning and which are in some fashion allowed to fall into disuse whenever they are not effectively and explicitly maintained in themselves. Well, it seems to me that our critical discourses of the last fifteen years have in effect discovered their essential force in this association between the buried knowledges of erudition and those disqualified from the hierarchy of knowledges and sciences.

In the two cases—in the case of the erudite as in that of the disqualified knowledges—with what in fact were these buried, subjugated knowledges really concerned? They were concerned with a *historical knowledge of struggles*. In the specialised areas of erudition as in the disqualified, popular knowledge there lay the memory of hostile encounters which even up to this day have been confined to the margins of knowledge.

What emerges out of this is something one might call a genealogy, or rather a multiplicity of genealogical researches, a painstaking rediscovery of struggles together with the rude memory of their conflicts. And these genealogies, that are the combined product of an erudite knowledge and a popular knowledge, were not possible and could not even have been attempted except on one condition, namely that the tyranny of globalising discourses with their hierarchy and all their privileges of a theoretical *avant-garde* was eliminated.

Let us give the term *genealogy* to the union of erudite knowledge and local memories which allows us to establish a historical knowledge of struggles and to make use of this knowledge tactically today. This then will be a provisional definition of the genealogies which I have attempted to compile with you over the last few years.

You are well aware that this research activity, which one can thus call genealogical, has nothing at all to do with an opposition between the abstract unity of theory and the concrete multiplicity of facts. It has nothing at all to do with a disqualification of the speculative dimension which opposes to it, in the name of some kind of scientism, the rigour of well-established knowledges. It is not therefore via an empiricism that the genealogical project unfolds, nor even via a positivism in the ordinary sense of that term. What it really does is to entertain the claims to attention of local, discontinuous, disqualified, illegitimate knowledges against the claims of a unitary body of theory which would filter, hierarchise, and order them in the name of some true knowledge and some arbitrary idea of what constitutes a science and its objects. Genealogies are therefore not positivistic returns to a more careful or exact form of science. They are precisely anti-sciences. Not that they vindicate a lyrical right to ignorance or non-knowledge: it is not that they are concerned to deny knowledge or that they esteem the virtues of direct cognition and base their practice upon an immediate experience that escapes encapsulation in knowledge. It is not that with which we are concerned. We are concerned, rather, with the insurrection of knowledges that are opposed primarily not to the contents, methods or concepts of a science, but to the effects of the centralising powers which are linked to the institution and functioning of an organised scientific discourse within a society such as ours. Nor does it basically matter all that much that this institutionalisation of scientific discourse is embodied in a university, or, more generally, in an educational apparatus, in a theoretical-commercial institution such as psychoanalysis or within the framework of reference that is provided by a political system such as Marxism; for it is really against the effects of the power of a discourse that is considered to be scientific that the genealogy must wage its struggle.

To be more precise, I would remind you how numerous have been those who for many years now, probably for more than half a century, have questioned whether Marxism was, or was not, a science. One might say that the same issue has been posed, and continues to be posed, in the case of psychoanalysis, or even worse, in that of the semiology of literary texts. But to all these demands of: "Is it or is it not a science?", the genealogies or the genealogists would reply: "If you really want to know, the fault lies in your very determination to make a science out of Marxism or psychoanalysis or this or that study." If we have any objection against Marxism, it lies in the fact that it could effectively be a science. In more detailed terms, I would say that even before we can know the extent to which something such as Marxism or psychoanalysis can be compared to a scientific practice in its everyday functioning, its rules of construction, its working concepts, that even before we can pose the question of a formal and structural analogy between Marxist or psychoanalytic discourse, it is surely necessary to question ourselves about our aspirations to the kind of power that is presumed to accompany such a science. It is surely the following kinds of question that would need to be posed: What types of knowledge do you want to disqualify in the very instant of your demand: "Is it a science?" Which speaking, discoursing subjects—which subjects of experience and knowledge—do you then want to "diminish" when you say: "I who conduct this discourse am conducting a scientific discourse, and I am a scientist"? Which theoretical-political *avant garde* do you want to enthrone in order to isolate it from all the discontinuous forms of knowledge that circulate about it? When I see you straining to establish the scientificity of Marxism I do not really think that you are demonstrating once and for all that Marxism has a rational structure and that therefore its propositions are the outcome of verifiable procedures; for me you are doing something altogether different, you are investing Marxist discourses and those who uphold them with the effects of a power which the West since Medieval times has attributed to science and has reserved for those engaged in scientific discourse.

By comparison, then, and in contrast to the various projects which aim to inscribe knowledges in the hierarchical order of power associated with science, a genealogy should be seen as a kind of attempt to emancipate historical knowledges from that subjection, to render them, that is, capable of opposition and of struggle against the coercion of a theoretical, unitary, formal, and scientific discourse. It is based on a reactivation of local knowledges—of minor knowledges, as Deleuze might call them—in opposition to the scientific hierarchisation of knowledges and the effects intrinsic to their power: this, then, is the project of these disordered and fragmentary genealogies. If we were to characterise it in two terms, then "archaeology" would be the appropriate methodology of this analysis of local discursivities, and "genealogy" would be the tactics whereby, on the basis of the descriptions of these local discursivities, the subjected knowledges which were thus released would be brought into play.

The course of study that I have been following until now—roughly since 1970/71—has been concerned with the *how* of power. [...]

This new mechanism of power is more dependent upon bodies and what they do than upon the Earth and its products. It is a mechanism of power which permits time and labour, rather than wealth and commodities, to be extracted from bodies. It is a type of power which is constantly exercised by means of surveillance rather than in a discontinuous manner by means of a system of levies or obligations distributed over time. It presupposes a tightly knit grid of material coercions rather than the physical existence of a sovereign. It is ultimately dependent upon the principle, which introduces a genuinely new economy of power, that one must be able simultaneously both to increase the subjected forces and to improve the force and efficacy of that which subjects them.

This type of power is in every aspect the antithesis of that mechanism of power which the theory of sovereignty described or sought to transcribe. The latter is linked to a form of power that is exercised over the Earth and its products, much more than over human bodies and their operations. The theory of sovereignty is something which refers to the displacement and appropriation on the part of power, not of time and labour, but of goods and wealth. It allows discontinuous obligations distributed over time to be given legal expression but it does not allow for the codification of a continuous surveillance. It enables power to be founded in the physical existence of the sovereign, but not in continuous and permanent systems of surveillance. The theory of sovereignty permits the foundation of an absolute power in the absolute expenditure of power. It does not allow for a calculation of power in terms of the minimum expenditure for the maximum return.

This new type of power, which can no longer be formulated in terms of sovereignty, is, I believe, one of the great inventions of bourgeois society. It has been a fundamental instrument in the constitution of industrial capitalism and of the type of society that is its accompaniment. This non-sovereign power, which lies outside the form of sovereignty, is disciplinary power. Impossible to describe in the terminology of the theory of sovereignty from which it differs so radically, this disciplinary power ought by rights to have led to the disappearance of the grand juridical edifice created by that theory. But in reality, the theory of sovereignty has continued not only to exist as an ideology of right, but also to provide the organising principle of the legal codes which Europe acquired in the nineteenth century, beginning with the Napoleonic Code.

Why has the theory of sovereignty persisted in this fashion as an ideology and an organising principle of these major legal codes? For two reasons, I believe. On the one hand, it has been, in the eighteenth and again in the nineteenth century, a permanent instrument of criticism of the monarchy and of all the obstacles that can thwart the development of disciplinary society. But at the same time, the theory of sovereignty, and the organisation of a legal code centred upon it, have allowed a system of right to be superimposed upon the mechanisms of discipline in such a way as to conceal its actual procedures, the element of domination inherent in its techniques, and to guarantee to everyone, by virtue of the sovereignty of the State, the exercise of his proper sovereign rights. The juridical systems—and this applies both to their codification and to their theorization—have enabled sovereignty to be democratized through the constitution of a public right articulated upon collective sovereignty, while at the same time this democratisation of sovereignty was fundamentally determined by and grounded in mechanisms of disciplinary coercion.

To put this in more rigorous terms, one might say that once it became necessary for disciplinary constraints to be exercised through mechanisms of domination and yet at the same time for their effective exercise of power to be disguised, a theory of sovereignty was required to make an appearance at the level of the legal apparatus, and to re-emerge in its codes. Modern society, then, from the nineteenth century up to our own day, has been characterised on the one hand, by a legislation, a discourse, an organisation based on public right, whose principle of articulation is the social body and the delegative status of each citizen; and, on the other hand, by a closely linked grid of disciplinary coercions whose purpose is in fact to assure the cohesion of this same social body. Though a theory of right is a necessary companion to this grid, it cannot in any event provide the terms of its endorsement. Hence these two limits, a right of sovereignty and a mechanism of discipline, which define, I believe, the arena in which power is exercised. But these two limits are so heterogeneous that they cannot possibly be reduced to each other. The powers of modern society are exercised through, on the basis of, and by virtue of, this very heterogeneity between a public right of sovereignty and a polymorphous disciplinary mechanism. This is not to suggest that there is on the one hand an explicit and scholarly system of right which is that of sovereignty, and, on the other hand, obscure and unspoken disciplines which carry out their shadowy operations in the depths, and thus constitute the bedrock of the great mechanism of power. In reality, the disciplines have their own discourse. They engender, for the reasons of which we spoke earlier, apparatuses of knowledge (*savoir*) and a multiplicity of new domains of understanding. They are extraordinarily inventive participants in the order of these knowledge-producing apparatuses. Disciplines are the bearers of a discourse, but this cannot be the discourse of right. The discourse of discipline has nothing in common with that of law, rule, or sovereign will. The disciplines may well be the carriers of a discourse that speaks of a rule, but this is not the juridical rule deriving from sovereignty, but a natural rule, a norm. The code they come to define is not that of law but that of normalisation. Their reference is to a theoretical horizon which of necessity has nothing in common with the edifice of right. It is human science which constitutes their domain, and clinical knowledge their jurisprudence.

In short, what I have wanted to demonstrate in the course of the last few years is not the manner in which at the advance front of the exact sciences the uncertain, recalcitrant, confused dominion of human behaviour has little by little been annexed to science: it is not through some advancement in the rationality of the exact sciences that the human sciences are gradually constituted. I believe that the process which has really rendered the discourse of the human sciences possible is the juxtaposition, the encounter between two lines of approach, two mechanisms, two absolutely heterogeneous types of discourse: on the one hand there is the reorganisation of right that invests sovereignty, and on the other, the mechanics of the coercive forces whose exercise takes a disciplinary form. And I believe that in our own times power is exercised simultaneously through this right and these techniques and that these techniques and these discourses, to which the disciplines give rise invade the area of right so that the procedures of normalisation come to be ever more constantly engaged in the colonisation of those of law. I believe that all this can explain the global functioning of what I would call a *society of normalisation*. I mean, more precisely, that disciplinary normalisations come into ever greater conflict with the juridical systems of sovereignty: their incompatibility with each other is ever more acutely felt and apparent; some kind of arbitrating discourse is made ever more necessary, a type of power and of knowledge that the sanctity of science would render neutral. It is precisely in the extension of medicine that we see, in some sense, not so much the linking as the perpetual exchange or encounter of mechanisms of discipline with the principle of right. The developments of medicine, the general medicalisation of behaviours, conducts, discourses, desires, etc., take place at the point of intersection between the two heterogeneous levels of discipline and sovereignty. For this reason, against these usurpations by the disciplinary mechanisms, against this ascent of a power that is tied to scientific knowledge, we find that there is no solid recourse available to us today, such being our situation, except that which lies precisely in the return to a theory of right organised around sovereignty and articulated upon its ancient principle. When today one wants to object in some way to the disciplines and all the effects of power and knowledge that are linked to them, what is it that one does, concretely, in real life, what do the Magistrates Union or other similar institutions do, if not precisely appeal to this canon of right, this famous, formal right, that is said to be bourgeois, and which in reality is the right of sovereignty? But I believe that we find ourselves here in a kind of blind alley: it is not through recourse to sovereignty against discipline that the effects of disciplinary power can be limited, because sovereignty and disciplinary mechanisms are two absolutely integral constituents of the general mechanism of power in our society.

If one wants to look for a non-disciplinary form of power, or rather, to struggle against disciplines and disciplinary power, it is not towards the ancient right of sovereignty that one should turn, but towards the possibility of a new form of right, one which must indeed be anti-disciplinarian, but at the same time liberated from the principle of sovereignty. It is at this point that we once more come up against the notion of repression, whose use in this context I believe to be doubly unfortunate. On the one hand, it contains an obscure reference to a certain theory of sovereignty, the sovereignty of the sovereign rights of the individual, and on the other hand, its usage introduces a system of psychological reference points borrowed from the human sciences, that is to say, from discourses and practices that belong to the disciplinary realm. I believe that the notion of repression remains a juridical-disciplinary notion whatever the critical use one would make of it. To this extent the critical application of the notion of repression is found to be vitiated and nullified from the outset by the two-fold juridical and disciplinary reference it contains to sovereignty on the one hand and to normalisation on the other.

CHAPTER 8

Revisiting Gramsci

Diana Coben

The problem for would-be radical adult educators in the 1990s—those who want change "from the root" and who see the education of adults as having the potential for progressive social purpose—is to envisage the directions that change from the root might take and the nature of those progressive social purposes, at a time when the very construction of the social and of the self is being called into question (McRobbie, 1994).

In these uncertain times I want to suggest that we should revisit the ideas of a Marxist revolutionary and victim of fascism who featured posthumously as a "radical hero" in the literature of adult education in the 1980s: Antonio Gramsci (1891–1937).[1]

Why Gramsci? The uncertainty of our times makes reading Gramsci, who struggled to make sense of what were to become catastrophic uncertainties in his own life and times, particularly apposite. Gramsci teaches us to see the education of adults as part of a wider political strategy requiring organisation and direction (for Gramsci, through the political party of the working class) as well as enthusiasm, commitment and hard work; to analyse the relations of power in a particular political conjuncture pertaining at a precise historical moment; to see the state and civil society as a complex set of institutions and forces, rather than as a monolithic entity.

I believe we can learn much from his notion of politics as a moral as well as a practico-political struggle to create and maintain hegemony among disparate groups; his is a politics of difference which presages many of the current debates within postmodernism and engages with adult educators' concern to respect the subjecthood of adult learners—and adult educators. His conceptualisation of the role of intellectuals offers a way of theorising what it means to teach a fellow adult which breaks with sterile debates about elitism. As Ireland shows in his analysis of popular education in Brazil (1987), Gramsci offers us analytical tools to understand the purpose and content of the education of adults in a wider political context. Furthermore, Gramsci's conception of politics as educative is attractive to radical adult educators who see their professional practice as a form of political activity. His broad interpretation of education as a lifelong process makes his ideas particularly interesting to adult educators, while his theory of intellectuals expresses the belief that is arguably the defining characteristic of the committed adult educator: the belief that everyone is an intellectual, that everyone can and does learn throughout life.

So who was Gramsci? He was born in Sardinia and grew up in poverty and in poor health. Despite his difficulties he won a scholarship for poor students to the University of Turin and there cut his political teeth as a leader of the Factory Council movement, organising occupations of the factories by the Turin proletariat in 1919. He was a founder-member and became leader of the Italian communist party and a prolific political journalist whose interests spanned the theatre, language, literature, education and folklore as well as the more usual, concerns of a communist leader with political tactics and strategy. Imprisoned by the fascist government for the last eleven years of his life, Gramsci struggled to develop his thought against a background of political defeat, censorship of his writing and his own physical deterioration. In his prison writings and in his political journalism, Gramsci advocates a revolutionary politics, organised through the revolutionary party of the working class and informed by rigorous study within an historical and dialectical framework, constantly relating theory and practice. His is an open, questioning Marxism, not at all of the "grand narrative" type.

However, this is just one among many different "Gramscis" which have emerged since his death: there is also Gramsci the Leninist; Gramsci the Eurocommunist; Gramsci the culturalist—to name but a few (see Forgacs, 1989, for a discussion of Gramsci's posthumous "career" in relation to Marxism in Britain). With the rise of interest in the ideas of Michel Foucault and other postmodernists in the 1990s, Gramsci has emerged as a precursor of post-Marxism (Laclau with Mouffe, 1990: 121) of postmodernist and feminist critical theory (Holub, 1992) and as the theorist of a new, post-liberal form of democracy (Golding, 1992).

This proliferation of interpretations has been encouraged by the fact that the Prison Notebooks, on which Gramsci's reputation as a major twentieth-century Marxist theorist largely rest, are peculiarly open to interpretation. Gramsci died before he was able to edit and organise his notes, which are fragmentary and often cryptic, written partly in code to deceive the prison censor. As a result, political, cultural and educational theorists and politicians of the left are still arguing over his legacy.

Gramsci's Concept of Hegemony

Gramsci's first mention of hegemony comes in the essay he was writing at the time of his arrest in 1926: "Some Aspects of the Southern Question" (SPW II: 441–462) about the relationship between the south and the north in Italy (an unresolved issue which has resurfaced recently with the emergence of the Northern League). Gramsci regarded the essay as short and superficial (LP: 79) and Ernesto Laclau and Chantal Mouffe point out that its logic is "still only of preconstituted sectoral interests" (Laclau and Mouffe, 1985: 66).

Gramsci developed the concept of hegemony in the Prison Notebooks (SPN: 52–120) as part of his elaboration of a strategy for revolution in situations where the state holds power in reserve, through the institutions of civil society, rather than through force alone. This strategy he calls "war of position," by contrast with the "war of movement" or direct assault on the state. The war of position entails a process of the establishment of hegemony during what might be a long period before the seizure of state power by the revolutionaries.

Gramsci was not the first Marxist to use the term hegemony, which was in common use by Russian Marxists from the early 1880s to denote a strategy through which a proletariat-led alliance, including intellectuals and peasants, would overthrow Tsarism. Lenin developed the notion in *What Is to Be Done?* in 1902, stressing the role of the revolutionary vanguard in developing leadership based on the most advanced theory (Lenin, 1947). Gramsci was certainly aware of Lenin's usage, which, he said, "gave new importance to the front of cultural struggle and constructed the doctrine of hegemony as the complement to the theory of the state as force" (Gramsci quoted by Buci-Glucksmann, 1980: 390).

In Gramsci's expanded usage in the Prison Notebooks, hegemony comprises the:

> "spontaneous" consent given by the great masses of the population to the general direction imposed on social life by the dominant fundamental group [i.e., class]; this consent is "historically" caused by the prestige (and consequently confidence) which the dominant group enjoys because of its position and function in the world of production. (SPN: 12)

However, Gramsci was no economic determinist and he rejects the simplistic idea of a purely instrumental class state. Instead, the state successfully maintains hegemony in so far as it succeeds in presenting dominant class interests as if they were universal:

> It is true that the state is seen as the organ of one particular class, destined to create favourable conditions for the latter's maximum expansion. But the development and expansion of the particular group are conceived of and presented, as being the motor force of a universal expansion, of a development of all the "national" energies. (SPN: 182)

For Gramsci, hegemonic leadership is always contested, never merely an automatic function of power. As Green points out, "A hegemonic order represents a temporary settlement, the ideological balance in favour of the ruling class, not the homogeneous substance of an imposed class ideology" (Green, 1990: 94). Hegemony must be actively maintained and in seeking to maintain hegemony, the state exercises an active, ethical function, an idea Gramsci borrowed from Benedetto Croce and which, ironically, was also used by Mussolini (SPN: 258f). For Gramsci, therefore,

> every relationship of "hegemony" is necessarily an educational relationship [and] every State is ethical in as much as one of its most important functions is to raise the great mass of the population to a particular cultural and moral level, a level (or type) which corresponds to the needs of the productive forces for development, and hence to the interests of the ruling classes. (SPN: 350)

Gramsci describes the parliamentary regime as a classical example of the normal exercise of hegemony

> characterised by the combination of force and consent, which balance each other reciprocally, without force predominating excessively over consent. Indeed, the attempt is always made to ensure that force will appear to be based on the consent of the majority, expressed by the so-called organs of public opinion—newspapers and associations (SPN: 80 n49).

In his exploration of ways in which an alternative, working-class hegemony could be established, Gramsci, for the first time, described the ways in which the ideas of the ruling class come to hold sway over subordinate classes to such an extent that they constitute the limits of common sense for most people most of the time—a situation described by Raymond Williams as "saturating the consciousness of a society" (Williams, 1973). Gramsci's concept of hegemony thus appears to echo Marx' and Engels' statement in *The German Ideology*:

> The ideas of the ruling class are in every epoch the ruling ideas, i.e., the class which is the ruling material force of society, is at the same time its ruling intellectual force (Marx and Engels, 1974: 64).

However, *The German Ideology* remained unpublished until 1932, six years into Gramsci's term of imprisonment, and there is no evidence that he knew of it. Instead, as Forgacs (SCW: 164) reports, Lo Piparo has argued that Gramsci's lifelong interest in historical linguistics may have been an important influence on his conception of hegemony. Lo Piparo's persuasive thesis is that Gramsci extended into the political sphere concepts developed to explain the process by which speakers of a language affect speakers of other languages with whom they come into contact. In other words, as Germino points out (1990: 30), Gramsci's theory of hegemony "had its roots prior to his intellectual encounter with Marx." Perhaps the truth is that Gramsci's concept of hegemony is so rich and multi-faceted precisely because it draws on more than one source.

For Gramsci, the antithesis of hegemony, "political government" or "direct domination," comes into play when consent is lacking. It is the

> apparatus of State coercive power which "legally" enforces discipline on those groups who do not "consent" either actively or passively. This apparatus is, however, constituted for the whole of society in anticipation of moments of crisis of command and direction when spontaneous consent has failed. (SPN: 12)

For a revolution to be successful necessitates victory in both the spheres of hegemony and direct domination and Gramsci is thus able to see the revolutionary process as an intellectual, moral and educational phenomenon, as well as a matter of practical politics. Indeed, Gramsci's expansion of the political, placing it, as Golding (1992: 131) says, "at the heart of all meaning," means precisely that intellectual, moral and educational phenomena are political phenomena.

Note

1. This article is based on extracts from my PhD thesis: 'Radical Heroes: Gramsci, Freire and the Liberal Tradition in Adult Education' (Coben, 1992). The thesis is to be published in an abridged form by Garland Publishing, New York. See Davidson (1977) for an excellent intellectual biography of Gramsci.

References

LIST OF ABBREVIATIONS OF WORKS CITED

LP

Letters from Prison by Antonio Gramsci, selected, translated and introduced by Lynne Lawner, Lawrence and Wishart, 1975

SCW

Selections from *Cultural Writings* by Antonio Gramsci, edited by David Forgacs and Geoffrey Nowell Smith, translated by William Boelhower, Lawrence and Wishart, 1985

SPN

Selections from the *Prison Notebooks* of Antonio Gramsci, edited and translated by Quintin Hoare and Geoffrey Nowell Smith, Lawrence and Wishart, 1971. Referred to throughout this article as the Prison Notebooks

SPW II

Selections from *Political Writings* (1921–26) by Antonio Gramsci, translated and edited by Quintin Hoare, Lawrence and Wishart, 1978

OTHER WORKS CITED

Buci-Glucksmann, C. (1980). Gramsci and the State, translated by David Fernbach, Lawrence and Wishart

Coben, D. (1992). 'Radical Heroes: Gramsci, Freire and the Liberal Tradition in Adult Education' unpublished PhD thesis, University of Kent at Canterbury

Davidson, A. (1977). Antonio Gramsci: Towards an Intellectual Biography, Merlin Press

Forgacs, D. (1989). 'Gramsci and Marxism in Britain', New Left Review No 176 July/August 1989, pp 70–88

Germino, D. (1990). Antonio Gramsci: Architect of a New Politics, Baton Rouge and London: Louisiana State University

Golding, S. (1992). Gramsci's Democratic Theory: Contributions to a Post-Liberal Democracy, Toronto: University of Toronto Press

Holub, R. (1992). Antonio Gramsci: Beyond Marxism and Postmodernism, Routledge

Ireland, T. D. (1987). Antonio Gramsci and Adult Education: Reflections on the Brazilian Experience, (Manchester Monographs), Manchester: The Centre for Adult and Higher Education, University of Manchester

Laclau, E. with Mouffe, C. (1990), 'Post-Marxism without apologies' in E. Laclau, New Reflections on the Revolution of Our Time, Verso

Laclau, E. and Mouffe, C. (1985). Hegemony and Socialist Strategy: Towards a Radical Democratic Politics, Verso

Lenin, V. I. (1947). What is to be Done?, Moscow: Progress Publishers

McRobbie, A. (1994). 'Feminism, postmodernism and the real me' in M. Perryman (ed), Altered States. Postmodernism, Politics, Culture, Lawrence and Wishart, pp 113–132

Marx, K. and Engels, F. (1974). The German Ideology, (2nd ed), edited and introduced by C. J. Arthur, Lawrence and Wishart

Williams, R. (1973). 'Base and superstructure in Marxist theory', New Left Review No 82, December 1973, pp 3–16

CHAPTER 9

Racial Formation in the United States

Michael Omi and Howard Winant

In 1982–83, Susie Guillory Phipps unsuccessfully sued the Louisiana Bureau of Vital Records to change her racial classification from black to white. The descendant of an eighteenth-century white planter and a black slave, Phipps was designated "black" in her birth certificate in accordance with a 1970 state law which declared anyone with at least one-thirty-second "Negro blood" to be black. The legal battle raised intriguing questions about the concept of race, its meaning in contemporary society, and its use (and abuse) in public policy. Assistant Attorney General Ron Davis defended the law by pointing out that some type of racial classification was necessary to comply with federal record-keeping requirements and to facilitate programs for the prevention of genetic diseases. Phipps's attorney, Brian Begue, argued that the assignment of racial categories on birth certificates was unconstitutional and that the one-thirty-second designation was inaccurate. He called on a retired Tulane University professor who cited research indicating that most whites have one-twentieth "Negro" ancestry. In the end, Phipps lost. The court upheld a state law which quantified racial identity, and. in so doing affirmed the legality of assigning individuals to specific racial groupings.[1]

The Phipps case illustrates the continuing dilemma of defining race and establishing its meaning in institutional life. Today, to assert that variations in human physiognomy are racially based is to enter a constant and intense debate. *Scientific* interpretations of race have not been alone in sparking heated controversy; *religious* perspectives have done so as well.[2] Most centrally, of course, race has been a matter of *political* contention. This has been particularly true in the United States, where the concept of race has varied enormously over time without ever leaving the center stage of US history.

What Is Race?

Race consciousness, and its articulation in theories of race, is largely a modern phenomenon. When European explorers in the New World "discovered" people who looked different than themselves, these "natives" challenged then existing conceptions of the origins of the human species, and raised disturbing questions as to whether *all* could be considered in the same "family of man."[3] Religious debates flared over the attempt to reconcile the Bible with the existence of "racially distinct" people. Arguments took place over creation itself, as theories of polygenesis questioned whether God had made only one species of humanity ("monogenesis"). Europeans wondered if the natives of the New World were indeed human beings with redeemable souls. At stake were not only the prospects for conversion, but the types of treatment to be accorded them. The expropriation of property, the denial of political rights, the introduction of slavery and other forms of coercive labor, as well as outright extermination, all presupposed a world view which distinguished Europeans—children of God, human beings, etc.—from "others." Such a worldview was needed to explain why some should be "free" and others enslaved, why some had rights to land and property while others did not. Race, and the interpretation of racial differences, was a central factor in that worldview.

In the colonial epoch science was no less a field of controversy than religion in attempts to comprehend the concept of race and its meaning. Spurred on by the classificatory scheme of living organisms devised by Linnaeus in *Systema Naturae*, many scholars in the eighteenth and nineteenth centuries dedicated themselves to the identification and ranking of variations in humankind. Race was thought of as a *biological* concept, yet its precise definition was the subject of debates which, as we have noted, continue to rage today. Despite efforts ranging from Dr. Samuel Morton's studies of cranial capacity[4] to contemporary attempts to base racial classification on shared gene pools,[5] the concept of race has defied biological definition.[...]

Attempts to discern the *scientific meaning* of race continue to the present day. Although most physical anthropologists and biologists have abandoned the quest for a scientific basis to determine racial categories, controversies have recently flared in the area of genetics and educational psychology. For instance, an essay by Arthur Jensen argued that hereditary factors shape intelligence not only revived the "nature or nurture" controversy, but raised highly volatile questions about racial equality itself.[6] Clearly the attempt to establish a *biological* basis of race has not been swept into the dustbin of history, but is being resurrected in various scientific arenas. All such attempts seek to remove the concept of race from fundamental social, political, or economic determination. They suggest instead that the truth of race lies in the terrain of innate characteristics, of which skin color and other physical attributes provide only the most obvious, and in some respects most superficial, indicators.

Race as a Social Concept

The social sciences have come to reject biologistic notions of race in favor of an approach which regards race as a *social* concept. Beginning in the eighteenth century, this trend has been slow and uneven, but its direction clear. In the nineteenth century Max Weber discounted biological explanations for racial conflict and instead highlighted the social and political factors which engendered such conflict.[7] The work of pioneering cultural anthropologist Franz Boas was crucial in refuting the scientific racism of the early twentieth century by rejecting the connection between race and culture, and the assumption of a continuum of "higher" and "lower" cultural groups. Within the contemporary social science literature, race is assumed to be a variable which is shaped by broader societal forces.

Race is indeed a pre-eminently *socio-historical* concept. Racial categories and the meaning of race are given concrete expression by the specific social relations and historical context in which they are embedded. Racial meanings have varied tremendously over time and between different societies.

In the United States, the black/white color line has historically been rigidly defined and enforced. White is seen as a "pure" category. Any racial intermixture makes one "nonwhite." In the movie *Raintree County*, Elizabeth Taylor describes the worst of fates to befall whites as "havin' a little Negra blood in ya'—just one little teeny drop and a person's all Negra."[8] This thinking flows from what Marvin Harris has characterized as the principle of *hypo-descent*:

> By what ingenious computation is the genetic tracery of a million years of evolution unraveled and each man [*sic*] assigned his proper social box? In the United States, the mechanism employed is the rule of hypo-descent. This descent rule requires Americans to believe that anyone who is known to have had a Negro ancestor is a Negro. We admit nothing in between.... "Hypo-descent" means affiliation with the subordinate rather than the superordinate group in order to avoid the ambiguity of intermediate identity.... The rule of hypo-descent is, therefore, an invention, which we in the United States have made in order to keep biological facts from intruding into our collective racist fantasies.[9]

The Susie Guillory Phipps case merely represents the contemporary expression of this racial logic.

By contrast, a striking feature of race relations in the lowland areas of Latin America since the abolition of slavery has been the relative absence of sharply defined racial groupings. No such rigid descent rule characterizes racial identity in many Latin American societies. Brazil, for example, has historically had less rigid conceptions of race, and thus a variety of "intermediate" racial categories exist. Indeed, as Harris notes, "One of the most striking consequences of the Brazilian system of racial identification is that parents and children and even brothers and sisters are frequently accepted as representatives of quite opposite racial types."[10] Such a possibility is incomprehensible within the logic of racial categories in the US.

To suggest another example: the notion of "passing" takes on new meaning if we compare various American cultures' means of assigning racial identity. In the United States, individuals who are actually "black" by the logic of hypo-descent have attempted to skirt the discriminatory barriers imposed by law and custom by attempting to "pass" for white.[11] Ironically, these same individuals would not be able to pass for "black" in many Latin American societies.

Consideration of the term "black" illustrates the diversity of racial meanings which can be found among different societies and historically within a given society. In contemporary British politics the term "black" is used to refer to all nonwhites. Interestingly this designation has not arisen through the racist discourse of groups such as the National Front. Rather, in political and cultural movements, Asian as well as Afro-Caribbean youth are adopting the term as an expression of self-identity.[12] The wide-ranging meanings of "black" illustrate the manner in which racial categories are shaped politically.[13]

The meaning of race is defined and contested throughout society, in both collective action and personal practice. In the process, racial categories themselves are formed, transformed, destroyed, and reformed. We use the term *racial formation* to refer to the process by which social, economic, and political forces determine the content and importance of racial categories, and by which they are in turn shaped by racial meanings. Crucial to this formulation is the treatment of race as a *central axis* of social relations, which cannot be subsumed under or reduced to some broader category or conception.

Racial Ideology and Racial Identity

The seemingly obvious, "natural" and "common sense" qualities which the existing racial order exhibits themselves testify to the effectiveness of the racial formation process in constructing racial meanings and racial identities.

One of the first things we notice about people when we meet them (along with their sex) is their race. We utilize race to provide clues about *who* a person is. This fact is made painfully obvious when we encounter someone whom we cannot conveniently racially categorize—someone who is, for example, racially "mixed" or of an ethnic/racial group with which we are not familiar. Such an encounter becomes a source of discomfort and momentarily a crisis of racial meaning. Without a racial identity, one is in danger of having no identity.

Our compass for navigating race relations depends on preconceived notions of what each specific racial group looks like. Comments such as, "Funny you don't look black," betray an underlying image of what black should be. We also become disoriented when people do not act "black," "Latino," or indeed "white." The content of such stereotypes reveals a series of unsubstantiated beliefs about who these groups are and what "they" are like.[14]

In US society, then, a kind of "racial etiquette" exists, a set of interpretative codes and racial meanings which operate in the interactions of daily life. Rules shaped by our perception of race in a comprehensively racial society determine the "presentation of self,"[15] distinctions of status, and appropriate modes of conduct. "Etiquette" is not mere universal adherence to the dominant group's rules, but a more dynamic combination of these rules with the values and beliefs of subordinated groupings. This racial "subjection" is quintessentially ideological. Everybody learns some combination, some version, of the rules of racial classification, and of their own racial identity, often without obvious teaching or conscious inculcation. Race becomes "common sense"—a way of comprehending, explaining, and acting in the world.

Racial beliefs operate as an "amateur biology," a way of explaining the variations in "human nature."[16] Differences in skin color and other obvious physical characteristics supposedly provide visible clues to differences lurking underneath. Temperament, sexuality, intelligence, athletic ability, aesthetic preferences, and so on are presumed to be fixed and discernible from the palpable mark of race. Such diverse questions as our confidence and trust in others (for example, clerks or salespeople, media figures, neighbors), our sexual preferences and romantic images, our tastes in music, films, dance, or sports, and our very ways of talking, walking, eating, and dreaming are ineluctably shaped by notions of race. Skin color "differences" are thought to explain perceived differences in intellectual, physical, and artistic temperaments, and to justify distinct treatment of racially identified individuals and groups.

The continuing persistence of racial ideology suggests that these racial myths and stereotypes cannot be exposed as such in the popular imagination. They are, we think, too essential, too integral, to the maintenance of the US social order. Of course, particular meanings, stereotypes, and myths can change, but the presence of a *system* of racial meanings and stereotypes, of racial ideology, seems to be a permanent feature of US culture.

Film and television, for example, have been notorious in disseminating images of racial minorities which establish for audiences what people from these groups look like, how they behave, and "who they are."[17] The power of the media lies not only in their ability to reflect the dominant racial ideology, but in their capacity to shape that ideology in the first place. D. W. Griffith's epic *Birth of a Nation*, a sympathetic treatment of the rise of the Ku Klux Klan during Reconstruction, helped to generate, consolidate, and "nationalize" images of blacks which had been more disparate (more regionally specific, for example) prior to the film's appearance.[18] In US television, the necessity to define characters in the briefest and most condensed manner has led to the perpetuation of racial caricatures, as racial stereotypes serve as shorthand for script-writers, directors, and actors, in commercials, etc. Television's tendency to address the "lowest common denominator" in order to render programs "familiar" to an enormous and diverse audience leads it regularly to assign and reassign racial characteristics to particular groups, both minority and majority.

These and innumerable other examples show that we tend to view race as something fixed and immutable—something rooted in "nature." Thus we mask the historical construction of racial categories, the shifting meaning of race, and the crucial role of politics and ideology in shaping race relations. Races do not emerge full-blown. They are the results of diverse historical practices and are continually subject to challenge over their definition and meaning.

Notes

1. *San Francisco Chronicle*, 14 September 1982, 19 May 1983. Ironically, the 1970 Louisiana law was enacted to supersede an old Jim Crow statute which relied on the idea of "common report" in determining an infant's race. Following Phipps's unsuccessful attempt to change her classification and have the law declared unconstitutional, a legislative effort arose which culminated in the repeal of the law. See *San Francisco Chronicle*, 23 June 1983.
2. The Mormon church, for example, has been heavily criticized for its doctrine of black inferiority.
3. Thomas F. Gossett notes:

> Race theory ... had up until fairly modern times no firm hold on European thought. On the other hand, race theory and race prejudice were by no means unknown at the time when the English colonists came to North America.

> Undoubtedly, the age of exploration led many to speculate on race differences at a period when neither Europeans nor Englishmen were prepared to make allowances for vast cultural diversities. Even though race theories had not then secured wide acceptance or even sophisticated formulation, the first contacts of the Spanish with the Indians in the Americas can now be recognized as the beginning of a struggle between conceptions of the nature of primitive peoples which has not yet been wholly settled. (Thomas F. Gossett, *Race: The History of an Idea in America* (New York: Schocken Books, 1965), p. 16.)

Winthrop Jordan provides a detailed account of early European colonialists' attitudes about color and race in *White over Black: American Attitudes Toward the Negro, 1550–1812* (New York: Norton, 1977 [1968]), pp. 3–43.

4. Pro-slavery physician Samuel George Morton (1799–1851) compiled a collection of 800 crania from all parts of the world which formed the sample for his studies of race. Assuming that the larger the size of the cranium translated into greater intelligence, Morton established a relationship between race and skull capacity. Gossett reports that "In 1849, one of his studies included the following results: The English skulls in his collection proved to be the largest, with an average cranial capacity of 96 cubic inches. The Americans and Germans were rather poor seconds, both with cranial capacities of 90 cubic inches. At the bottom of the list were the Negroes with 83 cubic inches, the Chinese with 82, and the Indians with 79" (Ibid., p. 74). On Morton's methods, see Stephen J. Gould, "The Finagle Factor," *Human Nature* (July 1978).
5. Definitions of race founded upon a common pool of genes have not held up when confronted by scientific research, which suggests that the differences within a given human population are greater than those between populations. See L. L. Cavalli-Sforza, "The Genetics of Human Populations," *Scientific American* (September 1974): 81–89.
6. Arthur Jensen, "How Much Can We Boost IQ and Scholastic Achievement?" *Harvard Educational Review* 39 (1969): 1–123.
7. Ernst Moritz Manasse, "Max Weber on Race,' *Social Research* 14 (1947): 191–221.
8. Quoted in Edward D. C. Campbell, Jr., *The Celluloid South: Hollywood and the Southern Myth* (Knoxville: University of Tennessee Press, 1981), pp. 168–70.
9. Marvin Harris, *Patterns of Race in the Americas* (New York: Norton, 1964), p. 56.
10. Ibid., p. 57.
11. After James Meredith had been admitted as the first black student at the University of Mississippi, Harry S. Murphy announced that he, and not Meredith, was the first black student to attend "Ole Miss." Murphy described himself as black but was able to pass for white and spent nine months at the institution without attracting any notice (ibid., p. 56).
12. A. Sivanandan, "From Resistance to Rebellion: Asian and Afro-Caribbean Struggles in Britain," *Race and Class* 23 (2–3) (Autumn–Winter 1981).
13. Consider the contradictions in racial status which abound in the country with the most

rigidly defined racial categories—South Africa. There a race classification agency is employed to adjudicate claims for upgrading of official racial identity. This is particularly necessary for the "coloured" category. The apartheid system considers Chinese as "Asians" while the Japanese are accorded the status of "honorary whites." This logic nearly detaches race from any grounding in skin color and other physical attributes and nakedly exposes race as a juridical category subject to economic, social, and political influences. (We are indebted to Steve Talbot for clarification of some of these points.)

14. Gordon W Allport, *The Nature of Prejudice* (Garden City, NY: Doubleday, 1958), pp. 184-200.
15. We wish to use this phrase loosely, without committing ourselves to a particular position on such social psychological approaches as symbolic interactionism, which are outside the scope of this study. An interesting study on this subject is S. M. Lyman and W. A. Douglass, "Ethnicity: Strategies of Individual and Collective Impression Management," *Social Research* 40 (2) (1973).
16. Michael Billig, "Patterns of Racism: Interviews with National Front Members," *Race and Class* 20 (2) (Autumn 1978): 161-79.
17. "Miss San Antonio USA Lisa Fernandez and other Hispanics auditioning for a role in a television soap-opera did not fit the Hollywood image of real Mexicans and had to darken their faces before filming. Model Aurora Garza said that their faces were bronzed with powder because they looked too white. 'I'm a real Mexican [Garza said] and very dark anyway. I'm even darker right now because I have a tan. But they kept wanting me to make my face darker and darker'" (*San Francisco Chronicle*, 21 September 1984). A similar dilemma faces Asian American actors who feel that Asian character lead roles inevitably go to white actors who make themselves up to be Asian. Scores of Charlie Chan films, for example, have been made with white leads (the last one was the 1981 *Charlie Chan and the Curse of Dragon Queen*). Roland Winters, who played in six Chan features, was asked by playwright Frank Chin to explain the logic of casting a white man in the role of Charlie Chan: "The only thing I can think of is, if you want to cast a homosexual in a show, and get a homosexual, it'll be awful. It won't be funny ... and maybe there's something there...." (Frank Chin, "Confessions of the Chinatown Cowboy," *Bulletin of Concerned Asian Scholars* 4 [3] [Fall 1972]).
18. Melanie Martindale-Sikes, "Nationalizing 'Nigger' Imagery Through Birth of a Nation," paper prepared for the 73rd Annual Meeting of the American Sociological Association, 4-8 September 1978, San Francisco.

SECTION 1D

RESEARCH METHODS

CHAPTER 10

General Research Orientations

Alan Bryman, James Teevan, and Edward Bell

Introduction

[...] It would be easy to "cut to the chase" by explaining how to choose among the various research procedures and describing how to implement them. But the practice of social research does not exist in a vacuum, sealed off from philosophical debates and contested assumptions. Several questions may arise, for example: Are people passive reactors to the social world or active creators of social reality? Can the methods of the natural sciences be applied to the social world or does social science need unique methods to deal with its subject matter? Must past research be the source for current research? The explanations scholars provide for social phenomena and their choice of research methods often depend on how they answer those sorts of questions.

Social research can arise from a variety of motives. Quite often, the goal is to assess the adequacy of a particular social theory, such as a theory of prejudice or crime. In other cases the aim is to gather information to create theories; for example, a sociologist may pose as a street person to find out how the homeless are treated by the public. Sometimes simple "fact-finding" or exploratory work is carried out. For instance, Milgram's (1963) famous study of obedience was done partly to see how far subjects would go in obeying an authority figure's commands, and the results were astounding—many people appeared to be willing to inflict pain on innocent others. [...]

In other instances, research is driven by what is seen as a pressing social problem. In fact the discipline of sociology came into being in the eighteenth and nineteenth centuries partly as a way of understanding the social crises associated with modern life, and that tradition continues to this day. Hier (2002), for example, investigated raves when they became an area of official concern following the 1999 ecstacy-related deaths of three young adults in Toronto. Yet another stimulus for research is personal experiences (Lofland and Lofland 1995). Sugiman (2004), who is a "sansei" or third-generation Japanese, investigated Japanese-Canadian women's experiences of internment during the Second World War after hearing about the personal histories of her family and friends.

Regardless of the motivation for doing research, the data gathered are usually viewed in relation to theories. That's because theories are an attempt to "make sense of it all," to find order and meaning in a seemingly infinite mass of information. How is that done?

Theory and Research

The connection between theory and research is not straightforward. There are several issues at stake here, but two stand out: first, the form of the theory; and second, the relationship between data and theory.

DEGREE OF ABSTRACTION

The term "theory" is used in a variety of ways, but its most common meaning is *an explanation of observed regularities or patterns*, such as the finding that schizophrenia is more common in the working class than in the middle class, or that more men than women are alcoholics. Theories are composed of interrelated and usually verifiable statements or propositions. The statements and propositions come in varying forms and different types that may be combined in the same theory. Here are some of the common components of a theory:

1. *definitions*, which specify what the key terms in the theory mean; for example, "Crime is any violation of the *Canadian Criminal Code* and includes arson, embezzling, etc.";
2. *descriptions of the phenomena of interest*; for example, "Arson involves the illegal setting of fires and is often done at night, either to abandoned buildings or houses when no one is home. There were 438 cases of arson last year, with estimated damage over 52 billion";
3. *relational statements*, which connect two or more variables; knowing the value of one variable conveys information about the other; for example, "As the economy experiences a downturn, the arson rate increases." [...]

There are different types of theories. One distinction that is sometimes made is between *theories of the middle range* (Merton 1967) and *grand theories*. The former are more limited in scope, and can be tested directly by gathering empirical evidence. For instance, Durkheim's (1952) theory of suicide, which maintains that suicide is a function of the level of social integration, is a theory of the middle range. One way to test it would be to compare suicide rates for married people with those for single, divorced, or widowed individuals. Grand theories, on the other hand, are more general and abstract. They include theories such as structural-functionalism, symbolic interactionism, [...] post-structuralism, and so on.

Grand theories generally offer few direct indications of how to collect evidence to test them. So, if someone were to try to test one, the level of abstraction would make it difficult to link the theory as a whole with the real world. [...]

Usually, then, it is not grand theory that directly guides social research—middle range theories are much more likely to be the focus of empirical inquiry. Merton's (1938) anomie theory, which suggests that crime is more common when a society instils a desire for wealth in everyone but provides insufficient means for all to achieve it, is another example of a theory of the middle range. Such theories fall somewhere between grand theories and particularistic explanations. They represent attempts to understand and explain a limited aspect of social life.

[...] Some social scientists are prone to reject research that has no direct connection to theory in either the grand or middle range sense of the term. However, [...] some non-theoretical work may provide qualitative insights that are useful or revealing in their own right. McKeganey and Barnard's (1996) research on British prostitutes and their clients is a case in point. The authors related their research findings to investigations of prostitutes in a number of other countries, and what they describe offers good illustrations of ideas that form an important part of the sociologist's conceptual toolkit. Although it is not possible to tell whether the authors had the concept in mind when they collected their data, their work offers real-life examples of Goffman's (1963) notion of "stigma" and the way in which stigmatized individuals, here prostitutes and clients, manage a spoiled identity. Their work also illuminates Hochschild's (1983) concept of "emotional labour," a term she coined to denote how flight attendants feign friendliness when dealing with difficult passengers. Similarly, it would be unwarranted to ignore the numerous studies that are directed towards providing data that could eventually be used to evaluate or devise a theory.

Our discussion of what theory is and what its importance is invites consideration of another question: What is the relationship between theory and research? Up to this point we have focused primarily on how theory can guide research, in particular on how the collection and analysis of data can be used to test theories. But this notion of research as essentially "theory testing" does not provide a complete picture of what social scientists do. Theory may also *follow upon* or *arise from* the collection and analysis of data. [...]

The next section examines some epistemological issues that impinge on the conduct of social research.

Epistemological Considerations

Those who do social research base their work on a number of epistemological assumptions—notions of what can be known and how knowledge can be acquired. One important epistemological issue in the social sciences concerns the question of what should be regarded as acceptable knowledge. A fundamental controversy in this context is whether the social world should be studied according to the same principles and procedures as those used in the natural sciences.

POSITIVISM

One epistemological position that affirms the importance of following the natural sciences is *positivism*. Although definitions of the term vary, positivism is generally taken to entail the following:

1. Only phenomena and regularities confirmed by the senses (such as sight and hearing) can be accepted as knowledge—the principle of *empiricism*. In other words, ideas must be subjected to the rigours of empirical testing before they can be considered knowledge.
2. A key purpose of theory is to generate hypotheses that can be tested and thereby allow explanations of observed laws and principles to be assessed (*deduction*).
3. Knowledge can also be arrived at through the gathering of facts that provide the basis for generalizations or laws (*induction*).
4. Science must (and presumably can) be conducted in a way that is value-free. Researchers used to call this *objectivity*; today they are more likely to call it *intersubjectivity*, meaning that different researchers, even those with different values, would reach the same conclusions given the same data.
5. There is a clear distinction between scientific statements, which describe how and why social phenomena operate the way they do, and normative statements, that outline whether certain acts or social conditions are morally acceptable. The former are held to be the true domain of science; the latter are seen as belonging in the realms of philosophy or religion, but not science. This idea is implied by point 1 above, because the truth of moral claims cannot be confirmed by the senses.

It is possible to see in these five points a link with some of the issues already raised about the relationship between theory and research. Positivism assumes a fairly sharp distinction between theory and research and includes elements of both deduction and induction. One role of research is to test theories and to provide information for the development of laws, somewhat similar to the laws of science like Boyle's law. There is also an implication that it is possible to collect observations in a manner not influenced by pre-existing theories, and to derive theories from those observations. Finally, theories and propositions not directly testable through empirical observation are often not considered to be genuinely scientific.

A common mistake is to treat positivism as synonymous with science and the scientific. In fact, philosophers of science and social science differ quite sharply over how best to characterize scientific practice, and since the early 1960s positivism has acquired some negative connotations. It began to be viewed with dissatisfaction partly because some researchers in the positivist tradition ignored some fundamental differences between human beings and the often inanimate or not fully conscious entities studied by natural scientists. Unlike subatomic particles or plants, for example, we humans have thoughts, feelings, and values, and according to some at least, we have some capacity for volition. Those aspects of human behaviour were often not addressed in the leading positivistic theories of the day. Also, dissatisfaction developed concerning the positivist idea that science can or should be value-free. Critics pointed out that "neutral" social scientists often took at least implicit moral positions on social issues—for example, theories that imply that social equilibrium or harmony are normal seemed to be saying that social change is not needed or desirable. Some critics went further and claimed that it is the duty of the social scientist to help bring about social change in order to create a better world.

INTERPRETIVISM

Interpretivism to some extent grew out of the epistemological critique of positivism, and provides an alternative to the sort of social science typically done by positivists. Interpretive researchers maintain that it is the role of social scientists to grasp the subjective *meanings* of people's actions. They make the point that people act on the basis of the meanings that they attribute to their acts and to the acts of others. Using their own common-sense constructs, individuals interpret the reality of their daily lives and it is these thoughts that motivate their behaviour.

Interpretivists claim that it is the job of the social scientist to gain access to the "common-sense thinking" of the people they study and hence to interpret people's actions and their social world from *the point of view of the actors*. Thus any thoughts constructed by the social scientist to grasp this social reality must be founded upon the common-sense interpretations of those they study: people living their daily lives within their own social world (Schutz 1962: 59). Many interpretive social scientists argue that the subject matter of the social sciences—people, groups, and institutions—is fundamentally different from that of the natural sciences. For them it follows that the study of the social world requires a different logic and research procedure, one that reflects what they see as the distinctiveness of humans as against other living things or inanimate objects. This clash reflects a division between an emphasis on the *explanation* of human behaviour that is the chief ingredient of the positivist approach to the social sciences, and the preference for an *empathetic understanding* and *interpretation* of human behaviour. This contrast reflects long-standing debates that preceded the emergence of modern social science, but find their expression in Max Weber's (1864–1920) notion of *Verstehen* (which means "empathetic understanding"). Weber described sociology as a "science which attempts the interpretive understanding of social action in order to arrive at a causal explanation of its course and effects" (1947: 88). Weber's definition seems to embrace both explanation *and* understanding here, but the crucial point is that the task of "causal explanation" is undertaken with reference to the "interpretive understanding of social action." This is a different emphasis from a more Durkheimian view in which the external forces that affect behaviour may not be perceived by those involved, or at least may have no meaning for them. For a Marxist view, see Box 10.1.

Symbolic interactionism is an example of a sociological perspective that falls under the heading of interpretivism. The ideas of the founders of symbolic interactionism, in particular those of George Herbert Mead (1863–1931), who maintains that one's *self-concept* emerges through an appreciation of the perceptions of others, have been hotly debated. Symbolic interactionists argue that interaction takes place in such a way that individuals are continually interpreting the symbolic meaning of their environment (including the actions of others) and acting on the basis of that imputed meaning (cf. Collins 1994). In research terms, according to Blumer (1962: 188), "the position of symbolic interaction requires the student to catch the process of interpretation through which [actors] construct their actions."

BOX 10.1 RESEARCH METHODS USED BY MARXISTS

Almost all who adopt a Marxist approach are critical of the positivist notion that social researchers should take a value-neutral stance regarding their subject matter. But they are also critical of narrowly interpretive perspectives on social life, arguing that social research has to go beyond acquiring knowledge of how people in society interpret their world. Marxists argue that those who own the means of production deceive, constrain, and exploit the weak. The masses could be free if social scientists, by asking embarrassing questions and making pointed arguments, would uncover exploitation, expose hypocrisy, and reveal to the general populace the nature and extent of their oppression. This would transform the masses from what Marx called a *class an sich* (a class in itself, an objective reality) into a *class für sich* (a class for itself, one with an awareness of its exploitation).

Marxists reject the idea that it is the role of the scientist to be detached. Instead, they see the role of social scientist as one of unmasking the unjust conditions in the world, thus allowing the downtrodden to see the sources of their ills. They maintain that research should be action-oriented, that it should involve *praxis*: putting one's theoretical and academic positions into practice. The idea of praxis is contained in Marx's famous dictum that "philosophers have only *interpreted* the world in various ways; the point, however, is to change it" (Marx 1998 [1845]: 574). Smashing myths and uncovering contradictions are just the first part of that process (cf. Neuman 2003).

Ontological Considerations

There are two ontological debates that are of particular interest to social scientists. The first is concerned with the following questions: Do social phenomena have an objective reality, one that is independent of our perceptions? Or is what passes for reality merely a set of mental constructions? If you answer "yes" to the first question, that puts you in the objectivist camp. People on this side of the debate maintain that there is such a thing as social reality, and that it is the job of social scientists to discover what that reality is. An affirmative answer to the second question means that you agree with the *constructionist* position. People holding this view are in sympathy with Nietzsche's (1910: 12) famous aphorism that there are no facts, only interpretations. Such people maintain that there is no objective social reality against which our conceptions and views of the world may be tested. [...] However, a middle ground or "soft constructionist" position is possible and is held by many. It maintains that there may be an objective social reality, but many of our ideas do not reflect that reality at all, but instead are constructed to justify or rationalize various forms of domination. [...]

A second debate revolves around these questions: Is social reality akin to how most people view the physical world—largely fixed and "out there," something that individuals and groups have to confront but over which they have little or no control, like a snowstorm? Or is social reality not necessarily pre-existing and fixed, but is instead created through our actions? A "yes" to the first question indicates support for a variant of objectivism, and agreement with the second affirms a kind of constructionism. [...]

Some social scientists suggest that social phenomena confront individuals as external facts beyond their reach or influence. For example, an organization has rules and regulations and adopts standardized procedures for getting things done. A division of labour assigns people to different jobs. There is a hierarchy of authority, a mission statement, and so on. Objectivists see any organization as possessing a reality external to any of the specific individuals who inhabit it; they may leave but it will stay. Moreover, the organization represents a social order in that it exerts pressure on individuals to conform to organizational requirements. People learn and apply the rules and regulations and follow the standardized procedures. They do the jobs to which they are appointed. If they do not do these things, they may be reprimanded or even fired. The organization is therefore a constraining force that acts on and inhibits its members. To a large extent, this is the "classic" way of conceptualizing an organization.

An alternative ontological position challenges the suggestion that things like an organization are external realities confronting social actors who have limited power to influence or change them. Strauss and colleagues (1973), for example, carried out research in a psychiatric hospital and proposed that its organization is best conceptualized as one of "negotiated order." Instead of viewing order as a preexisting characteristic, they argued that it is worked at and created to some extent, and that the rules are far less extensive and less rigorously imposed than might be supposed from an objectivist account of organizations.

Indeed, Strauss and colleagues viewed rules more like general understandings than as commands (1973: 308). Precisely because relatively little of the spheres of action of doctors, nurses, and other personnel is specifically set down or prescribed, the social order of a hospital is an outcome of agreed-upon patterns of action that are themselves the products of negotiations among the different parties involved. For instance, the official rules may say that only a doctor can increase medication; however, some nurses, though it is never actually stated in the regulations, are routinely given this power. The social order is in a constant state of change because the hospital is "a place where numerous agreements are continually being terminated or forgotten, but also as continually being established, renewed, reviewed, revoked, [and] revised.... In any pragmatic sense, this is the hospital *at the moment* [our emphasis]: this is its social order" (1973: 316–17). The authors argued that a preoccupation with the formal properties of organizations (rules, organizational charts, regulations, and roles) neglects the degree to which order in organizations has to be *accomplished* in everyday interaction. This *informal* organization arises because there cannot be rules for every possible contingency and the existing rules may be problematic, but this is not to say that the formal properties of organizations have *no* element of constraint on individual action.

Although Strauss and colleagues stressed the active role of individuals in the social construction of social reality, they did not push the argument to an extreme. For example, they did not claim that nurses can negotiate their roles to the point where they are allowed to operate on patients. But not all writers adopting a constructionist position are similarly prepared to acknowledge the existence or importance of an objective reality. [...]

The constructionist perspective that maintains that social reality can be negotiated also suggests that the concepts people employ to help them understand the natural and social world are social products whose meaning is constructed in and through social interaction. For example, a concept such as "masculinity" is treated as a social construction. This implies that, rather than a distinct, timeless, and universal entity, the meaning of masculinity is built up through interaction. That meaning is likely to be ephemeral, in that it will vary over time and place. [...] As Potter (1996: 98) observed: "The world ... is *constituted* in one way or another as people talk it, write it, and argue it." This sense of constructionism frequently leads to an interest in how social phenomena are represented.

Influences on the Conduct of Social Research

You can now see how social research is influenced by a variety of factors. Figure 10.1 summarizes the influences examined so far, but has added three more—the impact of *values, politics,* and *practical considerations.*

FIGURE 10.1: INFLUENCES ON SOCIAL RESEARCH

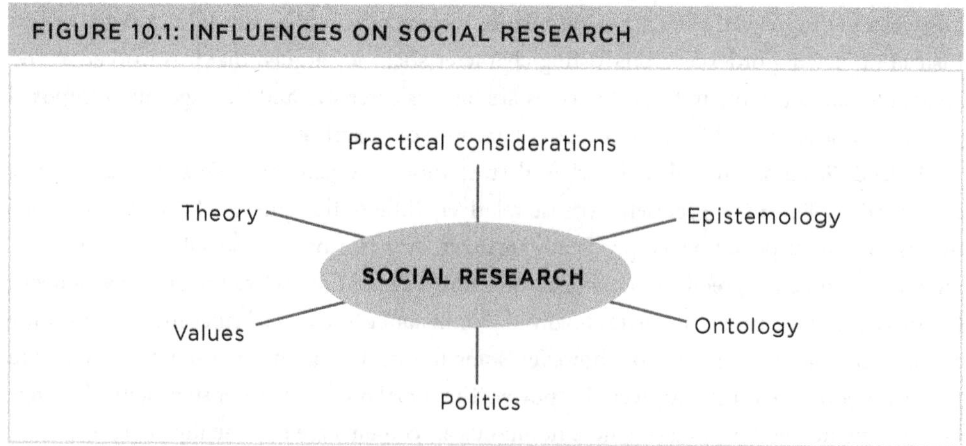

VALUES

How might the values, personal beliefs, and feelings of researchers affect their work? Perhaps one would expect social scientists to be completely value-free and objective in their studies. Research that simply reflects the personal views of its practitioners would be biased and invalid, and thus unscientific. Durkheim (1858–1917) wrote that *social facts* are objects whose study requires that all "preconceptions must be eradicated" (1938: 31). Since values are a form of preconception, his point implies that they should be suppressed when conducting research. But is that humanly possible? Values intrude in all phases of the research process, from the choice of a topic to the formulation of conclusions. This means that the social researcher is never working in a moral vacuum but is instead influenced by a range of ethical presuppositions that have implications for the conduct of social research. This view is increasingly accepted among social researchers. Indeed, it is now recognized that values can intrude at any or all points in the process of social research, such as:

- choice of research area;
- formulation of the research question;
- choice of method;
- formulation of the research design and data collection techniques;
- data collection;
- analysis of data;
- interpretation of data; and
- conclusions.

There are, therefore, numerous points at which bias and the intrusion of values can occur during the course of research. For example, a researcher may develop an affection or sympathy for the people being studied. It is quite common, for instance, for researchers working within a qualitative research strategy, in particular when they use very intensive interviewing, to become so close to the people they are studying that they find it difficult to disentangle their role as social scientists from their concern for their subjects' well-being.

Equally, social scientists may be repelled by those they study. In his research into an African society known as the Ik, a social anthropologist was appalled by what he saw: a loveless (and for him unlovable) group that left its young and very old to die (Turnbull 1973). Although he was able to point to the conditions lying behind these practices, he was very honest in his disgust for what he witnessed, particularly during his early time with them.

One way of dealing with the whole question of values and bias is to recognize that research cannot be value-free, and to try to ensure that values in the research process are acknowledged and made explicit. This is part of a larger process of *reflexivity* or self-reflection that researchers are encouraged to carry out. As Turnbull (1973: 13) put it at the beginning of his book on the Ik: "The reader is entitled to know something of the aims, expectations, hopes, and attitudes that the writer brought to the field [in his case, Western values about the family], for these will surely influence not only how he sees things but even what he sees." Researchers are increasingly prepared to forewarn readers of their biases and assumptions and to explain how these may have influenced their findings. There has been a growth since the mid-1970s in collections of inside reports of what doing a piece of research is really like, as against the generalities presented in social research methods textbooks (like this one). These collections frequently function as "confessions" about personal biases and reveal the pride researchers take in telling readers how open they are in revealing them.

Still another approach is to argue for consciously value-laden research. For some writers on social research, a "conscious partiality," as Mies (1993: 68) called it, is celebrated. For example, [...] this perspective allowed Pratt and Valverde (2002) to refer to a large Canadian newspaper as a "notorious tabloid" and "obsessed" with what it called bogus refugees. [...] In fact, among some feminist researchers, doing research on women in an objective, value-neutral way would be considered undesirable (as well as difficult to achieve) because it would be incompatible with their values. Instead, many feminist researchers extol the virtues of a commitment to women that exposes the conditions of their disadvantage in a male-dominated society. Some feminist writers argue that only research on women intended *for* women is consistent with the wider political needs of women.

The significance of feminism in relation to values goes further than this, however. In particular, several feminist social researchers in the early 1980s proposed that quantitative research is incompatible with feminist ideals. For writers such as Oakley (1981), quantitative research is bound up with the male values of *control*, as seen in the researcher's control of the research subject/respondent and of the research context and situation. Moreover, the research process is seen as one-way, in which researchers extract information from those studied and give little or, more usually, nothing in return. For many feminists, such a strategy borders on exploitation and is incompatible with feminism's values of sisterhood and non-hierarchical relationships.

The antipathy towards quantitative research resulted in a preference for qualitative research among certain feminists. Not only was qualitative research seen as more consistent with the values of feminism, it was portrayed as more adaptable to those values. Feminist qualitative research came to be associated with an approach in which the investigator denied a value-neutral approach and related to the people being studied as human beings rather than research instruments. This stance demonstrates how values have implications for the process of social investigation. In more recent years, there has been a softening of the attitudes of feminists towards quantitative research, especially when it is employed in conjunction with qualitative research (Oakley 1998). [...]

There are, then, different positions that can be taken in relation to values and value-free research. Fewer writers today subscribe to the position that the principle of objectivity can be put into practice fully. There is a greater awareness of the limits of objectivity, and some of the more categorical pronouncements on the subject, like those of Durkheim, have fallen into disfavour. At the same time, giving free rein to one's political beliefs and value positions can be problematic. Researchers today still have to fight the all too human propensity to demonize those whose values are different from their own, and struggle with the temptation to summarily reject research findings simply because the researcher's ideological or moral views are not compatible with their own.

POLITICS IN SOCIAL RESEARCH

Considerations of how values and moral positions can affect social research draw attention to how *politics* may influence research. The following points illustrate how social research may be political.

- Social researchers sometimes *take sides*, as we have seen. This is precisely what many feminist researchers do when they focus on women's disadvantages and on the possibilities for improving the position of women. But taking sides occurs among other researchers as well. For example, some social scientists may promote a greater role for government in society and globally; others may endorse the merits of the free market.
- A related issue involves research *funding*. Much social research is funded by organizations such as private firms and government departments that may have a vested interest in the outcomes of the research. The very fact that these organizations fund some research projects but not others opens the door to political influence. Such organizations may seek to invest in studies that will be useful to them or supportive of their operations and world views. Frequently, they launch a call for researchers to tender bids for an investigation in a certain area. When social researchers participate in such exercises, they are participating in a political arena because their research may be designed to please the funding body. As a result, as Hughes (2000) observed in relation to research in the field of crime, an investigation of gun crimes among the "underclass" is more likely to be looked upon favourably for funding than one concerned with state-related misdemeanours. Morgan (2000) pointed out that research funded by government is typically empirical and quantitative; it tends to be concerned with short-term costs and benefits of a policy or innovation; and it is generally uncritical in the sense that underlying government policies are not questioned, just the effectiveness of their implementation. Such features can be related to the fact that a funding agency itself may be involved in a political process of securing a continuous stream of government funding.
- Gaining *access* to research subjects and organizations is also a political process. Access is usually mediated by gatekeepers concerned not only about the researcher's motives but also about what the organization can gain from the investigation, what it will lose by participating in terms of staff time and other costs, and the potential risks to its image. Often, gatekeepers seek to influence how the investigation will take place: what kinds of questions can be asked; who can and cannot be a focus of study; the amount of time to be spent with each research participant; the interpretation of the findings; and the form the reports will take, even to the point of asking to approve drafts.
- Public institutions, such as police departments, schools, and hospitals, and most commercial firms, are concerned with how they are going to be represented in publications. Consequently, gaining access is almost always a matter of *negotiation* and as such inevitably turns into a political process. The results of this negotiation are often referred to as "the research bargain" and it turns out that the term really should be plural. Once in the organization, researchers often discover layers of gatekeepers with whom a constant process of negotiation and renegotiation of what is and is not permissible transpires. For example, let's say permission to talk to the boys in a group home is given by the provincial government. Before research can begin, the head of the home has to be brought onside, then the staff, and then the actual adolescents. Frequently, one of the staff is then given the responsibility of dealing with the fieldworkers. A suspicion that they are really

working for management then has to be overcome. And it is unwise to assume that simply because gatekeepers have given a researcher access, a smooth passage will ensue in subsequent dealings with the people to be studied. Perhaps the most powerful of the boys will turn out to be the key gatekeeper. Researchers may even find themselves used as pawns if subgroups attempt to enlist them in advancing a particular goal; and some research participants, because they doubt the utility of social research, may obstruct the research process.

- There may be pressure to restrict the *publication* of findings. Hughes (2000) cited a study of plea-bargaining in the British criminal justice system as a case in point. The researchers had uncovered what were deemed at the time to be disconcerting levels of informal plea-bargaining, concluding that the formal judicial process was being weakened. The English legal establishment sought to thwart the dissemination of the findings and was only persuaded to allow publication when a panel of academics confirmed the validity of the findings. Similarly, the editors of academic journals may refuse to publish pieces that do not conform to their own ideological or political preferences.

These are just a small number of ways in which politics intrudes in the research process.

PRACTICAL CONSIDERATIONS

There are also a number of *practical issues* to be confronted in carrying out our social research. [...] One important practical consideration is that the choice of research orientation, design, or method has to match the specific research question being investigated. For instance, if one is interested in measuring the impact of a number of possible causes of a social phenomenon, a quantitative strategy is probably appropriate. Alternatively, if the focus is on the world views of members of a certain social group, a qualitative research strategy—one sensitive to how participants interpret their social world—may be the way to go. If a researcher is interested in a topic on which no or little research has been done, the quantitative strategy may be difficult to employ because there is little prior literature from which to draw leads about its possible causes. A more qualitative, exploratory approach may be preferable because that type of investigation is typically associated with the generation rather than the testing of theory [...] and with a relatively unstructured approach to the research process.

Another dimension involves the nature of the topic and of the people being investigated. If a researcher wants to study individuals involved in illicit activities, for example, price fixing, shoplifting, or drug dealing, it is unlikely that a researcher could develop the rapport with them that is needed to conduct a social survey. [...]

Although practical considerations may seem rather mundane and uninteresting compared with the lofty realm inhabited by the philosophical debates surrounding epistemology and ontology, they are important. All social research is a coming together of the ideal and the feasible. The nature of the topic, the type of people one may be investigating, and the related constraints on a researcher loom large in decisions about how best to proceed.

RESEARCH QUESTIONS

The last practical consideration involves choosing a *research question*. Choosing a research question is in many ways like picking a destination before going hiking—the route to be taken and what you will experience along the way are largely determined by where you want to go. Similarly, what you stand to accomplish with a particular research study and how you will accomplish it are profoundly affected by your formulation of the research question.

What is a research question? A research question states the purpose of the study in the form of a question, which is very useful because a question may be more evocative and stimulating than a simple declarative sentence designed to do the same thing. A question arouses curiosity and challenges the researcher to find ways to answer it.

The process of formulating and assessing research questions is something of an art, but here are some general thoughts. Research often starts with the choice of a general area of interest, for example, male homosexuality. At this stage, a very general research question might be: How do people in general feel about gays? This broad research area has to be narrowed down, for example, to: How does the Canadian adult population react to the portrayal of gays on television dramas? But even that is too broad, so the next level of specification might be something like: Do straight, young men react differently than straight, young women to the portrayal of male gay romance on television program X? If so, can those differences be explained in terms of a more fluid sexual identity on the part of young women as compared to young men? Questions like the latter could be linked to larger theories of sex roles, sexual orientation acquisition, socialization, or the tolerance of difference in society.

A particular study cannot answer all the research questions that occur, but must select only a small number of them. This narrowing of the topic is not just a limit created by the time and cost of doing research. It is also due to the need for the project to have a clear focus.

As suggested above, the research question may change as the study progresses, for a number of reasons. The discovery of a new data source may change the focus a bit, as might some of the initial findings. For instance, if in the study of male homosexuality the researchers find that having a gay relative in one's immediate family makes a large difference in people's attitudes, the research question and the attendant methodology and theoretical orientation may be changed. The research question may also change because of limitations in time and other resources available to the researcher. [...]

Research questions set realistic boundaries for research. Having none or having poorly formulated research questions can result in unfocused and substandard research. It does not matter how well designed a questionnaire is or how skilled the interviewers are; clear research questions are required to avoid going off in unnecessary directions and tangents. Research questions are crucial because they guide:

- the literature search;
- decisions about the kind of research design to employ;
- decisions about what data to collect and from whom;
- the analysis of the data; and
- the writing up of the findings.

References

Blumer, H. (1962), "Society as Symbolic Interaction," in A. Rose (ed.), *Human Behavior and Social Processes* (London: Routledge & Kegan Paul).

Collins, R. (1994), *Four Sociological Traditions*, rev. ed. (New York: Oxford Univ. Press).

Durkheim, E. (1938), *The Rules of Sociological Method*, trans. S. Solavay and J. Mueller (New York: Free Press).

Durkheim, E. (1952), *Suicide: A Study in Sociology*, trans. J. Spaulding and G. Simpson (London: Routledge & Kegan Paul).

Goffman, E. (1963), *Stigma: Notes on the Management of Spoiled Identity* (Harmondsworth, UK: Penguin).

Hier, S. (2002), "Raves, Risks, and the Ecstasy Panic: A Case Study in the Subversive Nature of Moral Regulation," *Canadian Jour. of Sociology*, 27:33–57.

Hothschild, A. (1983), *The Managed Heart* (Berkeley and Los Angeles: Univ. of California Press).

Hughes, G. (2000), "Understanding the Politics of Criminological Research," in V. Jupp, P. Davies, and P. Francis (eds.), *Doing Criminological Research* (London: Sage).

Lofland, J., and Lofland, L. (1995), *Analyzing Social Settings: A Guide to Qualitative Observations and Analysis*, 3rd ed. (Belmont, CA: Wadsworth).

McKeganey, N., and Barnard, M. (1996), *Sex Work and the Streets* (Buckingham: Open Univ. Press).

Marx, K. (1998 [1845]), *The German Ideology Including Theses on Feuerbach and Introduction to the Critique of Political Economy* (Amherst: Prometheus Books).

Merton, R. (1938), "Social Structure and Anomie," *Amer. Sociological Rev.*, 3: 672–82.

Merton, R. (1967), *On Theoretical Sociology* (New York: Free Press).

Mies, M. (1993), "Towards a Methodology for Feminist Research," in M. Hammersley (ed.), *Social Research: Philosophy, Politics, and Practice* (London: Sage).

Milgram, S. (1963), "A Behavioural Study of Obedience," *Jour. of Abnormal and Social Psych.*, 67: 371–8.

Morgan, R. (2000), "The Politics of Criminological Research," in R. King and E. Wincup (eds.), *Doing Research on Crime and Justice* (Oxford: Oxford Univ. Press).

Neuman, W.L. (2003), *Social Research Methods* (Toronto: Pearson Canada).

Oakley, A. (1981), "Interviewing Women: A Contradiction in Terms," in H. Robert (ed.), *Doing Feminist Research* (London: Routledge & Kegan Paul).

Oakley, A. (1998), "Gender, Methodology, and People's Ways of Knowing: Some Problems with Feminism and the Paradigm Debate in Social Science," *Sociology*, 32: 707–31.

Potter, J. (1996), *Representing Reality: Discourse, Rhetoric, and Social Construction* (London: Sage).

Pratt, A., and Valverde, M. (2002), "From Deserving Victims to 'Masters of Confusion': Redefining Refugees in the 1900s," *Canadian Jour. of Sociology*, 27: 135–62.

Schutz, A. (1962), *Collected Papers I: The Problem of Social Reality* (The Hague: Martinus Nijhof).

Strauss, A., Schatzman, L., Ehrich, D., Bucher, R., and Sabshin, M. (1973), "The Hospital and Its Negotiated Order," in G. Salaman and K. Thompson (eds.), *People and Organizations* (London: Longman).

Sugiman, P. (2004), "Memories of the Internment: Narrating Japanese-Canadian Women's Life Stories," *Canadian Jour. of Sociology*, 29: 359–88.

Turnbull, P. (1973), *The Mountain People* (London: Cape).

Weber, M. (1947), *The Theory of Social and Economic Organization*, trans. A.M Henderson and T. Parsons (New York: Free Press).

CHAPTER 11

Becoming an Anti-oppressive Researcher

Karen L. Potts and Leslie Brown [1]

Beginning with Choices, Assumptions, and Tenets

Given the choice between being an oppressive or anti-oppressive researcher, hopefully we would all choose the latter. However, the choice is not really that simple or straightforward. A commitment to anti-oppressive research means committing to social justice and taking an active role in that change. It means that there is political purpose and action to our research work, whether that purpose is change on a societal level or within our own lives. Anti-oppressive research involves making explicit the political practices involved in creating knowledge. It requires making a commitment to the people you are working with, personally and professionally, in order to mutually foster conditions for social justice through research. It starts with paying attention to, and shifting, how power relations work in and through the processes of doing research.

Our own journeys to anti-oppressive research were fuelled by running into the same problem that perplexed another researcher committed to social justice, Patti Lather (1991): how is it that "our very efforts to liberate (through our research) perpetuate the relations of dominance" (p. 16)? Like Lather, we realized that the answer to that question required an examination of our own complicity in creating and sustaining oppression. This is not any easy task! Most of us recognize oppression when it occurs "out there" or when we are being oppressed ourselves, but can we also recognize how we are implicated in sustaining systems of inequality? This is often harder, especially if we are well-meaning people who espouse social justice ideals. But if we are committed to anti-oppression, we have to be prepared to critically analyze how oppression occurs through the various activities and social practices we engage in with others, including research activities. For example, as White women academics, we recognize that our ability to implement an anti-oppressive research approach rests (to some extent) on tapping into our privilege, and we acknowledge that researchers from the margins face different challenges in attempting to enable anti-oppressive research.

We want you to consider that anti-oppressive work, including research, is not contingent upon location. Social justice work can happen anywhere, including in dominant institutions such as governments, schools, and hospitals. The political nature of our environment is important to recognize and work with, but we do not have to have a job description that says "anti-oppressive researcher" (good luck waiting for that one!) before we can do anti-oppressive research. Anti-oppressive research is a commitment to a set of principles, values, and ways of working, and can be carried out anywhere—it's a matter of choice amid various constraints. We ask that you believe in your capacity for agency: you can act in ways that alter the relations of oppression in your own world. There are conversations among academics and activists that specifically interrogate the term *anti-oppressive* (McLaughlin, 2005). This chapter does not participate in these conversations. For us, we were attracted to and are using the term because we still feel challenged by it (in all our paradoxical and simultaneous, marginalized and dominant social locations) to "do" our research work in ways that move us closer toward social justice.

The purpose of this chapter is to explain our ideas about anti-oppressive research in ways that we hope will be helpful to all researchers, and to research students in particular. We start by outlining three key principles or tenets of anti-oppressive research. These are not discreet; rather, they are interrelated, and our articulation of them reflects how they inform one another. When we want to critically assess whether the research work we are doing is actually anti-oppressive research, it is these principles that we use to reflect on our topic, our methods, our relationships, our analysis, and our action. We then discuss what anti-oppressive research processes may look like.[...]

ANTI-OPPRESSIVE RESEARCH IS SOCIAL JUSTICE[2] IN PROCESSES AND OUTCOMES

Research can be a powerful tool for social change—and for maintaining the status quo. Research can be used to suppress ideas, people, and social justice—and it can be used to respect, empower, and liberate. Good intentions are never enough to ensure anti-oppressive processes or outcomes. Many research endeavours contribute to social justice outcomes, but are not necessarily anti-oppressive in their processes and procedures. The Canadian Centre for Policy Alternatives, for example, publishes important statistical research on poverty, taxation systems, and environmental degradation (www.policyalternatives.ca). While we applaud this work, there is an important difference between research that contributes to social justice and what we describe here as anti-oppressive research.

Choosing to be an anti-oppressive researcher means choosing to do research that challenges dominant ideas about research *processes* as well as research outcomes. This means that each step of the research work is carried out in a socially just way. For example, anti-oppressive research questions why we so easily think of researching those who are marginalized by reason of race, class, ability, gender, and so on while it is so difficult to think about researching dominance. "Reversing the gaze" on whom and what gets studied can be an important first step in anti-oppressive research. Similarly, we can ask how research participants can also be the researchers, and we can ensure equitable distribution of any money, credit, and direct benefits generated by the research work.

ANTI-OPPRESSIVE RESEARCH CONTENDS THAT ALL KNOWLEDGE IS SOCIALLY CONSTRUCTED, ALL KNOWLEDGE IS POLITICAL, AND, CURRENTLY, SHAPED BY THE NEO-LIBERAL CONTEXT

How do we know what we know? The answer to this epistemological question is key to understanding an anti-oppressive approach to research. From an anti-oppressive perspective, knowledge does not exist "out there" to be discovered. Rather, knowledge is produced through the interactions of people, and as all people are socially and politically located (in their race, gender, ability, class identities, and so on), with biases, privileges, and differing entitlements, so too is the knowledge that is produced socially located and political. Knowledge is neither neutral nor benign, as it is created within and through power relations between people. Knowledge can be oppressive in how it is constructed and utilized, or it can be a means of resistance and emancipation. Often, it is a complex combination of both.

Recognizing that knowledge is socially constructed means understanding that truth is created, rather than pre-existing and available to be measured and observed. Therefore, in anti-oppressive research, we do not look to prove or disprove a singular "truth" about the social or political world. We look for meaning, for understanding, for insights that can enable resistance and change. However, anti-oppressive researchers recognize that we live in a culture biased toward positivist research—that is, using natural science principles of counting, quantifying, and measuring to claim to understand social issues. As anti-oppressive researchers, we argue that we must trouble the dominance of positivism, because while counting, measuring, and quantifying can measure inequalities, the complex causes of injustice and inequity remain unexamined.

We contend that, in the present moment, positivism is part of the infrastructure that allows neo-liberalism to flourish and the transformation to a knowledge economy to occur. Recognizing knowledge as socially constructed means being politically astute about this context. Knowledge has been turned into a commodity in the new knowledge economy (David & Foray, 2002), and an increasing emphasis on patents, copyrights, and other regulations is restricting the free sharing of knowledge. Knowledge becomes a profitable commodity, and knowledge creation a profit-making endeavour, when knowledge can be made scarce or where access to knowledge can be limited and controlled (AUCC, 2001). Anti-oppressive research resists the commodification of knowledge and instead advocates "democratizing knowledge" by ensuring knowledge is accessible for the common good (Hall, 2011). As anti-oppressive researchers, we set out to construct emancipatory and liberatory knowledge that can be acted on, by, and in the interests of the marginalized and oppressed.

ANTI-OPPRESSIVE RESEARCH FOREGROUNDS RELATIONSHIPS

Consider the relationship in positivist research between the researcher and those who are being researched. In positivism, the researcher is the expert and is seen as being the primary, and often only, person with power and the ability to create knowledge, to act on that knowledge, and to profit from its creation. Those who are being studied, although they are not necessarily treated badly, are nevertheless objects; they are acted upon, without any input or real involvement or control in the process, and positivist research principles constrain researchers from having any interpersonal relationships with research participants. From a positivist perspective, there is usually no need to recognize these hierarchical and distant power relations, nor any attempt to change them. Researchers and participants are not equals: money paid to participants may be called an "inducement" or "honorarium," while money paid to researchers is usually called "wages" or "salary."

The problematic nature of researcher-researched relationships is not confined to positivism. Even in "empowerment"[3] approaches to research, the relationship between researchers and the researched may be hierarchical and paternalistic: members of the group being researched might conduct interviews or surveys, but otherwise have no control or involvement in research processes. Providing people with an opportunity to have their voices heard and hearing their stories can be exploitative or empowering, or a confusing mix of both.

In anti-oppressive research, key relationships and their attendant power relations are foregrounded, including relationships between the knower and known; groups of knowers; knowers and any outside researchers; and researchers and institutions. Constant attention is given to these relations, and care is taken to try and shift the balance of knowledge-creating power from outside researchers to those with lived experience of the issue under study (Ceglowski, 2000). As anti-oppressive researchers, we say that "we do not begin to collect data in a community until all the dogs know us." This is our way of saying, "No research without authentic relationships." Research relationships are not time specific or disposable (Huisman, 2008). Rather, we approach them as if we may be in relationship with people for life.

Re-thinking the Re-searching Process: Anti-oppressive Practice in the Process of Inquiry

There are some basic tasks that are common to most social science research processes. People come together with an issue. A question is articulated. A research design is drafted. An agreement about who will be involved and how people will work together is developed. Information to answer the question is captured. There is a meaning-making process to learn from the data. Some type of product, such as a write-up, is produced. These elements are present in anti-oppressive research, though they usually appear in particular ways. Anti-oppressive research is rarely a linear process, and few elements are determined at the outset. Anti-oppressive research is emergent, in that the issue under study, the people doing the studying, and the environments we are working within are constantly changing. The "tasks" of the research need to respond accordingly. For example, during the analysis we may realize we need to go back for more data. And sometimes, it is only after the analysis that we realize what the real question was that we answered.

Aside from the emergent nature of these research tasks, there are other activities that are a bit unique to anti-oppressive research. First is the time and attention given to relationship building. Second is the doing—the tasks that will come from making a commitment to acting and creating change from the research. This is much more than the authoring of a report to make action someone else's responsibility. We now turn our attention to these research tasks.

It Starts with Negotiating Who's Who

As a central tenet of anti-oppressive research, attending to relationships is foregrounded in all research tasks, and it is also the place we start. We spend time getting to know the people involved and the history and context of wherever the research will take place, and becoming savvy to the politics we will be immersed in. Before we can enter into authentic relationships with others, we need to be vigilant about our own biases and motivations, and attend to the gap between how we see ourselves (well meaning, caring, grounded in our own experiences of marginalization) and how others may see us (privileged, representing dominant institutions, not having as much at stake).

Anti-oppressive researchers are constantly negotiating their position along a continuum of insider-outsider relations. Insiders have epistemic privilege—that is, the intimate knowledge from lived experience of the issue under study. The outsider end of the continuum is the traditional academic researcher, positioned outside the situation, removed and in a position of studying "Others." Most of us on the journey toward becoming anti-oppressive researchers find ourselves somewhere in the middle of the continuum. Often we have a personal connection to the issue or topic, but we are also usually connected to government, human service, or academic institutions. In practice, negotiating and positioning ourselves as researchers is seldom as simple as declaring which position we hold. In some instances, we may think we are insiders only to find that others involved in the project (especially those providing data) see us as set apart, an outsider. Linda Tuhiwai Smith (2012) illustrates this when she talks about her experience doing research in her own Maori community:

> I was an insider as a Maori mother and an advocate of the language revitalization movement, and I shared in the activities of fund raising and organizing. Through my different tribal relationships I had close links to some of the mothers and to the woman who was the main organizer.... When I began the discussions and negotiations over my research, however, I became much more aware of the things which made me an outsider. I was attending university as a graduate student; I had worked for several years as a teacher and had a professional income; I had a husband; and we owned a car, which was second-hand but actually registered. As I became more involved in the project, interviewing the women about their own education stories, and as I visited them in their own homes, these differences became much more marked.... An interview with a researcher is formal. (Tuhiwai Smith, 2012, p. 139)

As Smith illustrates, outsider relations are established in the very declaration that a question is "research," with all its formal connotations.

Questioning

Questioning is the "mess-finding" stage in the research process, as well as the one that opens us up to possibilities and directs our gaze. What are the issues? What do we know already? What is our relationship to the issues and questions? What do other people know about it? What do we want to really understand?

There is enormous power in distilling the research question from a general research focus. The research question articulates what is and isn't explored and who is and isn't under scrutiny. Once a question has been put on the table, anti-oppressive researchers step back to critically consider: "Who says this is a question that needs to be studied, anyway?" And, "Whose interests are served by this research question being asked, and in this way?" Too frequently as researchers, we are influenced by funding, interest, curiosity, and previous research. Often, we have been trained to think of marginalized people as the "proper" objects of study and have given little consideration to studying those who are dominantly located. For example, if we are curious about racism, we are inclined to study visible minorities rather than White people. If we are concerned about accessibility for people with disabilities, we tend to study disabled people rather than the able-bodied. From an anti-oppressive perspective most research is organized with a gaze facing the wrong way, toward those who suffer from inequities rather than those who benefit from them or those who are indifferent. Our ability to shift the research gaze is often complicated by our connections to dominance. As well-intentioned, professional social justice workers, it is challenging to look at ourselves and our own positions as being complicit in creating and perpetuating oppression. But in anti-oppressive research, our complicity is an important focus for study. For example, instead of studying how the poor cope with poverty or homelessness, we might ask, "How do we (yes, you and I) contribute to the conditions creating poverty in our own community?" Reversing the gaze requires us to put dominance and power under scrutiny. We research "up." While it is also important to know the scope of inequality (for example, the number of homeless people), from a social justice perspective, perhaps it is more important to know how many buildings are left empty by land speculators waiting for prices to go up. Poverty is about a gap between the rich and the poor. But one side of the gap is more likely to be studied by the other side. Anti-oppressive research seeks to balance this.

To distill an issue into a guiding research question, anti-oppressive researchers do their homework. This involves finding out what knowledge is already available about the topic. Traditionally, this means checking the academic literature. As anti-oppressive researchers, we still do this, but we examine this existing knowledge critically to understand how, by whom, and for whose benefit it was constructed. And we do not stop there. We recognize knowledge from sources other than academic books and articles or reports published by governments and institutions. For instance, our lived experiences and those of others can provide valuable insights. Oral histories, blogs, and community conversations may also flesh out our starting point. Anti-oppressive research values diversity in knowledge. Critical assessment of many existing sources of knowledge on a topic and the credibility assigned to each source is part of the initial "questioning."

As important as it is to have a clear starting place, finding the question is seldom simple. Research questions are always political. Often, questions have to be extracted from our positivist and preconceived ideas about what a good research question "should" be. Sometimes questions are more like hunches, experienced tensions or disjunctures sensed in our own lives. But even when we get some initial clarity around the research question, this seldom lasts long. Questions usually change as the inquiry moves. Sometimes we never do find the question; instead, it finds us—at the end of the day, when the new knowledge from the analysis tells us what question we just answered. Keeping ourselves open to an emergent research process allows us to deepen our understanding about what it was we really wanted to know in the first place. But we have to be open to the art of the question through re-searching—the willingness to look again.

Designing, and Re-designing, a Plan to Study the Questions

More often than not, social justice research strives to be anti-oppressive in terms of purpose—that is, the desired outcomes are consistent with goals of social change. But this focus alone can replicate traditional research power relations, in which the dominant study the marginalized, with little shared control, relationships, or mutual benefits of participating in the research work. Because of this, we argue that we need the research process itself to be consistent with socially just and anti-oppressive values. Significant thought and strong relationships are integral to the designing and planning of an anti-oppressive research process. Given that most of us have been entrenched in Western scientific notions of research, doing research differently requires constant vigilance and support. A good plan always helps.

There are many questions that an anti-oppressive researcher asks in the ongoing process of articulating a research plan or design. Who has an interest, or stake, in the research? Who are we going to involve, and how? What are the ethical considerations? How are we going to collect data, and once collected, how are we going to interpret it? Who owns the data? What constraints and limitations do we face? What criteria will we use to judge the quality of our research? What do we do when things change or come up along the way?

The first question posed asks us to consider the various interests, power relations, and stakeholders in our research. We do not want the research work to be oriented toward external interests, but we do not want to be naïve about them, either. The interests of funders, target audiences, and hosting organizations should be considered. For example, if we are doing a research project as part of a university course, then we have to be aware of how the requirements of the assignment construct the research and constrain the possibilities. Or, if our purpose is to secure future funding for an addictions support program and we know that the funders want to know the extent of the problem, who needs to be served, and what alternative programs cost, we would not likely design a research project that interviewed one client in great depth about her experience as a drug user. Going back to our relationship work, it is useful to develop relationships with our potential audience and with those we are targeting for change. Politically, we have to consider when is the best time to get this stakeholder group engaged. There may be some merit to engaging this group throughout the research process in order to build rapport and possible support. There are a variety of ways to do this, including developing an advisory group or connecting the marginalized with the dominant through the research processes. Touraine, for example, achieved change in an organization through the process of putting labour and management representatives together in the same focus group in order to "reproduce social relationships in a research context, bringing together dominant and contesting actors in the same research groups" (McDonald, 2003, p. 248). Whatever the approach, the intention is that the actual process of the research becomes an intervention for change, rather than relying on changes coming through the research outcome or product.

At some point, decisions will need to be made to respond to the question of whom to involve in some or all of the research processes. This is what positivist researchers may call developing a sampling strategy. However, the goals for anti-oppressive research are very different, as involving people is done for purposes like community building, empowerment, and more nuanced understandings, rather than solely to achieve representativeness or validity. Sampling in anti-oppressive research is seldom random. Sampling is a power-laden decision, and is seen as one of many political acts in research. Ideally, an outsider researcher is never the sole source of invitations to participate; instead, it is a community of participants and insider researchers who do the inviting and including.

Ethical questions affect every research design. The ethics of anti-oppressive research reflect a commitment to and respect for people and relationships, as well as a commitment to action and social justice. The use of informed consent is one example. Constant renegotiation around a process of informed consent is important, as this highlights our commitments to the community, and our relationship to it, the data, and the process. Although most informed consent processes have become institutionalized for purposes of avoiding liability (Martin, 2007), we have reclaimed the concept of consent agreements to be a formal contract of our obligations to research participants, and a declaration of their ownership of the data, their right to a transparent research process, and their right to as much involvement or control as they choose. Certainly this way of working has led to some interesting situations for us (such as a community deciding to withdraw its data toward the end of a study), and as logistically difficult as these situations have been and can be, it does show that these processes work to shift power and ownership to the people living with the issues.

Respecting people and relationships also guides our responses to questions of ownership of data. The term *data* in its origins means "gift." From an anti-oppressive perspective, we see data as a gift that participants bestow, and we work to respect those gifts and treat them ethically. This means we must ask: Who owns the data, and what does ownership mean? If we (researchers) agree that participants own the data, and if after the research is completed the participants decide they don't like what we, the researchers, have said, what happens then?[4] Or if we hear the story of a participant that is compelling but filled with tangential comments and expressions we feel are distracting to what the research is saying, do we have the right to edit their story? Once edited, whose story is it? There are at least three voices in interpreting data: the participant who gave the story, the writer or researcher who records and retells it, and the reader who interprets it (Marcotte, 1995). We ask ourselves, "How are all these voices attended to?" Developing and attending to relationships, including those to data and data sources, are critical in anti-oppressive research.

Identifying the constraints to any design is important so that an anti-oppressive researcher can then identify the spaces within those constraints that can make the research less oppressive in its process, and ultimately in its outcome. The types of constraints you will encounter will be different and changing in every inquiry. However, there are some constraints that you can commonly anticipate, such as time, resources, and institutional and organizational structures. For example, if your research is connected with a university, you will be expected to submit your proposed study for approval to an ethics review committee and mould your research design to fit institutional regulations. Or, suppose the government has asked you to do some research. You will likely have a limited time frame and budget, and may face the constraints of having the research questions and possibly the design predetermined. But it is possible to engage in anti-oppressive processes even within constraints. For example, if we are confined to using a standardized survey questionnaire, we can still think about how to involve participants in the research, its process, and its outcome. Rather than designing the questionnaire yourself in isolation, it is possible to share control of question design and questionnaire administration with those being researched, or give control to them entirely. Similarly, rather than administer a questionnaire *to* participants, we could complete it *with* participants. This is more than just semantics; this shift in language produces a different relationship among the people involved in the research. It is also important that we never ask questions of others that we are not willing to answer and share ourselves.

Within the design, it is important to be clear about the criteria by which we want the quality of our research work to be evaluated, so that we can ensure there are methods in place to achieve them. It is the operationalization of "quality" that will make your research credible, publishable, actionable, and worth listening to. Without quality-assurance strategies, research can be dismissed as an opinion essay with no relevance for possible action. So what criteria are appropriate to judge the quality of anti-oppressive research, and who gets to decide this? Figuring this out requires attention to the perspectives of those who have an interest in the research, all within the framework of the tenets and ethics of anti-oppressive research.

And finally, there is the reality of implementing the research plan. When you are on a planned road trip, you often find you run across opportunities and obstacles that didn't exist on your map. Modifications to the plan are made, within the context of your purpose, the participants on the trip, how much time and money you have, and so on. Similarly, a research design is a dynamic plan that gets tweaked and altered along the way.

Collecting Data: Seeking, Listening, Learning

As anti-oppressive researchers, we strive to be perceptive, to pay attention to what we are in the midst of. However, this is hard work. We have to try to make what is usually invisible to us, visible. We have to find ways to see what we take for granted—the water we swim in. By paying attention, being creative, and being open, we can be responsive to seeing data, however it presents itself, in whatever forms are most meaningful to the people involved in the research. Data can be pictures, visuals, films, poems, music, numbers, or words. In our research classes we often encourage students to collect data on their own lives through mapping (Amsden & Van-Wynsberghe, 2005) and photovoice, a participatory research methodology first articulated by Caroline Wang and Mary Anne Burris (1997), in which research participants create, analyze, and discuss photos that represent their community (see also Castleden, Garvin, & Huu-ay-aht First Nation, 2008); these strategies are often meaningful for participants more comfortable with pictures than words. Sharing meaning between participants who speak different languages can help capture the materiality or embodiment of social issues, and it can help shake up those of us battling old biases about numbers and statistics being a superior form of data.

Regardless of the form our data takes, as all anti-oppressive research is relationship work, we still have to develop our political listening and critical reflecting skills. Mindfulness, being present, and being prepared to have the responsibility of witnessing are key skills. A good audio recorder, camera, or other technology can help to capture the details of the data, but it is the act of truly listening that propels the research forward. By articulating their experiences and thoughts, participants make meaning of their lives. By paying attention and listening, we become increasingly aware of contexts, histories, and social dynamics. Solidarity is nurtured. We can discover new opportunities for acting collectively that we had not foreseen or planned. Through paying attention and listening, research is reconceptualized and becomes an emergent, unfolding process, rather than a trip to a predetermined destination.

Making Meaning

Making meaning is often thought of as analyzing data. When doing anti-oppressive research, we assume that meaning-making is not restricted to any one part of the research process, but rather happens throughout the research process. As such, we pay attention to our processes of interpretation, reflection, and constructing meaning as the research journey unfolds.

While meaning-making is ongoing, we do have data to compile and make sense of, and this is the focus of this next part of the discussion. In practice, we have found that it is useful, as we begin to review our data, to revisit our research questions and design and consider how they have evolved and shifted from the original plan. By rearticulating our research design, we can open ourselves to understanding more specifically what we want to know and thus ask of the data. We can also become more aware of the kinds of data and data sources we have and our positioning in relation to the data. This clarity serves to ground our interpretations and analysis of the data. Our ways of gathering and working with data have probably been modified as the research process has unfolded. All these shifts and changes influence and determine what data we actually have and how we make sense of it.

There are a number of questions that we reflect upon as we plan for and engage in making meaning. These include issues of power and who does the analysis, as well as what concepts frame the analysis, who benefits from the meaning-making, and what analytic tools are appropriate.

Power lurks in all our reflections and decisions. Just figuring out who gets the privilege of making meaning is laden with issues of power. For us, research is a social process, and therefore the more positivist notion of one or two designated researchers who are responsible for analyzing the data is not our reality. Yet, even though we work collaboratively with participant-researchers, potential users of the research, and others in making meaning of our data, underlying hierarchies inherent in our relationships often challenge us. The analysis stage presents an opportunity for the social construction of knowledge to be facilitated in an intentionally liberatory way. Some people in the process are seen as experts in the topic of study, while others are seen as experts in particular data analysis techniques or in the lived experience of the data. Our collaborative meaning-making processes are influenced by the perceived and exercised power that we each bring to the process. These differences often become visible when there are disagreements about meanings or the importance of meanings. Further, while it may be ideal to have everyone possible involved in the meaning-making, the reality often is that not everyone has the time or interest to participate. Figuring out how to enable individuals to participate, as they would wish, is challenging.

Another point of reflection in planning and engaging in meaning-making concerns the conceptual framework that informs the research. Kirby and McKenna (1989, p. 32) challenge us to articulate our "conceptual baggage"—that is, the concepts, beliefs, metaphors, and frameworks that inform our perspective on and relationship to the research topic. The term *baggage* has a somewhat negative connotation, so we prefer to think about our "luggage." We carry our framework, which is not inherently good or bad, around with us, and it is through this framework that we view the data. Making the luggage visible is an individual and a collective process. Ensuring that everyone has had the opportunity to discuss the concepts that inform our perspectives helps to alleviate conflicts that can arise during the analysis around different perceptions of meaning and can expose contradictions in helpful ways. The conceptual framework that informed the project at the outset evolves during the project, and new or additional concepts, metaphors, and frameworks emerge. Winnowing through minutes of meetings about the topic or trying to explain to your friends what the research is about are often fruitful ways to discern the emergent frameworks. Discussing these frameworks with research participants can illuminate contradictions in concepts that may be held. Different concepts, metaphors, and frameworks produce different meanings and knowledge, and such discussions often bring up questions around which interpretation(s) is (are) seen as more valuable or believable than others, and why.

As researchers, we have found it particularly helpful to revisit the topic and questions in order to think through the fit between our approaches to analysis and what we really want to know. This revisiting is vital and informs the ability to make meaning and to extend the findings into conclusions and action.

The other point of reflection in the meaning-making process is thinking about who benefits from the chosen research process. What (and whose) purpose does the research serve?

There is an old saying that "figures don't lie, but liars can figure." The techniques of analysis, of making meaning of data, contribute to the meaning made. What is the intended outcome, and how is the data analysis, whether statistical or not, being constructed? What data is being included in the analysis and what is being left out? Why? If using interview data, who decides which quotations from participants to include, and by their inclusion, who is excluded? Again, knowledge is constructed, and paying attention to why and how it is constructed in certain ways is an ongoing challenge for anti-oppressive researchers.[...]

What kind of approach is to be taken? Some options include involving participants in analyzing the data or having those ultimately affected by the research (who may not be the participants) involved. What about having an advisory group to our research and having them conduct the analysis? Or finding a way to involve the people who will be responsible for making change as a result of the research? Whatever approach is used, consider how it will affect the results of the research and how those results could be used.

Posing Conclusions and New Questions, Taking More Action

> Knowing is not enough, we must apply. Willing is not enough, we must do.
>
> —Goethe

> Knowing without doing, isn't really knowing.
>
> —Fortune cookie

We continuously think about new questions, new realizations, and new applications of ideas as we travel the research journey. Yet at some point along the journey, there will be times when we are asked for conclusions and summary thoughts. Conclusions have a particular power in that they are the construction of knowledge that leads to recommendations and actions. As well, conclusions are often the sound bites in the research that an audience listens for. Sometimes, these consumers of our research are interested in our trip, the story of our process, but more often they are interested in what we have "found." How conclusions are constructed, therefore, has particular impact on how the audience will take up the research in their own lives.

Common practice is for research to be "written up" in a formal report, or perhaps turned into a journal article. This practice is inherently classist, exclusionary, and appropriative in that it requires translating marginal knowledges into the language of the elite. Written reports and journal articles are read by some audiences, but are they the audiences that will help mobilize our new knowledge into social justice? Other options are worthy of consideration. Brainstorming with co-researchers for options that could facilitate the goals of empowerment and social justice then becomes a key part of the work. For instance, would it be better to hold a community workshop to discuss the research, or write a letter to the editor, or put the findings into a popular theatre presentation, or convene a session of strategic planning, or produce a video or a website?

As we have noted throughout this paper, research happens in relationships between people. It is a site for practicing democracy. Recognizing our agency, our ability to make a choice in how something will be done, enables us to be purposeful in our anti-oppressive actions. As researchers, reframing research as part of our practice of knowledge democracy has helped us to move beyond the trap of oppositional thinking within anti-oppressive research. How we pose conclusions and devise actions is yet another opportunity to practice democracy and thereby make real our beliefs about power relations and social justice. Posing conclusions brings us to ask the critical question, "So what?" How will the research be used, and by whom? Who else could make use of it, and how? What uses could it have that were not intended? Remember that producing a product that sits on a shelf does not mean that the research, or the research report, does not fill a purpose. Too often, research is used to delay decision-making or distract attention from an issue. What is the professional obligation of the researcher in ensuring that the research is used for social change, not only throughout the process of conducting the research, but also after the research is concluded? We have found that by returning to our original discussions about the issues and what we wanted to know, we discover a nest of possibilities about what to do with the findings, who will use them, and how they will or could be used. Anti-oppressive action in the research process means taking up the processes and tools of research in ways that are congruent with the principles and values of empowerment and social justice wherever and whenever possible.

Identifying and Meeting the Challenges to Anti-oppressive Research

Anti-oppressive research is exciting, engaging, and critical. Why wouldn't we do anti-oppressive research all the time? In our efforts to become anti-oppressive researchers, we will come across a number of barriers and challenges—some of our own making, some external to us, and some that are a combination of both. Here we explain three significant challenges.

Dominant discourses: We live in a world with shared dominant myths that we encounter every day, and we need to make these visible in order to address them. Beliefs that continued economic growth is possible, desirable, and good for everyone, or that technology and science will save us from our current economic and environmental crises, have an unconscious influence on our lives and research work, shaping the research questions we pose, the methods we see as credible, and the value we place on the wisdom of the "oppressed" versus the "experts." Likewise, we need to acknowledge the current discourses that dominate human service research discussions. Outcome-based measurements and evaluation and evidence-based decision-making continue to be popular (Campbell & Ng, 1988). As a social justice worker, you will encounter these discourses, and it will be up to you to understand the deep positivist and neo-liberal epistemological roots they extend from. You will need to see how these discourses will try to construct and constrain your work. And most importantly, you will need to know how to engage anti-oppressive practices to try and produce social justice outcomes despite the constraints. For example, in program evaluation, empowerment or participatory evaluation approaches are a good place to start (Secret, Jordan, & Ford, 1999).

The project paradigm: Those of us trained to do research have been conditioned to think in terms of research "projects." This project paradigm sees research as a linear, time-limited, beginning-middle-end, textually based (proposal to report) process. Anti-oppressive research moves research into being part of a community-building, social change process. Anti-oppressive research needs to be entwined in the complex context, part of something larger, not an end in itself. The goal of anti-oppressive research is not a finished report, but an ongoing community-building enterprise helping us to develop complex understandings about our lives. Relationships and action are the prioritized components, not surveys and reports.

Funding: One factor that gets in the way of switching from the project paradigm is applying for and receiving money. A lot of good anti-oppressive research work can happen without money, but realistically, there are often costs to getting people together. Participants' time and work should be compensated. Money for meeting spaces and "getting the word out" can be a good thing. But most funding processes are geared to projects. Funders like time-limited, outcome-focused projects and rely on traditional proxies of proposals and reports as indicators of research work. To respond to funder guidelines, researchers are often transformed from community participants into research managers. However, it is possible to be accountable to community and run a fiscally responsible project! Strategies like negotiating time concessions or exploring non-traditional funding sources, such as credit unions or those interested in community-based work, can be explored. And, once money is obtained, sharing is an important principle for anti-oppressive research. Researchers taking the lion's share of the money out of the community as salaries or contracts are acting in ways that are counterproductive to community-building processes and social justice values.

Our own epistemology: Doing research differently requires a different acceptance of what counts as knowledge. While we all "know" there are different types of knowledges, most of us have been schooled in Western knowledge paradigms, and when it comes right down to it, most of us do not truly accept non-Western knowledges as equal. Most of us are still caught in valuing objectivity over subjectivity. We tend to believe that scientific, experimental knowledge is more valid than experiential knowledge. We tend to be biased toward large sample sizes versus seeing the value of learning from one person's "outlier" experience. We get caught up in looking for one truth instead of continually digging to find multiple perspectives. We still hope for one simple answer to questions when we have to learn to live with knowledge being ambiguous, temporal, and partial at best. These are tough challenges for us as researchers. But the good news is that we have the capacity within ourselves to meet these challenges.

A Few Concluding Thoughts ... for Now

By now you may be wondering: Is there a distinctive anti-oppressive method of inquiry? In a word, no. There is no fixed or bona fide set of methods or methodologies that is inherently anti-oppressive. Various emancipatory and critical social science research methodologies, such as feminist and Indigenous research and Freirian emancipatory or participatory research, are potential "allies" in doing anti-oppressive research. Many methodologies touch on some, but not necessarily all, of the tenets we are trying to foreground in anti-oppressive research. If anything, we are arguing that anti-oppressive research is not methodologically distinctive, but is epistemologically distinctive. We have come to believe that if we are to transform research into an anti-oppressive practice, then it is the epistemological underpinnings (e.g., relationships of the knower, the known, and those who want to know) that are key.

Part of the concept of agency that we have talked about is the ability to change one's self. This requires constant reflection and critique. In proposing the idea of anti-oppressive research, we do not want to create another dogma. In later life, Horkheimer critiqued the arrogance of any revolutionary tradition that can turn around and be itself oppressive (Ray, 2003, p. 164). Always being reflective about yourself and your work is not easy. Just when we think we're getting it right, we realize we're only getting it better. Becoming anti-oppressive is not a comfortable place to be. It means constantly reflecting on how one is being constructed and how one is constructing one's world. This chapter is part of our becoming. We hope it helps you in your research journey as well.

Notes

1. The authors acknowledge the University of Victoria social work students who have been with us on this journey toward anti-oppressive research, with special thanks to Christine and Andrea for their unique contributions.
2. For us, social justice work means transforming the way resources and relationships are produced and distributed so that all people can live dignified lives in a way that is ecologically sustainable. Our critical view of social justice includes economic justice, intergenerational equity, global justice, and eco-centric justice (Ife & Tesoriero, 2006). It takes direct aim at the sources of structural disadvantage, whether those are through institutions, like income security, or through human relations, such as racism. It is also about creating new ways of thinking and being, not only criticizing the status quo. Social justice means acting from the standpoint of those who have the least power and influence, and valuing the wisdom of the oppressed.
3. Empowerment is a problematic term because its meaning can be so variable. In this chapter, when "empowerment" appears in quotations, it is being contested as a term that often implies a feeling without real power, upward mobility, or individual self-confidence, or an illusion of real power. When we as authors truly speak of empowerment, we are using the term as Lather (1991) does, "drawing on Gramsci's (1971) ideas of counter-hegemony ... empowerment to mean analyzing ideas about the causes of powerlessness, recognizing

systemic oppressive forces, and acting both individually and collectively to change the conditions of our lives" (pp. 3–4).

4. Cultivating co-researchers is one way that many who try to be more anti-oppressive in their research engage the tenets of anti-oppressive work. As knowledge is socially constructed, and what is created through coming together as knowers is more than what each knew before, co-researching can become a way of producing knowledge and producing knowers. Yet such an approach is not without its own power issues. Too often, we have seen projects where insiders are co-researchers but are only given a token position within the research design. It posits the question: To what extent can research truly be anti-oppressive unless the people experiencing the issue under study *are* the researchers and are in control of the research decisions?

References

Amsden, J., & VanWynsberghe, R. (2005). Community mapping as a research tool with youth. *Action Research, 3*, 357–381.

AUCC. (2001). *The commercialization of university research.* Ottawa, ON: Association of Universities and Colleges of Canada.

Campbell, M., & Ng, R. (1988). Program evaluation and the standpoint of women. *Canadian Review of Social Policy, 22*, 41–50.

Castleden, H., Garvin, T., & Huu-ay-aht First Nation. (2008). Modifying photovoice for community-based participatory Indigenous research. *Social Science & Medicine, 66*(6), 1393–1405.

Ceglowski, D. (2000). Research as relationship. *Qualitative Inquiry, 6*(1), 88–103.

David, P. A., & Foray, D. (2002). An introduction to the economy of the knowledge society. *International Social Science Journal,* (171), 9–23.

Hall, B. (2011). Towards a knowledge democracy movement: Contemporary trends in community-university research partnerships. *Rhizome freirean, 9.*

Huisman, K. (2008). "Does this mean you're not going to come visit me anymore?": An inquiry into an ethics of reciprocity and positionality in feminist ethnographic research. *Sociological Inquiry, 78*(3), 372–396.

Ife, J., & Tesoriero, F. (2006). *Community development: Community-based alternatives in an age of globalisation.* Toronto, ON: Pearson Education Canada.

Kirby, S. L., & McKenna, K. (1989). *Experience research social change: Methods from the margins.* Toronto, ON: Garamond Press.

Lather, P. (1991). *Getting smart: Feminist research and pedagogy with/in the postmodern.* New York: Routledge.

Marcotte, G. (1995). "Metis c'est may nation. 'Your own people', Comme on dit": Life histories from Eva, Evelyn, Priscilla, and Jennifer Richard. Paper prepared for the Royal Commission on Aboriginal Peoples.

Martin, D. G. (2007). Bureacratizing ethics: Institutional review boards and participatory research. *ACME: An International E-Journal for Critical Geographies*, 6(3), 319–328.

McDonald, K. (2003). Alain Touraine. In A. Elliott & L. Ray (Eds.), *Key contemporary social theorists* (pp. 246–251). Oxford, UK: Blackwell Publishing.

McLaughlin, K. (2005). From ridicule to institutionalization: Anti-oppression, the state and social work. *Critical Social Policy*, *25*(3), 283–305.

Ray, L. (2003). Max Horkheimer. In A. Elliott & L. Ray (Eds.), *Key contemporary social theorists* (pp. 162–168). Oxford, UK: Blackwell Publishing.

Secret, M., Jordan, A., & Ford, J. (1999). Empowerment evaluation as a social work strategy. *Health & Social Work*, *24*(2), 120–127.

Tuhiwai Smith, L. (2012). *Decolonizing methodologies: Research and Indigenous peoples* (2nd ed.). London, UK: Zed Books.

Wang, C. & Burris, M. (1997). Photovoice: Concept, methodology, and use for participatory needs assessment. *Health Education and Behavior* *24*(3), 369-387

RETHINKING SECTION 1

Discussion Questions

Chapter 1

1. Why do people tend to view how society works in individual terms?
2. According to Mills, what are the benefits of employing one's sociological imagination?
3. Can you think of an example from your own life that you once thought of as an individual or private trouble that you now see as a public issue?

Chapter 2

1. In what ways does sociology challenge "our assumptions about ourselves as individuals and about the wider social contexts in which we live" as Giddens suggests?
2. What is the importance of theory in sociology and/or social research?
3. Giddens suggests that "social research doesn't and can't remain separate from the social world it describes. Is it problematic that sociologists cannot separate themselves from the world they describe in their works? Why or why not? What sort of ethical questions might this pose for social researchers?

Chapter 3

1. Are duties we perform as social actors external to individuals?
2. According to Durkheim, what is a social current?
3. How can we identify social facts?
4. What is the connection between power and social facts?

Chapter 4

1. Why do Marx and Engels assert that understanding one's present society requires an investigation into societies of the past?
2. What is class conflict? How is class conflict different from other forms of conflict (between individual people or nations)?

Chapter 5

1. How does Weber's analysis compare to Marx's materialist analysis that positions the forces of production as shaping the social world?

2. Outline the key characteristics of the Protestant ethic. How does Weber connect these characteristics to the development of capitalism?

Chapter 6

1. Who is generally considered the subject of sociology? How is a woman's world bifurcated?
2. How does the organization of public work depend upon men's alienation from their bodily and local existences? What does Smith argue this means for women?
3. Explain Smith's image of an alternative sociology. Where must the sociologist be situated?

Chapter 7

1. Why does Foucault view "genealogies" as anti-science?
2. How does Foucault understand "subjugated knowledges"?
3. In order to move beyond sovereignty and normalization as the mechanisms for exploration of social sciences, what does Foucault propose?

Chapter 8

1. How is the notion of consent important for hegemony?
2. What is the role of the dominant class in Gramsci's concept of hegemony?
3. Can you think of current applications for Gramsci's concept beyond class dynamics?

Chapter 9

1. Contemporary social sciences reject the idea of race as a biological concept in favour of considering race as a social construct. Why?
2. The article speaks of racial identity as a combination of both the racial assumptions made by individuals about themselves as well as the racial assumptions made by another person about them. How does this support viewing race as a social construct rather than a biological reality?

Chapter 10

1. Bryman et al. note that it is typically middle-range theories that directly guide social research. Can you think of examples where grand theory might be better suited?
2. What are the core differences between positivism and interpretivism? What are the core differences between objectivism and constructivism?
3. Why is transparency with regard to one's values so important to the social research process?

Chapter 11

1. How is social location important to anti-oppressive research? What social location(s) do you occupy, and how does this affect your claim to being anti-oppressive (should you choose to make this claim)?
2. Discuss the differences between positivist research and anti-oppressive research.
3. What are outsider-insider relations? How are power relations integral to these relations? What causes insider-outsider tensions? Can they be alleviated?

SECTION 2
MAJOR SOCIAL PROCESSES

The Readings

This section explores everyday social interactions, culture, and crime from a sociological perspective. Our first piece, by Jacqueline Lewis, explores the social process involved in learning to become an exotic dancer. Some of this learning takes place prior to becoming a dancer while much of it happens "on the job." Lewis also explores the relationship between being an exotic dancer and one's sexuality and sexual relationships.

Next we include another classic sociological piece. Here Erving Goffman explores how we present ourselves to others in our everyday lives. Goffman outlines two forms of communication: the expressions that we give and the expressions that we give off. We can use both forms of communication to learn about those we interact with.

Next we have a chapter that illustrates how social movements are both policed and repressed, with private security often serving as the catalyst for state action in the so-called interest of public order. The particular focus of this chapter is on the suppression of animal rights activists in Canada. The researchers, Walby and Monaghan, draw on both the Access to Information Act document request results and interviews with animal rights activists in their exploration of surveillance, policing, and social movements.

Last in this section is a chapter concerned with the social issue of woman abuse in Canada, by Walter S. DeKeseredy and Molly Dragiewicz. The authors trace past scholarly sociological research (since about the mid-1980s) on the topic as well as point to future directions of study. The authors take a political economy approach that emphasizes the social forces that both influence the form of research and limit research on woman abuse in Canada.

CHAPTER 12

Learning to Strip: The Socialization Experiences of Exotic Dancers

Jacqueline Lewis

Introduction

Entering any new job or social role requires a process of socialization where the individual acquires the necessary values, attitudes, interests, skills, and knowledge in order to be competent at her/his job. As with any new job or social role, becoming an exotic dancer requires a process of socialization. For exotic dancers, achieving job competence involves getting accustomed to working in a sex-related occupation, and the practice of taking their clothes off in public for money. In addition, in order to be a successful exotic dancer, women must also learn how to manipulate clientele and to rationalize such behaviour and their involvement in a deviant occupation.[1] For some dancers, the socialization process is partially anticipatory in nature, although, dancers reported that most of their socialization occurred once they had made their decision to dance and found themselves actually working in the strip club environment. In this paper, I explore the factors influencing entry into exotic dancing, the socialization experiences of exotic dancers, and the process of obtaining job competence.

Background

Since the late 1960s, exotic dancing and the experiences of exotic dancers have been the focus of academic inquiry (Boles & Garbin, 1974a, 1974b, 1974c; Carey, Peterson & Sharpe, 1974; Dressel & Petersen, 1982a, 1982b; Enck & Preston, 1988; Forsyth & Deshotels, 1997; McCaghy & Skipper, 1969, 1972; Petersen & Dressel, 1982; Prus, 1980; Reid, Epstein & Benson, 1994; Ronai & Ellis, 1989; Ronai, 1992; Skipper & McCaghy, 1971; Thompson & Harred, 1992). The relevance of some of the available literature to the present study is, however, limited by the focus of the articles. Within this literature on exotic dancers, only the articles by Boles and Garbin (1974b, 1974c), Carey et al. (1974), Dressel and Petersen (1982b), McCaghy and Skipper (1971), Prus (1980), Skipper and McCaghy (1972), and Thompson and Harred (1992) address the socialization experiences of dancers in any detail. Dressel and Petersen's (1982b) focus on the socialization of male exotic dancers makes their work of limited applicability to the present study.

Although much of this research was conducted over 15 to 20 years ago, some of it remains relevant to the work reported here. For example, the findings of Boles and Garbin (1974b, 1974c),

Carey et al. (1974), McCaghy and Skipper (1971), Prus (1980) and Skipper and McCaghy (1972) provide an historical point of comparison that indicates some consistency between past and current research findings on the occupational socialization of exotic dancers.

The literature on occupational socialization of exotic dancers emphasizes two basic themes: (1) the factors that influence entry into dancing; and (2) anticipatory and on-the-job socialization experiences. Two types of models have been advanced to explain entry into exotic dancing: (1) career contingency models (Skipper & McCaghy, 1972; Carey et al., 1974; Thompson & Harred, 1992); and (2) conversion models (Boles & Garbin, 1974b; Carey et al., 1974; Thompson & Harred, 1992). In some research reports, these models are used on their own (e.g., Skipper & McCaghy, 1972; Boles & Garbin, 1974b), and in others they are used in combination (Carey et al., 1974; Thompson & Harred, 1992). Although a variety of singular and combined models have been used to explain entry into exotic dancing, there are several common factors that are identified across the studies: (1) knowledge and accessibility of an opportunity structure that makes exotic dancing an occupational alternative (Carey et al., 1974; Skipper & McCaghy, 1972; Prus, 1980; Thompson & Harred, 1992); (2) an awareness of the economic rewards associated with being an exotic dancer (Boles & Garbin, 1974b; Carey et al., 1974; Dressel & Petersen, 1982b; Skipper & McCaghy, 1972; Prus, 1980; Thompson & Harred, 1992); (3) a recruitment process involving personal networks (Boles & Garbin, 1974b; Dressel & Petersen, 1982b; Thompson & Harred, 1992); and (4) financial need or a need for employment (Boles & Garbin, 1974b, 1974c; Carey et al., 1974; Prus, 1980; Thompson & Harred, 1992).

With respect to the anticipatory and on-the-job socialization experiences of dancers (Boles & Garbin, 1974c; Dressel & Petersen, 1982b; Thompson & Harred, 1992), early research found that most female dancers had either professional training in dance, music, or theatre, had been previously employed in the entertainment industry, or received extensive training in stripping prior to dancing before an audience (Boles & Garbin, 1974c; McCaghy & Skipper, 1972, Prus, 1980). However, despite their advanced (anticipatory) preparation, a large part of the occupational socialization dancers experienced occurred through informal channels after they had entered the occupation. Through observing and interacting with other subcultural members, dancers learned the tricks of the trade, such as how to: interact with customers for profit; manage their deviant lifestyle; and be successful at their job (Boles & Garbin, 1974c; Dressel & Petersen, 1982; McCaghy & Skipper, 1972; Thompson & Harred, 1992).

Method

This study used a combination of field observations inside strip clubs, and interviews with exotic dancers and other club staff to identify issues associated with the work and careers of exotic dancers. Observations were conducted at clubs in several cities in southern Ontario. Observational data were collected primarily to supplement interview data and to assist us in describing the work environment of exotic dancers, including: physical setting; contacts between those present in the club (employees and clients); and the atmosphere of different clubs.

Thirty semi-structured, in-depth interviews were conducted with female exotic dancers, club staff, and key informants. Participants were recruited either by the research team during field trips to the clubs or by dancers who had participated in the study. Each interview was audio taped and took place in a location chosen by the respondent (e.g., respondent's home, a research team member's office, a private space at a strip club, a local coffee shop). Interviews lasted anywhere from one to three hours, with the majority taking approximately one-and-a-half hours. All interviews were conducted informally to allow participants to freely express themselves, and to allow for exploration of new or unanticipated topics that arose in the interview.

The interviews explored each woman's work history, her perception of her future in the occupation, a description of her work, the various forms of interaction engaged in with clients, use of drugs and alcohol, current sexual practices, perception of risk for HIV and other STDs associated with dancing, sexual health-maintaining strategies, factors influencing risk and ability to maintain sexual health, and the presence and/or possibility of a community among exotic dancers. Interviews with other club employees were designed to tap their experiences in, and impressions of, club-related activities.

[...] The quotes that appear in this paper were selected as examples of the responses provided by the women interviewed that fit the various conceptual categories that emerged during data analysis.

Becoming an Exotic Dancer

Unlike other more conventional occupations with formally structured socialization programs, the socialization experiences of the women we spoke with were informal in nature. Dancers reported that they acquired the requisite skills for the job through informal socialization processes that were either: (1) anticipatory in nature, occurring prior to dancing; and/or (2) that occurred on the job, once they were employed to dance in a strip club.

ANTICIPATORY SOCIALIZATION

Early studies of female exotic dancers (see Boles & Garbin, 1974; McCaghy & Skipper, 1972) found that most dancers had fairly broad anticipatory socialization experiences, having been previously employed in an entertainment-related job, having some type of professional training in dance, music, or theatre, or having an agent who helped prepare them for the career of exotic dancing. In this study, we, however, found little indication of the latter two types of anticipatory socialization experiences. Although one woman had a background in drama, she talked about how it actually did little to prepare her for the job:

> I thought you know, O.K. being in Drama, ya, I'm kind of a freer person, whatever. But, like, actually taking off your clothes—nothing, nothing prepares you for it. Nothing. Seconds before I went up to go dance [for the first time], I'm thinking, oh my God, I can't do this, I can't do this. I can't do this. Then my music started play-

ing and I'm like, I guess I have to now. And you know, your stomach's all in knots and you just do it. There's no way to describe it. You just do it.

Although the experiences dancers reported during their interviews varied, the women we spoke with who reported engaging in anticipatory socialization, talked about spending time in strip clubs before deciding to dance. In recalling their entry into exotic dancing, some of the dancers we interviewed spoke of being curious about dancing, and wanting to find out if it was something they could do. These women reported that they sussed out and gained familiarity with dancing by going out to strip clubs on their own and talking to dancers or by going out to the clubs with friends who hung out at or worked in strip clubs.

> So, I read some more about it. I read a couple of books on the sex industry and strippers in particular and burlesque dancers. Um, and then I visited a lot of the clubs and tried to talk to the dancers about how they got interested in it and how they get paid and what the job entails. They were pretty open to talking to me about it.

The other women who had anticipatory socialization experiences reported experiencing a more gradual drift into dancing (Matza, 1992).[2] Instead of purposefully going to strip clubs and talking to people in the industry with the intention of sussing it out, these women drifted into dancing through associations they had with people in the industry or by working as a waitress in one of the clubs.

> I didn't start out dancing. First I was a waitress. Eventually, I quit waitressing and I went and started dancing at a strip club.

> I used to date this guy and some of his friends worked in the clubs, so we could go and hang out. He used to try to get me to try it [dancing], but I wouldn't. But, once we broke up, I decided to try it.

According to Ritzer and Walczak (1986), "[...] deviant occupational skills may be learned through involvement in different but related occupations or through nonoccupational activities" (p. 144). Through hanging out with people associated with the industry or by working in a strip club in some other capacity, these women experienced a form of anticipatory socialization that enabled them to view dancing as a viable job option. As noted by Matza (1992), "some learning is truly a discovery [for the individual], for until they have experimented with the forbidden, [... they] are largely unaware that infraction is feasible behavior" (p. 184).

> A lot of my friends and a lot of the group that I used to hang around with while I was waitressing were uh, we were all in the same circles with the guys from a strip club for women and uh, the two clubs were connected, and so they kept saying "try it" and, you know, "go to this bar, start there" and that's just how I ended up there.

The experiences of the women who drifted into dancing can be viewed as a form of recruitment or conversion process whereby the individual is gradually introduced/exposed to the inner world of a new role or career and gives up one view of that role, or one world view, for another (see Becker, 1964; Lofland & Stark, 1965; Prus, 1977). According to Lofland and Stark (1965), the reinforcement and encouragement made available through intensive interaction with subgroup members is necessary if the recruit is to experience a complete conversion process.

Regardless of how they began their process of occupational socialization, in providing themselves with time to think things through, and to learn to identify with the norms, values, and beliefs of the dancing subculture prior to entering it, these women were engaging in a form of role rehearsal and anticipatory socialization. Such efforts provided them with the opportunity to prepare themselves for the eventual reality of their new status, thereby easing the difficulties associated with the transition. Through engaging in anticipatory socialization, the women interviewed became accustomed to the strip club environment and the idea of taking their clothes off in public for money, thereby facilitating their entry into dancing.

ON-THE-JOB SOCIALIZATION

Similar to the socialization experiences of individuals in other occupations, novice dancers learn through interaction and observation while on the job. Since exotic dancers, however, have little, if any, formal training, learning through observation and interaction is crucial for attaining job competence (see Sanders, 1974). Although some of this learning may be anticipatory in nature and occurs prior to the initial dancing experience, it takes some time and experience to move from being a novice dancer to a seasoned pro. Since there is no formal certification structure, peers play an important role in this transformation process. During this period, novices can continue to acquire knowledge from those around them about how to be successful at their job. Experienced strip club staff can therefore play an important role in the socialization process of the novice dancer. As one woman noted:

> You learn as you go. Other people in the club give you advice. And, you know, you gradually learn about how to make more money and who to talk to and that kind of stuff as you go.

Through talking to and receiving advice about the job from other staff members, novice dancers learn how to handle situations that may arise while working in the club, and how to dance for profit.

> The DJ at the first club I danced at was very good. On my first night he was like, "Don't worry about it ... You know, just go up there and do your thing and you know, don't worry about it." And the other girls were kind of supportive, like, "Oh, you'll get used to it, it's not that bad after a while." You know, some of them kind of take you under their wing and sort of show you the ropes so to speak.

Other dancers play a particularly important role in the socialization process. As the following quotes illustrate, novices can learn how to dress, dance, and interact with customers for profit through observing and interacting with dancers more experienced than themselves.

> Most of the dancers are really nice, like, they're really understanding. They knew, you know, I hadn't danced for very long. Everybody was offering me advice. There were a few that were kind of like, stay away from me and I'll stay away from you sort of thing.

> I get ideas for my show from watching, you know, the ones that have been doing this [dancing] for a while.

RATIONALIZING PARTICIPATION IN A DEVIANT OCCUPATION

Since exotic dancing is viewed as a deviant occupation in our society, if novice dancers are to retain a valued sense of self, they must learn ways to justify their involvement in the strip club subculture. According to Sykes and Matza (1957), in order to deviate, people must have access to a set of rationalizations or neutralizations that allow them to reduce the guilt they feel about violating social norms. Neutralization makes norm violations "morally feasible since it serves to obliterate, or put out of mind, the dereliction implicit in it" (Matza, 1992, p. 182).

During interviews with dancers, it became apparent that dancers typically rely on several "techniques of neutralization" (Sykes & Matza, 1957) to justify their involvement in deviant behaviour. Similar to Thompson and Harred's (1992) research on topless dancers, we found that the dancers we interviewed tended to rely primarily on three of Sykes and Matza's (1957) techniques of neutralization. They denied injury or harm:

> Ya well, we pretend [that they like the customers], but what do they really expect? Do they really think we are there because we like them, that we like to dance for men—no. And really, who are we hurting?

> We may take their money, and although sometimes it may be a lot, but, they are adults, they should know better. And besides, it's just money.

They condemned the condemners:

> People may judge us and say that dancing is bad, but they seem to forget who it is we are dancing for—doctors, lawyers, sports figures. If it wasn't for them there would be no dancing—so maybe the focus is on the wrong people [the dancers rather than the customers].

And they appealed to higher loyalties[3]:

> Well, they say that you're not supposed to show your body to lustful men and that that's a sin. So I assume that like, obviously God wasn't gonna be very happy that I was doing something like this. But, the other way I looked at it was, I have a daughter who is two years old and the government really doesn't give you enough to survive, so I had to do something. And I figured that if it's a sin to take off your clothes and it's a sin to let your child starve, definitely, I would take care of the second one, and it's probably more normal.
>
> If you need to feed your kids, what are you going to do?

In addition to using some of Sykes and Matza's (1957) techniques of neutralization to justify their involvement in exotic dancing, we found that dancers used the technique of normalization. As the following quote illustrates, some women attempted to justify or neutralize their involvement in exotic dancing by refuting the deviancy associated with it.

> And I looked at the salaries these people were making and it was, you know, a thousand dollars a night, some nights, and it was really, really substantially helping with their tuition. And these were people working on Master's degrees and Doctorates and all kinds of things and I thought, "Wow, if they can do this, hey, maybe I can."

Despite the deviancy associated with being an exotic dancer and the negative aspects of the job, most of the women we spoke with seemed to be able to rationalize or justify their involvement in exotic dancing. In summarizing the use of justifications by exotic dancers, one woman said:

> You can justify it because you bring home money and at the end of the night that feels great. You don't reflect on, you know, how you were degraded, the leering and the other bad stuff. You know, you don't think about it because you've got a big wad of money in your hand.

In other words, the major incentive for entering dancing, money,[4] is also used as the main justification or rationale for continuing to do it. As with Hong and Duff's (1977) study of taxi-dancers, the neutralization techniques or rationalizations used by exotic dancers to downplay the norm-violating nature of their behaviour, soothe guilt feelings, and cope with the unpleasant aspects of their jobs, were learned during the informal socialization processes that occur on the job.

PUTTING ON A SHOW

Beyond acquiring the courage to take off one's clothes in public and learning how to justify one's actions, obtaining competence as an exotic dancer also requires learning to be good at the job. In order to become a successful exotic dancer, the novice dancer must learn how to put on a good show or performance. As with any successful performer, dancers need to learn how to use impression management skills to create an illusion that will allow them to control/manipulate their audience in order to achieve some specified goal, in this case the acquisition of money. In their interviews, the women talked about how their job required they put on a skilful performance that would lure men in and get them to spend their money on dancers.

> A dance is not just dancing, it is the way you present yourself, the way you talk to the customer, the way you introduce yourself ... If you gonna have a smile, right away it's gonna be easy [to make money].

> Sometimes you just look at a customer, the way he reacts ... I can tell what they like. I'm always doing things that flatter my body. I touch my boobs all the time. I touch myself all the time. It's kind of masturbation but in front of people ... It gets the men going and keeps them coming back.

As dancers reported in their interviews, learning how to control or manipulate an audience is acquired through observation and interaction with subcultural members within the club setting.

> I was really glad I waitressed before dancing. I got to overhear a lot of the conversations between the dancers and the customers. It was that way that I figured out how to operate and ways to play the men for their money.

Skill development, improvement, and job competence more generally were affirmed by coworkers through praise, and by customers through applause, requests for table dances, the development of a regular clientele, and increased take-home pay.

TYPOLOGY OF DANCERS

Although the women interviewed reported that they experienced a process of adjustment in becoming a dancer, this process differed somewhat according to the type of dancer each woman could be classified as. Based on the interview data collected, there appear to be two types of dancers: the career dancer and the goal-oriented dancer. Both types of dancers report money as the primary motivating factor for entry into dancing; however, they differ in the types of future they envision for themselves. Despite the fact that most of the women we spoke with told us that they never intended on making dancing a career, some ended up staying in the industry for many years, essentially making it one. Other women reported that they entered the world of dancing with the expectation that dancing would be their career for a while. Whether they intended on making dancing a career or not, the career dancers we spoke with tended to possess limited skill training and education. As a result, they saw dancing as an employment opportunity that enabled them to make a decent living that would otherwise be unavailable to them through other channels.

> This as a career for me, it's seventeen years. I don't want to stop this now. And besides, what other job could I get where I can earn this kind of money?

> There really are no jobs for women like me who have little education. At least none where I could make this much money.

In contrast with the career dancer, the goal-oriented dancer enters dancing with a specific goal in mind.

> I don't look at it like a career so it's kind of like a means to an end. You know how you put yourself on a program, like a five-year program. Get in there and make a whack of cash and then go on to something else. Like that can't be the only thing that I want to do for the rest of my life.

> Some dancers report being motivated to enter dancing in order to make the money they needed to get or stay out of debt.

> I'm getting my Honours Bachelor of Arts in Drama and I want to eventually open my own Drama Therapy Clinic. So, this is just a means of getting there because the money is really good and I'd like to start saving. You know, I've spent all my money on my education and I haven't put any aside for my future, so this would be a quick way to do it, cuz the money's really good and it's really fast.

> I don't want to do it, but you have to, I have to do it, I don't have a choice. I have a car payment, I have to pay my rent, I can't not do it. Nothing else will pay my bills. So that's it.

One specific group of goal-oriented dancers are the students. These women report that for them dancing is a short-term job that pays well and that can fit in with their class schedule.

> It's ideal when you're going to school because you just—you make your own schedules. When I have exam week I don't go at all. So, it fits in with school. So, I guess, I mean, I don't think I would work [as a dancer] once I finish school, unless I couldn't find a job or something.

The commonality among goal-oriented dancers is that dancing is seen as a short-term thing, a means to an end, once the end is achieved (e.g., they graduate from university, pay off their debts, etc.), the plan is to leave dancing. It is important to note though, that although many goal-oriented dancers reported planning on leaving, some spoke of difficulties exiting once they got used to the money they could earn.

> It's kinda hard once you get used to the money to leave [dancing]. I mean, like, I always said I would leave when I got out of debt, but the money draws you back.

> I've wanted out for so many years now and just didn't know how. You get so trapped in there and I didn't know what to do or what I could do.

The type of dancer one identifies as has implications for the socialization experiences of dancers. Women who see dancing as a career, rather than as a temporary job, tend to be more inclined to get involved in the "dancer life," develop relationships with other dancers and club employees, and become immersed in the strip club subculture. As a result, they are likely to experience a more complete socialization process than goal-oriented dancers. Goal-oriented dancers, in contrast, tend to limit their ties to others in the business. As the following quotes illustrate, they try to keep dancing and their private lives separate.

> I don't hang out with other dancers. When I leave here I go back to my other life.

> Although I try to be friendly to everyone here [at the club] I stick to myself as much as possible and when I leave [work], I try to leave it and everybody associated with it behind.

The implication of keeping the two aspects of their lives separate is that goal-oriented dancers have to contend with the stigma associated with dancing on their own and, as a result, often live very closeted/secretive lives.

> I work really hard at keeping this [dancing] a secret from my family. It is hard cuz I still live at home with my parents. So, I keep my costumes in the trunk of my car and I make sure I am the only one with a key.

> It's really hard because, you know, you're lying to your parents. Well, I am. And I'm close to my family. And I was lying to my friends and to my boyfriend at the time.

Without a community of supportive others, these women have limited access to competing definitions of reality and are therefore more likely to feel some sort of guilt and shame for choosing to dance. Since it is through interacting with other subcultural members that people learn rationalizations for their behaviour, these women are likely to have limited access to the techniques of neutralization used by other dancers that are important for the maintenance of a positive sense of self.

LIMITATIONS OF THE DANCER'S SOCIALIZATION PROCESS

Although both career and goal-oriented dancers felt they were able to experience successful occupational socialization that enabled them to achieve competence as exotic dancers, most of the women interviewed talked about how the socialization process inadequately prepared them for some of the realities of the life of an exotic dancer. *A Stripper's Handbook* (1997), a booklet written by several dancers in the Toronto region, nicely illustrates the benefits and limitations of learning about exotic dancing through informal channels. Although the booklet contains helpful information and advice about the job (e.g., where to get a licence, how much a license costs, how to save money on costumes, stage show rules, DJ fees, fines, freelancing vs. working on schedule, etc.), it also glosses over some of the negative effects the job can have on women's lives (e.g., relationship problems, inhibition of heterosexual desire, etc.). The tendency to overlook the negative is typical of the advice women reported being given by subcultural members, especially the women with limited ties to the subculture.

When discussing the limitations of their socialization experiences, the women we spoke with reported having little knowledge of, and therefore being unprepared for the impact of dancing on their private lives. The area of impact most often mentioned was relationships. In terms of relationships, women spoke of the difficulties of having and sustaining heterosexual relationships with males outside of the industry. For some women, relationship difficulties were tied to the problems men they date tend to have with their occupation (see Prus, 1980):

> I'd suggest to any girl that ever dances, unless your boyfriend's a male dancer, don't date someone when you're stripping. Most guys say they can handle it. They can't and then they start coming into clubs and causing bullshit.

Other women report that the difficulty of developing or sustaining heterosexual relationships was tied to the nature of their job (i.e., they usually work at night, in a bar, in a job that requires them be around and constantly interacting with customers, many of whom they don't like).

> Relationshipwise it's very hard. I think it's hard for someone to take a dancer seriously, it takes a certain type of guy that can look beyond that and ah, if I'm involved I have a really hard time doing my job. If I'm single I'm better with my job. It's hard to meet people cuz I work nights all the time. When I was working full time I was there a good 5 nights a week. On my night off I don't want to go to a bar or anything, I'm in one every day, so you never get a chance to meet people. It's pretty much taboo to date someone you meet at work, cuz you don't know who they are outside of there and they've been giving you money to strip in front of

> them all night, and they are like, "Ooh yeah, I want to take you on a date." And you are thinking, "Yeah, sure you do. For what, why?" So that's hard. And it's hard if you have a boyfriend, it's hard for them to deal with it.

Despite the difficulties exotic dancers confront in terms of developing and sustaining relationships, some of the women interviewed expressed an interest/desire to have a stable intimate heterosexual relationship. Others, however, talked about being disinterested in men.

> I'm kind of sick of, you know, the men and I just, I've always been a, you know, a big-chested person. So, I['ve] always gotten the yee-haw's and stuff walking down the street and I just kinda had it after a while, you know?

> I hate to be looked at. I don't like to be looked at by men. I don't like men very much.

One solution identified by dancers to the relationship difficulties and inhibited heterosexual desire dancers experience is pursuing relationships with other women. According to the women we interviewed, it is not uncommon for female exotic dancers to develop lesbian relationships, either because of a disinterest in heterosexual relationships stemming from dancing, or because relationships with women are just easier to develop and sustain while they are working as exotic dancers (see Carey et al., 1974; McCaghy & Skipper, 1969; Prus, 1980).

> I think a lot of girls end up bi ... I think it's convenient because it's easier to go out with another dancer, another girl than go out with a guy. You know what I mean? They understand your likes and a lot of guys that date dancers are ass-holes. So why deal with the hassle of going out? Why not just date a girl? I would have [dated women] if I met a nice girl. It's a lot easier to date a girl than to bother with going out. But I just happened to meet Paul who dances as well and fits into my lifestyle. But, if I wouldn't have met him I probably would date women. But I just never, I just never met any girl that I had enough in common with. A lot of the girls are [lesbian]. But a lot of people stereotype you. You know what I mean?

As noted by McCaghy and Skipper (1969), three conditions associated with the occupation are supportive of same-sex relationships: "(1) isolation from affective social relationships; (2) unsatisfactory relationships with males; and (3) an opportunity structure allowing a wide range of sexual behavior" (p. 266).

Conclusion

As other studies of exotic dancers have found, there are various factors influencing occupational entry into exotic dancing. This study provides support for a combined career contingency/conversion model. According to this model, four factors influence entry into the exotic dancing: (1) knowledge and accessibility of an opportunity structure that makes exotic dancing an occupational alternative; (2) an awareness of the economic rewards associated with being an exotic dancer; (3) a recruitment process involving personal networks; and (4) financial need or a need for employment. For the women interviewed, these factors played a significant role in their anticipatory socialization process and their movement in the direction of exotic dancing.

Although similar to earlier studies of exotic dancers (this study found evidence of a combined career contingency/conversion model for entry into exotic dancing), there were also some differences between the findings of this study and that of previous research in the area. For example, contrary to earlier studies, we found little indication of dancers having pre-job formal socialization experiences that involved professional training in entertainment-related fields, prior to entering dancing. This difference, however, may be tied to the evolution of stripping. Over the past 25 years or so, stripping has gone from a form of theatre or burlesque stage show, where complete nudity was rare and touching was prohibited, to the more raunchy table and lap dances performed today that often involve complete nudity, and sometimes physical and sexual contact between the dancer and the customer.

Despite some different findings in terms of the anticipatory socialization experiences of dancers, similar to other research in the area we found that once the decision to dance was made and they were employed as dancers, the women we interviewed continued to experience a socialization process through interacting with and observing other subcultural members. The on-the-job, informal occupational socialization the women reported experiencing enabled them to achieve job competence, even in a deviant occupation.

As social learning theories of deviance suggest, although most of us learn the norms and values of society, some of us also learn techniques for committing deviance and the specific motives, drives, rationalizations, and attitudes that allow us to neutralize our violation of normative codes. The socialization experiences of dancers fit with this framework. Learning occurs through observing and interacting with strip club employees, especially more experienced dancers. Through such observations and interactions, novice dancers learn techniques for rationalizing their involvement in the occupation, a process which enables them to stay in the job and succeed, while retaining a valued sense of self.

Although exotic dancers can experience socialization processes that result in job competence, their occupational socialization often inadequately prepares them for the potential impact of their job on their lives outside of the club. The most often mentioned area of concern was intimate relationships, due to the difficulties exotic dancers reported on developing and sustaining heterosexual relationships and desire.

Notes

1. According to Ritzer and Walczak (1986, p. 374), "an occupation will be treated as deviant if it meets one or more of the following criteria: (1) it is illegal; (2) one or more of the

central activities of the occupation is a violation of nonlegalized norms and values; and (3) the culture, lifestyle, or setting associated with the occupation is popularly presumed to involve rule-breaking behaviour."

2. According to Matza (1992, p. 29), "drift is motion guided gently by underlying influences. The guidance is gentle and not constraining. The drift may be initiated or deflected by events so numerous as to defy codification. But underlying influences are operative nonetheless in that they make initiation to … [deviant behaviour] more probable, and they reduce the chances that an event will deflect the drifter from his [/her deviant] … path. Drift is a gradual process of movement, unperceived by the actor, in which the first stage may be accidental or unpredictable."
3. Appeal to higher loyalties involves rationalizing deviant behaviour by couching it within an altruistic framework.
4. Although money is part of the motivation for anyone seeking employment, for dancers, it was the amount of money that could be earned dancing, compared with the amount that could be earned in more legitimate jobs, that motivated them to try dancing.

References

Boles, Jacqueline M. & Garbin, A.P. (1974a). The strip club and stripper-customer patterns of interaction. *Sociology and Social Research, 58*, 136–144.

Boles, Jacqueline M. & Garbin, A.P. (1974b). The choice of stripping for a living: An empirical and theoretical explanation. *Sociology of Work and Occupations, 1*, 110–123.

Boles, Jacqueline M. & Garbin, A.P. (1974c). Stripping for a living: An occupational study of the night club stripper. In C.D. Bryant (Ed.), *Deviant Behavior: Occupational and Organizational Bases*, (pp. 312–335). Chicago: Rand McNally.

Carey, S.H., Peterson, R.A. & Sharpe, L.K. (1974). A study of recruitment and socialization into two deviant female occupations. *Sociological Symposium, 8*, 11–24.

Dressel, P.L. & Petersen, D.M. (1982a). Gender roles, sexuality, and the male strip show: The structuring of sexual opportunity. *Sociological Focus, 15*, 151–162.

Dressel, P.L. & Petersen, D.M. (1982b). Becoming a male stripper: Recruitment, socialization, and ideological development. *Work and Occupations, 9*, 387–406.

Enck, G.E. & Preston, J.D. (1988). Counterfeit intimacy: A dramaturgical analysis of an erotic performance. *Deviant Behavior, 9*, 369–381.

Forsyth, C.J. & Deshotels, T.H. (1997). The occupational milieu of the nude dancer. *Deviant Behavior, 18*, 125–142.

Hong, L.K. & Duff, R.W. (1977). Becoming a taxi-dancer: The significance of neutralization in a semi-deviant occupation. *Sociology of Work and Occupations, 4*, 327–342.

Lofland, J. & Stark, R. (1965). Becoming a world-saver: A theory of conversion to a deviant perspective. *American Sociological Association, 30*, 862–875.

McCaghy, C.H. & Skipper, J.K. (1969). Lesbian behavior as an adaptation to the occupation of stripping. *Social Problems, 17,* 262–270.

McCaghy, C.H. & Skipper, J.K. (1972). Stripping: Anatomy of a deviant life style. In S.D. Feldman & G.W. Thielbar (Eds.), *LifeStyles: Diversity in American Society,* (pp. 362–373). Boston: Little Brown.

Petersen, D. & Dressel, P.L. (1982). Equal time for women: Social notes on the male strip show. *Urban Life, 11,* 185–208.

Prus, R.C. & Sharper, C.R.D. (1977). *Road Hustler: The Career Contingencies of Professional Card and Dice Hustlers.* Toronto: Lexington Books.

Prus, R.C. & Styllianoss, I. (1980). *Hookers, Rounders, and Desk Clerks: The Social Organization of the Hotel Community.* Toronto: Gage Publishing Limited.

Reid, S.A., Epstein, J.S. & Benson, D.E. (1994). Role identity in a devalued occupation: The case of female exotic dancers. *Sociological Focus, 27,* 1–16.

Ronai, C.R. (1992). The reflexive self through narrative: A night in the life of an erotic dancer/researcher. In C. Ellis and M.G. Flaherty (eds.), *Investigating Subjectivity: Research on Lived Experience,* (pp. 102–124). Newbury Park, CA: Sage Publications.

Ronai, C.R. & Ellis, C. (1989). Turn-ons for money: Interactional strategies of the table dancer. *Journal of Contemporary Ethnography, 118,* 271–298.

Sanders, C.R. (1974). Psyching out the crowd: Folk performers and their audiences. *Urban Life and Culture, 3,* 264–282.

Skipper, J.K. & McCaghy, C.H. (1971). Stripteasing: A sex-oriented occupation. In James M. Henslin (Ed.), *Studies in the Sociology of Sex,* (pp. 275–296). New York: Appleton-Century-Crofts.

Sykes, G.M. & Matza, D. (1957). Techniques of neutralization: A theory of delinquency. *American Sociological Review, 22,* 664–670.

Thompson, W.E. & Harred, J.L. (1992). Topless dancers: Managing stigma in a deviant occupation. *Deviant Behavior, 13,* 291–311.

CHAPTER 13

The Presentation of Self in Everyday Life

Erving Goffman

Introduction

When an individual enters the presence of others, they commonly seek to acquire information about him or to bring into play information about him already possessed. They will be interested in his general socio-economic status, his conception of self, his attitude toward them, his competence, his trustworthiness, etc. Although some of this information seems to be sought almost as an end in itself, there are usually quite practical reasons for acquiring it. Information about the individual helps to define the situation, enabling others to know in advance what he will expect of them and what they may expect of him. Informed in these ways, the others will know how best to act in order to call forth a desired response from him.

For those present, many sources of information become accessible and many carriers (or "sign-vehicles") become available for conveying this information. If unacquainted with the individual, observers can glean clues from his conduct and appearance which allow them to apply their previous experience with individuals roughly similar to the one before them or, more important, to apply untested stereotypes to him. They can also assume from past experience that only individuals of a particular kind are likely to be found in a given social setting. They can rely on what the individual says about himself or on documentary evidence he provides as to who and what he is. If they know, or know of, the individual by virtue of experience prior to the interaction, they can rely on assumptions as to the persistence and generality of psychological traits as a means of predicting his present and future behavior.

However, during the period in which the individual is in the immediate presence of the others, few events may occur which directly provide the others with the conclusive information they will need if they are to direct wisely their own activity. Many crucial facts lie beyond the time and place of interaction or lie concealed within it. For example, the "true" or "real" attitudes, beliefs, and emotions of the individual can be ascertained only indirectly, through his avowals or through what appears to be involuntary expressive behavior. Similarly, if the individual offers the others a product or service, they will often find that during the interaction there will be no time and place immediately available for eating the pudding that the proof can be found in. They will be forced to accept some events as conventional or natural signs of something not directly available to the senses. In Ichheiser's terms,[1] the individual will have to act so that he intentionally or unintentionally *expresses* himself, and the others will in turn have to be *impressed* in some way by him.

The expressiveness of the individual (and therefore his capacity to give impressions) appears to involve two radically different kinds of sign activity: the expression that he *gives*, and the expression that he *gives off*. The first involves verbal symbols or their substitutes which he uses admittedly and solely to convey the information that he and the others are known to attach to these symbols. This is communication in the traditional and narrow sense. The second involves a wide range of action that others can treat as symptomatic of the actor, the expectation being that the action was performed for reasons other than the information conveyed in this way. As we shall have to see, this distinction has an only initial validity. The individual does of course intentionally convey misinformation by means of both of these types of communication, the first involving deceit, the second feigning.

Let us now turn from the others to the point of view of the individual who presents himself before them. He may wish them to think highly of him, or to think that he thinks highly of them, or to perceive how in fact he feels toward them, or to obtain no clear-cut impression; he may wish to ensure sufficient harmony so that the interaction can be sustained, or to defraud, get rid of, confuse, mislead, antagonize, or insult them. Regardless of the particular objective which the individual has in mind and of his motive for having this objective, it will be in his interests to control the conduct of the others, especially their responsive treatment of him.[2] This control is achieved largely by influencing the definition of the situation which the others come to formulate, and he can influence this definition by expressing himself in such a way as to give them the kind of impression that will lead them to act voluntarily in accordance with his own plan. Thus, when an individual appears in the presence of others, there will usually be some reason for him to mobilize his activity so that it will convey an impression to others which it is in his interests to convey. Since a girl's dormitory mates will glean evidence of her popularity from the calls she receives on the phone, we can suspect that some girls will arrange for calls to be made, and Willard Waller's finding can be anticipated:

> It has been reported by many observers that a girl who is called to the telephone in the dormitories will often allow herself to be called several times, in order to give all the other girls ample opportunity to hear her paged.[3]

Of the two kinds of communication—expressions given and expressions given off—this report will be primarily concerned with the latter, with the more theatrical and contextual kind, the non-verbal, presumably unintentional kind, whether this communication be purposely engineered or not. As an example of what we must try to examine, I would like to cite at length a novelistic incident in which Preedy, a vacationing Englishman, makes his first appearance on the beach of his summer hotel in Spain:

> But in any case he took care to avoid catching anyone's eye. First of all, he had to make it clear to those potential companions of his holiday that they were of no concern to him whatsoever. He stared through them, round them, over them—eyes

> lost in space. The beach might have been empty. If by chance a ball was thrown his way, he looked surprised; then let a smile of amusement lighten his face (Kindly Preedy), looked round dazed to see that there *were* people on the beach, tossed it back with a smile to himself and not a smile *at* the people, and then resumed carelessly his nonchalant survey of space.
>
> But it was time to institute a little parade, the parade of the Ideal Preedy. By devious handlings he gave any who wanted to look a chance to see the title of his book—a Spanish translation of Homer, classic thus, but not daring, cosmopolitan too—and then gathered together his beach-wrap and bag into a neat sand-resistant pile (Methodical and Sensible Preedy), rose slowly to stretch at ease his huge frame (Big-Cat Preedy), and tossed aside his sandals (Carefree Preedy, after all).
>
> The marriage of Preedy and the sea! There were alternative rituals. The first involved the stroll that turns into a run and a dive straight into the water, thereafter smoothing into a strong splashless crawl towards the horizon. But of course not really to the horizon. Quite suddenly he would turn on to his back and thrash great white splashes with his legs, somehow thus showing that he could have swum further had he wanted to, and then would stand up a quarter out of water for all to see who it was.
>
> The alternative course was simpler, it avoided the cold-water shock and it avoided the risk of appearing too high-spirited. The point was to appear to be so used to the sea, the Mediterranean, and this particular beach, that one might as well be in the sea as out of it. It involved a slow stroll down and into the edge of the water—not even noticing his toes were wet, land and water all the same to *him!*—with his eyes up at the sky gravely surveying portents, invisible to others, of the weather (Local Fisherman Preedy).[4]

The novelist means us to see that Preedy is improperly concerned with the extensive impressions he feels his sheer bodily action is giving off to those around him. We can malign Preedy further by assuming that he has acted merely in order to give a particular impression, that this is a false impression, and that the others present receive either no impression at all, or, worse still, the impression that Preedy is affectedly trying to cause them to receive this particular impression. But the important point for us here is that the kind of impression Preedy thinks he is making is in fact the kind of impression that others correctly and incorrectly glean from someone in their midst.

There is one aspect of the others' response that bears special comment here. Knowing that the individual is likely to present himself in a light that is favorable to him, the others may divide what they witness into two parts; a part that is relatively easy for the individual to manipulate at will, being chiefly his verbal assertions, and a part in regard to which he seems to have little concern or control, being chiefly derived from the expressions he gives off. The others may then use what are considered to be the ungovernable aspects of his expressive behavior as a check upon the validity of what is conveyed by the governable aspects. In this a fundamental asymmetry is demonstrated in the communication process, the individual presumably being aware of only one stream of his communication, the witnesses of this stream and one other. For example, in Shetland Isle one crofter's wife, in serving native dishes to a visitor from the mainland of Britain, would listen with a polite smile to his polite claims of liking what he was eating; at the same time she would take note of the rapidity with which the visitor lifted his fork or spoon to his mouth, the eagerness with which he passed food into his mouth, and the gusto expressed in chewing the food, using these signs as a check on the stated feelings of the eater. The same woman, in order to discover what one acquaintance (A) "actually" thought of another acquaintance (B), would wait until B was in the presence of A but engaged in conversation with still another person (C). She would then covertly examine the facial expressions of A as he regarded B in conversation with C. Not being in conversation with B, and not being directly observed by him, A would sometimes relax usual constraints and tactful deceptions, and freely express what he was "actually" feeling about B. This Shetlander, in short, would observe the unobserved observer.

Now given the fact that others are likely to check up on the more controllable aspects of behavior by means of the less controllable, one can expect that sometimes the individual will try to exploit this very possibility, guiding the impression he makes through behavior felt to be reliably informing.[5] For example, in gaining admission to a tight social circle, the participant observer may not only wear an accepting look while listening to an informant, but may also be careful to wear the same look when observing the informant talking to others; observers of the observer will then not as easily discover where he actually stands. A specific illustration may be cited from Shetland Isle. When a neighbor dropped in to have a cup of tea, he would ordinarily wear at least a hint of an expectant warm smile as he passed through the door into the cottage. Since lack of physical obstructions outside the cottage and lack of light within it usually made it possible to observe the visitor unobserved as he approached the house, islanders sometimes took pleasure in watching the visitor drop whatever expression he was manifesting and replace it with a sociable one just before reaching the door. However, some visitors, in appreciating that this examination was occurring, would blindly adopt a social face a long distance from the house, thus ensuring the projection of a constant image.

This kind of control upon the part of the individual reinstates the symmetry of the communication process, and sets the stage for a kind of information game—a potentially infinite cycle of concealment, discovery, false revelation, and rediscovery. It should be added that since the others are likely to be relatively unsuspicious of the presumably unguided aspect of the individual's conduct, he can gain much by controlling it. The others of course may sense that the individual is manipulating the presumably spontaneous aspects of his behavior, and seek in this very act of manipulation some shading of conduct that the individual has not managed to control. This again provides a check upon the individual's behavior, this time his presumably uncalculated behavior, thus re-establishing the asymmetry of the communication process. Here I would like only to add the suggestion that the arts of piercing an individual's effort at calculated unintentionality seem better developed than our capacity to manipulate our own behavior, so that regardless of how many steps have occurred in the information game, the witness is likely to have the advantage over the actor, and the initial asymmetry of the communication process is likely to be retained.

In everyday life, of course, there is a clear understanding that first impressions are important. Thus, the work adjustment of those in service occupations will often hinge upon a capacity to seize and hold the initiative in the service relation, a capacity that will require subtle aggressiveness on the part of the server when he is of lower socio-economic status than his client. W.F. Whyte suggests the waitress as an example:

> The first point that stands out is that the waitress who bears up under pressure does not simply respond to her customers. She acts with some skill to control their behavior. The first question to ask when we look at the customer relationship is, "Does the waitress get the jump on the customer, or does the customer get the jump on the waitress?" The skilled waitress realizes the crucial nature of this question....
>
> The skilled waitress tackles the customer with confidence and without hesitation. For example, she may find that a new customer has seated himself before she could clear off the dirty dishes and change the cloth. He is now leaning on the table studying the menu. She greets him, says, "May I change the cover, please?" and, without waiting for an answer, takes his menu away from him so that he moves back from the table, and she goes about her work. The relationship is handled politely but firmly, and there is never any question as to who is in charge.[6]

When the interaction that is initiated by "first impressions" is itself merely the initial interaction in an extended series of interactions involving the same participants, we speak of "getting off on the right foot" and feel that it is crucial that we do so. Thus, one learns that some teachers take the following view:

> You can't ever let them get the upper hand on you or you're through. So I start out tough. The first day I get a new class in, I let them know who's boss.... You've got to start off tough, then you can ease up as you go along. If you start out easy-going, when you try to get tough, they'll just look at you and laugh.[7]

In stressing the fact that the initial definition of the situation projected by an individual tends to provide a plan for the co-operative activity that follows—in stressing this action point of view—we must not overlook the crucial fact that any projected definition of the situation also has a distinctive moral character. It is this moral character of projections that will chiefly concern us in this report. Society is organized on the principle that any individual who possesses certain social characteristics has a moral right to expect that others will value and treat him in an appropriate way. Connected with this principle is a second, namely that an individual who implicitly or explicitly signifies that he has certain social characteristics ought in fact to be what he claims he is. In consequence, when an individual projects a definition of the situation and thereby makes an implicit or explicit claim to be a person of a particular kind, he automatically exerts a moral demand upon the others, obliging them to value and treat him in the manner that persons of his kind have a right to expect. He also implicitly forgoes all claims to be things he does not appear to be[8] and hence forgoes the treatment that would be appropriate for such individuals. The others find, then, that the individual has informed them as to what is and as to what they *ought* to see as the "is."

One cannot judge the importance of definitional disruptions by the frequency with which they occur, for apparently they would occur more frequently were not constant precautions taken. We find that preventive practices are constantly employed to avoid these embarrassments and that corrective practices are constantly employed to compensate for discrediting occurrences that have not been successfully avoided. When the individual employs these strategies and tactics to protect his own projections, we may refer to them as "defensive practices"; when a participant employs them to save the definition of the situation projected by another, we speak of "protective practices" or "tact." Together, defensive and protective practices comprise the techniques employed to safeguard the impression fostered by an individual during his presence before others. It should be added that while we may be ready to see that no fostered impression would survive if defensive practices were not employed, we are less ready perhaps to see that few impressions could survive if those who received the impression did not exert tact in their reception of it.

In addition to the fact that precautions are taken to prevent disruption of projected definitions, we may also note that an intense interest in these disruptions comes to play a significant role in the social life of the group. Practical jokes and social games are played in which embarrassments which are to be taken unseriously are purposely engineered.[9] Fantasies are created in which devastating exposures occur. Anecdotes from the past—real, embroidered, or fictitious—are told and retold, detailing disruptions which occurred, almost occurred, or occurred and were admirably resolved. There seems to be no grouping which does not have a ready supply of these games, reveries, and cautionary tales, to be used as a source of humor, a catharsis for anxieties, and a sanction for inducing individuals to be modest in their claims and reasonable in their projected expectations. The individual may tell himself through dreams of getting into impossible positions. Families tell of the time a guest got his dates mixed and arrived when neither the house nor anyone in it was ready for him. Journalists tell of times when an all-too-meaningful misprint occurred, and the paper's assumption of objectivity or decorum was humorously discredited. Public servants tell of times a client ridiculously misunderstood form instructions, giving answers which implied an unanticipated and bizarre definition of the situation.[10] Seamen, whose home away from home is rigorously he-man, tell stories of coming back home and inadvertently asking mother to "pass the fucking butter."[11] Diplomats tell of the time a near-sighted queen asked a republican ambassador about the health of his king.[12]

To summarize, then, I assume that when an individual appears before others he will have many motives for trying to control the impression they receive of the situation.[...]

Notes

1. Gustav Ichheiser, "Misunderstandings in Human Relations," Supplement to *The American Journal of Sociology*, LV (September, 1949), pp. 6–7.
2. Here I owe much to an unpublished paper by Tom Burns of the University of Edinburgh. He presents the argument that in all interaction a basic underlying theme is the desire of each participant to guide and control the responses made by the others present. A similar argument has been advanced by Jay Haley in a recent unpublished paper, but in regard to a special kind of control, that having to do with defining the nature of the relationship of those involved in the interaction.
3. Willard Waller, "The Rating and Dating Complex," *American Sociological Review*, II, p. 730.
4. William Sansom, *A Contest of Ladies* (London: Hogarth, 1956), pp. 230–32.
5. The widely read and rather sound writings of Stephen Potter are concerned in part with signs that can be engineered to give a shrewd observer the apparently incidental cues he needs to discover concealed virtues the gamesman does not in fact possess.
6. W.F. Whyte, "When Workers and Customers Meet," Chap. VII, *Industry and Society*, ed. W.F. Whyte (New York: McGraw-Hill, 1946), pp. 132–33.
7. Teacher interview quoted by Howard S. Becker, "Social Class Variations in the Teacher-Pupil Relationship," *Journal of Educational Sociology*, XXV, p. 459.
8. This role of the witness in limiting what it is the individual can be has been stressed by Existentialists, who see it as a basic threat to individual freedom. See Jean-Paul Sartre, *Being and Nothingness*, trans. by Hazel E. Barnes (New York: Philosophical Library, 1956), p. 365 ff.
9. Goffman, *op. cit.*, pp. 319–27.
10. Peter Blau, "Dynamics of Bureaucracy" (Ph.D. dissertation, Department of Sociology, Columbia University, forthcoming, University of Chicago Press), pp. 127–29.
11. Walter M. Beattie, Jr., "The Merchant Seaman" (unpublished M.A. Report, Department of Sociology, University of Chicago, 1950), p. 35.
12. Sir Frederick Ponsonby, *Recollections of Three Reigns* (New York: Dutton, 1952), p. 46.

CHAPTER 14

Private Eyes and Public Order: Policing and Surveillance in the Suppression of Animal Rights Activists in Canada

Kevin Walby and Jeffrey Monaghan

Stop Huntingdon Animal Cruelty (SHAC) is a group that formed in 1999 with one explicit goal: to halt the operations of the animal-testing firm, Huntingdon Life Sciences (HLS). HLS is one of the world's largest animal testing firms, performing up to 500 vivisections a day. Having thousands of active members, solid funding, and an on-the-ground presence in several Western countries, SHAC has been one of the most resourceful and effective networks in animal rights activism to date. HLS and affiliated companies have lobbied for the enactment of legislation targeting animal rights activism in the USA and the UK. While extraordinary legal sanctions have been used against SHAC elsewhere,[1] the story concerning suppression and surveillance of SHAC-Canada is markedly different.

The SHAC campaign has developed numerous creative strategies to confront HLS.[2] One of these strategies involves pressuring secondary and tertiary companies, such as drug providers, drug developer clients, insurers, transport firms, and equipment providers to drop HLS as a business partner. In Canada, SHAC targets HLS customers through a diversity of tactics, including pickets, public outreach events, fax/phone jams, and the more militant strategy of home demonstrations. "Home demos" are loud, disruptive actions that occur at the home of a corporate CEO, used to bring public attention to the cruelties of animal testing.[3] SHAC's sidewalk actions do not involve trespassing or property destruction, so what makes the suppression of SHAC-Canada noteworthy is that its tactics are legal according to Canadian criminal law. Yet, because home demos disrupt the personal lives of the targeted corporate executives, elites have galvanized a response.

The regulatory response to SHAC-Canada has drawn upon a mixed economy of policing, including private security. We use the term private security to refer to a range of agents, including private security firms (e.g., Securicor, Securitas), as well as private detectives contracted out by individuals and corporations. With SHAC in Montréal, attempts at suppression began after complaints of Westmount elites concerning their property, but came to involve surveillance by a medical research firm security group, private detectives, the City of Westmount and their public security forces, and the Montréal police. It later involved national security and intelligence agencies who labeled SHAC members as "animal rights extremists." Global pharmaceutical corporations and business partners of HLS have been integral in efforts to counter SHAC campaigns. Novartis and AstraZeneca are two corporations targeted by SHAC-Canada. Private detectives employed by these corporations have joined the policing network, mixing public and private agents.

This article focuses on private security related to public order policing and social movement repression. Cunningham (2004) argued that scholarship on social movement repression does not account for the multiple scales of police involved in repression. Private repression remains an understudied field (Earl, 2004). We explore how typologies of social movement repression can be enriched by incorporating what has been identified by sociologists of policing as the rise of private security agents in public order maintenance. We emphasize the role of private agents in providing information to public police and the role of surveillance in coordinating policing projects that span from the local to the national scale. If social movement scholars drew more from the sociology of policing, three changes to existing typologies of social movement repression would result. First, scholars would investigate the direction of influence between private and public agents instead of assuming that state agencies are principally involved. Municipal and state police today are highly dependent on the information produced by private security (Lippert & O'Connor, 2006). Second, scholars would focus on the means of repression, not dwelling so much on one-off coercive events but instead accounting for protracted surveillance projects carried out by public and private agents. Third, scholars would focus on the scale of repression, and how private agents act as conduits for policing and intelligence agencies to operate across conventional boundaries.

Drawing from material obtained under the *Access to Information Act* and from interviews with SHAC-Canada members, we examine how agents representing multiple scales of policing have converged to suppress SHAC-Canada. First, we discuss the literature on repression of social movements, placing emphasis on the role of private security. We follow Boykoff (2007b), who argued that "suppression" offers a nuanced conceptualization of public *and* private repression. Second, we offer a note on our research method. Third, we discuss the suppression of SHAC in Montréal, detailing the involvement of private security and public police. We emphasize that private agents are not always acting at the behest of state agencies. We also discuss how the scale of suppression shifted, coming to involve national security agencies such as the Canadian Security Intelligence Service (CSIS) and the Royal Canadian Mounted Police (RCMP). Finally, with reference to the role of private eyes in public order policing, we discuss how our case study supplements Earl's (2003) and Boykoff's (2007b) typologies of repression and suppression. Our aim below is to enrich these typologies by focusing on how private security agents are catalysts in the policing and repression of social movements, particularly movements that confront dominant corporate actors and/or interests.

Keeping Track of Social Movements: Repression, Public Police, and Private Eyes

What would happen to typologies of social movement repression if they incorporated what sociologists of policing have written about the role of private security agents in public order maintenance? Before answering the question, we must review some key contributions to understanding social movement repression.

The literature concerning repression of social movements has hosted numerous debates as it regards cops, courts, and corrections. Marx (1979) contends that surveillance is the chief activity that police undertake. Barkan (2006) points to how criminal prosecution depletes resources and how police surveillance practices frame evidentiary submissions. For Meyer and Staggenborg (1996), regulation of social movement groups can emerge when an activist campaign shows signs of success, as well as when the campaign's goals threaten dominant political and economic interests. Other authors note that, despite the influence of national security agencies, local police are central to repressive responses (see Donner, 1990; Earl & Soule, 2006). de Lint & Hall (2009) have recently argued that intelligence from the national scale is increasingly used at the local scale of policing.

Though these contributions have been useful for studies of movement repression, numerous authors have called for further theoretical development. Cunningham (2003, p. 210) argued that the literature on social movement repression has been limited by a "predominant focus on overt policing of large public demonstrations." Similarly, Davenport (1995) argued that scholars interested in movement repression have mistakenly assumed that frequency of public protest is the most important factor influencing state repression. Earl (2006) and Ferree (2004) argued that the repression of social movements literature is state-centric.

Earl (2004) accounted for the role of private security. Focusing on private repression such as vigilantism, grassroots regulation, and elite-driven countermovements, Earl (2004) argued that the term "social control of protest" can be used to account for the range of public and private agents involved in repression. However, in a broad sense, the literature on repression of social movements focuses too much on politics as bound by sovereign states, too much on mass movements at the expense of affinity group organizing, and too much on public police. To address these limitations, Boykoff (2007a) argues that we should conceptualize regulatory actions as suppression. In Boykoff's typology, suppression is defined as "a process through which the preconditions for dissident action, mobilization, and collective organization are inhibited by either raising their costs or minimizing their benefits" (p. 12). State agencies are one set of agencies among many, operating on a particular scale. Scale refers to how people organize social space. National, regional, and local scales are not simply imagined, but provide a space for organizing relations, and a way of organizing surveillance and suppression (Boykoff, 2007c). The concept of "repression" is too close to what Snyder (1976) called "governmental coercion."[4] Compared to "covert repression," the term "suppression" highlights multi-scalar combinations of agencies that cooperate in attempts to neutralize activists.

Boykoff's (2007a) typology involves 4 social mechanisms as well as and 10 action modes. The action modes, which include use of direct force, prosecutions, surveillance, infiltration, harassment arrests, exceptional laws, mass media framing, and more, can lead to various mechanisms of suppression such as resource depletion, stigmatization, division, and intimidation. While the use of exceptional laws has been pivotal in the policing of SHAC in other countries (such as the *Serious Organized Crime and Police Act*, 2005, in the UK and the *Animal Enterprise Terrorism Act*, 2006, in the USA), Canada has not enacted specific laws to criminalize animal rights activism.[5] Nevertheless, suppression of SHAC-Canada does involve elements of Boykoff's (2007a) typology such as harassment arrests and surveillance.

Below we emphasize the pivotal role played by private security agents in supplying information to local police. Private security agents often provide initial reports about activists to public police. Hoogenboom (2006) used the idea of "grey intelligence" when referring to information swapped between public and private agencies. Information collected by a private security firm, which is communicated to municipal or state police, and then operationalized as intelligence, is an example of "grey intelligence." Grey intelligence practices are exemplified by CEOs in Montréal hiring private detectives to monitor SHAC activists and to pass on information to local police. Private security agents are now the largest provider of intelligence to municipal and state police in the Canadian province of Ontario (Lippert & O'Connor, 2006), a trend evident in other Canadian provinces as well.

Highlighting the role of private security in public order maintenance, we draw from the sociology of policing to expand existing explanations regarding private repression. In the sociology of policing literature, "policing" is not defined as the actions of municipal or state officers, but as any organizational attempt to maintain a semblance of security. This conceptualization moves beyond definitions that pin policing on public agencies alone or that tend to focus only on the local scale. As numerous authors (Shearing & Stenning, 1983; Johnston, 1992; Wakefield, 2008) have argued, there is an increasing differentiation of "police" themselves. Loader (2000, p. 323) described this process as the "pluralization of policing," where the delivery of policing, security services, and technologies are increasingly fragmented. Pluralization of policing, where public policing agencies come to cooperate with a host of private policing agents, raises issues of accountability and transparency (Loader, 2000; Newburn, 2001; Schönteich et al., 2004). A second related point is that public police cooperate with private security agents in ways that blur the line between public and private. The repression of social movements literature has tended to operate with an understanding of "policing" that focuses strictly on municipal or state officers.

The array of private security agents who are increasingly involved in repression has not received due attention. As Scott and McPherson (1971, p. 267) have argued, private security agents are overlooked in social science generally, because they "have not operated in the full light of publicity." The tasks that private security agents perform are similar to those carried out by local police (Brown & Lippert, 2007), and the nexus between public police and private security is well established in many countries (Trevaskes, 2007). The line between these agencies can be thin, as private security follows various protocols established by local police and vice versa (de Lint & Hall, 2009; Walby & Monaghan, 2010).

Sociologists of policing (Button, 2002; Lippert & O'Connor, 2006) claim that private security has increasingly assumed many of the functions of municipal and state police. Existing typologies of social movement repression need to be adjusted to place additional emphasis on how private agents are involved in public order policing. The issue is one of directionality, whereas the repression of social movements literature suggests that private security is activated through contracts and outsourcing by local police, we contend that private security is often contracted by other private agents (e.g., economic elites) and that local police are reliant on the grey intelligence that private security produces about activists.

We emphasize the instrumental role played by private agents in producing initial information reports that are communicated through networks of surveillance. Private policing informs subsequent interventions by other agencies. Our focus on this private dimension of public order maintenance combines literature on the repression of social movements with the sociology of policing to enhance existing typologies of social movement repression.

Note on Method

Several authors (see Koopmans, 1997; Davenport, 2005; Earl, 2006; Oliver, 2008) have called for context-specific, qualitative case studies to supplement broader typologies of social movement repression. As Earl (2009) notes, however, it is difficult to do research regarding policing agencies. Access is often closed off, especially since 11 September 2001. We were unsatisfied with the extent of information available in our initial web site and newspaper searches. We pursued access to information (ATI) requests, despite the numerous barriers involved in trying to access police planning documents and municipal government internal correspondence.[6] In Canada, the *Access to Information Act* allows individuals to request information from public institutions that would not otherwise be made public. These requests have been used by researchers to examine national security and immigration detention (Larsen & Piché, 2009), the staging and regulation of prison and jail tours (Piché & Walby, 2010), policing of park sex by conservation officers (Walby, 2009), and militarization of rural police agencies vis-à-vis nuclear response forces (Walby & Monaghan, 2010). With these access requests, we have attempted to get at some of what Marx (1984) calls "dirty data" produced behind closed doors in undercover policing. Beyond the theoretical contribution we make regarding private eyes and public order, we contribute to the development of ATI as a methodological field, with its emphasis on revealing government actions, decisions, and, in our case, relationships that public police have with private security.

Information was exempted from the results of our requests with reference to various sections of the *Access to Information Act*. Many reasons for exemption were predictable (e.g., personal information, ongoing lawful investigation). Some of the reasons, however, are telling. For instance, the Department of Justice exempted information using Sections 13(1)(a) and 15(1) of the *Act*.[7] The former has to do with "information obtained in confidence from the government of a foreign state" and the latter regards "international affairs and defense." Although the requests did not bare operational data, these references to inter-state coordination have substantiated our claims that this is an internationally coordinated preemptive policing effort developed in response to the SHAC campaign. We also conducted interviews with activist core members of SHAC-Canada. The interviews were helpful to pinpoint what kinds of texts to request through ATI, but also shed light on how activists experience (and sometimes try to counter) surveillance and suppression.

Suppressing SHAC: Private Security in Montréal

The primary targets of SHAC-Canada campaign were CEOs from Novartis and AstraZeneca. Novartis and AstraZeneca, producers of pharmaceutical drugs, hire HLS to test their products on animals. SHAC-Canada organized several home demos at the private residences of these CEOs on Roslyn and Victoria avenues in Westmount, a wealthy municipality carved into the middle of Montréal, Québec. Westmount boasts one of the highest per capita incomes of any residential area in Canada. On 22 September 2006, Karin Marks, Mayor of Westmount, distributed a leaflet to residents of the streets where the HLS-affiliated CEOs resided. The communiqué stated as follows:

> over the past few months, there have been many demonstrations on our streets … I appreciate that this has been unsettling to many of you, based on the number of calls that have been received at my office and the local police station.[8]

An information session followed in which Mayor Marks, the director of Public Security of Westmount, the Station 12 Police Commandant, and the District Councilors all met with the residents of the community. The purpose of the session was to "share with (Westmount residents) what we know about the cause of these demonstrations and what we can (and cannot) do to prevent and/or control them" (Westmount communiqué). The "and cannot" addition refers to how protests are legally protected under the *Canadian Charter of Rights and Freedoms* and could not simply be dispersed because of the discomforts of wealthy locals.

The SHAC demonstrations in Westmount were alarming to many residents, who were not accustomed to public gatherings and certainly not the black-clad aesthetics of a SHAC mobilization. As an article in the *Westmount Examiner* noted, "Demonstrators mask their faces and leaders shout out through bullhorns. There have also been reports of intimidating phone calls being made to the targeted individuals and that a home was vandalized with graffiti" (Barry, 2006). This article lamented the fact that SHAC actions were protected under the *Canadian Charter* and also noted that "the City of Westmount is currently considering what legal options can be used to restore tranquility on the streets." A letter to the editor in the *Westmount Examiner*[9] summed up anxious public sentiment:

> Imagine a horde of angry people running amok in front of your home, protesting a situation over which you have no control. Not only can this be very unsettling for children, but the mob mentality can be a dangerous thing—all it takes is one carelessly uttered word to set off a violent spree. (Larsen, 2006)

The location of social movement repression is key in terms of the resources that can be organized against dissent (Donner, 1990). In this case, private detectives were hired by local residents to trail the activists after demonstrations. Montréal police from Station 12 and Westmount Public Security officers were put on full-time alert. Several police and public security vehicles patrolled Roslyn and Victoria avenues when an action was suspected.

As sociologists of policing point out, private security collect information for public police and have assumed many of the public order maintenance duties of municipal and state officers (see Shearing & Stenning, 1983; Johnston, 1992; Rigakos, 2005; Lippert & O'Connor, 2006). The case of SHAC-Canada illustrates how private security agents become involved in repression processes as intelligence gatherers for public police. As mentioned, the targets of SHAC home demonstrations were the CEOs of AstraZeneca and Novartis, global pharmaceutical corporations with a close connection to HLS. In Westmount, a private security agency representing the vivisection industry was influential in suppressing SHAC. On 18 October 2006, the office of the pharmaceutical company AstraZeneca sent a fax to the director of Public Security of Westmount, Richard Blondin. The fax cover letter states that "as a follow up to our phone conversation in the afternoon," the representative of AstraZeneca had been provided information by their "security officer" regarding a SHAC action planned for Halloween outside the house of the Novartis president in Westmount. The fax included a SHAC flyer discussing the Halloween action. Also on 18 October 2006, an email sent by an unidentified person was distributed to City of Westmount officials. It speaks of a "pharma security managers group […] recently created (I'm a part of) to keep us inform[ed] on animal activists activities." Information about the Halloween action was gathered by the pharma security group, but information "that the target could be the house of the Novartis president who lives in Westmount" came from "the Montreal Police department (Security Intelligence section)." Here, we see "grey intelligence" (Hoogenboom, 2006) shared between private and public policing agents.[10] It is not only public police involved in the regulation of activists but it was also private detectives hired by Westmount residents and security clusters formed by target companies. Davenport (2005) argued that culturally condemned tactics often generate a regulatory response. Despite their nonviolent orientation, the tactics of SHAC were not viewed as an acceptable use of public space by Westmount elites. Westmount Mayor Marks said residents were becoming distressed and police response was needed. "Many of these people (in Westmount) have young children," said Marks. The Mayor also noted that "Sometimes the protesters have masks and are shouting slogans" (Morrison, 2006). Another Westmount resident said, "They use foul language, which deters people from taking them seriously," adding "there is a lot of noise and anger." Eventually, Westmount residents got their wish—several SHAC members were arrested preemptively before the commencement of a public demonstration. Municipal police were waiting for SHAC on the day of the arrests; officers were on hand when the group assembled at the Guy-Concordia metro station, although it is not certain whether the intelligence for this sting was prepared by public police or private security. The private security agency and the private detectives were not hired out by a state agency, but by the elites of Westmount, especially the pharmaceutical corporate executives, who galvanized an array of public and private agencies representing multiple scales of policing to engage in suppression of SHAC.

The Shifting Scale of Suppression: From Home Demos to National Security Threat

Radical groups are often linked to violence in ways that misrepresent their tactics and goals (see Scarce, 1990; Churchill, 2004). SHAC has tailored its tactics according to the letter of Canadian law, largely because of recent attacks on SHAC in the UK and the USA, which were coordinated using an array of legal and exceptional displays of state power (see Munro, 2005; Amster, 2006; Monaghan & Walby, 2008). Despite these legal framing efforts on the part of SHAC-Canada, the surveillance project initiated by Westmount elites created an institutional relationship between the local CEOs, private security, politicians, and public police.

The efforts directed against SHAC-Canada involved many traditional information-gathering methods used by public policing agencies highlighted by Marx (1979). These include infiltration, photo and video monitoring, wire and phone taps, and background checks with international intelligence and security agencies. Montréal police knew when and where protest actions would take place, because they had infiltrated the group and had undertaken a year-long surveillance operation that included home, car, and cellphone taps, as well as stake-outs. SHAC members became aware of the surveillance project when it was introduced as evidence in a court case against them.[11] Marx (1979) noted how longer-term surveillance programs are central aspects of attempts at social movement repression. Surveillance extends beyond policing of public demonstrations to bring the entire movement, including the daily activities of organizers and internal communications, into view (see also Davenport, 2005).

Overt forms of suppression that rely on harassment were components of this case. Police presence at home demos routinely included more than 50 officers (some in riot gear), police cruisers, and riot squad trucks.[12] Although protest is protected under the *Canadian Charter*, Section 2, concerning freedom of peaceful assembly, police began to block access into Westmount, take photos of activists and film at demos, break up their actions through force (e.g., hitting activists with car doors), and trail SHAC activists home. In addition to the home demos, SHAC regularly recruited, raised funds, and distributed educational materials at tabling sessions in downtown Montréal. Police targeted the tabling sessions, depleting SHAC resources and inhibiting recruitment efforts. Although early actions included hundreds of people, the result of this intense surveillance and targeting of resources meant that SHAC-Canada was soon reduced to a small number of core members.

The criminal justice system is often utilized to initiate onerous depletion of social movement resources (see Barkan, 2006). In late November 2006, Montréal police arrested and charged 13 people with breach of the peace after a protest outside a home in Westmount, one of the dozens of protests that had taken place over a 20-month period. The police used home and car raids to seize possessions having to do with animal rights, including flyers, clothing, magazines, as well as campaign materials such as bullhorns, posters, cameras, and money. Bail conditions included banishment from a 20 square mile area of Montréal, including downtown (where most of the activists tabled) and Westmount. As the example of banishment indicates, legal sanctions were used to suppress SHAC.

Of the dozens of charges laid against SHAC members, most have been dismissed. Only two court cases continue, which target key organizers who are facing multi-year prison terms. Contributing to what Fernandez (2008) called the "chilling out" of dissent, these charges have enabled police to deploy techniques of post-arrest control that have depleted resources and warranted continuation of surveillance (see also Barkan, 2006). Here, we see a slippage in the law that criminalizes SHAC-Canada members and their ostensibly "legal" home demo strategies, substantiating claims that criminal law is used in social movement policing for preventative security, not only for criminal prosecution (see Ericson & Doyle, 1999).

SHAC-Canada members were routinely subjected to extra-legal interventions. One example of extra-legal intervention concerns police destruction and confiscation of SHAC tabling materials on Montréal streets and in SHAC members' homes. Harassment arrests selectively target and criminalize group leaders for activities for which other citizens would not be arrested (Boykoff, 2007b). Without warrants, police entered homes of key figures in the group and destroyed and/or confiscated pamphlets and other educational and recruiting materials. Police continue to monitor SHAC in Montréal, handing out tickets at every tabling session that occurs and arresting activists for breach of bail conditions when they do attend animal rights rallies. When the group of SHAC-Canada activists moved to Vancouver, British Columbia, after police suppression in Montréal, this confiscation activity was continued by West Vancouver Police. As one SHAC-Canada member put it:

> We thought Montréal was bad ... first the Vancouver police confiscated all our material for our SHAC stall. We do tabling stalls downtown where we inform people about animal rights, gather petitions to shut down HLS and people can give us donations. [Police] seized the stall stating a bylaw. So we built a new one, which cost us $1500 ... they seized it a few days later. According to our lawyers the police are infringing our freedom of speech, but police do it so we have a harder time getting money. A day later we went to do a full day of home demos like we always do and Vancouver police seized all our demo stuff (the camcorder, banners, posters, megaphones, flyers), arrested all of us and ticketed us for mischief. They said "this is how it's going to be until you get out of BC!"

West Vancouver Police and the RCMP were waiting for the SHAC activists the day they arrived in Vancouver, some 3000 km from Montréal. In their operational plan for policing animal rights activism, West Vancouver Police included detailed write-ups concerning the SHAC activists likely provided by private security and public police in Montréal. These write-ups included names and addresses, close-up pictures, dates of birth, vehicle types, and details of the individuals' involvement with SHAC. These files were also organized as a slide show in PowerPoint, indicating that this information was used as a briefing material for investigators and officers.

The suppression of SHAC in Montréal was generated by local elites and was responded to by an array of private security and public policing agents. Private security provided the initial intelligence reports about the size, strategies, and location of SHAC. Yet, national security and intelligence agencies have also aligned with private security and public police to monitor SHAC in Canada. With the move of activists from Montréal to Vancouver and the development of a multi-scalar policing network, discourses of "extremism" were used by state security agencies to categorize the group. Our ATI request with Canada's national spy agency, the CSIS, procured a secret 2006 file entitled "Recent Incidents Related to Animal Rights and Environmental Extremism."[13] The introduction states that "animal rights and environmental extremists [...] unlike activists not prone to extremism, organize violent, direct-action campaigns or engage in illegal, often violent, acts, which range from vandalism, to arson and death threats." In a direct reference to SHAC, the document states "Montreal-region activists are motivated by international animal-rights campaigns." It adds that executives of pharmaceutical companies are "victims of noisy demonstrations at their homes" and warns that "in the case of animal rights extremism, the incidents are increasingly frequent and more violent." CSIS document conflates public demonstrations with illegal violence while clearly stating that the SHAC activists engaged only in noisy home demonstrations. In the USA, SHAC is often categorized with groups like the Animal Liberation Front (ALF), the Earth First!, and the Earth Liberation Front (ELF) (for an example of this conflation, see Liddick, 2006). Intelligence agents draw associations between these groups because they are organized non-hierarchically and embrace tactics of public demonstration.

Our broader point is that multiple scales of policing consolidate to suppress SHAC activists. The scale of this intelligence network now spans from private eyes on the ground to the Canadian government's national security and intelligence agencies. This CSIS document shows how animal rights activism in Canada is increasingly framed as "extremism." The involvement of CSIS in communicating intelligence concerning SHAC-Canada partially substantiates claims made by Earl (2009) that the regulation of social movements has been brought under the rubric of counterterrorism policing post 11 September 2001.[14]

The Discourse of Domestic Terrorism and the Role of International Intelligence

The project against SHAC started in the local site of disruption, literally on the street-fronts of the targeted CEOs. The elites of Westmount first turned to private security. Wealthy communities readily draw on private agents to address security concerns (see Isin, 2004; Brown & Lippert, 2007). Yet, the scale of suppression shifted, coming to involve numerous public police and eventually national security agencies. We discuss below how the scale of suppression targeting SHAC has shifted further to include international intelligence agencies and discourses of so-called domestic terrorism.

Discussing the violent assault on the MOVE house in Philadelphia, Wagner-Pacifici (1994) demonstrated how discourses of terrorism are used to justify repression of social movements. Only during the subsequent court cases has animal rights activism in Canada become framed as "Eco-Terrorism." When the juridical discourse of "Eco-Terror" entered the picture, the SHAC-Canada group was framed as a "terrorist" organization, legitimating police actions and intensive surveillance *post hoc*. During one court case, the prosecution showed videos of scorched cars and physical assaults, though these are tactics foreign to SHAC. The footage had no connection with any alleged actions in Montréal. Such legal fictions allow police the power of unaccountability in suppressing animal rights groups (see Amster, 2006). Application of this domestic terrorism discourse to SHAC-Canada demonstrates that policing of groups with any conceivable link to the animal/earth liberation movements—the ALF and ELF in particular— is increasingly influenced by the Green Scare politics from the USA. Like the Red Scare during early periods of the Cold War, the term Green Scare refers to a period in the USA beginning in the 1990s, where elements of the animal and environmental justice movement have been the target of hypervigilant policing, disproportionate criminal sentencing, and several antiterror inspired legislative initiatives (see Amster, 2006). The Federal Bureau of Investigation (FBI) has been central in this project and has publicly noted an interest in widening the policing net to include Canadian activists involved with SHAC-Canada. Eco-Terrorism "expert" John E. Lewis, of the FBI Counterterrorism Division, noted in 2006, at the *International Conference on Public Safety: Technology and Counterterrorism*, that the "eco-terrorist movement" has "become the most active criminal extremist element in the United States." Lewis added, "by way of example, today we are working with our Canadian counterparts and authorities in England to monitor SHAC's activities, both here and abroad." The FBI as well as CSIS has classified SHAC as an "extremist" element of the animal rights movement.

International intelligence risk designations trickle back down to the local scale of policing. For instance, the FBI works with a RCMP Integrated National Security Enforcement Team (INSET), created after 11 September 2001, specifically to police so-called "terrorism." INSET was created to coordinate antiterrorism intelligence among various agencies at the national and international levels. ATI requests from the West Vancouver Police Department indicates that Sgt Dennis Didyk, leader of the RCMP's "animal rights extremism" INSET team, was assigned to investigate SHAC in Vancouver during April 2007, immediately after the SHAC group moved to Vancouver following their banishment from Montréal.[15] When these police greeted protestors at home demos, they knew the names of SHAC activists from the information acquired by private security or from reading CSIS or Interpol files, demonstrating the transnational aspects of policing animal rights activism (see also Sheptycki, 1997). The addition of INSET to the multi-scalar policing network partially substantiates the claim of de Lint and Hall (2009) that intelligence from the national scale is now used in local policing.

Discussion: Repression, Suppression, and Surveillance of Social Movements

We have placed emphasis on the role that private security played in suppressing SHAC-Canada. Information was routinely swapped between the private pharmaceutical security group, private detectives, Westmount security, and Montréal police. Information collected by private eyes, we argue, feeds into public order policing. Information sharing leads to further networking, shifting the scale of suppression to a level of national security, which includes international intelligence agencies. Our analysis of SHAC-Canada adds to existing typologies of social movement repression by presenting a qualitative case study of unobserved suppression. This suppression was conducted by state agencies in conjunction with private agents, relying on resource depletion, arrests, and surveillance.

We have relied on the typologies provided by Earl (2003) and Boykoff (2007a) to frame our discussion, and we suggest that our analysis supplements their important typologies in four ways. First, Earl's typology frames movements in terms of mass mobilization, whereas many groups today organize in affinity groups that do not seek broad-scale collective action or public resonance *per se*.[16] SHAC is only concerned with targeted economic disruptions, using local home demos as one of its tactics. Earl, Soule, and McCarthy (2003) framed movement "strength" and "weakness" in terms of access to government officials and post-protest juridical routes to redress. But not all social movement groups organize in terms of government and juridical access— many reject such associations. Repression targeting groups not framed in terms of mass mobilization can be harsher, since these groups are not organized through institutionalized structures (see Gamson, 1975; Andrews, 2002). The character of the repressive actions taken against affinity groups has not yet been explored in a manner consistent with Earl's (2003) typology.

Second, although Earl (2004) has accounted for the role of private security in repression, her broader typology (Earl, 2003) places less emphasis on the private security agents who provide intelligence information to public police. Likewise, Boykoff (2007b, p. 12) used the term "outsourced suppression" to identify suppression carried out by private individuals or groups. What we emphasize is that private agents are not always acting at the behest of state agencies. Sometimes this relation between state and private agencies is inverted. The issue is directionality: private security agents are not simply activated by state agencies. In fact, the operations of state agencies rely heavily on the grey intelligence produced by private security. In the case of SHAC-Canada, multiple agencies were involved in ways that blurred traditional dichotomies of policing (e.g., private vs. public, domestic vs. international). National and international policing and security agencies later became involved, but the integral role played by the elite community of Westmount in spurring the response to SHAC cannot be understated. We have used the language of "suppression" since "covert repression" continues to denote state violence, neglecting multi-scalar combinations of agencies that can blur the line between public and private.

Third, Earl (2003) did not fully explain how crucial surveillance is to the regulation of social movements. All agencies involved in the regulation of SHAC-Canada are *networked through surveillance*. They engage in information gathering and sharing to cast a wider net of suppression. Surveillance not only captures information but also creates policing networks. For instance, the pharmaceutical security managers group was an informant for Westmount security, who, in turn, alerted Montréal police to make disruptions, arrests, searches, and seizures. Information generated by private agents was utilized by Vancouver police and within CSIS reports. Likewise, information from other state intelligence agencies was combed into CSIS and RCMP-INSET reports, flowing down into local police practices. Intelligence moves across the state/non-state divide, up and down the multiple scales of policing. Fourth, Earl (2003) discussed the role of national political elites and their proximity to policing and security agencies, but we place greater emphasis on the role of economic elites (such as the medical research executives targeted by SHAC) in galvanizing public police and private security responses. It is not only events involving political elites and internationally protected people that draw together policing and security agencies. It is not only heads of state that galvanize intervention into dissident groups. We also witness policing of dissent when movements threaten highly profitable enterprises and the expectations of comfort that are held by residents in an exclusive and wealthy community.

Conclusion

Suppression of SHAC-Canada has not involved mass round-ups of activists, multi-million dollar prosecutions, or political legislation tailored to the demands of the medical research lobby, as it has in the UK and the USA. In contrast, movement suppression took place through modest and coordinated efforts of policing entities to disrupt the day-to-day activities of the group. SHAC-Canada activists were thrown into jail, harassed, intimidated, and made subject to resource depletion, all for the purpose of incapacitation. For Humphrey and Stears (2006, p. 41), animal rights activism today:

> is associated with a whole series of political devices that appear to hover on the boundary of acceptability. Theirs is a politics of direct action, protest, even intimidation, in an age when those devices are increasingly critically received by political leaders concerned more with order and security than with dissent and political dynamism.

In the case of SHAC-Canada, the "boundaries of acceptability" have been demarcated by an affluent community with the material and political resources to galvanize private security and public police. Certainly, this is a product of SHAC's home demo tactics. SHAC has been targeted in the anticipation of future actions (see also Oliver, 2008), which is consistent with broader trends toward precautionary policing and cooperation of public police with private security (see Button, 2003; Lippert & O'Connor, 2006). This case also illustrates that, when private surveillance and intimidation fail to induce demobilization, contentious activism can be framed as "terrorism" and dragged through the courts.

We have shown that ATI requests can be used to collect the "dirty data" that policing agencies produce as it regards suppression of social movements. In fact, using ATI requests as a methodological tool is a corrective to research in social movement studies, surveillance studies, critical criminology, and the sociology of policing, which continues to rely primarily on the official discourse of police as well as easily accessible media articles. Social movement scholars should test how well ATI and freedom of information requests can be used in other countries to conduct research on policing, security, intelligence, and surveillance.

We have also supplemented existing typologies of social movement repression by demonstrating how the information produced by the surveillance practices of private security and detectives becomes actionable intelligence for local police and travels further up the policing network. Private security agents are often more involved in projects of suppression than first meets the eye. Public police and private security are contiguous insofar as they use both surveillance and resource depletion as methods of incapacitating movement participants.

Notes

1. In May 2007, Operation Achilles targeted SHAC-UK, involving several 100 police officers and the arrest of 32 SHAC members. The leadership of SHAC-UK faced numerous charges and was sentenced to multi-year prison terms. In March of 2006, six SHAC-USA members were charged under the *Animal Enterprise Protection Act*. The SHAC 7 activists are not only accused of having personally engaged in threatening acts but also of communications and organizing various promotions. The SHAC 7 activists faced multi-year prison terms. There have also been disproportionate sentences handed down to Eric McDavid, Rod Coronado, Jeffrey Luers, Peter Young, arrestees in "Operation Backfire," among others. Operation Backfire was the largest round-up of eco-activists in American history. Repercussions of the arrests are ongoing. The FBI-led efforts include infiltrations, paid informants, and present indications of other COINTELPRO-like tactics (Churchill & Vander Wall, 1988).
2. SHAC works in small affinity groups. Although there is a small central group based in the UK that coordinates the general direction of SHAC, geographic dispersion allows SHAC groups to organize autonomously. Each affinity group contains roughly a dozen people who act together (McDonald, 2002).
3. SHAC activists arrive to home demos and yell chants like "puppy killers" into megaphones. They hold posters depicting dead animals ripped open by vivisection. SHAC activists wear ski masks to remain anonymous and also to symbolize the executive's lack of accountability.
4. Goldstein's (1975) classic definition of repression focuses only on state violence and "government action."

5. Crafted at the behest of the well-funded animal research lobby, the Animal Enterprise Terrorism Act (AETA) was signed into law by President Bush on 27 November 2006. Like the *Patriot Act*, the AETA expands pre-emptive criminal law prohibitions against activities deemed suspicious by enforcement agencies. Section A of this legislation explicitly targets activities against any person or business with any "connection to an animal enterprise."
6. Originally, we requested information from the following federal departments: Canada Border Services Agency; Canadian Security Intelligence Service; Department of Justice Canada; Foreign Affairs and International Trade; Royal Canadian Mounted Police; and Public Safety and Emergency Preparedness Canada. When we realized that the policing of SHAC Montréal had more to do with the City of Westmount, we submitted a request to the City of Westmount in English and French. We filed similar requests with Montréal and West Vancouver Police (when SHAC was banned from Montréal they moved to Vancouver). We include below the request numbers for each request; using these request numbers, researchers can obtain the same information we did.
7. Department of Justice material was produced through request #A-2007-00089, received 17 August 2007.
8. All materials concerning the City of Westmount and Montréal police were produced through request #602-01-2007-047, received 24 September 2007. In a separate request to Montréal police, #07-2408, all information was withheld according to the ongoing investigation clause.
9. Marx's (1979) comment creation of an unfavorable public image as repression does not apply in the case of SHAC-Canada, since the goal of the group is to operate surreptitiously. While there was coverage in the *Westmount Examiner*, there was neither mass media coverage nor SHAC-Canada pursuing a media messaging campaign. The media are not a factor with this case or with many other examples of affinity group repression because neither the activists nor the police sought a media campaign to bolster their case.
10. Another connection between surveillance and private participation in public order policing has to do with ATI. Part way through our research, the City of Westmount hired a lawyer from a large private firm to take over as City Clerk and become the Access to Information Coordinator. Soon after, all sources of information about the case dried up (for a comparable case in the USA, see Earl, 2009).
11. At one trial, the prosecution used a 600-page document produced by Montréal police. The document reports in a detailed manner the comings and goings of SHAC members as chronicled by Montréal police. Within these police files, there is also data provided from private detectives hired by Westmount residents.
12. SHAC activists have attempted to counter police surveillance. At home demos, some members bring recording devices to capture police abuses in ways previously referred to as "countersurveillance" (see Huey et al., 2006).
13. All materials from CSIS were produced through request #117-2007-32, received 24 September 2007.
14. A whole array of activities from nonviolent demonstrations to labor organizing has been

subject to counterterrorism policing in the past several years, though this is not entirely new. Canadian scholars have provided excellent accounts of government surveillance campaigns as it regards the queer liberation movement (see Kinsman & Gentile, 2009) and socialist organizations during the Cold War (see McKay, 2005).

15. Material on the Vancouver Police was produced through request #07-2056A, received 3 December 2007.
16. Davenport (2007) argued that most literature on social movement repression has tended to portray movements as having a national orientation or a mass mobilization objective.

References

Amster, R. (2006) Perspectives on ecoterrorism: catalysts, conflations and casualties, *Contemporary Justice Review*, 9(3), pp. 287–301.

Andrews, K. (2002) Movement-countermovement dynamics and the emergence of new institutions: The case of "White Flight" Schools in Mississippi, *Social Forces*, 80(3), pp. 911–936.

Barkan, S. (2006) Criminal prosecution and the legal control of protest, *Mobilization*, 11(2), pp. 181–195.

Barry, M. (2006) Westmount to keep close eye on animal rights protestors, *Westmount Examiner*, 4 October.

Boykoff, J. (2007a) Limiting dissent: The mechanisms of state repression in the USA, *Social Movement Studies*, 6(3), pp. 281–310.

Boykoff, J. (2007b) *Beyond Bullets: The Suppression of Dissent in the United States* (Oakland, CA: AK Press).

Boykoff, J. (2007c) Surveillance, spatial compression and scale: The FBI and Martin Luther King Jr, *Antipode*, 39(4), pp. 729–756.

Brown, J. & Lippert, R. (2007) Private security's purchase: Imagining of a security patrol in a Canadian residential neighbourhood, *Canadian Journal of Criminology and Criminal Justice*, 49(5), pp. 587–617.

Button, M. (2002) *Private Policing* (Portland, OR: Willan Publishing).

Button, M. (2003) Private security and the policing of quasi-public space, *International Journal of the Sociology of Law*, 31(3), pp. 227–237.

Churchill, W. (2004) Illuminating the philosophy and methods of animal liberation, in: S. Best & A. Nocella (Eds) *Terrorists or Freedom Fighters? Reflections on the Liberation of Animals*, pp. 1–6 (New York: Lantern Books).

Churchill, W. & Vander Wall, J. (1988) *Agents of Repression: The FBI's Secret Wars Against the Black Panther Party and the American Indian Movement* (Boston, MA: South End Press).

Cunningham, D. (2003) The patterning of repression: FBI counterintelligence and the new left, *Social Forces*, 82(1), pp. 209–240.

Cunningham, D. (2004) *There's Something Happening Here: The New Left, the Klan, and FBI Counterintelligence* (Berkeley, CA: University of California Press).

Davenport, C. (1995) Multi-dimensional threat perception and state repression: An inquiry into why states apply negative sanctions, *American Journal of Political Science*, 39(3), pp. 683–713.

Davenport, C. (2005) Understanding covert repressive action: The case of the U.S. Government against the Republic of New Africa, *Journal of Conflict Resolution*, 49(1), pp. 120–140.

Davenport, C. (2007) State repression and political order, *Annual Review of Political Science*, 10(1), pp. 1–23.

de Lint, W. & Hall, A. (2009) *Intelligent Control: Developments in Public Order Policing in Canada* (Toronto: University of Toronto Press).

Donner, F. (1990) *Protectors of Privilege: Red Squads and Police Repression in Urban America* (Berkeley, CA: University of California Press).

Earl, J. (2003) Tanks, tear gas, and taxes: Towards a theory of movement repression, *Sociological Theory*, 21(1), pp. 44–67.

Earl, J. (2004) Controlling protest: New directions for research on the social control of protest, *Research in Social Movements, Conflicts, and Change*, 25, pp. 55–83.

Earl, J. (2006) Repression and the social control of protest, *Mobilization*, 11(2), pp. 129–143.

Earl, J. (2009) Information access and protest policing post-9/11: Studying the policing of the 2004 Republican National Convention, *American Behavioral Scientist*, 53(1), pp. 44–60.

Earl, J. & Soule, S. (2006) Seeing blue: A police-centered explanation of protest policing, *Mobilization*, 11(2), pp. 145–164.

Earl, J., Soule, S. & McCarthy, J. (2003) Protests under fire? Explaining protest policing, *American Sociological Review*, 69(5), pp. 581–606.

Ericson, R. & Doyle, A. (1999) Globalization and the policing of protest: The case of APEC 1997, *British Journal of Sociology*, 50(4), pp. 589–608.

Fernandez, L. (2008) Policing *Dissent: Social Control and the Anti-Globalization Movement* (Chapel Hill, NC: Rutgers University Press).

Ferree, M. (2004) Soft repression: Ridicule, stigma and silencing in gender-based movements, *Research in Social Movements, Conflicts and Change*, 25, pp. 85–101.

Gamson, W. (1975) *The Strategy of Social Protest* (Homewood, IL: The Dorsey Press).

Goldstein, R. (1975) *Political Repression in Modern America: From 1870 to the Present* (New York: Schenkman).

Hoogenboom, B. (2006) *Grey intelligence, Crime, Law & Social Change*, 45(4), pp. 373–381.

Huey, L., Walby, K. & Doyle, A. (2006) Cop watching in the downtown eastside: Exploring the use of (counter) surveillance as a tool of resistance, in: Torin Monahan (Ed.) *Surveillance and Security: Technological Politics in Everyday Life*, pp. 149–166 (London: Routledge).

Humphrey, M. & Stears, M. (2006) Animal rights protest and the challenge to deliberative democracy, *Economy and Society*, 35(3), pp. 400–422.

Isin, E. (2004) The neurotic citizen, *Citizenship Studies*, 8(3), pp. 217–235.

Johnston, L. (1992) *The Rebirth of Private Policing* (London: Routledge).

Kinsman, G. & Gentile, P. (2009) *The Canadian War on Queers: National Security as Sexual Regulation* (Vancouver: University of British Columbia Press).

Koopmans, R. (1997) Dynamics of repression and mobilization: The German extreme right experience in the 1990s, *Mobilization*, 2(2), pp. 149–164.

Larsen, M. & Piché, J. (2009) Exceptional state, pragmatic bureaucracy, and indefinite detention: The case of the Kingston Immigration Holding Centre, *Canadian Journal of Law and Society*, 24(2), pp. 203–229.

Larsen, W. (2006) Activists should demonstrate some fair play, *Westmount Examiner*, 4 October.

Liddick, D. (2006) *Eco-Terrorism: Radical Environmental and Animal Liberation Movements* (Westport, CT: Praeger).

Lippert, R. & O'Connor, D. (2006) Security intelligence networks and the transformation of contract private security, *Policing and Society*, 16(1), pp. 50–66.

Loader, I. (2000) Plural policing and democratic governance, *Social & Legal Studies*, 9(3), pp. 323–345.

Marx, G. (1979) External efforts to damage or facilitate social movements: Some patterns, explanations, outcomes and complications, in: M. Zald & J. McCarthy (Eds) *The Dynamics of Social Movements*, pp. 94–125 (Winthrop, MN: Winthrop Publishers).

Marx, G. (1984) Notes on the discovery, collection, and assessment of hidden and dirty data, in: J. Schneider & J. Kitsuse (Eds) *Studies in the Sociology of Social Problems*, pp. 78–113 (Norwood, NJ: Ablex).

McDonald, K. (2002) From solidarity to fluidarity: Social movements beyond "Collective Identity"—the case of globalization conflicts, *Social Movement Studies*, 1(2), pp. 109–128.

McKay, I. (2005) *Rebels, Reds, Radicals: Rethinking Canada's Left History* (Toronto: Between the Lines Press).

Meyer, D. & Staggenborg, S. (1996) Movements, countermovements and the structure of political opportunity, *American Journal of Sociology*, 101(6), pp. 1628–1660.

Monaghan, J. & Walby, K. (2008) The green scare is everywhere: The long reach of the war on "Eco-Terror," *Upping the Anti*, 6, pp. 93–112.

Morrison, J. (2006) Animal rights or wrongs?, *Ottawa Sun*, 7 December.

Munro, L. (2005) Strategies, action repertoires and DIY activism in the animal rights movement, *Social Movements Studies*, 4(1), pp. 75–94.

Newburn, T. (2001) The commodification of policing: Security networks in the Late Modern City, *Urban Studies*, 38(5–6), pp. 829–848.

Oliver, P. (2008) Repression and crime control: Why social movement scholars should pay attention to mass incarceration as a form of repression, *Mobilization*, 13(1), pp. 1–24.

Piché, J. & Walby, K. (2010) Problematizing carceral tours, *British Journal of Criminology*, 50(3), pp. 570–581.

Rigakos, G. (2005) Beyond public–private: Towards a new typology of policing, in: D. Cooley (Ed.) *Re-Imagining Policing in Canada*, pp. 260–319 (Toronto: University of Toronto Press).

Scarce, R. (1990) *Eco-Warriors: Understanding the Radical Environmental Movement* (Chicago, IL: The NoblePress, Inc.).

Schönteich, M., Minaar, A., Mistry, D. & Goyer, K. (2004) Private muscle: Outsourcing the provision of criminal justice services, *Institute for Security Study* (ISS) Monograph 93.

Scott, T. & McPherson, M. (1971) The development of the private sector of the criminal justice system, *Law & Society Review*, 6(2), pp. 267–288.

Shearing, C. & Stenning, P. (1983) Private security: Implications for social control, *Social Problems*, 30(5), pp. 493–506.

Sheptycki, J. (1997) Insecurity, risk suppression and segregation: Some reflections on policing in the transnational age, *Theoretical Criminology*, 1(3), pp. 303–315.

Snyder, D. (1976) Theoretical and methodological problems in the analysis of governmental coercion and collective violence, *Journal of Political and Military Sociology*, 4(3), pp. 277–293.

Trevaskes, S. (2007) The private/public security Nexus in China, *Social Justice*, 34(3–4), pp. 38–55.

Wagner-Pacifici, R. (1994) *Discourse and Destruction: The City of Philadelphia versus MOVE* (Chicago, IL: University of Chicago Press).

Wakefield, A. (2008) Private policing: A view from the mall, *Public Administration*, 86(3), pp. 659–678.

Walby, K. (2009) "He asked me if I was looking for fags … " Ottawa's National Capital Commission Conservation Officers and the Policing of Public Park Sex, *Surveillance & Society*, 6(4), pp. 367–379.

Walby, K. & Monaghan, J. (2010) Policing proliferation: On the militarization of police and atomic energy Canada Limited's nuclear response forces, *Canadian Journal of Criminology and Criminal Justice*, 52(2), pp. 117–145.

CHAPTER 15

Woman Abuse in Canada: Sociological Reflections on the Past, Suggestions for the Future

Walter S. DeKeseredy and Molly Dragiewicz

Since 1980, sociologists have made important empirical and theoretical contributions to the study of a variety of male assaults on current or former intimate female partners in Canada. Developments in the Canadian research have been shaped by outside forces. This is not surprising because Canada's economy, culture, and scholarship have been molded by foreign influences, especially from the United States, since its colonial beginnings (DeKeseredy, 2012a; Grabb, 2004). Yet, Canadian sociological work has also had a major impact on research in other countries. For example, Statistics Canada's Violence Against Women Survey (VAWS) was the world's first national survey specifically designed to investigate multiple types of male-to-female violence (Jacquier, Johnson, & Fisher, 2011). As a result, the VAWS yielded much higher rates of violence and abuse than earlier surveys designed to measure either crime or family conflict (Dobash & Dobash, 1995).[1] The impact of the path-breaking methodological developments made in this study is still felt today. The VAWS has been replicated in national studies in countries such as Australia, Finland, and Iceland (Walby & Myhill, 2001), as well as regional studies such as the Chicago Women's Health Risk Study (Block et al., 2000).

The Canadian national survey (CNS) of woman abuse in university/college dating was also the first countrywide study of its kind (DeKeseredy & Schwartz, 1998), expanding on the scope of earlier studies of sexual assault on campus (Koss, Gidycz, & Wisniewski, 1987). In addition, Canadian scholars such as Brownridge (2009) have been at the forefront of the examination of violence against women during and after separation and divorce.

This article chronicles Canadian sociological developments in the field that occurred since 1980 and suggests new directions in research, theorizing, and policy development. Many "highs" and "lows" emerged in the sociological journey that started over 30 years ago and more will come. Feminist sociologists, in particular, face significant challenges in the current neo-liberal political economic era characterized by a "well-oiled" counter-movement to degender the naming and framing of woman abuse (Bumiller, 2008; Johnson & Dawson, 2011). What will the future bring? According to historians, to answer this question, "We all need past knowledge ... It is all we have to guide us to the future" (Stearns, 2011, p. 1).

Looking Back[2]

There has been episodic concern with women's experiences with sexual assault, beatings, and the like in Canadian history, but such harms were not of major interest until recently to social scientists, practitioners, politicians, and the general public. It was, after all, only 40 years ago than an exhaustive bibliography on wife beating could be written on an index card (DeKeseredy & Dragiewicz, 2009). As Denham and Gillespie (1999) remind us, "Prior to the 1970s, there was no name for violence against women by their husbands or partners" (p. 6). Since then, mainly because of feminist efforts, many Canadians pay considerable attention to woman abuse during and after intimate relationships. Feminists also influenced the development of a spate of large- and small-scale studies, as well as the construction of several theories.

Empirical work specifically designed to determine the extent of woman abuse in Canada began with MacLeod and Cadieux's (1980) examination of transition house and divorce-petition data. Their study was "methodologically unsound" (Ellis, 1987), but these researchers concluded, "Every year, one in ten Canadian women who are married or in a relationship with a live-in lover are battered" (p. 17). Although not derived from a representative sample of the general population, this conclusion was not that far off the mark as demonstrated by subsequent studies, most of which showed that between 11% and 24% of Canadian women in marital/cohabiting relationships are physically assaulted at least once annually (Brinkerhoff & Lupri, 1988; Kennedy & Dutton, 1989; Smith, 1987). High rates of physical violence in university/college dating have also been uncovered. For example, of the 1,835 women who participated in the CNS, 22.3% indicated that they had been physically victimized by their dating partners in the past year. In addition, roughly 25% of the female respondents reported experiencing some type of sexual assault in the past 12 months (DeKeseredy & Kelly, 1993; DeKeseredy & Schwartz, 1998).

During the late 1980s and into the 90s, there were also studies of "post-separation woman abuse" and "intimate femicide" (e.g., Crawford & Gartner, 1992; Ellis, 1990; Ellis & Stuckless, 1993, 1996; Ellis & Wight, 1987; Sev'er, 1997). The results of this work supported "the widespread apprehension that wives often experience elevated risk when deserting a violently proprietary husband" (Wilson, Johnson, & Daly, 1995, pp. 340–341). This observation still holds true in Canada (Brownridge, 2009; Johnson & Dawson, 2011). In fact, throughout Canada, compared with women living with their male partners, separated women continue to run a sixfold risk of being killed (DeKeseredy, 2011a).

No review of Canadian woman abuse research done in the past is complete without mentioning another "key milestone" (Denham & Gillespie, 1999). In 1992, the Department of National Health (now called Public Health Agency of Canada [PHAC]) and the Social Sciences and Humanities Research Council funded the creation of five research centers on family violence and violence against women in response to the murder of 14 female students at the University of Montreal on December 6, 1989. This 5-year funding initiative ended in 1997, but the centers carried on with money from other sources. They also enhanced Canadians' awareness of woman abuse and generated useful information for policy makers and practitioners (Kettani, 2009). It should also be noted in passing that under yet another name (Health Canada), PHAC funded the CNS, VAWS, and Randall and Haskell's (1995) Toronto community-based survey of sexual and physical assault throughout women's lives.

Canadian theoretical developments did not keep pace with the expanding empirical literature. From 1980 until now, especially in the late 1980s and early 1990s, woman abuse research was guided mainly by "practical objectives" (Gelles, 1980). Most of the above-mentioned surveys were primarily concerned with answering two important questions: (a) "how many women are abused by their current or former male partners?" and (b) "what are the correlates of woman abuse" (DeKeseredy & Hinch, 1991, p. 28)? This is not to say that all of this work constituted "abstracted empiricism" (e.g., research divorced from theory; Mills, 1959). For example, using data from his Toronto woman abuse survey, Smith (1990) tested the feminist hypothesis that wife beating results from men's adherence to the ideology of familial patriarchy. Furthermore, Statistics Canada's VAWS and the CNS were heavily influenced by feminist theory (DeKeseredy & Schwartz, 1998; Johnson, 1996). Still, few original theories were crafted and tested by Canadian scholars. These include DeKeseredy's (1988) male peer support model, which has been revised and expanded over the past 24 years[3]; Ellis and DeKeseredy's (1989) dependency, availability, deterrence (DAD) model; and a sociological theory of separation/divorce femicide (Ellis & DeKeseredy, 1997). Furthermore, variations of feminist thought have always guided Canadian woman abuse research and still do today.

In sum, in approximately one decade, woman abuse emerged from a vacuum of silence to become a major issue for Canadian researchers. Today, however, it is no longer a priority for most politicians. In addition, while the empirical and theoretical work done since the mid-1980s provide an increasingly detailed picture of beatings, sexual assault, and the like, representative sample surveys such as the VAWS and CNS have provoked an anti-feminist backlash among those opposed to the findings (Crocker, 2010; DeKeseredy & Schwartz, 2003). Patriarchy is now being reasserted by conservative fathers' rights groups and other anti-feminist organizations (Dragiewicz, 2008). Increasingly, the Canadian federal government is sympathetic to anti-feminist initiatives.

The Current State of Affairs

A major shift in Canadian federal government responses to woman abuse started in the late 1990s, which, in turn, had a major impact on the research community. Statistics Canada moved away from developing feminist-informed surveys of woman abuse and is currently being influenced by political forces guided by anti-feminist groups and others with a vested interest in minimizing the pain and suffering caused by male-to-female violence (DeKeseredy, 2011a). Statistics Canada (2002, 2005, 2011) now uses less sophisticated measurement tools that fail to discern the differing contexts, meanings, and motives of male and female intimate violence. Government reports on the data now downplay significant differences in women's and men's experiences by aggregating data across sex categories and highlighting similar prevalence rates rather than dissimilar frequency, severity, and dynamics of violence (DeKeseredy,

2011a). In addition, on October 3, 2006, Bev Oda, then federal minister for the Status of Women Canada (SWC), announced that women's organizations would no longer be eligible for funding for advocacy, government lobbying, or research projects. SWC was also required to remove the word *equality* from its list of goals (Carastathis, 2006). To make matters worse, in early September 2007, Conservative Prime Minister Stephen Harper supported the anti-feminist agenda by cutting funds to the National Association of Women and the Law (NAWL), a non-profit women's group that tackles violence against women and other forms of female victimization.

On top of the above transitions, some prominent Canadian politicians, journalists, activists, and researchers minimize the alarming rates of woman abuse generated by surveys described in the previous section and launch biting critiques of feminist interpretations of these figures. For example, Dutton (2010) states that only a "minority of men are violent either outside or within relationships. There is no norm for wife assault—this is a sociological fiction and contradicted by surveys" (p. 8).

The PHAC used to prioritize violence against women, but now publishes "Family Violence Prevention E-Bulletins" such as the July 2011 issue,[4] which repeatedly reinforces the erroneous notions that women and girls are equally as violent as males and that rates of female violence are increasing. Moreover, gender-neutral terms, such as "intimate partner violence," "domestic violence," and "spousal violence" are rapidly replacing gender-specific ones (e.g., woman abuse) in federal government publications and in some academic circles. Many people who use such language selectively cite research that misleadingly characterizes violence as bi-directional, mutual, or sex symmetrical (DeKeseredy & Dragiewicz, 2009).

In this current era, many, if not most, people who attack feminist inquiry do not understand feminism. As Stanko (1997) puts it, "Those who make such accusations have not been reading the research carefully ... or not reading the research at all" (p. 79). Even so, it is the voice of anti-feminists, rather than that of feminists or abused women, that is the loudest. Ironically, this has a positive consequence on the social scientific community as feminists' studies are generally very rigorous because they know that they will be subject to heightened scrutiny and criticism for being "political" instead of scientific (Romito, 2008).

Often criticized, ignored, or even silenced, Canadian feminist sociological work on woman abuse persists. However, much of the recent research has been focused outside Canada. For example, University of Ottawa criminologist Holly Johnson helped conduct the International Violence Against Women Survey (Johnson, Ollus, & Nevala, 2008), and some Canadians continue to do collaborative research with U.S. colleagues on separation/divorce assault in urban and rural parts of the United States (e.g., DeKeseredy & Schwartz, 2009; Rennison, DeKeseredy, & Dragiewicz, 2013). It is also somewhat paradoxical that Molly Dragiewicz went to Canada from the United States to become one of the few feminist scholars there who studied Canadian fathers' rights groups, the anti-feminist backlash, and the experiences of abused Ontario women lacking legal representation in the family courts.[5]

Statistics Canada's recent renditions of the General Social Survey (GSS) are highly problematic and are used by anti-feminists to claim that women are as violent as men in intimate relationships. Brownridge (2009), however, has examined the woman abuse data from the 1999 and 2004 GSS and produced some valuable information on violence against women at the margins, such as those who are immigrants, disabled, or Aboriginal. Unfortunately, his analyses of GSS data receive much less public attention than GSS data showing sex symmetry. The same can be said about Fong's (2010) feminist anthology on woman abuse in ethnic, immigrant, and Aboriginal communities. Some feminists are doing intersectional analyses of violence in the lives of girls (Berman & Jiwani, 2002; Jiwani, 2006; Pajot, 2009). Intersectionality is also directly relevant to Canadian feminist interpretations of Internet pornography, which has become more violent and racist (Dines, 2010). DeKeseredy and Olsson (2011) show that cyberporn is also strongly associated with various types of woman abuse in intimate heterosexual relationships. Unfortunately, there is a giant market for hurtful sexual images, and the negative effects of pornography are being felt around the globe (Bridges & Jensen, 2011).

It may seem obvious, but worth stating nonetheless: Much more Canadian sociological empirical and theoretical work is necessary. The good news is that there are prolific researchers scattered across Canada and they will continue to make interesting and policy-relevant scholarly contributions in the near future. Nonetheless, they face numerous challenges over the next few years as Canada continues to move to the right of the political economic spectrum.

Future Challenges

At the end of the 1990s, based on interviews with roughly 50 Canadian people who worked on the issue of woman abuse since 1989, Denham and Gillespie (1999) stated that "this is a critical point in the evolution of our understanding of woman abuse" (p. 47). The same can be said today, but the circumstances are different. There was an anti-feminist backlash then, but it has become more deeply entrenched and mainstreamed (DeKeseredy, 2011a; Dragiewicz, 2008, 2011). For example, Springer Publishing Company now publishes the journal *Partner Abuse*. As stated on the journal's website,

> *Partner Abuse* seeks to advance research, treatment and policy on partner abuse in new directions. A basic premise of the journal is that partner abuse and family violence is a human problem, and that the particular role of gender in the etiology, perpetration and consequences of emotional and physical partner abuse cannot be assumed, but rather must be subjected to the same empirical scrutiny as any other factor. Just as treatment decisions ought to be based on sound assessment protocols, policies on partner abuse ought to be based on an understanding of the full range of available research, without regard to political considerations. (*Partner Abuse*, n.d.)

Despite the avowed commitment to recognizing "the full range of available research," the categorical dismissal of research that acknowledges the importance of gender to violence is a staple of the journal's content. The flagship article was a full-frontal attack on feminism, which claimed, "The gender paradigm is a closed system, unresponsive to major disconfirming data sets, and takes an antiscience stance consistent with a cult" (Dutton, 2010, p. 5). Indeed, the idea that a commitment to rigorous empirical research on violence is a "new direction" appears to indicate a lack of familiarity with the large extant literature, including multiple dedicated, selective, and widely read scholarly journals devoted to violence and abuse.

Certainly, major steps need to be taken to resist the degendering of one of Canada's most compelling social problems. One effective way of doing so is through social media such as Facebook and Twitter (DeKeseredy, 2011b). Launched in November 2009 by United Nations (UN) Women, Say No—Unite to End Violence Against Women is one example of a progressive global coalition that effectively uses social media to reach thousands of people around the world. Indeed, many people find it easier to join a social media group to make a political point than to protest in the streets. As well, it is much easier to get a few thousand people to join a Facebook group than to get a few hundred to show up at Canada's Parliament Hill with banners (Walker Rettberg, 2009). For instance, with the help of new electronic technologies, Say No—Unite managed to get 5,066,549 people to sign a call to make ending violence against women a top priority worldwide during its first phase (Say No—Unite, n.d.). Say No—Unite also engages in online media outreach and offers a range of useful web-based resources at www.saynotoviolence.org.

This initiative is a positive feature of information technologies, but there are also negative elements that contribute to patriarchal discourses and practices, including woman abuse (DeKeseredy, in press). For example, there are thousands of websites explicitly featuring adult women being degraded and abused in horrible ways. Actually, a common feature of new pornographic videos is painful anal penetration, as well as men slapping/strangling women and/or pulling hair while they penetrate them orally, vaginally, and anally (Bridges, Wosnitzer, Scharrer, Sun, & Liberman, 2010; Dines, 2010).

Effectively responding to hurtful media images of women constitutes a major challenge, given that there are over four million pornography sites on the Internet (Dines, 2010), with as many as 10,000 added every week (DeKeseredy & Olsson, 2011; Funk, 2006). Nevertheless, there are some effective initiatives that can be borrowed from activists in the United States. One novel method is the Clean Hotel Initiative developed by the Minnesota Men's Action Network: Alliance to Prevent Sexual and Domestic Violence. This involves strongly encouraging businesses, government agencies, non-profit organizations, and professional associations to hold conferences and meetings only in hotels that do not offer in-room pay-per-view pornography. Profit is a business's "bottom line" and boycotting is a tried and true way of influencing capitalist enterprises to stop using sexist and other harmful means of making money (DeKeseredy, 2011b).

Researchers and activists also need to target the mainstream media and engage in what Barak (2007) refers to as "newsmaking criminology." This involves constantly sharing information about progressive research, grassroots efforts, and policy work with newspaper and television journalists. That articles and letters written by feminists are periodically published by the mainstream press, and that some feminist scholars have been on television serve as evidence that the mainstream media do not totally dismiss or ignore progressive interpretations of gender violence (Caringella-MacDonald & Humphries, 1998; DeKeseredy, 2011b). For example, pioneering feminist Gloria Steinem's critique of the NBC series *The Playboy Club* recently appeared in the popular Canadian newspaper the *Toronto Star* (see Salem, 2011). Perhaps her statements had an impact because the series was terminated shortly after her remarks.

Canadian funding for academic woman abuse research is at an all-time low and will not improve soon. Under Prime Minister Stephen Harper's leadership, the Social Sciences and Humanities Research Council of Canada (SSHRC), which is the main funder of Canadian social science research, prioritizes business-related doctoral research (DeKeseredy, 2012a). Moreover, it is likely that the federal government will continue to influence Statistics Canada to produce data supporting the sexual symmetry of violence thesis. However, feminist projects funded by local community groups and provincial government agencies can be done, as demonstrated by scholars across the country. For example, we have developed a meaningful partnership with Luke's Place Support and Resource Center for Women and Children in Oshawa, Ontario, and jointly conducted studies of the needs of local battered women with funding from the Ontario Women's Directorate, Canadian Women's Foundation, and the Ontario Ministry of the Attorney General (Dragiewicz & DeKeseredy, 2008).

There will be even more intense competition for scarce grant money as governments at all levels downsize their budgets. Hence, researchers based at different institutions need to start thinking seriously about collaborating instead of competing with each other. Collaborations not only help "spread the wealth," but as Denham and Gillespie (1999) correctly point out, "They can create new opportunities for solutions that could not exist if groups worked in isolation" (p. 45).

Even though Canada is a bilingual country, an ongoing problem is the marginalization of Francophone social science, regardless of whether it is mainstream or feminist (Doyle & Moore, 2011; Dupont, 2011). Obviously, stronger relations between French- and English-Canadian scholars and activists need to be developed. In addition, more attention needs to be given to woman abuse in Aboriginal communities. And ethnic minorities' experiences, as well as those of immigrants and refugees, need to be an integral component of sociological work on woman abuse.

Theoretical work is just as important as empirical projects, and there is a need for new multivariate perspectives. As Kurt Lewin (1951), the founder of modern social psychology, stated, "There is nothing so practical as a good theory" (p. 169). The same can be said about good theories of woman abuse. Equally important is constructing and testing theories that focus on the broader social, political, cultural, and economic contexts in which woman abuse occurs, as this is a widespread problem. Although feminist scholars pay attention to the gendered dynamics of violence, more could be done to investigate and explain what we mean when we talk about gender and patriarchy. Theorizing these concepts continues to be important. Many criminologists still do not take gender into account and continue to develop putatively universal theories based on men's behavior. If there is anything the burgeoning literature on violence against women has decisively demonstrated, it is that context matters.

"Gender" is not simply a stand-in for "sex" or for "women." Women's and men's behavior and experiences are deeply gendered, and we need to do more to investigate how gender shapes violence and abuse. Sociologists cannot skirt the politics involved in talking about violence against women or patriarchy by using degendered language. Not only does this feed into incorrect assumptions about the nature of violence, as noted above, it impedes rather than enhances our understanding. Gender-inclusive theories of violence, that is to say theories that include and account for gender rather than obscuring it via gender-blind language, are still needed (Dragiewicz, 2009).

More than ever, crime control laws and policies transferred from the United States heavily influence some of Canada's modes of governance, as they do in the United Kingdom. Still, ironically, at a time when crime discussion is dominated by calls for harsher punishment and "what about the victim?," a market remains for belittling crime victims when they are women abused by current or former male partners (DeKeseredy, 2009). To make matters worse, victim blaming is very much alive and well. Note that in January 2011, metropolitan Toronto police officer Michael Sanguinetti told a personal security class at York University that "women should avoid dressing like sluts in order not to be victimized" (CBC, 2011). No wonder many sexual assault survivors still lack faith in the criminal justice system. Nevertheless, this officer's remark had an international effect and spawned a series of "slut walks" around the world in which scores of women marched to protest revictimization discourses and practices.

Protesting, lobbying, awareness campaigns, and other methods are constantly needed to make the criminal justice system more accountable and sensitive to the plight of abused women. Even so, prison and other punitive approaches cannot truly prevent woman abuse. Thus, it is time to contemplate progressive alternatives to reliance on traditional formal means of social control (Meloy & Miller, 2011). There are other reasons for doing so, including that the criminal justice system cannot deal with highly injurious behaviors that are not physically violent (e.g., coercive control and psychological abuse). Also, criminal justice policies and practices may prioritize the state's objectives over those of the targets of woman abuse (Bumiller, 2008; Goodmark, 2012).

Canada is taking a more punitive response to street crimes such as mugging (DeKeseredy, 2011a), but the Canadian Criminal Code (1985) lists "alternative measures" as a priority and recommends that all alternatives to imprisonment be contemplated. This advice is partially grounded in the long Canadian history of restorative justice practices, starting with Aboriginal/First Nations traditions and more recently with Mennonite strategies in the 1970s (Goel, 2000; Yantzi, 1998). Here, following Ptacek (2010a), restorative justice is defined as an approach that seeks "to decrease the role of the state in responding to crime and increase the involvement of personal, familial, and community networks in repairing the harms caused by crime" (p. ix). Restorative justice programs are subject to much debate in feminist communities and with good reason, given the harms caused by coercive mediation programs. Consider what happened to 34 abused Nova Scotia women:

> Abused women reported intimidation and revictimization in mediation regardless of the form of abuse: physical, sexual, emotional, psychological, or financial. Women reported that their mediator or conciliator minimized emotional, psychological, or financial abuse, or simply did not recognize certain behaviors as abusive. When women brought up the fact that their ex-partner was harassing, stalking, or otherwise continuing to abuse them during their mediation, their mediators did not terminate mediation. (Rubin, 2000, p. 8)

Unfortunately, experiences like this are not unique, highlighting the need to address issues for abused women beyond the criminal justice system. Although family court diversion programs are very widespread, there has been very little research on what actually happens to abused mothers in family court. Sociological research on every aspect of abused women's experiences in the family courts, as well as the outcomes for them and their children, is sorely needed.

Highly aware of the above and other problems with diversionary restorative justice practices, some feminists call for post-conviction restorative justice measures, such as the Victims' Voices Heard program examined by Susan L. Miller (2011). Best described by her, programs like this one:

> involve some kind of encounter between the victim and offender, a meeting that occurs only after extensive preparation. Sometimes letters are exchanged in preparation for a face-to-face meeting, and often victims and offenders select a support person to accompany them to such a meeting. Trained facilitators oversee these dialogues and use their skills to balance the concerns of all parties involved. Face-to-face meetings, letter exchanges, and other practices provide the opportunity for participants to explore what happened, for victims to receive answers to questions and assurances of safety to tell their stories and express their feelings, and for offenders to tell their stories, take responsibility for their actions, and display genuine remorse. Restorative justice provides a context for forgiveness, but there is no pressure to choose this path. (p. 8)

Evaluations of this and other feminist restorative justice programs that address woman abuse, such as RESTORE (Responsibility and Equity for Sexual Transgressions Offering a Restorative Experience) in Pima County, Arizona (Koss, 2010), found success in offender rehabilitation, as well as in survivor healing, satisfaction, and empowerment (Meloy & Miller, 2011). But, as is often said in social scientific circles, more research is necessary, which is why there is a call for a moratorium on new restorative justice programs for woman abuse in Canada (Johnson & Dawson, 2011).

Reforms within and outside the criminal justice system must accompany the ongoing quest for broader social transformation, and this involves emphasizing the role of prevention

(Meloy & Miller, 2011; Ptacek, 2010b). A long list of empirically informed suggestions could easily be provided here, including bystander intervention approaches, women's safety audits, and public education programs (Johnson & Dawson, 2011). Men, too, need to play a stronger role in the struggle to end all forms of woman abuse. It has been repeatedly stated over the past 20 years that more time and effort are needed to influence men and boys to join the feminist men's movement heavily guided by the internationally renowned White Ribbon Campaign. The December 6, 1989, murder of 14 women at the University of Montreal spawned the creation of the Campaign and similar organizations (DeKeseredy, Schwartz, & Alvi, 2000; Luxton, 1993), which, like other progressive collectives, face new challenges in the future.

Some earlier challenges, however, persist. For example, still today, most Canadian feminist men's groups mainly consist of males who are White, middle-class, and heterosexual (DeKeseredy, 2012b). This problem needs to be quickly resolved for several reasons, including that Canada is becoming more ethnically diverse, especially in metropolitan areas. By 2031, close to 28% of the country's population could be foreign-born. Moreover, more than 71% of the entire visible minority population will likely live in Toronto, Vancouver, and Montreal (Statistics Canada, 2010). Universities and colleges, too, will become more diverse in the near future. Consider that in March 2010, Ontario Premier Dalton McGuinty stated that his province's goal is to increase the number of foreign students by 50% in the following 5 years to 55,000 (Cohn, 2010). Needless to say, people from historically marginalized ethnic/cultural backgrounds, as well as other men and women at the margins, have much insight to offer feminist men's organizations. The same can be said about any movement aimed at ending woman abuse in Canada and around the world. We should always be conscious of who is absent from our gatherings and that we are not hearing their voices (Gilfus et al., 1999).

Conclusions

This article offers a brief history of sociological empirical and theoretical work on woman abuse in Canada. To be included in other chronicles will be contributions made by psychologists, anthropologists, social workers, and scholars from other disciplines. Their work is just as significant as sociological projects, and the intent of this article was not to try to elevate sociological offerings to a higher level of importance. Even so, to some extent, woman abuse as a social issue compels us all to become sociologists and to look at our whole society through the lens of a critical analyst. The challenge for us as sociologists is to continue to question the meaning of changes in the story of woman abuse and their unanticipated consequences to uncover the real meaning of change and the social meaning of woman abuse prevention (DeKeseredy & MacLeod, 1997).

Despite budget cuts, the anti-feminist backlash, and a host of other obstacles and challenges, men and women involved in the violence against women movement have achieved much over the past four decades (Johnson & Dawson, 2011). Abused women now have more resources to choose from, but they are not markedly safer (Dragiewicz & DeKeseredy, 2008). Without a doubt, separated/divorced women in Canada are still at high risk of being killed if they lived with abusive and/or controlling men (Cross, 2007; DeKeseredy, 2011a). Sadly, scores of women will continue to suffer in silence until the major causes of woman abuse are recognized, understood, and addressed by policy makers and the general public (Johnson & Dawson, 2011; Wolfe & Jaffe, 2001). We suggested some effective means of helping to achieve this goal and for making the feminist struggle to end woman abuse a "usual, rather than unusual part of public policy" (Hearn, 1998, p. 113).

Notes

1. See Johnson (1996) for more information on Violence Against Women Survey (VAWS) methods and the data gleaned by them.
2. This is a subheading in Section 1 of Denham and Gillespie's (1999) overview of Canadian initiatives and resources to end woman abuse.
3. See DeKeseredy (1990), DeKeseredy and Schwartz (1998, 2002, 2009, 2010), and Schwartz and DeKeseredy (1997) for in-depth reviews of the empirical and theoretical literature on the relationship between male peer support and woman abuse in various intimate heterosexual relationships.
4. See http://www.phac-aspc.gc.ca/ncfv-cnivf/EB/2011/july-juillet/e-bulletin-eng.php.
5. For more information on her recent Canadian work on these issues, see DeKeseredy and Dragiewicz (2007, 2009) and Dragiewicz and DeKeseredy (2008, 2012).

References

Barak, G. (2007). Doing newsmaking criminology from within the academy. *Theoretical Criminology, 11*, 191-207.

Berman, H., & Jiwani, Y. (Eds.). (2002). *In the best interests of the girl child.* Ottawa, ON: Status of Women Canada.

Block, C. R., Devitt, C. O., Fonda, D., Engel, B., Fugate, M., Martin, C., et al. (2000). *The Chicago women's health risk study, risk of serious injury or death in intimate violence: A collaborative research project.* Washington, DC: U.S. Department of Justice.

Bridges, A. J., & Jensen, R. (2011). Pornography. In C. M. Renzetti, J. L. Edleson, & R. Kennedy Bergen (Eds.), *Sourcebook on violence against women* (2nd ed., pp. 133-148). Thousand Oaks, CA: Sage.

Bridges, A. J., Wosnitzer, R., Scharrer, E., Sun, C., & Liberman, R. (2010). Aggression and sexual behavior in best-selling pornography videos: A content analysis. *Violence Against Women, 16*, 1065-1085.

Brinkerhoff, M., & Lupri, E. (1988). Interspousal violence. *Canadian Journal of Sociology, 13*, 407-434.

Brownridge, D. A. (2009). *Violence against women: Vulnerable populations.* New York: Routledge.

Bumiller, K. (2008). *In an abusive state: How neoliberalism appropriated the feminist movement against sexual violence*. Durham, NC: Duke University Press.

Canadian Criminal Code. (1985). *Revised statutes of Canada* (Chapter C-46, Section 718). Ottawa, ON: Government of Canada.

Carastathis, A. (2006, October 11). New cuts and conditions for Status of Women Canada. *Toronto Star*. Retrieved from http://www.dominionpaper.ca/canadian_news/2006/10/11/new_cuts_a.html.

Caringella-MacDonald, S., & Humphries, D. (1998). Guest editors' introduction. *Violence Against Women, 4*, 3-9.

CBC. (2011, April 3). *Toronto "slut walk" takes to city streets*. Retrieved from http://www.cbc.ca/news/canada/toronto/story/2011/04/03/slut-walk-toronto.html.

Cohn, M. G. (2010, March 30). Paying a price for selling our schools. *Toronto Star*, p. A17.

Crawford, M., & Gartner, R. (1992). *Woman killing: Intimate femicide in Ontario, 1974-1990. Report prepared for the Women We Honour Action Committee and the Ontario Women's Directorate*. Toronto, ON: Ontario Women's Directorate.

Crocker, D. (2010). Counting woman abuse: A cautionary tale of two surveys. *International Journal of Social Research Methodology, 13*, 265-275.

Cross, P. (2007, July 6). Femicide: Violent partners create war zone for women. *Toronto Star*, p. AA8.

DeKeseredy, W. S. (1988). Woman abuse in dating relationships: The relevance of social support theory. *Journal of Family Violence, 3*, 1-13.

DeKeseredy, W. S. (1990). Male peer support and woman abuse: The current state of knowledge. *Sociological Focus, 23*, 129-139.

DeKeseredy, W. S. (2009). Canadian crime control in the new millennium: The influence of neo-conservative policies and practices. *Police Practice & Research, 10*, 305-316.

DeKeseredy, W. S. (2011a). *Violence against women: Myths, facts, controversies*. Toronto, ON: University of Toronto Press.

DeKeseredy, W. S. (2011b). *Contemporary critical criminology*. London, UK: Routledge.

DeKeseredy, W. S. (2012a). History of critical criminology in Canada. In W. S. DeKeseredy & M. Dragiewicz (Eds.), *Routledge handbook of critical criminology* (pp. 61-69). London, UK: Routledge.

DeKeseredy, W. S. (2012b). Ending woman abuse on Canadian university and community college campuses: The role of feminist men. In J. A. Laker (Ed.), *Canadian perspectives on men and masculinities: An interdisciplinary reader* (pp. 69-89). Toronto, ON: Oxford University Press.

DeKeseredy, W. S. (in press). Patriarchy.com: Adult internet pornography and the abuse of women. In C. M. Renzetti & R. Kennedy Bergen (Eds.), *Understanding diversity: Celebrating difference, challenging inequality*. Boston, MA: Pearson.

DeKeseredy, W. S., & Dragiewicz, M. (2007). Understanding the complexities of feminist perspectives on woman abuse: A commentary on Donald G. Dutton's rethinking domestic violence. *Violence Against Women, 13*, 874–884.

DeKeseredy, W. S., & Dragiewicz, M. (2009). *Shifting public policy direction: Gender-focused versus bidirectional intimate partner violence. Report prepared for the Ontario Women's Directorate*. Toronto, ON: Ontario Women's Directorate.

DeKeseredy, W. S., & Hinch, R. (1991). *Woman abuse: Sociological perspectives*. Toronto, ON: Thompson Educational Publishing.

DeKeseredy, W. S., & Kelly, K. (1993). The incidence and prevalence of woman abuse in Canadian university and college dating relationships. *Canadian Journal of Sociology, 18*, 157–159.

DeKeseredy, W. S., & MacLeod, L. (1997). *Woman abuse: A sociological story*. Toronto, ON: Harcourt Brace.

DeKeseredy, W. S., & Olsson, P. (2011). Adult pornography, male peer support, and violence against women: The contribution of the "dark side" of the internet. In M. Varga Martin, M. A. Garcia-Ruiz, & A. Edwards (Eds.), *Technology for facilitating humanity and combating social deviations: Interdisciplinary perspectives* (pp. 34–50). Hershey, PA: IGI Global.

DeKeseredy, W. S., & Schwartz, M. D. (1998). *Woman abuse on campus: Results from the Canadian national survey*. Thousand Oaks, CA: Sage.

DeKeseredy, W. S., & Schwartz, M. D. (2002). Theorizing public housing woman abuse as a function of economic exclusion and male peer support. *Women's Health and Urban Life, 1*, 26–45.

DeKeseredy, W. S., & Schwartz, M. D. (2003). Backlash and whiplash: A critique of Statistics Canada's 1999 general social survey on victimization. *Sisyphe.org*. Retrieved from http://sisyphe.org/article.php3?id_article=1689.

DeKeseredy, W. S., & Schwartz, M. D. (2009). *Dangerous exits: Escaping abusive relationships in rural America*. New Brunswick, NJ: Rutgers University Press.

DeKeseredy, W. S., & Schwartz, M. D. (2010). Friedman economic policies, social exclusion, and crime: Toward a gendered left realist subcultural theory. *Crime, Law and Social Change, 54*, 159–170.

DeKeseredy, W. S., Schwartz, M. D., & Alvi, S. (2000). The role of profeminist men in dealing with woman abuse on the Canadian college campus. *Violence Against Women, 6*, 918–935.

Denham, D., & Gillespie, J. (1999). *Two steps forward ... one step back: An overview of Canadian initiatives and resources to end woman abuse 1989–1997*. Ottawa, ON: Family Violence Prevention Unit, Health Canada.

Dines, G. (2010). *Pornland: How porn has hijacked our sexuality*. Boston, MA: Beacon Press.

Dobash, R. P., & Dobash, R. E. (1995). Reflections on findings from the Violence Against Women Survey. *Canadian Journal of Criminology, 37*, 457–484.

Doyle, A., & Moore, D. (2011). Introduction: Questions for a new generation of criminologists. In A. Doyle & D. Moore (Eds.), *Critical criminology in Canada: New voices, new directions* (pp. 1–24). Vancouver, BC: University of British Columbia Press.

Dragiewicz, M. (2008). Patriarchy reasserted: Fathers' rights and anti-VAWA activism. *Feminist Criminology, 3*, 121–144.

Dragiewicz, M. (2009). Why sex and gender matter in domestic violence research and advocacy. In E. Stark & E. S. Buzawa (Eds.), *Violence against women in families and relationships: Criminal justice and law* (Vol. 3, pp. 201–215). Santa Barbara, CA: Praeger.

Dragiewicz, M. (2011). *Equality with a vengeance: Men's rights groups, battered women, and antifeminist backlash*. Boston, MA: Northeastern University Press.

Dragiewicz, M., & DeKeseredy, W. S. (2008). *A needs gap assessment report on abused women without legal representation in the family courts*. Oshawa, ON: Report prepared for Luke's Place Support and Resource Centre.

Dragiewicz, M., & DeKeseredy, W. S. (2012). Claims about women's use of non-fatal force in intimate relationships: A contextual review of the Canadian research. *Violence Against Women, 18*, 1008–1026.

Dupont, B. (2011). The dilemmas of "doing" criminology in Quebec: Curse or opportunity? In A. Doyle & D. Moore (Eds.), *Critical criminology in Canada: New voices, new directions* (pp. 31–54). Vancouver, BC: University of British Columbia Press.

Dutton, D. G. (2010). The gender paradigm and the architecture of antiscience. *Partner Abuse, 1*, 5–25.

Ellis, D. (1987). *The wrong stuff: An introduction to the sociological study of deviance*. Toronto, ON: Collier Macmillan.

Ellis, D. (1990). Marital conflict mediation and post-separation abuse. *Law and Inequality, 8*, 317–339.

Ellis, D., & DeKeseredy, W. S. (1989). Marital status and woman abuse: The DAD model. *International Journal of Sociology of the Family, 19*, 67–87.

Ellis, D., & DeKeseredy, W. S. (1997). Rethinking estrangement, interventions and intimate femicide. *Violence Against Women, 3*, 590–609.

Ellis, D., & Stuckless, N. (1993). *Marital separation, violence towards women and other outcomes: The Impact of mediation and lawyer negotiations*. North York, ON: LaMarsh Research Centre on Violence and Conflict Resolution.

Ellis, D., & Stuckless, N. (1996). *Mediating and negotiating marital conflicts*. Thousand Oaks, CA: Sage.

Ellis, D., & Wight, L. (1987). Post-separation woman abuse: The contribution of lawyers. *Victimology, 13*, 420-429.

Fong, J. (Ed.). (2010). *Out of the shadows: Woman abuse in ethnic, immigrant, and aboriginal communities*. Toronto, ON: Women's Press.

Funk, R. E. (2006). *Reaching men: Strategies for preventing sexist attitudes, behaviors, and violence*. Indianapolis, IN: Jist Life.

Gelles, R. J. (1980). Violence in the family: A review of research in the seventies. *Journal of Marriage and Family, 42*, 873-885.

Gilfus, M. E., Fineran, S., Cohan, D. J., Jensen, S. A., Hartwick, L., & Spath, R. (1999). Research on violence against women: Creating survivor-informed collaborations. *Violence Against Women, 10*, 1194-1212.

Goel, R. (2000). No women at the center: The use of the Canadian sentencing circles in domestic violence cases. *Wisconsin Women's Law Journal, 15*, 293-334.

Goodmark, L. (2012). *A troubled marriage: Domestic violence and the legal system*. New York: New York University Press.

Grabb, E. (2004). Economic power in Canada: Corporate concentration, foreign ownership, and state involvement. In J. Curtis, E. Grabb, & N. Guppy (Eds.), *Social inequality in Canada* (pp. 20-30). Toronto, ON: Pearson Prentice Hall.

Hearn, J. R. (1998). *The violences of men: How men talk about and how agencies respond to men's violence to women*. London, UK: Sage.

Jacquier, V., Johnson, H., & Fisher, B. S. (2011). Research methods, measures, and ethics. In C. M. Renzetti, J. L. Edleson, & R. Kennedy Bergen (Eds.), *Sourcebook on violence against women* (2nd ed., pp. 23-45). Thousand Oaks, CA: Sage.

Jiwani, J. (2006). *Discourses of denial: Mediations of race, gender, and violence*. Vancouver, BC: University of British Columbia Press.

Johnson, H. (1996). *Dangerous domains: Violence against women in Canada*. Scarborough, ON: Nelson Canada.

Johnson, H., & Dawson, M. (2011). *Violence against women in Canada: Research and policy perspectives*. Toronto, ON: Oxford University Press.

Johnson, H., Ollus, N., & Nevala, S. (2008). *Violence against women: An international perspective*. New York: Springer.

Kennedy, L., & Dutton, D. G. (1989). The incidence of wife assault in Alberta. *Canadian Journal of Behavioural Science, 21*, 40-54.

Kettani, A. (2009, June-July). Out from the shadows: Women's studies programs have changed how we view violence against women. *University Affairs*, p. 19.

Koss, M. P. (2010). Restorative justice for acquaintance rape and misdemeanor sex crimes. In J. Ptacek (Ed.), *Restorative justice and violence against women* (pp. 218-238). New York: Oxford University Press.

Koss, M. P., Gidycz, C. A., & Wisniewski, N. (1987). The scope of rape: Incidence and prevalence of sexual aggression and victimization in a national sample of higher education students. *Journal of Consulting and Clinical Psychology, 55*, 162-170.

Lewin, K. (1951). *Field theory in social science: Selected theoretical papers*. New York: Harper & Row.

Luxton, M. (1993). Dreams and dilemmas: Feminist musing on the men question. In T. Haddad (Ed.), *Men and masculinities* (pp. 347-374). Toronto, ON: Canadian Scholars' Press.

MacLeod, L., & Cadieux, A. (1980). *Wife battering in Canada: The vicious circle*. Ottawa, ON: Ministry of Supply and Services Canada.

Meloy, M. L., & Miller, S. L. (2011). *The victimization of women: Law, policies, and politics*. New York: Oxford University Press.

Miller, S. L. (2011). *After the crime: The power of restorative justice dialogues between victims and violent offenders*. New York: New York University Press.

Mills, C. W. (1959). *The sociological imagination*. New York: Oxford University Press.

Pajot, M. (2009). *Rethinking relationships: Engaging youth & connecting communities*. Toronto, ON: Ontario Women's Directorate.

Partner Abuse. (n.d.). Retrieved from http://www.springerpub.com/product/19466560.

Ptacek, J. (2010a). Editor's introduction. In J. Ptacek (Ed.), *Restorative justice and violence against women* (pp. ix-xviii). New York: Oxford University Press.

Ptacek, J. (2010b). Re-imagining justice for crimes of violence against women. In J. Ptacek (Ed.), *Restorative justice and violence against women* (pp. 281-286). New York: Oxford University Press.

Randall, M., & Haskell, L. (1995). Sexual violence in women's lives: Findings from the women's safety project, a community-based survey. *Violence Against Women, 1*, 6-31.

Rennison, C. M., DeKeseredy, W. S., & Dragiewicz, M. (2013). Intimate relationship status variations in violence against women: Urban, suburban, and rural differences. *Violence Against Women*. Advance online publication. doi:10.1177/1077801213514487.

Romito, P. (2008). *A deafening silence: Hidden violence against women and children*. Bristol, UK: Polity Press.

Rubin, P. (2000). *Abused women in family mediation: A Nova Scotia snapshot.* Halifax, NS: Transition House Association of Nova Scotia.

Salem, R. (2011, August 1). The sway of the '60s playboy. *Toronto Star,* p. E1.

Say No—Unite to End Violence Against Women. (n.d.). *About say no.* Retrieved from http://saynotoviolence.org/about-say-no.

Schwartz, M. D., & DeKeseredy, W. S. (1997). *Sexual assault on the college campus: The role of male peer support.* Thousand Oaks, CA: Sage.

Sev'er, A. (1997). Recent or imminent separation and intimate violence against women: A conceptual overview and some Canadian examples. *Violence Against Women, 3,* 566-589.

Smith, M. D. (1987). The incidence and prevalence of woman abuse in Toronto. *Violence and Victims, 2,* 173-187.

Smith, M. D. (1990). Patriarchal ideology and wife beating: A test of a feminist hypothesis. *Violence and Victims, 5,* 257-273.

Stanko, E. A. (1997). I second that emotion: Reflections on feminism, emotionality, and research on sexual violence. In M. D. Schwartz (Ed.), *Researching sexual violence against women: Methodological and personal perspectives* (pp. 74-85). Thousand Oaks, CA: Sage.

Statistics Canada. (2002, June 26). Family violence: Impacts and consequences of spousal violence. *The Daily.* Retrieved from http://www.statcan.gc.ca/daily-quotidien/020626/tdq020626-eng.htm.

Statistics Canada. (2005, July 14). Family violence in Canada: A statistical profile. *The Daily.* Retrieved from http://www.statcan.gc.ca/daily-quotidien/050714/dq050714a-eng.htm.

Statistics Canada. (2010, March 9). Study: Projections of the diversity of the Canadian population 2006-2031. *The Daily.* Retrieved from http://www.statcan.gc.ca/daily-quotidien/100309/dq100309a-eng.htm.

Statistics Canada. (2011). *Family violence in Canada: A statistical profile.* Ottawa, ON: Retrieved from http://www.statcan.gc.ca/pub/85-224-x/85-224-x2010000-eng.pdf.

Stearns, P. N. (2011). *Why study history?* Retrieved from http://www.historians.org/pubs/free/WhyStudyHistory.htm.

Walby, S., & Myhill, A. (2001). New survey methodologies in researching violence against women. *British Journal of Criminology, 41,* 502-522.

Walker Rettberg, J. (2009). Joining a Facebook group as political action. *jill/txt.* Retrieved from http://jilltxt.net/?p=2367.

Wilson, M., Johnson, H., & Daly, M. (1995). Lethal and non-lethal violence against wives. *Canadian Journal of Criminology, 37,* 331-362.

Wolfe, D., & Jaffe, P. (2001). Prevention of domestic violence: Emerging initiatives. In S. Graham-Bermann & J. Edleson (Eds.), *Domestic violence in the lives of children* (pp. 283-298). Washington, DC: American Psychological Association.

Yantzi, M. (1998). *Sexual offending and restoration*. Waterloo, ON: Herald Press.

RETHINKING SECTION 2

Discussion Questions

Chapter 12

1. Describe the difference between the techniques of neutralization and normalization.
2. Lewis puts forth two different types of socialization for exotic dancers: (1) anticipatory and (2) on the job. Provide examples for each. How do these processes (either individually or collaboratively) create "competent" dancers?
3. What does Lewis mean when she refers to "informal" socialization experiences? What are some examples of "formal" socialization processes? Why might these not be effective in exotic dancing?

Chapter 13

1. What is the difference between an expression a person "gives" and an expression a person "gives off"? What does this mean for his or her presentation of self?
2. How do projected definitions of self-presentation exhibit a distinctive moral character?
3. Reflect on your own personal presentation of self. What objectives have you had in mind and with what motives? Have you attempted to control the conduct of others through a defining of the situation?

Chapter 14

1. Traditionally, the sociology of policing has focused strictly on official agents of the state. Why do Walby and Monaghan argue that this must be expanded to consider the role of private agencies?
2. What shifts in policing tactics occur when activist activities are framed under the umbrella of domestic terrorism?
3. How does "grey information" play a role in blurring the lines between public policing and social movement repression by private agencies?

Chapter 15

1. What evidence do the authors present to support an anti-feminist backlash in public policy and funding for the study of woman abuse?
2. What is the impact of using degendered language when discussing woman abuse?
3. What are some of the challenges related to addressing woman abuse through the criminal justice system?

SECTION 3
MAJOR SOCIAL INSTITUTIONS

The Readings

SECTION 3A: FAMILIES

16. The Way We Weren't: The Myth and Reality of the "Traditional" Family, *Stephanie Coontz*

17. Neo-liberalism, Families, and Work-Life Balance, *Kate Bezanson*

18. Beyond Normalization: An Analysis of Heteronormativity in Children's Picture Books, *Anika Stafford*

SECTION 3B: THE ECONOMY AND LABOUR

19. Just Another Neo-liberal Worker: Tracing the State's Treatment of Low-Income Mothers, *Margaret Hillyard Little*

20. Does Citizenship Status Matter in Canadian Agriculture? Workplace Health and Safety for Migrant and Immigrant Laborers, *Kerry Preibisch and Gerardo Otero*

SECTION 3C: EDUCATION

21. Playing It Down/Playing It Up: Girls' Strategic Negotiations of Academic Success, *Rebecca Raby and Shauna Pomerantz*

22. Keeping the Ivory Tower White: Discourses of Racial Domination, *Carol Schick*

SECTION 3D: AGE, HEALTH, AND HEALTH CARE

23. "Old People Are Useless": Representations of Aging on *The Simpsons*, *Darren Blakeborough*

24. Gender, Race, and Health Inequalities, *Ann Pederson, Dennis Raphael, and Ellisa Johnson*

In Canadian society, there are many building blocks to social life. In this section, we consider the central institutions of families, the economy, education, health, and media. For each topic, we challenge the idea that there is something "natural" or functional about these social entities.

Families

"Family" is often considered to be the key site of our collective social life. It is within this social institution that children are usually first socialized, and within this social grouping that many of our norms and values are learned. But families—however they are defined and whatever their makeup—do not exist in isolation from other social institutions. Political forces and practices, trends in the macro-economy, and conditions of paid and unpaid work also affect and shape individuals. The social institutions in Canadian society exert profound positive and negative influences over our daily lives and, depending on one's social location, can be agents that liberate or oppress. One of the central tasks of sociological inquiry is to move beneath the surface of social relations to reveal the structure and consequences of "commonsense" ideas about society. "Family" is a subject that provokes heated debate as it is at once deeply personal and politically charged. The readings about family in this section challenge the idea of the male breadwinner model and suggest that families must be seen as both places of nurturing and care as well as places of subordination and inequality. They underline that there is no one family form, but rather that families come in many configurations and none should be prioritized over another.

Stephanie Coontz contrasts the ideal that many North Americans have about family life (often a happy, White, middle-class nuclear family with Dad working for pay and Mum at home with the kids) with historical evidence of the functions of marriage for society and gender divisions of labour within families. She asserts that the "revival" of a romanticized ideal of the "traditional" family form is narrow and serves few people. Coontz shows that while women are more autonomous and have greater equality today, families are not sites of equal sharing of work and responsibilities. She argues that the challenge is to build social institutions and values that meet the needs and realities of contemporary families.

The chapter by Kate Bezanson considers what happened to the Canadian economy in the fall of 2008 when the "great recession" began in Canada. She explains that a key cause of the recession was its foundations in neo-liberal political and economic thought. She then asks how families were faring before the crisis. She finds that their work and their home lives were in significant tension pre-crisis and that the effects of cuts in social spending because of budget deficits will have devastating effects on people. She provides a case study of one family in the Niagara region, and considers how their work lives and social supports intersect.

Anika Stafford considers the representation of queer families in children's storybooks. She examines a select grouping of books as they attempt to address and challenge homophobia and heterosexism. She considers these books within a broader cultural and political context that is often hostile to diversity in family forms. She concludes that the books sometimes promote the idea that queer families are just the same as other families, and that their messages are more about fitting into the mainstream than celebrating variety and differences in family forms.

The Economy and Labour

The chapters in this section consider how people are managing when work is insecure and when the social policy and economic environment often intensifies this insecurity. The first chapter by Margaret Little considers the contradictory ways in which the state (federal and provincial/territorial) in Canada understands poor women's unpaid caregiving work and their paid work. Little provides an important historical overview of policy developments related to motherhood and work. She finds that states adopting neo-liberal policies and practices now push women into an often low-paid and precarious workforce, but simultaneously blame women for not sufficiently attending to caregiving work.

The second chapter by Kerry Preibisch and Gerardo Otero considers workplace health and safety for migrant and immigrant labourers in Canada's agricultural sector. Through interviews with both temporary migrant guest workers as well as with immigrant workers (citizens or permanent residents), they find that both groups work in insecure and precarious circumstances, with significant effects on their health and safety. They argue, however, that citizenship status *does* make a difference in the extent of risks and the availability of social protections. They conclude that temporary migrant guest workers are among the most vulnerable workers in Canada and that significant changes are required of Canada's immigration system and labour laws.

These chapters give a sense of the significant, damaging, and far-reaching effects of changes in Canada's political, economic, and social policy environment. They also underline the complexities of labour market regulations, jurisdictional boundaries, and disputes in labour and social welfare laws, and the pervasive risks to those in vulnerable positions in the current labour market.

Education

Our first chapter takes education as the site for the identity work of "smart girls." Rebecca Raby and Shauna Pomerantz present wonderfully rich qualitative research on the active identity negotiation work of smart girls. Raby and Pomerantz draw from interviews with 51 smart girls in Canadian high schools. The researchers challenge assumptions that smart girls somehow sail through school without complications and complexities.

Schick's chapter moves us into the arena of higher education and considers the university as a site of racial privilege. Based on interviews with White students attending a cross-cultural course, she explores the processes through which students affirm their sense of entitled, racially based occupancy of university space.

Age, Health, and Health Care

In this section, questions of age and health care are explored. In the first chapter, Darren Blakeborough uses representations of aging in the cartoon *The Simpsons* to underline dominant views of the elderly in society, but also to challenge those same stereotypes. Drawing on scholarly approaches, he analyzes the use of parody and satire in *The Simpsons* to subvert the meanings of aging in North American culture.

The second chapter by Ann Pederson, Dennis Raphael, and Ellisa Johnson attends to health and health care in Canada. They consider the complexity of understanding the social determinants of health. While being sick and getting care might appear to be an equal opportunity experience, they make plain that social and economic vulnerability predispose particular populations, especially Aboriginal peoples and women, to significant risk.

Finally, Nick Mulé and Miriam Smith consider health policy in Canada, examining the understudied area of LGBTQ people in relation to federal health policy. This chapter builds on the insights provided by Pederson, Raphael, and Johnson (Chapter 24), providing a case study of the ways in which policy formulation systematically ignores LGBTQ issues, failing to place them accurately within an intersectional analysis of health. The diverse health needs of LGBTQ Canadians must be incorporated into a social determinants of health framework, but much work remains to be done.

Media

In our last section for our consideration of major social institutions, we have two qualitative chapters that explore the social power of media. First, Boyd explores how White, male heterosexuality gets inscribed and performed in the popular show *So You Think You Can Dance Canada*. The researchers argue that while other versions of masculinity are on offer on the show, it is a White, heterosexual masculinity that is normalized.

Second, Marwick and boyd present an interview-based exploration of teenager perspectives on the term "drama," which they define as "performative, interpersonal conflict that takes place in front of an active, engaged audience, often on social media." Through their analysis, they also examine the messiness of drama, how it plays out in the lives of teens, and how much of it takes place on social media.

SECTION 3A

FAMILIES

CHAPTER 16

The Way We Weren't: The Myth and Reality of the "Traditional" Family

Stephanie Coontz

Families face serious problems today, but proposals to solve them by reviving "traditional" family forms and values miss two points. First, no single traditional family existed to which we could return, and none of the many varieties of families in our past has had any magic formula for protecting its members from the vicissitudes of socio-economic change, the inequities of class, race, and gender, or the consequences of interpersonal conflict. Violence, child abuse, poverty, and the unequal distribution of resources to women and children have occurred in every period and every type of family.

Second, the strengths that we also find in many families of the past were rooted in different social, cultural, and economic circumstances from those that prevail today. Attempts to reproduce any type of family outside of its original socio-economic context are doomed to fail.

Colonial Families

American families always have been diverse, and the male breadwinner–female homemaker, nuclear ideal that most people associate with "the" traditional family has predominated for only a small portion of our history. In colonial America, several types of families coexisted or competed. Native American kinship systems subordinated the nuclear family to a much larger network of marital alliances and kin obligations, ensuring that no single family was forced to go it alone. Wealthy settler families from Europe, by contrast, formed independent households that pulled in labor from poorer neighbors and relatives, building their extended family solidarities on the backs of truncated families among indentured servants, slaves, and the poor. Even wealthy families, though, often were disrupted by death; a majority of colonial Americans probably spent some time in a stepfamily. Meanwhile, African Americans, denied the legal protection of marriage and parenthood, built extensive kinship networks and obligations through fictive kin ties, ritual co-parenting or godparenting, adoption of orphans, and complex naming patterns designed to preserve family links across space and time.

The dominant family values of colonial days left no room for sentimentalizing childhood. Colonial mothers, for example, spent far less time doing child care than do modern working women, typically delegating this task to servants or older siblings. Among white families, patriarchal authority was so absolute that disobedience by a wife or child was seen as a small form of treason, theoretically punishable by death, and family relations were based on power, not love.

The Nineteenth-Century Family

With the emergence of a wage-labor system and a *national* market in the first third of the nineteenth century, white middle-class families became less patriarchal and more child-centered. The ideal of the male breadwinner and the nurturing mother now appeared. But the emergence of domesticity for middle-class women and children depended on its absence among the immigrant, working class, and African American women or children who worked as servants, grew the cotton, or toiled in the textile mills to free middle-class wives from the chores that had occupied their time previously.

Even in the minority of nineteenth-century families who could afford domesticity, though, emotional arrangements were quite different from nostalgic images of "traditional" families. Rigid insistence on separate spheres for men and women made male-female relations extremely stilted, so that women commonly turned to other women, not their husbands, for their most intimate relations. The idea that all of one's passionate feelings should go toward a member of the opposite sex was a twentieth-century invention—closely associated with the emergence of a mass consumer society and promulgated by the very film industry that "traditionalists" now blame for undermining such values.

Early Twentieth-Century Families

Throughout the nineteenth century, at least as much divergence and disruption in the experience of family life existed as does today, even though divorce and unwed motherhood were less common. Indeed, couples who marry today have a better chance of celebrating a fortieth wedding anniversary than at any previous time in history. The life cycles of nineteenth-century youth (in job entry, completion of schooling, age at marriage, and establishment of separate residence) were far more diverse than they became in the early twentieth century. At the turn of the century a higher proportion of people remained single for their entire lives than at any period since. Not until the 1920s did a bare majority of children come to live in a male breadwinner–female homemaker family, and even at the height of this family form in the 1950s, only 60 percent of American children spent their entire childhoods in such a family.

From about 1900 to the 1920s, the growth of mass production and emergence of a public policy aimed at establishing a family wage led to new ideas about family self-sufficiency, especially in the white middle class and a privileged sector of the working class. The resulting families lost their organic connection to intermediary units in society such as local shops, neighborhood work cultures and churches, ethnic associations, and mutual-aid organizations.

As families related more directly to the state, the market, and the mass media, they also developed a new cult of privacy, along with heightened expectations about the family's role in fostering individual fulfillment. New family values stressed the early independence of children and the romantic coupling of husband and wife, repudiating the intense same-sex ties and mother-infant bonding of earlier years as unhealthy. From this family we get the idea that women are sexual, that youth is attractive, and that marriage should be the center of our emotional fulfillment.

Even aside from its lack of relevance to the lives of most immigrants, Mexican Americans, African Americans, rural families, and the urban poor, big contradictions existed between image and reality in the middle-class family ideal of the early twentieth century. This is the period when many Americans first accepted the idea that the family should be sacred from outside intervention; yet the development of the private, self-sufficient family depended on state intervention in the economy, government regulation of parent-child relations, and state-directed destruction of class and community institutions that hindered the development of family privacy. Acceptance of a youth and leisure culture sanctioned early marriage and raised expectations about the quality of married life, but also introduced new tensions between the generations and new conflicts between husband and wife over what were adequate levels of financial and emotional support.

The nineteenth-century middle-class ideal of the family as a refuge from the world of work was surprisingly modest compared with emerging twentieth-century demands that the family provide a whole alternative world of satisfaction and intimacy to that of work and neighborhood. Where a family succeeded in doing so, people might find pleasures in the home never before imagined. But the new ideals also increased the possibilities for failure: America has had the highest divorce rate in the world since the turn of the century.

In the 1920s, these contradictions created a sense of foreboding about "the future of the family" that was every bit as widespread and intense as today's. Social scientists and popular commentators of the time hearkened back to the "good old days," bemoaning the sexual revolution, the fragility of nuclear family ties, the cult of youthful romance, the decline of respect for grandparents, and the threat of the "New Woman." But such criticism was sidetracked by the stock-market crash, the Great Depression of the 1930s, and the advent of World War II.

Domestic violence escalated during the Depression, while murder rates were as high in the 1930s as in the 1980s. Divorce rates fell, but desertion increased and fertility plummeted. The war stimulated a marriage boom, but by the late 1940s one in every three marriages was ending in divorce.

The 1950s Family

At the end of the 1940s, after the hardships of the Depression and war, many Americans revived the nuclear family ideals that had so disturbed commentators during the 1920s. The unprecedented postwar prosperity allowed young families to achieve consumer satisfactions and socio-economic mobility that would have been inconceivable in earlier days. The 1950s family that resulted from these economic and cultural trends, however, was hardly "traditional." Indeed, it is best seen as a historical aberration. For the first time in 100 years, divorce rates dropped, fertility soared, the gap between men's and women's job and educational prospects widened (making middle-class women more dependent on marriage), and the age of marriage fell—to the point that teenage birth rates were almost double what they are today.

Admirers of these very nontraditional 1950s family forms and values point out that household arrangements and gender roles were less diverse in the 1950s than today, and marriages more stable. But this was partly because diversity was ruthlessly suppressed and partly because economic and political support systems for socially sanctioned families were far more generous than they are today. Real wages rose more in any single year of the 1950s than they did in the entire decade of the 1980s; the average thirty-year-old man could buy a median-priced home on 15 to 18 percent of his income. The government-funded public investment, home ownership, and job creation at a rate more than triple that of the past two decades, while 40 percent of young men were eligible for veteran's benefits. Forming and maintaining families was far easier than it is today.

Yet the stability of these 1950s families did not guarantee good outcomes for their members. Even though most births occurred within wedlock, almost a third of American children lived in poverty during the 1950s, a higher figure than today. More than 50 percent of black married-couple families were poor. Women were often refused the right to serve on juries, sign contracts, take out credit cards in their own names, or establish legal residence. Wife-battering rates were low, but that was because wife-beating was seldom counted as a crime. Most victims of incest, such as Miss America of 1958, kept the secret of their fathers' abuse until the 1970s or 1980s, when the women's movement became powerful enough to offer them the support denied them in the 1950s.

The Post-1950s Family

In the 1960s, the civil rights, antiwar, and women's liberation movements exposed the racial, economic, and sexual injustices that had been papered over by the Ozzie and Harriet images on television. Their activism made older kinds of public and private oppression unacceptable and helped create the incomplete, flawed, but much-needed reforms of the Great Society. Contrary to the big lie of the past decade that such programs caused our current family dilemmas, those antipoverty and social justice reforms helped overcome many of the family problems that prevailed in the 1950s.

In 1964, after fourteen years of unrivaled family stability and economic prosperity, the poverty rate was still 19 percent; in 1969, after five years of civil rights activism, the rebirth of feminism, and the institution of nontraditional if relatively modest government welfare programs, it was down to 12 percent, a low that has not been seen again since the social welfare cutbacks began in the late 1970s. In 1965, 20 percent of American children still lived in poverty; within five years, that had fallen to 15 percent. Infant mortality was cut in half between 1965 and 1980. The gap in nutrition between low-income Americans and other Americans narrowed significantly, as a direct result of food stamp and school lunch programs. In 1963, 20 percent of Americans living below the poverty line had never been examined by a physician; by 1970 this was true of only 8 percent of the poor.

Since 1973, however, real wages have been falling for most Americans. Attempts to counter this through tax revolts and spending freezes have led to drastic cutbacks in government investment programs. Corporations also spend far less on research and job creation than they did in the 1950s and 1960s, though the average compensation to executives has soared. The gap between rich and poor, according to the April 17, 1995, *New York Times*, is higher in the United States than in any other industrial nation.

Family Stress

These inequities are not driven by changes in family forms, contrary to ideologues who persist in confusing correlations with causes; but they certainly exacerbate such changes, and they tend to bring out the worst in all families. The result has been an accumulation of stresses on families, alongside some important expansions of personal options. Working couples with children try to balance three full-time jobs, as employers and schools cling to policies that assume every employee has a "wife" at home to take care of family matters. Divorce and remarriage have allowed many adults and children to escape from toxic family environments, yet our lack of social support networks and failure to forge new values for sustaining intergenerational obligations have let many children fall through the cracks in the process.

Meanwhile, young people find it harder and harder to form or sustain families. According to an Associated Press report of April 25, 1995, the median income of men aged twenty-five to thirty-four fell by 26 percent between 1972 and 1994, while the proportion of such men with earnings below the poverty level for a family of four more than doubled to 32 percent. The figures are even worse for African American and Latino men. Poor individuals are twice as likely to divorce as more affluent ones, three to four times less likely to marry in the first place, and five to seven times more likely to have a child out of wedlock.

As conservatives insist, there is a moral crisis as well as an economic one in modern America: a pervasive sense of social alienation, new levels of violence, and a decreasing willingness to make sacrifices for others. But romanticizing "traditional" families and gender roles will not produce the changes in job structures, work policies, child care, medical practice, educational preparation, political discourse, and gender inequities that would permit families to develop moral and ethical systems relevant to 1990s realities.

America needs more than a revival of the narrow family obligations of the 1950s, whose (greatly exaggerated) protection for white, middle-class children was achieved only at tremendous cost to the women in those families and to all those who could not or would not aspire to the Ozzie and Harriet ideal. We need a concern for children that goes beyond the question of whether a mother is waiting with cookies when her kids come home from school. We need a moral language that allows us to address something besides people's sexual habits. We need to build values and social institutions that can reconcile people's needs for independence with their equally important rights to dependence, and surely we must reject older solutions that involved balancing these needs on the backs of women. We will not find our answers in nostalgia for a mythical "traditional family."

CHAPTER 17

Neo-liberalism, Families, and Work-Life Balance[1]

Kate Bezanson

Introduction: A Wile E. Coyote Fall

In the late summer of 2008, classes were resuming and a federal election was in full swing. Canada seemed poised to continue its decade-long pattern of economic growth, high employment, and a general mood of prosperity. The crisp autumn air would bring more than a change in seasonal climate: the overheated Canadian economy was about to feel a chill like none experienced since the Great Depression of the 1930s. As the realities of the global economic crisis began to sink in, the scaffolding that had held together the expansion of the 1990s and 2000s was exposed and was found to be weak and built on unstable ground. This scaffolding was a neo-liberal market logic. Like Wile E. Coyote suspended in mid air with his legs still running before realizing his predicament and dropping like a stone, the contradictions and problems with neo-liberalism reached an inevitable crash in the fall of 2008. The consequences are deep and far-reaching. This chapter asks some fundamental questions about the economic crisis and its implications for work and families in Canada. It argues that the protections that might have shielded families and workers from the worst effects of this crisis were dismantled in the "Road Runner" capitalism years leading up to the fall of 2008.

The chapter proceeds in five stages. First, it explores what has happened in Canada since the crash of 2008. Second, it explains neo-liberalism, and how the logic of this kind of economic model left workers and families on shaky ground. Third, it considers social supports in the Canadian welfare state and argues that *before* the crisis of 2008, there were few supports to balance work and family and to offset income insecurity or shortfalls. Fourth, it profiles one family's story from a longitudinal case study of 49 families in Ontario who are balancing significant work and caregiving responsibilities. Lastly, the chapter concludes with a discussion of the future of work and family. It suggests that far from learning from the errors of neo-liberal market rule, we have entered into a new era of "strategic" neo-liberalism, intensifying the existing problems families face.

The Stormy Present: What Happened in the Fall of 2008?

In late September 2008, two headlines stood side by side and could not have been more at odds with one another. On the cover of the *Globe and Mail* (Scoffield, 2008, p. A1) was a photo of an oil rig in full production, with the caption: "Canadian Economy Booms in July." Directly underneath was the headline "Bush Urges Congress to Support Bailout" (Feller, 2008), with text describing the collapse of major financial institutions such as banks and insurance companies. In the United States and Europe, panicked discussions about economic bailouts by governments were underway. The doldrums between the sunny past and the stormy present were short-lived. For several months Canadians felt somewhat insulated from the effects of the meltdown in financial markets, mostly due to the more stringent regulatory environment in Canadian banks. Prime Minister Harper showed little concern in the early days of the economic meltdown when he stated during an election interview with the Canadian Broadcasting Corporation's flagship news program *The National* that "there are probably some great [stock] buying opportunities out there" (CBC Television, 2008). But by January 2009, layoffs were almost daily announcements and Ontario was particularly hard-hit as the meltdown in the U.S. auto sector travelled north. There were 387,000 full-time jobs lost in the seven months after the initial crash (Yalnizyan, 2009, p. 4). By the new year of 2009, there was no doubt that the effects of the economic recession were going to be devastating for Canada. This was underlined by the Harper Conservatives almost losing their minority government over their handling of the economic situation. In spite of the mounting evidence of Canada's economic vulnerability, in their fall 2008 economic update, there was no response to the global crisis to stem the tide of job loss and support industry, as other countries were doing. Almost overnight in the fall of 2008, banks in the United Kingdom and the United States were virtually nationalized and stimulus packages planned—by governments who days before would have laughed at the idea of deficit spending. In Canada, the opposition parties were so alarmed by the total lack of response on the part of the minority Conservatives that just weeks after an election, the government looked poised to fall over the issue of the handling of the economy. The opposition parties formed a coalition and called on the Governor General to recognize such a coalition in place of the Harper Conservatives. Rather than face the opposition, within weeks of the House of Commons resuming post-election, Prime Minister Harper asked the Governor General to suspend parliament. When the House returned in January 2009, Prime Minister Harper introduced a new budget, heavy on spending and more in line with the kind of responses governments of wealthy nations took around the world to attempt to remedy the crisis.

At the heart of this crisis was an under-regulated credit market that treated debt as assets. This played out most dramatically in the subprime mortgage market where the artificially inflated prices of homes allowed owners to access large amounts of credit (for a useful, easy to read review of the crisis, see http://www.economicshelp.org). It is hard for most of us to understand how bad mortgages in the U.S. could lead to a global economic meltdown. The organization of these mortgages and the more general level of credit offered by mortgage companies can be thought of as an elaborate house of cards. Once one or two cards at the bottom of the house became dislodged, it was not long before the building itself began to tumble. The house was built over a long period of time, but the biggest building boom happened in the early 2000s, after September 11, 2001 and the crash of Internet stocks. The U.S. economy, among others, faced the prospect of a recession (Canada also faced confirmed mad-cow cases beginning in 2003 along with Severe Acute Respiratory Syndrome in the same year), so interest rates were dropped dramatically. When interest rates drop, it is much cheaper to borrow money and to buy or refinance houses. More people bought houses and housing prices started to go up. Banks eased their lending policies. People with poor credit histories were able to get mortgages much more easily. People were able to leverage their homes to either purchase property or other goods, so they had huge debts. People were also given mortgages with great rates for the first one or two years. Counting on the continued appreciation of value in homes, financial institutions continued to buy up unsecured debt. When interest rates rose in 2006, many people were not able to meet their payments. New home construction continued while house prices started to drop and so the value of houses fell, although they were still mortgaged for more money than they were now worth and banks could not recoup the loans by selling the houses (*Guardian Weekly*, 2008; *New York Times*, 2009).

If we move up from the houses that are at the bottom of the proverbial house of cards, we find that reckless mortgage companies were backed by banks and other financial institutions. Big financial institutions like Bear Sterns, Morgan Stanley, AIG (an insurance company), and Lehman Brothers owned a lot of the bad debt. The U.S. Federal Reserve bailed out AIG in September 2008 to the tune of $85 billion but stock prices fell dramatically nonetheless (*New York Times*, 2009, p. 2). Banks could no longer lend money to one another as they normally did, and they began to sell off assets, making the problem worse. Confidence in the economy plummeted. Governments tried to buy up bad assets to get the financial system moving again. The U.S. government proposed a $700-billion plan to buy "toxic assets" from the affected banks (*New York Times*, 2009, p. 2). The toxicity spread across the globe, trade dropped, and the credit crisis decimated economies, notably those of Iceland and various Eastern European countries. According to an International Monetary Fund Estimate in April 2009, "writedowns of bad financial assets could reach $4 trillion worldwide, with two thirds of this incurred by banks" (IMF, 2009, p. xi). To illustrate what this number represents, consider that Canada's GDP for 2007 was just over $1.3 trillion (World Bank, 2009). In April 2009, at a meeting of the Group of 20 (G20) in London, leaders pledged $1.1 trillion to tackle the global financial crisis.[2] The public, contra the logic of the market rationally spreading risk and reward, is the backer of last resort for irresponsible financial practices and policies, the rebuilder of the house of cards.

There is much debate about what to do, what this means for workers, for families, and for entire sectors of the Canadian economy. What is clear [is] that the causes—which were not new nor were they unforeseeable—lay not only in the lack of regulation of financial capital but also in the widespread and widely accepted idea that markets would sort themselves out and that intervention meant interference. At the heart of the crisis is the question of neo-liberalism.

What Is Neo-liberalism?

As with understanding the house of cards built on risky credit, it is hard for most of us to understand how an economic and political *theory* can be the chief cause of massive job losses and the collapse of major banks and companies worldwide. Theory applied to practice—praxis—is powerful. Its power can be seen when praxis leads to a sense that there is no alternative to neo-liberalism, and when the key ideas of neo-liberalism come to be accepted by governments and citizens from across the political spectrum as common sense or hegemonic. Everyday experiences of neo-liberal theory are not abstract, although trying to understand the big picture of the historical, economic, and political forces at play can seem daunting.

There is a lot of debate about how to define neo-liberalism. Some argue that it is the catchphrase that has replaced globalization in discussions about economic policies, ideologies, and practices in the new millennium (Clarke, 2008). Others use it to refer more precisely to policies associated with organizations like the World Bank and International Monetary Fund that favour export-led growth and deep cuts in government spending (Stiglitz, 2008). Some (see Peck & Theodore, 2007) speak of it as an uneven and incomplete process—as neo-liberalization rather than neo-liberalism—to reflect its adaptability and variety. For our purposes here, we can talk about neo-liberalism as an approach that elevates the free market and advocates individualism and individual rights over any collectivism or group rights.

The kind of neo-liberalism that we must grapple with in trying to understand how we got to our stormy present is one rooted in the ideas of scholars like von Hayek and later Friedman and the Chicago School (see Braedley & Luxton, 2010; Connell, 2010). These thinkers, whose ideas were initially experimented with, and in some cases brutally imposed on Latin America and later all over the world, were deeply opposed to government intervention in the economy in ways that they argued constrained choice and trade. They were anti-regulation in the sense that they argued that constraints on markets crippled and distorted them. The kinds of regulations now being developed in response to the current crisis, like banking and credit oversight, are seen by neo-liberals as abhorrent, and even socialist. Nice catchphrases like "free markets create free people" (see, for example, Lott, 2007) linked the neo-liberal approach with democracy. Those who argued that markets were *not* self-regulating and that these markets often destroyed workers, communities, and cultures were positioned as somehow against freedom and democracy.

What made neo-liberalism such a risky approach, leading to such chaos? Neo-liberalism is about re-regulation, not de-regulation or self-regulation. What I mean here is that certain regulations—keeping wages low and making work more insecure, or making it easy to move capital out of countries—are very much a part of the project, but regulating *how* capital moves and how credit systems are overseen is interventionist because it is viewed as constraining to the goal of capital accumulation. Neo-liberalism is imposed by crisis and by force. It is opportunistic. It is in no way linked to democracy or freedom. The basic neo-liberal approach proceeded as follows through much of the 1980s, 1990s, and 2000s. A nation, say an African or a Latin American one, suffered an economic recession or crisis (there were many throughout this period). An international agency—usually the International Monetary Fund—would come in with loans, tied to conditions. These conditions were neo-liberalism in action because they hemmed the choices available to governments and created markets that usually did not serve the needs or interests of the country receiving the loans. The conditions included cutting social spending (reducing government and social services), reducing regulations on industry and trade (reducing particular kinds of regulation), usually focusing on export-led growth (so selling products on the world market, often of crops or other goods that might otherwise be used to feed people or at least diversify the economy), and generally disfavouring policies and practices that were social investments aside from infrastructure like roads for business purposes. Privatization—not collective ownership—was the mantra, so water, hydro, even education came to be delivered by for-profits as ways to put short-term cash into government coffers. The logic of neo-liberalism spread with a consensus emerging that free trade was good, and that the kinds of shocks and adjustments to neo-liberal policies would even out and create better lives for most people. This is the house of cards, built on a greed-is-good model of capitalism.[3]

What Has Happened to the Welfare State? How Were We Faring Before the Crisis?

In Canada, in the 1990s in particular, the logic of neo-liberalism was embraced as the federal and provincial governments faced a recession and began to privatize industries, cut social spending, and change labour laws. As McBride (2006, p. 260) aptly notes, for neo-liberalism "the chief impediment to the free operation of markets is the state, and a number of measures have been advanced to reduce its role." Government transfers and entitlements were cut over the 1990s and 2000s: family allowances were eliminated, Employment Insurance was made significantly less accessible and worth less money, transfers to provinces for housing, welfare, health, and education were altered significantly, and supports, such as training, were reduced (see Rice & Prince, 2000). There were some positive developments, such as the creation and expansion of the Canada Child Tax Benefit (Battle, 2006, 2008), but there was virtually no sustained movement on childcare and early learning (see Mahon, 2006). All of these elements—the fabric of the Canadian welfare state—matter enormously in buffering people against the unpredictability of capitalist crises and matter because they express a collective desire to share the risks and thus the costs of getting sick, being poor, or losing a job. This fabric was shredded by the logic of greed-is-good neo-liberalism and a shared social solidarity or sense of bringing up the floor was trampled. Political economist David Harvey (2006, pp. 154–56) contends that neo-liberal states like Canada transfer resources from those with less money to those with more money through means such as privatization, cutbacks in supports for things like social wages, and by changing tax codes and investment structures. "The state," he argues, "once transformed into a neo-liberal set of institutions, becomes a prime agent of redistributive policies, reversing the flow from the upper to the lower classes that had occurred during the era of social democratic hegemony" (2006, p. 155).

In people's work lives, a neo-liberal logic also played out. We now live in what one sociologist called a "political economy of insecurity" (Beck, 2000). The labour market of the 2000s is very different than the one of the 1970s and 1980s. Non-standard work, a term referring to work that does not match the post–World War II norm of a 40 hour per week full-time, full-year job, became increasingly normative (Vosko, 2004). Beaujot (2000, p. 129) asserts that by the mid 1990s, "only one-third of workers ha[d] what might be considered to be a typical pattern of one job, 35–48 hours per week, Monday to Friday during the day, working on a permanent basis for an employer at one place of work." The labour market in Canada since the 1990s has been characterized by significant increases in multiple job holding and in part-time, temporary, casual/on-call, and self-employment (Vosko, 2000). In its important review of labour law, the Law Commission of Canada (2004, p. 5) reflected on the problems with the rise of non-standard work:

> Among the problems associated with non-standard work are the following: poor pay, little job security, a lack of access to important statutory benefits and protections (such as Employment Insurance, employment standards protections, workers' compensation, the right to collective bargaining) and a lack of access to employer provided benefits such as dental, life and disability insurance.

As governments weakened labour market protections and supports making work lives more precarious, and as globalization altered the kinds of jobs and sectors in which people in Canada worked (increasing especially the service sector), the conditions under which most families were able to put together a living became more challenging. Moreover, women entered the labour market in record numbers, with 73 percent of all "women with children less than age 16 living at home ... part of the employed workforce" (Statistics Canada, 2007, p. 7) in 2006. There remain huge inequalities in the labour market, and many of these have intensified during this period of neo-liberal restructuring. Women and people of colour in particular are concentrated in low-wage, insecure, and often part-time work (Galabuzzi, 2006; Statistics Canada, 2007).

In Canada in the 2000s, a two-earner model is the norm. In 2008, 68 percent of couples were dual-earners in Canada (Marshall, 2009, p. 12). Yet while men and women are called into the labour market in order to meet their household income needs, the distribution of caregiving is not at all equal. A dual earner-female career model prevails (see Bezanson, 2006). What is particularly striking about this arrangement is that Canada has an abysmal record of investment in early childhood education and care (see OECD, 2006, for example). To illustrate, in 2004, for every 100 Canadian children requiring daycare, there were spaces for 12 in Canada (CCSD, 2009). In terms of early childhood services, Canada ties with Ireland for last place among economically advanced countries (see Table 17.1). Further, the combined effects of the gutting of social welfare supports like Employment Insurance and the neo-liberal push to get more people working and in more flexible arrangements have meant that work–life conflicts are especially high for women. Economic insecurity was already widespread even in a booming pre-2008 economy. The logic of the kind of neo-liberal restructuring of work and the welfare state meant that more work was shifted onto families, and usually onto women's labour within them. When services, like home care for the ill, were downloaded to lower levels of government or cut entirely, the need for the care did not disappear, but it was absorbed usually by women's unpaid work. As British economist Diane Elson (1998) has argued, this assumes that women's unpaid labour is infinitely elastic and can expand to meet needs given various states of social investment. The result is not simply much greater stress, anxiety, and imbalance in people's lives, but also a marked deterioration in the most important relationships in people's lives (see Bezanson, 2006; Luxton, 2006). Relying on loved ones for care can strain key relationships. Some carework simply does not get done, and the consequences are dire. The processes of neo-liberalism as they unfolded in Canada in the 1990 and 2000s, then, left many families in a precarious and stressed position before the market crash.

TABLE 17.1 EARLY CHILDHOOD SERVICES AMONG ECONOMICALLY ADVANCED COUNTRIES (2008)

Benchmark		1	2	3	4	5	6	7	8	9	10
	Number of benchmarks achieved	Parental leave of 1 year at 50% of salary	A national plan with priority for disadvantaged children	Subsidized and regulated child care services for 25% of children under 3	Subsidized and accredited early education services for 80% of 4 year-olds	80% of all child care staff trained	50% of staff in accredited early education services tertiary educated with relevant qualification	Minimum staff-to-children ratio of 1:15 in pre-school education	1.0% of GDP spent on early childhood services	Child poverty rate less than 10%	Near-universal outreach of essential child health services
Sweden	10	✓	✓	✓	✓	✓	✓	✓	✓	✓	✓
Iceland	9		✓	✓	✓	✓	✓	✓	✓	✓	✓
Denmark	8	✓	✓	✓	✓		✓	✓	✓	✓	
Finland	8	✓	✓	✓		✓		✓	✓	✓	✓
France	8	✓	✓	✓	✓	✓	✓		✓	✓	
Norway	8	✓	✓	✓	✓			✓	✓	✓	✓
Belgium (Flanders)	6		✓	✓	✓		✓			✓	✓
Hungary	6		✓		✓	✓	✓	✓		✓	
New Zealand	6		✓	✓	✓	✓	✓	✓			
Slovenia	6	✓	✓	✓		✓	✓				✓
Austria	5		✓		✓	✓		✓		✓	
Netherlands	5		✓	✓		✓	✓	✓			
United Kingdom*	5		✓	✓	✓	✓	✓				
Germany	4		✓		✓		✓	✓			
Italy	4		✓		✓	✓	✓				
Japan	4		✓		✓	✓					✓
Portugal	4		✓		✓	✓	✓				
Republic of Korea	4		✓			✓	✓				✓
Mexico	3		✓			✓	✓				
Spain	3				✓	✓	✓				
Switzerland	3					✓		✓		✓	
United States	3			✓			✓	✓			
Australia	2			✓			✓				
Canada	1						✓				
Ireland	1						✓				

* Data for the United Kingdom refer to England only. *Source:* UNICEF (2008) The Child Care Transition. Florence, Italy: UNICEF Innocenti Research Centre.

Case Study: Putting Together a Living and Balancing Significant Care Responsibilities

In 2006, along with a team of researchers, I began interviewing people with significant paid work responsibilities and significant caregiving responsibilities. The study, called "Ensuring Social Reproduction," aimed to uncover the gaps and tension in social and labour market policies and how these played out in people's day-to-day lives. Using a snowball sampling technique, we selected participants who lived in 49 households from a range of income backgrounds, household structures, geographic locations, ethnic/cultural origins, and caregiving types. We oversampled people with children under age six, creating a subcategory of women who were pregnant so that we could track them as they made decisions about parental leaves and childcare. We also interviewed people who were providing significant elder care. We did not include those caring for a dependant with a disability. We asked all members of the household to participate in the interviews if possible so that we could get a robust picture of a typical day, work lives and schedules, and how people reflected on their work–life balance. In most cases, where there were two adult members, only one (usually a woman) participated in both rounds of interviews. The interviews took place on average 12–18 months apart. Interviews were recorded, transcribed, and coded.

Participants were selected from four locations in Ontario—17 households lived in the Niagara region, 18 in the Greater Toronto Area (GTA), 13 were in central-north Ontario, and one was from eastern Ontario. We made efforts to include rural as well as urban households in our sample. We categorized the interviews conducted with the members of 49 households into three areas—30 had significant childcare responsibilities, 16 had significant elder care responsibilities, and three had both significant child and elder care responsibilities. The structure of the households also varied. As Table 17.2 shows, most lived in common-law relationships or were married. Income spreads among the participating household members ranged from very low income to very high income. Table 17.3 shows the income distribution for the 49 households for 2006. As a point of comparison, for Canada for 2006, average income after tax for families was $67,500 (Statistics Canada, 2009).[4] In our study, when those households with elder care responsibilities, who tend to be comprised of older participants with more years of labour market experience, are removed, the number of participating households below and marginally above the Statistics Canada Low Income Cut Off rises to almost 50 percent.

We also asked people to *self-report* their cultural or ethnic heritage. Table 17.4 shows the heritage of the primary respondents. Where there was more than one primary respondent in the household, both are reported, thus totalling more than 49 responses.

The collection of stories reveals a mixed and layered picture of love and devotion to children, parents, or friends alongside stress, sleeplessness, and worry. They depict the kinds of crises, particularly around finding and keeping good childcare, that can make or break paid work decisions and options. They also reveal that control over paid work and worktime is a crucial element for women in particular in order to meet caregiving roles. Social supports, especially extended kin providing assistance with unpaid work, were very significant in managing multiple roles. For the purposes of this chapter, and to illustrate how families were faring in the lead-up to our stormy present, one household's story is profiled below. Jade and her family give a glimpse into putting together a living in the Niagara region of Ontario while on maternity leave and subsequently, while re-entering the labour market with a small child in need of care, two school-aged children, and two careers. It shows how the need for childcare determines worklife and consequently income and divisions of labour. None of the adults in this household have significant job security nor do they have much control over their work hours or conditions of work.

TABLE 17.2 HOUSEHOLD STRUCTURE (2006)

Household Structure	Number of Households	Percentage
Common law/married	34	69.39
Single parent	4	8.16
Multigenerational	9	18.37
Other	2	4.08

* We followed Statistics Canada's definition of economic family in determining household categories, with several deviations based on how people identified the composition of their households and the pooling of resources.

TABLE 17.3 HOUSEHOLD INCOME (2006)

Income Range	Number of Households	Percentage
Below LICO	9	18.37
Marginally above LICO (within $5,000 per annum)	5	10.20
Middle income (> $5,000 above LICO to $100,000 taking into account community and household size)	25	51.02
High income (> $100,000)	10	10.41

* LICOs are Low Income Cut-Offs. We used 2006 Statistics Canada LICOs, which take into account community size and household size to determine low income.

TABLE 17.4 ETHNIC/CULTURAL HERITAGE, PRIMARY RESPONDENTS

Ethnic/Cultural Heritage	Number
Eastern European	3
Eastern European/Jewish	1
First Nations	2
First Nations/Irish/Scottish	3
First Nations/French	1
Jewish	2
Anglican	1
African	1
Black/Caribbean/English	1
Caucasian	3
Southern European	2
Northern European	13
South East Asia and China	3
French Canadian	3
Canadian	7
Other	1
No answer	3

JADE

In 2006 when we first met, Jade, a white woman who describes her ethnic origin as "Canadian," was living with her husband, two sons (7 and 9 years of age), and infant daughter.

Jade was on maternity leave from a permanent, full-time retail position. Jade had an arrangement with her employer in which she worked part-time while on maternity leave to, as she put it, "bank hours" because she anticipated that she would need days off to care for sick children and go to appointments when she returned to work. She began banking hours when her daughter was four weeks old. Her job had no benefits and she did not get paid for sick days. Her husband also worked in the service sector full-time, 40 to 60 hours per week. He had no dental or health benefits associated with his job and Jade said that his job was not terribly secure. Their combined household income for a family of five was about $60,000 for 2006. Jade had enough paid work hours to qualify for Employment Insurance (EI) while on maternity leave. EI covers 55 percent of earnings up to a maximum of a little over $400 per week. For Jade, this meant that for her year of leave, she received about $10,000. She decided to take the leave herself instead of sharing it with her spouse because she considered her job to be more secure and because her husband earned more money. While on leave, she worried and tried to plan about what she would do for childcare when she returned to work full-time.

> ... Just for (the baby), the only person I know is like thirty bucks a day, and that's a lot. My pay cheque is only ... under four hundred dollars a week ... I'm gonna do about half of it in child care. Just over a hundred and fifty a week, just for her, and then there will be something for the boys for after school care.

The year she gave birth to her daughter, the Harper government was elected. They eliminated the proposed national system of childcare and replaced it with a *taxable* monthly cheque worth $100 per child under six. Jade said the money—after taxes about $60 for her household—was handy for diapers. It could not make a dent in the cost of childcare nor was it sufficient to allow her not to work for pay.

By the second interview in 2007, Jade had changed jobs. Her employer, for whom she had been banking hours, did not have a full-time position for her because the business was not doing well. She took a position that paid a bit more and had benefits in another company and had daytime hours that more easily accommodated childcare, but had less flexibility in terms of taking sick days or providing other kinds of care. She continued to work on Saturdays at her previous job, extending her workweek to six days. Her spouse stopped working on Saturdays to provide childcare, but often worked 12-hour days until 8 p.m. to make up for lost worktime, so Jade managed pick-ups, sports, homework, meal preparation, and bedtime. Getting childcare for her one-year-old was very hard, as most centres don't have spaces for children under 18 months of age, despite the fact that maternity leave eligibility is 12 months. When she did find a space for her daughter with a home-based provider, she lamented that her prediction about the cost of childcare was accurate: "Half of my paycheque every week ... goes to childcare," she said. On days when her daughter was sick, she had to pay for daycare her daughter was not attending *and* hire a sitter to care for her daughter, thus negating her entire paycheque for the day. She reflected that despite this, she needed to work. During her maternity leave, she told us that:

> I had to borrow money from my aunt because our gas was disconnected. Twice. Which was hard ... Christmas was stressful until we had the flood ... that helped actually ... because a lot of the things that we got paid [from the insurance company], like that got damaged, we didn't replace. [Borrowing money was] embarrassing. Stressful. Hard. Very hard. Because my income wasn't a lot to begin with, so when it's cut in half, it was nothing every two weeks.

Even with two adults working full-time, they live paycheque to paycheque. Jade tells a story of her husband not getting a paycheque one night when it was expected and not being able to buy groceries.

Jade does the bulk of the household work, manages the household finances, and arranges childcare. She barters and trades household items and clothes, and worries constantly about meeting expenses. She notes that despite their total household income, she cannot pay all the bills each month so she alternates and carries household debt. She finished the last interview saying that "I wish we could be like Quebec and have ... $7 a day childcare ... That under an hour's worth of work, paid for me ... I'd actually *make* some money, instead of just squeak(ing) by."

DISCUSSION

Jade's family's story is a typical one for those interviewed with middle incomes in the sense that concerns about money and balancing work with caregiving are all being juggled at once. Despite their financial challenges and difficulties with childcare, however, they fare better than many middle-income households and most low-income households. Because self-employment has risen considerably since the 1990s in Canada, fewer Canadian women and men have insured earnings under the EI system and thus *do not qualify* for EI benefits for maternity/parental leaves. Jade has health benefits at her new place of employment, which offsets some household costs. Jade and her spouse also both have full-time hours mostly at one place of employment, though both work very long hours to make enough money to meet their family of five's needs. Their work is more *standard looking* than many Canadians' work, but it is characterized by Jade's having two jobs and her husband working 12-hour days so that she can work a six-day week. The supports that they need—quality, affordable childcare, well-paid parental leaves, more flexible work arrangements—are not available to them. The legacy of neo-liberal welfare restructuring and the effects of the last decade or so of changes in labour markets due to globalization have left this family without a strong net as the economy teeters.

Not So Different after All: The Future of Work and Family in a Not-So-Post-Neo-liberal Era

As the economic recession drives onward, a host of proposals are forwarded to redirect its course. None, thus far, proposes real investments in people, their worklives or their caregiving roles. After decades of retrenchment and rescaling of the Canadian welfare state and increased flexibility and precariousness in the labour market, Canadians face this downturn with the lowest level of protection in at least the last century (Yalnizyan, 2009). Recall that one of the key features leading to the crash of 2008 was record levels of household debt. This debtload compounds and makes even more intractable the economic risks families face.

There have been significant responses on the part of governments and international institutions, many hastily thrown together. At the core, however, are supports for financial institutions. The International Monetary Fund continues to respond to the economic crisis as it unfolds in developing countries with loans that are almost exactly the same as the structural adjustment policies that led to such massive debt crises throughout the developing world (Stewart, 2008). Moreover, the aim of investment is to return to an economy like the one that fell so spectacularly in 2008, by freeing up credit and getting people borrowing and buying again. Because neo-liberalism thrives on crisis, the time is ripe for a new variant of what seems like a particularly versatile virus.[5] Governments in Canada are not investing in building strong public sectors, childcare programs, or even in education spending, but rather in buildings and roads. The people who will clean the buildings, teach in them, or those who will drive the buses on the roads are not part of the equation. The stimulus is stimulating male employment in the construction trades, with some obvious spill-over into other kinds of jobs that support this industry.

One of the questions that has emerged in Canada as this particular recession has taken hold has been about the future of families. Many of the job losses thus far have been in traditionally male jobs. This is especially true because so many of the jobs have been lost in sectors related to the auto sector. Some have gone so far as to call this a "he-cession" (Pelieci, 2009). Will men, some wonder, become stay-at-home dads, and will roles reverse? While it may be the case that some men will do this, there are several problems with this logic and the question is too optimistic given the weight of evidence on the subject. This is the first recession in which women, and especially women with children, are already in the labour force in record numbers and most households rely on two incomes (see Yalnizyan, 2009). In past recessions, women often were called *into* the labour market to offset income shortfalls. Women are already in the labour market and thus this kind of buffer is reduced. It may be more likely that youth are called into the labour market in greater numbers, returning to a family model of work more characteristic of the early part of the last century. Further, the weight of evidence from economics, sociology, and anthropology indicates that during periods of economic downturn, men do not in significant numbers take on a greater share of social reproduction (see, for example, Elson, 1995; Scott, 2008). It would appear that absent any real investment in childcare, and given that the current session of parliament has already seen the Harper Conservatives rejecting as socialist efforts to make EI more accessible, the depth of the effects of income insecurity and family stress is only beginning to become plain. Successive neo-liberal governments who gutted income supports, labour regulations, failed to invest in carework, and failed to regulate risky credit markets, have left families facing a fraught future in what remains a neo-liberal political economy of insecurity.

Endnotes

1. The author wishes to thank the Social Sciences and Humanities Research Council for funding the research (grant number 410-2004-1786) reported on in the fourth section of this chapter. I also wish to thank Renee McKinley for her assistance with data analysis.
2. According to its website, the "Group of Twenty (G20) Finance Ministers and Central Bank Governors was established in 1999 to bring together systemically important industrialized and developing economies to discuss key issues in the global economy." Canada is one among the 20 nations in the group. See http://www.g20.org/about_what_is_g20.aspx
3. In 2008, Australian Prime Minister Kevin Rudd said, referencing a 1980s film about a Wall Street investment banker named Gekko: "It is perhaps time now to admit that we did not learn the full lessons of the greed-is-good ideology. And today we are still cleaning up the

mess of the 21st-century children of Gordon Gekko" (Rudd, 2008, retrieved from http://www.theaustralian.news.com.au/story/0,25197,24450662-7583,00.html).

4. As with LICOs, this number refers to economic families as defined by Statistics Canada. Average income after tax refers to total income, including government transfers, minus income tax (Statistics Canada, 2009).
5. As Klein (2007) and others (see, for example, Harvey, 2005 and Peck & Theodore, 2007) have powerfully illustrated, the adaptability and opportunism of the mechanisms inherent in a neo-liberal market logic make it particularly able to dramatically alter regulations pertaining to ownership, working conditions and protections, and wages in contexts of crisis. Klein uses the examples of massive privatization post-Hurricane Katrina in the United States and of the selling off of industry and financial systems in Iraq as part of the U.S. occupation strategy to map how expediently neo-liberalism approaches crises.

Works Cited

Battle, K. 2006. Modernizing the Welfare State. *Policy Options*, April–May 2006: 47–50.

Battle, K. 2008. *A Bigger and Better Child Benefit: A $5,000 Canada Child Tax Benefit.* Ottawa: Caledon Institute of Social Policy.

Beaujot, R. (2000) *Earning and Caring in Canadian Families.* Peterborough, Ont.: Broadview Press.

Beck, U. (2000) *The Brave New World of Work.* Cambridge: Polity.

Bezanson, K. (2006) *Gender, the State, and Social Reproduction.* Toronto: University of Toronto Press.

Braedley, S. and M. Luxton (2010) Introduction in S. Braedley and M. Luxton (eds) *Neo-liberalism and Everyday Life.* Montreal and Kingston: McGill-Queen's University Press.

CBC Television (2008) *The National with Peter Mansbridge.* Aired October 7, 2008.

CCSD (2009) *Families: A Canadian Profile.* Retrieved online May 25, 2009 at: http://www.ccsd.ca/factsheets/family/

Clarke, J. (2008) Living with/in and without neo-liberalism. *Focaal, 51* (1): 135–147.

Connell, R.W. (2010) Understanding Neoliberalism in S. Braedley and M. Luxton (eds) *Neo-liberalism and Everyday Life.* Montreal and Kingston: McGill-Queen's University Press.

Elson, D. (1995) *Male Bias in the Development Process.* Manchester: Manchester University Press.

Elson, D. (1998) The Economic, the Political, and the Domestic: Businesses, States, and Households in the Organization of Production. *New Political Economy,* 3 (2). P. 198–207.

Feller, B. (2008) Bush, Candidates Urge Congress to Support Bailout. September 30, 2008.

Retrieved online on September 30, 2008 at http://www.reportonbusiness.com/servlet/story/RTGAM.20080930.wbush0930/BNStory/Business/home

Galabuzzi, G. (2006) *Canada's Economic Apartheid: The Social Exclusion of Racialized Groups in the New Century.* Toronto: Canadian Scholars' Press Inc.

Guardian Weekly (2008) *Weekly Review. The Guardian Weekly*, October 31, 2008: 26–28.

Harvey, D. (2005) *A Brief History of Neoliberalism.* New York: Oxford University Press.

Harvey, D. (2006) Neo-liberalism as Creative Destruction. *Geografiska Annaler 88 B* (2): 145–158.

International Monetary Fund (2009) *Global Financial Stability Report: Responding to the Financial Crisis and Measuring Systemic Risks* (Washington, April). Retrieved May 6, 2009 from http://www.imf.org/external/pubs/ft/gfsr/2009/01/pdf/text.pdf

Klein, N. (2007) *The Shock Doctrine: The Rise of Disaster Capitalism.* Toronto: A.A. Knopff.

Law Commission of Canada (2004) *Is Work Working? Work Laws That Do a Better Job.* Ottawa: Law Commission of Canada.

Lott, J.R. (2007) *Freedomnomics: Why the Free Market Works and Other Half Baked Theories Don't.* Washington: Regnery Publishing Inc.

Luxton, M. (2006) Friends, Neighbours, and Community: A Case Study of the Role of Informal Caregiving in Social Reproduction in K. Bezanson and M. Luxton (eds.) *Social Reproduction: Feminist Political Economy Challenges Neo-liberalism.* Montreal and Kingston: McGill-Queen's University Press.

Mahon, Rianne (2006) The OECD and the Reconciliation Agenda: Competing Blueprints in J. Lewis (ed) *Children in Context: Changing Families and Welfare States* London: Edwin Elgar.

Marshall, K. (2009) The Family Work Week. *Perspectives on Labour and Income*, April 2009. Ottawa: Statistics Canada.

McBride, S. (2006) Domestic Neoliberalism in V. Shalla (ed) *Working in a Global Era.* P. 257–277. Toronto: Canadian Scholars' Press Inc.

New York Times (2009) Credit Crisis: The Essentials. *New York Times*, May 7, 2009: 1–11. Retrieved May 9 at topics.nytimes.con/topics/reference/timestopics/subjects/c/credit_crisis/

OECD (2006) *Starting Strong: Early Childhood Education and Care.* Paris: OECD.

Peck, J. and N. Theodore (2007) Variegated Capitalism. *Progress in Human Geography, 31* (6): 731–772.

Pilieci, V. (2009) "He-cession" Hits Men's Jobs Harder. *Winnipeg Free Press*, April 11, 2009. Retrieved online April 20, 2009 at: http://www.winnipegfreepress.com/business/he-cession-hits-mens-jobs-harder-42843302.html

Rice, M. and J. Prince (2000) *Changing Politics of Canadian Social Policy.* Toronto: University of Toronto Press.

Rudd, K. (2008) The Children of Gordon Gekko. *The Australian*, October 6, 2008. Retrieved May 13, 2009 at http://www.theaustralian.news.com.au/story/0,25197,24450662-7583,00.html

Scoffield, H. (2008) Canadian Economy Booms in July. *The Globe and Mail.* September 30, 2008: A1.

Scott, J. (2008) *Paid and Unpaid Work: A Retreat in Gender Role Egalitarian Attitudes* Paper presented at the annual meeting of the American Sociological Association Annual Meeting, Sheraton Boston and the Boston Marriott Copley Place, Boston, MA . Available online May 23, 2009 from http://www.allacademic.com/meta/p242289_index.html

Statistics Canada (2007) *Women in Canada: Work Chapter Updates.* Ottawa: Statistics Canada.

Statistics Canada (2009) Average Income after Tax by Economic Family Types 2003–2007. *The Daily.* June 2, 2009. Ottawa: Statistics Canada.

Stewart, L. (2008) New World, Same Old Ideology. *The Guardian Weekly,* November 7, 2008: 18.

Stiglitz, J.E. (2008) The End of Neo-liberalism? *Project Syndicate Commentary*, July, accessed at www.project-syndicate.org

UNICEF (2008) *The Child Care Transition.* Florence, Italy: UNICEF Innocenti Research Centre.

Vosko, L. (2000) *Temporary Work.* Toronto: University of Toronto Press.

Vosko, L. (2004) Precarious Employment: Towards an Improved Understanding of Labour Market Insecurity in L. Vosko (ed) *Precarious Employment: Understanding Labour Market Insecurity in Canada.* Montreal and Kingston: McGill-Queen's University Press.

World Bank (2009) *World Development Indicators Database*, revised April 24, 2009. Retrieved May 6, 2009 at http://siteresources.worldbank.org/DATASTATISTICS/Resources/GDP.pdf

Yalnizyan, A. (2009) *Exposed: Revealing the Truths about Canada's Recession.* Ottawa: Canadian Centre for Policy Alternatives.

CHAPTER 18

Beyond Normalization: An Analysis of Heteronormativity in Children's Picture Books

Anika Stafford

Over the past twenty years, one of the most fascinating sites of struggle with regard to queer families has been children's storybooks. Since the late 1980s, there has been a growing body of books that depict families with same-sex parents (or other relatives in same-sex relationships). From *Heather Has Two Mommies* by Leslea Newman (1989) to *Mom and Mum Are Getting Married* by Ken Setterington (2004), the emphasis has been on same-sex relationships as "normal" and "healthy." Despite their unthreatening tones, these books have been highly contested and often banned. The most notorious Canadian example took place in Surrey, B.C., when the Surrey School Board banned three such books. The case began in the late 1990s and dragged on for years, in local and supreme courts. Intensely polarized reviews of these books had some reviewers warning potential readers that the books in question dealt with *unnatural* relationships, while others praised the books for honouring *diversity*. Unaddressed in both these perspectives are the ways that power, privilege, and heteronormativity are reproduced or challenged in these books. The highly polarized debate also pays little attention to the ways that literary quality is often sacrificed in order to make a political point.

In this essay, I examine some of these children's books to show how they attempt to break down homophobia and heterosexism. Many of these picture books focus on convincing a homophobic public that "homosexuality" and same-sex relationships are normal. It is important to examine the literary and political implications of this trend. Below, I analyze some of the nuances involved in creating anti-oppressive politics and how literary form can help or hinder a political message.

The framework from which I analyze these books has been shaped by current queer and anti-racist feminist theory as well as by children's literary criticism. Often, discussions of children's literary criticism and discussions of anti-oppressive politics take place in isolation from one another. The result is that children's literary criticism has a tendency to discuss literary quality while ignoring issues of systemic power and privilege; while books that actively engage with anti-oppressive politics can ignore the way didactic political messages can compromise not only literary quality but also the effectiveness of the message itself (more on this below). My framework takes into account the ways in which this isolation can be problematically reflected in children's books that challenge homophobic norms when illustrating meanings of family. Central to my analysis is the assertion that an intentional engagement with anti-oppressive politics does not have to be done at the expense of literary quality; rather, that a combination of theories is useful in assessing ways in which quality children's literature can challenge normative regulation of relationships/identity so that gay and lesbian relationships can be more fully developed and represented in this literature.

With the poverty of resources depicting queer families, queer communities have been quick to defend any children's books which include same-sex couples. Children's stories, so often repeated, can begin to shape values and expectations. It is important that we take a closer look at the messages in the still-growing literature that deals with queer families so that we can understand what they are saying and how they are saying it.

Questions for Analysis

The first step in my analysis was to compile a list of critical questions that I could use to analyze children's picture books with characters in same-sex relationships. To do so, I drew on political theory by authors such as Kevin Kumashiro, Shane Phelan, and Himani Bannerji. I also drew on the literary works of such critics as Hazel Rochman, Sheila Egoff, Deidre Baker, and Ken Setterington. The following political and literary questions guided my overview and critiques:

POLITICAL QUESTIONS

- Do the picture books recreate power hierarchies from the dominant culture such as gender expression, race, and class in order to normalize homosexuality (for privileged populations of LGBT/queer people)? How is this reflected in the illustrations?
- Is the LGBT/queer reader "othered"? Is the education structured in a way that assumes the reader is heterosexual and homophobic to the point where LGBT/queer readers are excluded as potential readers?
- Is homophobia dealt with in a way that shows homophobia as the problem to be challenged as opposed to families with same-sex relationships needing to justify that they are healthy and not damaging their children?
- Is the family validated for homophobic reasons; for example, are they framed as acceptable because their children are straight, or because the child has straight friends, or because they have positive role models of the other sex?

LITERARY QUESTIONS

- Are the pictures visually stimulating? Do they ignite the imagination? Do they draw the reader further into the story?
- Is the story told in an interesting way? Is the only event the fact that there are same-sex relationships, or is there something happening to these characters that the reader can come to care about?

- Is the use of language engaging for a picture book (that is generally meant to be read out loud)? Can the reader be drawn in through lyricism, rhythm, or patterns?
- Are the characters in the story distinct individuals or static symbols? Does the reader get to know them in ways that show their uniqueness, their humour, their quirks? Can the reader identify with them?
- Does the theme come through as an engaging story or is it merely an explicitly stated "moral message"?

How "Gay Is Normal" in Children's Picture Books

When I began researching children's picture books with "gay" characters, I was glad to see that there were close to forty books that could be grouped into this category. It was my hope that among this number there would be books that depicted a wide range of individuals with family structures departing from hetero-nuclear family norms. I was dismayed by the number of books that replicated normative conceptualizations of family and gender (more on this below). Many books focused on the assertion that "gay is normal" at the expense of enthralling story lines, multi-faceted characters, enticing language, and other elements of literary quality.

For example, in *Daddy's Roommate* by Michael Willhoite, the young boy narrator's parents got divorced the year before the story opens. His dad now has a "roommate," an obvious euphemism for partner/lover/spouse. The boy's dad and his roommate "live together, eat together, sleep together, shave together, and times even fight together. But they always make up."

The pictures are cartoonish and oversimplified, depicting conservatively gendered, white, middle-class norms. There is truly nothing else in the story besides a description of how gay people can eat, sleep, shave, and so on, just the way real (a.k.a straight) people do. If difference (from the mainstream) is depicted as okay because it is actually sameness, the underlying message becomes that difference is really not okay.

Similarly, in another book by Michael Willhoite, *Uncle What-Is-It Is Coming to Visit*, a brother and sister find out that their uncle is coming to visit. When they ask if he has a girlfriend, they find out that he is gay. Not knowing what that means, they ask homophobic people in their neighbourhood who tell them tales about gay people being leather people and drag queens. The children get so terrified by this that they don't know if they want their uncle to visit after all. In the end, he is just an "unthreatening," conservative man who doesn't like Brussels sprouts just like them. The cartoonish pictures depict 1950s-style gender roles with the parents and children. The uncle is unthreatening because he looks like a white, middle-class, gender-normative man. The homophobic bullies appear to be working class, probably mechanics. This book definitely falls into the category of those that do more to uphold the status quo than contesting it. Adding conservative, middle-class, white, gay men to the margins of what is acceptable does not necessarily do much to break down barriers and embrace difference.

In my research, I grouped the books into two categories: books explaining how a family can include people in a same-sex relationship (expository books), and books with the same-sex relationship as the background, but not the focal point, of the story (background books). While expository books tend to focus didactically on messages that the family is "normal," background books tend to use storylines and illustrations to create an environment in which the background characters in same-sex relationships are as close to the heteronormative mainstream as possible. Both categories often position the reader as heterosexual and homophobic—thus denying the possibility of gay and lesbian readership. As a result, the same-sex relationship, as opposed to homophobia, is usually positioned as the aberration to be studied.

Within the expository category there is a trend towards explicitly stated moral messages. Unfortunately, the didactic nature of the message shifts the focus away from the characters as individuals as they become symbols of something to accept, as opposed to specific and interesting people with whom a reader can connect. For example, the daycare teacher at the end of Leslea Newman's *Heather Has Two Mommies* (1989) gathers her students around her and tells them, "It doesn't matter how many mommies or how many daddies your family has ... it doesn't matter if your family has sisters or brothers or cousins or grandmothers or grandfathers or uncles or aunts. Each family is special. The most important thing about a family is that all the people in it love each other." In *How My Family Came to Be: Daddy, Papa, and Me* by Andrew Aldrich (2003), the main character describes how he and his family "play, talk, read, hug and sometimes fight, just like other families." The repetition that all families are the same does not leave room for families with cultural differences and for families with "gay" members to be part of non-mainstream countercultures. This detracts from the message of "diversity" and of valuing difference, because conforming to the mainstream is the trait that makes the family acceptable; the capacity for sameness rather than difference is what is honoured. The reader is also positioned as heterosexual and homophobic through the constant assurance that the family is okay, implicitly suggesting that the reader would have originally thought otherwise. The reader is not engaged in the overall storyline or drawn into an appreciation for the characters as individuals.

Background books often begin with long explanations of everyday things that gay families do together. In *Anna Day and the O-Ring* (Wickens, 1994), the main character, a young boy with two moms, tells the reader that he has sleepovers and eats cookies. *Gloria Goes to Gay Pride* begins with a rundown of how Gloria and her moms celebrate Valentine's Day, Halloween, Mother's Day, and Hanukkah (Newman, 1991). In both books, the preambles do not further an overall plot nor are they worded in particularly engaging ways. The reader is again assumed to be both heterosexual and homophobic; children or adults who know individuals in same-sex relationships would already be aware that their families do everyday things together. When the audience is presumed to be homophobic and heterosexual by default, those whose identities fall outside of heterosexist norms are not positioned as a potential readership. Consequently, these readers are "othered" because they are situated not as subjects but as objects to be studied. In addition to perpetuating exclusion, this limits the potential of the books to challenge heterosexist assumptions of potentially homophobic readers as they replicate heterosexist frameworks in the way in which the reader is positioned.

The exclusion does not end with "othering" gays and lesbians. Another aspect of the relentless normalization of characters in same-sex relationships is that often families are exemplified for the ways in which they uphold the status quo in all ways except for this one exception. The four books I have discussed thus far primarily feature white, middle-class characters. Books that include characters of colour generally do so in the context of "hypernormal," suburban, nuclear families. For example, in *Molly's Family* by Nancy Gordon, the story follows a plot similar to stories previously seen on this subject, such as *Asha's Moms* and *Heather Has Two Mommies*. When Molly draws a picture of her family for a kindergarten open house, some of her peers tell her that she can't have two moms. The teacher and her moms help validate Molly and her family. In the end, Molly puts her picture up on the wall for the open house. The illustrations depict conservatively gendered and mostly white characters, reinforcing dominant power structures. People of colour, poor, working-class individuals, and those whose familial structures do not replicate nuclear family norms are "othered" when whiteness, class privilege, and normative family structures are used as sites through which select families with people in gay and lesbian relationships are validated. Additionally, such familial depictions detract from the book's literary quality as characters become stereotypes and their cultures lack the specificity that makes for engaging setting and scenery.

The trend of defending families with same-sex relationships on the basis of their conformity to mainstream standards can result in the replication of homophobic norms. For example, in *Zack's Story* (Greenberg, 1996), Zack reassures the reader that he plans on marrying a woman when he grows up (assuring the reader of his future heterosexuality) despite the fact that he has two moms. Would there be something wrong with him or his family if he, too, grew up to be gay? The overarching message of the story is that Zack has a good family; however, the attempt to normalize him results in Zack's potential heterosexuality becoming homophobic reinforcement of what validates his family—his family is okay because he is straight. Similarly in *How My Family Came to Be*, the reader is reassured that the (nameless) main character has female parental role models and friends from straight families. Again, this reiterates the notion that families with same-sex parents are inadequate in comparison to families with heterosexual parents. From a literary perspective, within this context of normalization, families with same-sex parents are generalized and lose the individualism that makes the members of a family amusing or interesting as characters in the story.

In both expository and background stories, there is a propensity for the same-sex relationship to cancel out any specific attributes the characters have. As a result, the same-sex relationship subsumes all other aspects of a person's identity in ways that a heterosexual relationship does not. The implications of such a trend counteract the explicit goal these books often have—to challenge homophobia.

However, not every picture book reflects the trends that I have critiqued. While the overall trends show a tendency towards problematic politics and literary shortcomings, there are examples of both background and expository books that do more to engage the reader and challenge oppression than those I have discussed.

One example in the category of background books is Bobbie Combs's *ABC: A Family Alphabet Book* (2001), which reflects a broader range of characters than the books previously discussed. In *ABC*, each letter of the alphabet is depicted in bright, original, and captivating illustrations. The letters are paired up to depict same-sex couples having fun with children. The different genders, ethnicities, and personalities expressed by the alphabet characters break up the emphasis on normalization that is commonly found in books depicting characters in same-sex relationships. The text that accompanies the illustrations describes what is going on in the picture: the couples and the kids are going to the zoo, the kids are waking up moms in the morning with big musical instruments, and so on. The images portray a wide enough range of activities that the depictions of the families move away from stock characters set up as normalizing role models.

Another example of a book in which the same-sex relationship is clear while not defaulting to a "moral message" is *And Tango Makes Three* by Justin Richardson and Peter Parnell (2005). *Tango* (for short) tells a true story about two male penguins who partner-up and make a nest together at the New York City Park Zoo. Whereas *ABC* shows a range of different familial networks in order to move away from heteronormative characters, *Tango* uses specificity in a way that alleviates the same-sex family from the responsibility of having to normalize all families outside the heterosexual mainstream. In the story, the two male penguins sit on rocks and other egg-shaped objects hoping that they will hatch. When a zookeeper eventually finds an egg in need of care, he gives it to them. Together, they take turns sitting on the egg until it hatches into a baby penguin, their little daughter, Tango. The illustrations bring the penguin characters to life, particularly little Tango, and successfully draw the reader into the story.

Within the expository category, Johnny Valentine's *One Dad, Two Dads, Brown Dads, Blue Dads* (1994) describes a family with two dads in a way that challenges homophobia. In *One Dad, Two Dads*, Lou, who "has two dads who both are blue," is asked questions by a friend who doesn't think anyone can have blue dads. After being asked "If they hug you too hard will the color come off?" and other allegorical questions, Lou shakes his head and wonders why his friend can ask such silly things. Lou replies, "They were blue when I got them and blue they are still." He declares that although "it is hard to see blue dads against a blue sky," his dads are "remarkable wonders" and their lives are just fine. It is a humorous Dr. Seuss-style explanation about how dads are dads in all their varieties.

The illustrations feature bold colours and combine images of the dads going about their activities and images of Lou's friend's silly questions about how the dads became blue. The story is amusing and there is a greater attention to language, cadence, and rhythm than in other books, which makes it entertaining to read out loud to audiences of younger children. Additionally, it is the questions Lou is asked and not Lou's family that are positioned as the problem. The focus is less heterosexist because the book does not assume the reader and the reader's family and friends are heterosexual and homophobic. However, despite these positive attributes, conflating issues of racism with "appreciating different colours" is problematic. It risks perpetuating the idea that anti-racism is about being "colour blind," which can subsequently erase considerations of white power and privilege. As well, the emphasis on appreciating difference because "we are all the same" can negate the celebration of difference. While this book successfully avoids homophobic traps, it would be strengthened by a deeper questioning of the systemic power of racism.

The normalizing trends within children's picture books depicting characters in same-sex relationships often shortchange literary quality and the ability to effectively convey a political message. Analyzing the books from both a literary and political framework, I found the concept of difference is often used in a problematic way. While espousing a politic of valuing diversity, the message frequently asserted is, conversely, that those outside the heterosexual mainstream are "okay" because they are *normal* and *just like everyone else*. If difference is only celebrated because it matches the status quo, then it is assimilation rather than difference that is actually being celebrated.

The nature of privilege is often invisible to those who have it. It is what is taken for granted. One of the ways in which privilege manifests itself is that those who hold it rarely have to question their place as subjects of their own experience, as opposed to objects for others to study. Children's picture books with characters in same-sex relationships continue to overwhelmingly position relationships outside the heterosexual mainstream as objects to be studied. The emphasis on these populations as "normal" turns individuals into stereotypes. While this may be done as an attempt to end homophobia, when one is turned into a symbol, one is no longer in the position of being a fully complex person or of inhabiting a culturally specific space. Creating an anti-oppressive political framework is a multifaceted task informed not only by ideologies but also by the pedagogical forms in which such ideologies are conveyed. Children's picture books that seek to end homophobia and heterosexism provide a rich landscape for examining how the form in which a politic is conveyed can be as crucial to challenging or reinforcing an ideology as the explicit politic itself. They are valuable examples of the multi-layered ways oppressive norms can be reiterated even as they are resisted. Such contradictions need to be addressed in order to understand how family structures outside the heteronormative mainstream are not yet being fully and effectively depicted in diverse and inclusive ways within children's picture books.

References

Alden, Joan. Illustrated by Catherine Hopkins. *A Boy's Best Friend*. Boston: Alyson Wonderland, 1992.

Aldrich, Andrew. Illustrated by Mike Motz. *How My Family Came to Be: Daddy, Papa, and Me*. Bel Air, CA: New Family Press, 2003.

Baker, Deidre, and Ken Setterington. *A Guide to Canadian Children's Books*. Toronto: McClelland and Stewart, 2003.

Bannerji, Himani. "But Who Speaks for US: Experience and Agency in Conventional Feminist Paradigms." In H. Bannerji et al., eds., *Unsettling Relations: The University as a Site of Feminist Struggles*. Toronto: Women's Press, 1991.

Combs, Bobbie. Illustrated by Danamarie Hosler. *ABC: A Family Alphabet Book*. Ridley Park: Two Lives Publishing, 2001.

Greenberg, Keith Elliot. Photographs by Carol Halebian. *Zack's Story*. Minneapolis: Lerner Publishing Group, 1996.

Kumashiro, Kevin K. "Against Repetition: Addressing Resistance to Anti-oppressive Change in the Practices of Learning, Teaching, Supervising, and Researching." *Harvard Educational Review* 72 (Spring 2002): 67–92.

Newman, Leslea. Illustrated by Russell Crocker. *Gloria Goes to Gay Pride*. Boston: Alyson Wonderland, 1991.

———. Illustrated by Diana Souza. *Heather Has Two Mommies*. 1st ed. Boston: Alyson Wonderland, 1989.

Parnell, Peter. Illustrated by Justin Richardson. *And Tango Makes Three*. New York: Simon and Schuster Children's Publishing, 2005.

Phelan, Shane. "(Be)Coming out: Lesbian Identity and Politics." In J. Dean, ed., *Feminism and the New Democracy*. Thousand Oaks, CA: Sage, 1997.

Rochman, Hazel. *Against Borders: Promoting Books for a Multicultural World*. Chicago: American Library Association, 1993.

Setterington, Ken. Illustrated by Alice Priestly. *Mum and Mum Are Getting Married*. Toronto: Second Story Press, 2004.

Valentine, Johnny. Illustrated by Lynette Schmidt. *One Dad, Two Dads, Brown Dad, Blue Dads*. Boston: Alyson Wonderland, 1994.

Wickens, Elaine. *Anna Day and the O-Ring*. Boston: Alyson Wonderland, 1994.

Willhoite, Michael. *Uncle What-Is-It Is Coming to Visit*. Boston: Alyson Wonderland, 1993.

———. *Daddy's Roommate*. Boston: Alyson Wonderland, 1990.

SECTION 3B

THE ECONOMY AND LABOUR

CHAPTER 19

Just Another Neo-liberal Worker: Tracing the State's Treatment of Low-Income Mothers

Margaret Hillyard Little

Historically poor single mothers in liberal democratic states were recognized for their caring work, receiving some state support, however minimal. In the last two decades, neo-liberal governments are no longer willing to recognize poor single mothers' caring work. Instead these governments have enacted a number of welfare reforms that see poor single mothers as workers. Workfare and other welfare tied to employment often ignore or minimize the enormous amount of caring work poor single mothers undertake. Through an examination of Canadian welfare policy, this paper explores the growing gap between what poor single mothers do on a daily basis and the state's expectations as revealed by neo-liberal welfare regulations.

Low-income mothering has never been adequately supported by the 20th-century liberal democratic welfare state. And yet, if we trace the last century of liberal democratic welfare states we see that some low-income single mothers who were considered morally and financially deserving received some state support (however inadequate) to permit them to reduce or reject paid work and concentrate on their mothering. Now, during a neo-liberal era, we have witnessed a tectonic shift in the liberal democratic welfare state's understanding of low-income mothering, which concentrates on women's paid versus unpaid work. This article examines the changes in Canadian welfare policy to demonstrate that the neo-liberal state increasingly ignores the mothering responsibilities of low-income mothers and attempts to view these mothers as just more potential workers to join many others in the precarious labour force. As such, mothering, particularly low-income mothering, is no longer viewed as a legitimate claim for state support.

When Low-Income Mothers Were Mothers First: The Canadian Historical Context

The introduction and development of welfare for single mothers in Canada during the early 1900s occurred during what is often termed the "maternal" era of state reform. In political and popular discourse, it was generally agreed that women's maternal duties made the genders quite distinct. During this period, the state and influential societal organizations defined women's role as deeply influenced by their imagined or real maternal responsibilities. Claims for women to obtain the vote or state financial support—through workers' compensation, mothers' allowances, or government supplements to the Canadian Patriotic Fund—were generally couched in maternal language (Little, 1998: 7-17). All of these policies supported a family wage model that assumed a male worker with dependent wife and children, or granted government support to the dependants if the male worker was absent or injured. This family wage model promoted a maternal ideology that assumed that a mother's first role was to care for her children, and this arrangement should be state-supported under certain circumstances.

The campaign across Canada for mothers' allowance clearly illustrated the maternal underpinnings of the call for state payments to low-income single mothers. Both male and female lobbyists promoted the notion of gender difference, advocating that women's "natural" role in life was that of caregiver, whereas men were "naturally" economic providers. Women's experiences as caregivers made them uniquely able to nurture both their families and society at large. It was argued that, if possible, every child needed his or her mother's constant attention and influence, and the state should provide financial support for this. Thereby, it was determined that low-income single mothers of "worthy" character should be encouraged to stay home and raise their children through regular state payments, as opposed to working full-time and having their children raised by others or placed in an orphanage. Of course, there was some disagreement about just which single mothers should be financially supported by the state and which ones were considered unworthy; race, ethnicity, religion, number of children, and moral character all played a role in this deliberation.

This maternalist ideology was gendered, but it was also elitist and racist. There has been some debate among American feminist scholars about whether this maternalist ideology crossed class and race divisions in the United States. But research of Canadian campaigns for mothers' allowances suggests that the debate in Canada was predominantly elitist. Labour and working-class advocates joined the lobby for mothers' allowances, promoting a similar familial model to their bourgeois counterparts—that of a working man with dependent wife and children. But labour and working-class lobbyists supported mothers' allowance policies for distinctive reasons. Whereas bourgeois lobbyists were concerned about poor children being abandoned in orphanages and poor women unable to afford to stay home and care for these children, labour lobbyists had different concerns. They were concerned with shoring up the male wage and believed that a policy that would deter working-class and poor mothers from working would help achieve this aim. Even though they had different aims most of the mothers' allowance lobbyists in Canada espoused a maternalist philosophy that assumed that a mother's primary responsibility was to provide care for her children. For instance, these lobbyists clearly opposed collective childcare, which would have freed poor women to engage in full-time employment, while they promoted mothers' allowance (Little, 1998; Strong-Boag, 1979; Ursel, 1992). Also, most of these mothers' allowance lobbyists had a similar race agenda. They clearly demonstrated their concern about the fragility of the White race and advocated a racist policy that shored up the White single-mother-led family at the expense of most ethnic minority and Aboriginal single mothers (Little, 1998).

More recently American historians have determined that not all maternalist reformers held the view that low-income mothers must remain at home full-time with their children. For instance, African-American maternalist reformers had a more realistic sense of how low-income African-American mothers juggled paid and unpaid work. As a result, these African-American maternalist reformers lobbied for a wider range of policy options, including low-cost childcare that more clearly met the real needs of many African-American mothers and their children (Boris, 1993). In Canada, we have yet to adequately explore the extent to which ethnic-minority maternal feminists of the early 1900s lobbied for a wider range of policies to support low-income women's paid and unpaid work than the White, bourgeois maternal feminists. It is also important to recognize that despite the motivations of early White maternal feminists to have low-income mothers remain in their homes, the policies adopted were often inadequate and consequently required low-income mothers to enter the paid workforce in order to survive (Goodwin, 1997; Little, 1998). We do know that many poor mothers protested vehemently against their need to take on paid work. They believed it was crucial that they stay at home to raise their children or to care for other dependants, and through letters to politicians, [...] and angry encounters with early state administrators they used a maternalist rhetoric in an attempt to have their concerns heard (Abel, 1998; Christie, 2000, 131–159; Little, 1998).

The welfare policy for low-income single mothers established in most provinces and eventually the territories was entrenched in this maternalist philosophy. In the 1920s, five of Canada's provinces had established a mothers' allowance policy, and all of these policies encouraged the female recipients to see mothering as their primary responsibility (Little, 1998). The majority of mothers' allowance lobbyists, steeped in maternalist values, favoured policies that would not require mothers to work outside the home. Despite the rhetoric, mothers' allowance payments were insufficient on their own and required mothers to conduct some part-time paid work. Mothers' allowance administrators vehemently discouraged full-time work, advising part-time work that was carefully monitored. As a result, mothers' allowance recipients tended to be involved in low-paid, female-ghetto jobs. It was clear that their first job was to be in the home and that they would obtain financial security only through remarriage. As a result, this policy encouraged a maternal ideal that met White middle-class standards rather than the long-term interests of its recipients. Women were persuaded to undertake part-time paid work and unpaid domestic work—neither of which would lead to economic security.

Administrators advised mothers on just what type of work they could do to earn money and still receive their allowance. Part-time work in the home that utilized the "natural" domestic skills of the mother was the preferred option. In fact, policy administrators insisted that single mothers refuse factory work in favour of domestic work such as selling pies, sewing, and laundry, even though factory work paid substantially more (Little, 1998).

The rise of male unemployment in the 1930s did little to dramatically challenge the maternalist underpinnings of mothers' allowance policy in Canada. Feminist historians argue that this was a period of gender crisis, as both masculine and feminine prescribed roles were challenged by the economic difficulties of the era. Gender boundaries were under enormous stress as men's jobs disappeared and the female labour force expanded. Margaret Hobbs argues that these gender identities underwent perhaps their biggest challenge of the modern industrial period during the Depression era (Hobbs, 1993a, 1993b; Gordon, 1994; Light and Pierson, 1990). Mothers' allowance rates across the country remained woefully inadequate during this difficult time. As in the past, single moms were forced to find some paid work to supplement their allowance. There is evidence from case files to demonstrate that mothers' allowance administrators reinforced traditional gender roles over the economic needs of the family. There were complaints from the public that mothers' allowance recipients were taking jobs away from others who could not receive public assistance. So although there was considerable gender slippage in "women's" and "men's" work in the larger community, the traditional definitions of women's work were carefully maintained by the mothers' allowance administrators. In the case of mothers' allowance recipients, their paid work was never to interfere with their primary responsibility: the care of their children. As in the 1920s, it remained clear in the 1930s that mother work was their first and most important job (Little, 1998).

The Second World War and the immediate postwar period raised new challenges about the role of women in society. Social programs such as Family Allowances (1944) and Unemployment Insurance (1940) demonstrated that the Canadian wartime and immediate postwar welfare state would be premised on a family-wage model where men were assumed to be the primary breadwinners and women remained in the home providing unpaid domestic care. Unprecedented employment opportunities characterized the war years and had a dramatic impact on welfare programs. Those considered employable who were unable to find work during the Depression were quickly absorbed into the expanding war economy. Even marginal workers, namely the partially disabled, single mothers, and even seniors, were attractive to employers during this economic boom. Increased employment opportunities also led to increased surveillance. In Ontario, the mothers' allowance administrators became suspicious of the possibility of mothers and children secretly doing paid work while collecting their mothers' allowance cheques. Consequently, the Ontario government almost doubled its number of mothers' allowance investigators in the early 1940s to ferret out single mothers or their children who were doing paid work (Little, 1998).

Through financial regulation of women and children in the postwar era, the nuclear family unit was remodelled. During this period of rapid social and economic change, the family model was used to quiet anxieties and achieve both political and personal goals. On the political front, this model was to exemplify the success of capitalism and Western democracy. And, personally, a home filled with children was to create a feeling of warmth and security—a haven from threatening social, economic, and political forces outside the door (May, 1988).

Mothers' allowance regulation reflected this desire to preserve and bolster the nuclear family model. Although the policy extended eligibility to new groups of single mothers, regulations continued to favour the male-breadwinner family. Administrators did send mothers outside the home in search of paid work, but this action did not threaten the male-breadwinner family model as the ideal familial unit. Mothers were not encouraged to take jobs that would lead to long-term financial security. Rather, they were urged to reinforce their domestic skills through paid work. The mothers' allowance policy assumed that these single mothers were only temporarily in the labour force and would return to their domestic subservient role if and when the right male breadwinner came along. Simultaneously, mothers' allowance amendments concerning children encouraged the young to extend their time as familial dependants and, consequently, prolong a mother's duties within the home. Also in support of this familial ideal, the mothers' allowance administration offered rehabilitation services for incapacitated husbands by the mid-1950s so that they could once again become the breadwinners (Little, 1998).

The 1960s and 1970s saw the consolidation of the Canadian welfare state—some existing programs were expanded, including Unemployment Insurance, as was subsidizing of post-secondary education, while certain new universal policies were introduced, such as medicare and seniors' benefits. And the Canada Assistance Plan committed the federal government to 50/50 unlimited cost-sharing with the provinces for health care, education, and welfare, as well as the creation of federal guidelines for these programs that perceived welfare as a right to all those in economic need. These programs helped to solidify a popular belief that the Canadian state could and should help to improve the socio-economic lives of its citizens. Although this is considered the golden age of the Canadian welfare state, large groups of ethnic minority men and women did not benefit equally from the arrangement. Those without full-time employment did not receive the full benefit of these more generous welfare state entitlements. Thus, the maternal ideology of a previous era was not significantly challenged by the war and postwar welfare state. An ideology that promoted the female-caretaker norm fit well with the more generous state benefits for the (male) full-time worker (Fudge and Vosko, 2003). Although single mothers were not granted state support to the same degree as full-time male workers, and in fact the family-wage model worked to perpetuate gender inequalities, there was still a recognition that these women should be acknowledged, however inadequately, for their maternal responsibilities.

The history of mothers' allowance in Canada from its introduction in the early 1900s to the early 1980s demonstrates that the state saw low-income single mothers' first responsibility as their unpaid domestic work. Despite dramatic changes in the labour market during this period, a maternalist philosophy continued to influence much of Canadian welfare for single mothers through the 1920s, the unemployment crisis of the 1930s, and the demand for female workers during the Second World War and the immediate postwar period. During this entire period, welfare payments to single mothers were inadequate. Because the payments did not begin to meet the real needs of single mothers, it was assumed that these women would supplement their government cheques with paid employment. But welfare administrators were adamant that this employment not interfere with mothering responsibilities. In addition, administrators permitted only the most gendered employment. It is only in the mid-1990s and the early twenty-first century, when a neo-liberal regime was entrenched, that this belief that single mothers are first and foremost mothers was dramatically challenged.

Neo-liberalism: Mothers Are Workers

The neo-liberal era has heralded seismic changes in the way the Canadian state views mothering, particularly for low-income single moms. Neo-liberalism is an ideology that dramatically changes how we perceive the role of the state, the economy, and the individual. It advocates decreased state regulation of capital and often increased state regulation of the marginalized—that is the poor, criminals, immigrants, and others. It glorifies competition as the best method to produce social good. And it understands human rights and equity concerns as the rights and equality to compete, ignoring or minimizing the fact that everyone does not meet at the starting line with the same abilities or equipment to compete fairly. Neo-liberalism promotes lower direct taxation and increased individual and market responsibility for various services. And through more punitive and restrictive social policies, the neo-liberal state blames the individual, rather than the market, for poverty and unemployment (Bakker, 1996; Bezanson and Luxton, 2006; Braedley and Luxton, 2010; Brodie, 1996). Such dramatic changes in state policy have affected the distribution of goods in a manner that intensifies inequities of gender, race, and class. These policy changes have affected all women, but especially those most dependent on the state, such as low-income single mothers.

Under a neo-liberal regime, women are predominantly viewed as gender-neutral workers. The male breadwinner-female caregiver model assumed by the Canadian state in the immediate postwar Keynesian welfare state era is no longer. Instead, the majority of women, both with and without young children, are involved in paid work. For example, in 2001, almost 70 per cent of mothers with children under six were in the labour force, and the majority was working full-time (Bezanson and Luxton, 2006). Yet, the Canadian state virtually ignores the mothering responsibilities of women in the workforce. Year after year, the federal government has refused to establish a national affordable, quality childcare program. Federal-provincial agreements such as the Canada Assistance Plan and the Established Programs Financing Act were replaced with the Canada Health and Social Transfer, which reduced funding to the provinces and encouraged them to place restrictions on eligibility. This policy change has had a tidal effect on most provincial social policies and services. First, numerous efforts to support workers and families from health care and education to community services and welfare have been scaled back in the neo-liberal era. Although there is some innovation in childcare and early childhood education by the provinces, especially Quebec, the federal government has remained intransigent in this arena. The result is that much caring work continues to be privatized, with middle- and upper-income workers employing low-paid precarious women workers, often women of colour, to fulfill caring responsibilities (Bakan and Stasiulis, 2005; Mahon, 2009). And at the same time, policies that receive the least popular support, namely benefits and services for the most marginalized, are the ones most vulnerable to cuts and eligibility restrictions.

These changes in the economy-family-state nexus have implications for all women but particularly for the most marginalized. Welfare policy across Canada, from the early 1900s to the 1980s, implicitly recognized mothering as the first duty of poor single mothers. This is no longer the case for most contemporary welfare policy in Canada. In the late 1980s, there were attempts in various provinces to place more emphasis on paid work for these single mothers. For instance, in 1989, the Ontario Liberal government established the Supports to Employment Program (STEP) to help ease the transition from welfare to paid work. STEP increased earning exemptions, provided special exemptions for training allowances, provided for the first months' costs of childcare, and offered start-up benefits for people starting new jobs. And the New Democratic Party government that followed produced a report that recommended that each single mother on welfare have an employment counsellor who would establish an "opportunity plan," an agreement about how a single mother planned to transition to full-time work (Little, 1998). Other provinces went even further to move low-income single mothers toward employment. Among the most ambitious projects were New Brunswick Works (NB Works) and the Self-Sufficiency Project in New Brunswick and British Columbia. NB Works, which ran in the 1990s, provided long-term training compared with most programs for welfare recipients, thereby allowing low-income women to gain academic upgrading and skills training that would make them able to compete for stable jobs at living wages. Participants, 84 per cent female, were provided with allowances at least equal to their previous welfare cheques and a childcare allowance. They participated in a community work placement following academic upgrading and training of their choice (McFarland and Mullaly, 1996). The Self-Sufficiency Project, which ran from 1992 to 1995, supplemented the wages of single mothers who were welfare recipients for up to three years, provided they were employed a minimum of thirty hours a week and remained off welfare. The purpose of these self-sufficiency projects was to financially supplement the earnings of the participants for a certain period, thereby lifting these people out of working poverty. This supplement helped single mothers pay for childcare, transportation, and other employment-related expenses. It was assumed that the participants were being trained in employment-related skills while on the job. It was also assumed that these women would be able to find better-paying jobs once the program ended.

But most of these retraining and wage-supplement programs specifically designed for poor single mothers did not lead to employment. The 1980s and early 1990s was a period of high unemployment; despite some retraining or supplements to their wages, poor single mothers generally could not find permanent employment. NB Works participants found that they were not able to complete their educational goals before the program disbanded. And some participants of the Self-Sufficiency Project had difficulty finding employment and were concerned that they would not be able to meet their childcare and other employment-related expenses once the supplement to the poorly paid job ended (Ford et al., 2003: ch. 2 and 4; McFarland, 2003: 201). Consequently these programs did very little to remove single mothers from poverty. Instead of investing in job opportunities so that single mothers would have a light at the end of the retraining tunnel, government abandoned the entire project of retraining poor single mothers. Today, there is virtually no training program across the country specifically designed for poor single mothers (Little, 2005).

Although the Self-Sufficiency Project and NB Works provided low-income single mothers with a choice of whether to enter training or employment, the writing was on the wall. Through these programs, a single mother could choose to spend the majority of her time in unpaid caring work, or she could choose to juggle unpaid and paid work. But even these choices were limited given that these welfare policies did not adequately appreciate the realities of women's paid and unpaid work responsibilities. It is hardly a choice to participate in an employment program if the alternative is to try to survive on welfare payments that do not meet basic needs. However, today, most neo-liberal welfare policies no longer present even these limited choices. Instead, single mothers are forced to be in the workforce and, in many cases, they can be denied welfare if they are not conducting some type of paid or volunteer work outside the home. In Quebec, the welfare benefit is reduced when a mother's youngest child enters school. The Ontario Conservative government in 1997 established workfare, which ties most welfare to employment or employment-related activity. Single mothers with children four years or older are expected to be involved in workfare activities or paid work and can be cut off all welfare payments if they do not comply. Some provincial welfare programs are more severe. Both Saskatchewan and Alberta welfare programs consider a mother to be employable when her youngest child is *six months old.* And British Columbia's welfare program states that an applicant must prove two years of prior work experience before she or he can be eligible for welfare (Little and Marks, 2010). Welfare programs that emphasize a current or previous attachment to the workforce clearly erode a single mother's choice to stay at home full-time and raise her children. For the first time in the history of welfare in Canada, poor single mothers are now considered paid workers, in some instances completely interchangeable with single childless adults. This development is what some feminist scholars call the gender-blind nature of neo-liberal policy. For now, welfare does not appreciate single mothers as having considerable unpaid caring responsibilities. Instead, these responsibilities are increasingly ignored as these women are treated as employable, requiring few if any supports to enter the paid-work world.

The main feature of welfare-tied-to-employment programs is their focus on individual characteristics such as educational level, job-seeking skills, work habits, the ability to write resumés, interviewing skills, and interpersonal presentation skills (Baker and Tippin, 1999). Increasingly, there is little recognition of mothering responsibilities that might interfere with a mother's time and commitment to paid work. Where previous welfare programs attempted to pay some lip service to childcare needs for mothers, and the better ones helped financially compensate low-income working mothers for their childcare costs, the situation has changed. Most low-income mothers transitioning from welfare to paid work receive less financial compensation for childcare expenses than before. Interviews with such women demonstrate time and again that these mothers are forced to place their children in substandard childcare arrangements because of the prohibitive costs and limited availability of state-regulated daycare (Little and Marks, 2010). Mothers transitioning from welfare to paid work are most often part of the precarious part-time employment sector, with work shifts that vary from day to day and week to week and do not fit the nine-to-five timeframe of most licensed childcare. These mothers constantly worry about their childcare arrangements as they shuffle their children from one unregulated space to another, juggling the irregularity of multiple part-time jobs and inconsistent work shifts (Little, 2001). Neither their unpaid caring responsibilities nor the responsibilities of those who replace them in these duties are addressed by welfare policies that focus on transitioning people from welfare to paid employment regardless of the monetary or intangible costs to the mother or the next generation. As workfare and welfare tied to employment have become the norm in this neo-liberal age, so has the increasing invisibility of caring work conducted by mothers and their replacements.

The Canadian state is not without contradictions in its treatment of mothering. Even though there is a general trend toward the invisibility of mothering, there are small pockets of policy where the state recognizes and reaffirms mothering. The federal government does recognize some caring responsibilities through tax-based incentives and certain social policies, but these have been dramatically scaled back in the neo-liberal era. For more than three decades, Ottawa provided the monthly Family Allowances to all families with children.[1] This has been replaced with the National Child Benefit (NCB), a benefit for low- and moderate-income families (McKeen and Porter, 2003). However, many provinces claw back the NCB from parents on welfare. This has the effect of the state recognizing this unpaid caring work for working poor families but not acknowledging this role among welfare poor families. Clearly, such policies demonstrate that the state is choosing which types of parenting to support and which to ignore. As well, Employment Insurance (EI) eligibility has been severely restricted. The proportion of the unemployed receiving EI has dropped from 83 per cent in 1989 to 42 per cent in 1997. Among those who have become ineligible are the more marginal workers who are employed less than full-time, with little job security (McKeen and Porter, 2003; Porter, 2003). This describes many working-class and working-poor women. The federal government's childcare contribution of $100 per month per child under six years old recognizes unpaid childcare at the same time as it makes it impossible for low-income parents to rely solely on this income to care for a child. Thus, the Canadian state recognizes some mothering but, at the same time, policies have restricted just which mothers should be financially supported and under what conditions.

At the same time that the Canadian state has re-shaped social policy to minimize its support of low-income mothering it has simultaneously increased its regulation of these mothers. The state has rationalized this surveillance of marginalized families as necessary to ensure the social, psychological, and physical health of Canadian children. By shifting state discourse from "mothers" to "children" the state has increased the invisibility of mothering work. In the name of promoting healthy children, a number of Children's Aid Societies in Canada now include poverty as a form of child abuse and neglect and a reason to apprehend children. Increasingly, staff at women's and domestic violence shelters must report to the state families where they believe poverty may affect the health of the child (Bumiller, 2008; Krane and Carleton, 2011). And many jurisdictions in Canada have established centres to promote healthy children where the staff at these centres are encouraged to conduct visits to low-income homes to promote the healthy development of children (McKeen, 2007). While much of this social work is done in the name of being "helpful" to children and their marginalized families, this help is intrusive and often moralistic, embued with White middle-class values of parenting. Many of the so-called "problems" that these state social workers will find in these marginalized homes are due to the fact that these families are in economic crisis and mothers are forced to attempt to balance part-time work or workfare placements with full-time parenting responsibilities. If welfare rates were at a level that met the needs of low-income families, some of these social, psychological health problems of children and their mothers would disappear. Thus, through a discourse that focuses on children's health and ignores unpaid mothering work the neo-liberal state has justified increased surveillance of low-income mothers.

Conclusion: The Neo-liberal Dilemma for Low-Income Mothers

Over the last 30 years of neo-liberal social policy making we have seen a dramatic shift in the state's commitment to low-income mothering. During the hey-day of maternalism in the early 1900s the Canadian state introduced policies such as mothers' allowance, which recognized low-income mothers as mothers first and foremost. These maternal policies did not sufficiently support low-income mothers nor did it recognize all low-income mothers but it did endorse a philosophy that recognized that low-income mothers who were deemed "worthy" did considerable unpaid care work and that this work should be acknowledged by the state, however inadequately. One hundred years later the neo-liberal Canadian state no longer has a commitment to recognize low-income mothers' unpaid care work. Instead, state policy strongly encourages low-income mothers to make their first priority their participation in the workforce. And yet at the same time, state administrators are quick to blame these mothers when they are not able to adequately carry out their unpaid caring responsibilities in the home. This creates new challenges for low-income mothers who are attempting to raise their children with woefully inadequate state support while juggling paid work that does not fully recognize their parenting responsibilities. Such is the neo-liberal dilemma for low-income mothers that has not been adequately addressed by mainstream feminists, social workers, or politicians.

Note

1. One exception to this universal policy was the federal government's treatment of Inuit people. Instead of a monthly allowance cheque, families received food and staples that were insensitive to Inuit culture; see Kulchyski and Tester, 1994.

References

Abel, Emily (1998). A Valuing Care: Turn-of-the-Century Conflicts between Charity Works and Women Clients. *Journal of Women's History*, 10(3) (Autumn) 34-50.

Bakan, Abigail, and Daiva Stasiulis (2005). *Negotiating Citizenship: Migrant Women in Canada and the Global Context.* Toronto: University of Toronto Press.

Baker, Maureen, and David Tippin (1999). *Poverty, Social Assistance, and the Employability of Mothers: Restructuring Welfare States.* Toronto: University of Toronto Press.

Bakker, Isabella (Ed.) (1996). *Rethinking, Restructuring: Gender and Change in Canada.* Toronto: University of Toronto Press.

Bezanson, Kate, and Meg Luxton (Eds.) (2006). *Social Reproduction: Feminist Political Economy Challenges Neo-Liberalism.* Kingston: McGill-Queen's University Press.

Boris, Eileen (1993). The Power of Motherhood: Black and White Activist Women Redefine the Political. In Seth Koven and Sonya Michel (Eds.), *Mothers of New World: Maternalist Politics and the Origins of Welfare States* (pp. 215-245). New York: Routledge.

Braedley, Susan and Meg Luxton (Eds.) (2010). *Neoliberalism and Everyday Life.* Kingston: McGill-Queen's University Press.

Brodie, Janine (Ed.) (1996). *Women and Canadian Public Policy.* Toronto: Harcourt Brace.

Bumiller, Kristin (2008). *In an Abusive State: How Neoliberalism Appropriated the Feminist Movement Against Sexual Violence.* Durham: Duke University Press.

Christie, Nancy (2000). *Engendering the State: Family, Work and Welfare in Canada.* Toronto: University of Toronto Press.

Ford, Reuben, David Gyarmati, Kelly Foly, Doug Tattrie with Liza Jimenez (2003). *Can Work Incentives Pay for Themselves?* Ottawa: Social Research and Demonstration Corporation.

Fudge, Judy and Leah F. Vosko (2003). Gender Paradoxes and the Rise of Contingent Work: Towards a Transformative Political Economy of the Labour Market. In Wallace Clement and Leah F. Vosko (Eds.), *Changing Canada: Political Economy as Transformation* (pp. 183-209). Montreal: McGill-Queen's University Press.

Goodwin, Joanne (1997). *Gender and the Politics of Welfare Reform: Mothers' Pensions in Chicago, 1911-1929.* Chicago: University of Chicago Press.

Gordon, Linda (1994). *Pitied But Not Entitled: Single Mothers and the History of Welfare.* New York: Free Press.

Hobbs, Margaret (1993a). Rethinking Antifeminism in the 1930s: A Response to Alice Kessler-Harris. *Gender & History*, 5(1): 4-15.

Hobbs, Margaret (1993b). Equality and Difference: Feminism and the Defence of Women Workers During the Great Depression. *Labour/Le Travail*, 32: 201-223.

Krane, Julia and Rosemary Carleton, Practising at the Crossroads: Understanding Women as Mothers in Shelter Settings. Conference Paper, Violence Against Women: Complex Realities and New Issues in a Changing World, Montreal, May 31, 2011.

Kulchyski, Peter and Frank Tester (1994). *Tammarniit (Mistakes): Inuit Relocation in the Eastern Arctic, 1939-63.* Vancouver: University of British Columbia Press.

Light, Beth and Ruth Roach Pierson (1990). *No Easy Road: Women in Canada 1920s to 1960s.* Toronto: New Hogtown Press.

Little, Margaret Hillyard (1998). *No Car, No Radio, No Liquor Permit: The Moral Regulation of Single Mothers in Ontario.* Toronto: Oxford University Press.

Little, Margaret Hillyard (2001). A Litmus Test for Democracy: The Impact of Ontario Welfare Changes on Single Mothers. *Studies in Political Economy*, 66(Autumn): 9-36.

Little, Margaret Hillyard (2005). *If I Had a Hammer: Retraining that Really Works.* Vancouver: University of British Columbia Press.

Little, Margaret Hillyard and Lynne Marks (2010). Ontario and British Columbia Welfare Policy: Variants on a Neoliberal Theme. *Comparative Studies of South Asia, Middle East and Africa*, 30(2): 192-203.

Mahon, Rianne (2009). Canada's Early Childhood Education and Care Policy: Still a Laggard? *International Journal of Childcare and Education Policy* 3(1): 27–42.

May, Elaine Tyler (1988). *Homeward Bound: American Families in the Cold War Era.* New York: Basic Books.

McFarland, Joan (2003). Public Policy and Women's Access to Training in New Brunswick. In Marjorie Griffin Cohen (Ed.), *Training the Excluded for Work* (pp. 193-213). Vancouver: University of British Columbia Press.

McFarland, Joan and Bob Mullaly (1996). NB Works: Images vs. Reality. In Jane Pulkingham and Gordon Ternowetsky (Eds.), *Remaking Social Policy: Social Security in the Late 1990s* (pp. 202-219).Halifax: Fernwood Press.

McKeen, Wendy (2007). The National Children's Agenda: A Neoliberal Wolf in Lamb's Clothing. *Studies in Political Economy*, 80(Autumn): 151-173.

McKeen, Wendy and Ann Porter (2003). Politics and Transformation: Welfare State Restructuring in Canada. In Wallace Clement and Leah F. Vosko (Eds.), *Changing Canada: Political Economy as Transformation* (pp. 119-122). Kingston: McGill-Queen's University Press.

Porter, Ann (2003). *Gendered States: Women, Unemployment Insurance, and the Political Economy of the Welfare State in Canada, 1945-1997.* Toronto: University of Toronto Press.

Strong-Boag, Veronica (1979). Wages for Housework: Mothers' Allowances and the Beginning of Social Security in Canada. *Journal of Canadian Studies*, 4(2): 24-34.

Ursel, Jane (1992). *Private Lives, Public Policy.* Toronto: Women's Press.

CHAPTER 20

Does Citizenship Status Matter in Canadian Agriculture? Workplace Health and Safety for Migrant and Immigrant Laborers

Kerry Preibisch and Gerardo Otero

Introduction

Like most advanced capitalist countries in the "global age of migration" (Castles and Miller 2009), Canada has dramatically increased its noncitizen, migrant population since the 1970s. In 2011, Canada welcomed a historically high number of migrants on temporary employment authorization, marking a significant policy shift for a nation with "an unusually strong immigration tradition" (Cornelius, Martin, and Hollifield 1994:119). Unlike the United States, where unauthorized immigrants add some 8.3 million workers to the labor force (Passel and Cohn 2009), or the European Union, where the common labor market resulted in significant movement from eastern to western member states following the 2004 enlargement (Holland 2012), Canada's large increases in labor migration have occurred largely through the country's suite of temporary migration programs. The latest rise in temporary migration has been most pronounced in the West, where temporary worker entries began outpacing those of permanent residents by 2007 in Alberta and 2008 in British Columbia (Citizenship and Immigration Canada 2012). Rising numbers of temporary workers have been opposed by anti-immigrant campaigners (Centre for Immigration Reform 2013; Immigration Watch Canada 2012) and the general public (Tomlinson 2013), but most forcefully by a growing social movement that identifies a range of exploitative practices emerging from the citizenship and immigration restrictions placed on migrants excluded from the rights and entitlements granted to citizens and permanent residents (Alberta Federation of Labour 2009; Justicia for Migrant Workers 2013; Migrant Workers Alliance for Change 2013; United Food and Commercial Workers of Canada and Agriculture Workers Alliance 2011). At the heart of this movement is the demand to grant migrant workers permanent resident status on arrival, that is, a removal of conditions on their right to remain.

[...] Although policymakers laud the benefits of managed migration schemes (see Hennebry and Preibisch 2010), scholars have pointed to their overly exploitative nature (Bakan and Stasiulis 2003; Binford 2009; Griffith 2006; Mannon et al. 2012). Canada's Temporary Foreign Worker Program, an umbrella program encompassing numerous initiatives, has been criticized for creating a system of legislated inequality (Lenard and Straehle 2012) and even global apartheid (Sharma 2006; Walia 2010). Critics allege that temporary migrants should be theorized as unfree participants in the national labor market (Bakan and Stasiulis 2003; Basok 2002; Satzewich 1991; Sharma 1995). The principal basis of migrants' unfreedom is their categorization as "foreign workers," a move that allows the state to legally deny them the rights and entitlements associated with citizenship and to impose restrictions on their labor mobility, such as closed permits or requirements to live in or on their employer's property (Bakan and Stasiulis 2012; Sharma 2006). For migrant workers in low-skilled occupations, these restrictions are compounded by poor working conditions and substandard wages (Piper 2008). Migrant employment tends to reinforce these jobs as low-paid, difficult, and dangerous (Saucedo 2006; Waldinger and Lichter 2003). It has also allowed employers to exercise labor arrangements that would be difficult to implement with an all-citizen labor force (Rogaly 2008). Since citizens also work in these occupations, researchers have thus cautioned against associating extreme forms of labor exploitation exclusively with migrant status (Goldring and Landolt 2012; Scott, Craig, and Geddes 2012). Indeed, the employment of migrants may [have] consequences for all workers, including those with formal citizenship or landed immigrant status, who may find it difficult to exit these jobs no matter how undesirable they become.

In this article, [...] we explore the comparative consequences in health and safety for two groups of farmworkers in Canada: migrants from Mexico under the Seasonal Agricultural Workers Program (SAWP) and immigrants from India holding Canadian citizenship or permanent residency. "Migrant" here refers to foreigners on temporary employment authorization, unless specified otherwise, and "immigrant" refers to foreign-born naturalized citizens or permanent residents (landed immigrants). Unauthorized migrants compose a marginal segment of the agricultural labor force so were not included (Basok and Rivas 2012). We conducted field research in British Columbia, Canada's westernmost province and fourth largest agriculture and food processing labor market, which only began hiring Mexican migrants in 2004. Since British Columbia's agricultural employers had been prevented from using the SAWP before this date due to provincial government attempts to protect the domestic labor market that, until then, was almost exclusively composed of South Asian immigrants, this case study allowed us to study migrant incorporation at the outset. Although there are other immigrant and Canadian-born farmworkers employed in agriculture, including whites, our study comprises the bulk of the workforce.

The research took place between 2007 and 2009 and included face-to-face questionnaires with 200 farmworkers (100 Mexican migrants, 100 South Asian immigrants), 53 in-depth interviews with stakeholders (farmworkers, growers, industry representatives, Canadian and Mexican civil servants, and advocacy groups), and a detailed review of secondary data. [...] Since no list of the total farmworker population exists, precluding random sampling, we recruited participants from the three valleys that together account for nearly three quarters of British Columbia's horticultural farms. We contacted Mexican participants at churches, supermarkets, or migrant support centers and South Asian farmworkers through service providers. Our research team conducted interviews and questionnaires in Spanish, Punjabi, or

English, fostering rapport through shared language, skills of empathetic listening, and a conversational approach. [...]

We first chart changes in temporary migration in Canada with respect to agriculture and food industries. Second, we situate agricultural employment as precarious work, explore the nascent Canadian literature on migrant health, and position our research within the literature on precarious legal status. We then turn to our field results on workplace health and safety, where we explore a range of findings regarding coercive labor practices, working hours, and labor intensity; workplaces, transportation, and housing; training and language barriers; and access to health care.

Canadian Immigration Policy and Agrifood Labor Markets

Since the mid-1970s, a significant shift in migration to Canada has been the relative decline in numbers of new permanent residents alongside rising numbers of migrants on temporary employment authorization, in other words, from a flow of people to a flow of labor power (Arat-Koc 2009; Sharma 2012). This trend has become pronounced in recent years: since 2000, temporary migrant entries have more than tripled to reach a high of 300,211 in 2011 as a result of policies to expand the authorized use of migrants in jobs designated as low-skilled (Citizenship and Immigration Canada 2012:59). Prior to 2002, agriculture and domestic work were the only occupations classified as low-skilled that had formalized temporary migration programs designed to admit migrant workers. Migrant farmworkers entered Canada through the SAWP, a postwar, sector-specific guest worker program that began in 1966 with a bilateral agreement between Canada and Jamaica and subsequently expanded to include 11 Caribbean countries and Mexico. Owing to its seasonal policy intent and sectoral focus, the SAWP runs from January 1 to December 15, issues work permits for a maximum of eight months, and is available only to producers of specific commodities considered on-farm, primary agriculture. In 2002, the government launched the Stream for Low-Skilled Occupations, a unilateral immigration initiative that allowed approved employers from any sector to recruit migrant workers into jobs categorized as low-skilled. This initiative simultaneously enabled a broader range of agrifood industries access to temporary migrants and, since it was not bound by bilateral agreements, permitted migrants from a broader range of countries access to the Canadian labor market. Further policy adjustments meant that, by 2012, agrifood employers could hire temporary migrants under four different initiatives, all of which were experiencing growth.

Canadian agricultural production has a long history of immigrant and migrant employment that began before (and has consolidated alongside) formalized temporary migration programs. In British Columbia, Lanthier and Wong (2002) document the labor incorporation and exodus between 1880 and 1960 of racialized immigrants and migrants, including Pacific Northwest indigenous, Chinese, Japanese, Doukhobor, and Portuguese farmworkers. In the 1960s, the removal of racist criteria favoring white settlement from Canada's immigration policy led to increased immigration from the Indian subcontinent that again altered the social composition of the province's agricultural workforce. By 2003, some 98 percent of British Columbia's 6,000 farmworkers were South Asian immigrants with limited or no English proficiency (BC Public Service Agency 2003). Most were newcomers; Runsten et al. (2000) found that two-thirds of workers employed by farm labor contractors (FLCs) had entered Canada less than three years before. This workforce is, and has consistently been, predominantly female (Fairey et al. 2008; Sharma 2012), reflecting in part the workers' migration trajectory as family-class immigrants, a category that allows Canadian citizens or permanent residents to sponsor the immigration of parents and children. Among family-class immigrants, women outnumber men three to two (Citizenship and Immigration Canada 2008:148).

The social composition of British Columbia's labor force started to shift again in 2004 when the provincial government allowed growers to access the federal SAWP. In the ensuing five years, migrant employment skyrocketed. While just 47 Mexican workers arrived in 2004, by 2008 they numbered almost 3,000. Since the contracted farmworker population composed predominantly of South Asian immigrants remained more or less stable in that period, this means that in five years Mexican migrants came to represent half of British Columbia's seasonal agricultural labor force. In 2011, most Mexican migrants were employed in fruit or vegetable production and some 96 percent were male (Moral del Arbona 2011). By 2011, British Columbia accounted for 14 percent of all approved SAWP positions countrywide, just under 4,000 jobs (Employment and Social Development Canada 2013).

Agricultural Labor Markets and Precarious Employment

Agrifood employment is located at the bottom of Canada's occupational hierarchy, with most jobs in the sector exhibiting indicators of precarious work [...] (Goldring and Landolt 2012; Rodgers and Rodgers 1989; Vosko 2006). First, farm labor tends not to involve contracts.[1] Across Canada, but particularly in British Columbia, FLCs provide the bulk of seasonal labor. Second, work schedules on many farms involve significant seasonal variation and hours that are inconsistent, demanding, and unconventional (Lanthier and Wong 2002; Sergeant and Tucker 2009). Third, wage structures vary between hourly wages and piecework, with few salaried full-time positions. A 2008 study found that British Columbia's immigrant farmworkers lacked secure income and were often paid piece rates and below the minimum wage (Fairey et al. 2008). Fourth, benefits are scarce or nonexistent; in British Columbia, farmworkers lack overtime pay and other benefits enjoyed outside the industry such as paid statutory holidays, paid rest periods, and annual vacation (Fairey et al. 2008). Fifth, farmworkers' place of work can also shift between multiple sites, particularly for those contracted by FLCs. Finally, few farmworkers are unionized and in some provinces (which in Canada have jurisdiction over labor standards and health) it is illegal for them to do so (Tucker 2012). Like the United States and other high-income countries (Getz, Brown, and Shreck 2008; Luna 1998), Canada has excluded farmworkers from laws that set standards for working conditions and protect most workers historically (Tucker 2012).

Agriculture is [...] one of the most dangerous [job sectors] (Pickett et al. 1999; Sharpe and Hardt 2006). Workers' compensation figures depict a hazardous occupation in which workers take longer to recover from injuries sustained at work and have a higher serious injury rate than the all-industry average (WorkSafeBC 2012). Research on farmworker health, however, remained limited prior to 2000 (Bolaria, Basran, and Hay 1988; Bolaria, Hay, and Basran 1992), when rising migrant employment sparked new scholarly interest (Duarte and Sánchez 2008; Hennebry, Preibisch and McLaughlin 2010; McLaughlin 2009; Otero and Preibisch 2010; Pysklywec et al. 2011; Tucker 2006). [...]

This emerging research identifies the principal occupational risks for farmworkers as exposure to agrochemicals, plants, soil, insects, sun, and climatic extremes; hazards posed by machines, vehicles, and confined spaces; and repetitive and stressful ergonomic positions (Hennebry et al. 2010; McLaughlin 2009). Repetitive motion and accidents constitute some of the principal occupational exposures in agriculture that can present acute problems and long-term disabilities (Hennebry 2008). Some farmworkers perform tasks that involve constantly breathing in particles or work in poorly ventilated, enclosed spaces; in 2008, three workers at a British Columbia mushroom farm were killed and another two left with severe brain damage after being overcome by toxic gas in a composting shed (*CBC News* 2012).

In addition, unsafe transportation constitutes a significant occupational health hazard, particularly for farmworkers hired by contractors who are known to use unsafe vehicles and careless, tired, untrained, or unlicensed drivers (Fairey et al. 2008). A coroner's report into a major traffic accident in 2007 that resulted in the deaths of three greenhouse workers found that the 15-passenger van had faulty brakes and poor tires, was overloaded, and was equipped with only two seatbelts (*CBC News* 2009). In a second major accident in 2012 that killed ten farmworkers (nine of them Peruvian migrants) and the driver of the oncoming vehicle, police found that the driver transporting the farmworkers was not properly licensed (Ontario Provincial Police 2012). Poor living conditions constitute a further principal health risk. Rural housing is often low quality, underserviced, and overcrowded. In addition, chemical overspraying or drift poses hazards for those who live on, or adjacent to, their worksites (Arcury et al. 2005; Quandt et al. 2006). Poor hygiene and sanitary conditions at the workplace and in farmworker housing have also been identified as key hazards, including compromised access to adequate drinking water and hand-washing, toilet, and laundry facilities (Hennebry et al. 2010).

[...] Migrant farmworkers face substantial barriers to addressing health concerns, including limited information regarding health services and resources as well as legal protection and health insurance coverage (McLaughlin 2009; Preibisch and Hennebry 2011). Language barriers further compromise access to and quality of treatment. Moreover, both immigrant and migrant farmworkers lack secure income and thus may be unwilling to forfeit wages by taking time off from work (Downes and Odle-Worrell 2003; Fairey et al. 2008; Preibisch and Hennebry 2011). Farmworkers also tend to refrain from using health services and fail to report work-related illnesses or injuries to their employers in order to protect their employment or immigration status (Fairey et al. 2008; Hennebry et al. 2010; Sergeant and Tucker

2009). In addition, immigrant and migrant farmworkers' social and geographical isolation acts as a barrier to health care, particularly when some employers resist their requests for medical treatment (Verduzco and Lozano 2003). Undeniably, wage labor in agriculture is not only highly precarious but carries significant health and safety risks for workers, particularly those with less-than-full citizenship status. Because migrant workers are separated from their families and communities while in Canada, they have an incentive to work as much as possible. This fact plays well into employers' own incentives to extort as much labor from as few workers as possible.

Farmworker Health and Safety in British Columbia

Across high-income countries, immigrant and migrant farmworkers carry out many of the same tasks, often on the same kinds of farms, but with contrasting relationships to (and positions within) multiple and overlapping social relations of power (gender, race or ethnicity, age, sexuality, rural or (sub)urban location, state citizenship, class). Such differences have consequences for the structural realities of their lives and their ability to exercise their rights. For migrant guest workers, precarious legal status stems primarily from time-limited, employer-specific work permits that highly constrain their labor mobility and, consequently, dampen their bargaining power. Crucially, employers can deport workers or give them a negative evaluation at the end of the season, thus jeopardizing future job placements. Thus, the lack of a dismissal review process in their contracts or the right to be rehired each year before new workers, along with sending-country practices of labor control (e.g., worker evaluations or compulsory savings schemes), constitutes migrants as a highly disciplined, vulnerable workforce. Other coercive features of temporary migration programs include forced rotation, obliging migrants to return home at the end of their contracts as a precondition for subsequent employment. Migrant farmworkers in Canada are offered no route to permanent residency and policies are in place to discourage or prohibit them from bringing their dependants, a factor that shapes their willingness to accept longer, antisocial hours (Basok 2002; Preibisch and Binford 2007). This disciplinary tactic is reinforced by recruitment policies that privilege married applicants with dependants. Furthermore, temporary migrants reside on property owned or rented by their employer, living arrangements known to foster personal labor relations and extend employers' control beyond the sphere of work (Wall 1992). The architecture and operation of Canada's guest worker programs ensure that while temporary migrants share many of the same rights as domestic workers, they face challenges to exercising them.

While immigrant farmworkers enjoy permanent residency or full citizenship, the nature of their immigration trajectories also positions them precariously in the labor market. They fall within the definition of precarious status because their categorization as family-class immigrants subordinates them to the person who sponsors their entry into Canada—often a son, son-in-law, or husband (Oxman-Martinez et al. 2005). Sponsors agree to financially support their dependants for 10 years (even if the sponsored immigrant becomes a Canadian citizen in that period), including repaying any social assistance they may incur (Ontario Ministry of

Community and Social Services 2013). Family-class immigrants constitute a more vulnerable segment of the workforce if they feel compelled to repay their families for bringing them to Canada and supporting them, at times remaining in employment despite poor working conditions, ill health, or old age (Fairey et al. 2008; Oxman-Martinez et al. 2005).

Furthermore, while immigrants in this category have the right to move freely in the labor market, their mobility is hindered by language ability, age, suburban location, and often their gendered responsibilities for social reproduction. Because of this limitation, family-class immigrants come to depend heavily on the farm labor contracting system for employment, an institution notorious for its exploitative labor practices (Bush and Canadian Farmworkers Union 1995; Moore 2004). FLCs act as intermediaries between workers and growers, supplying laborers, arranging wages, and providing transportation, thus linking a predominantly suburban-sited, immobile group to the agricultural labor market.[2] FLCs are these workers' formal employer, rather than farm owners or operators. Strong kinship ties, with origins in the Punjab region of India, further shape workers' loyalty to contractors, even when these relationships are abusive (Bush and Canadian Farmworkers Union 1995). Growers continue to rely on FLCs, despite their history of flaunting employment standards and violating safety regulations (Fairey et al. 2008; Moore 2004). Moore (2004) reports that 69 percent of FLCs involved in site visits by provincial authorities in 2003 were in contravention of "core issues," including entitlements to payment of wages and adhering to the minimum wage and had fraudulent payroll records. Overall, labor contracting has multiple implications for the employment relationship, including the potential to discourage growers from training contract workers and, consequently, increase the risk of accidents (Guadalupe 2003). [...]

The social contours of our survey participants corroborated existing descriptions of the workforce. On average, South Asian immigrant farmworkers were older, married women who came from India as family-class immigrants and now held Canadian citizenship (65 percent) or permanent residence (35 percent). Most had very little formal education: more than a fifth lacked primary school education. Conversely, Mexican migrants were most often young, married men and had completed junior high school or higher. The majority were from the most populous (and poorest) central and southern states of Mexico and more than half spoke an indigenous language, a strong indicator of indigeneity. [...]

Coercive Labor Practices, Working Hours, and Labor Intensity

Our research found a labor regime in agriculture characterized by coercive employment practices occurring in a weak regulatory environment, with serious consequences for workplace health and safety, even for those who had achieved formal citizenship. To begin, a principal finding was that farmworkers' fear of losing hours or jeopardizing their current or future employment led both groups to accept work or transportation they perceived as unsafe, to work long hours, to work while ill or injured, and, in the case of migrants, to acquiesce to poor housing. A common perception among Mexican migrants was that questioning their employers, let alone refusing work or long hours, would risk their current and long-term employment in the SAWP through a negative evaluation, failure to be recalled, or premature dismissal or deportation. The following remarks by a Mexican migrant illustrate migrants' reticence to raise concerns: "the tractors don't have signal lights and the brakes are failing. Sometimes you have to drive on the highway when you're going from one field to another, and this worries me. But if [my employer] says the signal lights or brakes are working, I'm not going to contradict him." South Asian immigrants similarly feared that speaking out could result in losing both income and their jobs. As one former farmworker turned advocate explained, "today if I speak something against the contractor, the next day I'm not going to be picked up. He'll say, 'Fine, stay at home. You'll come to know.' "

Fear of losing hours or jeopardizing future employment led both immigrants (79 percent) and migrants (69 percent) to work when ill or injured or avoid reporting health concerns. Our interviews included statements such as these from two Mexican migrants: "We tolerate the pain and don't say anything"; "there are people who have injured themselves horribly, and even so they keep working." In addition to short-term economic motivations such as losing hours for working while ill or injured was a general fear of employer reprisals. When respondents were asked to agree or disagree with the statement, "On my farm there are coworkers who work when they are ill because they are afraid to tell the boss," 48 percent of Mexican migrants responded affirmatively, as did 44 percent of South Asian immigrants. The following statements illustrate this view: "You don't want to stop working because you think maybe they [employers] won't ask for me [next year] if they see me complain and because I'm hurt" (Mexican migrant); "I'm still in pain, but I've decided not to say anything because I'm ashamed [and] afraid the boss will send me back to Mexico" (Mexican migrant); "I have felt sick a few times at work, but I was afraid that the owner may get angry at me if I asked for a holiday" (South Asian immigrant). Farmworker advocates said that a common employer response to illness or injury among migrants was firing the individual and arranging his or her deportation. This practice has been widely documented in eastern Canada (Basok 2002; Hennebry 2006; McLaughlin 2009; United Food and Commercial Workers Canada 2005).

Fear was also fostered through degrading treatment. Study participants reported receiving verbal aggression (yelling, insults, racist remarks) and even physical violence. When asked to rate activities they carried out on the job in terms of the perceived risk to their health and safety on a scale of 1 to 10 where 1 indicated very low risk and 10 indicated very high risk (hereafter the "risk scale"), 44 percent of the Mexican migrants and 22 percent of South Asian immigrants rated "working with an aggressive boss or supervisor" as high-risk (≥7). Thus while both groups perceived aggressive management as a risk, it was of considerably greater concern to Mexican migrants.

Fear of jeopardizing their employment is also inducing both groups to acquiesce to long shifts. Mexican migrants, however, worked significantly longer shifts than their South Asian counterparts. Our survey found that during high production, Mexican migrants worked an average of 12 hours on weekdays and 8 hours on Saturday and Sunday, while South Asian respondents averaged 9 hours on weekdays and 5 hours Saturday and Sunday. [...]

Amendments in 2001 to British Columbia's Employment Standards Act, which governs minimum wage, hours of work, and holiday pay, have likely exacerbated the already long shifts that characterize seasonal farm work. Farmworkers lost their entitlement to overtime pay and had to work longer to compensate for wages they lost through other mechanisms, such as cuts to the minimum piece-rate wage. In 2008, a study calculated that Canadian farmworkers on piece rates were earning just over $5.00 per hour (Fairey et al. 2008) at the time that Mexican migrants were making $8.90 per hour. The self-disciplining character of piece rates operates in a distinct institutionalized context of social protection whereby eligibility for employment insurance in the off-season (an entitlement denied to migrant workers) requires recent labor market entrants to accumulate a minimum of 910 hours the first season and a minimum of 700 hours in following years (Fairey et al. 2008). Because employment opportunities in agriculture diminish substantially in the winter, Canadian workers often rely heavily on employment insurance payments to complement their income (Fairey et al. 2008). Immigrant farmworkers may thus acquiesce to prolonged work hours, consequently placing themselves at an increased risk of workplace injuries and accidents, or work while ill or injured. Guest workers are protected from this form of wage theft since their employers are contractually obliged to pay them annually negotiated hourly rates. [...]

In agriculture, the occupational health hazards of fatigue (Lilley et al. 2002) occur in workplaces that involve physically demanding tasks carried out at an intense pace (Basok and Rivas 2012). Study participants perceived that unreasonable productivity targets, piece-rate wage systems, and pressure from management intensified the production process to an extent that was increasing their risk of workplace injury. As one Mexican migrant recounted: "Since we use very sharp knives and they ask us to cut very quickly, there's always a risk. They ask us to cut 13 boxes of [green peppers] per hour per person, so you have to work very fast, and I've cut myself twice." To further illustrate, a South Asian immigrant argued that "To make work safer, I feel that we should receive three breaks per day and not get pushed so hard by our contractor to work faster." Employers were also using ethnic or national competition as a disciplinary tactic to increase productivity or gain acquiescence and were intimidating South Asian farmworkers with their potential replacement by Mexican migrants and vice versa. With the spectacular growth of the SAWP, these threats need little reinforcement among South Asians. However, labor replacement also constitutes a threat for Mexican migrants. The year after a group of Mexicans became the first migrant agricultural workers to unionize in British Columbia, their employer rehired only a dozen migrants of the original 38 and complemented the workforce with 28 Canadians (Sandborn 2009).

Workplaces, Transportation, and Housing

Immigrant and migrant farmworkers also worked in environments they perceived to be unsafe. Respondents described poorly maintained equipment and worksites that presented hazards such as falling from heights, cuts from dull knives, or injury from machinery. Inadequate hygiene and sanitation on some farms also poses health and safety risks. Fourteen percent of our respondents reported lacking access to bathrooms. Interviewees reported withholding urine and stool for extended periods, being reprimanded for using toilets outside scheduled breaks, and the indignities of lacking bathroom facilities in a mixed-gender workplace. One Mexican migrant said, "If I feel like going to the bathroom, I go, but my coworkers say they wouldn't do it because they fear they'll be fired." Thirty-one percent of respondents rated the risk of working without access to a bathroom as a high-risk activity. Twenty-three percent also reported lacking hand-washing facilities at their worksites, amplifying their risk of exposure to infectious diseases and chemicals. Interviewees reported being unable to wash their hands before eating after using the toilet, handling chemicals, or working with soil. One Mexican interviewee related, "Sometimes we cannot wash our hands as we'd like to and this causes stomach ailments. Many of us have fallen ill. It's what we get the most." Finally, more than a third of migrants and a quarter of immigrant farmworkers indicated lack of drinking water as a high risk.

Transportation also presents a risk to both groups. For immigrant workers dependent on the FLC system, unsafe transportation may constitute their most serious occupational hazard (Bush and Canadian Farmworkers Union 1995). One South Asian participant explained why she drove to work: "It was common knowledge in the field that contractors did not offer their workers adequate seat belts, the van was overloaded, and it was being driven too fast." Among survey respondents transported to their worksites, an astounding 27 percent reported an insufficient number of seat belts. Further, 24 percent of our South Asian immigrant respondents disagreed with the phrase "I felt safe when being transported from my home to my workplace." Respondents reporting insufficient number of seat belts were more likely to be traveling in vans or buses driven by a FLC and to work on larger farms. While Mexican migrants tend to live on farm premises, they are exposed to transportation hazards traveling between worksites, often sitting or standing in trailers, wagons, or tractors, some of which are not roadworthy. Both groups also face risks when working in remote areas, since some employers fail to provide a vehicle or cell phone for emergencies. One interviewee reported carrying an injured coworker 30 minutes before reaching a telephone.

Housing was also a specific concern for migrant workers. Thirty-seven percent of Mexican survey respondents disagreed that "the state of my housing does not present any risk to my health" and reported shortcomings in facilities such as inadequate sanitation, with some dwellings lacking indoor plumbing and potable water (see Table 20.1). Farmworker and advocate interviewees emphasized concerns of overcrowding, as well as insufficient facilities: "People are living nine, ten, eleven to a house with access to one bathroom; without even a stove but three or four electric hotplates for nine people," said one advocate. "No washer, no dryer. There are houses that ... are not even adequate for human abode." Despite SAWP guidelines indicating that a laundry facility should be provided for every 15 occupants, 19 percent of migrants had no washing machine and 25 percent had no tumble dryer, a significant concern considering the importance of washing clothes to mitigate pesticide exposure. Further, inadequate refrigeration space is troubling, given that migrants' access to supermarkets is generally limited to one day per week. The risks of gastrointestinal problems are exacerbated by insufficient cooking elements that impede migrants' ability to heat meals adequately, if at all. The existence of poor housing conditions indicates both inconsistent employer compliance with the SAWP agreement and regulatory deficiencies in monitoring and enforcement.

TABLE 20.1 SURVEY RESULTS OF AVAILABILITY OF HOUSING FACILITIES FOR MEXICAN MIGRANTS

	% Yes	% No
Drinking water within the dwelling	97	3
Functioning toilets inside the dwelling	93	7
Portable toilets outside the dwelling	71	29
Running water inside the dwelling	96	4
Kitchen separated from the toilet	88	12
Stove separated from sleeping area	72	28
Sufficient refrigerator space for all occupants	79	21
Sufficient cooking elements for all occupants	75	25
Washing machine	81	19
Tumble dryer	75	25
Heating in cold weather	86	14
Windows with insect screens	75	25

Training and Language Barriers

A further principal finding was that most farmworkers—74 percent of Mexican migrants and 70 percent of South Asian immigrants—did not receive health and safety training for their jobs at their principal worksite. One South Asian woman, age 30, who became a farmworker in Canada at age 9, asserted, "Throughout my agricultural career, I haven't received much training from my different bosses. In agriculture you learn from your coworkers and through experience. Your boss or supervisor doesn't have the time to train you properly and doesn't want to [pay] to have someone else train you." Even when workers did receive some occupational health and safety training, our research did not find a significant association between training and a decreased likelihood of occupational injury: workers were just as likely to get injured whether they received training or not. This could indicate that training is inadequate, corroborating our qualitative findings. [...]

In addition to insufficient training, farmworkers confronted language barriers in their jobs that held consequences for workplace health and safety. Our study found that workers whose self-assessed English proficiency is poor or very poor were more likely to have sustained a work-related injury. Among South Asian immigrants, we found a strong relationship between language skills and work-related injuries; 75 percent of South Asian workers who reported work-related injuries rated their English proficiency as poor or very poor. [...] Although the survey did not find statistically significant results for Mexican migrants, it is noteworthy that 82 percent of those who reported a work-related injury also reported poor or very poor English skills. [...]

Access to Health Care

Language barriers also constitute one of multiple barriers to health care identified in this study, particularly for Mexican migrant workers. This barrier is compounded by geographical isolation and poor rural transportation, as most migrants live on farms in rural, sometimes remote areas. Long, antisocial work shifts further hamper their access to health care. Moreover, migrants are not eligible for provincial public health care until they have resided in British Columbia for three months; they also depend on their employers to register them. In our study, only 8 of 100 migrants surveyed had been enrolled in public health care. Although migrant workers have private insurance for the intervening period, its coverage is limited: at the time of the study, some clinics and hospitals were not recognizing it and, consequently, either refused to treat migrants or required a prepayment, something migrants were unwilling or unable to finance. For South Asian immigrants, the three-month qualifying period for public health care also applies to newcomers, thus increasing their dependency on their sponsors.

In addition to insurance-related problems, access to health care was impeded by employers and supervisors who did not respond immediately or at all to farmworkers' concerns: "The delay it takes—it's as if they don't believe us immediately," a Mexican migrant said. "One of my coworkers has been waiting a month, and they [Mexican Consulate employees] told him that they're going to come visit him today to see if they take him to the doctor. They'll probably send him [back] to Mexico." Immigrant farmworkers also asserted that FLCs denied requests for medical care on the job. A South Asian immigrant said:

> If we have an accident at work, we'll be left to take care of ourselves. Another problem with the contractor is that they don't pay attention to anyone who gets hurt. They will never offer to take someone to the hospital if they get injured or are feeling ill. They may offer the person a ride home, but more often they'll tell you to wait in the lunchroom until the day is over.

[...] Employers' failure to respond to farmworkers' requests for medical care may generate feelings of despair, hopelessness, and having been discriminated against—factors identified by researchers as stressors for higher rates of mental distress and psychiatric difficulties among migrants (Arcury and Quandt 2007; Lee 2008; Magaña and Hovey 2003). Such failure is also a violation of provincial occupational health and safety legislation and the current SAWP agreement.

Discussion and Conclusions

[...] Our research on workplace health and safety provides insights into the intersection between precarious work and precarious legal status through a novel and empirically rich comparison of migrant and immigrant farmworkers. As we have demonstrated, migrants on tied work permits are subject to highly coercive forms of labor discipline that rest principally on their deportability. The fear of losing the opportunity to obtain Canadian wages, fostered as a result of their precarious legal status as highly deportable, temporary labor market entrants, compels them to acquiesce to working conditions and housing that many perceive as unsafe or damaging to their health, to accept exceptionally long hours, or to work while ill or injured. Family-class immigrants experience precarious legal status in other ways. These older, predominantly female workers, living in (sub)urban centers, face challenges to their economic integration into the wider workforce. They thus rely on the FLC system to link them to the agricultural labor market, where they face a remuneration system that induces them to accept undesirable working conditions if they are to qualify for social protection during the low season. They face specific risks linked to the FLC system, including that the contractor rather than the farm owner is their formal employer, a factor that may affect the amount and quality of the health and safety training they receive. [...] As we have shown in our comparison of two legalized groups of immigrant and migrant workers, precarious migratory status shapes labor regimes in distinct, complex, and paradoxical respects.

[...] One of the principal contributions of our study is a snapshot of the wretched labor regimes that characterize contemporary food and agricultural production in a postindustrial economy. Farmworkers continue to face a number of indignities at work, such as verbal and physical aggression, including racially based aggression; exacting productivity standards that have intensified the work process; and dangerous environments for which they have received little health and safety training and in which they often do not understand the language of the "shop floor." Among risks to their bodily integrity are unsafe transportation to their jobs and unsanitary, underequipped, and overcrowded housing. Migrant farmworkers in particular work incredibly long shifts, averaging an astonishing 76 hours per week without a day of rest in periods of high production.

Immigrants with partial or full formal citizenship, however, have greater opportunities to escape agriculture's brutal labor regime. Entitled to labor mobility and state-funded language classes, they can potentially improve their labor market attachment and find work outside the sector. At the very least (although unlikely) they can also withdraw from the labor market to rely on their family members physically located in Canada and, for those landed for more than ten years, gain access to the (diminished) social protection offered by the state (e.g., welfare). Being supplementary rather than primary economic providers for their households is one factor that may allow them greater latitude to work fewer hours than guest workers in what is a physically exacting job. Finally, for those immigrants who cannot leave agriculture or "choose" to remain in the sector, formal citizenship rights afford them greater ability to pursue claims against their employers, notwithstanding the barriers we identified in the FLC system. [...]

[These findings] underscore the need for two equally ambitious policy changes to address labor injustices in Canada's food and agricultural system. [...] First, Canada should adopt a national strategy to commit provincial governments and other stakeholders to address serious shortcomings in the legislation protecting agricultural labor, strengthen monitoring and enforcement, and find new solutions to improving employer compliance. Second, since formal citizenship can mitigate an important dimension of vulnerability, we argue for a restructured immigration system that would accept applications for permanent residency from a broader range of skill sets, including manually skilled agricultural workers. Such a reform would better reflect the country's labor needs and obviate the need for temporary migration programs. At the very least, migrants should be offered untied, sectoral work permits to enable their mobility within the agricultural labor market, thus removing the principal source of their unfreedom.

Notes

1. In the case of migrant guest workers, however, employers must create a contract.
2. Immigrant farmworkers belong to households located predominantly outside rural areas, owing to the greater concentration of co-ethnic persons, cultural and religious infrastructure, and employment opportunities in cities.

References

Alberta Federation of Labour. 2009. *Entrenching Exploitation: The Second Report of the Alberta Federation of Labour Temporary Foreign Worker Advocate*. Edmonton, AB: Alberta Federation of Labour.

Arat-Koc, Sedef. 2009. "The Politics of Family and Immigration in the Subordination of Domestic Workers in Canada." Pp. 428–52 in *Family Patterns, Gender Relations*, edited by B. Fox. Don Mills, ON: Oxford University Press.

Arcury, Thomas A. and Sara A. Quandt. 2007. "Delivery of Health Services to Migrant and Seasonal Farmworkers." *Annual Review of Public Health* 28:345–63.

Arcury, Thomas A., Sara A. Quandt, Pamela Rao, Alicia M. Doran, Beverly M. Snively, Dana B. Barr, Jane A. Hoppin, and Stephen W. Davis. 2005. "Organophosphate Pesticide Exposure in Farmworker Family Members in Western North Carolina and Virginia: Case Comparisons." *Human Organization* 64(1):40–51.

Bakan, Abigail and Daiva Stasiulis. 2003. *Negotiating Citizenship: Migrant Women in Canada and the Global System*. Houndsmill, England: Palgrave-Macmillan.

———. 2012. “The Political Economy of Migrant Live-in Caregivers: A Case of Unfree Labour?” Pp. 202–26 in *Legislated Inequality: Temporary Migrant Workers in Canada*, edited by P. Lenard and C. Straehle. Montreal, QC: McGill-Queen’s University Press.

Basok, Tanya. 2002. *Tortillas and Tomatoes: Transmigrant Mexican Harvesters in Canada*. Montreal, QC: McGill-Queen’s University Press.

Basok, Tanya and Eloy Rivas. 2012. *Choosing to Become Unauthorized: A Case Study of Mexican and Central American Migrant Workers in Leamington*. Toronto, ON: CERIS—Ontario Metropolis Centre.

BC Public Service Agency. 2003. *Multi-jurisdictional Team Raises Employment Standards for Agricultural Farm Workers*. Vancouver, BC: BC Public Service Agency.

Binford, Leigh. 2009. “From Fields of Power to Fields of Sweat: The Dual Process of Constructing Temporary Migrant Labour in Mexico and Canada.” *Third World Quarterly* 30(3):503–17.

Bloomekatz, Rachel. 2007. “Rethinking Immigration Status Discrimination and Exploitation in the Low-Wage Workplace.” *UCLA Law Review* 54:1963–2010.

Bolaria, B. Singh, Gurcharn S. Basran, and David Hay. 1988. “The Health Effects of Powerlessness: The Case of Immigrant Farm Labour.” Pp. 109–24 in *The Political Economy of Agriculture in Western Canada*, edited by G. S. Basran and D. A. Hay. Toronto, ON: Garamond Press.

Bolaria, B. Singh, David A. Hay, and Gurcharn S. Basran. 1992. “Farm Labour, Work Conditions, and Health Risks.” Pp. 228–45 in *Rural Sociology in Canada*, edited by D. A. Hay and G. S. Basran. Toronto, ON: Oxford University Press.

Bush, Murray and Canadian Farmworkers Union. 1995. *Zindabad! A History of the Canadian Farmworkers Union*. Surrey, BC: Canadian Farmworkers Union.

Castles, Stephen and Mark Miller. 2009. *The Age of Migration: International Population Movements in the Modern World*. 4th ed. Basingstoke, England: Palgrave Macmillan.

CBC News. 2009. “3-Death Crash Inquest Told Previous Inquest ‘Ignored.’ ” December 9. Retrieved June 3, 2010 (http://www.cbc.ca/canada/british-columbia/story/2009/12/09/bc-highway-van-crash-inquest-sinclair.html).

———. 2012. “Mushroom Farm Coroner’s Jury Urges Training, Inspections.” May 16. Retrieved November 10, 2012 (http://www.cbc.ca/news/canada/british-columbia/story/2012/05/16/bc-mushroom-farm-inquest-recommendations.html).

Centre for Immigration Reform. 2013. “Aims and Objectives.” Retrieved November 15, 2013 (http://immigrationreform.ca/english/View.asp?x=883&id=650).

Citizenship and Immigration Canada. 2008. *Facts and Figures: Immigration Overview Permanent and Temporary Residents*. Ottawa, ON: Minister of Public Works and Government Services Canada, Research and Evaluation Branch.

———. 2012. *Canada Facts and Figures: 2011 Immigration Overview: Permanent and Temporary Residents*. Ottawa, ON: Citizenship and Immigration Canada.

Cornelius, Wayne A., Philip L. Martin, and James Frank Hollifield. 1994. *Controlling Immigration: A Global Perspective*. Stanford, CA: Stanford University Press.

Downes, Andrew and Cyrilene Odle-Worrell. 2003. *Barbados, Trinidad and Tobago, OECS Workers' Participation in CSAWP and Development Consequences in the Workers' Rural Home Communities*. Ottawa, ON: North-South Institute.

Duarte, Angela and Ana Sánchez. 2008. "Being Free of Tuberculosis: Not Just a Matter of Health." Presented at the International Conference on Emerging Infectious Diseases, March 16–19, Atlanta, GA.

Employment and Social Development Canada. 2013. "Labour Market Opinion (LMO) Statistics—Annual Statistics 2008–2011." Retrieved November 15, 2013 (www.hrsdc.gc.ca/eng/jobs/foreign_workers/lmo_statistics/annual2011.shtml#h2.10).

Fairey, David, Christina Hanson, Glenn MacInnes, Arlene Tigar McLaren, Gerardo Otero, Kerry Preibisch, and Mark Thompson. 2008. *Cultivating Farmworkers' Rights: Ending the Exploitation of Immigrant and Migrant Farmworkers in BC*. Vancouver, BC: Canadian Centre for Policy Alternatives BC Office, Justicia for Migrant Workers, Progressive Intercultural Community Services, and BC Federation of Labour.

Getz, Christy, Sandy Brown, and Aimee Shreck. 2008. "Class Politics and Agricultural Exceptionalism in California's Organic Agriculture Movement." *Politics and Society* 36(4):478–507.

Goldring, Luin and Patricia Landolt. 2012. *The Impact of Precarious Legal Status on Immigrants' Economic Outcomes*. Montreal, QC: Institute for Research on Public Policy.

Griffith, David C. 2006. *American Guestworkers: Jamaicans and Mexicans in the U.S. Labor Market*. University Park, PA: Pennsylvania State University Press.

Guadalupe, Maria. 2003. "The Hidden Costs of Fixed Term Contracts: The Impact on Work Accidents." *Labour Economics* 10(3):339–57.

Hennebry, Jenna L. 2006. "Globalization and the Mexican-Canadian Seasonal Agricultural Worker Program: Power, Racialization and Transnationalism in Temporary Migration." PhD dissertation, Department of Sociology, University of Western Ontario, London, ON.

———. 2008. *International Agricultural Migration and Public Health: Examining Migrant Farm Worker Health and the Public Health Implications of Agricultural Temporary Migration*. Ottawa, ON: Public Health Agency of Canada.

Hennebry, Jenna L. and Kerry Preibisch. 2010. "A Model for Managed Migration? Re-examining Best Practices in Canada's Seasonal Agricultural Worker Program." *International Migration* 50(S1):e19–e40. doi:10.1111/j.1468-2435.2009.00598.x.

Hennebry, Jenna L., Kerry Preibisch, and Janet McLaughlin. 2010. *Health across Borders—Health Status, Risks and Care among Transnational Migrant Farm Workers in Ontario*. Toronto, ON: CERIS—Ontario Metropolis Centre.

Holland, Dawn. 2012. "The Impact of Transitional Arrangements on Migration in the Enlarged EU." *FMW Online Journal on Free Movement of Workers* 4:18–25.

Immigration Watch Canada. 2012. "What Is Good for Tim Horton's Is Often Not Good for Canada." Retrieved November 15, 2013 (http://www.immigrationwatchcanada.org/2012/12/07/what-is-good-for-tim-hortons-is-not-good-for-canada/).

Justicia for Migrant Workers. 2013. "About Us." Retrieved November 15, 2013 (http://www.justicia4migrantworkers.org/justicia_new.htm).

Lanthier, Mario and Lloyd Wong. 2002. *Ethnic Agricultural Labour in the Okanagan Valley: 1880s to 1960s*. Vancouver, BC: Royal BC Museum.

Lee, Jungwhan. 2008. "Migrant Workers and HIV Vulnerability in Korea." *International Migration* 46(3):217–33.

Lenard, Patti T. and Christine Straehle. 2012. *Legislating Inequality: Temporary Labour Migration in Canada*. Montreal, QC: McGill-Queen's University Press.

Lilley, Rebecca, Anne-Marie Feyer, Patrick Kirk, and Philippa Gander. 2002. "A Survey of Forest Workers in New Zealand: Do Hours of Work, Rest, and Recovery Play a Role in Accidents and Injury?" *Journal of Safety Research* 33(1):53–71.

Luna, Guadalupe T. 1998. "An Infinite Distance? Exceptionalism and Agricultural Labor." *University of Pennsylvania Journal of Labor and Employment Law* 1(2):487–510.

Magaña, Cristina G. and Joseph D. Hovey. 2003. "Psychosocial Stressors Associated with Mexican Migrant Farmworkers in the Midwest United States." *Journal of Immigrant Health* 5(2):75–86.

Mannon, Susan E., Peggy Petrzelka, Christy M. Glass, and Claudia Radel. 2012. "Keeping Them in Their Place: Migrant Women Workers in Spain's Strawberry Industry." *International Journal of Sociology of Agriculture and Food* 19(1):83–101.

McLaughlin, Janet. 2009. "Trouble in Our Fields: Health and Human Rights among Mexican and Caribbean Migrant Farm Workers in Canada." PhD dissertation, Department of Anthropology, University of Toronto, Toronto, ON.

Migrant Workers Alliance for Change. 2013. "Our Demands." Retrieved November 15, 2013 (http://www.migrantworkersalliance.org/about-us/demands/).

Moore, Graeme. 2004. *Hand-Harvesters of Fraser Valley Berry Crops: New Era Protection of Vulnerable Employees*. Vancouver, BC: BC Federation of Labour.

Moral del Arbona, Euclides 2011. "Programa de Trabajadores Agricolas Temporales México—Canadá: Temporada 2011." Presented at the Foro Nacional sobre los Asuntos Internacionales de los Gobiernos Locales, November 26, Queretaro, Mexico.

Ontario Ministry of Community and Social Services. 2013. "Ontario Works Policy Directives." Retrieved June 4, 2013 (http://www.mcss.gov.on.ca/en/mcss/programs/ social/directives/directives/OWDirectives/3_11_OW_Directives.aspx).

Ontario Provincial Police. 2012. "Update—Multi Fatal OPP Investigation." News release, February 8. Retrieved November 10, 2012 (http://www.opp.ca/ecms/index.php?id=405&nid=758).

Otero, Gerardo and Kerry Preibisch. 2010. *Farmworker Health and Safety: Challenges for British Columbia*. Vancouver, BC: WorkSafeBC.

Oxman-Martinez, Jacqueline, Jill Hanley, Lucyna Lach, Nazilla Khanlou, Swarna Weerasinghe, and Vijay Agnew. 2005. "Intersection of Canadian Policy Parameters Affecting Women with Precarious Immigration Status: A Baseline for Understanding Barriers to Health." *Journal of Immigrant Health* 7(4):247–58.

Passel, Jeffrey S. and D'Vera Cohn. 2009. *A Portrait of Unauthorized Immigrants in the United States*. Washington, DC: Pew Hispanic Center.

Pickett, William, Lisa Hartling, Robert J. Brison, and Judith R. Guernsey. 1999. "Fatal Work-Related Farm Injuries in Canada, 1991–1995." *Canadian Medical Association Journal* 160(13):1843–48.

Piper, Nicola. 2008. "Feminisation of Migration and the Social Dimensions of Development: The Asian Case." *Third World Quarterly* 29(7):1287–303.

Preibisch, Kerry and Leigh Binford. 2007. "Interrogating Racialized Global Labour Supply: An Exploration of the Ethnic Replacement of Foreign Agricultural Workers in Canada." *Canadian Review of Sociology and Anthropology* 44(1):5–36.

Preibisch, Kerry and Jenna Hennebry. 2011. "Temporary Migration, Chronic Effects: The Health of International Migrant Workers in Canada." *Canadian Medical Association Journal* 183(9):1033–38.

Pysklywec, Michael, Janet McLaughlin, Michelle Tew, and Ted Haines. 2011. "Doctors within Borders: Meeting the Health Care Needs of Migrant Farm Workers in Canada." *Canadian Medical Association Journal* 183(9):1039–42.

Quandt, Sara A., María A. Hernández-Valero, Joseph G. Grzywacz, Joseph D. Hovey, and Melissa Gonzales. 2006. "Workplace, Household, and Personal Predictors of Pesticide Exposure for Farmworkers." *Environmental Health Perspectives* 14(6):943–52.

Rodgers, Gerry and Janine Rodgers. 1989. *Precarious Jobs in Labour Market Regulation: The Growth of Atypical Employment in Western Europe*. Brussels, Belgium: International Labour Organisation.

Rogaly, Ben. 2008. "Intensification of Workplace Regimes in British Horticulture: The Role of Migrant Workers." *Population, Space and Place* 14(6):497–510.

Runsten, David, Raúl A. Hinojosa Ojeda, Kathleen Lee, and Richard Mines. 2000. *The Ex-*

tent, Pattern, and Contribution of Migrant Labor in the NAFTA Countries: An Overview. Los Angeles, CA: North American Integration and Development Center.

Sandborn, Tom. 2009. "Setback for Historic Effort to Unionize Guest Farm Workers." *Tyee*, June 29. Retrieved September 29, 2009 (http://thetyee.ca/News/2009/06/29/FarmUnionSetback/).

Satzewich, Vic. 1991. *Racism and the Incorporation of Foreign Labour: Farm Labour Migration to Canada*. New York: Routledge.

Saucedo, Leticia. 2006. "The Employer Preference for the Subservient Worker and the Making of the Brown Collar Workplace." *Ohio State Law Journal* 67(5): 961–1022.

Scott, Sam, Gary Craig, and Alistair Geddes. 2012. *Experiences of Forced Labour in the UK Food Industry*. York, England: Joseph Rowntree Foundation, University of Bristol.

Sergeant, Malcolm and Eric Tucker. 2009. *Layers of Vulnerability in Occupational Health and Safety for Migrant Workers: Case Studies from Canada and the United Kingdom*. Toronto, ON: Comparative Research in Law and Political Economy.

Sharma, Nandita. 1995. "The True North Strong and Unfree: Capitalist Restructuring and Non-immigrant Employment in Canada, 1973–1993." MA dissertation, Department of Sociology and Anthropology, Simon Fraser University, Vancouver, BC.

———. 2006. *Home Economics: Nationalism and the Making of Migrant Workers in Canada*. Toronto, ON: University of Toronto Press.

———. 2012. "Enforcing 'Difference' in Canada: Re-organizing Canadian Immigration Policy during Late Capitalism." Pp. 26–47 in *Legislated Inequality: Temporary Migrant Workers in Canada*, edited by P. T. Lenard and C. Straehle. Montreal, QC: McGill-Queen's University Press.

Sharpe, Andrew and Jill Hardt. 2006. *Five Deaths a Day: Workplace Fatalities in Canada, 1993–2005*. Ottawa, ON: Centre for the Study of Living Standards.

Tomlinson, Kathy. 2013. "RBC Replaces Canadian Staff with Foreign Workers." *CBC News*, April 6. Retrieved November 11, 2013 (http://www.cbc.ca/news/canada/britishcolumbia/rbc-replaces-canadian-staff-with-foreign-workers-1.1315008).

Tucker, Eric. 2006. "Will the Vicious Circle of Precariousness Be Unbroken? The Exclusion of Ontario Farm Workers from the Occupational Health and Safety Act." Pp. 256–76 in *Precarious Employment: Understanding Labour Market Insecurity in Canada*, edited by L. Vosko. Montreal, QC: McGill-Queen's University Press.

———. 2012. "Farm Worker Exceptionalism: Past, Present, and the Post-Fraser Future." Pp. 30–56 in *Constitutional Labour Rights in Canada: Farm Workers and the Fraser Case*, edited by F. Faraday, J. Fudge, and E. Tucker. Toronto, ON: Irwin Law.

United Food and Commercial Workers Canada. 2005. *The Status of Migrant Farm Workers in Canada*. Rexdale, ON: United Food and Commercial Workers.

United Food and Commercial Workers of Canada and Agriculture Workers Alliance. 2011. *The Status of Migrant Farm Workers in Canada, 2010–2011*. Rexdale, ON: United Food and Commercial Workers of Canada.

Verduzco, Gustavo and María Isabel Lozano. 2003. *Mexican Workers' Participation in CSAWP and Development Consequences in the Workers' Rural Home Communities.* Ottawa, ON: North-South Institute.

Vosko, Leah F. 2006. *Precarious Employment: Understanding Labour Market Insecurity in Canada*. Montreal, QC: McGill-Queen's University Press.

Waldinger, Roger and Michael I. Lichter. 2003. *How the Other Half Works: Immigration and the Social Organization of Labor*. Berkeley, CA: University of California Press.

Walia, Harsha. 2010. "Transient Servitude: Migrant Labour in Canada and the Apartheid of Citizenship." *Race and Class* 52(1):71–84.

Wall, Ellen. 1992. "Personal Labour Relations and Ethnicity in Ontario Agriculture." Pp. 261–75 in *Deconstructing a Nation: Immigration, Multiculturalism and Racism in '90s Canada*, edited by V. Satzewich. Halifax, NS: Fernwood.

WorkSafeBC. 2012. "Agriculture Statistics (2007–2010)." Retrieved October 2, 2012 (http://www2.worksafebc.com/portals/agriculture/statistics.asp).

SECTION 3C

EDUCATION

CHAPTER 21

Playing It Down/Playing It Up: Girls' Strategic Negotiations of Academic Success

Rebecca Raby and Shauna Pomerantz

Introduction

> Sometimes ... I don't go full out brainiac. I gotta tone it down a bit.[1] (Christy, age 14)

The last two decades have been rife with reports of girls' pervasive high achievement as they flourish in school and outshine boys in test scores (DiPrete and Buchmann 2013). This ubiquitous storyline is sustained by two popular discourses. The *Globe and Mail*'s series "Failing Boys" reflects the first, arguing that while historically boys tended to fare better in school than girls, they have more recently fallen behind (Abraham 2010).[2] The parallel narrative concentrates on the Supergirl, contending that girls today are excelling in school, suggesting that girls are no longer thwarted by gender inequality but instead have the power to do and be anything they want (see Ringrose and Walkerdine 2008). Such gendered shifts in academic achievement are frequently explained through assertions that the classroom has become a gendered space that favours the feminine while boys' masculine tendencies have become unwelcome and problematized (Kindlon and Thompson 2002).

This article counters the notion that girls engage their academic identities easily, naturally, and without struggle. Dominant essentializing constructions of both girlhood and the classroom render smart girlhood impossibly simple, without recognizing the incompatibilities between prominent conceptualizations of smartness and girlhood (Walkerdine 1990), the ambiguity inherent in all identity construction (Hall 1996), and girls' active negotiation of such ambiguity (Gonick 2006). Instead, we draw out the complexities of smart girlhood as an identity that entails careful negotiation when being a socially successful girl entails performing femininity in a way that is often in tension with academic success (Renold and Allan 2006; Skelton, Francis, and Read 2010; Walkerdine, Lucey, and Melody 2001).

Our study examines how a diverse group of Canadian self-declared "smart girls" described strategically performing smart girlhood in order to balance negative characteristics associated with being a smart girl alongside the rewards of academic success. On the one hand, these girls sought to avoid the danger in being too focused on school, introverted, or a know-it-all, by playing down being smart (Renold and Allan 2006). On the other hand, the girls placed a great deal of value on their academic success and played up their own achievement as a form of validation and cultural capital in the present and/or their imagined futures. And generally, girls did both—playing it up or down depending on the risks and rewards of being seen as studious at any given time or place, illustrating how girls' high academic performance is neither easily embraced nor unambivalently accepted, but is carefully and consciously navigated. Girls are also distinct in their intersecting identities and contexts, a diversity that affects the ease with which they experience and negotiate their smartness (Skelton, Francis, and Read 2010; Walkerdine, Lucey, and Melody 2001).

In what follows, we cite literature which suggests that the classroom is a feminized space and countering research illustrating the incommensurability of successful girlhood with high academic achievement. The latter foregrounds the complexity of doing smart girlhood. As Judith Butler (1990, 1993) explains, gender is neither innate nor natural but the gelling together of acts that cohere as an identity. In this regard, gender is performative, "not as an act of intentionality, but as a performance already set up by a pre-scripted rehearsal" (Hey 2006, 444). Our use of the expression "doing smart girlhood" signals this socially constructed understanding of gender as something that girls "do" as a set of repeated acts within a larger field of discursive constraint. But as we explore, while smart girls are positioned to play particular social roles in the school, they are also able to re-position themselves as agentic subjects whose subjectivities are creatively used to offset the limiting features of discursive construction. We conclude that doing smart girlhood is a complex form of agency for girls in the school and is a practice much more challenging than depicted in accounts that feminize education and thus represent smart girls as beyond struggle.

GENDERING ACHIEVEMENT

Gendered patterns of school failure and success have elicited diverse academic theorizing. From one perspective, concern about Failing Boys is linked to a homogenized, essentialized male energy and aggression that clashes with classroom settings premised on feminine cooperation, especially as they are dominated by female teachers at the primary and junior levels (Kindlon and Thompson 2002; see also Ringrose 2013). In response, researchers such as Kindlon and Thompson argue that girls are thriving, but that boys' inclinations to kinaesthetic, visual, and competitive learning are neglected, thus fostering boys' trouble in school.

The implication is that the ideal students in such settings are girls, who are thought to share inherent feminine traits ideal for the current organization of education.

Others counter that masculine traits are not inherent but cultivated, and it is boys' pursuit of hegemonic masculinity, currently premised on aggression, competition, compulsory heterosexuality, and the denigration of anything feminine (Pascoe 2007), which is the problem. Through such gender theory, hegemonic masculinity is not inherent in boys but a constructed ideal, making it unstable, and complicated by boys' diverse identifications (Frosh, Phoenix, and Pattman 2002). Those working from this position contend that hegemonic masculinity must shift toward more inclusive forms of masculinity (Kimmel 1999). Despite this important aim to broaden acceptable masculinities, critical examinations of the anti-intellectualism of hegemonic masculinity and its denigration of a presumed feminine studiousness also conflate academic success with femininity (see Mac an Ghaill 1994; Sadker and Sadker 2002).

Girls are similarly understood to be flourishing in school within the discourse of the Supergirl (see Ringrose and Walkerdine 2008). This narrative has been critiqued for presuming a post-feminist context in which girls no longer experience gender inequality and are, instead, thriving (see Harris 2004; McRobbie, 2004). Indeed, while the boys flounder, the Supergirl is thought to be doing extremely well in the classroom as well as extra-curricular activities, relationships, and work life. Constructed as the perfect neo-liberal subject based on feminine flexibility, the Supergirl seems able to adapt to the needs of the market without seeming to succumb to stress or confusion (see Harris 2004; Pomerantz, Raby, and Stefanik 2013). As they no longer have to struggle against sexism or compete with "less ambitious" boys, girls now seem free to embrace their academic success unimpeded and without ambivalence (Kindlon 2006)

In opposition to the claims above, studies have shown the incommensurability of academic success and dominant femininity. As Skelton, Francis, and Read (2010, 187) suggest, being an "acceptable girl" is not in harmony with being a successful, academic achiever: the former involves passivity, accommodation, a concern with social relations and projecting feminine "desirability," whilst the latter demands hard-nosed determination, singularity, and concern with mental/intellectual (rather than social) pursuits.

Skelton, Francis, and Read found that, far from "having it all" (2010, 192), the girls in their study led lives circumscribed by gender, leading to a delicate balancing act between "doing girl" and "managing achievement" (2010, 186). Through interviews and observations with high-achieving 12-year-old to 13-year-old students, they concluded that girls manage their smartness by conforming to conventional femininity (see also Francis, 2009). Based on the same study, Francis, Skelton, and Read (2010, 336) detail the potentially "arduous identity work" required for these girls to maintain academic success alongside their popularity. [...]

In our own pilot study of smart girl identities in Canada (Pomerantz and Raby 2011), high school girls saw smartness as a multifaceted category that demanded far more than being "good at school." The girls noted that smartness included being book, street, and socially smart, upping the ante for girls' performances of success. Adding street and social smarts to book smarts facilitated their identities as "worldly" and "social" girls with lots going on besides schoolwork (2011, 556). While these girls maintained that they were "handling" these demands, they also discussed the stress of needing to be "smart, demonstrate leadership, get into the best college, all while being thin, pretty and wearing expensive designer jeans" (Rimer 2007, 1).

These studies illustrate that girls are not simply the winners of an educational climate that resonates with their femininity, but are struggling to negotiate their identities within highly contradictory expectations that demand careful and conscious thought. In performing girlhood and academic success, the girls in these studies understand the discursive limitations of each identity category, sometimes playing one against the other, downplaying their intelligence, or using a rigorous citation of dominant femininity to offset potential problems. We suggest that doing smart girlhood thus offers an interesting and complex example of girls' agency that demands further scrutiny.

DOING SMART GIRLHOOD

The concept of doing smart girlhood draws attention to the constructed nature of gender and academic success. Also, it suggests "girls' active role in creating their social presence" (Currie, Kelly, and Pomerantz 2009, 3). Doing smart girlhood therefore entails making oneself intelligible in the school as both a girl and a high academic achiever by being aware of, and vigilantly navigating, the risks and rewards of academic success. Such constraints and possibilities can be complicated, shifting, and contradictory. As such, they did not fully determine the girls' identities. Smart girls drew on various resources to tinker with, negotiate, or even reject how they were perceived by others. Doing "smart girl" identities thus offered the girls in our study at least the possibility of shaping, or resignifying, who and what a smart girl can be.

To theorize how girls "do" smart girlhood, we draw on a feminist post- structural reconceptualization of agency, particularly evident within the sociology of education (Currie, Kelly, and Pomerantz 2009; Davies 2006). While some post-structural thinkers have rejected agency as incompatible with post-structuralism given its humanist baggage (Jones 1997; Ringrose 2013), we view agency in its reconfigured form as useful for examining girls' understanding of their power to shape how others view them in the school. One way of thinking about agency assumes an autonomous individual unfettered by structural constraints that "places its own point of view at the origin of all historicity—which in short, leads to a transcendental consciousness" (Foucault 1970, xiv). This way of thinking about agency is contingent upon a pre-discursive self, outside socio-cultural context. But as Stuart Hall (1996) notes in relation to identity, agency must operate under erasure, or "in the interval between reversal and emergence; an idea which cannot be thought in the old way, but without which certain key questions cannot be thought at all" (1996, 2). Based on the Foucauldian concept of subjectification, or being formed and enacted at the same time, Judith Butler (1997) resignifies agency as an effect and not the origin of subjecthood. Butler theorizes that power "acts on the subject in at least two ways: first, as what makes the subject possible ... and second, what is taken up and reiterated in the subject's own acting" (1997, 14). This doubleness creates "the very terms in which agency is articulated and becomes culturally intelligible" (Butler 1990, 187). The subject is produced through power, but this production simultaneously grants subjecthood and thus gives us the ability to think and act beyond our subjection. Butler calls this ambivalence between formation and regulation "a fundamental dependency" (1997, 2) that creates the "bind of agency" (1997, 13), as agency is dependent upon the very thing that would seem to preclude it. But this fundamental dependency also offers promise, enabling the subject to "reflexively and critically examine their conditions of possibility and in which they can both subvert and eclipse the powers that act on them and which they enact" (Davies 2006, 426). Post-structural agency is thus a critical reflexivity of our own discursive production, enabling us to read and re-write the "texts of [our] selving" (Davies 1997, 274).

Because the subject is enacted as a subject through power, post-structural agency is always partial and mitigated by the socio-cultural forces that discursively produce the self. For example, while the girls in our study understood themselves as able to offset the stereotypes concomitant with academic identities by conceptualizing smartness as a form of capital, they did not have carte blanche to impact the way others viewed them. In recognizing their discursive production as smart girls, the girls had the ability to position themselves differently, but not to the exclusion of broader discursive frameworks. As such, not all girls were able to engage all strategies successfully. Social, gendered, and class-based positionings contributed to how effective girls were at negotiating academic success.

Methodology

[...] We draw on interviews with 51 girls (12–18 years old) living within the Niagara Region of Ontario, Canada, a de-industrializing area increasingly drawing on the service industry for employment. These girls were located through local advertising and snowball sampling in which we sought self-identified smart girls who "do well in school, or could if they tried."

The girls had the choice to be interviewed either individually or with a smart friend, resulting in 12 interview pairs, one trio, and 23 solo interviews. Overall the participants included 40 white girls and 11 non-white girls (10 with an Asian background) from 16 different schools, seven of which were middle schools and nine high schools. Two of these schools were private and six were religious. The girls came from a diversity of class backgrounds and self-identified across a range of locations in terms of popularity. While we recognize that identities are complexly layered and intersectional, this article focuses specifically on the impact of gender in relation to academic success. [...]

With a digital recorder running, we sat across from girls in their living rooms and in coffee shops asking them about how they experienced their smartness in school, including how they defined smartness, what they liked about being smart, how their academic work was supported within their families, what peers knew of their smartness, and how being smart affected their negotiations of school social structures and relationships. [...] For this paper, we selected dominant codes that addressed the fine line that girls negotiated to manage their academic success. These codes were then coded yet again to identify emerging sub-themes as well as moments of tension and contradiction in girls' narratives. [...]

Playing It Down: Smart Girlhood as a Liability

I'm basically a popular girl trapped inside a smart girl's body. (Virginia)

It is not surprising that the girls in our study placed a great deal of importance on being smart, as it was this self-identification that led to their involvement in this study. Almost all of the participants noted varieties of intelligence but focused primarily on grades as the indication of their smartness. Academic performance was central to their identities and almost all of the girls were proud of their grades and framed them positively. Yet as we progressed with most interviews, the apparent ease of academic success was fractured by the need to contain it. For example, many participants noted an incompatibility between a strong investment in school and sociality: the "problem" with smart students is that they are obsessed with school and consequently considered anti-social. As Anna (age 14) noted, "Well sometimes the smart kids are always talking about school, so sometimes it's nicer to not hang out with smart kids...." Similarly, Bella (age 14) explained: "I don't think the boys would consider you popular if you are so single-minded and focused on work ... I think some guys would consider them un-dateable because they are boring." And Kaitlyn (age 16) added: "Some people can be a little off because all they want to talk about is school. A lot of people kind of like edge away from them."

These comments followed intriguing patterns. First, the girls talked about such smart students as "Others," even though they themselves were self-declared smart girls for this study; thus many smart girls' performative positioning was to distance themselves from even the idea of being school-centred smart girls to manage the risks associated with smart girlhood. Second, Othered smart students were commonly held individually responsible for their consequent ostracism, thus framing it outside of potentially relevant structural hierarchies, such as gender, class, or problematic peer relations. For example, Maggie (age 12) felt sorry for socially awkward students focused on their school work, but her co-interviewee Darlene (age 14) countered: "They aren't making an effort to be friends." Darlene's position—that it is the smart student's own fault that she or he is not popular—was dominant within our data. Third, by focusing on school instead of socializing, these students were positioned as outside teenaged peer cultures (Milner 2004). Positioning problematically smart students as responsible for their own isolation and failing at acceptable teenagehood was explicitly gendered when it was linked to girls' attractiveness to boys and prioritizing good looks over their intelligence. As Haley stated in weighing the value of attractiveness versus intelligence at her school: "Our school definitely goes for pretty."

GRADE SILENCE

In response to this danger of going "too far" with one's high achievement, many girls in our study managed their smartness by containing it through down-playing their academic performance, even when this tactic sometimes undermined their classroom success. For Sarah (age 15), containment was a crucial feature of her smart girlhood performance: "I do [feel proud] but I don't try to flaunt it. I'm proud but I don't say it." Christy (age 14) also felt strongly about quietly performing success: "Sometimes I won't raise my hand in class as often and definitely don't share my marks. [...] you really have to watch it. You don't want to be the know-it-all." Similarly, Chuchos Valdes (age 15) ensured that others did not see her as a bragger: "I don't want to say I'm smart and sound cocky." To avoid seeming too cocky, too proud or too "in your face," the girls consciously opted to be nice and self-effacing about their academic achievement in a manner that has been similarly described in the research projects of Francis (2009) and Renold (2006). As Renold states: "Girls continue to hide, downplay, or deny rather than celebrate and improve upon their successes and feel the pressure to conform to normative cultural representations of (hetero) femininity" (2006, 459).

[...] Mauve (age 15), Emma (age 14), and Audrey (age 14) talk about the way they hide their smartness through containment so as not to annoy others or be judged negatively by their peers. Their self-restraint is therefore about managing others' feelings and ensuring the perception of modesty. They also critically note, however, that there are certain other ways that girls can successfully show off—by being physically affectionate with boys, for example, and by partying, both of which were seen as hallmarks of popularity.

We have illustrated how many girls sought to contain their smartness in a number of ways. While terms like "nerd" or "geek" were less of a threat in our study than in others (for example, Francis 2009), a few participants were concerned with the possibility that they might be called nerds. But more girls talked about how "nerd" was used as playfully teasing than anything else. Instead, the more consistently isolated and stigmatized position was "loner." The loner was not necessarily someone smart, but someone who was socially isolated and consequently stigmatized. Not only the lure of popularity, but the fear of becoming a loner seemed to lead many girls to contain their focus on school.

DUMBING DOWN

The containment of the girls' smartness was most pronounced and most gendered when the girls talked about "dumbing down," or pretending that they are not smart. This practice was strongly evident in our data. Some girls said that they had downplayed their own intelligence at some point during their schooling, and many others lamented friends or peers doing so. While we encountered the odd story of a boy dumbing down, in our data this was overwhelmingly something that girls did. According to our participants, a main reason to dumb down was to be popular. While some girls in our interviews felt that it was possible to be "out" about their smartness and to be popular, particularly within certain schools (see Skelton, Francis, and Read 2010; Raby and Pomerantz forthcoming), many argued that popular girls are not school smart, or must pretend not to be. Anna (age 14) explained that if popular girls are smart, "They don't portray it, like I don't know what their grades are, but they act really giggly and everything, so I don't know if they are smart, but they don't really portray being smart." Virginia (age 16) further described the incompatibility of smartness and popularity: "It's a very rare species of person who is smart and popular ... being popular essentially means you are slightly dumb [...] they project the idea that they aren't good in school."

As well as dumbing down to be popular, girls also did so to be attractive to boys. As Anna further observed:

> A lot of girls in my class [think it is more important to get a guy than to be smart]. My one friend goes around purposely acting dumb and will go around asking the guys if they know the answer even though she just told me the answer, soooo.

[...] The fact that so many girls talked about others (and sometimes themselves) dumbing down for popularity and/or for boys makes it clear that their smartness and academic skills are not thoroughly accepted or easy to negotiate, suggesting that sexism prevails, despite many girls' assertions of gender equality (Pomerantz, Raby, and Stefanik 2013) and pervasive post-feminist discourse of girls' easy academic success. Furthermore, girls who intentionally hold back in the classroom complicate assertions that current classrooms are more dominantly "feminine." Finally, the prominence of dumbing down illustrates how some girls consciously and strategically mediate their smartness. This negotiation is also evident when girls refuse to go so far in the name of popularity or dating, however. Anna, for instance, who described herself as being "in the middle" in terms of popularity, was critical of other girls' "dumbing down" by drawing on a narrative of authenticity: "Well, you aren't being yourself, so you really shouldn't do that. If you are dumb, go ahead. If you are smart, show them what you are, be smart." Anna later added that if a boy does not like it that she is smart, then "there is no reason in liking him." Here, she acknowledges potential trade-offs that girls might make when they are "out" about their academic success, but refuses to compromise in order to please popular peers.

Dumbing down is a strategy that girls deploy, but the association between dumbing down and popularity was not ubiquitous. Girls would avoid being too "in your face" with their smartness, but many refused to dumb down as a matter of personal pride, authenticity, and also to reap some of the contrasting benefits that came to them as a result of their high achievement. Thus they made clear decisions in navigating their identities as smart girls that suggest a reflexive negotiation of the contextual risks and rewards before them.

Playing It Up: Smart Girlhood as a Resource

> I like to be smart, I like to be successful, I like to be liked by teachers and people. (Wren, age 14)

Despite the challenges girls faced between performing their smartness problematically or acceptably, the girls we talked to were also aware of ways that their smartness worked well for them, particularly as a resource for earning status, freedom, and future success. Consequently girls sometimes "played up" their academic success, appreciating what it could bring in the present and in the future (see also Renold and Allan 2006).

For many girls, their smart identity was a source of validation and status within their family, with their teachers, and sometimes with their peers. Wren (age 14) explained that "[being smart] is actually valued [at my school]. People admire people with higher grades." Anna (age 14) also noted that "[t]eachers will respect you, and adults like your parents [and] you definitely get respected [by peers], like if you aren't a total airhead or always goofing off." And Christy (age 14) was pleased to be singled out for being smart: "Well at grade eight graduation, when they were giving out awards and the teachers were giving little speeches about the students, I felt proud because they had nice things to say about me....' In a possible gesture towards desires to please that have been inflected as feminine (see Walkerdine 1990), many participants talked about enjoying the positive reinforcement they received from their parents' pleasure in their work. The girls also enjoyed validation from teachers and the school through awards and praise, but also sometimes through perks such as leniency or extra attention. This positive feedback from a variety of sources, as well as their own self-satisfaction with high marks, helped the girls to invest in maintaining their grades.

Some girls also talked about enjoying certain freedoms that came with a smart identity, disrupting a more passive femininity. Their smartness was rewarding because its associated competency increased their sense of agency, independence, and freedom. For example, when asked why smartness was important to her, Ella (age 12) prioritized independence: "I think it's just a good thing to be, like, a smart individual and just be your own person and not have to rely on someone else." While some smart girls spent an incredible amount of time on schoolwork, others felt that their smartness provided them with spare time to pursue their interests because they could do their schoolwork more quickly. The girls' competency was similarly thought to generate options such as additional extra-curricular opportunities. As McLovin (age 15) explained:

> Well, for one thing, being a smart girl has allowed me to get into the programs I'm in, like, allowing me to do this interview. I get into jobs without trying. It's like, "oh I'm a 90% average student" and they're like, "oh you're in."

This appreciation of options was particularly marked when the girls talked about choices they felt would be available to them in the future. As Bella (age 14) noted: "If I have good grades then I change my mind [about a career]. I'll be able to go with what I want. So it leaves me [with] options." Even if linked to unpopularity in the present, confidence that their smartness was a resource for future privilege and success bolstered some of the girls in the face of social ostracism. As Haley (age 14) explained: "It doesn't bother me if someone calls me [a nerd]. I'd rather be a nerd than not smart. [Being smart] will help me in the future, I'll get a good career and they won't." Chanel (age 15), too, saw being smart as an advantage: "Those who do try to insult someone for their intelligence usually just don't go very far cuz, like, 'Oh, they're smart. They're going to get a better job than you when they're older, oh that sucks so much!'" These girls were thus aware that their smartness was a future resource—they knew they had something that would probably become valuable and they utilized this promise to manage ostracism in the present.

CULTURAL CAPITAL AND ECONOMIC CAPITAL

One way to conceptualize how these girls strategically and optimistically embraced their academic success is through recognizing the perceived value of this smartness within various forms of capital, or what Bourdieu terms the "accumulated labor [...] that, when appropriated on a private, that is exclusive, basis by agents or groups of agents, enables them to appropriate social energy in the form of reified or living labor" ([1983] 2001, 96). This capital is the accumulation of work in oneself, or one's group, through skills, credentials, and connections, which can be translated into economic capital later. These forms of capital may also vary by field, or the regulated social setting in which people are interacting. The school is one such field. A peer culture can also be considered a field, one that can be both distinct from, and interact with, the school.

In this article we have been arguing that the girls have a self-understanding as subjects with agency, and perform this agency through their strategic and conscious negotiation of their smart identities. Resonant with this analysis is how people identify and deploy what they perceive and experience to be resources, or capitals, in their interpersonal interactions and negotiations, as we see with the girls in our study. The girls adopted a conceptualization of their smartness (including their intelligence, academic skills, and investment in hard work) that acted as a form of cultural capital, both the "dispositions of the mind and body [and] educational qualifications" that are rewarded within a field (Bourdieu [1983] 2001, 98). The girls assumed they would be able to convert this accumulation of dispositions and qualifications into future economic capital, a confidence facilitated by neo-liberal discourses of individualized, meritocratic success (see Harris 2004; Pomerantz, Raby, and Stefanik 2013).

A minority of girls identified their smartness as an immediate resource operating in their relationships with their peers, facilitating social standing, and reflecting a peer culture that meshed well with the field of the school. We see this deployed resource in the example of McLovin, for instance, who cited her current school culture as a haven for being what she called "geeky." As Mendick and Francis (2012) argue, in Mendick's research "boffins/geeks" were not totally delegitimated categories in that there are "geek capitals" that young people can access, although usually it is white, middle-class boys who benefit from qualifications, teachers' validation, and media popularization of male nerds. Similarly, McLovin's successful smart girl performance is bolstered by her feminine good looks, athleticism, and middle-class background, all of which were also clearly linked to popularity at her school.

For most smart girls, negotiation of the present more so included faith in building cultural capital to ensure economic capital in the future, as they were acquiring the skills and credentials that they believed would later be converted into a good job (Bourdieu [1983] 2001, 98). This narrative provided them with a discourse of self-actualization and endurance within the school, even in the face of peer challenges. This understanding of their capacities is both a recognition of ongoing scholarly rewards that eventually come to be linked to economic success and a faith in the individualizing discourses of neo-liberalism, which suggest that, through sheer skill and hard work, girls can become successful. This understanding of future success was one significant resource that the girls drew upon as they made choices within their day-to-day peer interactions.

Negotiating Smartness

> If you are smart, good at sports, and attractive, then no one will bother you. (Lisa, age 15)

The girls that we spoke with were "doing smart girlhood" in a variety of ways, with friends, in class, and at home with their families, but within broader discursive contexts of popular femininity and neo-liberalism, and the distinct contexts of school and peer cultures. Most talked about doing some kind of relational work around performing smartness so that they did not stand out too much, did not seem too anti-social and did not become ostracized, but did not completely undermine their grades or their identities as smart girls. This work can be understood as traditionally feminine and heterosexual in its inclination towards self-effacement and its management of others, particularly to ensure that they fit in with other girls and were considered attractive to boys, but also as subverting these expectations in their scholarly ambitions. There were some girls who had an easier time negotiating their smartness in school, however, and others who more comfortably sacrificed some social acceptance for the promise of cultural capital.

SUPERGIRLS AND OTHER POPULAR GIRLS

There were eight girls in our study who could be described as Supergirls. Notably, these girls were exclusively white and mostly middle class or upper middle class, indicating the role of privilege in some girls' ability to excel as both popularly feminine and academic (Francis, Skelton, and Read 2010). They were almost all conventionally attractive, and every one of them was involved in a number of extra-curricular activities that included some kind of athletics. These girls also had strong social skills. Some could excel in school without much studying, or easily organized their time so that they could consciously and successfully balance socializing and school. Such balancing was given significant priority, with several specifically noting that sometimes they hide their smartness, and several others talking about the supportive cultures of their schools. Julia (age 16) was one such Supergirl. She was well dressed in a preppy style, came from an upper-middle-class family and grew up in a large home in a small community in the Niagara Region. She was involved in piano, percussion band, jazz band, synchronized skating, and swimming. She also worked six hours a week in a part-time job. To Julia, having good looks helped girls to be both smart and popular, although it was also important to be social, and to be at a school where smartness was valued and you did not "see people who have high marks going down [in their grades] to fit in."

Like Julia, most of these girls also had the right look, dress, and the economic resources to achieve these things. Skelton, Francis, and Read (2010) found that girls who were smart and popular were socially connected, good looking, stylish in their dress, and conventionally gendered. They suggest that the girls' feminine attractiveness balances out their smartness, making it more palatable, a pattern reflected in current "post-nerd" popular culture (Pomerantz and Raby forthcoming). This link was corroborated by several of our participants who suggested that some smart students were unpopular because of how they looked (Smarty Pants, age 17) and that for girls in particular "it's harder for someone who is not pretty as a girl to be popular" (Bella, age 14). For girls like Julia, a smart identity was often presented as easy. Other popular girls worked more consciously at playing down their academic success. Allie (age 12), for instance, also saw herself as popular but talked about how she tried to both hide her smartness and to stand up for herself and embrace her smartness if others bothered her about it—a tricky balancing act. For girls such as Allie, social success was important and they were aware that within their school environments it was linked to containing smartness. They were more willing and able than some other girls to play down their smartness to fit in.

REJECTING POPULAR FEMININITY

In contrast, there were some other girls, like Anna, who securely rejected dumbing down and the teen social life focused on gendered popularity, instead enjoying a smaller circle of friends, recognition from parents and teachers, and the promise of future success. The ability to fully embrace their smartness in this way was in part made possible by having like-minded friends, which was often linked to a certain kind of school culture, or at least a strong enough sub-group within a school that the girls felt supported. As we have noted elsewhere (Pomerantz and Raby 2011; Raby and Pomerantz forthcoming), and with regard to McLovin, a diverse school environment that promotes and values academic success and thus draws stronger students can provide an environment that is more positive for smart girls. As Elizabeth (age 14) also describes: "[My school] is a very academic school so it's not a bad thing to be smart." Such environments are, of course, often linked to class (Francis 2009). Elizabeth's school had specialized programmes for strong students and was seen by other participants as a particularly positive place for smart girls to be. It was also a large school in a prosperous neighbourhood.

Almost every girl in the study also spoke of a parent or parents who were supportively invested in their scholarship, and this was particularly the case for those girls refusing to contain their smartness in the interests of popularity. A culture of intellectual engagement and support at home helped them negotiate the consequent challenges they faced. For instance, after a friend suggested that she should try to "dumb it down" a little, Erin sought family advice from her mom:

> I spoke to my mom about it, and she's like "no, never dumb it down, obviously you shouldn't, if you need to dumb it down for your friends that's not a good thing."

Erin also talked about how supportive her parents were in terms of reviewing her schoolwork. Anna, the girl who sought peer respect over popularity, similarly stated that her parents "are really proud. Every time I get an A, my mom is like 'yay, good job!'" Many girls discussed a range of ways in which their parents invested in their daughters' academic identities. Several girls also spoke of their religion guiding them to embrace their smartness, such as Smarty Pants (age 17), whose commitment to getting a good education was connected to serving God.

Finally, there were a few girls who drew on a more structural, overtly political analysis in their rejection of a popular femininity premised on girls containing their smartness. Lisa, for example, was very critical of girls feeling the need to dumb down because "guys are supposed to be dominating. Society tells us without actually telling us. [...] We think about feminism and prejudice against women as a thing of the past but I think it's all really prevalent in our society." McLovin and her sister, Carmel Latte, similarly argued that it is degrading to act dumb and suggested that it takes us "back" to an era of gender inequality.

These smart girls, and the Supergirls discussed above, all articulated their thoughtful and overt negotiations of smart girlhood within peer cultures, school contexts, and broader social environments. In this process they drew on the resources or tools available to support or facilitate them, resources that were not always available to other girls. In this way we are reminded that agency is not unfettered or limitless, but bounded and contextual, and that agency is produced within discursive constraints that do not evaporate upon being acknowledged, but still enable subjects to actively engage in their own discursive positioning (Butler 1997; Davies 2006).

The Pleasures and Hazards of Doing Smart Girlhood

Despite post-feminist arguments that girls are now easily surpassing boys within schools and beyond, our data suggest otherwise by highlighting a knot of narratives that complicate the idea that girls' academic success is simple and smooth. These findings resonate with those of researchers such as Skelton, Francis, and Read (2010), Francis (2009), Ringrose (2013), and Renold (2006), who suggest that girls' experiences of academic success are gendered, intersectional, and complicated. We have also illustrated how girls can be conceptualized as agentically "doing smart girlhood" as they consciously negotiate the complex challenges and promises of their academic success, both within their immediate school and peer environments, and beyond into the future. Finally, some girls have resources—financial, social, and academic—that facilitate an easier negotiation in balancing their high achievement with social success. Many of these resources are linked to structural patterns of class and gender performance, with some able to invest in and accomplish a presentation of popular smart girlhood and others supported through close friends and family to provide a smart resilience in the face of peer pressures. And yet, despite overt references to such resources, most of the girls focused on individualized skill or personality as an explanation for how it is that some girls can successfully combine smartness and popularity, and that some cannot, reflecting the current post-feminist climate of individual responsibility and inherent talents.

Our findings do not negate the role of masculinity in shaping boys' experiences of schooling, nor do they address classroom pedagogy, but they successfully complicate a number of assumptions embedded in popular assertions about successful, academic girlhood. The notion that smart girls suddenly breeze through school is unwarranted when we attend to the challenges girls face as they negotiate their smartness in school. Conflations between academic success and femininity fail to account for ways in which girls' acquiescence to traditional femininity can undermine their academic success. Further, easier negotiations of smartness are not solely about inherent talents and will, but about present and future resources that girls bring to bear on their specific peer and school cultures. We demonstrate how girls perform their smartness by showing their understanding of the discursive constraints that limit how they are perceived by others, and how they navigate these constraints by playing down or playing up their academic success. While such negotiations were not always rewarded or praised, the girls in our study seemed well aware of how they were performing their smart identities and how they wanted to be seen by others. Finally, our research points out some troubling patterns of girls dumbing down and limiting their classroom participation in order to contain their smartness. These findings raise concerns about girls feeling the need to hold back to be accepted, one of many unrecognized issues in the dominant narrative of girls' academic successes.

Notes

1. Brainiac is a colloquial term for someone who is very smart, and cares about school and getting good grades.
2. This popular assertion fails to take into consideration the intervening variables of race and class, and fails to recognize that girls' successes do not lead to greater career prospects than boys' (Harris 2004; Ringrose 2013).

References

Abraham, Carolyn. 2010. "Part 1: Failing Boys and the Powder Keg of Sexual Politics." In *The Globe and Mail*, October 15.

Bourdieu, Pierre. [1983] 2001. *"The Forms of Capital" in the Sociology of Economic Life*. 2nd ed., 96–111. Cambridge MA: Westview Press.

Butler, Judith. 1990. *Gender Trouble: Feminism and the Subversion of Identity*. New York: Routledge.

Butler, Judith. 1993. *Bodies That Matter: On the Discursive Limits of "Sex."* New York: Routledge.

Butler, Judith. 1997. *The Psychic Life of Power: Theories in Subjection*. Stanford, Calif.: Stanford University Press.

Currie, Dawn H., Deirdre M. Kelly, and Shauna Pomerantz. 2009. *"Girl Power": Girls Reinventing Girlhoods*. New York: Peter Lang.

Davies, Bronwyn. 1997. "The Subject of Post-Structuralism: A Reply to Alison Jones." *Gender & Education* 9 (3): 271–284.

Davies, Bronwyn. 2006. "Subjectification: The Relevance of Butler's Analysis for Education." *British Journal of Sociology of Education* 27 (4): 425–438.

DiPrete, Thomas, and Claudia Buchmann. 2013. *The Rise of Women: The Growing Gender Gap in Education and What It Means for American Schools*. New York: Russell Sage Foundation.

Foucault, Michel. 1970. *The Order of Things*. London: Tavistock.

Francis, Becky. 2009. "The Role of the Boffin as Abject Other in Gendered Performances of School Achievement." *The Sociological Review* 57 (4): 645–669.

Francis, Becky, Christine Skelton, and Barbara Read. 2010. "The Simultaneous Production of Educational Achievement and Popularity: How Do Some Pupils Accomplish It?" *British Educational Research Journal* 36 (2): 317–340.

Frosh, Stephen, Ann Phoenix, and Rob Pattman. 2002. *Young Masculinities: Understanding Boys in Contemporary Society*. Hampshire: Palgrave.

Gonick, Marnina. 2006. "Between 'Girl Power' and 'Reviving Ophelia': Constituting the Neoliberal Girl Subject." *NWSA Journal* 18 (2): 1–23.

Hall, Stuart. 1996. "Introduction: Who Needs 'Identity'?" In *Questions of Cultural Identity*, edited by, S. Hall and P. Du Gay. London, Thousand Oaks, Calif: Sage.

Harris, Anita. 2004. *Future Girl: Young Women in the Twenty-First Century*. New York: Routledge.

Hey, Valerie. 2006. "The Politics of Performative Resignification: Translating Judith Butler's Theoretical Discourse and Its Potential for a Sociology of Education." *British Journal of Sociology of Education* 27 (4): 439–457.

Jones, Alison. 1997. "Teaching Post-Structuralist Feminist Theory in Education: Student Resistances." *Gender & Education* 9 (3): 261–269.

Kimmel, Michael. 1999. "'What about the Boys?' What the Current Debates Tell Us (and Don't Tell Us) about Boys in School." *Michigan Feminist Studies* 14: 1–28.

Kindlon, Dan. 2006. *Alpha Girls: Understanding the New American Girl and How She Is Changing the World*. Emmaus, PA: Rodale Books.

Kindlon, Dan, and Michael Thompson. 2002. "Thorns among Roses: The Struggle of Young Boys in Early Education." In *The Jossey-Bass Reader on Gender in Education*, 153–181. San Francisco: Jossey-Bass.

Mac an Ghaill, M. 1994. *The Making of Men: Masculinities, Sexualities and Schooling*. Buckingham: Open University Press.

McRobbie, Angela. 2004. "Notes on Postfeminism and Popular Culture: Bridget Jones and the New Gender Regime." In *All About the Girl: Culture, Power and Identity*, edited by A. Harris, 3–14. New York, London: Routledge.

Mendick, H., and B. Francis. 2012. "Boffin and Geek Identities: Abject or Privileged?" *Gender and Education* 24 (1): 15–24.

Milner, Murray. 2004. *Freaks, Geeks, and Cool Kids: American Teenagers and the Culture of Consumption*. New York, London: Routledge.

Pascoe, C. J. 2007. *Dude You're a Fag: Masculinity and Sexuality in High School*. Berkeley:

University of California Press.

Pomerantz, Shauna, and Rebecca Raby. 2011. "'Oh, She's So Smart': Girls Complex Engagements with Post/Feminist Narratives of Academic Success." *Gender & Education* 23 (5): 549–564.

Pomerantz, Shauna, and Rebecca Raby. Forthcoming. "The Post-Nerd: Reading Smart Girls in Post-Feminist Popular Culture." In *Girls, Texts, Cultures*, edited by C. Bradford and M. Reimer. Waterloo: Wilfrid Laurier University Press.

Pomerantz, Shauna, Rebecca Raby, and Andrea Stefanik. 2013. "Girls Run the World? Caught between Sexism and Post-Feminism in the School." *Gender & Society* 27 (2): 185–207.

Raby, Rebecca, and Shauna, Pomerantz. Forthcoming. "Landscapes of Academic Success: Girls, Location, and the Importance of School Culture." In *Girlhood Studies and the Politics of Place*: Contemporary Paradigms for Research, edited by C. A. Mitchell and C. Rentschler. New York, Oxford: Berghahn Books.

Renold, Emma, and Alexandra Allan. 2006. "Bright and Beautiful: High-Achieving Girls Ambivalent Femininities and the Feminisation of Success." *Discourse: Studies in the Cultural Politics of Education* 27 (4): 457–473.

Rimer, Sara. 2007. "For Girls, It's Be Yourself, and Be Perfect, Too." New York times.com (June 28, 2009), http://www.nytimes.com/2007/04/01/us/01girls.html.

Ringrose, Jessica. 2013. *Postfeminist Education? Girls and the Sexual Politics of Schooling*. London: Routledge.

Ringrose, Jessica, and Valerie Walkerdine. 2008. "What Does It Mean to Be a Girl in the Twenty-First Century? Exploring Some Contemporary Dilemmas of Femininity and Girlhood in the West." In *Girl Culture: An Encyclopedia*, edited by C. A. Mitchell and J. Reid-Walsh, 6–15. Westport, CT: Greenwood Press.

Sadker, Myra, and David, Sadker. 2002. "The Miseducation of Boys." In *The Jossey-Bass Reader on Gender in Education*, 182–203. San Francisco: Jossey-Bass.

Skelton, Christine, Becky Francis, and Barbara Read. 2010. "Brains before 'Beauty'? High Achieving Girls, School and Gender Identities." *Educational Studies* 36 (2): 185–194.10.1080/03055690903162366.

Walkerdine, Valerie. 1990. *Schoolgirl Fictions*. London, New York: Verso.

Walkerdine, Valerie, Helen Lucey, and June Melody. 2001. *Growing up Girl: Psychosocial Explorations of Gender and Class*. Houndmills, Basingstoke, Hampshire: Palgrave.

CHAPTER 22

Keeping the Ivory Tower White: Discourses of Racial Domination

Carol Schick

As a marker of difference and an indicator of respectability, space cannot be underestimated as a sign of personhood and legitimacy. This chapter examines a university space that remains dominated by those who identify as white. It examines how discourses in this university space function in ways that privilege whiteness, so that whiteness persists as what is worth knowing and as an identification worth performing. Ironically, the efforts to maintain the university space as white-dominated were instigated by the presence and acknowledgement of diverse populations in the university as well as a potential shift in power relations within the academy which was brought on by alternative political thought.

At the education faculty in the Canadian university in which this study is set, racial privilege was used to reconfirm the space as white in the midst of and, in part, because of the introduction of a compulsory cross-cultural course in a pre-service teacher-training program. I conducted semi-structured interviews with twenty-one white pre-service teachers who had attended this course. By applying a discourse analysis[1] to the interviews, I examined processes by which white identification is affirmed and supported by educated white participants who claim liberal values of equity and tolerance. My research indicates that racial identification processes, to which these participants have access, establish them as "rightful occupants" of university space. In many examples drawn from their discourses, participants perform themselves as belonging "in here," a place characterized by abstraction, objectivity, and rationality; quite unlike "out there," where others belong and which participants describe as political, embodied, and not necessarily rational. In their association with the university as a site of white domination, participants reinforce their identities, a process that further supports their performance of whiteness in other teaching arenas.

My understanding of how space produces subject identifications is drawn from the work of Sherene Razack,[2] whose analysis argues that space produces identities of both privilege and degeneracy. As a production of difference, the designation of space constructs and contains identities that are said to belong in a particular site. Social relations that converge in specific sites mark out places of privilege and elite formation against contamination by an outside Other. Since spaces produce identities, continuous surveillance is necessary to prevent the loss of privilege and respectability. My research findings illustrate that the surveillance and disciplinary practices that support the production of dominant identifications also produce intellectual identities in this site. Participants from this education faculty struggle to establish themselves as legitimate occupants of this white space in which their own claims to whiteness are insecure. In describing the multicultural course, they use the intellectual discourses of the university so that the influence *of* the Other is turned into discourse *about* the Other. These participants come to know themselves as knowledgeable, innocent, and in control; and their access to privilege is measured by how they use this compulsory multicultural course to confirm their rightful place in the university.

Spatial Arrangements

In 1988, the College of Education at the University of Saskatchewan accepted the proposal of the Subcommittee on Multicultural Teacher Education, which acknowledged that newly graduated teachers could expect to meet a diverse ethnic, racial, and minority student body within the province. The proposal constituted the framework for the motion passed at Academic Affairs (University Council), which required a compulsory course in multicultural education for all pre-service teachers with a specific focus on Aboriginal culture. The proposal's rationale reflected "the changing nature of the responsibilities of teachers and teacher educators in a country in which multiculturalism and human rights have become the cornerstones of Canadian citizenship."[3]

Multicultural education, framed as an issue that was "not going to disappear," was described as "consonant with the changing balance among ethnocultural groups in this country." The rationale and philosophical ethic of the proposed course were "concerned with equality of educational opportunity and outcome," and the "creation of multiculturally literate citizens who respect and promote linguistic and cultural diversity, social equality, racial harmony, and national cohesiveness as cornerstones of Canadian society." Finally, the compulsory course would ensure that graduates would "be able to function effectively in situations requiring cross-cultural perspectives, understandings and competencies."[4] After many course proposals and incarnations of the committee, a course was finally piloted in 1993–94.

In the multicultural course under discussion, over 90 per cent of students were white. Although Saskatchewan is a province made up of widely diverse ethnocultural groups, it is Aboriginal peoples whose critical mass most sharply challenges the discourses of hegemonic whiteness at all intersections of personal and institutional contact. Though the overarching view was to produce teachers who can teach "students from majority and minority backgrounds,"[5] and despite the variety of populations at this particular Canadian university, a significant purpose of this course was to produce white teachers who would "know something about" Aboriginal culture.

Since 1988, the course has become a requirement without which pre-service education students cannot graduate. Each year, several sections of the course are taught by both Aboriginal and white teachers. What, then, is produced by this compulsory multicultural course in a setting where students already perform dominant subjectivities? How is the setting contained and strengthened as an elite white space through the development of a compulsory curriculum that requires multicultural, cross-cultural learning of all its students?

Desiring Whiteness

The research participants were interviewed following their completion of the course. It is hardly surprising that the participants' greatest desire is to be accepted as legitimate entrants into a professional college of education and as successful teacher candidates. Many of the students are of non-Anglo European ancestry and from working-class origins; many have direct contact with older relatives for whom English is not a first language. Gaining access to norms and values formed in the privileged space of the university allows these participants to claim a "toehold on respectability."[6] The security of their white identities is dependent upon their construction of themselves as not-Other. As white-ethnic minority participants, they claim entitlement by moving closer to the centre of white norms and values by means of "dominance through difference." They need the credentials the university will give them and the ideological training to "become a teacher."

I am not assessing participants' interviews for particular racist or non-racist claims, nor suggesting that they express some essential white identity. I am examining their discursive practices for the processes they use to perform their subject identities in spite of, and perhaps because of, compulsory multicultural education. This includes tactics by which participants justify their university attendance as normal and appropriate. These discursive practices are not necessarily peculiar to a particular geographic location or a particular individual, but rather they are peculiar to a community of speakers in which the discourses are easily understood. I explore some of the discursive practices participants use to access the elite space of the university: specifically, their knowledge of how domination is organized and produced in this site.

For example, participants use discursive practices to justify their own positionings as respectable, innocent, and "well-intended." Kim pointed out that "when you see someone else getting stepped on ... your heart goes out to them because you know, hey, I've had it happen to me."[7] At other times, however, his identity as defender of the oppressed conflicts with his delight in experiencing the privileges of his educated white male status. He can hardly conceal his pleasure, for example, when describing how surprised he was, on a trip to the Philippines, to be called "Sir" by elders. Even though he suggests that others are elitist, this same position has become available to him as a university-educated white male.

Because participants' own dominant identities are not yet fixed, they require the university to uphold the racial configurations of a white teaching profession. By aligning themselves with this elite space, they secure their own legitimacy and respectability. Before I address the substantive issue of how participants produce themselves as white subjects in this elite space, it is necessary to discuss the contexts in which their claims to legitimacy are considered the norm.

Threatening Ideas

Cross-cultural, multicultural initiatives—also called anti-racist or oppositional—frequently meet with resistance. Difficulty in implementing and teaching such courses suggests that they pose some kind of threat in the spaces where they are introduced. Equity initiatives appear to be inevitably disruptive, no matter how carefully worded or ideologically mild the agenda. What is being endangered by a cross-cultural course in this white-dominated university of the Canadian Prairies? What are anti-oppressive courses up against? How might multicultural, cross-cultural stories implicitly undermine claims of white entitlement? What common-sense assumptions do they disturb?

From the very beginning, the compulsory nature of the cross-cultural course was considered an affront, even though it was by no means the only mandatory course in the participants' program. Margaret Wetherell and Jonathan Potter indicate that "[t]o define something as compulsory is, in terms of the liberal discourse of freedom and human rights, to define it negatively. Compulsion is automatically rhetorically bad."[8] Many view cross-cultural matters as a private affair and therefore resent the suggestion that they require preparation in a public space before they can encounter their racialized Other in the classroom.

The compulsory nature is also at odds with a popular Canadian persona: the laissez-faire individual who has no particular ideology except to allow others to live with their differences. The participants treat the course as an objectifying, intellectual exercise akin to mathematics and language instruction. However, their negative responses in describing the effects of the course indicate that they actually have had very little success at maintaining objective distance, suggesting instead the extent to which the experience of the course was more of a moral and ethical issue for many participants. They attempt to distance themselves by saying: "I really felt alienated in that class," "I was taking it to be almost a form of forced reverse discrimination," and "Why is this being shoved in our face all the time?"[9] By describing the course in such negative terms, participants can dismiss any effects the course may have had on them.

Multicultural education also threatens Canadian stories of immigration in which Europeans produce a national narrative that establishes them as the "original inhabitants." Heroic tales of successful occupation by white settlers are narratives that legitimize European, especially Anglo, claims of entitlement. Another part of the national narrative, however, one which is more conveniently "forgotten," is the colonizing process that threatens Aboriginal people with geographic, cultural, and economic erasure. The notion of historic Anglo entitlement shapes Canada as a white space in which Aboriginal land claims need not be taken seriously; this spatial configuration—which is a *dis/placement*—establishes European immigration as instrumental in the founding of Canada. The claims of Aboriginal people are ignored in the celebratory heroism attached to immigration mythology, and the construction of dominant white-identified people is established through the production of Aboriginal peoples as Other. The control of space, on which domination depends, also requires a relationship with another whom it is necessary to designate as abject and Other. Lenore Keeshig-Tobias describes the necessity of the Other for the production of dominant Canadian identities in her poem "O Canada":

> We have always walked on the edge/of your dreams, stalked/you as you made wild your way/through this great land/generation after generation/And, O Canada, you have always been/Afraid of us, scared, because you know/you can never live without us.[10]

In Western Canada, both degeneracy and privilege are produced as effects of spatialization. White entitlement is produced and rationalized as survey lines, deeds, boundaries, purchase prices, and mortgages—signs of ownership and belonging.[11] White entitlement is also produced relationally against the Otherness of original habitants. Production of the space as white, therefore, is never complete, and the identities that depend on the legitimacy of domination are forever insecure.

What else is challenged by a compulsory course on multicultural education? The proposal from the University of Saskatchewan refers to the recommendations of "definitive Canadian and international texts which implicitly critique the historical context of discrimination and racism"[12] in Canada. Canadian institutions are subject to the Canadian Charter of Rights and Freedoms, the Constitution, and the Universal Declaration of Human Rights, in which the rights of minorities are defended. Responding to diverse populations is not simply an act of conscience or a desire to "do the right thing." Mandating a multicultural course "reflects the changing nature of the responsibilities of teachers and teacher educators."[13] In an increasingly pluralist society, elite institutions can no longer maintain race, class, and gender barriers, that is, they cannot keep out the Other. Diverse populations and legal documents that protect minority interests may motivate multicultural studies, yet diverse bodies of knowledge on university campuses threaten the knowledge and space of the elite. David Sibley describes how alternate knowledge threatens established hierarchies and power structures in academia:

> There are certain parallels between the exclusion of minorities, the "imperfect people" who disturb the homogenized and purified topographies of mainstream social space, and the exclusion of ideas which are seen to constitute a challenge to established hierarchies of knowledge and, thus, to power structures in academia. In both cases, there is a distaste for mixing expressed in the virtues of pure spaces and pure knowledge. In both cases, it is power—over geographical space or over the territory marked out by groups within an academic discipline—which is under threat.[14]

How is this threat to "power structures in academia" averted or at least contained? One way is to offer a multicultural course. This course may forestall demands the Other might make on white space, contain challenges of racism and discrimination brought against the white spaces, and limit accusations that the academic space is exclusionary. Being supportive of diverse bodies of knowledge is consistent with inquiry and open-mindedness, the cornerstones of white liberalism. Ironically, while the multicultural course may be threatening, it strengthens the space as liberal and as one in which whites welcome the Other. The multicultural course threatens participants because it presents symbolic reminders of the Others' demands. Participants' whiteness and "toehold on respectability" are always insecure and they rely on their exclusive access to elite spaces to produce themselves as dominant. They also rely on the university space as a site for the reaffirmation of their bourgeois, racialized identity as the not-Other.

Space as a major metaphor in participant discourses is indicated by the often-repeated expressions "fit in" and "out there." The desire to fit in is protected against the unconstrained, illogical space where unpredictable, potentially harmful, outdated, and contrary knowledge resides. Participants are very much aware that "that kind of knowledge is *out there*"; even the "real" world of teaching is contaminated space. Participants take great care to keep their knowledge and identities safe so that they themselves are not "outed." They want to "fit into" an elitist knowledge centre with its access to a "regime of truth," which is characterized by middle-class status, whiteness, ability, normative sexuality, post-secondary education, up-to-date training, possession of cross-cultural knowledge (politically correct attitudes), assumptions of moral superiority, idealism, and innocence.

In the next section, I show how participants' discourses indicate that educational institutions work to their advantage in the formation of their entitlement. In these central places of education and learning, participants attempt to distinguish themselves from "other" ways of life found "out there." What is already in place to make these discourses understandable? To which discourses do white pre-service teachers already have access in the construction of white privilege?

Securing White Entitlement

RATIONALITY RULES

There are two techniques that participants use to secure white entitlement. The first is the identification with ideological space of rationality and objectivity. As a source of white bourgeois legitimacy, the university, like no other place, represents the establishment and practice of that most distinguishing trait of white male legitimacy: rationality.[15]

Participants use a variety of rhetorical strategies to claim this ideological space, including reporting the reactions of classmates, objectifying self- and others' reactions, making disclaimers, claiming credentials as a feminist sympathizer, offering evidence of supportive actions, and offering extensive qualification of negative remarks.[16] These strategies produce participants as utterly reasonable people, ones who understand the necessity of civility, rationality, and self-control. Participants have an interest in claiming these identities because logic and reasoning are not only highly prized in the teaching profession, they are also markers of civility and the right to govern. Their claims create a distinction between "us" and "them" around the ownership and distribution of emotions and intellect. In possession of intellectual control, participants offer their own rationality and moderation as the basis for dismissing other remarks with which they disagree; their demonstration of what is considered rational and reasonable maintains their identities as non-prejudiced supporters of tolerance.

Participants express negative remarks about the course in a variety of ways—not as biased opinions, but as statements of reasoned fact. For example, the course content is questionable because it implicates white participants in a racist history. This revised history undermines the participants' positions as neutral players; it calls into question issues of knowledge—who holds it? how is it constituted? what knowledge can be considered legitimate? Their conclusions lead them to believe that the "facts" of the course, which do not necessarily present a flattering image of racially dominant people, are merely a point of view or a particular slant; they are unfounded notions that need not be taken seriously. Participants also report that issues were forced on them, either by means of materials or by the professor's methods. Some hold that it was mildly coercive and others that it was outright manipulative: "I didn't like what the class was doing to me because it was changing how I felt and it wasn't changing it in a really positive manner." "This class was very much directed at trying to get you to believe, focus on cultural ideas and make you think those ideas."[17]

The expression "make you think those ideas" may be intellectually impossible, but does suggest that some kind of coercion is at work. Participants defend themselves against the implications of the course by describing it as something forced on them, further evidence of its emotional, irrational, and unreasonable premises. Both presentation and course material are suspect: "The Native focus was a little too Native."[18] The phrase "too Native" implies abandonment of all that is rational and civil while retaining the potential to *go Native*, a prospect that must be guarded against.

Even though the course is seen as unfairly emotional and irrational, the participants see their hostile reactions as completely justified and reasonable because they have been provoked. As Chris points out: "I really thought that [the course] was a travesty in many ways because I thought there was some really ... uncalled for situations that we were placed into."[19] Justification of their emotional responses signals participants' assertion of dominance. Even though their emotional response is a deviation from reasonableness, the contradiction goes unacknowledged. Instead, their manipulation of "rationality" indicates their insider knowledge about conditions under which deviations may occur. By rejecting the course, participants declare authority or superiority over it; similarly, their performance of a credible, dominant identification includes the authority to pronounce that their own extreme actions are reasonable. Citing that other classmates were similarly affected is further evidence of credibility.

These discourses rely on the university as the home of official white rationality and knowledge—the markers by which a taxonomy of difference may be established and where "different from" means "unequal to." Here is the mythological, safe, and pure place of abstraction and objectivity; the world of knowledge and theory; a place for the "disembodied" mind. There is no awareness of the university as a site where power relations exist. The assumption is that knowledge and intellectual teachings are objective and neutral and need not be challenged. Chris expresses her dissatisfaction when issues in the classroom became political and were no longer objective:

> I know there's problems that go beyond the university class. Like there's *problems with politics and things like that and I think that those are being brought into the classroom* rather than being sort of left at the door, and we were all people, looking for a better, some sort of a solution. *But those problems weren't left at the door, they were brought in.*[20]

The real-world politics of gender, culture, and classroom management are strongly resisted. When this intrusion happens—when an issue becomes too personal for comfort—participants use their indignation to re-establish their dominant identities and central positions. The space must be maintained; the identities—those who are in control and those who are not—cannot be confused. If participants' reactions are described as unreasonable, their authority and their ability to discern what is reasonable are undermined.

TAKING PLACE

The second technique participants use to secure white entitlement is to identify themselves with the physical space and with the normative designation of who is likely to be found there. It is hardly surprising that participants desire identification with the university. The attendance of people who do not fit any of those categories does not belie the claim that the university is a white, elite, male-dominated place. Indeed, the point of interest is how these hegemonic European values are maintained in spite of the presence of others who are neither male nor European. Criticism of university elitism is typically managed by suggesting that such arguments are one sign of the university's legacy of liberalism and rationalism as evidenced in its capacity for tolerance and open debate. Pat describes one of the attractions of the university in comparison to his workplace:

> If I took this class and I went back to [my trucking job], I wouldn't be able to go in and say, "You know, you can't really call the, you know, the Hispanic janitor, you know, a spic. You can't do that. That's bad." That part wouldn't go over very well in the coffee room full of, you know, huge stereotypical truck drivers. *At university you can discuss these things and talk about them....*[21]

Participants are very interested in associating themselves with the university; they look to it for the legitimating function it offers to those who do not necessarily come from the ranks of the social elite. In exchange, the speed with which participants are able to comply with the normative values and requirements determines how well they are prepared to "fit in" with university life and performance. For Pat, university is a place of privilege where learning takes place with intellectual types who are his equals: "You get spoiled at university, I find, because you're with a certain type of people all the time." The university is a rational place where differences on issues of race and gender can be discussed as intellectual topics. The social, economic, and intellectual gulf between the truckers' coffee room and the university is well marked; it is unreasonable to expect that the coffee room can accommodate what participants consider the same high standards of behaviour found in the pure space of the university. Pat, however, considers himself a liberal thinker and agrees that the ideas in the cross-cultural course should be taught to all university students, no matter what their course of study:

> Actually I'm saying that every course should be happening across the disciplines but this course in particular because we're talking about it; because when you step *out in the street in Canada* you can't get away from issues of culture or gender. They're all around you so to not integrate them I think is an *injustice to the very ideas.*[22]

Pat has indicated that he is a moderate in all things, therefore he is willing to discuss "culture and gender," which he assumes are part of what he will meet "out in the street in Canada." He identifies this street venue as separate from where he now resides. This meeting on the street will not be voluntary, but forced; and in a place that lacks order and control such as the street, one will have to expect such irrationalities as "culture and gender." In the pure white space of the university, these issues can be discussed as intellectual topics so as not to do "injustice to the very ideas." In his position as a privileged insider, he can assume that these are disembodied "ideas" that do not touch him personally and are separate from the life he now lives.

This participant offers himself as innocent and naive; he is shocked to learn that his levels of self determination and rationality are not experienced by all people. Although he is perhaps even more naive in his ignorance than he would care to claim, he is proud of his arrival at liberal thought and the level of control and autonomy he describes. He finds himself in a dilemma; he says that his liberal, autonomous outlook—characterized by such qualities as "saying whatever I like"; "having common sense, being rational"; "being a strong, independent thinker"; "being in charge of one's own destiny"—is not unique but neither is it a widely held belief. Furthermore, he assumes these qualities are his personal possession, his property, and warrant him taking up his position of privilege. These are the possessions that mark his dominance and of which he is proud. His expression of surprise that these qualities are not widely circulated or in general use does not completely cover his pride that his possession of them affords him a unique and powerful status.

The dilemma he faces is in trying to appear both humble about his access to elite space and, at the same time, maintaining that his privileges are available to everyone. He resolves his dilemma by claiming innocence and naïveté as well as by referring to his associations with other people from other cultures to refute any notion that his own access is culturally enhanced. Aída Hurtado suggests that "most [whites] can detect when whiteness is being questioned and its potential privilege dismantled."[23] The response is to de-emphasize its function as a group while at the same time universalizing its privilege by saying, like Pat, that "anybody" can achieve merit,[24] pretending that the value attached to being white does not exist. The contradictions in participants' discourses are most interesting for the use participants make of them and the tension participants produce by holding these conflicts.

Pat struggles continually, through many rhetorical devices, to keep himself in a good light, which is defined by objectivity, rationality, the life of the mind, and an uninvolved stance separate from gender and culture. He is the "anti-imperialist" "seeing-man"[25] who claims to be supportive of the cross-cultural course because it fits his liberal philosophy. He has figured out the "correct way" to think about Otherness; he knows what an anti-racist stance should sound like. Maintaining this particular identity as a sympathetic white male enhances his credibility in and entitlement to this dis/embodied white space. The university site recuperates whiteness and accomplishes the very successful performance of this participant identity in a way that cannot easily be questioned.

Beings in Outer Spaces

Yet there are those in the university whose identities—such as the representative Aboriginal professor—who are perceived as being "out of place." Her embodied presence poses a dilemma for many of the participants; some of their greatest hostility is reserved for her. For, if she can be a legitimate authority in this site, and if participants' own legitimacy is dependent on their whiteness, the presence of the Aboriginal female professor undermines their entitlement. The Aboriginal professor triggers conflicting desires such as authority/subordination in the professor–student relationship. Some participants find it confusing and some reassuring that even though at a distance they reject the professor's authority, they find her agreeable one-on-one. Chris displays a distinct lack of control, however, in that she both desires the professor for her difference and is repelled by her attraction:

> Before the class … *I had respect for the Native culture* and I understood the issues…. But *after the class I felt resentful in some way*. It wasn't … a growing experience. To me, it was a diminishing experience because I felt I became more narrow-minded. And since I've taken that class I've tried to put the class out of my mind because it wasn't a good experience. *And I think a lot of it had to do with the professor.*[26]

Chris rejects and anticipates the presence of the Aboriginal body as it is positioned to provide her with an experience of Western culture that is not otherwise available to her. For Bev, however, the smooth objectification of cultural knowledge is continually interrupted by personal relations:

> The professor at the university was not liked by our class as a whole. *We didn't like her because we felt she didn't like us….* It wasn't enjoyable to go to class because of the instructor. We challenged what she had to say. *We didn't accept everything she said word for word. We spoke our minds* and I don't think she liked that much….[27]

Participants consider their rejection of the professor as reasonable because it is in response to the professor's unreasonableness. That participants don't accept "everything she said word for word" indicates that they are discerning and rational, not slavish believers of what anybody tells them.

Jan, who reacts to contested spaces, has portrayed herself as credible and sympathetic by means of her personal interest in cross-cultural issues as well as her voluntary enrolment in a number of Native Studies courses. She frequently refers to her "place" in her interview, speaking of "out there" and "coming back," wondering where she and others "fit in."

Jan is caught in a dilemma of her own making. She is a supporter of Aboriginal issues and of what she calls "differences." But now that Aboriginal people are claiming the sites of their children's education for themselves—by organizing more band-controlled schools and hiring more Aboriginal teachers—Jan suggests that differences don't really matter that much. At the same time that she doesn't want her whiteness to be held against her or to exclude her from a job, she continues to rely on her white privilege for access to jobs in an Aboriginal school—a space that has never belonged to her and that has only recently been denied to her. She is very confused about her "place" and finds that her question of where she fits in is her greatest concern:

> Even after the information, I'm seeking it out, there's people out there that are saying well *you don't fit in*. I've had profs where I've asked that question in Native Studies or otherwise and got told well we don't want your help.... And as far as I'm concerned *I have to try to fit in*, and I mean maybe one day I'll be the minority. You know, *I want to fit in. I don't want to have no rights like you [Natives] had no rights.* Like, if one day I'm to come to Saskatchewan and you [Native] people make up the majority of the population, which could very well be, I'd like to know that *I'm going to fit in* somewhere. *I don't want to be treated the way you've been treated*, you know.[28]

The circle of benefits leads back to white control, even when the sense of place is not clear. The question "Where do I fit in?" must be answered so that white identity, as a condition of its privilege, will be secure. There is a strong sense of place in describing the "pure" and the "impure," but she questions how white dominant people are to "take their place" "out there" in areas where white privilege may be less secure than in the white space of the university. Even at times when sense of place may be uncertain, white participants assume that they will maintain their place as identity keepers and definers in their own lives and those of Aboriginal peoples.

An assumption that presupposes the contradictions and dilemmas of these participants is that cultures and identities are "settled," separate, and real. They rely on a realist approach when it supports their entitlement to attend the clean, well-lighted space of the university, or when they wish to secure the teaching job of their choice, or when they are granted privilege in hiring practices. In contrast, when participants explain their need for further entitlement to space to which they may not have ready access—such as teaching in Aboriginal-run schools—they eschew the notion of separate and divided identities. They assume that their privilege need not be a barrier to access because, with privilege, comes the ability to change at will the significance of their embodied status. Participants assume that they can transform their identities as required by performing themselves, in chameleon-like fashion, as "not really white." When coming up against the walls of contested space, white participants imagine they can pass through the walls by leaving their bodies behind.

These participants, as do many others, position themselves at the centre of a place-knowledge-privilege repertoire of self-definition. This repertoire occurs most often in the distinctions participants make between "here," where the participants are, and "out there." "Here" typically refers to a university environment, which is mainly white, middle-class, elite, straight, privileged, and often liberal in rhetoric if not in action. "Here" is a protected, enlightened, and enlightening place in the middle of raging storms of prejudice, unrealistic claims, and misinformation. By definition of quantity, "here" may be considered a minority position; but in these circumstances, adopting a minority position marks the exclusive rather than the excluded. This exclusive access supports participants in the performance of their roles as reliable witnesses in which they claim that various life circumstances have provided them with unique and unclouded perspectives. These unique positions are contrasted with participants' illustrations of how others have failed to be rational, moderate, knowledgeable, and fair.

When this self-referential place-knowledge-privilege cycle is interrupted by experiences such as found in the cross-cultural course, the participants struggle to re-establish their central positions. It is the disruption of the cycle that makes visible the norms that support it. Pat describes now the contested site of white privilege is neither exclusive nor secure: the "in here" place of the university is not completely pure, having among its members some aberrant character types:

> The things that happened in the course, I think, are a reflection of character … for good or for bad…. When you go into the washroom and you see somebody scrawling some racial or gender slur on the wall, I'm actually a little bit surprised about that because you think, geez, I mean, in university and they didn't even spell … that word right. What's going on? Oh, they didn't flush the toilet either, that doesn't surprise me. But when you get outside the walls of this institution, you're exposed to it everyday. I think I'm going to see it.[29]

That the university space has been invaded and contaminated by unreliable characters is an indication that white privilege and its power to exclude and define are continuously under siege. The contamination is an exception in this place where the walls typically act as borders between space that is rational and the space "out there" where disorder cannot be contained. Pat suggests that it is not rational to be racist and sexist, that evidence of discrimination and prejudice in the university would seem to be a problem of irrationality and an individual's bad character. Because whiteness signals innocence, it is inconceivable that this contagion could be from someone who "belongs" here.

The notion of secure spaces for the production and control of identities is a myth and an impossibility. Michel Foucault's illustration of the production of sexuality offers a good analogy of the production of racial identity.[30] He claims one is mistaken to assume that identities can be controlled or limited or that contagion is from without. In the case of sexuality, it is false to assume that everything learned about sexuality within the family is normative, proper, and "safe." On the contrary, as Ann Laura Stoler points out, the family is the site where sexuality acquires social meaning, where we begin to identify as sexual beings; as the family is the site where sexuality is learned, it is not a haven from "sexualities of a dangerous outside world, *but the site of their production*."[31]

I suggest that the same is true regarding the production of whiteness in university spaces. Like the familial context, these white places produce identities in which codes and expectations of proper white behaviour are vigorously enforced by reiterative, normative practices and designations of what is worth knowing. It is inconceivable to Pat that white privilege and racism are what one *learns* at university. He must maintain that elite white space is safe from contamination and innocent of racism because, tautologically, university space is elite and white. It is in these ideologically coded spaces that the performance of whiteness is most thoroughly embodied and reinforced as normative, especially in the midst of a course on multicultural education. Sexuality, class, ability, and ethnicity are learned through whiteness as the embodiment of what the Other is not. Here is the site where the performativity of whiteness coheres—in the "unsettled and unsettling"[32] population of the discursively absent Other.

Self-Preservation

The division of identities into site-specific locations supports a "grid of intelligibility"[33] through which a white bourgeoisie comes to define itself. Participants' access to white-identified spaces does not necessarily follow from racist practices or confrontations or from particular events. Rather, access is gained through using "historical discourse as a strategic weapon of power."[34] For example, class-and-race-specific sites of education—such as universities that are instrumental in the production of white identities—are one tactic for maintaining distinct spaces in Canadian society.

The participants' responses are reactions to a cross-cultural studies course, as I have tried to make clear, do not represent individual racist actions per se. Yet as Stoler explains, there are ways in which current discursive practices are used to "work up" and "assemble" older forms of racism already in place. Following Foucault, Stoler provides this understanding of racism:

> [R]acism is more than an ad hoc response to crisis; it is a manifestation of *preserved possibilities*, the expression of an underlying discourse of permanent social war, nurtured by the biopolitical technologies of "*incessant purification*." Racism does not merely arise in moments of crisis, in sporadic cleansings. It is internal to the biopolitical state woven into the weft of the social body, threaded through its fabric.[35]

The assumption that society must at all times be protected from the biological dangers of its ever-present "sub-race" produces an "internal racism," requiring "incessant purification" as one of the fundamental dimensions of social normalization.[36] Participants desire "incessant purification" as a justification for their claim to innocence.

"Preserved possibilities," which remain available for reproduction of the social order, can be contrasted with the effects of university space on the construction of Aboriginal students' identities. Rick Hesch describes the process of social reproduction in a teacher-education program for Aboriginal students attending a Prairie university. Hesch states that in spite of the affirmative nature of the program, Aboriginal students' experiences are racialized, gendered, and classed in ways that contribute significantly to their overall problem of staying in the university and completing their programs. Describing students' decisions to leave as a "choice" is ironic considering the exclusionary nature of the institution. Hesch continues, however, that even the successful completion of the program—constrained as it is by a university environment—"both enables and limits the possibilities for the development of [A]boriginal teachers."[37] At the same time, the affirmation of white identities in this site continues apace in that any lack of success Aboriginal education students may have in the university system leaves those jobs and the ideological spaces they might have filled still available for prospective white teachers. Through these spatial arrangements and preserved possibilities, the entitlement and belonging of white students is affirmed.

The "preserved possibilities" of the white participants are their rights to reject or access anything they choose such as the knowledge of cross-cultural teachers, positions in Aboriginal-controlled schools, or proprietorial status at a university. These "preserved possibilities" were in place long before they participated in their cross-cultural course, which for some participants was a moment of crisis.

For most of the participants, their interactions with the course placed them in contradictory positions which they struggled to explain: they defend their dominant subjectivities against the implications of the cross-cultural course and the anger and uncertainty it arouses; they affirm their identities as non-prejudiced, liberal individuals. They support their liberal identities by claiming their responses are rational and unemotional, quite unlike the responses of anyone with whom they might disagree. Participants justify their own emotional responses by implying that it is only what reasonable people would do when provoked by the unreasonableness of others. Participants rely heavily on a particular understanding of rationality and emotional control to mark them as self-determining individuals. Regardless of their own conduct or that of others, it is their description of the events that performs participants as insiders and demonstrates their control of the definition of rationality which is, perhaps, the single, most highly prized claim of white bourgeois subjects.

In ideologically white spaces such as university campuses, identities are produced both inside and outside the specific site. The maintenance of domination is actively supported by white students, as the participants in my project demonstrate. Their grasp on bourgeois white identification relies on their allegiance to prestigious white space and their access to privilege and social respectability. They depend on university processes and make full use of a mandatory multicultural course to support white domination so that they may establish and produce their own legitimacy as "good" teaching bodies and "respectable" Canadian citizens.

Notes

1. See Margaret Wetherell and Jonathan Potter, *Mapping the Language of Racism: Discourse and the Legitimation of Exploitation*. New York: Columbia University Press, 1992.
2. See Sherene Razack, "Race, Space, and Prostitution: The Making of the Bourgeois Subject," *Canadian Journal of Women and the Law* 10, 2, (1998): 338.
3. The Subcommittee on Multicultural Teacher Education, *Multicultural Teacher Education: A Proposal for a Multicultural Teacher Education Component for the Incorporation into the Program*. Saskatoon, SK: University of Saskatchewan College of Education, 1988, 5.
4. Ibid., 9, 13.
5. Ibid., 9.
6. See M.L. Fellows and Sherene Razack, "The Race to Innocence: Confronting Hierarchical Relations among Women," *Iowa Law Review* I, 2 (1998): 335.
7. Kim, interview with author, 10 November 1995. All names of interviewees are pseudonyms.
8. Wetherell and Potter, *Mapping the Language of Racism*, 189.
9. Responses are drawn from interviews with participants in November 1995.
10. Lenore Keeshig-Tobias, "O Canada (bear v)," in C. Fife, ed., *The Colour of Resistance: A Contemporary Collection of Writing by Aboriginal Women*. Toronto: Sister Vision Press, 1993, 69–70.
11. C. Harris, "Whiteness as Property," *Harvard Law Review* 106, 8 (1993): 1707.
12. The Subcommittee on Multicultural Education, *Multicultural Teacher Education*, 10.
13. Ibid., 5.
14. David Sibley, *Geographies of Exclusion: Society and Difference in the West*. London: Routledge, 1995, 116.
15. See David Goldberg, *Racist Culture: Philosophy and the Politics of Meaning*. Oxford: Blackwell, 1993.
16. See Wetherell and Potter, *Mapping the Language of Racism*.
17. Drawn from interviews with participants in November 1995.
18. Ibid.
19. Chris, interview with author, 12 November 1995.
20. Ibid. Emphasis added.
21. Pat, interview with author, 15 November 1995. Emphasis added.
22. Ibid. Emphasis added.
23. Aída Hurtado, *The Color of Privilege: Three Blasphemies on Race and Feminism*. Ann Arbor: University of Michigan Press, 1996, 149.
24. See Harris, "Whiteness as Property."
25. See M.L. Pratt, *Imperial Eyes: Travel Writing and Transculturation*. London: Routledge, 1992.
26. Chris, interview with author, 4 November 1995. Emphasis added.
27. Bev, interview with author, 4 November 1995. Emphasis added.
28. Jan, interview with author, 12 November 1995. Emphasis added.

29. Pat, interview with author, 15 November 1995.
30. See Michel Foucault, *The History of Sexuality: An Introduction*, trans. R. Hurley, vol. I. New York: Vintage Books, 1990.
31. Ann Laura Stoler, *Race and the Education of Desire: Foucault's History of Sexuality and the Colonial Order of Things*. Durham, NC: Duke University Press, 11995, 110. Emphasis added.
32. See Toni Morrison, *Playing in the Dark: Whiteness and the Literary Imagination*. New York: Vintage, 1993.
33. Stoler, *Race and the Education of Desire*, 53.
34. Ibid., 54.
35. Ibid., 69. Emphasis added.
36. Ibid.
37. See Rick Hesch, "Cultural Production Cultural Reproduction in Aboriginal Service Teacher Education," in L. Erwin and D. MacLennan, eds., *Sociology of Education in Canada: Critical Perspectives in Theory, Research and Practice*. Toronto: Copp Clark Longman, 1994, 200.

SECTION 3D

AGE, HEALTH, AND HEALTH CARE

CHAPTER 23

"Old People Are Useless": Representations of Aging on *The Simpsons*

Darren Blakeborough

HOMER: Hmm … sorry, Dad. You're too old.
ABE: [*Stammers.*] Too old? Why, that just means I have experience. Who chased the Irish out of Springfield village in aught four? Me, that's who!
IRISH MAN: And a fine job you did, too.
HOMER: Aw, Dad. You've done a lot of great things, but you're a very old man now, and old people are useless. [Tickles Abe.] Aren't they? Aren't they? Huh? Yes they are! Yes they are! Tee hee—
ABE: Stop it! That's a form of abuse. (Swartzwelder & Reardon, 1994)[1]

As words on a piece of paper, Homer Simpson's response to his aging father Abraham Simpson[2] could sound callous and derogatory. When Homer exclaims, "[Y]ou're a very old man now, and old people are useless," it is a sentiment—or at least representative of a sentiment—about aging that is increasingly echoed in North American culture. Cultural stereotypes abound that portray elderly people as senile, feeble, frail, financially distressed, lonely, non-productive members of society, or as the site of some other social problem. Existing research and numerous communications theories indicate that the mass media are largely responsible for helping to construct and transmit the ideologies that shape the attitudes of both young and old toward the aging process. This can pose problems in many different areas of society, as some report that "factual information about aging is rarely … presented in popular media" (Weaver, 1999,

p. 479). Many elderly people cite this as a primary problem with media representations of old age.

The exclusion of what is seen as a realistic portrayal of aging can leave many of our elders feeling that their lives and their wealth of lived experience are not accurately depicted in movies, television, print, music, or advertising. Others feel that they not only are portrayed unrealistically but actually have had their voices ignored altogether (Healey & Ross, 2002). Many are beginning to express concern that the media are presenting a reality that excludes the aging and are having an unfavourable influence over viewers. As a major socializing agent, TV helps to convey the images and ideals that ultimately help to construct our social fabric (see, e.g., Gerbner, Gross, Signorielli & Morgan, 1980). If the media exclude, stereotypically portray, show them as less than active members of society, or misrepresent elderly people in another fashion, this is the message the majority of the viewing public internalizes.

The argument that media images of aging are evolving into a more positive look at older adults is beginning to emerge, together with the notion that these positive images of the elderly are directly tied to consumer culture and product consumption (Bradley & Longino, 2001; Gerstel, 2007). The elderly—at least the young-old—are viewed as an attractive emerging market, consumers with burgeoning resources and little debt (Sawchuk, 1995; Tulle-Winton, 1999). Featherstone and Hepworth (1995) identify a new ideal emerging, where the idea of the elderly is not a sufficient label for all purposes, particularly marketing, and thus, this group has been bifurcated into *young-old* and *old-old* (and may potentially be divided further). This is important when marketing to the young-old, as the media "rarely depict(s) the old-old associations between 'deep old age', terminal illness, and death" (Featherstone & Hepworth, 1995, p. 44). So it is important to take from this the idea that the new breed of positive imagery does nothing to dispel the negative discourse on aging; it simply suggests how a good or a service can seemingly help to subvert this "horrible" process.

Stereotypes are generally negative, feeding off of small truths and exploiting irrational fears. When watching an episode of *The Simpsons*, it would be easy simply to look at the visual representation and ignore the context or even the audio, deciding that this is an ageist representation. There are many who take this approach. A colleague mentioned that he did not watch *The Simpsons* with any regularity, as he found its view of aging negative. The example that he chose to demonstrate this occurred in the episode "The Mansion Family" (Swartzwelder & Polcino, 2000), in which the aging Mr. Burns went to the Mayo Clinic for a check-up after winning an award as Springfield's oldest resident. While he is getting his physical, the doctor goes to take some blood. He plunges the syringe in Mr. Burns's left arm and it passes all the way through. Amazed, the doctor exclaims, "Well, isn't that odd? It's like poking through meringue," to which Burns responds, "Try this arm. I saw some blood in there the other day." After his test results come back, Burns meets with his doctor and this exchange takes place:

BURNS: Well, doc, I think I did pretty well on my tests. You may shake my hand if you like.
DOCTOR: Well, under the circumstances, I'd rather not.
BURNS: Eh?

DOCTOR: Mr. Burns, I'm afraid you are the sickest man in the United States. You have everything.
BURNS: You mean I have pneumonia?
DOCTOR: Yes.
BURNS: Juvenile diabetes?
DOCTOR: Yes.
BURNS: Hysterical pregnancy?
DOCTOR: Uh, a little bit, yes. You also have several diseases that have just been discovered—in you.
BURNS: I see. You sure you haven't just made thousands of mistakes?
DOCTOR: Uh, no, no, I'm afraid not.
BURNS: This sounds like bad news.
DOCTOR: Well, you'd think so, but all of your diseases are in perfect balance. Uh, if you have a moment, I can explain.
BURNS: Well … [*Looks at his watch. The DOCTOR puts a tiny model house door on his desk.*]
DOCTOR: Here's the door to your body, see? [*Brings up some small fuzz balls with goofy faces and limbs from under the desk.*] And these are oversized novelty germs. [*Points to a different one as he names each disease.*] That's influenza, that's bronchitis [*Holds up one.*] and this cute little cuddle-bug is pancreatic cancer. Here's what happens when they all try to get through the door at once. [*Tries to cram a bunch through the model door. The "germs" get stuck.*] [*Three Stooges-like.*] Woo-woo-woo-woo-woo-woo-woo! Move it, chowderhead! [*Normal voice.*] We call it, "Three Stooges Syndrome."
BURNS: So what you're saying is, I'm indestructible!
DOCTOR: Oh, no, no, in fact, even a slight breeze could—
BURNS: Indestructible.

While he was arguing that this was a stereotype of older adults as infirm and constantly in need of health care, it could also be argued that the irony in this scene helps to demonstrate the truly ridiculous nature of the images employed. This example demonstrates how a reading can differ between individuals and how irony can, in fact, be missed.

Is there an avenue for positive images of aging to exist outside of the consumption model? Relying primarily on theoretical writings, beginning with Frederic Jameson's (1984, 1991) postmodern aesthetic and Linda Hutcheon's (1985, 1989) work on parody and irony, this article will demonstrate how television's *The Simpsons* can be looked at as such an avenue.

Frederic Jameson's work is central to most investigations of postmodern aesthetics. Jameson's work in *postmodernism*, or the cultural logic of late capitalism, ushered in a new era in both Marxist and postmodern thought. Perhaps most influential is his thesis that postmodernism exists as more than simply a title for a specific historical period. Jameson (1991) counters this simplification using Marx's mode of production model to label postmodernism a new social epoch within a capitalist schema, which, it can be argued, moves somewhat from the production mode into the equally capitalist consumption mode. His views echo the writings of Jean Baudrillard as a paradigmatic shift occurs in neo-Marxist writings changing from a focus on production to consumer determinants (Duvall, 1999). Jameson sees capitalism as having three distinct eras, each with a different *cultural dominant*. He begins in the nineteenth century, with what he refers to as the age of *market capitalism*, also called *aesthetic realism*. His second epoch begins in the early twentieth century, with *monopoly capitalism* as the cultural dominant; this is also seen as the modernist era. It follows, then, that postmodernism would come next, and does, with what Jameson calls *late capitalism*.

He sees late capitalism as a multinational era, in which we operate on a global scale, as opposed to what others commonly call a *post-industrial* age (Kellner, 1997). While we seem to be moving away from an industrial cultural dominant, many still rely on the industrial model to a great extent. We are clearly not free of this dependence. Perhaps that is why Jameson eschews the term *post-industrial*. His packaging of late capitalism accepts the industrial model as well as recognizing that newer technological and theoretical imperatives exist, as all are able to inhabit simultaneously his concept of the cultural dominant. It is within this framework that Jameson expounds his ideas of postmodern aestheticism.

Linda Hutcheon's work on postmodernism emerges here, rejecting Jameson's approach to a certain extent and taking some of his ideas further, politicizing them, if you will. So while their views at times are conflicting and oppositional, I feel that it is both helpful and appropriate to utilize both because, as John Duvall (1999), explains, "Jameson's postmodernism focuses on the consumer, while Hutcheon's originates with the artist as producer" (p. 372). So, while they often purport to be writing about the same thing, they have inherently different approaches to similar topics. Duvall explains this by showing how Jameson views postmodern narrative as not having an historical reference in that it is a pastiche of imagery and aesthetic forms, which, at best, present history as degraded. Hutcheon, meanwhile, sees Jameson's "pastiche" as missing the mark, at least historically. Rather than being ahistorical, pastiche is parody, an historical fiction that, through the use of irony and satire, serves to politicize history and serves as a cultural critique.

To Linda Hutcheon (1989), irony is the ingredient that transforms the aesthetics of postmodernism from Jameson's pastiche of images or "blank parody" into a parodic textual entity that points out and questions the conventional. The decoding abilities of the reader (or viewer) incorporate the sense of agency missing from Jameson's aesthetic model, allowing for the politicization and historicization of the text. As she explains, one of the overarching tenets of postmodernism is its historicizing and politicizing of texts, making them available for critiquing. Postmodernism takes the form of

> self-conscious, self-contradictory, self-undermining statement. It is rather like saying something whilst at the same time putting inverted commas around what is being said. The effect is to highlight, or "highlight," and to subvert, or "subvert," and the mode is therefore a "knowing" and an ironic—or even "ironic"—one. (p. 1)

It is the subversion of the concept of "natural" that Hutcheon (1989) feels is postmodern;

she points out that representations are not, in fact, natural but are culturally constructed. This realization gives postmodern irony its strength. Drawing on postmodern theorist Victor Burgin (1986), the *politics of representation* recognizes the ideological grounding in all forms of representation and is cognizant that the "the self-reflexive, parodic art of the postmodern" serves to underline this with its ironic qualities (p. 55). This is the intrinsic political component of postmodernism.

Hutcheon (1989) takes Roland Barthes' notion of *doxa* as public opinion or "The Voice of Nature" (p. 3) and suggests that the postmodern serves to *de-doxify* or denaturalize the inherent politics of our cultural representation. The aesthetics of postmodern texts demonstrates the political dimension of our representations and ultimately serves to critique them. This allows us to recognize that everything we experience is "cultural"; in other words, "mediated by representations" (Hutcheon, 1989, p. 34). According to Hutcheon's (1989) definition, postmodernism is the means by which we question our reality, our representations, and our meanings; these include representations of older adults in our population. On the basis of these insights we can look closer at parody and how it operates within this postmodern schema.

Parody, according to Hutcheon (1985, 1989), is central to theories of postmodern aestheticism as it borrows from the past to show how the representations of our present have evolved, where they began, and what the ideological implications are. Borrowing from the past, parody uses irony as a "value-problematizing, de-naturalizing form of acknowledging the history ... of representations" (Hutcheon 1989, p. 94) as well as the political implications of those representations. Answering her critics, Hutcheon addresses their conviction that parody is nothing more than a pastiche without power, of imagery that does not take into account original contexts and history and thus falls short of becoming political. Hutcheon counters that postmodern parody does not disregard the context of the past representations it cites but uses irony to acknowledge the fact that we are inevitably separated from that past today—by time and by the subsequent history of those representations (Hutcheon 1989, p. 94).

So postmodern representation cannot ignore the context and the history of past representations: In acknowledging the past, it cannot help but showcase the passage of time and maintain the continuum that some theorists believe is missing from parody.

Hutcheon (1985) speaks of parody as being more than a simple intertextual reference. There is the implication in parody of "intention to parody another work (or set of conventions) and both a recognition of that intent and an ability to find and interpret the backgrounded text in its relation to parody" (Hutcheon, 1985, p. 22). When *The Simpsons* parodies other texts, like movies, books, TV shows, or even paintings, it does so in a manner that recognizes the history, showcases the passage of time, while adding a political colouring and uses irony in an attempt to create an arena for criticism.

Irony takes representations, highlights the contradictions, the processes of production, and calls attention to them, asking for a critique. As with ironic readings, parodic readings (which, of course, often include ironic elements) require the participation of the audience. Parody offers us a look at the representations of the past; by "giving it [the past] a new and often ironic context, it makes similar demands upon the reader, but these are demands more on his or her knowledge and recollection than on his or her openness to play" (Hutcheon, 1985, p. 5). Thus, the reader's knowledge base dictates which parodic and ironic devices are available to subvert the history of representations. This is how *The Simpsons* utilizes ironic parody.

Parody borrows from past texts and through this historicization shows the evolution in our representations and their ideological implications. Answering critics who suggest that parody is simply a pastiche of old images with no inherent political power, Hutcheon (1985, 1989) shows that, by highlighting the passage of time and subsequent historical representations, parody meets the criteria for the political. While satire is utilized in *The Simpsons*, and effectively so, parody recognizes, pays respect to, and ultimately serves to authorize the original text. As Chatman (2001) notes, it is seemingly a respect for the original text that results in its parodization. Parody simultaneously ridicules as it pays respect and homage. Irony functions within this schema to showcase the contradictions and asks for a critical evaluation. *The Simpsons* utilizes ironic parody in such a way that representations are afforded a new contextual positioning, demanding that readers access their own base of knowledge in decoding the text. In his essay "Local Satire with a Global Reach," Beard (2004) agrees with this thesis, as he writes that the use of parodic representations on *The Simpsons* is purposeful and critiques American cultural ideals. Perhaps this helps to explain *The Simpsons*' popularity outside of the United States, as the show offers other nations a chance to view contentious representations of American culture with a decidedly superior attitude. As well, Beard (2004) suggests that the use of satire also helps to undermine "media-generated stereotypes through an interrogatory utilization of these same stereotypes with subversively ironic intent" (p. 288). Far from being the first media vehicle to use irony and parody, or to frame issues of aging, *The Simpsons* builds on a strong generic history in animation, situation comedies, and even jokes as it occupies terrain laid out by *The Flintstones*, *All in the Family*, *Golden Girls*, and *Roseanne* to bring together multiple approaches to visual representation. These representations are thus problematized, deprived of the badge of "natural" and thus open to a critical reevaluation. This article uses a case study of an episode from *The Simpsons* to meld all these elements into a singular cohesive account that shows the relations inherent in differing ideals. Through this approach, it will examine how *The Simpsons* creates a positive site for looking at aging.

Case Study

In order to illustrate postmodern theory and how it applies to *The Simpsons*, the following section looks at one complete episode, as well as instances from other individual shows, demonstrating how the theoretical underpinnings uncover a positive representation of age. An analysis of instances of irony, parody, and satire, will establish how, according to Linda Hutcheon's theoretical model, these serve to subvert the stereotypes they seem to employ. The episode being analysed here is "Old Money" (Kogen & Wolodarsky & Silverman, 1991). This particular episode has been selected for examination because it focuses on elderly characters, and there are many overt references to aging and to stereotypes associated with age. "Old Money" also makes parodic references to many other texts—including the 1936 film *Mr.*

Deeds Goes to Town, starring Gary Cooper; the 1932 film *If I Had a Million*, also starring Gary Cooper; and the 1963 film *Tom Jones*—as well as alluding to scenes from *A Christmas Carol* and Neil Diamond's *The Jazz Singer*.

The family drops Grampa off at the retirement home after another miserable third-Sunday-of-the-month outing. The sign out front reads, "Springfield Retirement Castle—Where the elderly can hide from the inevitable."

HOMER: Dad, next time we see you we'll do something more fun.
ABE: Ohhhhhhh. What could be more fun than today's trip to the liquor store? [*Angrily*] Thanks for the beef jerky!
MARGE: Say goodbye to Grampa, everyone.
BART and LISA: BYE! [*Homer speeds away.*]
BART: Ya know, Grampa kinda smells like that trunk in the garage where the bottom's all wet.
LISA: Nuh-uh. He smells more like a photo lab.
HOMER: Stop it! Both of you. Grampa smells like a regular old man, which is more like a hallway in a hospital.
MARGE: Homer, that's terrible. We should be teaching the children to treasure the elderly. (Kogen & Wolodarsky & Silverman, 1991)

The episode begins with this scene; the family drops Grampa off after their monthly visit. After returning Grampa to the Springfield Retirement Castle, the family speeds off, and the discussion turns to what Grampa smells like. Bart feels that Grampa smells "like that trunk in the garage where the bottom's all wet." Lisa believes Grampa smells more like "a photo lab." Homer chastises his children with a loud and abrupt "Stop it! Both of you." As we prepare for Homer to remind the kids to respect their elders or that Grampa is his father and their flesh and blood and that thus their comments are mean and hurtful, his admonishment is that Grampa "smells like a regular old man, which is more like a hallway in a hospital." So rather than stopping the children, or explaining that elderly people are to be respected, he simply corrects their stereotypes with another, that old people are antiseptic and smell like hospitals. This is, of course, where Marge assumes her role as the "responsible" parent. She chides her husband, reminding him that, as parents, they should be "teaching the children to treasure the elderly. You know, we'll be old someday." And there is the ultimate irony, of course, lost on Homer until now. Instantly fearful that what he has done to his father may happen to him, Homer gasps and asks, "You kids won't put me in a home like I did to my dad, will ya?" Bart has to think this over as it may have appeal. Like father, like son. This, of course, greatly worries Homer, fearful that his actions may come full circle later in life. Marge suggests that they need to set a positive example with Grampa, and Homer readily agrees. He is not doing this out of any altruistic feelings for his father; rather, he simply hopes to avert being placed in a retirement home by his children. Wanting to create a more positive family excursion, they make the decision that, next time, they will all go to Discount Lion Safari.

We next see Abe as he enters his room, angrily mumbling about his day with the family. He opens the top drawer in his dresser, slams the beef jerky into it, and closes the drawer. This is not the first time his family day has consisted of a trip to the liquor store; his drawer is overflowing with beef jerky. Then the residents are lined up like cattle at the dispensary window to receive their daily medication. Abe is given the wrong cup of pills and, through this mix up, meets Beatrice Simmons. While he tries to explain the error to the nurse by pointing out that he should have "two red ones for my back spasms, a yellow one for my arrhythmia, and two of … ," he looks to his right and notices Bea, "the bluest eyes I've ever seen in my life." After they have the situation righted and notice an initial attraction between them, they sit down and begin a seductive pill-taking campaign, an allusion to the famous dining scene in the movie *Tom Jones* but with less seduction and more medication. After much awkwardness—they lament that "you'd think this would get easier with time" and point out how they are acting "like a couple of stupid punk teenagers"—they make a date.

Looking around at the background as Grampa walks down the hallway to Bea's room and also in the other scenes from the retirement home, you cannot help but notice that plaster is cracked, ceilings are crumbling, wallpaper is peeling off, and there is a general feeling of deterioration in the building. None of the characters, however, take notice, as that is just the way that things are. Abe picks up Bea, they go dancing, and they sing to each other, and, while the same song plays, we are shown scenes of subsequent dates where they feed pigeons in the park, share a milkshake at the malt shop, and stroll along the beach. The scenes help to create different feelings about the couple, and about the aged.

The first scene shows them dancing and laughing and makes no overt references to their age as they float across the dance floor, nimbly and effortlessly. The scene in the malt shop hearkens back to the stereotypical date of the 1950s, at least as it has been presented in movies, TV, and even comic books. This lends a period feeling to the piece, establishing a specific era for the characters and demonstrating the ideal put forward by Bultena and Powers (1978) with their "denial of aging" theory. The characters in this situation, rather than falling into the stereotypical roles that the elderly are often seen in, deny their age by reverting to something from their youth, namely a date at a malt shop. The same can also be said of their walk on the beach, often the mantra for young people attempting to attract a member of the opposite sex through a singles ad. This creates a juxtaposition with their other activity—sitting on a bench feeding birds. Countless movies have used the stereotype to show lonely elderly people. But they are not alone; they are together, and they are happy. Does this subvert the stereotype? Does it at least cause us to question the history of these representations? And even though they are strolling hand-in-hand down the beach, in this scene, they wear Hawaiian print shirts and Abe is wearing shorts, looking like the prototypical representation of an elderly tourist. They both have a lot of skin showing and it is wrinkly. Perhaps excessively so. As well, as they stroll along, they are passed by a large turtle. An irony in this situation is that, while it demonstrates how slow they are (perhaps because of their age, and the notion of old and slow comes up again later in this episode), turtles live a long time, longer than most other animals. Apparently, old turtles are still quicker than old humans. The scene ends with them back at the home. Abe is playing the piano, both are singing, the floor is lifting, and the walls are peeling. We then jump to a new day.

It is Bea's birthday and Abe needs to buy a special gift for his girlfriend. Unfortunately, the only store he knows is the military surplus store, so he goes in looking for a gift. Unable to find a suitable gift, he is shown the store across the street that may be more appropriate, Grandma's World. The signs over the aisles name stereotypical items associated with old ladies, such as "hard candies," "doilies," "picture frames," "sea-shell soap," "sachets," and "potpourri." Abe decides on a wool shawl. The clerk has to check the "active wear" department to get a price check. The idea of a wool shawl conjures images of an old lady in a rocking chair knitting a blanket. Is that what we see as "active" for seniors?

While Abe is preparing for his date with Bea by wrapping her gift, Homer barges into the room, reminding his father that it is the third Sunday of the month again, the one day it would seem when the Simpson family feels obligated to spend time with the aging Simpson. Grampa is wrapping the present and not so politely tells his son that he "can't go, it's my girlfriend Bea's birthday," to which Homer mockingly replies, "Ohhhh, you have a girlfriend! Hee hee hee! Well, Happy Birthday, Bea," as he talks to an empty chair. Homer's assumption, in this instance, is that his father is senile and has an imaginary girlfriend. Despite his protests, Grampa is hauled away and forced to participate in the outing. While they drive along in the car, he tries to open the door and escape, only to curse the child-proof doors. This should be seen as ironic, as Grampa is the oldest and the patriarch of the Simpson family and he is being treated like a child, but so are many elderly people, so the irony is seemingly lost. While at the Discount Lion Safari, the family gets lost, gets stuck, is surrounded by lions, and is forced to spend the night in the park. This means Grampa will get home too late for his date. (When one of the park security members arrives on the scene in the early morning, he fires his shotgun and watches the lions scramble. This alerts the family, and, after rolling down his window, Homer is greeted with "Mr. Simpson, I presume," an allusion to the reporter who travelled to Africa to find the famous explorer David Livingstone and, upon finally meeting him in the jungle, uttered the now famous, "Dr. Livingstone, I presume"—another example of how *The Simpsons* utilizes parodic references as an inter-textual device.

When Grampa returns from this disastrous family outing, he runs into the Springfield Retirement Castle, exclaiming:

ABE: Outta my way, I've got a date with an angel.
JASPER: You don't know how right you are, Abe.
ABE: What?
JASPER: Ummm, sorry to be the one to tell you this, but, uh, Bea passed away last night.
ABE: Ohhhhhhhhh no.
JASPER: It was her ticker. Doc said her left ventricle burst.
ABE: Oh no, Jasper. They may say she died of a burst ventricle, but I know she died of a broken heart.

The viewer here, at least the viewer who took grade nine human biology, knows that a "burst ventricle" is, for all intents and purposes, a broken heart. We fade to black—which is important, as *The Simpsons* rarely uses fade to black as a transitional device—perhaps reflecting here the death of a character. We next see family and friends at the gravesite for the funeral. The rain is falling as six elderly men struggle to pull the casket out of the hearse and carry it to the grave.

ABE: I can tell she really cared for me; she didn't make me a pallbearer.
HOMER: I can't tell you how sorry I am, Dad.
ABE: Is someone talking to me? I didn't hear anything.
HOMER: OH NO! Dad's lost his hearing.
ABE: No, you idiot, I'm ignoring you. You made me miss the last precious moments of Bea's life. I'll never speak to you again. I haavvvve nooo soooonnn. [*Rips jacket.*]
[*Homer cries.*]

The admonishment that "I have no son" is a direct allusion to *The Jazz Singer*, starring Neil Diamond.[3] In this movie, the main character (played by Diamond) defies his strict Jewish father and pursues his dream of being a popular singer. The same movie is parodied in even more detail in the episode "Like Father, Like Son," where we, as viewers, learn that Krusty the Klown is really named Herschel Krustofsky and has defied his rabbi father by becoming an entertainer. Krusty and his father are estranged and the Simpsons set out to get them back together, at which time Rabbi Krustofsky also uses the "I have no son" line. Parodic references are not restricted to references to film or television texts either.

In "Old Money," as Grampa walks the streets of Springfield thinking about whom to give his money to, he looks around to see the homeless, the dilapidated "Pub-ic Lib-ary," and the other needy groups and individuals. Needing time to think, he stops at a diner for a cup of coffee and, in a shot reminiscent of the famous Edward Hopper painting *Nighthawks*, Grampa is sidled up to the diner counter as we see in from outside. This parody of the original painting serves a few purposes. First, it reminds the viewer of the original, and the feeling of emptiness or loneliness that it invokes. The figures in the diner of the original, looking contemplative and seemingly lost in their own thoughts, give us a window into what Grampa is presumably feeling at this time. The allusion also helps to establish the context and the history of the original painting. As the painting was created and placed in the 1940s, it hearkens back to a different time, ironically a time when a younger Grampa might have been seated, drinking coffee and thinking about the war. Obviously, Grampa is older, and that removal from the time of the original text juxtaposed with the now highlights and shows the history of both texts, rather than ignoring or ahistoricizing, as Jameson might claim. This is what Hutcheon (1985) refers to as "trans-contextualization" (p. 8). An original work, Hopper's painting *Nighthawks* has been incorporated into another medium, television animation, and works within the original context to create an ironic difference. *The Simpsons* regularly references other texts in each episode. Often as many as 10 or 15 overt references can be found, as these parodic and intertextual references help to place the program on a larger continuum of cultural programming from early TV, film, music, and animation, and that, in turn, despite what James claims, helps to give historical referents to both *The Simpsons* and the texts that they parody.

We find out from Bea's attorney that Abe has inherited $106,000 from his girlfriend. Unsure of what exactly to do with the sudden windfall, Grampa decides to give the money to "truly needy causes." In the movie *Mr. Deeds Goes to Town*, the main character, Longfellow Deeds, also inherits a large sum of money and decides to give it to needy causes. In both cases, characters are lined up and, one at a time, make a proposal to their potential benefactors for funding. In the movie, *If I Had a Million*, an aging millionaire is upset with those around him, family and otherwise, so, before he dies, he randomly picks eight people from the city directory to whom he will give his money. One of the lucky eight is a resident of a decaying retirement home, who uses the windfall to restore the building as well as gain control in order to implement softer rules. In "Old Money," Abe Simpson ultimately uses his money to do the same thing. However, shortly after he has been informed of his windfall, the director of the Springfield Retirement Castle comes in to schmooze with Grampa Simpson.

DIRECTOR: [*Opening door to Grampa's room.*] Mr. Simpson?
ABE: AHHHHHH! What is it?
DIRECTOR: I couldn't help overhearing about your newfound fortune and, uh, let me assure you that here at the Springfield Retirement Castle, money does make a difference.
ABE: Ehhhhh?
DIRECTOR: I mean, there are rubdowns, and then there are rubdowns.
ABE: Listen you, bloodsucker. Has it ever occurred to you that old folks deserve to be treated like human beings whether they have money or not?
DIRECTOR: Yes, but it passes.
ABE: [*Mumbling as he exits his room.*] … son of a …

In a situation like this, humour is used to present what can be a real issue in elder care when residents deal with retirement-home owners or directors. When Grampa lashes back at the director, he presents an argument that may be on the minds of many elderly. The exchange also parodies *If I had a Million*. In the film, the retirement-home resident randomly picked to get money has been having issues with her home director and, by putting the money into the home, is ultimately able to subvert the director's authority and change her position, to the benefit of all the residents. In *The Simpsons*, Grampa plans to use the money to fix up the old folks' home, and funds will then be available to treat old folks like human beings, whether they have money or not. The postmodern aesthetic devices present this issue in such a way that the reader is allowed to interrogate it—interrogate its history and its authenticity. This is what makes possible a political critique of the representation, not only our feelings as a society towards the elderly, but also of our concern with money, so that individuals with money are cared for, and about, differently than others. This idea is carried further, and the episode uses more stereotypes of aging, when Grampa realizes that he does not have enough money to help all those who need help. So what does he do? Apparently, what all old people in the United States do—he goes on a seniors' gambling junket.

Homer has figured out where his father is heading, and, hoping to prevent him from losing the money, he sets off in a desperate high-speed pursuit. Driving rapidly down the highway, eyes focused intently on the road, Homer gasps and goes into a power slide in his vehicle, as he tries desperately to make a last-second left-hand turn. He must have seen something, something important, the bus perhaps. As he screeches and squeals, he completes the turn and pulls into … a Krusty Burger Fast Food Drive-Thru. He hurriedly orders "a double cheeseburger, onion rings, a large strawberry shake, and for God's sake, hurry!!" He makes it to the casino, and screaming "noooooooooo," he watches his father win big at roulette. Trying to convince his father to quit while he's ahead, Homer is momentarily silenced by his father's impassioned speech.

GRAMPA: I think Rudyard Kipling said it best: If you can make one heap of all your winnings and risk it on one turn of pitch-and-toss, and lose, and start again at your beginnings [*by this point, soft emotional music is playing and the entire casino appears to have stopped to listen*] and never breathe a word about your loss, yours is the earth and everything that's in it, and, which is more, you'll be a man, my son.
HOMER: You'll be a bonehead!
GRAMPA: Put it all on 41. [*Nudges Homer.*] I've got a feeling about that number.
ROULETTE MAN: The wheel only goes to 36, sir.
GRAMPA: Okay, put it all on 36.
[*Nudges Homer.*] I've got a feeling about that number.
[*Homer stops his father from betting on 36, saving Grampa all his money. The ball ultimately ends up falling into the 00 slot.*]

This scene references a portion of the inspirational Rudyard Kipling poem "If," and Abe is reciting it, in this instance as well, for inspirational purposes. An irony at work here is that Homer has saved his father's money by ignoring this inspirational plea, and, as Abe goes on to say, "[F]or the first time in my life, I'm glad I had children." And, despite Homer's happiness at reconnecting with his father, he will simply take him back to the home and continue to ignore him in each subsequent episode.

As the program draws to a close, Homer sits outside on a bench, eating, while his father sits all downtrodden, suitcase between his legs, overflowing with money. In between bites, Homer asks, "So, uh … have you figured out who gets the money?" Watching his fellow Retirement Castle residents filing back onto their bus with their blue hair, shuffle steps, and walkers, Grampa pauses to stare at his wrinkled hands. We see them close up, from his perspective. He stretches and clenches them before folding them and turning to his son. "Yes, Homer, I have."

We see a shot of the aged home, falling apart and weatherbeaten. The roof is a patchwork quilt of materials, the awning hangs in tatters, and the yard is overgrown and unwieldy. A title appears across the screen that says "SIX MONTHS LATER," as the home slowly begins to morph into a bright, fantastic, and restored version of what it once was. Residents frolic in the front yard, light cascades off the shiny windows, and, perhaps most importantly, a new Springfield Retirement Castle sign hangs proudly, sans the "hide from the inevitable" tag line.

We go inside and see happy residents all sitting in new recliners, walls painted and adorned with colourful artworks, and a new big-screen TV playing. The pool table is fixed, the ceiling is not leaking, and books line the bookshelves—the opposite of how things were six months ago. A shiny gold plaque on the door reads "The Beatrice Simmons Memorial Dining Hall," in honour of Grampa's late girlfriend. The doors swing open to reveal an ornate room filled with tables and beautiful settings. Grampa steps up and announces to the crowd, "Come on in. Dignity's on me, friends!" Thanks to *The Simpsons* and its ultimately positive look at aging, dignity is available for all aging people. Interestingly, and perhaps even intentionally, dignity is tied to consumption and related to economics.

The representations of elderly people in "Old Money" conform to rigid stereotypes and expectations, to the point of helping to show just how ridiculous these are. This is often the result of the satirizing of these beliefs. For example, the sign in front of the retirement home that says, "Where the elderly can hide from the inevitable," mocks the idea that elderly people, at least those in homes, have no purpose left and are simply waiting for death's embrace. As we all know, while there are elderly people with health issues, others are still spry, alert, and contributing to society. Painting an entire group with one ludicrous brush of homogeneity shows, in a humorous fashion, how wrong this portrayal ultimately is. The irony, of course, is that Abe's new girlfriend does not manage to hide from the inevitable, as she passes away shortly after their first meeting.

The Simpsons uses ironic parody and satire as a tool for criticizing the values and representations shown and, despite Jameson's claims to the contrary, for helping to historicize them. By recognizing the history of these representations, by questioning their past and their legitimacy, the show offers more than simple imitation; it offers a political critique that opens the door for these representations to be undermined or subverted. Why have we looked at the elderly as frail, as helpless, as lonely, and as a burden? *The Simpsons* portrays them as such, some of the time at least, but the use of parodic and ironic devices within the show's postmodern aesthetic allows the viewer to see these portrayals with a critical eye. But what about people who do not get irony or parody?

Wayne Booth (1974) sees irony as moving "from the known to the unknown" or as "saying one thing and meaning the opposite" (p. 34). In his estimation, this leaves the reader with the task of having to reconstruct the sense of the ironic text, and such reconstruction, of course, requires competence on the part of the decoder—in the case of *The Simpsons*, not a reader but a viewer. Booth (1974) also explains how, because competence is required, irony can succeed or ultimately fail, and that is a risk that the author or producer must take. As a result, irony "risks disaster more aggressively than any other device. But if it succeeds, it will succeed more strongly than any literal statement can do" (pp. 41–42). As K.J.H. Dettmar (2004) suggests, *The Simpsons* succeeds for many reasons, not the least of which is that it encourages a critical evaluation of our world. As Ryan (1992) notes, "irony can be an elusive element—hard to pin down, not easily defined" (p. 59). Thus, decoding ironic texts can be problematic for various reasons. One of these, according to Dettmar (2004), is that irony is often "used primarily to reinforce and reinscribe an 'in-group' (wink-wink, nudge-nudge)" (p. 85). This position on irony runs counter to the views of most theorists, including Hutcheon. Dettmar is saying that, rather than being overtly political or truly critiquing texts, irony frequently serves only as an affirmation to the hip and cool of their hipness and coolness—a notion of irony that coincides with the modernist ideal of irony in all its elitism. To a literal thinker, then, the often (not so) subtle nuances of irony fall flat or are simply dismissed as being incorrect. By definition, postmodernism and postmodern irony are subversive of this ideal because, as Dettmar explains, they are "more democratic, more inclusive, more open and fluid" (p. 86). It is the element of subversion that gives postmodern irony its strength at creating oppositional meaning.

So *The Simpsons* employs what can be considered negative representations of the elderly, the same representations railed against in the literature and research. While these familiar stereotypes exist within the larger social structure and are repeated *ad nauseam* in our cultural texts, there exists a means by which such representations can be historicized, contextualized, probed, questioned, undermined, and subverted: With the opening of a critical discourse through the satiric and ironic parodizations of such representations on *The Simpsons*, we can look into the ideology that drives these portrayals in the mass media and our culture. We can look at representations of our elderly, question them, fight them, and—as we understand better their basis in ideology—dispel them. It was Homer Simpson who said that "old people are useless." Why does this feeling exist, and how can we change it? Stay tuned for the next episode of *The Simpsons*; an answer may be found there.

Notes

1. All quotes and/or scripts used throughout this paper are either transcribed by the researcher directly from video or DVD or else taken from the exhaustive Simpsons Archive: Episode Capsules at http://www.snpp.com/ unless otherwise noted.
2. Grampa Simpson, Abraham Simpson, Abe, and Grampa will all be used interchangeably to refer to the same character.
3. The original *The Jazz Singer* starred Al Jolson and was released in 1927. Considered one of the movies ultimately responsible for the demise of the silent pictures, it was mostly musical numbers with a limited number of conversational sequences. The parody in *The Simpsons*, and this line in particular, is thus to the Neil Diamond version.

References

Beard, D.S. (2004). Local satire with a global reach: Ethnic stereotyping and cross-cultural conflicts in *The Simpsons*. In John Alberti (Ed.), *Leaving Springfield: The Simpsons and the possibility of oppositional culture*. Detroit, MI: Wayne State University Press.

Booth, W. (1974). *A rhetoric of irony*. Chicago: University of Chicago Press.

Bradley, D.E. & Longino, C.F. (2001). How older people think about images of aging in advertising and the media. *Generations, 25*(3), 17–21.

Bultena, G.L. & Powers, E.A. (1978). Denial of aging: Age identification and reference group orientation. *Journal of Gerontology, 33*, 748–754.

Burgin, V. (1986). *The end of art theory: Criticism and postmodernity*. Atlantic Highlands, NJ: Humanities Press International.

Chatman, S. (2001). Parody and style. *Poetics Today, 2*(1), 25–39.

Dettmar, K.J.H. (2004). Learning irony with *The Simpsons*. In John Alberti (Ed.), *Leaving Springfield: The Simpsons and the possibility of oppositional culture*. Detroit: Wayne State University Press.

Duvall, J. (1999). Troping history: Modernist residue in Fredric Jameson's pastiche and Linda Hutcheon's parody. *Style, 33*(3), 372–390.

Featherstone, M. & Hepworth, M. (1995). Images of positive aging: A case study of *Retirement Choice Magazine*. In M. Featherstone & A. Wernick (Eds.), *Images of aging: Cultural representations of later life* (pp. 29–47). New York, NY: Routledge.

Gerbner, G., Gross, L., Signorielli, N. & Morgan, M. (1980). Aging with television: images of television drama and conceptions of social reality. *Journal of Communication, 30*, 37–47.

Gerstel, J. (2007, February 3). Sexy sells, senior doesn't. Columnists. *Toronto Star*. Retrieved February 3, 2007 from http://www.thestar.com/article/176903

Healey, T. & Ross, K. (2002). Growing old invisibly: Older viewers talk television. *Media, Culture, and Society, 24*, 105–120.

Hutcheon, L. (1985). *A theory of parody: The teachings of twentieth-century art forms*. London: Methuen.

Hutcheon, L. (1989). *The politics of postmodernism*. New York: Routledge.

Jameson, F. (1984). Postmodernism or, the cultural logic of late capitalism. *New Left Review, 146*, 53–91.

Jameson, F. (1991). *Postmodernism or, the cultural logic of late capitalism*. Durham, NC: Duke University Press.

Kellner, D. (1997). Fredric Jameson. In M. Groden & M. Kreiswirth (Eds.), *The John Hopkins guide to literary theory and criticism*. Baltimore, MD: John Hopkins University Press.

Kogen, J. & W. Wolodarsky (Writers) & D. Silverman (Director). (1991, March 28). Old money. [Television series episode]. In J.L. Brooks, M. Groening & S. Simon (Executive Producers), *The Simpsons*. New York: Twentieth Century Fox.

Ryan, A.J. (1992). Postmodern parody: A political strategy in contemporary Canadian Native art. *Art Journal, 51*(3), 59–65.

Sawchuk, K.A. (1995). From gloom to boom: Age, identity, and target marketing. In M. Featherstone & A. Wernick (Eds.), *Images of aging: Cultural representations of later life.* New York: Routledge.

Swartzwelder, J. (Writer) & M. Polcino (Director). (2000, January 23). The mansion family. In J.L. Brooks, M. Groening & S. Simon (Executive Producers), *The Simpsons.* New York: Twentieth Century Fox.

Swartzwelder, J. (Writer) & J. Reardon (Director). (1994, January 6). Homer the vigilante. In J.L. Brooks, M. Groening & S. Simon (Executive Producers), *The Simpsons.* New York: Twentieth Century Fox.

Tulle-Winton, E. (1999). Growing old and resistance: Towards a new cultural economy of old age? *Ageing and Society, 19*, 281–299.

Weaver, J.W. (1999). Gerontology education: A new paradigm for the 21st century. *Educational Gerontology, 25*(6), 479–491.

CHAPTER 24

Gender, Race, and Health Inequalities

Ann Pederson, Dennis Raphael, and Ellisa Johnson

Introduction

Health is grounded in the context of men's and women's lives: It arises from the roles we play, the expectations we encounter, and the opportunities available to us based upon whether we are women or men, girls or boys. Whether one is a man or a woman affects one's health status, use of health services, experience of illness, and engagement in health-related activities such as caring for others or participation in sports. However, while all societies are divided along the "fault lines" of sex and gender (Papanek 1984), there are other dimensions of social location such as race and ethnicity that also contribute to health through social processes of racialization, historical practices of exclusion and marginalization, and/or challenges in overcoming barriers in accessing care. Racialized discrimination against some immigrant groups in Canada and Aboriginal peoples has contributed to serious inequalities in health in both, but through different pathways.

When the combined effects of gender and race are considered, Aboriginal women—of which there were just under a half million in 2001—are among the most vulnerable members of Canadian society (Health Canada 2003b). For Aboriginal women, it is crucial to understand that the implementation of colonialism, which combined patriarchal practices with racism, shaped institutions, laws, legislation, and policies that have had a long-lasting negative effect on their health (Kubik, Bourassa, and Hampton 2009).

This chapter delves briefly into issues of gender, race, and health. In the first section, we consider women's and men's health comparatively, but also independently, with particular emphasis on women's health given the continued need to argue for its inclusion as a separate area of study, research, and practice. We argue that gender is a marker of social and economic vulnerability that manifests in inequalities in access to health and health care (Standing 1997). For women, income inadequacy and caregiving responsibilities are major contributors to health. The second part of the chapter looks more closely at how race and ethnicity contribute to health in Canada. We consider how the analysis of race and health is still in its infancy through two examples: (1) recent immigrants to Canada and (2) the health of Aboriginal peoples in Canada. Recent evidence suggests that while the health of recent immigrants to Canada is excellent, over time health status deteriorates, especially among immigrants of non-European descent. This may be due to the poor living conditions to which these immigrants are subjected. Research documents significant differences in health status and access to the determinants of health among many

Aboriginal peoples in Canada. At the end of the chapter we introduce gender-based diversity analysis—that is, the systematic examination of an issue from the perspective of gender and other social locations, including race, as a strategy to be incorporated into health research and policy development as a means to understand and improve health.

Gender and Health

KEY CONCEPTS

It can be useful to distinguish between "sex" and "gender" in discussing men's and women's health. "Sex" refers to biological aspects of being male or female. While sex is perhaps most visible in terms of reproduction, there are underlying physiological processes and anatomical features that are typically different in males and females. "Gender," on the other hand, refers to the social attributes commonly ascribed to males or females. All societies are organized in ways that reflect constructions of women and men as different kinds of people, with respective roles, responsibilities, and opportunities, including access to resources and benefits. As a social construct, the particular expressions and understandings of gender can vary over time and place and among communities. Behaviours, customs, roles, and practices are flexible and more variable across societies than the sex-related hormonal, anatomical, or physiological processes that typically characterize male and female bodies.[1]

Gender is a relational concept and involves not only the ascribed attributes that are systematically assigned to each sex, but also relations between women and men (Health Canada 2000), including gender power. For example, the legal codes that frame social relationships—such as marriage, divorce, and child custody—have important implications for relations between women and men (as well as for relations between partners of the same sex) by the ways that they shape access to or responsibility for employment, income, housing, child care, and social benefits. Such practices enshrine social norms and values and contribute to individual expectations and personal as well as social identities. These social processes, in turn, contribute to physical and mental well-being through access to resources, opportunities, and power. Thus, sex and gender interact to create health conditions, situations, and problems that are unique to one sex or that vary in terms of prevalence, severity, risk factors, or interventions for women or men (Greaves et al. 1999).

Sex and gender also interact with the other determinants of health discussed in this volume such as socio-economic status, paid and unpaid work, and disability (Janzen 1998). Patricia Monture-Angus (1985: 178) describes the interconnectedness of race and gender:

> I am not just woman. I am a Mohawk woman. It is not solely my gender through which I first experience the world, it is my culture (and/or race) that precedes my gender. Actually if I am the object of some form of discrimination, it is very difficult for me to separate what happens to me because of my gender and what happens to me because of my race and culture. My world is not experienced in a linear and com-

> partmentalized way. I experience the world simultaneously as Mohawk and as woman. It seems as though I cannot repeat this message too many times. To artificially separate my gender from my race and culture forces me to deny the way I experience the world. Such denial has devastating effects on Aboriginal constructions of reality.

Standing (1997: 2) describes gender as a marker of vulnerability in two senses in the global context:

> First, women are found disproportionately among the most vulnerable population groups. They tend to be poorer than men on average, to have less access to income earning opportunities and other resources, including health care, and to be more dependent on others for their longer term security.... Second, access to and utilization of health services are importantly influenced by cultural and ideological factors, such as the embargoes on consulting male practitioners, lack of freedom to act without permission from husbands or senior kin and low valuation of the health needs of women and girls compared to that of men and boys.

In Canada, women's health and men's health similarly reflect important sex- and gender-related opportunities and vulnerabilities.

HEALTH STATUS

According to Statistics Canada, average life expectancy at birth in 1999 was 79.0 years. Broken down by sex, however, women had an average life expectancy of 81.7 years, while men had an average life expectancy of 76.3 (Health Canada 2002). This breakdown illustrates the value of even basic sex-disaggregation of data as the overall figure masks the differences in life expectancy between women and men. However, as noted earlier, differences among women or men are also important to understanding the health of Canadians. Average life expectancy at birth in 1999 for First Nations people, living on and off reserve, was estimated to be 76.6 years for women and 68.9 years for men, sobering evidence of inequalities in Canada (Health Canada 2002). In 2005, life expectancy at birth for Aboriginal women was 76.8 years—over five years less than for non-Aboriginal women, whose life expectancy was an average of 82 years (Assembly of First Nations 2007a).

The main causes of death among women and men in Canada are similar: coronary heart disease, cancer, and chronic lung disease; however, an analysis of potential years of life lost (PYLL) indicates that a larger number of PYLL are attributable to accidents for men as opposed to cancer for women (DesMeules, Manuel, and Cho 2003). Further, the size of the difference in PYLL between women and men in Canada varies across the lifespan, "with the largest discrepancy between men and women emerging in early and middle adulthood, where death from external causes (e.g., motor vehicle accidents) occurs at a much greater rate for men" (Janzen 1998: 21).

Women's apparent health advantage is reduced when morbidity and health care utilization are examined. For example, women report more frequent long-term disability and more chronic conditions than men (DesMeules, Turner, and Cho 2003). Ruiz and Verbrugge (1997), among others, suggest that the higher mortality rate and lower life expectancy of men compared to women have been misinterpreted to mean that women enjoy superior health, completely ignoring, they contend, the higher prevalence of chronic conditions in women, particularly in later life. Moreover, women's health status may be converging with that of men's: Data suggest a narrowing of the gender gap in longevity in industrialized countries, most of it due to improvements in men's life expectancy (Trovato and Lalu 1996). Just as women's life expectancy increased dramatically in the middle of the 20th century as a result of reductions in maternal mortality, the current pattern of life expectancy observed between women and men may not hold in the future.

"Women are sicker, men die quicker" used to be an adage that supposedly summarized sex differences in health in Western industrialized countries such as Canada. Janzen (1998: ii) warns, however, that recent evidence of the complexity and variability of gender differences in health suggests that "broad generalizations about health-related gender differences are inappropriate." Let's consider at least six ways that sex and gender are important in shaping health and health care needs (Donner and Pederson 2004; Greaves et al. 1999).

First, there are sex-specific conditions, including the full spectrum of reproductive issues. These include birth control for women, pregnancy, childbirth, menstruation, menopause, and female infertility, as well as cervical cancer screening. For men, sex-specific conditions include prostate and testicular cancer and other diseases of the reproductive system, as well as male infertility and related problems. Second, there are conditions more prevalent among women or men, such as breast cancer, eating disorders, depression, and self-inflicted injuries in women and substance use, schizophrenia, and HIV/AIDS in men. Third, there are conditions that appear to be sex-neutral, such as heart disease, but where the signs, symptoms, and appropriate treatment may be different in women and men (Grace 2003). Fourth, there are the ways in which women's gendered roles in our society influence their health, including women's caregiving responsibilities; the sex-segregation of the labour force (both in general and within health care in particular); the demands of women's caregiving responsibilities, which contribute to their own ill health; women's average lower incomes; and women's greater responsibilities for combining paid work with child care or caring for other family members.

Fifth, gender stereotypes within the health care system itself may negatively affect women's health. These include both stereotypes about women's use of care and stereotypes about women's caregiving roles. For example, women are often assumed to use health care services more than men, but there is good evidence that this is related to sex-specific care and not to male stoicism or to women's predisposition to seek help. For example, in Manitoba in 1994–1995, the per capita cost of providing females with health care services funded by the medicare system was approximately 30 percent higher than for men. However, after the costs of sex-specific conditions were removed, and considering costs for both physicians' services and acute hospital care, the costs of insured health care services for women were about the

BOX 24.1 WOMEN, POVERTY, AND MINIMUM WAGE

Part of the reason that the wage gap is still as big as it is in Canada is because women make up two-thirds of minimum-wage earners. In Canada, minimum-wage earnings do not provide people with a fair income. In fact, minimum-wage earnings fall well below the poverty line. For example, Manitoba's minimum wage of $8.75 per hour (as of May 1, 2009) falls well below both the Low-Income Cut-Off (LICO), a formula determined by Statistics Canada that often acts as Canada's unofficial poverty line, and the Acceptable Living Level (ALL), a poverty line determined by anti-poverty organizations in Winnipeg.

TABLE 24.0

	Before Tax Low-Income Cut-off (Urban)	*Minimum-Wage Earnings	Acceptable Living Level (Pre-tax) in Winnipeg
Family of one	$21,666	$18,200	$15,430
Family of two (one adult, one child)	$26,972	$18,200	n/a
Family of three (one adult, two children)	$33,159	$18,200	$33,471
Family of four (two adults, two children)	$40,259	$36,400	$36,996
Family of four (one adult, three children)	$40,259	$18,200	n/a

*40 hours per week, 52 weeks per year, no allowance for sick days, holidays, or periodic layoffs. *Sources:* Statistics Canada, *Before Tax Low Income Cut Offs* (Ottawa: Statistics Canada, 2007); Social Planning Council of Winnipeg, *Acceptable Living Level* (Winnipeg: Social Planning Council of Winnipeg, 2003). Minimum wage rates were current as of May 2009.

What this means:

- According to LICO, a single person earning minimum wage falls 16 percent below the poverty line.
- According to LICO, a family of three in which the adult works 40 hours per week every week of the year and earns minimum wage falls 45 percent below the poverty line.
- According to the LICO, a family of four (two adults, two children) in which both adults work full-time all year, earning minimum wage, falls 10 percent below the poverty line.

Source: Women & the Economy. A Project of United Nations Platform for Action Committee. Available online at http://unpac.ca/economy/wompoverty4.html.

same as for men (Mustard, Kaufert, Kozyrskyj, and Mayer 1998). It has also been suggested that negative stereotypes about women lead to women receiving negatively differential treatment in everything from the use of life-saving drugs during heart attacks (Grace 2003) and the secondary prevention of ischemic heart disease (Hippisley-Cox, Pringle, Crown, Meal, and Wynn 2001) to physicians being more likely to assume women's physical symptoms are psychological in origin (McKie 2000).

Finally, there is the overmedicalization of normal aspects of women's lives, including pregnancy, childbirth, and menopause (Conrad 2007). This practice of framing normal life events as medical problems has been challenged by the women's health movement for over 40 years with some successes (for example, the reintroduction of midwifery into Canada and its organization as a licensed profession, and challenges to the view of menopause as an estrogen-deficiency disease). Recent marketing campaigns for products to manage erectile dysfunction and male-patterned hair loss suggest that men are not immune to this trend of overmedicalization either.

Some Issues Affecting Men's and Women's Health in Canada

SMOKING AND TOBACCO USE

While overall tobacco use has declined in Canada, the decline in smoking prevalence among men has been more pronounced than the decline in smoking prevalence for women, with men's prevalence having declined from 61 percent to 25 percent between 1965 and 2001, while women's smoking prevalence declined from 38 percent to 21 percent during the same time period (Kirkland, Greaves, and Devichand 2003). Moreover, smoking rates among teenaged girls are comparable to, or exceed, those of teenaged boys, and there is evidence that girls start to smoke earlier than boys (Kirkland et al. 2003). Aboriginal peoples have the highest rates of smoking in Canada (62 percent of First Nations peoples and 72 percent of Inuit were smokers in 1997 compared to 29 percent of the general Canadian population) (Reading 1999). Pearce et al. (2005) suggest that there are important gendered patterns within these overall data that link Aboriginal women's tobacco use to poverty, child-care responsibilities, few employment opportunities, and poor housing, among other factors.

INCOME ADEQUACY AND POVERTY

Poverty is one of the most pressing issues for women in Canada. Women are more likely to be poor than men in Canada, given current patterns of child-bearing, child custody following divorce, and women's employment over the lifespan. Families headed by lone mothers are particularly vulnerable to poverty, both in terms of incidence (56 percent were poor in 1997) and depth (incomes for poor lone-mother families were, on average, $9,046 *less* than the low income cut-off poverty line in 1997) (Ross, Scott, and Smith 2000). The situation among First Nations' households is even more serious. For example, of Nunavut's 30,000 Inuit, 13,000 live in decaying and overcrowded social housing and endure the "worst housing crisis in Canada" (Government of Nunavut and Nunavut Tunngavik Inc. 2004: 8). Although Nunavik's overcrowding rates are slightly higher at 58 percent than Nunavut's 54 percent, these numbers are still substantially higher than First Nations at 19 percent and the mainstream Canadian population at 5 percent.[2]

CHILD CARE AND CAREGIVING

The availability of child care is an important contributor to the quality of life of women as it is essential for the support of women's equality (Doherty and Friendly 2004). It assists women in their role as primary child-rearers and facilitates employment outside the home (Palacio-Quintin 2000). Similarly, home health and supportive care are important to Canadian women because women are the most likely recipients of such care, the most likely to be employed as formal caregivers, and serve as the primary caregivers of family members (National Coordinating Group on Health Care Reform and Women n.d.). As such they are most likely to be affected when such care is not available or accessible (Morris, Robinson, and Simpson 1999). These two issues typify how governmental policy directions affect the quality of life for women (Fast and Keating 2000; Friendly 2008).

Among First Nations families, the legacies of such experiences as residential schooling and forced removal from the land challenge many families to care for their children. According to the Canadian Incidence Study of Reported Child Abuse and Neglect, one in four First Nations children live in poverty, as opposed to one in six non-Aboriginal children (Trocme et al. 2000). Physical neglect as a result of poverty, poor housing, and substance abuse is the key factor for placing First Nations children in care. There are currently over 27,000 First Nations children in the care of the child welfare system across Canada. First Nations children are taken into care at a rate of one in 10, whereas non-Aboriginal children are taken into care at a rate of one in 200 (First Nations Child and Family Caring Society of Canada 2005).

VIOLENCE

Experiences of violence differ for women and men, although they report similar rates of victimization (Statistics Canada 2001a). As detailed by Eichler (1997), a man is more likely to experience violence on the street whereas a woman is more likely to experience violence from a family member in her own home. Men report higher rates of robbery and assault, but sexual assaults are more likely to be perpetrated against women than men (see Figure 24.1) (Statistics Canada 2001a). The meaning of these gender differences for the physical and psychological safety of women and girls is profound because often "home" does not provide them with security. While violence does affect men in the home, it is a tiny proportion of the violence experienced by men (2.3 percent), whereas it is the single largest type of violence experienced by women (27.5 percent) (Health Canada 2003a). Responses to "family" or "domestic violence" must reflect these gendered patterns if they are to be of any value in reducing the incidence of violence against women.

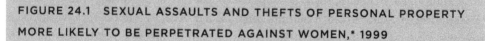

FIGURE 24.1 SEXUAL ASSAULTS AND THEFTS OF PERSONAL PROPERTY MORE LIKELY TO BE PERPETRATED AGAINST WOMEN,* 1999

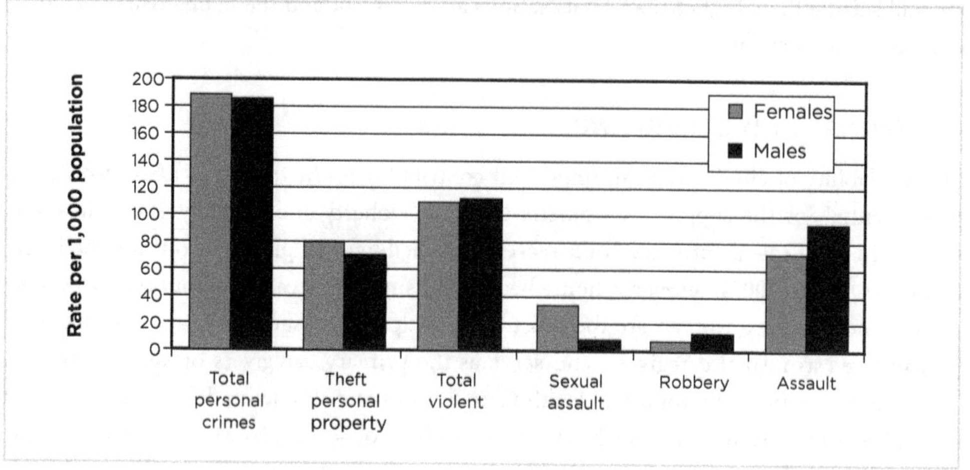

* Includes incidents of spousal physical and sexual assault.
Source: Statistics Canada, *Women in Canada*, Canadian Centre for Justice Statistics Profile Series (Ottawa: Statistics Canada, 2001): 7.

MENTAL HEALTH AND ILLNESS

Mental health and illness also offer interesting illustrations of sex and gender differences in Canada. Sex differences have been noted in the prevalence of specific mental health problems. For example, women are nearly twice as likely as men to be diagnosed with depression (Health Statistics Division 1998) and anxiety (Howell, Brawman-Mintzer, Monnier, and Yonkers 2001), particularly young women (Canadian Council on Social Development 1998). "In fact, according to the Canadian Community Health Survey on Mental Health and Well-being conducted in 2002, women of all age groups, and particularly young women aged 15–24, are more likely than men to perceive their mental health as fair or poor" (Statistics Canada 2005: 67). The highest prevalence of depression is found, however, among Aboriginal women, in part as a result of living in impoverished conditions (Health Canada 2003b).

According to the Assembly of First Nations, one in three (33.4 percent) First Nations women living on reserve have thought about committing suicide (suicide ideation) at least once in their lifetime; this is about the same rate as men (28.5 percent) (Assembly of First Nations 2007b). However, the relative difference increases significantly when lifetime attempted suicides are considered. Nearly one in five (18.5 percent) First Nations women reported to have attempted suicide at least once in their lifetime; this rate is over 40 percent higher than the reported rate for men (13.1 percent). This gender difference is apparent from the time First Nations individuals are in their teens: One in five (20.7 percent) girls between 15 and 17 reported having attempted suicide at least once in their lifetime, a rate that is almost three times the rate for boys aged 15–17 and over three times higher for girls aged 12–14.

Among men, in contrast to women, schizophrenia, certain personality disorders, and substance abuse are the most commonly diagnosed mental health problems (Culbertson 1997). Women and men also have different patterns of access to and use of mental health services, with women accessing the system more frequently, receiving treatment more often, and having higher rates of hospitalization for psychiatric problems than men (Federal–Provincial and Territorial Advisory Committee on Population Health 1996; Rhodes and Goering 1994).

Mental illness is associated with experiences of violence and trauma, and being mentally ill puts both men and women at risk for abuse, but women are typically more vulnerable than men (Anderson and Chiocchio 1997). Poverty and homelessness are associated with serious mental illness for both men and women in Canada, but less is known about homelessness in women than men, in part because the patterns of being without shelter manifest differently for women. Women are more likely, for example, to "couch surf" or stay temporarily with friends and family when they are without shelter, one effect of which is that fewer women appear in homeless shelters and in homelessness research, despite women's higher levels of poverty. Differences such as these have led analysts such as Morrow (2003) to call for a comprehensive policy response to women's mental health in Canada.

OCCUPATIONAL HEALTH

Occupational health research and practice remains largely gender-blind (Messing 1998). The labour force remains largely sex-segregated in some areas, despite the influx of women into many "traditionally" male occupations in the past 40 years. Interestingly, repetitive strain injury is equally reported by both men and women, but there is some evidence suggesting that the percentage of women affected by these problems is rising, particularly women in traditionally male-dominated occupations. Possible explanations include psychosocial aspects of the workplace, as well as poorly designed work stations, deadlines, and self-reported stress. In addition, many women's occupational health issues remain hidden in the household because women's labour in this setting is not recognized as work, and the health risks associated with unregulated activities in individual households are seldom the target of policy interventions.

Each of these issues illustrates the various ways that sex and gender influence patterns of health and illness among women and men in Canada. Sometimes the effects of sex and gender on health illustrate dramatic differences between women and men; sometimes the analysis shows that women and men share a similar experience of health or illness. In addition, the data suggest that among women and among men, some men and women experience these health challenges at higher rates than others. In particular, in Canada, Aboriginal women and men have a greater likelihood of living in poverty, with all its attendant problems. Sex- and gender-based diversity analysis supports better understanding of these issues and helps to highlight the specific ways that women and men are affected by health challenges and *which* women and men are particularly affected. These gender-related differences in health present a call for action from policy-makers, researchers, and clinicians.

Addressing Gender-Based Inequalities in Health

Canadian policy-makers have made numerous commitments to gender equality, as exemplified by Canada being a signatory to international conventions such as the 1981 United Nations *Convention on the Elimination of All Forms of Discrimination against Women* (Waldorf and Bazilli 2000) and the *Platform for Action*, which arose from the Fourth World Conference on Women in Beijing in 1995 (Health Canada 2003a). Canada has also taken many steps to support an expanded evidence base on women's health through, for example, supporting a women's health strategy and the Centres of Excellence for Women's Health, establishing a women's health theme within the Canadian Health Network (an electronic resource on health topics), introducing an Institute on Gender and Health as part of the national health research funding infrastructure (Canadian Institutes for Health Research), and developing training in gender-based analysis specific to the health field.

Evidence is not always available to facilitate gender-based analysis. For example, Statistics Canada's (2001b) *Access to Health Care Services in Canada* contains only sex-aggregated data. The production, analysis, and reporting of sex-disaggregated data is an important step toward understanding gender and health issues. However, it is not sufficient to understand these issues. Gender-based diversity analysis, "which wrestles with issues of women's social location, gender-related power and access to resources, is needed in addition to sex-disaggregated data to fully understand women's lives" (Donner and Pederson 2004: 18). Such analyses rest on an understanding of intersectionality (Weber and Parra-Medina 2003)—that is, an understanding of the multiple social processes underlying social experiences, including experiences of gender and race.

Many governments, health authorities, non-governmental organizations, and advocacy groups have developed women's health plans or strategies to address the specific health concerns of women in their communities. However, many of these efforts focus on aspects of care and are consequently addressing health outcomes rather than addressing the underlying social and economic structures that shape women's (and men's) health. Action on these more deeply embedded elements of the social structure may require action far beyond the health sector. Moreover, such strategies need to be developed with an awareness of women's lives so that women are truly able to benefit from the initiative. Financial support for caregiving, for example, is currently part of the Employment Insurance scheme in Canada. Unfortunately, access to this program is limited to people who work full-time and therefore many of the people who need this assistance the most—women—are unable to access the program because they do not qualify.

Race, Ethnicity, and Health

Despite a long-standing concern with the health status of Aboriginal peoples in Canada, analysis of the relationship of race and ethnicity with health remains in its infancy in Canada. Increasing attention in Canada is being paid to racial and ethnic issues in health as changing patterns of immigration see increasing numbers of members of visible minority groups.

These Canadian efforts—much of which is being carried out within an immigration studies focus—are directed at two issues: (1) the relationship of race and ethnicity to health status and (2) analysis of the quality of various social determinants of health experienced by racial and ethnic groups in Canada. A particularly important focus of this work is examining the health status and economic and social conditions associated with various "racialized groups."

This section discusses issues of race and health in Canada, with particular emphasis on the situation of two important but distinct groups: Aboriginal peoples and non-European immigrant groups. In Canada, these immigrants of non-European descent are often called "visible minorities" or "racialized groups," but may also include immigrants from the Middle East or North Africa who are, strictly speaking, White. "Racialization" is a term that considers how groups of individuals come to be treated in inferior ways than the dominant group (Allahar and Cote 1998).

Differences in health status among Aboriginal peoples in Canada and non-Aboriginal peoples are striking, as noted in earlier portions of the chapter. However, differences in traditional indicators of health status between racialized immigrant groups and non-racialized groups have, until recently, found few differences; frequently the health status of racialized groups is superior to that of Canadians of European descent. Two recent studies find, however, that the health status of non-European immigrants in Canada appear to deteriorate over time. In addition, recent research finds profound differences in economic and social conditions among racialized—especially recently immigrating—groups. This is important as difficult economic and social conditions are frequently precursors to poor health status, and these racialized immigrant groups represent a significant proportion of the population living in Canadian urban areas.

There is a well-developed sociological literature that concerns itself with the definition of race, ethnicity, and related issues (McMullin 2004). Clear consensus exists, at least among academics in the social sciences, that race and ethnicity are social constructions representing dominant or mainstream groups' historical attempts to maintain control and power over those identified as members of "other" races or groups. However, some health researchers and health workers do not share this view, and for them race and ethnicity are indicators of biological disposition to disease or a convenient marker to identify targets for public health interventions (Cruickshank et al. 2001). These differences in understandings of "race" as a biological or social construct are often reflected in research, policy, and practice.

Public health interventions frequently remain focused on modifying behavioural risk factors for disease such as tobacco use, physical inactivity, or poor diet, or improving access to health care. Less common is a public health concern with addressing the social and economic conditions that members of different racial groups are exposed to and working to modify these risk conditions through public policy. The concern in the discussion here is to consider two questions: How has the race concept been applied to understanding health and its determinants? What is known about health inequalities among members identified as being of different "racial" groups?

Key Concepts

Lee, Mountain, and Koenig (2001: 58) point out that: "Historically, race, genetics, and disease have been inextricably linked, producing a calculus of risk that implicates race with relative health status." Rather than view the greater incidence of a disease among a group as potentially reflecting social and economic conditions that result from discrimination and prejudice, these associations can be attributed to genetic causes. Duster (2003) argues that when the association between race and illness is viewed through a "prism of heritability," environmental and class-related causes of illness among specific racial groups tend to be ignored or suppressed. Similarly, Krieger (2003: 195) states that: "Myriad epidemiological studies continue to treat 'race' as a purely biological (i.e., genetic) variable or seek to explain racial/ethnic disparities in health absent consideration of the effects of racism on health." A social determinants of health view of "race" focuses attention on social explanations for observed differences and challenges the view that such differences are inherently biological.

For example, racial differences in health status can be attributed to exposures to specific material conditions of life that result from both membership in specific social and occupational classes, as well as the systematic experience of discrimination and prejudice. Members of racialized groups in Canada are overrepresented in lower status occupations and experience greater incidence of poverty and low income (Galabuzi 2005, 2008). There is increasing evidence that such overrepresentation is due to discrimination reflecting racism in Canadian society.

Jones (2000) outlines three forms that racism can take, all of which will have impacts on health. *Institutionalized racism* is concerned with the structures of society and may be codified in institutions of practice, law, and governmental inaction in the face of need. *Personally mediated racism* is defined as prejudice and discrimination, and can manifest itself as lack of respect, suspicion, devaluation, scapegoating, and dehumanization. *Internalized racism* is when those who are stigmatized accept these messages about their own abilities and intrinsic lack of worth. This can lead to resignation, helplessness, and lack of hope. These concepts are clearly applicable to Canadian society (Galabuzi 2005, 2008).

ABORIGINAL PEOPLES IN CANADA

Systematic reviews of health issues facing Aboriginal peoples in Canada are available (Health Canada First Nations and Inuit Health Branch 2003; Smylie 2008). Aboriginal peoples overall show significantly greater incidence of a range of afflictions and premature death from a variety of causes. These issues result from the poor state of any number of social determinants of health (e.g., income, housing, food security, employment and working conditions, social exclusion, etc.), and reflect a history of social exclusion from Canadian society.

There is a large gap in mortality between the Aboriginal and the general Canadian population. In 1996–1997, mortality rates among First Nations and Inuit people from eastern and western Canada and the prairie provinces were almost 1.5 times higher than the national rate. During this same period, infant mortality rates among First Nations peoples were close to 3.5 times the national infant mortality rates. Neonatal death rates are double the general Canadian rates, and post-neonatal mortality rates almost four times higher.

Further, off-reserve Aboriginal peoples rate their health status lower than the overall Canadian population (Tjepkema 2002). For every age group between 25 and 64, the proportion of Aboriginal peoples reporting fair or poor health is double that of the total population. The effect is more pronounced among Aboriginal women. For example, 41 percent of Aboriginal women aged 55–64 reported fair or poor health compared with 19 percent of women in the same age group in the total Canadian population. Among those aged 65 and over, 45 percent of Aboriginal women reported fair or poor health compared with 29 percent in the total female population. Poor economic and social conditions are responsible for these differences in health.

NON-ABORIGINAL PEOPLES IN NORTH AMERICA

UNITED STATES

Health disparities among racial and ethnic minorities is the focus of numerous research initiatives, national and state public health agendas, and local public health activity. Indeed, the focus on racial and ethnic disparities is so great in U.S. research that issues of health differences related to income and wealth, social class, and gender are frequently downplayed or neglected. As a result, a great amount of evidence is available concerning racial and ethnic differences in health status among Americans. The U.S. Department of Health and Human Services (2004: 1) provides the most recent information on these differences, which can be succinctly summarized as follows: "There are continuing disparities in the burden of illness and death experienced by African Americans, Hispanic Americans, Asian/Pacific Islanders, and American Indians/Alaska natives, as compared to the U.S. population as a whole."

In most cases, these racial/ethnic differences exist in life expectancy, infant mortality, and virtually every other indicator of health status. The predominant focus on the causes of these disparities is unduly focused on access to health care and behavioural risk factors with rather less attention paid to the economic and social conditions of these groups and the public policies that spawn these conditions. The precarious economic and social conditions under which these minority groups live are well documented, but these issues take a back seat to traditional health care and public health concerns with behaviour and lifestyle modifications (Raphael 2003).

CANADA

Canadian concern with issues of race and health as it relates to immigrant groups has been spurred by changing immigration patterns over the past 20 years. While previously a large proportion of immigrants to Canada were of European descent, Galabuzi (2008: 255) points out that: "There has been a significant change in the source countries with over 75% of new immigrants in the 1980s and 1990s coming from the Global South." Racialized (or visible minority) groups now constitute significant proportions of those living in many urban areas

TABLE 24.1 AGE-ADJUSTED PREVALENCE CONDITIONS, BY IMMIGRANT STATUS, CANADIAN-BORN AND IMMIGRANT, CANADA, 1994–1995

				European Immigrants Years in Canada			Non-European Immigrants Years in Canada		
	Total[a]	Canadian -Born	All Immigrants[b]	Total[c]	0–10	11+	Total[d]	0–10	11+
Any chronic condition	55.5	56.8	50.3d	55.3	46.7	57.7	44.7	37.2d	51.2
Sex									
Men	51.7	53.0	46.6d	51.1	39.8	54.7	40.8	33.8d	46.7
Women	59	260	553.8d	59.3	52.3	60.5	48.1	40.1d	55.6
Annual household income									
Less than $30,000	57.6	59.7	51.3d	57.4	46.3	59.5	45.8d	37.4d	55.5
$30,000 or more	53.9	54.7	49.8d	54.0	46.4	56.8	44.6d	39.0d	48.7
Education									
Less than secondary	55.5	56.3	52.5	57.7	55.2	58.8	45.7	37.0d	58.3
Secondary graduation or more	54.9	56.2	49.6d	54.4	45.8	57.0	44.6d	35.8d	50.1
Specific chronic conditions									
Joints	23.9	24.5	21.7d	24.9	28.1	25.7	16.4d	10.9d	20.0
Allergy	18.9	19.5	16.4d	17.3	-	19.6	16.0	11.2d	20.0
Hypertension	9.7	9.7	9.6	10.0	-	10.2	8.9	6.8	10.3
Headaches	7.3	7.2	7.4	9.1	-	9.4	5.4	<d	7.0
Asthma	5.6	6.0	4.1d	4.6	-	5.1	3.6d	<d	-
Heart/Stroke	4.9	5.0	4.6	5.2	-	5.4	3.3	<d	3.9
Sinusitis	4.3	4.7	3.2d	3.5	-	3.9	2.7d	-	-
Ulcers	3.5	3.5	3.2	3.7	-	4.0	-	-	-
Diabetes	3.4	3.5	3.2	2.8	-	2.9	4.2	-	4.3
Bronchitis	3.0	3.5	1.6d	2.2d	-	2.4	<d	<d	<d
Cancer	1.7	1.7	1.7	2.0	-	2.1	-	-	-
Urinary incontinence	1.1	1.2	0.9	1.1	-	1.1	<d	-	<d

Notes: (a) Includes unknown immigrant status, (b) Includes unknown country of birth (c) Includes unknown years in Canada, (d) Difference compared with Canadian-born significance at 95% confidence level, < or > Value significantly greater or smaller than that of Canadian-born, but not shown because of large sampling error. *Source:* National Population Survey, 1994–1995. Reproduced in J. Chen, R. Wilkins, and E. Ng, "Health Expectancy by Immigrant Status, 1986 and 1991," *Health Reports 8*(3): 29–38, Catalogue no. 82-003-XIE (Ottawa: Statistics Canada, 1996).

(e.g., Toronto, 36.8 percent; Vancouver, 36.9 percent; Calgary, 17.5 percent; Edmonton, 14.6 percent; Ottawa, 14.1 percent; Montreal, 13.6 percent; Winnipeg, 12.5 percent, etc.). Of particular concern is emerging evidence that the social and economic conditions under which members of racialized groups are living are distinct threats to health.

Unlike the situation in the U.S., there is little evidence—outside of studies of Aboriginal peoples—of health differences between racial groups (McMullin 2004). Much of this may be due to what has been termed the "healthy immigrant effect" whereby immigrants to Canada show superior health status to that seen for those born in Canada (Hyman 2001). Since a significant proportion of visible minority Canadians are relatively newly arrived in Canada and subject to health screening, it is not surprising that many studies find that non-White status really should have something that qualifies the terminology of "White" and "non-White" used throughout the document (Hyman, 2001) is not associated with poorer health status. Table 24.1 shows a very well-quoted study that shows that immigrant—both more recently arrived and those from earlier periods—show evidence of health status that is superior to those born in Canada.

However, the recent availability of both cross-sectional and longitudinal data from the National Population Health Survey (NPHS) provides compelling evidence that the health of immigrants to Canada—especially non-European immigrants—shows deterioration over time as compared to Canadian-born residents and European immigrants. Newbold and Danforth (1993) found that immigrants to Canada were more likely to rate their health as poor or fair than non-immigrants, and that this was especially the case for those who have been in Canada for longer periods of time.

A more nuanced and recent analysis is provided by longitudinal analysis of NPHS data (Ng, Wilkins, Gendron, and Berthelot 2005). They categorized respondents into four groups: (1) recent (10 years or less) European immigrants, (2) recent non-European immigrants, (3) long-term (more than 10 years) European immigrants, and (4) long-term non-European immigrants. They then examined the likelihood that individuals reported a transition from good, very good, or excellent health to either fair or poor health.

They found that, as compared to the Canadian-born population, recent non-European immigrants were twice as likely to report a deterioration in health from 1993/1994 to 2002/2003. Long-term non-European immigrants were also more likely to report such deterioration. There was no effect for either of the two European immigrant groups (Figure 24.2). Of importance was the finding that non-European immigrants were 50 percent more likely to become frequent visitors to doctors than the Canadian-born population.

The additional predictors of transition to lower health status included a number of factors best described as social determinants of health. These were low income adequacy, less education, and low support. As the authors commented: "Findings from the literature on immigrants' integration in Canada have shown that those with non-European origins have low-paid jobs that require little education. Because immigrants with European origins share a similar culture with the Canadian-born, they may encounter fewer social, economic, and lifestyle barriers than do those from non-European countries" (Ng, Wilkins, Gendron, and Berthelot 2005: 6). We now turn to these issues.

FIGURE 24.2: NON-EUROPEAN IMMIGRANTS WERE MORE LIKELY THAN THE CANADIAN-BORN TO REPORT A DETERIORATION IN HEALTH

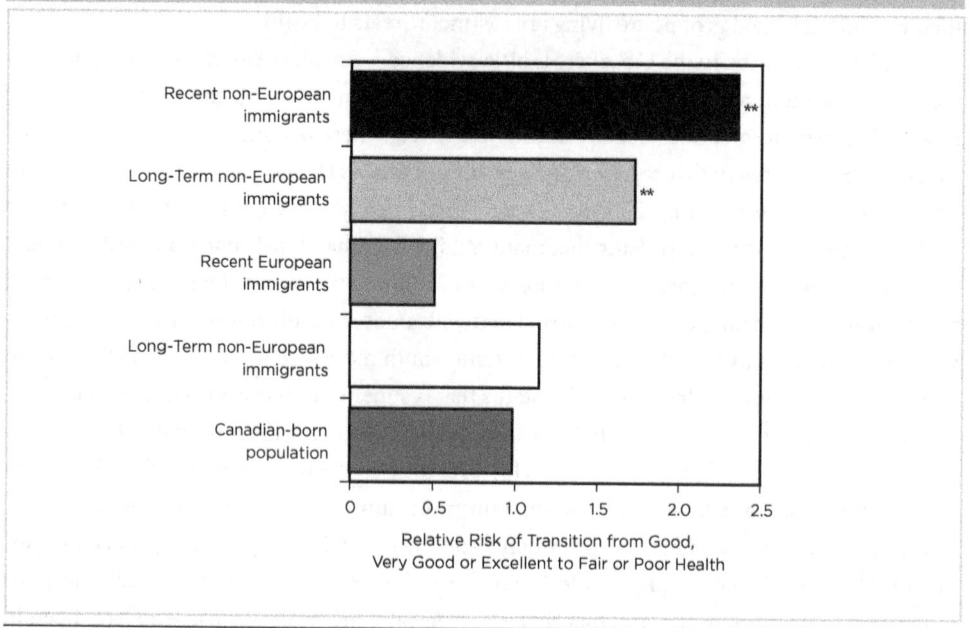

Data Source: 1994/95 to 2002/03 National Population Health Survey, longitudinal file.
Note: Analysis, based on individuals reporting good, very good, or excellent health in 1994/95; controls for age, sex, income adequacy, education, smoking, inactive leisure, social support/social involvement and body mass index in 1994/95.
**Significantly different from estimate for Canadian-born ($p<0.01$)
Source: E. Ng, R. Wilkins, F. Gendron, and J.-M. Berthelot, *Healthy Today, Healthy Tomorrow: Findings from the National Population Health Survey* (Ottawa: Statistics Canada, 2005): 3.

RACIAL AND ETHNIC DIFFERENCES IN SOCIAL DETERMINANTS OF HEALTH

Extensive scholarship is identifying profound differences in the material conditions of life among Aboriginal and visible minority immigrants, and non-White Canadians. These are clearly related to social determinants of health such as income, employment and working conditions, housing, and educational and recreational opportunities. Indeed, these differences are so profound as to require application of the broad concept of social exclusion as both process and outcome of various societal factors driving these differences (Galabuzi 2008).

Galabuzi (2005, 2008) provides evidence concerning the economic and social-status of racialized immigrant groups in Canada. Concerning the latter, these include: (1) 30 percent income gap in 1998 between racialized and non-racialized groups; (2) higher than average unemployment, with unemployment rates two to three times higher than non-racialized groups; (3) deepening levels of poverty; (4) overrepresentation in lower paying and lower status jobs; (5) differential access to housing; (6) increasing racial and economic concentration in Canadian urban areas; and (7) disproportionate contact of racialized groups with the Criminal Justice system (Ornstein 2000; Pendakur 2000; Reitz 2001).

Ornstein also provides evidence that the situation of recent racialized immigrants is profoundly less favourable as compared to Canadians of European descent than was the case 10–20 years ago (Ornstein 2006). This is the case for employment and unemployment rates, income levels, and poverty rates. Evidence is also accumulating that recent immigrants of colour are likely to experience greater incidences of mental health problems, lower incomes and lack of employment opportunities, greater contact with the police and justice systems, and housing and food insecurity than Canadians of European descent (Colour of Poverty 2009; Wallis and Kwok 2008).

Statistics Canada has documented differences in income and employment status of recent and earlier immigrants to Canada (Picot 2004). There is a consistent finding that the rate of low income among immigrants (particularly recent immigrants) has been rising during the 1990s while falling for the Canadian-born. Picot attempted to identify the factors responsible for the deteriorating economic welfare of immigrants and found that the rise in low-income status affected immigrants in all education and age groups, including the university educated (Picot 2004). The study found that the economic returns to recent immigrants for their work experience and education were diminished as compared to that seen for earlier immigrants. Considering that 75 percent of these recent immigrants were members of racialized groups, the hypothesis that racism and discrimination were responsible for these diminishing returns must be considered.

As noted, to date health status differences among racialized and non-racialized groups are not apparent. There is evidence from more in-depth studies of members of racialized groups in Canada that these members are encountering significant threats to physical and mental health that are not easily detected by traditional health status measures or are mediated by the "healthy immigrant" effect (Beiser, Hou, Hyman, and Tousignant 2002; Canadian Research Institute for the Advancement of Women 2002; Noh, Beiser, Kaspar, and Rummens 1999). However, international research indicates that exposure to adverse economic and social conditions are reliable precursors to disease. While in the past immigrants to Canada gradually reached income and employment levels comparable to the Canadian-born, this may not continue to be the case.

The pattern of increasing economic and racial concentration in Canadian urban areas suggests cause for concern (Hatfield 1997; Myles, Picot, and Pyper 2000; United Way of Greater Toronto 2004). Such concentration of visible minority groups has been associated in the U.S. with poor health and increasing social disintegration (Ross, Nobrega, and Dunn 2001). This process may well be underway in many Canadian urban centres, but to date there is little research that has concerned itself with the lived experience of members of racialized groups in Canada.

We also know nothing about the experience of discrimination and racism and their effects upon members of racialized groups. We would expect that such studies would replicate findings that refugees who reported the experience of racial discrimination had higher depression levels than those who did not (Noh et al. 1999). Research on the effects of discrimination in the U.S. and the U.K. suggest that attention to this area is needed (Karlsen and Nazroo 2002; Krieger 2003).

Conclusion

This chapter describes evidence of the relationships between gender, race, and health in Canada. Discussions of gender and health, and race and health, share the same challenge of competing explanations. To what extent are gender and race biological and/or social constructs? We believe that these concepts represent the effects of economic and social forces that then determine how these issues are construed by governments, academic researchers, and the public. To the extent that alternative views are held, the dominance of particular understandings will shape the research agenda and practical approaches for dealing with these issues.

This chapter describes evidence of the relationships between gender, race, and health in Canada. Regardless of the issue, it is apparent that probing for the possibility of sex differences is an important first step in analyzing health status, health service utilization, and health policies. Further analysis that considers the potential contribution of sex, gender, and their interaction in accounting for differences in health conditions, outcomes, experiences, and needs for services is useful and can help direct policy-makers, program developers, health care providers, and researchers.

A focus on the issue of gender and health can result in a tendency to treat "sex" and "gender" only in comparative terms and to reify the distinctions between men and women at the risk of understanding similarities and of recognizing that facets of the human experience, such as sexuality, are more diverse than is sometimes implied by the focus on "women" and "men." As work on gay, lesbian, bisexual, transgendered, and queer health grows, we learn more about not only the specific health problems of these people, but also how issues such as sexual orientation interact with constructs of gender in everyday life, affecting access to opportunities for health as well as health care (Mule et al. 2009).

While it is important to study health comparatively, as we have seen throughout this chapter, the study of women's or men's health independently remains important and necessary. Moreover, the differences among women and among men, as exemplified by the discussion that follows on racialization and health, are critically important because, as this article has illustrated, the determinants of health interact in the lives of individual men and women. Social structures and processes such as heterosexism, racism, ageism, and class call for critical diversity analyses in addition to gender-based analysis, as illustrated by the discussion that follows on race, ethnicity, and health (Jackson et al. forthcoming). Finally, sex and gender are linked to health inequalities in profound ways worldwide, far beyond Canada, which has implications for Canada's role as a global actor as well as for people who come from all over the world to Canada as immigrants and refugees. Indeed, women's health status is a central factor in measuring progress toward gender equity globally. As Doyal (2004: 162) argues, much remains to be done:

> Currently, less than 10% of current global funding for research is spent on diseases that afflict more than 90% of the population. This is referred to as the 10/90 gap in health research, and efforts to close it are mounting as part of the wider equity agenda

> in health. Increasingly, it is being recognized that gender issues must be central to these efforts, since women comprise the majority of the world's poor. The health of these women is affected not just by their poverty and by failures to meet many of their sex-related (i.e., biological) and reproductive health needs, but also by the wider gender (i.e., social) inequalities that continue to shape their lives. Men's health can also be negatively affected by their masculinity, with the poorest often at the greatest risk. Health researchers will need to take these factors just as seriously as more widely accepted determinants of health such as race, class, and ethnicity.

Research into race and health is a growing area of study. The Canadian Institutes of Health Research support sex- and gender-sensitive health research, though methodological issues remain. Yet much remains to be learned about the effects of sex, gender, and their interaction in order to understand the health of Canadian women and men, girls and boys. The literature on the effects of economic and social conditions suggests cause for concern regarding the health of members of racialized groups in Canada, many of whom are recent immigrants.

The economic situation of these individuals—many of whom are concentrated in urban areas—is clearly inferior to the situation of earlier arrived immigrants and the Canadian-born. Findings that these increased levels of poverty, unemployment, and social and economic exclusion are more persistent than that seen for earlier arrived immigrants is disturbing. The sources of these differences appear to reside in a general deterioration of Canadian social and economic environments that interacts with processes of racial discrimination directed toward newly arrived members of racialized groups (Krieger 2000; Williams, Neighbors, and Jackson 2003). As argued by Galabuzi:

> At a time when Canada's population growth and stability are increasingly dependent on immigration, with racialized group members now forming 13.5% of the population and growing and immigrants now 18.4% and projected to account for 25% of the population by 2015, these issues represent an important area of health policy and research. (Galabuzi 2008: 253)

Any attempts to include the health of Canadians must seriously address the key issues faced by women, recent immigrants, and people of colour in Canada. These issues include economic vulnerability, ingrained attitudes that prejudice the life chances of these groups, and public policy decisions that increase conditions of risk. Research must consider how increased economic and social insecurity interacts with gender and racial and immigrant status to influence health and well-being. At the same time, concrete actions need to be taken to address these conditions of risk and encourage actions that will promote the health of Canadians in general and members of these groups in particular.

Notes

1. On the other hand, research continues to grow, indicating the vast variability in the human body, including its structures and functioning. Despite our customary belief in two sexes, wide variability exists among individuals with respect to the presentation of sex-based physical characteristics, and research has demonstrated the complicated nature of sexual classification systems. One in 2,000 infants are born with so-called ambiguous genitalia, with sometimes dramatic results. Parents in North America, for example, are typically encouraged to decide upon the sex of their child very quickly and then to raise the child according to sex-appropriate norms. Such practices illustrate the tremendous significance of sex and gender in everyday life. People commonly want to know how to identify and label other individuals, and sex-based criteria are a major element of such practices.
2. Government of Nunavut and Nunavut Tunngavik Inc., *Nunavut's Ten Year Housing Action Plan* (Iqualuit: Government of Nunavut, Nunavut Housing Corp., September 2004): 8.

References

Allahar, A., and J. Cote. (1998). *Richer and Poorer: The Structure of Inequality in Canada*. Toronto: Lorimer.

Anderson, C., and K. Chiocchio. (1997). "The Interface of Homelessness, Addictions, and Mental Illness in the Lives of Trauma Survivors." In *Sexual Abuse in the Lives of Women Diagnosed with Serious Mental Illness*, edited by M. Harris and C. Landis, 21–38. Amsterdam: Overseas Publisher's Association.

Assembly of First Nations. (2007a). *Regional Health Survey (2007)*. Available online at http://www.rhs-ers.ca/english/phase1.asp.

———. (2007b). *Fact Sheet: The Health and Wellbeing of Women in First Nations Communities*. Ottawa: Assembly of First Nations.

Beiser, M., F. Hou, I. Hyman, and M. Tousignant. (2002). "Poverty, Family Process, and the Mental Health of Immigrant Children in Canada." *American Journal of Public Health* 92(2): 220–227.

Canadian Council on Social Development. (1998). *The Progress of Canada's Children, Focus on Youth*. Ottawa: Canadian Council on Social Development.

Canadian Research Institute for the Advancement of Women. (2002). *Women's Experience of Racism: How Race and Gender Interact*. Ottawa: Retrieved January 30, 2005 from Canadian Research Institute for the Advancement of Women.

Chen, J., R. Wilkins, and E. Ng. (1996). "Health Expectancy by Immigrant Status, 1986 and 1991." *Health Reports* 8(3): 29–38, Catalogue no. 82-003-XIE. Ottawa: Statistics Canada.

Colour of Poverty. (2009). *Fact Sheets from the Colour of Poverty Project*. Available online from http://cop.openconcept.ca.

Conrad, P. (2007). *The Medicalization of Society: On the Transformation of Human Conditions into Treatable Disorders*. Baltimore: Johns Hopkins University Press.

Cruickshank, J., J. Mbanya, R. Wilks, B. Balkau, N. McFarlane-Anderson, and T. Forrester. (2001). "Sick Genes, Sick Individuals, or Sick Populations with Chronic Disease? The Emergence of Diabetes and High Blood Pressure in African-Origin Populations." *International Journal of Epidemiology 30*(1): 111–117.

Culbertson, F.M. (1997). "Depression and Gender: An International Review." *American Psychologist 52*(1): 25–31.

DesMeules, M., D. Manuel, and R. Cho. (2003). "Health Status of Canadian Women." In *Women's Health Surveillance Report: A Multi-dimensional Look at the Health of Canadian Women*, 17–22. Ottawa: Health Canada, Canadian Population Health Initiative.

———, L. Turner, and R. Cho. (2003). "Morbidity Experiences and Disability among Canadian Women." In *Women's Health Surveillance Report: A Multi-dimensional Look at the Health of Canadian Women*, edited by M. Desmeules, 19–20. Ottawa: Health Canada, Canadian Population Health Initiative.

Doherty, G., and M. Friendly. (2004). *OECD Thematic Review of Early Childhood Education and Care*. Ottawa: Government of Canada.

Donner, L., and A. Pederson. (2004). *Beyond Vectors and Vessels: Women and Primary Health Care Reform in Canada*. Prepared for the National Workshop on Primary Care and Women, February 6–7, Winnipeg. Sponsored by the National Coordinating Group on Health Care Reform and Women and the Prairie Women's Health Centre of Excellence.

Doyal, L. (2004). "Gender and the 10/90 Gap in Health Research." *Bulletin of the World Health Organization 82*(3): 162.

Duster, T. (2003). *Backdoor to Eugenics*. New York: Routledge.

Eichler, M. (1997). *Family Shifts: Families, Policies, and Gender Equality*. Toronto: Oxford University Press.

Fast, J., and N. Keating. (2000). *Family Caregiving and Consequences for Careers: Towards a Policy Research Agenda*. Ottawa: Canadian Policy Research Networks.

Federal–Provincial and Territorial Advisory Committee on Population Health. (1996). *Report on the Health of Canadians: Technical Appendix*. Toronto: Federal–Provincial and Territorial Advisory Committee on Population Health.

First Nations Child and Family Caring Society of Canada. (2005). *Wen'de: We Are Coming to the Light of Day*. Available online at www.fncfcs.com.

Friendly, M. (2008). "Early Childhood Education and Care as a Social Determinant of Health." In *Social Determinants of Health: Canadian Perspectives* (2nd ed.), edited by D. Raphael, 128–142. Toronto: Canadian Scholars' Press Inc.

Galabuzi, G. E. (2005). *Canada's Economic Apartheid: The Social Exclusion of Racialized*

Groups in the New Century. Toronto: Canadian Scholars' Press Inc.

———. (2008). "Social Exclusion." In *Social Determinants of Health: Canadian Perspectives* (2nd ed.), edited by D. Raphael, 252–268. Toronto: Canadian Scholars' Press Inc.

Government of Nunavut and Nunavut Tunngavik Inc. (2004). *Nunavut's Ten Year Housing Action Plan.* Iqualuit: Government of Nunavut, Nunavut Housing Corp.

Grace, S. (2003). "Presentation, Delay, and Contraindication to Thrombolytic Treatment in Females and Males with Myocardial Infarction." *Women's Health Issues 13*(6): 214–221.

Greaves, L., et al. (1999). *CIHR 2000: Sex, Gender, and Women's Health*. Vancouver: British Columbia Centre of Excellence for Women's Health.

Hatfield, M. (1997). *Concentrations of Poverty and Distressed Neighbourhoods in Canada*. Retrieved July 2002, from http://www.hrdc-drhc.gc.ca/sp-ps/arb-dgra/publications/research/w-97-1e.pdf.

Health Canada. (2000). *Health Canada's Gender-Based Analysis Policy*. Ottawa: Minister of Public Works and Government Services Canada.

———. (2002). *Healthy Canadians: A Federal Report on Comparable Health Indicators 2002*. Retrieved January 30, 2005, from http://www.hc-sc.gc.ca/iacb-dgiac/arad-draa/english/accountability/indicators.html.

———. (2003a). *Exploring Concepts of Gender and Health*. Ottawa: Women's Health Bureau, Health Canada.

———. (2003b). *The Health of Aboriginal Women*. Ottawa: Health Canada.

Health Canada First Nations and Inuit Health Branch. (2003). *A Statistical Profile on the Health of First Nations in Canada*. Ottawa: Health Canada, First Nations and Inuit Health Branch.

Health Statistics Division. (1998). *National Population Health Survey Overview, 1996/97*. Ottawa: Statistics Canada.

Hippisley-Cox, J., M. Pringle, N. Crown, A. Meal, and A. Wynn. (2001). "Sex Inequalities in Ischaemic Heart Disease in General Practice: Cross-sectional Survey." *British Medical Journal 322*(7290): 832.

Howell, H. B., O. Brawman-Mintzer, J. Monnier, and K. A. Yonkers. (2001). "Generalized Anxiety Disorders in Women." *Psychiatric Clinics of North America Journal 24*(1): 165–178.

Hyman, I. (2001). *Immigration and Health*. Retrieved July 2002, from http://www.hc-sc.gc.ca/iacb-dgiac/arad-draa/english/rmdd/wpapers/Immigration.pdf.

Jackson, B., A. Pederson, P. Armstrong, M. Boscoe, B. Clow, K. Grant et al. (forthcoming). "'Quality Is Like a Carton of Eggs': Using a Gender-Based Diversity Analysis to Assess Quality of Health Care." *Canadian Woman Studies*.

Janzen, B. L. (1998). *Women, Gender, and Health: A Review of the Recent Literature*. Winnipeg: Prairie Women's Health Centre of Excellence.

Jones, C. (2000). "Levels of Racism: A Theoretic Framework and a Gardener's Tale." *American Journal of Public Health 90*(8): 1212–1215.

Karlsen, S., and J. Y. Nazroo. (2002). "Relation between Racial Discrimination, Social Class, and Health among Ethnic Minority Groups." *American Journal of Public Health 92*(4): 624–632.

Kirkland, S., L. Greaves, and P. Devichand. (2003). "Gender Differences in Smoking and Self-Reported Indicators of Health." In *Women's Health Surveillance Report: A Multi-dimensional Look at the Health of Canadian Women*, 1–8. Ottawa: Health Canada, Canadian Population Health Initiative.

Krieger, N. (2003). "Does Racism Harm Health? Did Child Abuse Exist before 1962? On Explicit Questions, Critical Science, and Current Controversies: An Ecosocial Perspective." *American Journal of Public Health 93*(2): 194–199.

Krieger, N. A. (2000). "Refiguring 'Race': Epidemiology, Racialized Biology, and Biological Expressions of Race Relations." *International Journal of Health Services 30*(1): 211–216.

Kubik, W., C. Bourassa, and M. Hampton. (2009). "Stolen Sisters, Second-Class Citizens, Poor Health: The Legacy of Colonization in Canada." *Humanity and Society 33*(1/2): 18–34.

Lee, S. S., J. Mountain, and B. Koenig. (2001). "The Meanings of Race in the New Genomics: Implications for Health Disparities Research." *Yale Journal of Health Policy, Law, and Ethics 1*(1): 33–75.

McKie, R. (2000). "Moaning Men Push Women to Back of Health Queue." *U.K. Observer* (May 7).

McMullin, J. (2004). *Understanding Social Inequality: Intersections of Class, Age, Gender, Ethnicity, and Race in Canada.* Toronto: Oxford University Press.

Messing, K. (1998). *One-Eyed Science: Occupational Health and Women Workers.* Philadelphia: Temple University Press.

Monture-Angus, P. (1985). *Thunder in My Soul: A Mohawk Woman Speaks.* Halifax: Fernwood.

Morris, M., J. Robinson, and J. Simpson. (1999). *The Changing Nature of Home Care and Its Impact on Women's Vulnerability to Poverty.* Ottawa: Status of Women Canada.

Morrow, M. (2003). *Mainstreaming Women's Mental Health: Building a Canadian Strategy.* Vancouver: British Columbia Centre of Excellence for Women's Health.

Mule, N., L. Ross, B. Deeprose, B. Jackson, A. Daley, A. Travers et al. (2009). "Promoting LGBT Health and Wellbeing through Inclusive Policy Development." *International Journal for Equity in Health 8*(1): 18.

Mustard, C., P. Kaufert, A. Kozyrskyj, and T. Mayer. (1998). "Sex Differences in the Use of

Health Services." *New England Journal of Medicine 338*(23): 1678.

Myles, J., G. Picot, and W. Pyper. (2000). *Neighbourhood Inequality in Canadian Cities.* Retrieved July 2002, from http://www.statcan.ca/english/research/11F0019MIE/11F0019MIE2000160.pdf.

National Coordinating Group on Health Care Reform and Women. (n.d.). *Women and Home Care: Why Does Home Care Matter to Women?* Retrieved January 30, 2005, from http://www.cewh-cesf.ca/healthreform/publications/homecare.html#homecare.

Newbold, K. B., and J. Danforth. (2003). "Health Status and Canada's Immigrant Population." *Social Science and Medicines 57*(10): 1981–1995.

Ng, E., Wilkins, R., Gendron, F., and Berthelot, J-M. (2005). *Healthy Today, Healthy Tomorrow: Findings from the National Population Health Survey.* Ottawa: Statistics Canada.

Noh, S., M. Beiser, V. Kaspar, and J. Rummens. (1999). "Perceived Racial Discrimination, Depression, and Coping: A Study of Southeast Asian Refugees in Canada." *Journal of Health and Social Behavior 40*(3): 193–207.

Ornstein, M. (2000). *Ethno-racial Inequality in the City of Toronto: An Analysis of the 1996 Census.* Toronto: Access and Equity Unit, Strategic and Corporate Policy Division, Chief Administrator's Office.

———. (2006). *Ethno-racial Groups in Toronto: A Demographic and Socio-economic Profile.* Toronto: York University Institute for Social Research.

Palacio-Quintin, E. (2000). "The Impact of Day Care on Child Development." *Isuma 1*(2): 17–22.

Papanek, H. (1984). *Women in Development and Women's Studies: Agenda for the Future.* East Lansing: Office of Women in International Development, Michigan State University.

Pearce, D., D. Schwartz, and L. Greaves. (2005). *No Gift: Tobacco Policy and Aboriginal People in Canada.* Vancouver: British Columbia Centre of Excellence for Women's Health.

Pendakur, R. (2000). *Immigrants and the Labour Force: Policy, Regulation, and Impact.* Montreal: McGill-Queen's University Press.

Picot, G. (2004). *The Deteriorating Economic Welfare of Immigrants and Possible Causes.* Ottawa: Statistics Canada.

Raphael, D. (2003). "A Society in Decline: The Social, Economic, and Political Determinants of Health Inequalities in the U.S.A." In *Health and Social Justice: A Reader on Politics, Ideology, and Inequity in the Distribution of Disease*, edited by R. Hofrichter, 59–88. San Francisco: Jossey Bass.

Reading, J. (1999). *The Tobacco Report: First Nations and Inuit Regional Health Surveys.* Winnipeg: Northern Health Research Unit, University of Manitoba.

Reitz, J. G. (2001). "Immigrant Skill Utilization in the Canadian Labour Market: Implications of Human Capital Research." *Journal of International Migration and Integration 2*(3): 347–378.

Rhodes, A., and P. Goering. (1994). "Gender Differences in the Use of Outpatient Mental Health Services." *Journal of Mental Health Administration 21*(4): 338–347.

Ross, D., K. Scott, and P. Smith. (2000). *The Canadian Fact Book of Poverty*, 2000. Ottawa: Canadian Council on Social Development.

Ross, N., K. Nobrega, and J. Dunn. (2001). "Income Segregation, Income Inequality and Mortality in North American Metropolitan Areas." *GeoJournal 53*(2): 117–124.

Ruiz, M. T., and L. M. Verbrugge. (1997). "A Two-Way View of Gender Bias in Medicine." *Journal of Epidemiology and Community Health 51*(2): 106–109.

Smylie, J. (2008). "The Health of Aboriginal Peoples." In *Social Determinants of Health: Canadian Perspectives* (2nd ed.), edited by D. Raphael, 280–304. Toronto: Canadian Scholars' Press Inc.

Social Planning Council of Winnipeg. (2003). *Acceptable Living Level.* Winnipeg: Social Planning Council of Winnipeg.

Standing, H. (1997). "Gender and Equity in Health Sector Reform Programmes: A Review." *Health Policy and Planning 12*(1): 1–18.

Statistics Canada. (2001a). *Women in Canada: Canadian Centre for Justice Statistics Profile Series.* Ottawa: Statistics Canada.

———. (2001b). *Access to Health Care Services in Canada.* Ottawa: Statistics Canada.

———. (2001c).*Women in Canada.* Canadian Centre for Justice Statistics Profile Series. Ottawa: Statistics Canada.

———. (2005). *Canadian Community Health Survey—Mental Health and Well-being.* Ottawa: Statistics Canada.

———. (2007). *Before Tax Low Income Cut Offs.* Ottawa: Statistics Canada.

Tjepkema, M. (2002). "The Health of the Off-Reserve Aboriginal Population." *Health Reports* (Supplement) 13.

Trocme, N., et al. (2000). *Canadian Incidence Study of Reported Child Abuse and Neglect Final Report.* Ottawa: Public Health Agency of Canada.

Trovato, F., and N. M. Lalu. (1996). "Narrowing Sex Differentials in Life Expectancy in the Industrialized World: Early 1970s to Early 1990s." *Social Biology 43*(1–2): 20–37.

United Way of Greater Toronto. (2004). *Poverty by Postal Code: The Geography of Neighbourhood Poverty, 1981–2001*. Toronto: United Way of Greater Toronto.

U.S. Department of Health and Human Services. (2004). *Health, United States 2004.* Washington: U.S. Department of Health and Human Services.

Waldorf, L., and S. Bazilli. (2000). *The CEDAW Impact Study*. Toronto: York University Centre for Feminist Studies.

Wallis, M., and S. Kwok, eds. (2008). *Daily Struggles: The Deepening Racialization and Feminization of Poverty in Canada*. Toronto: Canadian Scholars' Press Inc.

Weber, L., and D. Parra-Medina. (2003). "Intersectionality and Women's Health: Charting a Path to Eliminating Health Disparities. In *Advances in Gender Research*, edited by M. Texler Segal, V. Demos, and J. Kronenfeld, 181–230. Oxford: Emerald Group Publishing.

Williams, D. R., H. W. Neighbors, and J. S. Jackson. (2003). "Racial/Ethnic Discrimination and Health: Findings from Community Studies." *American Journal of Public Health* 93(2): 200–208.

Women & the Economy. A Project of United Nations Platform for Action Committee. Available online at http://unpac.ca/economy/wompoverty4.html.

CHAPTER 25

Invisible Populations: LGBTQ People and Federal Health Policy in Canada

Nick J. Mulé and Miriam Smith

Gender and diversity have become central issues in health policy-making. Increasingly, health policy analysis is grounded in population health or social determinants of health approaches that define particular populations as objects of policy intervention and that consider the impact of social inequality on health status and outcomes (Orsini 2007). This approach calls attention to the role of factors such as gender, social class, indigeneity, and race in health policy outcomes. Despite the increasing attention to gender and diversity in health policy over the 2000s, however, there continues to be a systematic lack of attention to lesbian, gay, bisexual, transsexual, transgender, two-spirit, queer and questioning (LGBTQ)[1] health issues. This paper explores this lacuna, pointing to the exclusion of systematic and explicit consideration of sexual orientation, gender identity, gender expression, and LGBTQ health, in federal health policy discourse.

The exclusion of LGBTQ issues from federal health policy discourse is important for a number of reasons. A wave of recent research has highlighted the extent to which the social location of LGBTQ communities and the discrimination and stigmatization experienced by these populations may influence health outcomes in a range of other ways, including higher rates of certain cancers, alcohol and tobacco use, reproductive health issues, sexually transmitted infections (STIs), barriers to accessing health care, lack of knowledge of medical professionals, and specific mental health concerns (Canadian Rainbow Health Coalition 2004; 2006; Jackson et al. 2006; Lehavot and Simoni 2011; Mulé et al. 2009: 20–21). LGBTQ health is most often referenced in relation to HIV/AIDS, which, from its emergence in the early 1980s, affected gay men more frequently than other groups. More recently, health issues affecting trans people have also been the subject of public discussion, as several provinces, including Ontario, have debated the funding of Sexual Reassignment Surgery (SRS) and other publically funded medical treatments for trans people such as hormone therapy. Aside from these areas, there has been little public debate in Canada about the distinctive health needs of LGBTQ populations.

Moreover, over the period from 2004 to 2011, the LGBTQ community has repeatedly called attention to health issues. A number of non-governmental organizations have been formed to push the agenda of LGBTQ health. [...] Therefore, in addition to recent research that shows the gaps in LGBTQ health provision, there is also political demand from LGBTQ stakeholders for increased recognition in health policy-making and delivery. [...]

In this article, we specifically examine federal health policy discourse and action, focusing on the major federal department that is responsible for health—Health Canada—as well as the Public Health Agency of Canada, charged with responsibility for public health. These federal bodies are responsible for national discourses, models, and perspectives that shape concepts of health and health care in Canada with international influence. Our purpose is to evaluate the extent to which federal policy discourse incorporates LGBTQ health issues. While the federal government is not responsible for the direct delivery of health services to most Canadians, it does play a lead role in macro-level discourse and health care strategies that influence health care delivery at the provincial and territorial level, where health care is administered. We then explain the methodology we used to evaluate the government's discourse, and we then present our findings that suggest LGBTQ interests are marginalized and silenced in federal health policy.

Methodology

In order to evaluate the federal government commitment to LGBTQ health, we surveyed policy and research documents produced by Health Canada and the Public Health Agency of Canada (PHAC) since 2004 and sought interviews with Health Canada and PHAC officials. While policy documents and research reports do not provide complete information on the implementation of federal health policy, they do furnish a reasonable basis for evaluating the federal government's health policy discourse. The government's policy agenda is defined and shaped by what it says about its own policies and research reports in publicly available websites, policy and research documents, and interviews. Even when research reports are not written by government staff, but commissioned from outside consultants or produced in partnership with other agencies, this research reflects the parameters and priorities set by the government departments and agencies that fund the research.

In order to develop a well-grounded picture of federal government health policy, we searched the publicly available documents authored or published by Health Canada and PHAC as well as searching the documents available on the Health Canada and PHAC websites. Health Canada is the main federal health ministry and PHAC is the main agency responsible for public health. Given the range of health issues that have been raised in biomedical research and in advocacy on LGBTQ health over the course of the 2000s as well as the expansive recognition of LGBTQ rights in Canadian law over the same period (for example, through the passage of the same-sex civil marriage legislation in 2005), we expected that Health Canada and PHAC would offer some recognition of LGBTQ interests in health. In addition to Health Canada and PHAC, we included some documents that were authored, co-authored, or published by the Health Council of Canada, the Canadian Institute of Health Information, and Statistics Canada. [...]

In order to conduct the document analysis, we used the York University library to collect Health Canada and PHAC-authored documents published in English from 2005 to August 2011.[...]As the purpose of the sample was to evaluate the extent to which and the ways in which LGBTQ health was discussed in federal policy discourse, the sample was culled to include only publications on topics that could be defined as potentially relevant to LGBTQ health. Topics were considered to be potentially relevant to LGBTQ health if they had been identified in reports of biomedical research, identified by LGBTQ stakeholder organizations such as the Canadian Rainbow Health Coalition, identified in secondary literature, or covered in the media. These issues included access to health care, the (lack of) cultural competence of health care professionals, higher rates of certain cancers (for example, breast cancer for lesbians), domestic violence, sexual reassignment therapy, hormone therapy, reproductive and sexual health, parenting, HIV/AIDS, and mental health and addiction (see Canadian Rainbow Health Coalition 2011 for an overview of LGBTQ health issues). In addition, discussion of specific populations such as Aboriginal people, youth, children, the elderly, racialized minorities and migrants, immigrants or refugees were included in the sample in order to see if LGBTQ people were mentioned or considered to be part of these populations.[...]

Finally, we sought interviews with officials from Health Canada and the Public Health Agency of Canada who were positioned in departments and units that could potentially address policies related to LGBTQ health. The intent was to target key policy makers at the intermediate and senior levels. Within Health Canada five divisions were identified and nine policy makers and one ministry official therein were approached to participate in the study. Four divisions within PHAC were identified and five policy makers were approached. Some indicated a lack of availability during the data collection time period. Others indicated that they did not have any knowledge of LGBTQ populations and/or that their work did not expose them to these communities, and as such did not see themselves being useful for our purposes, clearly indicating the absence of policy attention to our subject matter. It is also possible that the pending federal election of May 2011 may have dampened the response rate for interview requests. In addition, the Harper government has exerted strong and centralized control over the management of information and this may have shaped the challenges we faced in obtaining interviews (Delacourt 2011; Kozolanka 2009: 227–232). Nevertheless, we were able to undertake interviews with two Health Canada civil servants, both of whom were interviewed in person at their departments in Ottawa, as well as one civil servant from PHAC based in BC, who was interviewed by phone in March 2011, and we include their insights here.

Findings

OVERALL RESULTS IN CONTEXT

Table 25.1 presents the number of documents in the culled sample of 62 that included LGBTQ search terms such as "sexual orientation," "gender identity," "gay," "lesbian," "bisexual," "transgender(ed)," or "queer." Of these documents, 14.5% contained at least one of the keywords. Table 25.2 indicates whether or not the reference to LGBTQ keywords was substantive. [...] After a careful review of the document sample, the results in Table 25.2 show that LGBTQ health was substantively mentioned in only 8% of the total document sample.

TABLE 25.1 TOTAL LGBTQ KEYWORDS IN A SAMPLE OF HEALTH CANADA AND PHAC PUBLICATIONS, 2005–2011

	Total Keywords	
Keyword	**# of Documents That Mentioned Keyword**	**As % of Total Document Sample (62 Documents)**
gay	9	14.5
lesbian	8	12.8
bisexual	6	9.6
transgender	3	4.8
two spirit	2	3.2
queer	2	3.2
sexual orientation	3	4.8
gender identity	3	4.8
total*	9	14.5

*Most of the keywords appear together in the same document. Therefore, the totals do not add up. *Source:* Health Canada and PHAC document sample taken from York University library catalogue, August 2011.

[...] Given that the sample reviewed was culled to focus on LGBTQ health and included issues of concern to LGBTQ communities or issues identified as important for LGBTQ health in the biomedical literature and by LGBTQ stakeholders, this result clearly demonstrates that LGBTQ health issues have not been systematically taken up by Health Canada and PHAC in their published policy discussions.

To put this result into perspective, we reviewed the same set of documents for references to gender and gender-based analysis. Over one-quarter of the documents mentioned gender (if only in terms of the gender binary) and exhibited awareness that health research, needs, and outcomes might be different for women than for men. However, only about 10% of the document sample mentioned or engaged in gender-based analysis, showing the weak level of commitment to GBA in the practice of Health Canada and PHAC's documentary discussions and research reports. Nonetheless, there was more discussion of gender and gender-based analysis in this sample than of sexual orientation, gender identity, or any single LGBTQ keyword. [...]

Our interviews with federal civil servants parallel the content and website findings. LGBTQ people are not recognized for their broad health and well-being issues in federal health policy, funding and programming, nor as a designated population outside of STIs. [...]

TABLE 25.2 SUBSTANTIVE VERSUS NON-SUBSTANTIVE DISCUSSION OF LGBTQ KEYWORDS IN A SAMPLE OF HEALTH CANADA AND PHAC PUBLICATIONS, 2005–2011

	Substantive		Not substantive	
Keywords	**# of Documents That Mentioned Keyword**	**As % of Total Document Sample (62 Documents)**	**# of Documents That Mentioned Keyword**	**As % of Total Document Sample (62 Documents)**
gay	5	8	4	6.5
lesbian	5	8	3	4.8
bisexual	5	8	1	1.6
transgender	2	3.2	1	1.6
two spirit	2	3.2	0	0
queer	2	3.2	0	0
sexual orientation	2	3.2	1	1.6
gender identity	2	3.2	1	1.6
total*	5	8	4	6.5

*Most of the keywords appear together in the same document. Therefore, the totals do not add. *Source:* Health Canada and PHAC document sample taken from York University library catalogue, August 2011.

SUBSTANTIVE CONTENT

The marginalization of LGBTQ health in these documents is even more pronounced when the substantive content of the discussions is considered. All of the documents that mentioned LGBTQ keywords in the sample were qualitatively reviewed in order to assess the quality and nature of the discussion of LGBTQ health, producing a short list of a few documents that contained such substantive discussions. These documents included PHAC's two pamphlets on sexual orientation and gender identity in schools (PHAC 2010a; 2010b), the population studies of HIV/AIDS (PHAC 2009a; PHAC 2011) and one other document produced for the Mental Health Commission of Canada that mentioned LGBTQ health needs, although without explicit discussion of the specific needs of trans people (O'Hagan et al. 2010). Therefore, of the sample, only five documents substantively discussed LGBTQ health over the course of the decade.

Overall, most policy documents and research reports were resolutely heteronormative and gender-normative; that is, they implicitly or explicitly assumed an opposite-sex definition of couples and a heterosexual sexual orientation (heteronormative) and failed to mention gender beyond the traditional binary, thus excluding gender variant and trans people. [...] A PHAC document on pregnancy and childbirth presents information on how to manage risks of childbirth with repeated references to the "husband or partner" but without mentioning female partners or gay fathers, thus eliding the reality of the growth of queer parenthood (PHAC 2009d: 1, 7; see also McCourt 2005; on queer parenthood in the Canadian context, see Epstein 2009). [...]

Moreover, there were areas in which we have expected the incorporation of LGBTQ interests in health, given the identification of these health issues in the biomedical literature as well as their identification by LGBTQ health advocacy organizations, and yet they were not discussed. For example, several biomedical studies have identified the fact that bisexual and lesbian women (or women who have sex with women—WSW) have higher rates of breast cancer than heterosexual women (Kavanaugh-Lynch et al. 2002; Dibble, Roberts, and Nussey 2004; Brandenburg et al. 2007). Yet, a PHAC guidebook on breast cancer screening discusses breast cancer risk factors without mentioning lesbian and bisexual women or the terms "sexual orientation" and "gender identity" (PHAC 2009b). A guidebook on cervical cancer does not mention gender, lesbian, or bisexual women (PHAC 2009c). Discussions of women's health equity from a population health perspective listed ethnicity, income, education, and geography as important factors within each gender category (male and female) without further reference to gender identity or sexual orientation (Bierman 2006). A discussion of street-involved youth and the health risks of their sexual behaviour did not mention same-sex sexual behaviour or LGBTQ people (PHAC 2006a; see also PHAC 2007a; 2007b). Publications on access to care (that is, the ability to access a knowledgeable family doctor), a major concern for LGBTQ communities (Ryan, Brotman, and Rowe 2000), did not refer to these communities (Statistics Canada 2006; Health Council of Canada 2010). Many other areas in which the LGBTQ communities might be expected to have specific concerns and interests such as assisted human reproduction (Health Canada 2006); addiction (Ahmad 2008), cancer (Canadian Cancer Society 2007; Canadian Cancer Society 2010), public and stakeholder communication about health risk (PHAC 2006b), and palliative, chronic, and elder care (Health Canada 2007; Zierler and Health Council of Canada 2010; Health Council of Canada 2007; Health Council of Canada 2009b), did not include any mention of LGBTQ people. The population-based reports on HIV/AIDS in the Black and Caribbean communities and among First Nations provide some of the only examples of intersectionality (PHAC 2009a; PHAC 2011). [...]

The most common frameworks for health policy discussion excluded sexual orientation and gender identity. [...] LGBTQ communities are submerged from view in government-sanctioned health research, even when such research is explicitly undertaken using a social determinants or population health approach and even when it is based on a participatory model of research. [...]

There were also examples in the sample of policy and reports that took up an explicitly gender-based analysis without mention of sexual orientation or gender identity or with only passing mention, reflecting the extent to which S/GBA itself has been based on and has replicated the heteronormative assumptions and the gender binary. For example, a discussion of the development of women's health indicators moves beyond GBA to diversity-based analysis, emphasizing "the interaction between gender and the social determinants of health" (Bierman 2006: vii). While the author argues that "gender and equity analyses should be routinely incorporated into all Canadian health indicator reporting initiatives" (Bierman 2006: vii), "gender" is understood in binary terms and used interchangeably with "sex." In keeping with the focus on SGBA, the author deploys gender-based analysis to show men's health situation, as they are more prone to binge drinking and other conditions. The author is critical of previous work that has mentioned gender but did not undertake a gender-based analysis. Ethnicity, income, education, and geography are all identified as important factors within each gender category (male and female). This document was one of the few to incorporate an extensive discussion of race, using the terms "race" and "migration," but gender was not deemed to include the LGBTQ populations, either on their own, or as subsets of other groups (Bierman 2006: 2–7). [...]

The discussion of HIV/AIDS is a key example of the way in which LGBTQ health is currently situated in federal policy. While HIV/AIDS is a longstanding issue in the LGBTQ communities, sparked the establishment of early queer health organizations such as the AIDS Committee of Toronto (ACT), and continues to affect a large number of gay and bisexual men, their status in HIV/AIDS health research and service delivery is contested. Despite the fact that these men are disproportionately affected by HIV/AIDS (Jaffe, Valdiserri, and De Cock 2007; Sullivan et al. 2009), gay, bisexual, and other men were not singled out as a population according to the document search. Moreover, in an attempt to focus on behaviour rather than identity for purposes of public health, HIV/AIDS research and policy sometimes deploys the epidemiological terminology of men who have sex with men (MSM) and, at times, writes of HIV/AIDS and of same-sex sexual behaviour without ever referring to LGBTQ identity (Mulé 2005; Young and Meyer 2005). [...]

WEBSITES

In order to obtain another view of the public discussion of LGBTQ communities by the federal government and in order to validate our results from the document search, we also used Google to search the Health Canada and PHAC websites. Websites are an important aspect of the public presentation of health discourse and may contain additional resources that are not captured by formally published government documents. We used Google's Advanced Search to conduct site-specific searches for LGBTQ keywords as well as comparator keywords over the period 2004 to August 2011 on the Health Canada and Public Health Agency of Canada websites. There were 17,500 mentions of the word "health" on the Health Canada website, but only 45 mentions of the word "gay," 34 mentions of the word "lesbian," 19 mentions of the word "bisexual," 14 mentions of the term "transgender," 6 mentions of the term "gender identity," and 25 mentions of the term "sexual orientation." Most mentions of lesbians and all mentions of bisexuals and transgender people occurred as part of the umbrella term "LGBTQ," rather than as a discussion of specific lesbian, bisexual, or transgender health issues. The search of the Public Health Agency of Canada website covering the same period found better representation of LGBTQ populations. There were 131 mentions of the word "gay" on the PHAC website; however, 90 of them mentioned gay men in relation to HIV/AIDs or other sexually transmitted infections. Interestingly, PHAC links gay men with HIV/AIDS through its website. Yet, like Health Canada, it fails to do so in its more comprehensive documents that impact health policy. The other 41 documents on the PHAC website mentioned gay men (usually as part of the LGBTQ group, rather than on their own) in relation to a few other health issues, including mental health, domestic partner abuse, and, in one case, homophobic bullying of gay youth. Many other health-identified issues were not mentioned, however. For specifically lesbian issues, there were only 11 mentions, most of them on intimate partner violence, certainly an important issue, but far from the only public health issue affecting lesbian women, according to the secondary literature and according to LGBTQ stakeholder organizations. For bisexuals, there was only one specific mention, aside from their inclusion under the umbrella of LGBTQ, and this was a substantive discussion of the risk of intimate partner violence for bisexual men compared to straight men. Tellingly, the term "transgender" had the lowest number of total hits on the PHAC website, at 36, most of them overlapping with the LGBTQ category and all but three focussing on HIV/AIDs. Only one document on the PHAC website specifically discussed trans health issues. These findings confirm the results of the document analysis and the exclusion of discussion of broad LGBTQ health issues from the public presentation of Canadian health policy by Health Canada and by the Public Health Agency of Canada.

Interview Results

Several key themes emerged from the data gathered from interviews with three federal civil servants that provide relevant insights into the development of LGBTQ-sensitive policy. The interview subjects confirmed that, at best, LGBTQ communities are thought to be included in illness-based HIV/AIDS/STI policies or diversity-based policies, the latter of which focuses strictly on "sexual orientation," ignoring trans issues. The interview participants questioned the influence of GBA in the federal government and argued that, if anything, it appears that community-based groups and organizations contribute to shaping policy and programming based on their feminist analysis and mandates more so than the government's commitment to GBA. Regarding the Social Determinants of Health model, one interviewee questioned why the government has not captured LGBTQ populations within it, given the obvious fit.

Although respondents were clearly in touch with the LGBTQ communities and did receive issues and concerns regarding their health and wellbeing, what is lacking is a formal governmental systemic vehicle with which to address the broad health concerns raised by the LGBTQ communities. Recommendations from final reports of federal government-funded community-based LGBTQ health research studies were neither formally followed up, nor was an environment created that encouraged policy makers to do so. These recommendations essentially called for governmental recognition of broad health issues, needs, and concerns of LGBTQ people with corresponding education, research, policy, programming, and funding. Many called for a formalized government-backed systemic initiative that would ensure these components are properly resourced and implemented. This lack of priority and minimized recognition meant that LGBTQ individuals were generally consulted regarding HIV/AIDS/STIs but not regarding other health issues. In this way, the interview participants confirmed the federal government view of the LGBTQ communities as illness-based rather than socially located or positioned. Despite numerous federal government-funded community-based LGBTQ health research studies, health-based LGBTQ funding was not extended for broad health and wellbeing issues. Yet, funds were extended for public awareness campaigns regarding STIs codifying the LGBTQ communities as sexualized and dangerously so. The interview participants also pointed to the role of fear and ignorance in limiting attention to and inclusion of LGBTQ communities. In sum, the interview results were consistent with the findings of the document analysis and website searches.

Conclusions

Despite federal policy templates such as population health and the social determinants of health and the commitment to undertake a Sex and Gender-Based Analysis (S/GBA) in policy development, LGBTQ communities are, for the most part, absent from federal health policy. Although S/GBA is now official policy at the federal level, its traditional assumption of binary notions of the genders falls far short of even beginning to adequately address the complex and diverse health-related issues affecting LGBTQ populations. Where LGBTQ people are acknowledged tends to be in HIV/AIDS/STI- specific initiatives, with an emphasis on MSM. Although these illness-based policies entail funding, programming, and services that by extension benefit gay and bisexual men, they further marginalize the health needs of lesbians, bisexual women, and the transgender populations, not to mention the broader health and wellbeing issues of LGBTQ communities in general. It is well established that LGBTQ communities experience a series of distinct health and wellness issues and concerns as found in the formal and grey literature, and has become a focus for organizing and political action within the LGBTQ movement over the past 12 years. Yet, federal health policy discourse, with few exceptions, has all but ignored these needs. [...]

A future study might also seek to explore the reasons for the federal neglect of LGBTQ issues, a neglect that has spanned both Liberal and Conservative governments. As a minority group that is not able to mobilize substantial electoral pressure, the LGBTQ community has benefitted from political alliances with Liberals, and especially, with the federal NDP over the years. Yet, most of the main changes in federal and provincial policies toward the LGBTQ community in Canada, especially on issues such as same-sex marriage and relationship recognition, occurred as a result of litigation, as the LGBTQ movement was able to exploit the political opportunities created by an empowered judiciary in the wake of the constitutional entrenchment of the Charter of Rights (Smith 1999; 2008). The integration of LGBTQ interests into other aspects of policy-making is a challenge in the absence of electoral or legal pressure. The project of explaining the position of LGBTQ communities in Canadian health policy naturally flows from this paper, which has presented an empirically based description of the absence of the community from federal health policy discourse.

As a population that has suffered years of discrimination and marginalization, the LGBTQ movement fought for equitable representation and recognition, including protection on the basis of sexual orientation in human rights legislation (this battle continues on the gender identity and gender expression front). Yet, as demonstrated in this study, the federal health system has not adequately taken up these issues in a manner that would effectively address LGBTQ health needs. Given that health care is administered at the provincial and territorial level, future research can explore whether these populations are better recognized at that meso level. Nonetheless, the role of federal health programs is not to be underestimated in setting a pan-Canadian health discourse as a guide for the provinces and territories to follow. The Canadian federal government can redress this situation by allowing for a more inclusive, diversified approach to its health care perspectives encapsulating the LGBTQ populations.

Note

1. For the purposes of this paper, LGBTQ denotes lesbian, gay, bisexual, transgender, trans-sexual, two-spirit, queer and questioning people. This encompassing acronym captures sexual orientation regarding those sexually attracted to the same sex (lesbians, gay men) and both sexes (bisexuals); gender identity and gender expression (transgender, trans-sexual) that involves identifying with a gender that differs from the biologically assigned gender at birth (which may or may not conform to binary genders and may or may not involve sex reassignment surgery); the sometimes contested Aboriginal notion of two genders within one person (two spirit); the politicized identity of queer that celebrates difference and resists heteronormativity; and those questioning their sexuality, gender identity, or gender expression.

References

Ahmad, Nadya. 2008. *Canadian Addiction Survey (CAS)*. Ottawa: Health Canada. Available at: http://epe.lac-bac.gc.ca/100/200/301/hcan-scan/cdn_addiction_survey_focus_gender-e/ H128-1-07-519E.pdf.

Bierman, Arlene S. 2006. *Equity and Women's Health*. Ottawa: Health Canada.

Brandenburg, Dana L., Alicia K. Matthews, Timothy P. Johnson, and Tonda L. Hughes. 2007. "Breast cancer risk and screening: A comparison of lesbian and heterosexual women." *Women & Health* 45 (4): 109–30.

Canadian Cancer Society. 2007. *Canadian Cancer Statistics 2007*. Toronto: Canadian Cancer Society.

———. 2010. *Canadian Cancer Statistics 2010*. Toronto: Canadian Cancer Society.Canadian Institute of Health Information (CIHI). 2011. *Vision and Mandate*. Available at: vision+and+mandate/cihi010703. Accessed 12 September 2011.

Canadian Rainbow Health Coalition. 2004. *Health and Wellness in the Gay, Lesbian, Bisexual, Transgendered and Two-Spirit Communities*. Available at: http://www.rainbow-health.ca/ documents/english/health%20and%20wellness.pdf. Accessed 22 April 2011.

———. 2006. *Rainbow Health-Improving Access to Care*. Report to Primary Health Care Transition Fund, Health Canada. Ottawa. Available at: http://www.rainbowhealth.ca/documents/english/Final_Report-July_4_2006.pdf. Accessed 22 April 2011.

———. 2011. *Canadian Rainbow Health Coalition*. Available at: http://www.rainbowhealth.ca/english/index.html. Accessed 2 July 2012.

Delacourt, Susan. 2011. "Show us your face, say profs at centre of information war." *Toronto Star* (February 12): A4.

Dibble, Suzanne L., Stephanie A. Roberts, and Brenda Nussey. 2004. "Comparing breast cancer risk between lesbians and their heterosexual sisters." *Women's Health Issues: Official Publication of the Jacobs Institute of Women's Health* 14 (2): 60–8.

Epstein, Rachel (ed.) 2009. *Who's Your Daddy?: And Other Writings on Queer Parenting*. Toronto: Sumach Press.

Health Canada. 2006. *Gender-Based Analysis and Wait Times: New Questions, New Knowledge: Final Report of the Federal Advisor on Wait Times*. Ottawa: Health Canada.

———. 2007. *Canadian Strategy on Palliative and End-of-Life Care: Final Report of the Coordinating Committee, December 2002 to March 2007*. Ottawa: Health Canada.

Health Council of Canada. 2007. *Canadians' Experiences with Chronic Illness Care in 2007*. Toronto: Health Council of Canada.

———. 2009b. *Getting It Right: Case Studies of Effective Management of Chronic Disease Using Primary Health Care Teams*. Toronto: Health Council of Canada.

———. 2010. *Decisions, Decisions: Family Doctors as Gatekeepers to Prescription Drugs and Diagnostic Imaging in Canada*. Toronto: Health Council of Canada.

Jackson, Beth, A. Daley, D. Moore, N. Mulé, L., Ross, A. Travers, and E. Montgomery. 2006. *Whose Public Health? An Intersectional Approach to Sexual Orientation, Gender Identity, and the Development of Public Health Goals for Canada*. Discussion Paper submitted to Health Canada by the Rainbow Health Network (RHN) and the Coalition for Lesbian and Gay Rights in Ontario, CLGRO. Available at: http://www.rainbowhealth.ca/documents/english/ whose_public_health.pdf. Accessed 18 April 2011.

Jaffe, H.W., R.O. Valdiserri, and K.M. De Cock. 2007. "The reemerging HIV/AIDS epidemic in men who have sex with men." *The Journal of the American Medical Association* 298 (20): 2412–4.

Kavanaugh-Lynch, Marion H.E., Emily White, Janet R. Daling, and Deborah J. Bowen. 2002. "Correlates of lesbian bsexual orientation and the risk of breast cancer." *Journal of the Gay and Lesbian Medical Association* 6 (3–4) (December): 91–5.

Kozolanka, Kirsten. 2009. "Communication by stealth: The new common sense in government communication." In *How Ottawa Spends 2009–10: Economic Upheaval and Political Dysfunction*, edited by Alan M. Maslove. Montreal and Kingston: McGill-Queen's University Press, pp. 241–61.

Lehavot, K., and J.M. Simoni. 2011. "The impact of minority stress on mental health and substance use among sexual minority women." *Journal of Consulting and Clinical Psychology* 79 (2): 159.

McCourt, Catherine, and Public Health Agency of Canada. 2005. *Make Every Mother and Child Count: Report on Maternal and Child Health in Canada.* Ottawa: Public Health Agency of Canada.

Mulé, Nick J. 2005. "Beyond words in health and wellbeing policy: 'Sexual orientation'—From inclusion to infusion." *Canadian Review of Social Policy* 55: 79–98.

Mulé, Nick, J.L.E. Ross, B. Deeprose, B.E. Jackson, A. Daley, A. Travers, and D. Moore. 2009. "Promoting LGBT health and wellbeing through inclusive policy development." *International Journal for Equity in Health* 8: 18–29.

O'Hagan, Mary, Céline Cyr, and Heather McKee. 2010. *Making the Case for Peer Support: Report to the Peer Support Project Committee of the Mental Health Commission of Canada.* Ottawa: Mental Health Commission of Canada.

Orsini, Michael. 2007. "Discourses in distress: From health promotion to population health to 'You are responsible for your own health.'" In *Critical Policy Studies*, edited by Michael Orsini and Miriam Smith. Vancouver: University of British Columbia Press, pp. 347–63.

Public Health Agency of Canada. 2006a. *Street Youth in Canada.* Ottawa: Public Health Agency of Canada.

———. 2006b. *Strategic Risk Communications Framework for Health Canada and the Public Health Agency of Canada.* Ottawa: Public Health Agency of Canada.

———. 2007a. *Hepatitis C Virus Infection in Canadian Street Youth: The Role of Injection Drug Use.* Ottawa: Public Health Agency of Canada.

———. 2007b. *Canadian Street Youth and Substance Use.* Ottawa: Public Health Agency of Canada.

———. 2009a. *Population-specific HIV AIDS Status Report People from Countries Where HIV*

Is Endemic, Black People of African and Caribbean Descent Living in Canada. Ottawa: Public Health Agency of Canada.

———. 2009b. *Information on Mammography for Women Aged 40 and Older: A Decision Aid for Breast Cancer Screening in Canada*. Ottawa: Public Health Agency of Canada.

Public Health Agency of Canada. Cervical Cancer Prevention & Control Network (Canada). 2009c. *Performance Monitoring for Cervical Cancer Screening Programs in Canada*. Ottawa: Public Health Agency of Canada.

Public Health Agency of Canada. 2009d. *Mothers' Voices: What Women Say About Pregnancy, Childbirth and Early Motherhood*. Ottawa: Public Health Agency of Canada.

———. 2010a. *Questions & Answers: Gender Identity in Schools*. Ottawa: Public Health Agency of Canada.

———. 2010b. *Questions & Answers: Sexual Orientation in Schools*. Ottawa: Public Health Agency of Canada.

———. 2011. *Population-Specific HIV AIDS Status Report Aboriginal Peoples*. Ottawa: Public Health Agency of Canada.

Ryan, Bill, Shari Brotman, and Bill Rowe. 2000. *Access to Care: Explaining the Health and Well-Being of Gay, Lesbian, Bisexual and Two-Spirited People in Canada*. Montreal and Ottawa: McGill School of Social Work and Health Canada.

Smith, Miriam. 1999. *Lesbian and Gay Rights in Canada: Social Movements and Equality-Seeking, 1971–1995*. Toronto: University of Toronto Press.

———. 2008. *Political Institutions and Lesbian and Gay Rights in the United States and Canada*. New York: Routledge.

Statistics Canada. 2006. *Access to Health Care Services in Canada, January to June 2005*. Ottawa: Statistics Canada.

Sullivan, P.S., O. Hamouda, V. Delpech, J.E. Geduld, J. Prejean, C. Semaille, J. Kaldor, C. Folch, E. Op de Coul, U. Marcus, G. Hughes, C.P. Archibald, F. Cazein, A. McDonald, J. Casabona, A. van Sighem, K.A. Fenton, and Annecy MSM Epidemiology Study Group. 2009. "Re-emergence of the HIV epidemic among men who have sex with men in North America, Western Europe, and Australia, 1996–2005." *Annals of Epidemiology* 19 (6): 423–31.

York University Library. 2011. *Policies and Procedures for External Libraries*. Available at: http://www.library.yorku.ca/ccm/ResourceSharing/ForOtherLibraries/

Young, Rebecca M., and Ilan H. Meyer. 2005. "The trouble with 'MSM' and 'WSW': Erasure of the sexual minority person in public health discourse." *American Journal of Public Health* 95 (7): 1144–9.

Zierler, Amy, and Health Council of Canada. 2010. *Beyond the Basics: The Importance of Patient-Provider Interactions in Chronic Illness Care*. Toronto: Health Council of Canada.

SECTION 3E

MEDIA

CHAPTER 26

"You Bring Great Masculinity and Truth": Sexuality, Whiteness, and the Regulation of the Male Body in Motion

Jade Boyd

"Is reality TV ready for a gay icon? Some think *American Idol* and *So You Think You Can Dance* could be the last bastions of homophobia." So begins Canada's Broadcasting Corporation (CBC) radio host Jian Ghomeshi on the popular syndicated national arts program Q on June 1, 2009. Ghomeshi, Canadian journalist Rachel Giese, and "Canadian dance legend," ballet dancer Rex Harrington, debate reality TV judges' confounded and homophobic reactions to two men samba dancing together during an audition in the fifth season of the popular Emmy Award-winning American reality dance series *So You Think You Can Dance* (*SYTYCD*). CBC's debate is illustrative of ongoing anxieties surrounding male dancers and popular debates about sexuality and masculinity. These anxieties are present in contemporary Canadian popular discourse and represented in the first season of the Canadian version of *SYTYCD*, which aired in 2008. This paper draws on *So You Think You Can Dance Canada* (*SYTYCDC*) as a case study to explore representations of sexuality, whiteness, authenticity, and the male dancer. I argue that though the presence of male dancers in the (often feminized) representational realm has the potential to challenge static heteronormative dichotomies of masculine/feminine, reality dance television in this case plays with, yet ultimately reaffirms, heteronormative masculinity and does so relationally, through the juxtaposition of racialized dance contestants (both men and women) over the span of a series. While it is not surprising that a reality show depends heavily upon heteronormative stereotypes, these discursive mechanisms are rendered invisible, in this case, when couched in a discourse of authenticity, technical ability, and dance aesthetics, resonating beyond the context of television, into the ways we think about dance practice.

Dance and cultural theorist Jane Desmond (2001) points out that dance is a particularly productive arena in which to explore gender and sexuality because of the shared emphasis on the physical body and body practices. She explains that, "how one moves, and how one moves in relation to others, constitutes a public enactment of sexuality and gender" (6), thus the study of dance provides insight into how gender and sexuality are embodied and represented. Dance, an art form that moves outside the privileged, hegemonic modes of literate and verbal discourse (Carol Brown 1997), has long been associated with sexuality and desire, whether perceived as lascivious, illicit, and depraved, or earnestly articulated as non-sexual and/or chaste in efforts to counter erotic associations intertwined with the body (Susan Foster 2001). Christy Adair (1992) accounts for the marginalization of dance in Western society to an emphasis on the verbal as well as to the Judaeo-Christian tradition that demonizes the body, sexuality, and dance by extension. However, since 2005, American reality dance shows have become popular transnational cultural products.

Dance and Masculinity

As Michel Foucault (1977) has made clear, power relations are often centralized on the body, as the subject of control and regulation through subtle processes of normalization, judgment, and surveillance. Ramsay Burt (2001) argues that with the rise of the bourgeoisie in nineteenth-century Europe, coupled with the development of scientific and rational thought, definitions of masculinity changed as part of shifting attitudes towards gender and the body. Definitions of what constituted normative male bodily display and expression became limited and homophobia developed as a means for regulating male behaviour; the spectacle of the male body began to disappear from both art and the concert stage (Burt 2001). Women, on the other hand, were, and continue to be, celebrated as both spectacle and object on (and off) stage, as bearers of male desire (Helen Thomas 2003). In accordance with prevailing gender codes, the "erotic motivation behind looking in an objectifying way at women" supported (rather than challenged) the dominant heteronormative male gaze (Burt 2001, 51). Though dancers themselves may experience their bodies in motion quite differently from how a spectator might view them, it is important to note that "the ways we look at dance [and dancers] are profoundly partial and social at the same time: they are inscribed in and through a chain of signifying practices and cultural codes through which we make sense of the world … " (Thomas 2003, 161–162). As the dance stage became coded in popular Western thought as a feminine space, the male dancer came to *represent* a "feminized presence on the concert stage" (Gay Morris 2001, 245), and was essentially queered amidst notions that "real men" (i.e., normal, straight men) do not dance (Cynthia Weber 2003). Male dancers, by their very presence in the representational realm, became suspect.

Because it is a distinct body-based expressive form, dance is often associated with truth, "realness," or authenticity despite being highly codified (see Jade Boyd 2012, 2014; Jane Desmond 1999). The search for "authentic" tourist experiences has also extended to dance performance, often staged to satisfy consumer desires for perceived authenticity while serving to reinforce cultural stereotypes, particularly in relation to the commodification of representations of the Other (Desmond 1999; Ning Wang 1999). "Authenticity," while often used as a descriptor, is nevertheless situated and socially defined. It is not aesthetic but rather ideological, in that it reflects ideologies about what is assumed to be genuine or real as opposed to artificial or fake. It suggests that there exists an original source or an essence and/or core of truth or naturalness. Theorists such as Michel Foucault (1980) and Judith Butler (1990, preface) have exposed "foundational" identity categories (such as race and gender) as effects of specific formations of power, wherein seemingly natural or innate categories are revealed as socially constructed (through institutions, practices, and discourses). Thus discourses that demarcate (in)authenticity of movement and identity (delineating "real" men and how they move from presumably "false" enactments) are imbued with power, while suggestive of innateness.

The representational realms of television and film also participate in discourses surrounding both authenticity and the male body as spectacle. Steven Cohan and Ina Rae Hark (1995/1993), for example, argue that analyses of the "spectacle of men" can serve to destabilize classic representational systems that frame masculinity as secure and unitary, revealing it as a fictive construct. Beginning with the presumption that masculine identities are wide-ranging, contradictory, fluid, multiple, and experienced relationally (to concepts of femininity and to axes of difference such as ethnicity, race, class, sexuality, ability, and age), it is nevertheless important to note the considerable cultural investment in particular homogeneous visual and narrative representations of masculinity. Though there exists a plurality of masculinities, there is also a hierarchy of masculinity. That is to say, representations, discursive practices, and enactments of masculinity that conform to current normative, hegemonic conventions are afforded more power through the maintenance and rewards of patriarchy than other more subordinated masculinities (Raewyn Connell and James W. Messerschmidt 2005).

As critical studies on the social construction of gender have emphasized, masculinity is not a given feature of the historicized male body; it must also be (re)enacted and (re) embodied (see Butler 1990; Raewyn Connell 1995). Cultural practices, including body movement, signify particular forms of masculinity (Michael Kimmel 2006); those that emphasize culturally idealized attributes such as strength, activity, rationality, heterosexuality, competitiveness, and dominance (Connell 1995; Christian Alexander Vaccaro 2011) while soliciting difference are most readily rewarded. As Connell and Messerschmidt (2005, 851) argue, it has long been recognized "that hegemonic masculinity is related to particular ways of representing and using men's bodies." However, as previously noted, representations of the male body on physical display also offer a "threat of disempowerment" through an invitation of the gaze (Laura Mulvey 2009) that engenders the possibility of homoeroticism (Amelia Yeates 2013, 115). Richard Dyer (1997) extends analyses on masculinity in his exploration of how whiteness is paradoxically implicated in the cinematic spectacle of men.

Dyer (1997) argues that in film, non-white bodies are continually on physical display, whereas the spectacle of the white male body is less often seen. The white body on display threatens the authority of white male power, as it risks revealing the instabilities and inadequacies of whiteness predicated on difference. Nevertheless, Dyer (1997, 146) argues, "there is value in the white male body being seen" in reaffirming its superiority and dominance—an assertion that particularly resonates in the context of "'underachieving' masculinity" (147). Dyer's argument extends to dance television, where representations of (gendered) bodies in motion are on critical physical display and (white) masculinity continually risks being called into question.

At the same time, the spectacle of non-white male (and female) bodies to perform as stereotyped representations of the exotic Other has dominated popular film and television (S. Coltrane and M. Messineo 2000; Dyer 1997; Stuart Hall 1997). Indeed critical scholars point to the history of the burden of the "Other" to perform. In *Black Skin, White Masks* (1967), Franz Fanon decrees the power and violence of racial representation and stereotyping noting the over-visibility of the black male body in popular culture represented as over-sexed and reducibly corporeal (172–176). Fanon's highly quoted phrase, "I am overdetermined from without" (116), speaks to the way in which every action is historically understood within the context of the racializing stereotypes that already exist and define him based on his epidermal schema.

The black body has consistently been compelled to involuntarily perform acts of degradation for white audiences for entertainment, scientific analysis, and fetishistic consumption (Coco Fusco 1995, 2001; Jose Esteben Muñoz 1999). Hall (1997, 262) outlines the ways in which a repertoire of stereotyped representations of black masculinity, which "has been forged through histories of slavery, colonialism and imperialism," continues to persist in contemporary film, television, and advertising, despite counter-hegemonic images. Two common seemingly oppositional (yet mutually constitutive) representational strategies that resonate include: (1) infantilization, wherein the black man is symbolically castrated, never quite a man; and (2) representations of black men as overly aggressive and sexually insatiable (225–279). While conventional depictions of black masculinity dominate popular media, the black male presence in music, dance, and entertainment has been naturalized, in part, through their association with nature, emotion, and physicality (Hall 1997). Thus, the body is a site for naturalizing racialized difference, often evoked in claims of authenticity in performance and in reality television. Reality television, grounded in both spectacle and much critiqued documentary claims of "reality" and the ordinary (see Zoe Druick and Anastasia Kotsopoulos 2008; Linda Grindstaff 2002; Sue Holmes 2004; Kathleen LeBesco 2004; Beverley Skeggs 2009), and dance reality television in particular, because of its emphasis on the body (Boyd 2012; Mark A. Broomfield 2011), provide a privileged representational space to explore dominant ideologies implicated in visual performative enactments of gender, sexuality, and also race.

Through an examination of narrative and accompanying visuals, the following outlines how within the context of *So You Think You Can Dance Canada* (2008), normative gender conventions are naturalized relationally, between men and women contestants and also between men, in their failures and successes to live up to the series' expectations and narrow conceptions of masculinity. Implicated in these relational naturalizing choreographies of representation are racializing processes, interlocked with concepts of gender, sexuality, and authenticity. In the West, dance, particularly theatrical dance, has been routinely gendered as a feminine cultural practice, as an expressive, non-verbal, body-based practice featuring bodies on display, and offering little in terms of financial security (Sally Banes 1998; Desmond 2001; Julia L. Foulkes 2001; Eluned Summers-Bremner 2000). Therefore, the work required in the maintenance of masculine heteronormative expression is significant here, as the male dancer is already easily implicated in discourses of non-normative sexuality and homosexuality in the popular imagination (Burt 2001; Desmond 2001; Morris 2001; Weber 2003). Indeed, part of what makes the spectacle of dancing particularly compelling in the context of popular media is the representational disjunction of heteronormative masculinity in the feminized space of dance performance.

Method and Context

This paper draws from a larger study of *So You Think You Can Dance Canada*'s four seasons (2008–2011), the US multi-series of *SYTYCD* (2005–2011), and the series' related media. The initial study explores dominant repetitive and thematic categories within the visual and narrative framework of the show. The emergence of thematic findings surrounding gender, sexuality, embodiment, citizenship, nationalism, and neo-liberalism shape the overall study. Drawing from socio-cultural perspectives, dance theory, and feminist and critical qualitative research methods, this article specifically explores dance narratives of whiteness, masculinity, authenticity, and heteronormative conventions through the juxtaposition of season one's three key competitors, and a few auditioning dancers. Though key chosen competitors and auditioning dancers shape how dancers are perceived, this paper is primarily attentive to the narratives following three key contestants, as it is their scenes that dominate the first season.

Case studies, though often bounded by a particular point in time, allow for a nuanced and detailed focus where the developments of themes, concepts, and patterns are connected to a broader sociological framework (Helen Simons 2009; Gary Thomas 2011). As such, the analysis is intended to have an impact beyond the parameters of the study itself (Sharlene Nagy Hesse-Biber and Patricia Leavy 2010). Case studies allow in-depth analysis of how discourses also make possible certain forms of representations. Hall (1997), drawing from Foucault in his exploration of how power relations function in the construction of images, argues that representation is both active and productive. He states that power is "productive in the constitution of masculinity through specific visual codes" (Hall 1997, 303). This study primarily explores narrative frames but some visual contextualization is included. Season one (2008) of *SYTYCDC* is analysed as a case study because of its very popular reception and also because it established the basis for the subsequent three seasons. Season one (2008) also proved a rich site to explore some of the work underpinning the maintenance of heteronormative gender norms and whiteness within the context of dance and to explore some of the ways in which the male dancing body is offered up for televisual consumption.

Sexuality, as a significant aspect of thinking through dance, emerged as a dominant theme in the research, and is evident, as a regulatory discursive trope, throughout the series. The examples highlighted in the following sections are representative of how the series generally mobilizes sexuality, as it connects to concepts around whiteness and masculinity, and they are also significant in that the interrelationship of these particular examples offers an extended exploration of how masculinity (and sexuality by extension) is constituted throughout the first season.

SYTYCDC stems from the popular international franchise (a co-production between American and British companies, created by Simon Fuller and Nigel Lythgoe) that began in 2005 in the US. The Canadian version (like many of the other national adaptations of the series) follows a format closely aligned with the US version, and US guest judges and choreographers often appear as guests on the show. The format of the show, broadcast in Canada on the Canadian Television Network (CTV), is fairly consistent. The first series begins with a host of dance auditions that take place in several of Canada's major cities, after which twenty selected dancers (ten men, ten women, aged between eighteen and thirty) compete to become "Canada's favourite dancer."

A panel of "expert" judges and audience call-in votes serve to determine which of the selected dancers are to be eliminated from the show. Leah Miller, a minor Canadian MTV celebrity, hosts the show week to week. Throughout the season, dancers compete individually and with partners chosen by the judges. The dancers are expected to perform a number of dances in different popular dance styles such as ballroom, hip hop, contemporary, and jazz. In addition, video clips of contestants partnering while working with choreographers prior to each televised duet provides context, offering the viewer insider knowledge of the daily trials and "personality traits" of each contender. After each weekly performance, judges comment upon the success and failures of each contestant and his or her dancing abilities. Though the series was cancelled in 2011 due to dwindling viewership, the first season premiered with 3.7 million Canadians watching at least part of the two-hour episode (CNW Group 2008) and the series remained a top primetime contender throughout the season with a 1.4 million weekly viewership (CNW Group 2009).

The Relational Fortification of Heteronormative Masculinity: A Case Study

Weber (2003) argues that the seeming lack of fit between prevalent ways of reading contemporary dance and the presence of male dancers in popular film serves as a popular trope in many mainstream dance films (e.g., *Billy Elliot* 2000; *Strictly Ballroom* 1992; *The Full Monty* 1997), and that heteronormative masculinity is often secured in, through, or in relation to dance performances that do not live up to dominant heteronormative expectations—what she terms "queer dance performances," in "that they confuse meaning, the norm, normativity." Her argument can easily be extended to representations of dance on television, as the following case study illustrates.

In *SYTYCDC* season one auditions, which preface the series, Canadian ice skating champion and contestant Emanuel Sandhu is chastised by the judges for going down a "girly lane" and urged to offer "sincerity." Similarly, Troy Miller is told by guest judge Melissa Williams that he has to be "well-rounded": "you have to dance like a dude." Guest judge Dan Karaty adds, "Can you rough it up a bit?" to which Troy Miller responds with a playful growl. Neither dancer makes it to the top twenty.

That the judges repeatedly call auditioning male dancers' masculinity into question exposes deep-rooted anxiety about the male dancing body, which effectively serves to regulate performances, reinforcing gender norms while simultaneously limiting the range of expressiveness afforded male dancers on the *SYTYCDC* series (Broomfield 2011, 125). Indeed, the regulations of expressive movement for male dancers exceed the boundaries of the show and are reinforced by normative comments such as that made by Canadian ballet icon Rex Harrington, recurring judge on the series, aspiring judge for the US series *SYTYCD* (John R. Kennedy 2012), and also artist-in-residence at the National Ballet School of Canada. Commenting on the controversy noted at the outset of this article surrounding two male samba partners who auditioned in season five of the US series, Harrington states: "Whether you are gay or straight, I don't like to see effeminate dancing on stage" (CBC 2009), a sentiment that is perhaps representative of the shows' apparent efforts to sell dance to straight male audiences. This is a difficult task for, as Burt (2001, 53) points out in his discussion of prevailing attitudes around the body and gender within the West's profoundly homophobic society, "all male dancers are placed under suspicion with the result that, as it is widely recognized, fewer boys and men are involved in the dance world than girls and women."

The seeming incongruence of the male dancing body occurs throughout the first season, while the recuperation of heteronormative masculinity develops relationally, emerging slowly over the course of twenty-two episodes. The series' expectations around the embodiment of male gender norms in particular become narratively more pronounced when observed in the juxtaposition of three *SYTYCDC* performers: male contemporary dancers Izaak Smith (age nineteen) and Nico Archambault (age twenty-three); and Cuban-born, twenty-one-year-old contemporary female dance contender, Arassay Reyes. Significantly, most of the overt discussions of masculinity by the judges occur when Nico and Izaak have the same dance partner, Arassay Reyes—who is represented throughout the show as uncontainable in her sexualized Latino exoticness and therefore serves as a counterpoint, through her filmed performances (or perhaps choreographies) of hyper-femininity, to reflections of masculinity. The following section includes three representational scenes/narratives that reflect how masculinity and dance are framed on *SYTYCD Canada* in the first season.

Dance contender Izaak Smith is a tall, dark-haired, brown-skinned, youthful man with a medium build. Being one of the youngest male contestants of the season, he is also the youngest man to make it so close to the show's finale (as one of the top three male dancers). Izaak begins the season quite impressively. His audition solo is a lyrical, yet powerful contemporary/hip hop dance for which he is complimented for his movement abilities by the show's panel of "expert" judges, and he is expedited to the final round of audition eliminations. His masculinity is also assessed by guest judge Sean Cheesman, who comments: "It's nice to see a man dance, and look like a man." As the season progresses, however, Izaak is often emasculated, coded as effeminate in descriptions of his dance, particularly through comments by the judges about his lack of strength, his cuteness, his inability to dominate his female dance partners (spatially, physically, emotionally), and most interestingly, as lacking in authenticity. Much of this critique of his masculinity is shrouded in the form of discussions of technical measure from the panel of judges.

For example, in episode seventeen, Izaak and Arassay dance a punk rock Lindy Hop that host Leah Miller calls "from the war zone" to the song "Welcome to the Black Parade" by My Chemical Romance and choreographed by Benji Schwimmer. The dancers wear running shoes and their costumes, which are considerably less revealing than most on the show, are matching with small gender-specific differences (he in jeans, she in a short ruffled skirt and leggings, both in dark sport coats with what appear to be army bands on their sleeves). The performance itself mirrors the militarized costume in that the dancers perform together in unison for much of the dance with small differences (e.g., Izaak does most, but not all, of the lifting). The dance choreography is youthful, playful, and somewhat underwhelming.

After the performance the first judge and resident choreographer Mia Michaels comments:

> It was a little sloppy, for me. Arassay, you're a beast, in a good way—in a good way, you're a beast. Amazing. Um Izaak, you need to step up if she's your partner. You got to step way up. You're adorable, but you're not dancing, *you're a man*, you should be as physical—you should be *more physical* than the lady. And she was way more physical than you. You need to step it up, the physicality of it. And just, the *reality* of your performance needs to step up for sure. But overall, wow.

In this segment, Michaels makes it clear that Izaak fails to embody her concept of what a "real" man is (a concept aligned with the show), hence his enactments of masculinity are considered inadequate for Canada's favourite dancer and the reality of his performance is questioned. He is deemed inauthentic. In fact, because of his perceived failure to perform masculinity, his dancing ability is rendered immeasurable; in Michaels' words he is "not dancing" and his performance lacks "reality." Because masculinity appears to be shorthand for heterosexuality within the series, Izaak's sexuality becomes somewhat suspect in his inability to embody their norm. His racial markers as a man of colour, though not commented upon, further serve to emasculate him, as Izaak does not fit the stereotype of the "eroticized primitive" black male dancer (Morris 2001, 251) that so easily aligns with hyper-sexualized representations of men of colour in the media (Hall 1997). The judges' repetitive comments over the course of the season suggest a desire for Izaak to change his representative identity from (perceived) passive feminized object to a more active (perhaps stereotypically aggressive) masculinized (black) subject, in order "to contest the stereotype of male dancer as weak and effeminate" (Morris 2001, 250) and by association, essentially queer (while simultaneously encouraging a dominant caricature of black masculinity).

Dance theorist Gay Morris (2001, 244) lists three intersecting forms of demasculation that are useful for considering how normative masculinity is constructed and maintained: (1) as previously stated, the male dancer is considered less of a man when in the feminized space of the dance stage; (2) in dominant white society, men of colour are considered lacking, as less than a "real" man (as discussed by Hall [1997] above), as they are never fully "accorded a white man's power," the power of white patriarchy; and (3) within regimes of compulsory heterosexuality, gay men are less than men in their inability to reproduce (Morris 2001, 244). Izaak is demasculated through each of these intersecting forms in the course of season one. Izaak is not the only male dancer in the season whose masculinity is regulated but his case is significant because of his longevity in the season and because he becomes a project of transformation for the judges. Potential accusations of effeminacy are certainly an anxiety shared by some other male dancers on the show, as alluded to by dance contender Nico during season one (which I will return to shortly).

Arassay Reyes, on the other hand, is represented as a bubbly, sexy, and enthusiastic woman who emigrated from Cuba to Canada three months prior to her audition. Much of the "back story," which frames her narrative in the competition through video clips, centres on her immigration story and celebrates the new successes she is being offered by both Canada and the series—presumably as spaces of inclusion. From the outset Arassay is framed in her audition segment as different, exotic, and explicitly sexy. Referring to both her Cuban accent and ability to "shimmy," one male judge expresses a rolling growl of the letter "rrrrrr" before describing her as the "full package." Arassay is deemed the "Cuban shaker," and as the example with Izaak demonstrates, she is often described as a "beast." Not surprisingly, Arassay's relationship to dance and femininity is never questioned. Rather, she is repeatedly called upon to (re)mark her ethnicity in the season, a tactic that serves to re-eroticize her as a racialized commodity.

Representations of Arassay within the series uphold an appearance of naturalness and truth because they fit easily with sustained Western popular media stereotypes that reduce Latina women from multiple cultures and countries into a single knowable construct (Molina Guzmán and Angharad N. Valdivia 2004). Latinas are represented as hot, over-sexed, as sexual objects, inviting, exotic, flamboyant, excessive, dangerous, voluptuous, and particularly in touch with their bodies and body movement, to name a few characteristics (see Mary Beltran 2002, 82; Guzmán and Valdivia 2004, 21; Gary D. Keller 1994; Dana E. Mastro and Elizabeth Behm-Morawitz 2005, 125; Debra Merskin 2007). These stereotypes are also sustained relationally to constructs of whiteness. Michelle Fine, Lois Weis, Linda C. Powell, and L. Mun Wong (1997, 57) suggest we take some time to "witness whiteness" by averting our gaze from the discriminations, deficits, and inequalities experienced by people of colour to an awareness of how whiteness accrues power, privilege, dignity, status, and resources. Decentring whiteness can also assist in countering celebratory multiculturalisms and liberal pluralisms in their various national manifestations (see Floya Anthias and Nira Yuval-Davis 1992; Himani Bannerji 2000; Ruth Frankenberg 1993; Chandra Talpade Mohanty 2003), similar to the discourses that surround Arassay on the series. Though Arassay is a celebrated contestant on the show (making it to the top eight), her role serves as a normalizing counterpoint to many of the men and women on the series in two interlinked ways: as marked racialized outsider (though celebrated as evidence of Canada's liberal multicultural and pluralist success), and consequently, as a means by which to measure masculinity (as a representational embodiment of eroticized hyper-femininity), as the previous and following examples with Izaak and Nico (respectively) demonstrate.

Season one's winner, Nico Archambault, is a white, medium-build man of average height with a trendy hairstyle and a French Canadian accent. Unlike Izaak, Nico comes to embody a more successful representation of heteronormative masculinity, secured, in part, in relation to Izaak's failures in this regard. Nico is coded within the show quite differently than Izaak; his movement is described by the show's judges as powerful, athletic, sexual, and masculine, just enough so that he can also safely be both emotive and delicate in movement, and, according to the judges, ultimately authentic in his embodiment of truth.

For instance, in episode nine, season one, Nico and Arassay dance to "Let Me Leave" by Marc Broussard, a contemporary piece by choreographer Blake McGrath. A dance that the choreographer describes to the camera as being "about a guy who's just at his wits end in the relationship and he's basically telling this woman that it's over and you have to let me leave and she is not having it at all." The accompanying musical lyrics mirror the story line:

> Let me be who I am/Let me leave while I can/ [...] Why is it that I'm as bad as I am [...] Why do you still love me/When all I have done is to lie and deceive? [...] And I tried my best to be a man.

Nico and Arassay are featured dancing together several times in the series suggesting a visual and narrative emphasis by the producers on their compatibility as performers, dance partners, and potential sweethearts—a theme repeated in this particular dance performance. The dance primarily consists of Arassay, barefoot in a short blue slip dress and purple underwear, repeatedly flinging herself upon, chasing and clinging to Nico, tearing off his tank top, and performing moments of frustration when spatially separated from him (looking down and convulsing). Nico, now topless and barefoot in ripped jeans, continues to physically reject Arassay, by lifting, pushing, and shaking her, and, unlike Arassay's more introverted spatial solo, runs towards the audience when released from Arassay's grip, and to the lyrics "let me be who I am" emotively enacts a plea to the viewer for his individuality, with arms and legs spread wide. To the lyrics "I try my best to be a man," he flexes both his arms, like an angry muscle-builder. They then both tumble and roll around in sexual embrace, until Nico finally pins her down and then walks away, leaving Arassay at the end of the piece, as if rejected and alone, crawling on the floor, head down.

Unlike the previously described more playful and somewhat unison-based choreography of Benji Schwimmer that Izaak and Arassay danced to, the choreography of McGrath in this instance draws upon familiar narratives of romantic heterosexual love (including spousal violence) that emphasize opposing characteristics and distinctions between men and women, a dominant choreographic format within the show. Nico's gaze towards the audience, similar to his movement, is active and powerful; his choreographed and embodied adherence to conventional representational codes of dominant (white) masculinity (Ramsay Burt 1995; Cohan and Hark 1995/1993; Dyer 1997) serve to resist easy objectification. Arassay, on the other hand, is easily eroticized as object. Though she appears powerful in her attempts to contain Nico in her embrace, her body movements are often resisted and manipulated by Nico as she is lifted and flung about. She concludes the dance on her knees looking down and away from the viewer in a performance of bodily submission. Burt argues that,

> the ways in which the male dancer's presence succeeds or fails in reinforcing male power is clearly central to an understanding of representations of masculinity in theatre dance. How spectators read dancers' presence is determined partly by visual cues. Some of these cues are given by the dancers, through the way they present themselves to the audience, and in the way they themselves focus their gaze. (1995, 50)

The visual cues Nico provides the audience in this case (through physicality and intent) effectively situate him as an embodiment of male power. The dance performance draws upon heteronormative gender roles through the music, the costumes, the movement, and the choreographed dance narrative. Arassay is characterized as the desperate temptress, while Nico is characterized as a man seeking solitude, resisting female temptation, and bombarded by feminine desperation. Despite the dance's heavy reliance on conventional stereotypes, the performance itself is quite exciting to watch: it is highly physical, emotive, has a broad use of space, creates tension through kinesthetic energy, and is well performed. Nico's movement is simultaneously powerful and elegant. These pleasurable, skill-based attributes along with the audience's possible invested interest in the couple's success seductively invite the viewer to collude in the maintenance and naturalization of gendered heterosexual norms.

Preceding the performance, much fuss is made about Nico breaking his nose during rehearsal for the piece, which is represented to viewers via video montage. Nico's manliness is again reaffirmed as viewers witness the rehearsal video of him casually pushing his nose back into place, despite the perceived yet (expressively absent) pain. Men in sports where physical pain is common are accorded esteem and their masculine status is maintained by concealing, downplaying, disregarding, and depersonalizing injuries (Michael Messner 1989; Steven Schacht 1996; Pablo Schyfter 2008; Vaccaro 2011; Kevin Young, William Mcteer, and Philip White 1994). Such tactics allow for the representation of an active body that is in control, attributes central to discourses of dominant masculinity.

Following the rehearsal video and Nico and Arassay's "live" performance, judge Kenny Ortega enthusiastically proclaims while pointing excitedly at Nico and Arassay:

> Viva Cuba. You know, talk about blood on the dance floor. This kind of choreography is difficult and to become able to own it and to find it, you do get hurt. [...] You're the reason why guys dance, you're the reason why guys like to dance.

Nico responds:

> It's such an important comment for me.

Judge Kenny Ortega continues:

> *You bring great masculinity and truth* and, and you're grounded and you're powerful and strong, you're beautiful partner to this exquisite young lady. Really I think it was the most powerful dancing I've seen all evening (emphasis added).

Nico, demonstrating his awareness of popular conceptions of dance as a queer and feminized space, responds:

> Thank you so much. What you just said is really important 'cause it's really hard for guys to grow up in the dance world—I'm not gonna make a drama here, you do it because you like it and we're all happy that we're here, but it's not easy. Thanks for saying that. 'Cause, you have to find who you are as a guy. So …

This construct of opposition between male/female and heterosexual embodiment's of masculinity and femininity is also apparent in judge Jean Marc Generoux's further comment to Nico and Arassay when he states: "You know you are an amazing force of nature coming from two different worlds but united as one. You are fusion in motion, I love you." This comment, perhaps referring to sexual union, can also be read as an emphasis on nationality and ethnicity set up earlier in previous episodes of the show (Nico being white French Canadian and Arassay a recent immigrant from Cuba) (Boyd 2012).

Nico's masculinity is secured through his "authentic" performance of heterosexual opposition to dance partner Arassay Reyes, and also relationally to Izaak's failure to fully embody the kind of heteronormative masculinity expected on the show. While Nico's performance of masculinity is naturalized (e.g., "great masculinity and truth"), Izaak, according to the judges, does not perform his "true self," thus his performance remains "inauthentic" (e.g., "the *reality* of your performance needs to step up").

Because of his perceived whiteness, Nico also embodies a particularly "believable" form of heteronormative masculinity. This is because male heteronormativity and whiteness work together as mutually affirming unmarked norms through which privilege is naturalized (Dyer 1997). While Nico, as "Canada's favourite dancer," certainly possesses both technique and charisma, his performances are attributed with authenticity by the judges in a way that eludes most of the other contestants, including Izaak. This authentic status potentially serves a considerable advantage in terms of technical dance ability, in that it affords Nico more fluidity and creative versatility in his movement vocabulary, as his movements are less likely to be interpreted as a challenge to the (already established yet continually threatened) masculine norm.

Yeates' (2013) discussion of how visual representations frame and police (hetero) sexuality is relevant here. Using representations of David Beckham as her subject, she notes:

"In an empowered position afforded by his sexuality, Beckham can perform 'queer' in ways unavailable to homosexual male athletes, pointing to the limitations of hegemonic masculinity's assimilation of queerness" (117). Similarly, Nico, in his empowered position afforded by his perceived heterosexuality and I would argue his whiteness, can perform (femininity) in ways that queer and non-white male contestants in the first season cannot. This serves as an example of how hegemonic masculinities are mutable and adaptive despite being associated with the singular and static (John Beynon 2002; Yeates 2013). His whiteness further enables a performance of masculinity that is less likely to be attributed with a menacing hyper-sexuality historically associated with black masculinity. While Nico's relationship to dance and masculinity (and implicitly, sexuality) becomes part of the season's narrative, his whiteness remains unacknowledged. Nico, as a dancer and television character, enacts the value of being seen for which Dyer (1997, 146–147) relates—in the context of "underachieving" masculinity he does not reveal the instability of the heterosexual white male body but rather *reaffirms* its dominance.

Auditions/Resistant Bodies?

The audition segment of the *SYTYCDC* series provides insight into the social process behind the choosing of the contestants, but is also significant in that it seems to offer the most potential, in terms of confounding some of the normalizing representations of the dancing body. In this section, the audience is introduced to a wider range of dancing bodies, performances, and choreographies that can potentially exceed, defy, and confound the narrowly defined parameters of dance on the series. This includes differently-abled bodies, those exceeding normative gender boundaries, including those whose movement is deemed by the show to be too effeminate or too masculine, those who appear transgendered and/or queerly disruptive; dancers performing choreographies outside the scope of the show, such as folk dance, traditional, and ceremonial dance, and some particularly creative dancers who have not been formally trained.

It is during the auditions that these rebellious dancing bodies are also most critiqued and regulated in that these are the bodies that do not make it into the competition based on their inability to conform. They are highlighted for their entertainment value, emphasized often for dramatic effect (as an act of charity, bravery, and personal sob-story), and/or as part of what that show defines itself against—what it is emphatically not. Harmanie Shairp's audition, for instance, consists of two white women dancing together, one on foot, one in a wheel chair. The segment is framed as an inspirational anomaly, with the help of slow-motion footage, tears, and a voiceover by Shairp stating:

> I heard once that if you walk you can dance. And I was sitting there in my wheelchair thinking that was the most ridiculous thing I've ever heard in my whole entire life, because if you have a heartbeat, you have a rhythm, and if you have a rhythm, you can dance. So I want to challenge everybody to realize that everybody can dance.

Though her challenging words and performance are both featured and celebrated, the impact is ultimately negated within the series as a whole, for only "able-bodied" performers are chosen to become "Canada's favourite dancer." The judges declare such boundary-pushing performances as immeasurable or unjudgeable, as is implied by their reactions to Shairp's performance. Nevertheless, these performances, in their public existence and representation, have power to a small degree (despite it being ultimately negated within the context of the show), as "[d]ance displays, in the very ways that bodies are placed in motion, traces of the forces of contestation that can be found in society at large" (Randy Martin 1998, 6). These moments of confounding performance extend mainstream boundaries of dance to a larger viewership.

Conclusion

An exploration of some of the discursive practices through which the dancing body is articulated assists in the destabilizing of theories of sexual difference dependent upon the concept of a stable, "natural," and unitary body (Thomas 2003). Further, claims to authenticity of movement and identity are implicated in the reinforcement of race and gender-based stereotypes. Because (perceived) authenticity is valued, how the judges on the show define it serves to confer legitimacy on particular dancers and dances, identities and movement qualities.

This paper offers one example of how male heterosexuality is inscribed, performed, and (re)choreographed in dance media. This case study has wider implications for analyses of how heterosexuality and whiteness work together in the embodied social practice of dance and the representational realm of television. The status accrued from both constructs of whiteness and masculinized expressions of heterosexuality remain often unacknowledged and unproblematized, maintained and normalized through cultural practices and discourses. Popular media representations offer insight into contemporary ideals surrounding masculinity, which often come to be defined relationally, by what it is not. While new forms of masculinities emerge within popular representational realms that point to changing conceptions of how masculinity is valued (such as popularity of graceful male dancers on primetime television), heteronormative limits are maintained.

In season one of *So You Think You Can Dance Canada* heteronormative expectations of the white male dancing body became naturalized through a number of visual, auditory, physical, and narrative devices as well as through "expert" discourses of embodied authenticity and truth (for which conceptions of gender and race are implicated) couched in a rhetoric of technical ability and choreographic intent. This leaves little room for male dancers on the show to negotiate the heterosexual norms imposed by the series and the culture at large. Dance is enjoyable, emotional, and it is also seductive. Because of these qualities it is easy to presume that it is also apolitical or an unfettered expression of freedom; however, it participates subtly yet insidiously in our ideological culture and this is precisely why it is important to study. As Foucault (1977) has demonstrated, the body, body movement, and bodily expressions are always implicated in our regimes of "truth, knowledge and power."

References

Adair, Christy. 1992. *Women and Dance: Sylphs and Sirens*. New York: New York University Press.

Anthias, Floya, and Nira Yuval-Davis. 1992. *Racialized Boundaries: Race, Nation, Gender, Colour, and Class and the Anti-Racist Struggle*. London and New York: Routledge.

Banes, Sally. 1998. *Dancing Women: Female Bodies on Stage*. New York: Routledge.

Bannerji, Himani. 2000. *The Dark Side of the Nation: Essays on Multiculturalism, Nationalism and Gender*. Toronto: Canadian Scholars' Press.

Beltran, Mary. 2002. "The Hollywood Latina Body as Site of Social Struggle: Media Constructions of Stardom and Jennifer Lopez's 'Crossover Butt.'" *Quarterly Review of Film and Video* 19 (1): 71–86.

Beynon, John. 2002. *Masculinities and Culture*. Buckingham and Philadelphia, PA: Open University Press.

Billy Elliot. 2000. Film. Directed by Stephen Daldry. Universal.

Boyd, Jade. 2012. "'Hey, We're From Canada but We're Diverse, Right?': Neoliberalism, Mulitculturalism and Identity on So You Think You Can Dance Canada." *Critical Studies in Media Communication* 29 (4): 259–274.

Boyd, Jade. 2014. "'I Go to Dance, Right?' Representation/Sensation on the Gendered Dance Floor." *Leisure Studies* 33 (5): 491–507.

Broomfield, Mark A. 2011. "Policing Masculinity and Dance Reality Television: What Gender Nonconformity Can Teach Us in the Classroom." *Journal of Dance Education* 11 (4): 124–128.

Broussard, Marc. 2004. "Let Me Leave." Song on *Carencro*, Music Album. Island Records.

Brown, Carol. 1997. "Dancing Between Hemispheres: Negotiating Routes for the Dancer-Academic." In *Knowing Feminisms*, edited by Liz Stanley, 132–143. London: Sage Publications.

Burt, Ramsay. 1995. *The Male Dancer: Bodies, Spectacle, Sexualities*. London: Routledge.

Burt, Ramsay. 2001. "The Trouble with the Male Dancer …." In *Moving History/Dancing Cultures: A Dance History Reader*, edited by A. Dils and A. C. Albright, 44–55. Middletown: Wesleyan University Press.

Butler, Judith. 1990. *Gender Trouble: Feminism and the Subversion of Identity*. New York: Routledge.

Canada's Broadcasting Corporation (CBC) Radio One. 2009. "Is North American Reality TV Ready for a Gay Icon?" Q Podcast. Accessed January 23, 2010. http://www.cbc.ca/q/

CNW Group. 2008. "So You Think You Can Dance Canada Debuts at No. 1 on CTV With 1.25 Million Viewers." Accessed February 14, 2014. http://www.newswire.ca/en/story/330445/so-you- think-you-can-dance-canada-debuts-at-no-1-on-ctv-with-1-25-million-viewers

CNW Group. 2009. "So You Think You Can Dance Canada Delivers Highest Audience of Season with 1.4 Million Viewers on CTV." Accessed September 8, 2009. http://www.newswire.ca/en/releases/archive/August2009/26/c7905.html

Cohan, Steven, and Ina Rae Hark, eds. 1995/1993. *Screening the Male: Exploring Masculinities in Hollywood Cinema*. London and New York: Routledge.

Coltrane, S., and M. Messineo. 2000. "The Perpetuation of Subtle Prejudice: Race and Gender Imagery in 1990s Television." *Sex Roles* 5 (6): 363–389.

Connell, Raewyn. 1995. *Masculinities*. Sydney: Allen and Unwin.

Connell, Raewyn, and James W. Messerschmidt. 2005. "Hegemonic Masculinity: Rethinking the Concept." *Gender and Society* 19 (6): 829–859.

Desmond, Jane. 1999. *Staging Tourism: Bodies on Display from Waikiki to Seaworld*. Chicago: University of Chicago Press.

Desmond, Jane, ed. 2001. "Introduction. Making the Invisible Visible: Staging Sexualities through Dance." In *Dancing Desires: Choreographing Sexualities On & Off the Stage*, edited by J. Desmond, 3–32. Madison, WI: University of Wisconsin Press.

Druick, Zoe, and Anastasia Kotsopoulos, eds. 2008. *Programming Reality: Perspectives on English-Canadian Television*. Waterloo, Ontario: Wilfrid Laurier University Press.

Dyer, Richard. 1997. *White*. London and New York: Routledge.

Fanon, Franz. 1967. *Black Skin, White Masks*. New York: Grove Press.

Fine, Michelle, Lois Weis, Linda C. Powell, and L. Mun Wong. 1997. *Off White: Readings on Race, Power, and Society*. New York: Routledge.

Foster, Susan. 2001. "Closets Full of Dances: Masculinity and Sexuality in American Modern Dance." In *Dancing Desires: Choreographing Sexualities On & Off the Stage*, edited by J. Desmond, 147–208. Madison, WI: University of Wisconsin Press.

Foucault, Michel. 1977. *Discipline and Punish: The Birth of the Prison*. London: Allen Lane.

Foucault, Michel. 1980. "Body/Power." In *Power/Knowledge: Selected Interviews and Other Writings 1972–1977*, edited by Colin Gordon, 55–62. New York: Pantheon.

Foulkes, Julia L. 2001. "Dance Is for American Men: Ted Shawn and the Intersection of Gender, Sexuality and Nationalism in the 1930s." In *Dancing Desires: Choreographing Sexualities On & Off the Stage*, edited by J. Desmond, 113–146. Madison, WI: University of Wisconsin Press.

Frankenberg, Ruth. 1993. *White Women, Race Matters: The Social Construction of Whiteness*. Minneapolis: University of Minnesota Press.

Fusco, Coco. 1995. *English Is Broken Here: Notes on Cultural Fusion in the Americas*. New York: New Press.

Fusco, Coco. 2001. *The Bodies That Were Not Ours: And Other Writings*. London and New York: Routledge.

Grindstaff, Linda. 2002. *The Money Shot: Trash, Class, and the Making of TV Talk Shows*. Chicago, IL: University of Chicago Press.

Guzmán, Molina, and Angharad N. Valdivia. 2004. "Brain, Brow, and Booty: Latina Iconicity in US Popular Culture." *The Communication Review* 7: 205–221.

Hall, Stuart, ed. 1997. *Representation: Cultural Representations and Signifying Practices*. Thousand Oaks, CA: Sage Publications.

Hesse-Biber, Sharlene Nagy, and Patricia Leavy. 2010. *The Practice of Qualitative Research*. London: Sage Publications.

Holmes, Sue. 2004. "Reality Goes Pop! Reality TV, Popular Music, and Narratives of Stardom in Pop Idol." *Television New Media* 5 (2): 147–172.

Keller, Gary D. 1994. *Hispanics and United States Film: An Overview and Handbook*. Tempe, AZ: Bilingual Review Press.

Kennedy, John R. 2012. "Rex Harrington Kicks Off Social Media Campaign to Land on US Show." Global News. Accessed January 2, 2013. http://www.globalnews.ca/entertainment/rex%2Bharrington%2Bkicks%2Boff%2Bsocial%2Bmedia%2Bcampaign%2Bto%2Bland%2Bon%2Bus%2Bshow/6442698135/story.html

Kimmel, Michael. 2006. Manhood in America: A Cultural History. New York: Oxford University Press.

Lebesco, Kathleen. 2004. "Got to Be Real: Mediating Gayness on Survivor." In *Reality TV: Remaking Television Culture*, edited by S. Murray and L. Ouellette, 271–287. New York: New York University Press.

Martin, Randy. 1998. *Critical Moves: Dance Studies in Theory and Politics*. Durham and London: Duke University Press.

Mastro, Dana E., and Elizabeth Behm-Morawitz. 2005. "Latino Representation on Primetime Television." *Journalism and Mass Communication Quarterly* 82 (1): 110–127.

Merskin, Debra. 2007. "Three Faces of Eva: Perpetuation of the Hot-Latina Stereotype in Desperate Housewives." *Howard Journal of Communications* 18 (2): 133–151.

Messner, Michael. 1989. "Masculinities and Athletic Careers." *Gender and Society* 3 (1): 71–88.

Mohanty, Chandra Talpade. 2003. *Feminism without Borders: Decolonizing Theory, Practicing Solidarity*. Durham: Duke University Press.

Morris, Gay. 2001. "What He Called Himself: Issues of Identity in Early Dances by Bill T. Jones." In *Dancing Desires: Choreographing Sexualities On & Off the Stage*, edited by J. Desmond, 243–263. Madison, WI: University of Wisconsin Press.

Mulvey, Laura. 2009. *Visual and Other Pleasures*, 2nd edn. Basingstoke: Palgrave MacMillan.

Muñoz, Jose Esteben. 1999. *Disidentifications: Queers of Color and the Performance of Politics*. Minneapolis: University of Minnesota Press.

My Chemical Romance. 2006. "Welcome to the Black Parade." Music Single. Reprise Records.

Schacht, Steven. 1996. "Misogyny On and Off the 'Pitch'—The Gendered World of Male Rugby Players." *Gender and Society* 10 (5): 550–564.

Schyfter, Pablo. 2008. "Tackling the 'Body Inescapable' in Sport: Body-Artifact Kinesthetics, Embodied Skill and the Community of Practice in Lacrosse Masculinity." *Body and Society* 14 (3): 81–103.

Simons, Helen. 2009. *Case Study Research in Practice*. London: Sage Publications.

Skeggs, Beverley. 2009. "The Moral Economy of Person Production: The Class Relations of Self-Performance on 'Reality' Television." *Sociological Review* 57 (4): 626–644.

So You Think You Can Dance. 2008–2011. Television Series. Seasons 1–4. CTV.

So You Think You Can Dance Canada. 2005–present. Television Series. Seasons 1–11. Fox.

Strictly Ballroom. 1992. Film. Directed by Baz Luhrmann. Miramax.

Summers-Bremner, Eluned. 2000. "Reading Irigaray, Dancing." *Hypatia—A Journal of Feminist Philosophy* 15 (1): 90–124.

The Full Monty. 1997. Film. Directed by Peter Caltaneo. Twentieth Century Fox Film Corporation.

Thomas, Gary. 2011. "A Typology for the Case Study in Social Science Following a Review of Definition, Discourse, and Structure." *Qualitative Inquiry* 17 (6): 511–521.

Thomas, Helen. 2003. *The Body, Dance and Cultural Theory*. New York: Palgrave Macmillan.

Vaccaro, Christian Alexander. 2011. "Male Bodies in Manhood Acts: The Role of Body-Talk and Embodied Practice in Signifying Culturally Dominant Notions of Manhood." *Sociology Compass* 5 (1): 65–76.

Wang, Ning. 1999. "Rethinking Authenticity in Tourism Experience." *Annals of Tourism Research* 26 (2): 349–370.

Weber, Cynthia. 2003. "'Oi. Dancing Boy!': Masculinity, Sexuality, and Youth in Billy Elliot." *Genders* 37.

Yeates, Amelia. 2013. "Queer Visual Pleasures and the Policing of Male Sexuality in Responses to Images of David Beckham." *Visual Studies* 28 (2): 110–121.

Young, Kevin, William McTeer, and Philip White. 1994. "Body Talk Male-Athletes Reflect on Sport, Injury, and Pain." *Sociology of Sport Journal* 11 (2): 175–194.

CHAPTER 27

"It's Just Drama": Teen Perspectives on Conflict and Aggression in a Networked Era

Alice Marwick and danah boyd

Introduction

> Victoria (15, Nashville): His girlfriend, Brittany, cheated on him and she went and partied really hard and got drunk and cheated. And then it was all over Formspring. A lot of people are like, "You can do better than that slut" and stuff. And people would write on hers, "You're such a cheating whore" and blah, blah, blah. And so, that was like drama and stuff. And like, I know Brittany Martinez. If I saw her, I'd be like, "Hey, what's up?" But I don't know her personally. And so, I wouldn't go talk to her about it. But I read that and I could know about it. So it was kind of just like drama I could [see] and stuff.

The vast majority of American teenagers (95%) are Internet users, and 85% use social media (Lenhart et al. 2011). The popularity of social media sites like Facebook and Twitter among teenagers has prompted serious concerns about "cyberbullying" (Hinduja and Patchin 2008; Kowalski, Limber, and Agatston 2008) and online harassment (Ybarra and Mitchell 2004) as conflict moves from the schoolyard to online environments. But asking young people about online bullying or harassment often obscures other negative experiences they encounter; in a recent survey, only 19% of teens reported being bullied in the last year, although 88% had witnessed mean or cruel behavior on social media (Lenhart et al. 2011). Meanwhile, qualitative studies have found that teenagers often use the term "drama" when asked about aggressive online behavior, typically to describe girls' online conflict (Allen 2012; Veinot et al. 2011). Drama shares elements with other models of youth aggression and conflict, such as relational and indirect aggression, bullying, cyberbullying, and gossip, but appears distinct from each (Allen forthcoming). To understand the relationship between youth conflict and social media sites, a closer look at drama, and its relationship to related terms, is warranted.

While much of the meanness and cruelty that young people experience online does not fit into the frame of "cyberbullying," this concept is predominantly used when discussing online conflict (Burgess-Proctor, Patchin, and Hinduja 2010; Livingstone et al. 2011). Rather than simply mapping offline bullying to online spaces, scholars must study how widespread use of social media alters dynamics of aggression and conflict. As Erving Goffman conceptualized a "front stage" and a "back stage" for interpersonal interaction and identity presentation, drama typically takes place on a stage organized around high school (1959). In most American high schools, social media have replaced the street or coffee shop as the "place" where much discussion, interaction, and "hanging out" between teens goes on (boyd 2014). Drama appears to exist both offline and online, and may illuminate the effects of widespread social media use, and its properties of performance, visibility, and participation, on teen sociality.

This paper analyzes unstructured face-to-face interviews with 166 American teenagers in an attempt to deepen theoretical conceptions of the term "drama." We investigate how teenagers define the term; the relationship between drama and social media; and the implications drama has for understanding teenage conflict online in terms of gender and discourse.

Methods

This paper draws on interviews collected from 2006 to 2011 across the United States as part of an ongoing ethnographic project to understand American teenage use of social media (boyd 2014; boyd and Marwick 2011). This project consists of two sets of qualitative interviews, two focus groups, and online and offline participant observation. The first set of interviews (n = 106) was conducted with teenagers in 14 states during 2006–2009 and focused on general teenage use of social media (boyd, forthcoming). The second set of interviews (n = 60) was conducted with teenagers in 2010–2011 in five states focusing on privacy. A different protocol was used for each set of interviews, although neither protocol included specific questions about "drama." Participants in both sets brought up "drama" in the course of the interview, and thus, both sets of interviews produced data relevant to this paper.

INTERVIEWS

The corpus includes 166 semi-structured interviews conducted in 17 states with participants ranging in age from 13 to 19 (we use the terms "teenagers" and "youth" interchangeably in this study to refer to participants in this age range). Participants under 18 needed a guardian's permission to participate in the study. Each participant was given information sheets about the study before confirming participation. We worked with community organizations in each location to recruit interview subjects, including after-school programs, public libraries, a youth homeless shelter, and public and private high schools.

Before each interview, subjects signed a consent form and filled out a questionnaire including open-ended demographic questions, household makeup, technology ownership and access, social media services used, and media consumption. Interviews took place in schools, libraries, coffee shops, after-school programs, and participants' homes, and were typically 90 minutes long, although they ranged from 60 minutes to 2 hours. Subjects were compensated $30 in cash during the first set of interviews and $40 in cash during the second set for their participation.

The first set of interviews focused on general teenage use of social media. The second set of interviews consisted of concept-driven data collection (Corbin and Strauss 2007, 145–149) to focus on two themes that emerged from the first set: bullying and privacy. While the interview protocol for the second set of interviews asked specific questions about these issues, all interviews used a semi-structured interview method (Wengraf 2001) to ask about a range of topics, including interests, friends, and technology use. Neither protocol included questions about drama; we asked about drama in response to the language our participants had used. For example, we asked one participant "How would you describe the kids at [your high school]?" She answered, "I think they all like to start unnecessary drama." The interviewer followed up with "You said you feel like kids at [your high school] like to cause unnecessary drama. What causes drama?" This use of participants' emic terms follows an ethnographic approach to interviewing, in that we listened to how teenagers explained and conceptualized their lives rather than attempting to determine the veracity of their statements. We focused on cultural meaning-making, language use, description, and experience (Spradley 1979).

During interviews, we asked participants to clarify with concrete examples and took screenshots of their Facebook, MySpace, Twitter, and Formspring profiles. The interviewers digitally recorded each interview. A transcription company transcribed all recordings, and a research assistant double-checked the transcripts for accuracy.

Finally, each author conducted one focus group focused on drama with a convenience sample of three female participants in the Boston area in 2011. Because drama was not the focus of previous interviews, we used these group discussions as theoretical sampling to clarify ideas about drama that arose during data analysis (Corbin and Strauss 2007, 145–149). The all-female focus groups allowed for explicit discussion of drama and gender.

Participants were not compensated for these discussions, which were digitally recorded by interviewers and transcribed by a transcription company. Although any discussion of peer conflict raises questions of values, morals, and ethics, no notable issues emerged during the interviews conducted for this study. For more information on the ethics procedures used for this study, see boyd (forthcoming).

PARTICIPANTS

We recruited a diverse sample by visiting a variety of communities and working with organizations that served differing demographics. To give a sampling of the diversity of our interview subjects, out of the 166 interviews, 94 were female and 72 were male. Racially, 86 identified as White; 39 as Black, African-American, or biracial Black/White; 22 as Hispanic, Chicano, Latino, or biracial Hispanic/White; 13 as Asian, Indian, or Pakistani descent; 3 as Native American; and 3 as Middle Eastern or Egyptian. The ages of our participants ranged from 13 to 19 with an average age of 16. Forty-five teens had at least one parent with a graduate or professional degree, 50 teens had at least one parent with a BA or some college, and the parents of 35 teens had only a high school diploma or less; 36 reported that they didn't know their parents' education level. This sample thus reflects a variety of experiences and backgrounds. All names and identifying information have been changed to protect the privacy of our informants.

DATA ANALYSIS

In the field, "drama" was frequently mentioned when asking about privacy or online conflict. Our theory of drama was formulated throughout data collection and analysis in an iterative approach. After finishing fieldwork, both authors read through the corpus line by line. The first author coded for instances of drama using the qualitative data analysis program Atlas.ti; a passage was coded for drama only when the term "drama" was used by a participant. The second author wrote ethnographic memos of particular incidents that demonstrated emergent themes. As our understanding of "drama" deepened, the first author returned to the corpus and coded for related concepts, specifically "gossip" and "bullying." As before, a passage was coded for "gossip" or "bullying" only if the term was used by a participant. Due to the iterative nature of coding and analysis, coding was ongoing.

Drawing on experiences in the field and the coded interview data, the authors began formulating a theoretical understanding of "drama" through discussions and perusal of previous research on related topics. During the writing process, our understanding of "drama" developed based on findings that problematized our original theories. We incorporated different perspectives from informants into our findings, such as acknowledging that our interviewees had a diverse array of definitions for drama. Once we had formulated a basic theory of "drama," we held two focus groups. These functioned as concept-driven data collection to validate our thoughts on drama and explore the strengths and weaknesses of our argument.

LIMITATIONS

This study is specific to American youth. Understandings of "bullying," for instance, are culturally situated, and may be experienced quite differently elsewhere. Future studies could focus on other cultural and national contexts. Moreover, studying social media is always a moving target. Since this research took place, new forms of social media, such as Tumblr, Snapchat, and Instagram have grown in popularity. The differences between social network sites like MySpace and Facebook and mobile, visual, or ephemeral social media sites should be taken into account by other scholars.

We begin by defining "drama" and its many components, and compare it to extant concepts in the literature, namely bullying, relational aggression, and gossip. We discuss two implications for future research and policy: the relationship between drama and more prevalent conceptions of young people's online aggression; and the ways in which "drama" reproduces normative conceptions of gender and aggression.

Findings: Defining Drama

Defining drama is not easy, as its conceptual slipperiness is part of its appeal. To the teens we talked with, drama was like Justice Potter Stewart's definition of obscenity: you know it when you see it. When asked to define drama, teens typically gave examples. For instance, Seong, 17, from Los Angeles, said, "They would be bad mouthing someone [online] and then they would see it and then people would fight and take sides and stuff like that, a lot of bad comments coming back and forth." Jenna, 17, from North Carolina, said, "One time a boy wrote something where it didn't say her name but it said enough that everyone in the school knew they were talking about her and all of the senior girls didn't like her. So they all started liking it. So there was 50 likes on a comment a boy said about this one girl." These examples ranged widely and included posting what teenagers often refer to as "inappropriate" videos and photos on social media and the resulting fallout; conflicts that escalated into public standoffs; cries for attention; relationship breakups, makeups, and jealousies; jokes; and a vast array of aggressive or passive-aggressive interactions between friends, enemies, or "frenemies."[1] After consolidating responses, we define drama as "*performative, interpersonal conflict that takes place in front of an active, engaged audience, often on social media.*"

Drama is social and *interpersonal*, about other people and relationships, and intrinsically involves *conflict*. This takes various forms, from moral evaluation of other people's behavior to minor disagreements that escalate. Drama is performative, in that participants are aware that they are in front of others, and often strategically act to appeal to their peers. Drama thus involves an *active, engaged audience*. As Carmen (18, Boston) said, "You can't have drama by yourself." Other teens talked about the involvement of other people "with no lives" who jumped into arguments "where they didn't belong." This is consistent with the findings of Allen, who argues that "drama often moves beyond the original individuals to include others who may have little stake in the original situation" (2012, 110). *Social media* plays a critical role in how drama is constructed in contemporary teen life. Several young people mentioned that the visibility of social media compounds interpersonal conflict. Cachi (18, Iowa) said, "I don't like to comment that much. Everybody can see that and it's just annoying because what if there's something private to one of your guy friends and he has a girlfriend. What's gonna happen? The girlfriend is gonna go to the guy's page and she's gonna, 'Oh, who was that girl leaving you comments and like that?' It's just drama." Furthermore, social media allows additional opportunities for participation, including adding comments and "liking" status updates, illustrating the blend of online and offline that exists in many teenagers' lives.

While investigating bullying, Kathleen Allen found that "drama" emerged as a prevalent concept from focus groups and interviews. She states that it "seemed to be distinct from conflict and bullying, yet it was related to these themes because of overlapping features" (forthcoming, 12). Allen defines drama as social interaction with the following attributes: (1) conflict; (2) excessive emotionality; (3) excessive time and attention; and (4) practices that overlap with bullying, gossip, and aggression (2012, 109–110). We concur with Allen's definition that it involves conflict and practices that overlap with bullying, gossip, and aggression, but we believe that the "excessive emotionality" and "excessive time and attention" imply normative judgments. Some teenagers may judge others' involvement as excessive, but others may not. The indication of "excessive emotionality" may have a gendered component, as "drama" is often conceptualized by teenagers as a female behavior (boyd and Marwick 2011).

Other components of drama differ across communities. Rashna, a 16-year-old from Chicago, gave us her perspective:

> The definition varies from friend group, like where the school is. I think each community has its own sense of drama. Like her [*Naila, another girl in the room*] sense of what is drama, like the fact that fights go on, that doesn't happen at my school. And I think that drama will vary based on where it is, like the suburb or city, like geographically, maybe how much money the school has, and how much people they have in school. So I don't know if you'll ever be able to pin [it] down.

In a group interview, Rashna, Naila, and Carmen agreed that drama differed between their schools. In Naila's school, drama included physical aggression, while Carmen and Rashna saw fighting and drama as distinct. We also found definitional differences within schools, suggesting that young people view drama differently depending on their social status and friend group norms. Our definition of drama attempts to bring clarity to something that is not necessarily clear to teenagers.

WHAT DRAMA IS NOT

Drama resembles other social processes like gossip, bullying, and relational aggression. While researchers conceptualize these three terms separately, the teenagers we talked with often struggled to differentiate one from another. Drama functions as an umbrella term that can encompass elements of all three but is seen by teenagers as different from each.

BULLYING

One commonly used definition of bullying defines it as aggressive behavior that is (1) unwanted; (2) repeated over time; (3) intentional; and (4) unbalanced in power (Olweus 1994, 2011). Bullying is repeated while other forms of aggression can be singular; bullying implies a power imbalance whereas other aggressive forms can take place between two persons of equal power (Dooley, Pyzalski, and Cross 2009). Most scholars conceptualize bullying similarly (Nansel et al. 2001; Salmivalli et al. 1996).

None of the teenagers we spoke with conflated drama and bullying; they viewed them as separate concepts. Carmen distinguishes drama from bullying by defining drama as involving active, agented subjects:

> Drama is more there's two sides fighting back. I guess the second you fight back, it's—you're not allowed to call it bullying because you're defending yourself, I guess. But like, for example, my gay friend, these people spit tobacco in his locker. And I would consider that bullying, not drama, because like these are people who don't have a beef with him. Like they don't know him. They just know he's gay, and [think] "I'm going to spit tobacco in his locker."

For Carmen, drama is bidirectional, while bullying is directed with an aspect of differential power. The tobacco-spitting kids are targeting her friend to demonstrate that he is "other."

The *participatory* aspects of drama appear to differentiate it from the unidirectional model of bullying, which involves a bully and a victim.

Many teenagers told us that bullying had declined as they grow older, "more of a middle school kind of thing" that they had "grown out of." Caleb (17, North Carolina) said, "Once you get to high school is when the bullying really just like stops." When we asked Aarti, a 17-year-old from North Carolina, why this was, she remarked: "People don't care anymore." Caleb concurred: "It just stops because people realize that there's no point. If we're not gonna be friends, we're not gonna be friends and there's no point of getting all into it." However, only one teenager we talked to claimed that drama was a "middle school" thing. The others agreed that in high school, drama was ever-present. Indeed, scholarly research suggests that bullying peaks during middle school years before declining (Wang, Iannotti, and Nansel 2009), even though meanness and cruelty in online settings do not appear to decline in high school (Lenhart et al. 2011).

Even when drama might meet the scholarly definition of bullying, teenagers eschewed it as a descriptive category.

Author: How big an issue is bullying at your school?

Chloe (15, Atlanta): Not big, because we're a Christian school, so our teachers always tell us to be nice to each other and stuff, and no one's ever mean to anyone. Or unless someone says something rude to someone on accident. They're, like, "Oh, I'm so sorry," and you know.

Author: Is there ever issues with rumors spreading?

Chloe: Oh, yeah, all the time.

Author: How does that play out?

Chloe: Well, someone starts a rumor and then someone else finds out and they're like—and they, everyone just changes the story around. And once it gets around to the person that it's about, they hate this person. It's just ...

Vicki (15, Atlanta): Whoever started it.

Chloe: A bunch of gossip, yeah.

While Vicki and Chloe defended their school from bullying or "mean" behavior, they admitted it was full of rumors, gossip, and drama.

RELATIONAL AGGRESSION

Relational aggression is defined by Crick and Grotpeter as "harming others through purposeful manipulation and damage of their peer relationships" (1995, 710) and has been extensively investigated by researchers (Björkqvist, Lagerspetz, and Kaukiainen 1992; Card et al. 2008). According to scholars, girls engage in relational aggression because it is socially and contextually unacceptable for them to engage in physical aggression. Because women and girls are judged harshly for anger and aggression, their use of teasing, gossip, and ostracization allows them to express these feelings in a socially condoned way (Ness 2010). However, a meta-analysis of scholarly studies did not find support for the increased incidence of relational aggression in girls or direct aggression in boys (Card et al. 2008). This suggests that relational aggression is viewed as a female practice regardless of the genders of actual practitioners.

While both drama and relational and indirect aggression are considered "female" and involve the interpersonal, they are distinct. Indirect aggression, which Björkquist et al. define as "a type of behavior in which the perpetrator attempts to inflict pain in such a manner that he or she makes it seem as though there has been no intention to hurt at all" through means including gossip, "backbiting," and social manipulation (1992, 118), implies aggression with an unknown perpetrator, but the visible, participatory nature of drama makes this impossible. However, many examples of drama illustrated that participants in drama manipulate social ties, popularity, and status, just as those engaging in relational aggression do. For example, Wolf (18, Iowa) described the drama caused by MySpace:

> My sister and her friends, when they get angry at each other, they'll try to post the most provocative pictures they can, the ones that will make their friends the most angry. And that's what they do back and forth, and when it gets bad, they'll comment to each other and it's almost as bad as instant messaging. By the end of the day, they're ready to tear each other to bits.

The fact that drama takes place in front of an audience often means that, like relational aggression, it involves the manipulation of interpersonal relationships.

While it is tempting to categorize drama as simply a form of relational aggression, other examples were quite different. Naila's (18, Boston) story illustrates this point:

> There's this one girl, she posted a picture on Facebook. And she has two different groups of friends. She has her really like hoity-toity white friends. And then she has her school friends. And so she had like new Jordans on. So her really like hoity-toity friend was like, "Oh, it's a cute picture, but what the hell is on your feet?" And this one girl from school who's a really good friend of hers was like, "Clearly, they're Jordans. And they're like that expensive, and they're like this and that." And this other girl, her white friend was like, "Excuse me, who invited you into this conversation? I was clearly commenting on X-Y-Z, my best friend's photo, and where I come from, Jordans are ghetto." And they just kept going for like—it got to like 53 comments.

In this case, an inoffensive picture posted to Facebook sparked drama between two groups of teens with different norms. To Naila's school friends, expensive sneakers were recognized as a status symbol. But to the "white girls" from the other side of town, they were tacky and racially marked. The use of the word "ghetto" incited both class and racial tension in the comments section. This example shows that drama does not necessarily involve close friends or even acquaintances. Naila's friends were acting aggressively, but not using peer relationships to do so.

In other instances, drama was not intrinsically aggressive. Many participants characterized drama as fun or entertaining. Samantha (18, Seattle) explained that social media "is fun to use when you're bored. It's a way to start drama because people use it to check up on other people." Camille (15, North Carolina) explained further:

> Camille: Everybody will use a quote that somebody said, and then they'll be like, that's so stupid or something, who is she, and then another person will say it, and then they'll respond to something else, and kind of making fun of them indirectly, fighting.
>
> Author: So why do you think someone would do that?
>
> Camille: I don't know, it's drama, kind of entertaining.

To Camille, actively participating in drama is a form of entertainment. This suggests that the stakes in this drama are relatively low, even for the instigators.

GOSSIP

Gossip was often mentioned as an element of drama.

> Author: And for you, are you seeing drama?
>
> Chelsea (15, Nashville): Yes. It seems like when one person doesn't like somebody else then they have their whole group of friends not liking that one person. And they'll all talk about what that person did two days ago, yesterday or what they were wearing or what they looked like. Just basically gossip and talking about the other person.

This distinction seemed blurry, but many participants defined them differently:

> Carmen: I like to think of gossip as more like passive-aggressive. Drama is like it's happening now, and it's like, "Oh, my god, it's explosions!" And gossip, I think more like, "Oh, my gosh! Did you hear about this?" It's not like, "I'm going to go fight that person now, because they did this, this, and this." And you gossip about drama.
>
> Naila: Or in my case, gossip is more removed from yourself. Like someone will be like, "Oh, my gosh! Do you have any gossip?" And it'll be like, "So-and-So broke

> up with So-and-So." But it's not something that's happening drama towards you, I guess. It's not like, well, gossip is more like, "Oh, you know that perfect couple that isn't in my group that's kind of over there, they broke up."

Anthropologist Gary Fine writes that gossip is a "form of discourse between persons discussing the behavior, character, situation, or attributes of absent others" (1997, 422). In other words, gossip requires its subjects to be elsewhere (Ayim 1994) and typically takes place in tiny, intimate groups (Altman and Taylor 1973), thus serving to strengthen social bonds and affection between group members (Ben-Ze'ev 1994). Similarly, Carmen, Naila, and Abigail distinguish drama from gossip based on participation. Gossip is detached, whereas Carmen's description of drama as "explosions" shows the importance and closeness of drama.

Folami (18, Tennessee) and Mei Xing (17, Tennessee) reveal another element of participation in their discussion of relationships online:

> Folami: Facebook is fun when there's Facebook drama on somebody's Facebook status. That's like, I don't know, it makes it even more fun when people start acting ridiculous on Facebook and everyone can see it.
>
> Author: So what's an example of Facebook drama?
>
> Folami: I think like when people have statuses there about someone or their boyfriends.
>
> Mei Xing: About relationships.
>
> Folami: In relationships. And you can't really—even though they don't put names on it you know who they're talking about and everyone sees it.
>
> Mei Xing: I love seeing the little hearts on Facebook because it's always like someone just got in a relationship or someone just broke up.

To these girls, information that a relationship began or ended is typical gossip. Once people post veiled, negative status messages about relationships, these comments become public drama and involve others. In such situations, the performative and audience involvement of drama become salient when distinguishing it from gossip.

Drama and Social Media

Drama is a performative set of actions undertaken to involve an audience. By *performative*, we mean the heightened dramaturgical awareness caused by digital media users' "need to deliberately write self into being, an activity that requires both technical skills and reflexivity about what is required to enact embodiment" (Markham 2013). Thus, the integration of social media into teenage interaction enhances the performative aspect of interpersonal conflict (Van House 2011). Due to social media's ubiquity, teenagers know that an audience of peers is watching, and use the technical affordances of social media to appeal to them (Papacharissi 2009). The publicity enabled by sites like Facebook or Twitter affects how conflict plays out in teenage social groups.

In virtually every town where we conducted fieldwork, it was typical for teens to "friend" everyone in their class or school. This results in large potential audiences for Facebook messages that can involve people far beyond the original participants. Thus, when teens interact using social media, conflicts often take place in front of a highly distributed networked audience of classmates and acquaintances, who can participate in situations they were not originally a part of, fostering drama. Amira (15, Tennessee) related an example of drama:

> There was this girl and she put up a picture [on Facebook] and I guess it was like she was making a Botox face like where your eyes are like this [half-closed] and you like try to make your lips look bigger. And so this girl commented to her and she's like, "Botox much?" And then the other girl comments on it and then they just start cussing each other out. And then the next thing you know everyone jumps in and they're like cussing each other and it's all this is really funny because like in person they'll just walk past each other and they won't do anything.

Audience members make their presence known by commenting on the argument in progress on Facebook. Similarly, Ashley (14, North Carolina) says:

> I see people post—I don't know—as their status like "I don't know what blah, blah, blah is talking," "I don't know what she," they won't even say a name. They'll say like, "People need to mind their own business what I do with blah, blah, blah, isn't any of yours." And I'm just like, not everybody needs to see this. This is a personal thing so don't make it public. Some people want to cause drama.

Ashley explains that such thinly veiled messages are intended for a public audience. In another interview, Heather (16, Iowa) offered the story of her friends Erin and Anya, who were fighting over a boy. Erin argued with Anya on her Facebook wall so that "everyone [would] back her up." Heather sighed, "I guess things are just more dramatic if they're on the wall, and Anya wants everyone to see how unfairly she's being treated." Many teenagers take arguments to Facebook to make them visible and accrue support for their point of view.

Moreover, several teenagers we interviewed gave us examples of drama that involved the participatory properties of social media.

> Author: How does it [drama] come out on Facebook?
>
> Alicia (17, North Carolina): Well, there's a girl from [high school] that got in an

> argument with a girl from [high school] and they were at a party. So then when I looked on Facebook the next day there were all of these comments on [there] like "I love you, I don't think you're a—" whatever the girl called her. So it's all really immature and they'll put statuses up like "oh my gosh I'm so over this." So that's how drama gets on Facebook.

Alicia's story shows how the technical affordances of Facebook can be used to demonstrate public support for one side of a conflict. The status update "oh my gosh I'm so over this" is intended to elicit attention from friends and classmates. In the example given previously by Jenna, the audience "weighed in" on one side of an argument by "liking" a comment. Twitter's "retweet" feature and Tumblr's "reblog" feature are other technical affordances that let audiences take sides in a dramatic incident.

Drama also illustrates the incorporation of social media into all aspects of teenage life, revealing the inadequacy of an "online/offline" dichotomy (Baym 2009). In Alicia's earlier anecdote, drama began at a party and moved to Facebook, becoming visible to a larger audience. In Amira's story, drama started in the comments on a Facebook photo, but the participants ignored each other in person. Other dramas may turn into offline confrontations, as Brandy (16, Washington, DC) explains:

> Author: How does Facebook play a role in drama?
>
> Brandi: I mean, like if somebody makes a comment on their status, or have a status and if somebody comments it, and another person, like, "Why would you say that?" Then that starts something. Then somebody's going to say somebody's name, and that's going to roll, and then somebody's going to comment on that. And then that's going to go back to school or back to the streets.

While Facebook is sometimes thought of as a separate, distinct environment, social media sites more frequently serve as extensions to unmediated spaces like school and parties.

> Rashna: There's no removal from what happens at school. Cause it can always continue on Facebook, and you have access to that at your home. Which previously was considered somewhere where you don't have to deal with everything that's going on in school.

Rumors, gossip, and drama circulate on Facebook and Twitter while moving back and forth between the school corridor and instant messenger, texts, and written notes. Drama exists beyond a single media into what Haythornthwaite (2001) calls a multiplexity of communicative methods.

Because social media has the property of persistence, it can serve as an archive of interactions and comments that can be used in conflict. Most examples of drama given involved social media in one way or another. Jared (17, Tennessee) explains:

> All of this drama ... It's not that it takes place in person. It's just that technology didn't really influence it other than making communication possible. I mean, without [people] stalking around Facebook—or them sifting through the text messages—then there wouldn't be a written record for them to go through and look at.

To Jared, the persistent property of social media increases the likelihood of drama. This integration suggests that models of youth aggression must incorporate the prevalence of social media to understand how it changes and modifies aggressive behavior.

Discussion

THE CULTURAL WORK OF DRAMA

Beyond its practical manifestation, the use of "drama" does significant cultural work for teenagers. It allows teens to blur the boundaries between real conflict and jokes, and hurt and entertainment. This makes it possible for young people to frame their own engagement with social conflict in ways distinct from the perpetrator/victim subjectivities of bullying narratives, which are often set and defined by adults. This serves as an empowerment strategy for teens who can dismiss a hurtful joke by labeling it as "drama." While none of the teenagers we interviewed explained this cultural work in their own narratives, analyzing their anecdotes and explanations makes it clear that "drama" has a function beyond a popular slang term.

By using the term "drama" rather than gossip, bullying, or any related practice, teens can disengage with adult models of peer aggression and create and participate in their own narratives. As mentioned previously, some forms of drama involve acts that adults may identify as bullying or relational aggression, suggesting that they are synonymous. Instead, by using the language of drama to refer to an array of different practices—some emotionally devastating, others lightweight and fun—many teenagers we spoke with attempted to protect themselves from the social and psychological harm involved in drama.

The public rhetoric surrounding bullying suggests there are "bullies" and "bullied," which can be problematic. Some scholars argue that the bully-victim dyad does not reflect the realities of peer participation in bullying (Hawkins, Pepler, and Craig 2001), while others have criticized this binarism (Davies 1998; Farrell 1999). Many examples of drama lacked a clear perpetrator and victim or an obvious power or status imbalance. We found that teens gain little by identifying as a "bully" or "victim." The emphasis on status in youth culture discourages teens from identifying themselves as weak, while others are unwilling to admit that they purposefully hurt others. While some teenagers talked about being bullied in the past, few young people in our sample admitted to currently being bullied, or called someone else out as a bully. The teens we interviewed and observed who were least likely to admit being bullied were those most likely to lose social status from being labeled as weak: street-smart, inner-city boys (Ness 2010; Pascoe 2007). Even youths who might admit privately to being bullies or victims appeared unlikely to publicly engage with an anti-bullying program. The few teens who acknowledged currently being bullied were socially marginalized, clearly lower on the popularity spectrum in their schools. Since teenagers position bullying as "immature" or childish, teens who identify with it as perpetrator or victim risk framing themselves as juvenile.

In North Carolina, we met Morgan, a 16-year-old target of extensive aggression by a female classmate, Cathy. Cathy's boyfriend had pursued Morgan and lied to Cathy about it. Jealous and angry, Cathy began tormenting Morgan, blaming her instead of her boyfriend. Morgan explained:

> I have these kids that I don't really know and they come up to me and they're like "Yeah, I heard about you." And I'm like "I don't even know you. How'd you hear about me?" I told her that I don't want drama and I don't want her to talk about me and I'm not going to talk about her. But she continues to say things about me. I'm trying to leave it alone but it's kind of hard. She'll text one of my friends and say "Morgan's a skank," and I'll be like "What? What'd I do." And then they'll show me the text message and I'll confront her back, and she'll be like "No, I never said that." And then she'll stick stuff on Facebook.

Morgan told us she was doing nothing to further the drama, which escalated as Cathy sought support from her peers. Cathy's ongoing text messages, Facebook updates, and rumors about Morgan might be defined by adults as "bullying," but Morgan used the term "drama." When recounting what was happening, she attempted to save face by minimizing the conflict's impact, while framing Cathy as immature and desperate for attention. Still, this did not diminish the situation's seriousness, as Morgan was so disturbed that she contemplated leaving school. Despite her face-saving to us and her peers, it was clear that this situation was taking a serious psychological toll.

Similarly, young people who others identify as "bullies" rarely see themselves as aggressors. Ashley, a ninth grader, has gotten into trouble at school for bullying others. In our interview, she expressed strong disapproval of people trying to get attention, of teens drinking and partying, and of classmates acting "ghetto." Her sister Abigail—whom we also interviewed—described Ashley as judgmental towards friends, acquaintances, and classmates alike. When Ashley recounted an incident on Facebook, we saw this judgmental attitude in action.

> I think it's kind of annoying when people dye their hair so much. You'll see on Facebook "I just dyed my hair" and you'll see pictures and stuff. Can't you just make it simple, just leave it as it is. Because I know just like I think they kind of do it for attention. I know girls who cut their hair every two weeks or something and they're like, "Look at my new bangs," "Look at this, look at this." And it's kind of like stick with something. Have that be your something.

Ashley dismisses her older sister's claims that she is a bully, but uses gossip and aggression as tools to enforce her own moral code. This has caused tensions between the two sisters, as

Abigail has tried to intervene with little success. Meanwhile, Ashley continues to engage with others in ways she sees fit, ignoring both her sister and her parents. Instead, Ashley argues that she is unfairly treated by others and is justified in her attitude and actions. She describes others' reactions to her interactions as baseless. "Some people want to cause drama," she explains.

"Drama" allows for a kind of blurriness and liminality in teen practice that is not afforded by the terms "bullying," "relational aggression," or "gossip." Drama incorporates a spectrum of seriousness, which includes joking, "talking trash," and serious anger. The very fact that drama constitutes a wide variety of different practices—and the ambiguity of their meaning—is central to what makes drama a valuable concept for teens. By lumping these different interactions into the single category of drama, teens can discursively minimize the pain they feel from being left out or made fun of. Furthermore, by intentionally downplaying its significance, teens use drama to distance themselves both from entertaining situations and events that cause serious emotional pain. The slipperiness of drama lets teens frame the social dynamics and emotional impact of conflict as unimportant, letting them save face as an alternative to feeling like a victim—or a bully themselves.

THE GENDERED WORK OF DRAMA

Drama is *gendered*. Regardless of the actual participants in a dramatic situation, "drama" in the abstract is conceptualized, dismissively, as a "girl thing." Alicia said, "Drama? Just it's mostly between girls. Guys' drama is not really." Mark (15, Seattle) explained, "[Girls] always take it more seriously." Luke (15, Washington, DC) said, "Girls are just drama" (we heard this sentiment from several other boys). When asked why his peers would respond to mean questions on Formspring, Matthew, a 17-year-old from North Carolina, explains:

> The people who do it it's the attention [they] crave, for sure. It's the only way I can say it. The girls who do that are the girls who watch "Gilmore Girls" or "Gossip Girl" better yet. So it's like those girls who love a little drama in their life or something.

This is concurrent with Allen's finding that drama is considered a feminine practice (Allen, forthcoming).

Drama is often dismissed as unimportant because it is about traditionally feminine subjects like dating, gossip, and friendships, which scholars have argued tend to be viewed publicly as frivolous or insignificant (Jones 1980; Lorber 1994). Christopher (15, Iowa) concurs dismissively:

> Author: Does dating create much drama?
>
> Christopher: Amongst the girls it does but not the dudes.
>
> Author: In what kind of ways does it create drama for the girls?
>
> Christopher: Like, "Oh my gosh, this happened" and like they cry a lot.

Author: And the dudes are like eh?

Christopher: Yeah, whatever.

The implication of "drama" captured by Allen, that drama includes excessive emotion and reaction, serves to underplay the seriousness of girls' concerns. While young people characterize girls as the ones who *do* drama, boys are often the cause of drama, following the script of high school popularity, which pins a girl's popularity on her relationships and desirability (Brown 2005). Thus, the expression and perpetration of drama crystallizes conventional sex roles that police teen behavior along heteronormative gender lines.

The majority of teenagers we talked with saw participating in drama as un-masculine. Several girls told us that if two boys had an argument, they would physically fight or forget it within a few days, whereas drama between girls could drag on. In practice, we witnessed situations in which boys had long-term conflicts with each other; in some inner-city schools, we heard about "beefs" between boys, which could last years and be based on a real or perceived insult. Dylan (18, Nashville) and Amira unpack these differences in their discussion:

Dylan: Like, I've never gone [on Facebook] and been like oh what's this going on? What's this drama going on?

Amira: Well, you're a guy.

Dylan: I mean yeah, but that's like the difference, I guess, between the sexes. Like girls they constantly are on Facebook. I'll get on after school just to see what's going on with me but I don't go and be like going on about, oh who does Tara like? Or who does Abby like?

Despite these disavowals, Dylan then discussed a lengthy dramatic incident between two boys:

> Like this guy Matt, he … [and David] were arguing about who is a better football team. And Matt was "Vanderbilt sucks." And then David was like "No they don't. Tennessee has six national championships," or something like that, I don't know. And then Matt got off what it was supposed to be about and started attacking David's ex-girlfriend Taylor. Matt was like, "The reason that she left you was because you weren't good enough for her and that you were too ugly." Everybody found out … We looked up exactly the comments on the wall post and saw every single one of them.

This account exemplifies the ways in which boys engage in their own forms of social conflict and gossip. Given that boys and girls engage in relational aggression at fairly similar rates—but the practice is overwhelmingly female-gendered (Card et al. 2008)—the perception of drama as a "girl thing" may not match up to the reality of practice.

When we talked with boys about conflict, we more frequently heard them talk about "pranking" and "punking" where they used social media to play jokes on each other. Debby Phillips argues that "punking" is synonymous with bullying and is used to police masculine norms and maintain status hierarchies (2007). Like drama, we found that "punking" or "pranking" were often used by boys as liminal terms that encompassed both serious aggression and light-hearted jokes. Matthew, who actively dismisses the kinds of dramas that girls engage in, doesn't recognize that the pranks he and his friends play on one another have a similar valence.

> So my friend took my phone and my phone has Facebook on it. So he goes on there and he makes an incredibly realistic status, like, "Just got suspended for five days because I—" real mature, but he's like, "I have a boner and I was walking in class and I turned to the left and I knocked some kid's book off the table," or something like that, something that was really funny. But now I'd say literally five weeks later, I'm at work with my coworker, who I don't know at all, but she's like, "I saw on your Facebook that you got suspended. Is that true?" I was like, "Oh no! Not true at all."

Although this particular incident of being "punked" caused only a small amount of social embarrassment for Matthew, other pranks are more harmful. As with girls' drama, boys' acts of punking and pranking blur the line between what is hurtful and what is simply funny (see also Phillips 2007). Although the intention behind the prank is often what makes the difference, this can be difficult to determine.

High school is an environment in which appropriate gender policing is taken very seriously; the casual homophobia among teenage boys is a way to delineate clear markers between acceptable and unacceptable ways of enacting masculinity (Pascoe 2007). Drama is a way to encapsulate and define a host of behaviors—including gossiping, romance, and relational aggression—as things that boys do not engage in. Given that gender is a social construct (Kessler and McKenna 1978), the hyper-conformist gender environment of high school is brought into being through such types of classification. But despite these seemingly solid boundaries, it is clear that many boys do involve themselves in drama, at least as spectators and sometimes as participants. Labeling drama as "girl stuff" is a way for boys to distance themselves from behavior they see as feminine and simultaneously diminish the concerns of their female classmates as unimportant. Girls and boys have different rules regulating the language that they believe to be appropriate for navigating social conflicts, revealing how gendered norms are reproduced and solidified through arguments and quarrels. These strict gender norms explain why many models of youth aggression are gendered, including relational aggression and bullying. This suggests that addressing the underlying gender dynamics is a necessary component of combating youth conflict.

Conclusion

> Stan (18, Iowa): You'd actually be surprised how little things change. I'm guessing a lot of the drama is still the same, it's just the format is a little different. It's just changing the font and changing the background color really.

While teen conflict will never disappear, social media has changed how it operates. "Drama" is a messy process, full of contradictions and blurred boundaries, but it opens up spaces for teens. While the lack of definitional clarity around "bullying" or "cyberbullying" may be academically problematic, we found the lack of clarity of "drama" illuminating. As a concept, drama lets teens theorize and understand how their social dynamics have changed with the emergence of social media. The persistence and involvement of audiences in environments like Facebook engender a performative, participatory model of youth aggression. We present our definition and explanation of drama as an additional model of youth conflict that uses young people's own vocabulary to theorize the effects of the prevalence of social media on American teenage life.

Understanding how "drama" operates is necessary to recognize teens' own defenses against the realities of aggression, gossip, and bullying in social media. Drama allows teens to carve out agented identities for themselves even when embroiled in social conflict. They use a strict gender dichotomy to understand aggression, even when it does not map to the realities of practice. Social media increases the visibility of young people's conflict, heightening public awareness and prompting public anxieties about teen bullying. Yet, we are concerned that the focus on "bullying" may ignore the very real hurt caused by drama. To support youth as they navigate aggression and conflict in a networked society, adults must begin by understanding teenage realities from teenage perspectives.

Note

1. A "frenemy" is someone who appears to be a friend but with whom there is distrust and uncertainty about the relationship.

References

Allen, K. P. 2012. "Off the Radar and Ubiquitous: Text Messaging and Its Relationship to 'Drama' and Cyberbullying in an Affluent, Academically Rigorous US High School." *Journal of Youth Studies* 15 (1): 99–117. doi:10.1080/13676261.2011.630994.

Allen, K. P. forthcoming. "'We Don't Have Bullying, But We Have Drama.' Understandings of Bullying and Related Constructs within the Social Milieu of a US High School." *Journal of Human Behavior in the Social Environment.*

Altman, I., and D. A. Taylor. 1973. *Social Penetration: The Development of Interpersonal Relationships*. New York: Holt, Rinehart & Winston.

Ayim, M. 1994. "Knowledge through the Grapevine: Gossip as Inquiry." In *Good Gossip*, edited by R. F Goodman and A. Ben-Ze'ev, 85–99. Lawrence: University of Kansas Press.

Baym, N. K. 2009. "A Call for Grounding in the Face of Blurred Boundaries." *Journal of Computer-Mediated Communication* 14 (3): 720–23. doi:10.1111/j.1083-6101.2009.01461.x.

Ben-Ze'ev, A. 1994. "The Vindication of Gossip." In *Good Gossip*, edited by R. F Goodman and A. Ben-Ze'ev, 11–24. Lawrence: University of Kansas Press.

Björkqvist, K., K. M. J. Lagerspetz, and A. Kaukiainen. 1992. "Do Girls Manipulate and Boys Fight? Developmental Trends in Regard to Direct and Indirect Aggression." *Aggressive Behavior* 18 (2): 117–27. doi:10.1002/1098-2337(1992)18:2%3C117::AID-AB2480180205%3E3.0. CO;2-3.

boyd, d. 2014. *It's Complicated: The Social Lives of Networked Teens.* New Haven, CT: Yale University Press.

boyd, d. forthcoming. "Making Sense of Teen Life: Strategies for Capturing Ethnographic Data in a Networked Era." In *Digital Research Confidential: The Secrets of Studying Behavior Online*, edited by E. Hargittai, and C. Sandvig. Cambridge, MA: MIT Press.

boyd, d., and A. Marwick. 2011. "Social Privacy in Networked Publics: Teens' Attitudes, Practices, and Strategies." *The Oxford Internet Institute Decade in Internet Time Symposium*, Oxford, September 22. http://papers.ssrn.com/sol3/papers.cfm?abstract_id=1925128.

Brown, L. M. 2005. *Girlfighting: Betrayal and Rejection among Girls.* New York: New York University Press.

Burgess-Proctor, A., J. W. Patchin, and S. Hinduja. 2010. "Cyberbullying and Online Harassment: Reconceptualizing the Victimization of Adolescent Girls." In *Female Crime Victims: Reality Considered*, edited by V. Garcia and J. Clifford, 162–176. Upper Saddle River, NJ: Prentice Hall.

Card, N. A., B. D. Stucky, G. M. Sawalani, and T. D. Little. 2008. "Direct and Indirect Aggression During Childhood and Adolescence: A Meta-Analytic Review of Gender Differences, Inter-correlations, and Relations to Maladjustment." *Child Development* 79 (5): 1185–1229. doi:10.1111/j.1467-8624.2008.01184.x.

Corbin, J., and A. Strauss. 2007. *Basics of Qualitative Research: Techniques and Procedures for Developing Grounded Theory.* 3rd ed. Thousand Oaks, CA: Sage.

Crick, N. R., and J. K. Grotpeter. 1995. "Relational Aggression, Gender, and Social-Psychological Adjustment." *Child Development* 66 (3): 710–722. doi:10.2307/1131945.

Davies, B. 1998. "The Politics of Category Membership in Early Childhood Settings." In *Gender in Early Childhood*, edited by N. Yelland, 131–148. London: Routledge.

Dooley, J. J., J. Pyzalski, and D. Cross. 2009. "Cyberbullying versus Face-to-Face Bullying."

Zeitschrift Für Psychologie/Journal of Psychology 217 (4): 182–88. doi:10.1027/0044-3409.217.4.182.

Farrell, M. 1999. "Bullying: A Case for Early Intervention." *Australia and New Zealand Journal of Law and Education* 4 (1): 40–46.

Fine, G. A. 1997. "Gossip." *In Folklore: An Encyclopedia of Beliefs, Customs, Tales, Music, and Art*, edited by Thomas A. Green, 422–423. Santa Barbara, CA: ABC-CLIO.

Goffman, E. 1959. *The Presentation of Self in Everyday Life*. New York: Doubleday.

Hawkins, L. D., D. Pepler, and W. Craig. 2001. "Naturalistic Observations of Peer Interventions in Bullying." *Social Development* 10 (4): 512–527. doi:10.1111/1467-9507.00178.

Haythornthwaite, C. 2001. "Exploring Multiplexity: Social Network Structures in a Computer-Supported Distance Learning Class." *The Information Society* 17 (3): 211–226. doi:10.1080/01972240152493065.

Hinduja, S., and J. W. Patchin. 2008. "Cyberbullying: An Exploratory Analysis of Factors Related to Offending and Victimization." *Deviant Behavior* 29 (2): 129–156. doi:10.1080/01639620701457816.

Jones, D. 1980. "Gossip: Notes on Women's Oral Culture." *Women's Studies International Quarterly* 3 (2–3): 193–198. doi:10.1016/S0148-0685(80)92155-7.

Kessler, S. J., and W. McKenna. 1978. *Gender: An Ethnomethodological Approach*. Chicago: University of Chicago Press.

Kowalski, R. M., S. P. Limber, and P. W. Agatston. 2008. *Cyber Bullying: Bullying in the Digital Age*. Malden, MA: Blackwell.

Lenhart, A., M. Madden, A. Smith, K. Purcell, K. Zickuhr, and L. Rainie. 2011. *Teens, Kindness and Cruelty on Social Network Sites*. Washington, DC: Pew Internet & American Life Project. http://pewinternet.org/Reports/2011/Teens-and-social-media.aspx.

Livingstone, S., L. Haddon, A. Görzig, and K. Ólafsson. 2011. *Risks and Safety on the Internet: The Perspective of European Children: Full Findings*. London: London School of Economics, EU Kids Online. http://eprints.lse.ac.uk/33731/.

Lorber, J. 1994. *Paradoxes of Gender*. New Haven, CT: Yale University Press.

Markham, A. N. 2013. "The Dramaturgy of Digital Experience." In *The Drama of Social Life: A Dramaturgical Handbook*, edited by Charles Edgley, 279–294. Burlington, VT: Ashgate.

Nansel, T. R., M. Overpeck, R. S. Pilla, W. J. Ruan, B. Simons-Morton, and P. Scheidt. 2001. "Bullying Behaviors among US Youth." *JAMA: The Journal of the American Medical Association* 285 (16): 2094–2100. doi:10.1001/jama.285.16.2094.

Ness, C. 2010. *Why Girls Fight: Female Youth Violence in the Inner City*. New York: New York University Press.

Olweus, D. 1994. "Bullying at School: Basic Facts and Effects of a School Based Intervention Program." *Journal of Child Psychology and Psychiatry* 35 (7): 1171–1190. doi:10.1111/j.1469-7610.1994.tb01229.x.

Olweus, D. 2011. "What Is Bullying? Definition, Statistics & Information on Bullying." *Olweus Bullying Prevention Program*. http://www.olweus.org/public/bullying.pa0067e.

Papacharissi, Z. 2009. "The Virtual Geographies of Social Networks: A Comparative Analysis of Facebook, LinkedIn and ASmallWorld." *New Media & Society* 11 (1–2): 199–220. doi:10.1177/1461444808099577.

Pascoe, C. J. 2007. *Dude, You're a Fag: Masculinity and Sexuality in High School*. Berkeley: University of California Press.

Phillips, D. A. 2007. "Punking and Bullying." *Journal of Interpersonal Violence* 22 (2): 158–178. doi:10.1177/0886260506295341.

Salmivalli, C., K. Lagerspetz, K. Björkqvist, K. Österman, and A. Kaukiainen. 1996. "Bullying as a Group Process: Participant Roles and Their Relations to Social Status within the Group." *Aggressive Behavior* 22 (1): 1–15. doi:10.1002/(SICI)1098-2337(1996)22:1%3C1::AID-AB1%3E3.0.CO;2-T.

Spradley, J. P. 1979. *The Ethnographic Interview*. New York: Harcourt Brace Jovanovich.

Van House, N. A. 2011. "Feminist HCI Meets Facebook: Performativity and Social Networking Sites." *Interacting with Computers* 23 (5): 422–429. doi:10.1016/j.intcom.2011.03.003.

Veinot, T. C., T. R. Campbell, D. Kruger, A. Grodzinski, and S. Franzen. 2011. "Drama and Danger: The Opportunities and Challenges of Promoting Youth Sexual Health through Online Social Networks." In *Proceedings of the American Medical Informatics Association (AMIA) 2011 Annual Symposium*, 1436–45. Washington, DC. http://www.ncbi.nlm.nih.gov/pubmed/22195207.

Wang, J., R. J. Iannotti, and T. R. Nansel. 2009. "School Bullying among Adolescents in the United States: Physical, Verbal, Relational, and Cyber." *Journal of Adolescent Health* 45 (4): 368–375. doi:10.1016/j.jadohealth.2009.03.021.

Wengraf, T. 2001. *Qualitative Research Interviewing: Biographic Narrative and Semi-Structured Methods*. Thousand Oaks, CA: Sage.

Ybarra, M. L., and K. J. Mitchell. 2004. "Online Aggressor/Targets, Aggressors, and Targets: A Comparison of Associated Youth Characteristics." *Journal of Child Psychology and Psychiatry* 45 (7): 1308–1316. doi:10.1111/j.1469-7610.2004.00328.x.

RETHINKING SECTION 3

Discussion Questions

Chapter 16

1. Coontz suggests that referring to "traditional" family forms and values to solve the problems experienced by families today is problematic. How is "traditional" family defined? Is it problematic to define family in this way? Is there an alternative method to alleviate families of some of the stresses they incur?
2. Discuss some of the key shifts to the dynamics of "family" over time (from colonial families to the post-1950s family).
3. How is the concept of "family" related to the state, the market, and the mass media?

Chapter 17

1. Bezanson emphasizes neo-liberalism as a political theory. Why?
2. How is Jade's story illustrative of the effects of neo-liberalism on Canadian families?
3. How can future proposals to dismantle neo-liberalism include "real investments in people, their work lives and their care giving roles"?

Chapter 18

1. Given the aim of Stafford's analysis, do you think the political and literary questions she used to guide her overview and critiques were adequate? Were there any that you would add? Leave out?
2. Stafford suggests that when the audience of children's books are presumed to be homophobic and heterosexual, "those whose identifies fall outside of heterosexist norms are not positioned as a potential readership" and they are therefore "othered" because they are situated not as subjects but as objects to be studied. Do you agree with this analysis?
3. How might some of the contradictions Stafford posits be addressed in children's literature?

Chapter 19

1. According to Little, how did a traditional familial model influence early Canadian policy on mothers' allowance to be "racist and elitist"?
2. Little notes that under a neo-liberal regime, women are viewed as gender-neutral workers. What are some consequences to state supports at the individual level as a result of this shift?
3. When viewed through a gender-blind lens by the state, how is the transition from welfare to work made more challenging for women with caregiving responsibilities?

Chapter 20

1. Scholars have called Canada's temporary foreign workers "unfree participants in the national labour market." In what ways are foreign workers determined to be unfree?
2. What factors contribute to an assessment of Canada's agrifood jobs as being among the most precarious in the nation?
3. In what ways does the absence of permanent resident or citizenship status allow for employment standards to be ignored in agrifood labour practices?
4. While both seasonal agricultural migrant labourers and immigrant labourers were found to be at increased risk in agrifood jobs, how does permanent legal status in Canada reduce some of the risk for immigrants in ways unavailable to migrants?

Chapter 21

1. What are some of the ways in which smart girls balance "performing femininity" with being academically successful?
2. The authors challenge viewing the "Supergirl" exclusively through a post-feminist lens. Why?
3. What conclusions do the authors draw from the fact that self-proclaimed smart girls broadly discuss smart girls in general under the framework of Other?

Chapter 22

1. What is White privilege?
2. Discuss the connection between university space and White privilege.
3. Why might there be resistance to a compulsory course on multiculturalism? How would you react to such a course? Why?
4. How do experiences of Aboriginal faculty relate to relations of White privilege?

Chapter 23

1. Blakeborough uses the perspectives of both Jameson and Hutcheon whose "views at time are conflicting and oppositional." Comment on this methodology choice. Was it effective in illustrating how postmodern theory applies to *The Simpsons*?
2. In addition to representations of age, what other representations might surface from the episodes we are introduced to by Blakeborough?
3. How does Blakeborough answer the question: "But what about people who do not get irony or parody?" Is this answer to your satisfaction?
4. While *The Simpsons* might "encourage a critical evaluation of our world," what happens to those who do not engage in such an evaluation?

Chapter 24

1. Given the apparent sex-specific health conditions provided in the chapter, what consequences could arise from ignoring sex and gender when discussing health and medicine?
2. How is socio-economic status linked to gender and race? How does this affect health? Provide specific examples.
3. Discuss the debate between the varying definitions of "race" and "ethnicity." Is it problematic to have conflicting definitions between the social sciences and the field of medicine? If so, how?

Chapter 25

1. While Gender-Based Analysis has been implemented in federal health policy, the authors note that it is only along a gender binary. Why is this approach identified as excluding certain populations?
2. What conclusions are offered about the government's efforts to include LGBTQ populations in its policy considerations?
3. What are some examples of specific health needs of LGBTQ populations that are not explicitly addressed in current federal health policy?

Chapter 26

1. Dance is often considered a feminized space. In what ways does the assumed femininity of dance impose a requirement of hyper-masculinity on male dancers?
2. How do heteronormativity and Whiteness work together to affirm and naturalize privilege?
3. The author cited multiple examples of male dancers being critiqued over their perceived "authenticity." How is authenticity challenged by a White, heteronormative expectation of male dancers?

Chapter 27

1. Based on the ways teens identified and discussed "drama," what are some ways in which drama differs from bullying?
2. How do social media enhance the performative nature of drama?
3. Drama is often viewed as gendered. What arguments supporting and challenging this position were found by interviewing study participants?

SECTION 4

SOCIAL INEQUALITIES

The Readings

SECTION 4A: SOCIAL CLASS

28. Building Their Readiness for Economic "Freedom": The New Poor Law and Emancipation, *Anne O'Connell*
29. "Too Much of That Stuff Can't Be Good": Canadian Teens, Morality, and Fast Food Consumption, *Deborah McPhail, Gwen E. Chapman, and Brenda L. Beagan*
30. Class and Power: The Major Themes, *John Porter*

SECTION 4B: GENDER AND SEXUALITIES

31. Our Bodies Are Not Ourselves: Tranny Guys and the Racialized Class Politics of Incoherence, *Jean Bobby Noble*
32. Sexual Ethics and Young Women's Accounts of Heterosexual Casual Sex, *Melanie A. Beres and Panteá Farvid*
33. "Real Fast and Tough": The Construction of Canadian Hockey Masculinity, *Kristi A. Allain*

SECTION 4C: ETHNICITY AND RACE

34. "Canadian-First": Mixed Race Self-Identification and Canadian Belonging, *Jillian Paragg*
35. African-Centred Education: Situating the Tradition, *George Dei and Arlo Kempf*
36. "Born" Freaks, "Made" Freaks, and Media Circuses: Systemic Management of Race and Gender in the Reena Virk Case, *Nicole Pietsch*

Despite important gains in some areas, Canada remains an unequal society. In this section, individual and intersecting axes on inequality are explored. None of the forms of inequality discussed here stand alone. Rather, we find that women are more likely to be poor than are men; people of colour are more likely to be overrepresented in low-wage employment; and among the elderly, poverty is overwhelmingly female. The readings in this section represent a snapshot of important debates and evidence in sociological examinations of stratification.

Social Class

We begin with social class. Anne O'Connell's lucid historical account of the racialization of poverty in Canada is woven into her analysis of the poor laws and their most recent incarnation, welfare laws in Ontario. She presents a careful review of the ways in which the history of social welfare in Canada is bounded together with the creation of a White bourgeois society. She assesses current approaches to social welfare in Canada and finds that this historical backdrop continues to frame the racialization of poverty in Canada.

McPhail, Chapman, and Beagan consider social class from the vantage point of Canadian teens and fast food. Via interviews with Canadian teens in urban and rural settings, they challenge the commonly held idea that teens eat (or do not eat) fast food because it is available or because of their social class location. Their research and conversations with teens show a nuanced picture of how teens navigate food cultures, and complicate the view that rising levels of obesity are due to the clustering of fast-food restaurants in poor and working-class neighbourhoods.

John Porter's classic piece on social class and power in Canada underlines a belief that recurs in Canada today: Canada is a classless or, at best, a middle-class society. Porter's article challenges this myth and suggests that social class and power are intimately connected in Canada.

Gender and Sexualities

Gender and sexualities are dimensions of social inequality. Noble, Beres and Farvid, and Allain offer different approaches to gender inequality and sexualities. Noble draws on his own biography to explore transsexual issues as labour—the making of a "self"—and how that labour can be harnessed to disrupt the sex/gender system. He also explores the connections between trans men and feminist communities.

Beres and Farvid consider how young Canadian and New Zealand women experience heterosexual casual sex. Drawing on Foucault's work on ethics and sexuality, they explore through interviews how the gendered construction of women's sexuality affects how they understand, negotiate, and experience casual sex.

Kristi A. Allain shifts our attention to how masculinity is constructed in Canadian hockey. Through interviews and media analysis, as well as through the ways in which gender is performed and represented by players and the hockey association, Allain reveals how a distinctly *Canadian* hockey masculinity is constructed and maintained. Here, gender and masculinity are deeply entwined with physical aggression, but are increasingly challenged by non–North American players providing alternative visions of hockey masculinity.

Ethnicity and Race

Ethnicity and race are crucial dimensions of social stratification in Canada. Paragg considers how young adults of mixed race in Western Canada understand and experience their identities as "Canadian"; Dei and Kempf examine African-centred pedagogy, theory, education, and schooling in Canada; and Pietsch considers how race, space, and place are implicated in the murder of Reena Virk.

First, Paragg presents findings from interviews with young adults about self-identification and claiming "Canadian" as an identity. She finds that her study participants use the frame of "Canadian" in three ways: stating that they are "Canadian first"; suggesting that "Canadian" tends to mean "White"; and using the term "Canadian" strategically in interactions. This chapter troubles understandings of Whiteness, Canadian-ness, and multiculturalism.

Next, Dei and Kempf provide an historical, theoretical, and applied analysis of African-centred education in Canada. They begin by reviewing the literature relevant to African-centred schooling. They consider the theory, and the theory applied to practice—or praxis—of African-centred schooling and education, showcasing the visions and goals of Afrocentricity and African-centred education. They conclude by examining the challenges and issues that arise in applying theory to educational practice and pedagogy.

Finally, Pietsch examines the media construction of the murder of Reena Virk through a feminist post-structural lens. She pays particular attention to the construction of the category of "girlhood" and what happens to those who cannot claim membership in such a category.

SECTION 4A

SOCIAL CLASS

CHAPTER 28

Building Their Readiness for Economic "Freedom": The New Poor Law and Emancipation

Anne O'Connell

[...] In this paper, the author maps out the entwined relationship between poor relief, slavery, and racial thinking in our historiography of social welfare. By exploring these historical ties, the author shows how contemporary debates about the retraction of the welfare state and the "discovery" of the racialization of poverty are necessarily altered.

Poor Law Reform—The Great Transformation(s)

The history of social welfare in North America draws from the British literature on the poor laws and notions of the deserving and non-deserving poor. In addition, scholars have noted how welfare reform in Canada and the United States mirrors the type of policymaking and social disruption that ushered in the New Poor Law in Britain (1834). The retraction of social assistance and the increased surveillance of recipients are often traced to this time period. In Britain, "the principle of a legal, compulsory, secular national system of poor relief was established in a series of enactments that were consolidated in the celebrated statute known as the 43rd Elizabeth of 1601" (Englander, 1998, p. 2). Specified types of relief existed for various classes of the needy—"alms and almshouses for the aged and infirm, apprenticeship for children, work for the able-bodied and punishment for the work-shy" (Englander, 1998, p. 2). The three basic features that developed in the fifteen and a half thousand parishes in England

and Wales consisted of the workhouse, outdoor relief, and settlement regulations (Englander, 1998, p. 2). Outdoor relief was administered outside of the workhouse and embraced all those employed and unemployed whose income fell below a minimum subsistence level. Those who were unable or unwilling to work were sent to workhouses.

Population growth, deteriorating living conditions, new technologies, and the end of the Napoleonic wars in 1815 brought about an increase in need and insecurity among the laboring poor. By the 1820s, the cost of poor relief became a flashpoint for philosophers, scientists, and politicians who hammered away at a supposedly dependency-creating system that, in their accounts, turned laborers into paupers. Providing outdoor relief was thought to make laborers less disposed to subject themselves to the discipline of the emerging wage economy, which adversely affected the labor market and reduced productivity. Instead, the morally superior approach of voluntary charity was promoted (Lees, 1998; Poynter, 1969; Rose, 1971).

The Reform Act of 1834 resulted in the abolition of outdoor poor relief to the able-bodied and those who were constituted as dependents for almost the whole of the next century (Dean, 1991). If they were without work, the able-bodied and their dependants would be forced to enter the workhouse. The principle of less eligibility was applied, through which the condition of the pauper in the workhouse was kept well below that of the poorest independent laborer. The logic was if brutal conditions were maintained in the workhouse, only the truly destitute would enter. Karl Polanyi dubbed the Poor Law Reform *The Great Transformation*, a social policy intervention that gave rise to a national capitalist labor market (Dean, 1991, p. 172). Abolishing outdoor relief would force the pauper to accept any employment, it would reduce taxes, improve wages, increase productivity, reduce crime rates, and increase morality and frugality. The New Law included the famous Bastardy Clauses, in which unmarried mothers were forced to accept full responsibility for their children, relieving fathers from all liability. Clark (2000) describes how this official policy could not be put in practice due to local resistance and the complications of its implementation.

The Pauper and Slave Subject

If one looks at this time period with a lens attuned to race and the colonies, one sees how Britain was engaged in building the empire, in colonizing and enslaving peoples in distant lands, and in establishing itself as the leading slave-trading nation. [...]

Anti-colonial theorists and current studies on imperial histories direct us towards examining the ways in which the New Poor Law and the Total Abolition of Colonial Slavery deeply influenced one another. As local unrest in Britain and slave rebellions in the colonies grew, debates in parliament were focused on the conduct of the pauper and slave subject and their readiness for economic "freedom." Both populations could not simply inhabit this freedom. Each population had to be examined in order to set in place the various reforms and policies required for their improvement and amelioration. The supposed characteristics of the pauper and slave subjects were often contrasted in political battles over the elimination of poor relief, the slave trade, and emancipation. A proliferation of writings, studies, and parliamentary hearings were conducted for the forty years prior to the passing of both acts.

Social scientists, Christian evangelicals, political economists, liberal reformers, and parliamentarians attempted to document the daily lives of the pauper and slave population(s) and measure their ability to be improving economic subjects. Townsend's *A Dissertation on the Poor Laws* (1787) immediately made population a contested domain, tied to the economy. Applying the laws of determinism, he argued that the poor law system itself led to poverty and overpopulation. In the same year of Townsend's dissertation, Prime Minister William Pitt recommended to William Wilberforce that he lead a parliamentary campaign for the Abolition of the Slave Trade (1787). For twenty years the campaigns produced statistics from an endless series of government publications on population, migration, capital, labor, production, and trade, used by both abolitionists and the plantocracy. Both the abolitionists and the planters had an interminable series of expert witnesses who spoke before generations of official investigative committees, which resulted in a multi-volume series of Parliamentary Papers.

Wilberforce's first abolition bill (1792) was struck down in parliament and replaced by an amendment introduced by Henry Dundas (Pitt's Home Secretary) that would call for gradual abolition. Amelioration policies were introduced during the slave trade and emancipation debates in order to improve and civilize the slave. In this racist configuration, the African slave was debased and targeted as a separate race, compared to the improved creole slaves, who were "generally believed to be more submissive, more efficient, and less of a security threat to plantation enterprises" (Fergus, 2000, p. 176). [...] If abolitionists were keen to lament the horrors of the slave trade, support for Black emancipation and an independent Black modern state was another story. During the first bill, plans to import Chinese labor to Trinidad were drafted and later initiated. Extending the racial taxonomy further, the Chinese were described as a "free race of cultivators [...] distinct from the Negroes." Chinese laborers were expected to identify with White proprietors, acting as a "buffer population" that would protect the British colonies from further insurrection (Fergus, 2000, p. 189).

At the Second Reading of the Abolition Bill in the House of Commons (1806–1807), there emerged a new publication that had burst on the scene of social science–public policy: *An Essay on the Principle of Population, as It Affects the Future Improvement of Society* (1798). Thomas Robert Malthus' thesis blamed the poor laws for encouraging improvident marriages and the proliferation of children, which in turn led to lower living standards and high relief levels. Designed to target the political problem of the teeming poor in London, Malthus' population principle—that populations grow at a geometrical rate versus subsistence that only grows at an arithmetical rate—became a central technology in the battle about the future of the poor laws and the abolition of the slave trade.

Depicted as anti-social, degenerate, and insinuating themselves into the natural order of political economy, paupers were not considered as rational subjects or granted fully human status. Viewed as a separate and contaminated race, this representation drew on imagery from Africa or often turned to the Irish, whose history of colonization positioned them in the nineteenth century as non-White (Loomba, 1998). Malthus pointed to the Irish as an uncivilized group capable of contaminating the "general" population. The containment of this problem was concerned with maintaining White bourgeois power at home and throughout the Empire—a racial purity that was threatened by destitute White women breeding without restriction.

In relation to the slave trade, the planters utilized the population principle for their own purposes. The planters argued that if the population principle was natural and inevitable, then slavery itself did not determine the population dynamics of any country. In this view, the plantocracy—hoping amelioration would assuage political pressure—argued that the slave trade and the loss of African life was a normal illustration of Malthus' scientific principle (Drescher, 2002). Nonetheless, the *Slave Trade Bill of 1807* originated in the House of Lords and the king himself was credited for the achievement in celebration of the jubilee year of his reign. Although influenced by war, resistance, revolt, petitions, public clamor, and threatened boycotts, the bill heightened the belief that in England "a righteous question needs only to be fully revealed and understood to be carried" (Davis, 1975, p. 446). As the drive for emancipation moved along and poor relief concerns grew, various studies and the writings of political economists remained central. Each population was considered for their levels of dependency, degeneracy, and their willingness to labor and participate in a free labor market. Were the pauper and slave subject ready for economic "freedom?" What was required in order to assist these subjects into economic freedom?

Political economists who advanced notions of free labor were faced with numerous contradictions at home and in the colonies. As the category of free and enslaved labor began to impinge on one another as political problems, the demand for clearer distinctions escalated. Adam Smith weighed in on the debate, casting his well-worn phrase that a *free laborer doubled the output of a slave*. Although sceptical of his pronouncement, political economists capitalized on his distinction between free and unfree labor to attack poor relief, even though Smith never spoke against the poor laws (Drescher, 2002). For Burke and Townsend, slavery was an impediment to the free market and an artificial restriction on enterprise, just like the poor laws. Townsend argued that slavery and poor relief were a threat to the natural motive to labor. In this way, slavery entered the poor law debate as a discursive strategy to help split the respectable laborer from the less desirable pauper. Poor law officials and administrators mobilized the apparent characteristics of the slave to help explain the behaviour of relief recipients. Reformers argued that poor relief took away responsibility and fostered a *slave mentality* in which support from the state was seen as a right (Clark, 2000). Nassau Senior, author of the Poor Law Report, concluded that the poor laws entitled men to "all a slave's security for subsistence without his liabilities to punishment" (Kern, 1998, p. 428).

[...] The same capitalist class in Britain was using the labor of children in the Lancashire mills to produce the textiles exported to Africa for the purchase of slaves. When destitute parents were "admitted to the parish workhouses, their children were taken from them and compulsorily bound apprentice to the cotton manufacturers" (Fryer, 1988, p. 15). These overlapping debates were further complicated by the demands injected by the Black resistance movement.

The Black Poor and Black Resistance Movement

Slaves, ex-slaves, and Black loyalists living in London, Bristol, Liverpool, and Glasgow (about 17,000 in the 1790s) brought practical links between the poor laws and emancipation to the fore (Killingray, 2003). African sailor Olaudah Equiano helped create an abolitionist movement in London by enlisting people like Granville Sharp to study law and represent those in London attempting to resist re-enslavement. The Black resistance movement forced Britain to face the system of racial slavery it had attempted to confine to the slave colonies. Fugitive slaves, such as Jonathan Strong, John and Mary Hylas, and Thomas Lewis, launched a number of legal cases, including the famous Somerset Case, a case where Granville Sharp successfully argued that it was illegal for masters to compel their slaves to leave the country. This decision helped reposition slavery as an alien innovation from the colonies, which contrasted with and reaffirmed the long established law, custom, and constitution of England (Lorimer, 1992). This was beneficial to theorists conceptualizing and promoting notions of free labor and private property at the time.

These domestic cases were crucial for identifying the cause of anti-slavery with notions central to political economists: liberty, free labor, and private property, all part of England's prized social order. In this way, Black resistance continued to threaten Empire, yet it also became folded into upholding British standards for White liberal reformers and philanthropists. Political economists objected to the personal proprietorship, which gave the master control over the body of a slave, thereby producing dependence. This deprived the slave of the freedom of selling his labor and removed his self-interest in a reasonably free market (Davis, 1975). However, this concern did not translate the notion of selling one's labor into the right to wages in England. Entering into a contract with a slave, at this time, implied the slave was a free person and thereby was an act of manumission. As Lorimer argues, the courts never came to a clear decision on this issue, which plagued the slave-servants' fight for payment of wages and eligibility for poor relief (1992, pp. 68–69).

Since the poor law left paupers to rely on the support of their parish of origin, destitute Blacks were denied relief. For the few that managed to fulfill residency requirements, the slave's wage-less state could not prove a hiring had occurred, thereby again rendering them ineligible for relief (Lorimer, 1992). Instead, the concerns for this population came under the scrutiny of abolitionists, Christian reformers, and philanthropists who ran private charities and started a movement to send London's destitute Blacks back to Africa. Depending on the literature, the Sierra Leone project was either an example of pan-Africanism led by Olaudah Equiano, a project run by White philanthropists committed to ridding London of this degenerate population, or a paternalistic and racist experiment in cheap Black labor that might be a handy substitute for slavery (Drescher, 2002; Linebaugh & Rediker, 2000; Lorimer, 1992).

Abolitionists capitalized on this opportunity to prove that Blacks could become free laborers and reach a level of natural reproduction. Awash in debates about dependency that borrowed heavily from the poor law discourse, the pro-slavery opinion was eager to portray ex-slaves as incapable of self-reliance. London's destitute Blacks, whose loyalist attachment and military service to Great Britain were quickly forgotten, became tied into West African colonization. Distressed that so few were willing to go in 1787, one philanthropist requested that all forms of charity to Black paupers be stopped. In typical imperial-economist prose, he argued that charity would blind them to their own self-interest.

The Poor Whites and White Supremacy

While the *Black Poor* became central to colonization experiments in West Africa, in the slave colonies it was the poor Whites that were a growing problem. Viewed as a social problem in terms of class, gender, and sexuality, poor Whites threatened to destabilize the legitimacy of White supremacy—in the colonies and the metropole. While White elites had little sympathy for lower-class Whites, poor relief measures were instituted when anti-slavery activities increased and White colonial society was beginning to fracture. The main criterion for poor relief eligibility was not poverty per se, but the possession of *White skin*. Poor relief delineated the social and sexual boundaries between free Whites and unfree Blacks. Impoverished White women represented the largest group of poor relief claimants in Barbados and Jamaica. Poor relief programs were a way to regulate the conduct and sexuality of poor White women in an attempt to secure White solidarity, White supremacy, and the legitimacy of the slavocracy. Any suspicions of sexual and conjugal unions with Black men meant that poor White women were immediately disqualified from assistance (Jones, 1998). Black men faced dismemberment, castration, and execution for having sexual relations with White women, in order to limit the size of the free non-White group in colonized society while sustaining an enslaved labor force (Beckles, 1999). While wealthier White women were slaveholders, destitute White women became a symbol of the breakdown of White patriarchal family structures "critical to the formation and maintenance of a newly emerging White identity" (Jones, 1998, p. 26).

The practice of poor relief was connected to the extension of White supremacy, a policy used to facilitate clearer class, gender, and race boundaries through notions of the deserving and non-deserving poor. Responsibility for the welfare of old, sick, and infirm Blacks rested with planters. When it came to the presence of impoverished Blacks in the colonies, Beckles describes how the poor laws were used to deny their freedom. In order to prevent the freeing of slaves, an annuity was added to the manumission fee. Poor law officials insisted on this "as one way to prevent slave owners from freeing old and infirmed persons who could not reasonably be expected to earn their subsistence" (Beckles, 1999, p. 33). By the mid-1820s, increased efforts to alleviate poverty, strengthen ties with White paupers, and to police more strenuously the interactions between Whites and people of color were necessary to the unification of Whites and [the] preservation of racial segregation (Newton, 2003). Authorities refused to extend poor relief to non-Whites, a policy that remained in effect until well after emancipation. Further connections between poverty and racial supremacy occurred post-emancipation.

While the New Poor Law saw a more central role for the workhouse system in Britain, in the colonies, it took on an even larger role. Once the emancipation act was passed, workhouses sprung up in efforts by the plantocracy to sustain output levels and create a docile and obedient workforce. While paupers (racially coded as non-White) at home were a danger to domestic security, poor Whites in the colonies struck at the legitimacy of a regime of racial subjugation.

The bill for the *Total Abolition of Colonial Slavery throughout the British Dominions* was passed, taking effect on August 1, 1834. The bill enacted an eight-year apprenticeship system for former slaves, higher sugar duties, and a grant of twenty million pounds to appease the planters. Poor conditions remained in the colonies and apprentices were still liable to corporal punishment. Advocates continued to push until the apprenticeship program was cut short by two years before the fixed date. The twenty million pounds represented 40% of the government's annual average income at the time, and it was three times England's annual expenditure on the poor laws. Working-class radicals like William Cobbett were outraged that poor Britons would be paying for the freedom of "comfortable" West Indian slaves (Himmelfarb, 1983). While many viewed apprenticed labor as slavery under another name, the colonial secretary argued that it had merely been borrowed from the kind of contract labor and the metropolitan apprentices that existed in England (Drescher, 2002, p. 138).

The *Poor Law Reform* of 1834 led to the abolition of outdoor relief to the able-bodied, the confinement of violators in the workhouse, and the creation of a centralized administration. While Bentham's plan to build workhouses was rejected, his idea did receive support from abolitionists such as Wilberforce. Hundreds of Houses of Industry, based on the panopticon principles of central surveillance and regimentation, could resolve the domestic labor problem. Connections between slavery and the poor laws did not end in 1834. In fact, the relevance of the poor law system in the slave colonies only increased as a way to secure the labor market. Britain's 540,559 Black slaves in the Caribbean did not become "free" overnight as apprenticeship, along with the systematic export of Indian labor to the Caribbean, was used by planters to save the sugar economy and contribute to Britain's overseas wealth (Fryer, 1988; Bolaria & Li, 1988). A system of Trespass and Vagrancy Acts became key to the transformation to free labor. In this case, these policies remain strategies for prolonging slave labor and White patriarchal capitalism through the increased surveillance and criminalization of those in and outside of the labor market.

White Settler Societies and the Racialization of Poverty

Social policy theorists and social historians have embraced Britain's historical narrative—and its absences—as a framework from which relief policies in North America can be understood. We reproduce the argument about the deserving and non-deserving poor and the separation of the respectable laborer from the degenerate pauper. A rich scholarly literature debates whether the New Poor Law of 1834 was an epochal shift in which the old class compact of poor relief was broken, ushering in an unregulated market (Fox-Piven & Cloward, 1998; Kern, 1998; Wood, 1998). In addition, this analysis is extended by theories that debate the degrees to which pauper emigration to Upper Canada was central to relieving Britain of its superabundant poor. In this way, we replicate a class-based history that severs poor relief policies from Britain's colonial practices and our own racial colonial project of establishing a White settler society.

Poor relief and pauper emigration gathered its political coherence alongside ideas and studies about racial hierarchies that were not simply imposed upon the colonies. Upper Canadians participated in the debates about the poor laws, slavery, and Aboriginal populations at home and in Britain. They were particularly influential as experts and witnesses in Parliamentary Reports concerned with reforming and saving Aboriginal peoples. Upper Canadians were instrumental in how notions of Britishness would be constructed back home. As Stoler (1997) reminds us, Victorian settlers had well-inscribed notions of class that were constructed on a racial nomenclature whose primary reference was the colonial encounter. In this view, class formation and bourgeois sensibilities were organized by ideas about race, racial superiority, and Britain's relationship to its colonies.

DEBATES OVER THE PAST AND ITS INTERPRETATION ARE NEVER LIMITED TO HISTORY

Historical arguments are resurrected in order to explain current phenomena. The history of social welfare we ascribe to is used to situate policy shifts today, including the retraction of the welfare state and the emergence of the racialization of poverty. For example, in Ontario, since 1995, the 21.6% cut to welfare benefits, administrative regulations that have disqualified thousands, the reintroduction of workfare programs, and the Spouse in the House rule are policies that harken back to the New Poor Law. Just as the Poor Law Reform was key to industrialization, welfare reforms today are considered instrumental to the entrenchment of a corporate transnational global economy. In the United States, for example, Kern has argued that Clinton's welfare bill was an integral part of what he calls the *Great Capitalist Restoration Project* (Kern, 1998). To retrieve this history to make sense of globalization blinds us to the relationship between racial thinking and poverty in our past and present social policies. This discussion views the New Poor Law outside of its colonial counterpart and ensures that globalization is similarly disconnected from its colonial roots. Contemporary studies that stress the racialization of poverty do not capture or productively theorize the colonial and racial underpinning of social welfare.

While connections between race and poverty have been debated in various ways in the United States, in the last few years researchers have tracked the rise of poverty among racialized groups in Toronto, Ontario, and Canada more generally (Galabuzi, 2006; Halli, 1998; Ornstein, 2000, 2006). The racialization of poverty is a new term that scholars and policy analysts have introduced to reveal the material deprivations of people of color and how widespread everyday racism contributes to economic, social, legal, and political exclusion. While studies that stress the quantitative matter of population breakdown are important, they tend to present race and racism as new or newly problematic. Unlike the United States, where race has been featured in social welfare debates, it still positions class against race. This is evident in the White working class backlash against affirmative action programs.

In Canada, a race-absent narrative deeply penetrates our national story. An increase in the number of racialized poor becomes tied to the increase of immigrants of color to Canada since World War II. This approach reproduces the idea that race is solely about non-White residents who are always considered recent members of the nation-state. The history of European immigration remains race-less and often disconnected from the forms of genocide and land theft policies experienced by Aboriginal populations—all crucial to the making of a White settler society. As Razack (2002) argues, "European settlers thus *become* the original inhabitants and the group most entitled to the fruits of citizenship" (p. 2).

If we look closely, however, these historical dynamics can be revealed when contemporary studies on poverty attend to people's experience of racism and views on race. In a recent study of low-income families in Ontario, low-income White women who felt attacked by social assistance workers never invoked race as one of the instruments of their exclusion (Neysmith, Bezanson & O'Connell, 2005). Either the invisibility of Whiteness or the partial membership into White bourgeois society ensures that these women (and others) aggressively reject racism as an important variable in understanding poverty. Racial thinking continues to be structured by and through views about poverty and social welfare. Indeed, poverty in White communities is often upheld as evidence of the lack of racism in society. For women of color the experience of welfare surveillance was inseparable from the racist construction and denigration of their communities.

In *Telling Tales* (Neysmith, Bezanson & O'Connell, 2005), it was clear how White Euro-Canadians were naturalized as citizens, while participants of color, in spite of their country of birth or generations here, pointed to their always-questioned status as Canadians. When responding to demographic questions in our study the term "purebred 100% Canadian" was invoked by a number of participants to signify Canadian-born, White, and English-speaking. Terms such as purity, breeding, and the notion that identity can be quantified echo earlier Victorian practices that attempted to define and measure populations at home and in the colonies, highlighted so starkly by the eugenics movement (McLaren, 1978). Current manifestations of making identity something knowable and measurable can be found in the new resident card and the variety of biometric schemes that attempt to capture exact eye color in place of previous preoccupations with skull size (Stepan, 1982).

Discussions about identity intensified when discussions turned to the allocation of state resources. One family that identified itself as purebred Canadian was distressed about being overrun by immigrants of color who are offered the best jobs and education opportunities, and are able to drain our welfare system. Ironically, the family's declaration that "White people are under attack" finally acknowledges its racial status of Whiteness. A woman in the study who described herself as African Canadian put a different spin on this. She remarked on the double humiliation of participating in mandatory training programs for those on social assistance, attended by many new immigrants. Not only did it elide her fifth-generation presence as a Canadian citizen, but the new immigrants viewed her presence in the program as her failure to capitalize on the advantage of being English-speaking and Canadian-born.

In another situation, an Aboriginal man noted how Native peoples in northern Ontario were pitted against the Francophone community when attempting to access federal funding. His analysis was also formed in relation to what he perceived as the unwarranted claims of the Métis peoples, since in his mind you were either Native or not. Many of these characterizations are rooted in Britain's colonial history, the building of a White settler society, and in contemporary policies that attempt to celebrate multiculturalism. The weight of historical and colonial practices is ever-present yet at the same time absent in contemporary studies that stress the racialization of poverty.

Conclusion

In order to understand the retraction of the welfare state we must attend to the colonial and racial antecedents of social welfare. These show us how racial categories are politically active, constructed, and calculated over time in relation to studies and policies about poverty. By viewing systems of oppression and notions of race and class as separate structures, disciplining the poor appears unrelated to racial subjugation, racial slavery, and White supremacy. The extensive and connected terrains through which empire circulates, and how it works to define and secure White bourgeois power in metropolitan and colonial sites need to be scrutinized. Histories of social welfare that focus primarily on class formation or studies that view class and race as separate phenomena really miss how mutually constitutive these relations continue to be. Meanwhile, the contemporary application of the racialization of poverty adds to the elision of the racial history of social welfare. While the numbers of people living in poverty require urgent attention we must also interrogate how the making of racial subjects, including White bourgeois subjects enlisted into colonial and settler projects, are part of our historical and contemporary analysis of poverty.

References

Beckles, H.M. (1999). *Centering woman: Gender discourses in Caribbean slave society*. Kingston: Ian Randle.

Bolaria, S.B. & Li, P. (1988). *Racial oppression in Canada*. Toronto: Garamond.

Clark, A. (2000). The new poor law and the breadwinner wage: Contrasting assumptions. *Journal of Social History, 34*(2), 261–281.

Davis, D.B. (1975). *The problem of slavery in the age of revolution, 1770–1823*. New York: Cornell University Press.

Dean, M. (1991). *The constitution of poverty: Toward a genealogy of liberal governance*. London: Routledge.

Drescher, S. (2002). *The mighty experiment: Free labor versus slavery in British emancipation*. New York: Oxford University Press.

Englander, D. (1998). *Poverty and poor law reform in Britain: From Chadwick to Booth,*

1834–1914. New York: Addison Wesley Longman.

Fergus, C. (2000). War, revolution, and abolitionism 1793–1806. In H. Cateau & S.H.H. Carrington (Eds.), *Capitalism and slavery after fifty years* (pp. 173–196). New York: Peter Lang.

Fox Piven, F. & Cloward, R.A. (1998). Eras of power. *Monthly Review, 49*(8), 11–23.

Fryer, S. (1988). *Black people in the British Empire: An introduction*. London: Pluto Press.

Galabuzi, E.-G. (2006). *Canada's economic apartheid: The social exclusion of racialized groups in the new century*. Toronto: Canadian Scholars' Press.

Halli, S. (1998). The plight of immigrants: The spatial concentration of poverty in Canada. *Canadian Journal of Regional Science, 20*, 1.

Himmelfarb, G. (1983). *The idea of poverty: England in the early industrial age*. New York: Random.

James, C.L.R. (1938). *The Black Jacobins: Toussaint L'Ouverture and the San Domingo Revolution*. New York: Vintage.

Jones, C. (1998). Mapping racial boundaries: Gender, race, and poor relief in Barbadian plantation society. *Journal of Women's History, 10*(3), 9–31.

Kern, W.S. (1998). Current welfare reform: A return to the principles of 1834. *Journal of Economic Issues, 32*(2), 427–432.

Killingray, D. (2003). Tracing people of African origin and descent in Victorian Kent. In G.H. Gerzina (Ed.), *Black Victorians/Black Victoriana* (pp. 51–70). Piscataway: Rutgers University Press.

Lees, L.H. (1998). *The solidarities of strangers: The English poor laws and the people, 1700–1948*. Cambridge: Cambridge University Press.

Linebaugh, P. & Rediker, M. (2000). *The many-headed hydra: Sailors, slaves, commoners, and the hidden history of the revolutionary Atlantic*. Boston: Beacon Press.

Loomba, A. (1998). *Colonialism/Postcolonialism*. London: Routledge.

Lorimer, D.A. (1992). Black resistance to slavery and racism. In J.S. Gundara & I. Duffield (Eds.), *Essays on the history of Blacks in Britain* (pp. 58–80). Aldershot: Ashgate.

McLaren, A. (1978). *Our own master race: Eugenics in Canada, 1885–1945*. Toronto: McClelland & Stewart.

Newton, M.J. (2003). *The King v. Robert James, a slave, for rape: Inequality, gender, and British slave amelioration, 1823–1834*. Toronto: Unpublished manuscript.

Neysmith, S., Bezanson, K. & O'Connell, A. (2005). *Telling tales: Living the effects of public policy*. Halifax: Fernwood Press.

Ornstein, M. (2000). *Ethno-racial inequality in the city of Toronto: An analysis of the 1996 census*. Toronto: City of Toronto, Access and Equity Unit, Strategic and Corporate Policy Division, Chief Administrator's Office.

Ornstein, M. (2006). *Ethno-racial groups in Toronto, 1971–2001: A demographic and social profile*. Toronto: Institute for Social Research.

Poynter, J.R. (1969). *Society and pauperism: English ideas on poor relief 1795–1834*. Toronto: University of Toronto Press.

Razack, S. (2002). When place becomes race. In S. Razack (Ed.), *Race, space, and the law: Unmapping a White settler society* (pp. 1–20). Toronto: Between the Lines.

Rose, M. (1971). *The English Poor Laws 1780–1930*. New York: Barnes and Noble.

Stepan, N. (1982). *The idea of race in science: Great Britain in 1800–1960*. London: The McMillan.

Stoler, L.A. (1997). Carnal knowledge and imperial power: Gender, race, and morality in colonial Asia. In R.N. Lancaster & M.D. Leonardo (Eds.), *The gender/sexuality reader* (pp. 1–36). New York: Routledge.

Williams, E.F. (1944). *Capitalism and slavery*. Chapel Hill: University of North Carolina Press.

Wood, E.M. (1998). Class compacts, the welfare state, and epochal shifts (a reply to Francis Fox Piven and Richard A. Cloward). *Monthly Review, 49*(8), 24–43.

CHAPTER 29

"Too Much of That Stuff Can't Be Good": Canadian Teens, Morality, and Fast Food Consumption

Deborah McPhail, Gwen E. Chapman, and Brenda L. Beagan

Introduction

The idea that an increase in obesity rates is due to "obesogenic environments" has gained credence not only with the Canadian popular press, but within public health policy and obesity science nationally and internationally (Beaulac, Kristjansson, & Cummins, 2009; Black, Macinko, Dixon, & Fryer, 2010; Black & Macinko, 2010; Cummins, McKay, & MacIntyre, 2005; Health Canada, 2006; Jago, Baranowski, Baranowski, Cullen, & Thompson, 2007; Larson, Story, & Nelson, 2009; Moore & Roux, 2006; Powell, Auld, Chaloupka, O'Malley, & Johnston, 2007a; Powell, Caloupka, & Bao, 2007b; World Health Organization, 2000). The relationship between rates of obesity and obesogenic environments—spaces in which a confluence of beliefs, behaviors, and the simultaneous over-availability of processed "junk" foods and unavailability of fresh healthy foods lead to the spread of obesity—is debated (Beaulac et al., 2009; Smith & Cummins, 2008). Yet more popular sources and public health discourses make simple correlations between environment and obesity. Most often, these sources focus on the prevalence of "food deserts" in low-income areas where fewer supermarkets offer fresh produce and other healthy foods and where there is a high concentration of fast food restaurants, leading to skyrocketing obesity rates (Beck, October 14, 2009; Crush, November 20, 2009; Papemy, February 16, 2010). This argument has taken on particular salience with respect to childhood and adolescent obesity, as not only are teenagers perceived as liking and therefore consuming more convenience and fast foods than adults (Bugge, 2011), but these foods are often marketed to teenagers (Bugge & Lavik, 2010; Goren, Harries, Schwartz, & Brownell, 2010; Powell, Szczypka, & Chaloupka, 2010).

In this paper, we draw on data from our qualitative study of food consumption practices in five urban centers and four rural areas in Canada to further explore the relationship between fast food restaurants and teenagers' eating and, by extension, teens' interactions with the obesogenic environment. Our interview data problematizes discussions of teen fast food consumption by demonstrating the complex and contradictory meanings our teenaged participants associated with fast foods and the multiple discourses they drew on in resisting and/

or choosing to eat fast food. Using Lamont's (1992, 2000) concept of "moral boundary work," this paper explores how the Canadian teenagers in our study constructed themselves as "bad" or "good" through articulating perceptions of fast food and those who consume it.

Fast food, Obesity, and Morality

Previous scholarship in Western contexts has demonstrated perceived links between food consumption and morality, between "judgments about 'good' and 'bad' [eating] behaviors" and "judgments about 'good' and 'bad' individuals," which are generally based in assumptions and presumptions about healthy eating (Backett, 1992, p. 261; see also Bourdieu, 1984; Johnston & Baumann, 2010; Lupton, 1996). In an era in which obesity is of great public health concern, obesity and the eating practices thought to lead to it are particularly harshly judged as unhealthy and, therefore, "bad"; people considered to be obese are imagined to be "bad" citizens who have made "bad" food choices, becoming a drain to healthcare systems and government dollars (Burrows, 2009; Colls & Evans, 2008; Gard & Wright, 2005; Gilman, 2010; Herndon, 2005, 2010; Rail, 2009). As Murray (2009) argues, "[there is a] tacit assumption that 'obese' subjects are 'immoral subjects.' In a secular Western world, bodily maintenance has become the most visible signifier of morality and one's adherence to the dictates of an ethical lifestyle" (pp. 80–1).

At the same time that obesity is regarded as bad or amoral because it is the perceived culmination of unhealthy eating, critical obesity scholars have argued that health moralities regarding obesity rest on the simplification of statistics and overstatements about the health risks of body fat (Campos, 2004; Ernsberger, 2009; Gard & Wright, 2005). They maintain that obesity is a discursively constructed category—and not simply a bio-medical condition—that interacts with and re-enforces norms concerning gender, race, class, sexuality and space, helping to maintain inequitable power relations and social structures (Evans & Colls, 2009; Gard, 2011; Gard & Wright, 2005; LeBesco, 2004; Monaghan, 2008). In this view, obesity science, anti-obesity policy and programming, and discourses about "healthy eating" and morality disproportionately regulate the bodies of working-class, poor, and racialized populations, positioning them as "bad people" (Burrows, 2009; Everett, 2009; Fee, 2006; Herndon, 2005; Poudrier, 2007). As Rich and Evans (2009, p. 162) suggest, "the idea that health problems are essentially the fault of certain individuals (especially the poor, working class and ethnic minorities)" is endemic in obesity discourse.

Discriminatory health moralities tied to obesity are particularly evident in conversations about fast food consumption (Everett, 2009; Johnston & Baumann, 2010). Discourses of healthy eating and fast food paint a picture in which primarily working-class, poor, and racialized people live in obesogenic environments where low-cost fast food outlets are concentrated (Ernsberger, 2009). As a result, poor and racialized people are defined almost ubiquitously as fast food eaters, "obese," and, therefore, inherently and essentially "Other" (Said, 1979) to or less than the normative white, middle-class (slender) subject. Critical obesity scholars do not suggest that fast food is "healthy" for the body, but they do maintain that ideas about who primarily consumes fast food are socially destructive (c.f. Campos, 2004).

Teens, Fast Food, Obesity, and Morality

About a third of Canadian teenagers consume fast food (Garriguet, 2004). The consumption of fast food by Canadian teens has purportedly increased over recent decades (Riediger, Shooshtari, & Moghadasian, 2007). Canadian statistics mimic those for adolescents in other Western countries, such as the UK, Norway, and the US (Bugge, 2011; Powell et al., 2010; Schneider, 2000). Even as teenagers seem to be eating more fast food more often, qualitative research has shown that they take up moralistic discourses about healthy eating in general discussions of food habits (Colls & Evans, 2008; Rail, 2009; Wright, O'Flynn, & Macdonald, 2006), and judge fast food consumption particularly harshly. In a qualitative study of UK teens carried out by Wills, Backett-Milburn, Lawton, and Roberts (2009), moral judgments about fast food were steeped in the classism noted above. Middle-class teens avoided fast food not only to be healthy but also to formulate themselves as "good" middle-class citizens who took up the "'authentic' health and dietary messages sanctioned by experts" in contrast to "those who more frequently eat in fast food restaurants (i.e., the working classes)" (pp. 65, 66). In Norway, a recent study of teenagers' food consumption found "no one was more negative about fast food than the upper-middle/upper class" (Bugge, 2011, p. 82). Importantly, this class identity was mitigated by a type of nationalism, as it was specifically "American" fast food chains teens most vehemently opposed (Bugge, 2011). In both studies, then, teenagers used moralistic binaries about healthy eating and fast food consumption to reinforce, convey, or create class identities. These findings are an important antidote to simplified notions of teen interaction with fast food, which suggest that teens eat fast food mindlessly without concern for health (Koehly & Loscalzo, 2009; Taylor, Evers, & McKenna, 2005; Weeks, 2009).

Building on the UK (Wills et al., 2009) and Norwegian (Bugge, 2011) studies, and drawing from the insight that fast food consumption is now regarded as an amoral act, in this paper we examine how teens employ health morals through fast food. We analyze teens' accounts of healthy eating and fast food using Lamont's (1992, 2000) concept of "moral boundary work" whereby subjects distinguish from or align with particular social groups, "[defining] their identity in opposition to that of others by drawing symbolic boundaries" (1992, p. 233). Whereas Wills et al. (2009) focused on morality in fast food consumption among middle-class teens, we follow Lamont's approach to explore how class identities are also forged through moral boundary marking among middle-class and lower/working-class teens. Lamont argues that class location shapes what can be legitimately drawn upon to construct oneself as a "good" person. Based on Lamont, we examine how class influenced our teen participants' moral judgments about fast food environments and consumption, and how their moral boundary marking concerning fast food related (or not) to class location or identity.

Method

This paper is based on analysis of interviews carried out between 2007 and 2009 with 132 teenagers (77 girls and 55 boys, ages 13–19 years) from five urban areas and four rural areas across Canada. The interviews were carried out as part of the Family Food Practices study, a cross-national project exploring how food consumption, production, and preparation practices of Canadian families are shaped by social and geographic location. All methods were approved by five university ethics boards. The research sites included two neighborhoods in Toronto, and one in each of Vancouver and Edmonton, three of Canada's largest cities. The smaller cities of Halifax, Nova Scotia, and Kingston, Ontario, were included, along with four rural areas comprised of farming communities, small towns, and villages: Kent County, British Columbia; Athabasca County, Alberta; Prince Edward County, Ontario; King's County, Nova Scotia.

In each site approximately ten families were recruited through advertisements in local papers, posters placed in public places such as grocery stores and cafés, and word-of-mouth. Research assistants interviewed at least one adult and one teen from each family, using semi-structured interview guides. No questions included in the interview guide were specifically about fast food, and often the topic was raised by participants when answering the second question in the interview guide: "Can you describe a typical day's eating for you?" Teen participants might also discuss fast food when asked by the interviewer whether lunch was brought to school or bought at a cafeteria or other restaurant. Other questions that elicited responses about fast food were: "When you think about your food habits overall, what do you like about how you eat?"; "To what extent do you think people in this area tend to eat in particular ways? How does the way you eat compare to others you know? Family, friends, people from other places?"; and "What does the term 'healthy eating' mean to you? How 'healthy' do you think your eating habits are? Is this an issue for you?" Each participant was interviewed twice for approximately one hour. Interviews were digitally recorded, transcribed, and coded using Atlas.ti. Teen participants were offered an honorarium of $20.00. [...]

We engaged in purposeful sampling to attract families from a variety of social classes. We developed class categories based on a combination of Lamont's (1992) approach and the Gilbert-Kahl model of class distinction (Gilbert, 2008). We therefore devised the following class categorizations based primarily on occupation and education: Upper-class, who live off the earnings from their own capital, and are generally the top 3–5% of a population in terms of income (Gilbert, 2008); upper-middle-class, who include university-educated managers and professionals, such as doctors, lawyers, professors, registered nurses, social workers, librarians, school teachers, administrators, and self-employed professionals; lower-middle-class, who are lower managers and administrators, lower-status white collar and some highly skilled blue- or pink-collar workers such as executive assistants, licensed practical nurses, and skilled tradespeople (e.g., cabinet makers); working class, who work manual and clerical jobs (blue and pink collar), which require less formal skills, training, and education; and working poor and underclass, those who perform precarious work or receive income assistance and have insecure incomes that fall at or below the poverty line as defined by Statistics Canada's "low-income cut off" for each city (Statistics Canada, 2009). In cases where partners in a couple were of different classes, we classified the family according to the higher class parent. Teenagers were categorized according to the class of the parents. In total, 25 working-poor/underclass teens, 22 working-class teens, 34 lower-middle-class teens, 49 upper-middle-class teens, and two upper-class teens were interviewed.

Findings

Of the 132 teenagers we interviewed, most brought up fast food in their interviews, in some instances solicited by the interviewer but often not. This suggests that fast food consumption is something that the teens in our study actively thought about and is an issue that is important to them. According to Wills et al. (2009), fast food is significant to teenagers because it is one of the few types of food that teenagers can afford to purchase outside of the home and therefore (ostensibly) beyond the influence of their families. Fast food can thus become a form of self-expression for teenagers as they struggle to assert their autonomy apart from their family's food identity. Fast food has social meanings beyond the context of the individual family, however, and teens' fast food consumption or avoidance is also a response to, and negotiation with, social discourses associated with fast food (Bugge, 2011).

In line with Bugge's study of Norwegian teens' fast food consumption (2011), teens in our study appeared to be thinking about fast food and health in part because of the ubiquitous discourse of adolescent obesity and fast food consumption. Many signaled their awareness of this discourse by citing Morgan Spurlock's (2004) *Supersize Me*—a documentary that explores the dangers of obesity precipitated by a McDonald's-only diet—while discussing their reasons for avoiding fast food, particularly the food served at McDonald's. As one Toronto girl said: "I watched *Supersize Me* a while ago, which kind of made me stop [eating at McDonald's]. I've heard so much bad things about it, so I'm trying to stop eating that."

Fast food may also have been a concern for teens in our study because most encountered it on a regular basis. Despite the belief that rural residents do not consume much fast food because these establishments do not exist in their areas of residence (Galloway, 2006), both urban and rural teens in our study described a variety of fast food restaurants in their environments, though the number of places and how close they were differed according to location. Teens in Edmonton, for example, described a wide variety of fast food outlets such as McDonald's and KFC in their immediate environments, while teens from the rural community of Athabasca two hours north had minimal access to fast food places. Many small rural communities did, however, have at least one or two fast food places. In the District of Kent, for example, teens spoke of choosing between the Subway and the A&W (an international chain of fast food restaurants known for its root beer, which also sells hamburgers, French fries, and so on). In King's County, teens contended with "Dairy Queen, Pizza Delight, McDonald's, A&W, Subway" (King's County girl) along a 12 km stretch of highway that joins three small towns. Some rural teens therefore encountered fast food every day, often "right across from [the] school" (Kent boy).

Since the discourse of obesogenic environments suggests that access to fast food equates with the consumption of fast food, especially in the case of poor and working-class people (Block, Shribner, & DeSalvo, 2004; King, Kavanagh, Jolley, Turrell, & Crawford, 2006; Moffat et al., 2005; Reidpath, Burns, Garrard, Mahoney, & Townsend, 2002), one might assume that the teens in our study who lived in urban areas with the most fast food availability would eat more fast food, particularly if they were working poor or working class. On the whole, however, access to fast food was not the sole determinate of whether or how our participants related to fast food, and there was no real spatial pattern of reported fast food consumption. Nor was there a general class pattern, as participants of all class categories said that they did and did not eat fast food to more or less the same degrees. Though we analyzed the data repeatedly looking for patterns by social class status, we generally found no apparent class patterns, which suggests that class does not predict responses to fast food, indicating instead an overall complexity in how teens across classes regarded fast food consumption. We therefore argue that teens in our study approached fast food consumption with a complex collection of social factors, individual preference, and, in particular, moral dictates. This is not to say that place and class were not important to food choice for our participants, but that moralistic notions of health—teens' conceptions of fast food as unhealthy and therefore "bad"—were more salient in their consumption choice. Nonetheless, we do attend to the class of participants throughout our analysis, given the prevalence of class stereotyping in dominant discourses of the obesogenic environment and the pervasive perception that poor and working-class people eat fast food more regularly than the middle class.

Health morals framed participants' responses to fast food in three ways, explored in detail below: first, some teens regarded fast food as unhealthy and avoided it altogether; second, even though some teens regarded fast food as unhealthy they would consume it but felt bad for doing so; third, some teens regarded fast food as unhealthy, consumed it because they liked it, and felt no guilt or remorse.

FAST FOOD, HEALTH, AND MORALITY

Colls and Evans (2008) have argued that much obesity research assumes that children and teens are either "incapable" of making or "unwilling" to make healthy food choices (c.f. Stead, McDermott, MacKintosh, & Adamson, 2011), therefore failing "to explore the possibility that [they] can be 'healthy-eating bodies'" (Colls & Evans, 2008, pp. 628–9). In contrast, we found that teens were quite well aware of what constitutes "healthy eating" in dominant discourse, especially as it related to fast food consumption. It is important to note, however, that 25 of the 132 teens we interviewed had no problem with fast food consumption, and regarded it as neither healthy nor unhealthy but simply as good tasting. Unlike discourses of obesity that posit the poor to eat more fast food, and in contrast to Wills et al. (2009), who argue that fast food consumption is regarded as unhealthy by the middle class (see also Johnston & Baumann, 2010), the greatest number of teens who happily ate fast food without regard to health in our study were in fact upper-middle class. For example, one upper-middle-class girl from Edmonton related that she and her friends went out to "McDonald's or ... Burger Baron [a local eatery] because it's convenient and it's fast. It's relatively cheap." She was also one of the only participants who professed, without guilt: "I like McDonald's." As another example, an upper-middle-class Kingston teen ate fast food for health reasons: he had a peanut allergy and felt safest in fast food restaurants because "they tend not to use peanuts ... because they want as many customers as they can possibly get."

The majority of teens in our study, however, regardless of class category, thought of fast food as unhealthy and bad. For example, when asked by the interviewer what he considered healthy food to be, one Kent boy stated: "All five food groups.... Grain, dairy, desserts, meat, vegetables, fruits, you know." When asked what he considered unhealthy, he named "Junk food. Pizza, chips, pop. (Interviewer: Okay, so fast food as well?) Yeah." Fast food was also described as "super greasy" and "disgusting" (Prince Edward County boy), "greasy and just not very good food for you" (Toronto boy), "the most unhealthiest thing you could probably eat" (Toronto boy), "gross" and "nasty" (Vancouver boy), "packaged ... [and] fatty" (Vancouver boy), and "not part of healthy eating" (Athabasca girl). As another Athabasca girl put it, "too much of [that] stuff cannot be good."

Because they regarded fast food as "not good," it is therefore not surprising that participants judged negatively those who consumed it. One teen boy from Toronto replicated dominant discourses when he spoke about fast food:

> [Fast foods are] all unhealthy. They're all kind of greasy.... I feel like just in general, teenagers have more reckless abandon for their health than adults do.... Especially since a lot of these foods are the ones I find around my school, as well, I just see people eating this stuff all the time.

When asked why he thought teens ate fast food, another Toronto teen boy stated: "Well, lack of experience, lack of knowledge.... Some people do know what's in the food but then they can't control, they can't deny the convenience. Or they can't deny the taste.... A lot of teenagers will just eat anything." One Halifax girl noted about teens in her area:

> You walk downtown and you see everyone in pizza places and McDonald's and KFC. And you think "Why didn't you just bring a sandwich?" They could avoid McDonald's and foods like that, and go to ... Soup Sergeant [a local eatery], because you can get healthier choices [there]. But most of the time they don't, they just choose to go to a fast food restaurant, probably just because it tastes good. Lots of fat and salt.

A girl from King's County related how fast food had caused her sister to gain "quite a bit of weight." She saw her own eating habits as much more healthy than her sister's, whom she described quite negatively: "Just watching her eat that, it kind of disgusts me." Similar sentiments were expressed by a teen boy, also from Halifax, who vehemently stated:

> They eat like shit, most [people in Halifax]. Most of them do the McDonald's once every couple of days or every day. Health is not pressed in terms of nutrition around here. I mean, yeah they put up the god damn food guide that tells you to eat like enough to kill an elephant every day. And that's crazy. They just want you to buy more food. But I don't know. People eat really horribly. The obesity rates

around here, you can just look at them, it's out of control. The heart disease rate, it's obvious.

Thus, teens engaged in moral boundary work when speaking of fast food, positioning themselves against those groups of people who ate fast food—teenagers in general, their peers, family members, and other residents living in their area, many of whom were thought to be obese. The fact that teens regarded fast food as unhealthy and judged those who ate it as "unknowledgeable," "out of control," "disgusting" people that made poor and unhealthy food choices did not translate neatly into behavior; some teens who believed fast food to be unhealthy and bad avoided fast food, while other teens, even though they also judged fast food as unhealthy, ate it frequently.

COMPLETE FAST FOOD AVOIDANCE

Very few participants claimed to never eat fast food. As a whole, no obvious class pattern existed in the complete rejection of fast food. For example, one upper-middle-class pair of sisters from Toronto had not darkened the door of a McDonald's or Burger King in recent memory. Both sisters preferred fresh, local, organic foods to processed foods, as they believed fresh foods were more healthy. "We never ate fast food as kids," one sister said, "and now the media and everything are big on how bad fast food is for you and stuff ... so we just don't." Even though there were "a few fast food places" around their school, the sisters "don't go there." A teen boy from King's County similarly stated: "The only thing I won't eat is fast foods.... Greasy, disgusting stuff—McDonald's or KFC." This working-class participant, much like the Toronto sisters, classified processed foods in general as unhealthy. One upper-middle-class girl from Prince Edward County, who discussed her abhorrence of processed foods at length, also noted that she "never went to McDonald's ever ... I honestly don't remember the last time I went to McDonald's."

GUILTY FAST FOOD CONSUMPTION

Most teens in our study fell into the category of believing fast food to be unhealthy, but consuming it nonetheless to varying degrees. When teen participants who perceived fast food as unhealthy did eat it, they would often negatively judge their own behaviours using the same moralistic health-based discourse they employed when judging others' fast food consumption. One teen boy from Toronto said, for example: "I find some days I'll eat like really healthy for like two weeks and then there'll be a week where I just go completely out and eat only fast food and it's just really bad. I try not to do it but..." ... One girl from Kingston said that she would "never eat" at the local McDonald's, and then guiltily admitted to having gone: "Well, I've eaten there once with my friend ... and we just got an ice cream. And then once I went with my choir at the end of the year and [the conductor] bought us milk-shakes." She then quickly re-established her identity as someone who did not eat fast food by stating: "But I really, really don't like the idea of it....Their things are processed so much." A Toronto girl similarly noted: "I used to eat [at McDonald's] a lot, but I've been trying to stop a bit." Lamenting that the food "draws me back in every time," she noted, "it's really bad." Another girl, from King's County, when asked what she had eaten the night previous to the interview, admitted: "Last night I didn't eat healthy. I ate McDonald's and then I came home at five in the morning and made Smores.... It's probably not the best...."

One Kent girl and her brother talked about the physical manifestations of "feeling bad" after the consumption of fast food, as the grease made them feel ill. They both believed it best to stick with the "five food groups" as a result. Similarly, one Athabasca teen girl noted: "I went through a change where whenever I ate [fast food] I'd get sick. I just couldn't stomach it." In contrast, one teen boy from Halifax expressed disdain for his own eating habits, but at the same time spoke with a sense of relish for the taste and texture of fast foods. He began speaking of his regular fast food consumption by providing family context:

> I wasn't allowed to go to McDonald's 'till I was eight. It was out of the question, not fast food. But now ... Maybe I was so used to eating this wholesome stuff as a kid that I'm trying to get all the junk I can subconsciously.... I love the flavor [of fast food]. I love grease and crispy fries.... I will almost certainly have a heart condition due to what I'm eating.... I have a hamburger four times a week.... I'm serious. I have to stop, actually, or I'm going to die. But I love them.

Thus, although participants who believed fast food to be unhealthy also ate it, they seemingly could not do so without an act of guilty self-discipline, or without some sense that the consequences of fast food consumption were "bad." They therefore reified moralistic assumptions of fast food as "bad" and unhealthy, even as they ate it.

Employing a technique that has been previously identified by other researchers as "healthy fast food" consumption (Bugge & Lavik, 2010; Wills et al., 2009), many of our participants who felt bad for eating fast food redrew their moral boundaries and recovered their identities as "good" and healthy eaters by choosing to eat the healthiest foods at particular fast food restaurants, or by going to fast food places they perceived to be "better" and healthier than other places. While there was no real class pattern in who considered fast food to be unhealthy, and the extent to which teens ate fast food did not differ by class, one important class difference was evident in what kinds of fast foods people were eating in order to assuage their guilt. This moral hierarchy of fast foods, whereby hamburgers and French fries from McDonald's were generally considered the worst types of fast foods while Subway sandwiches were the best, was a process undertaken primarily by the upper-middle and lower-middle classes. This supports Wills et al.'s (2009) claim that eating so-called healthy fast food is a function of middle-class identity, whereby the middle class can have its fast food and its claims to moral superiority, too.

Most commonly, teens employed the hierarchy of fast food by ranking fast food chains, and then claiming that they preferred the healthier places mentioned. Two sisters in Toronto, for example, stated that while they would never eat any fast food, they would go to Tim Horton's, a Canadian fast food and doughnut shop chain, because it is healthier than other places. One sister argued: "The only fast food we ever eat is Tim Horton's.... I've never been to Burger King, I've never been to a lot of those places." Tim Horton's was, in general, spoken of as a healthy fast food place, as was Wendy's. One teen boy in Edmonton noted: "I like Wendy's way better [than McDonald's].... I don't find their burgers so greasy.... They put ... a lot more vegetables and stuff in it."

Subway, however, was unquestionably the restaurant most participants considered to be the best in terms of health. (It is probably not a coincidence that Subway also markets itself as a healthy choice that even helps to fight childhood obesity. See: Subway International, n.d.). A girl from Prince Edward County captured the sentiment that Subway sells healthy fast food from all four food groups, stating: "I normally go to Subway because it's not as ... fried, it's just a sub with the grain, the vegetables, the meat, and the dairy because they put cheese on it so ... as opposed to a Big Mac or something from McDonald's." A teen boy from Kent, when rating the restaurants in his area in terms of health, stated: "A&W is not that healthy. Chevron's [a gas station with some fast food options] not that healthy. Subway's alright. Subway is probably the healthiest out of all the fast food places." A Toronto girl lamented that she did not eat well when not at home, with the exception of Subway: "When my mom makes my foods they're okay. But when it's me buying my foods then that's not good choices, like the only good choice I would say that I make is going to Subway.... Everything else is not good. Like there's a lot of McDonald's in this area." When asked about whether she and her friends ate fast food, a girl from Kent demonstrated how ranking fast food could be a gendered process related to the well-documented pressures that girls in particular often feel to be slim (Wright et al., 2006): "A lot of [the girls at school] won't eat like certain things, 'Oh we'd get fat' or something. I don't really care as long as I just keep in shape.... Sometimes we'll go to Subway but other than that."

While good and bad fast food restaurants existed for participants, so did good and bad foods within particular restaurants. Some participants would go to places that served burgers and fries, but they would choose what they considered to be healthy options such as salads and baked potatoes while there. Two teen brothers from Kent demonstrated this by noting: "Wendy's has baked potatoes and stuff. [Second Brother:] Yeah, there's like healthier alternatives." Similarly, an Athabasca girl who worked at a fast food restaurant said she tried not to eat there because the food was unhealthy, but if she did she would "just eat the salad."

Apart from eating what teens perceived to be healthy choices at otherwise unhealthy fast food places, some teens employed other strategies at establishments deemed as "bad." For example, a teen boy from Prince Edward County related that he felt fine about eating at McDonald's, as long as he balanced their bad food with eating good healthy food throughout the day: "If I've had enough healthy food or good food, and I have like, not room but, if I've eaten all healthy during the day so I could have a snack of ice cream or ... if I went out for breakfast to like, McDonald's or something, I wouldn't go again to McDonald's for lunch or dinner" (see Backett, 1992 for a discussion of similar strategies employed by adults).

Not all teens felt better about themselves by practicing the hierarchy of fast food. A Kingston girl, for example, expressed doubt regarding the notion that fast food could be healthy, stating:

> When we're driving, say to Toronto, we stop at Tim Horton's a lot. And I don't know, I like their stuff. I know it's probably … not the healthiest but … I guess we think, oh, Tim Horton's is healthier than McDonald's or something like that. But maybe it's not, but it's just, I don't know, it feels that way. And it makes you feel better eating there.

FAST FOOD CONSUMPTION WITHOUT REGRET

Very few participants talked about fast food as unhealthy, but then spoke of consuming it with an almost defiant sense of complacency about eating these bad foods. This reaction was rare. Again, no obvious class pattern existed. A lower-middle-class teen girl from King's County, for example, after noting that her family did not "really eat a lot of fast food anymore," then insisted: "Something we can't kick though is Timmie's [Tim Horton's]. We would never—Tim Horton's [is a] lifeline.… For me and [my brother], French Vanilla Icecaps [iced cappuccinos], we're drinking them until [we] die." Another girl from King's County, from a working-poor family, noted throughout her interview that fast food was not healthy, but stated: "I guess when I'm out with my friends or something I don't really think about the healthy side of it. Just whatever's cheapest at A&W I guess."

Discussion and Conclusions

In a cross-national qualitative study of Canadian food practices, we found teens engaged in what Lamont has called "moral boundary work" through their discussions of fast food consumption and avoidance, not primarily to draw class distinctions but first and foremost to articulate themselves as healthy or unhealthy, and therefore good or bad. Teens from all classes in our study positioned themselves within moralist narratives of healthy eating by reciting three basic fast food-related narratives: teens believed fast food to be unhealthy, and claimed to completely avoid fast food for health reasons; teens regarded fast food as unhealthy, and claimed to consume fast food but feel guilty and bad for doing so; and less often, teens claimed to consume and enjoy fast food without feelings of guilt or concerns for health, even while knowing fast food was bad and unhealthy. Through moral pronouncements about health and, specifically, about the unhealthful nature of fast food, teen participants from across Canada and from different social class backgrounds articulated themselves and others as successful or unsuccessful subjects.

Teens in general believed fast food to be unhealthy, and drew lines between "good" and "bad" eating, and "good" and "bad" people, based on fast food consumption. The moral boundary work that teens performed through talk of fast food consumption therefore helped them to articulate a sense of self and who they were as people—a good person who never ate fast food or ate only healthy fast food, a good person who made mistakes sometimes and ate fast food occasionally but knew it was "wrong" and felt bad about it, or, less frequently, a bad person who bucked social norms and did not care about health and ate fast food without concern or feeling guilty. This type of moral boundary work was not endemic to a particular class, but was evident among teens from all class groups in our study. Nor was moral boundary work through fast food discourse specific to a particular region in our study, or connected to proximity to obesogenic, fast food-prevalent settings. One can see from the variety of examples we used to demonstrate teens' moral boundary work that it occurred across Canada, across class, in both rural and urban spaces.

The fact that all classes of teens in our study from all regions made complicated decisions about fast food consumption that were based in moralist notions of healthy eating, good eating, and good eaters is an important interruption to mainstream discourses, which posit obesity to be a disease of the lower/working classes primarily who live in obesogenic urban environments. We therefore maintain that easy conflations among social class, teens' access to fast food, and consumption of fast food as suggested by the discourse of obesogenic environments are troubling in their lack of specificity and nuance, and their failure to take into consideration the complexity of teens' practices of subjectivity in relation to understandings of healthy eating and fast food consumption.

Because our study is based on a volunteer sample, it could be biased toward people who think about food and healthy eating more than others (although more often the parents "volunteered" the family as participants). We therefore cannot conclude that our analysis about teen fast food consumption can be generalized to the Canadian teen population at large. Our data do, however, take a step toward understanding teens' decision-making regarding fast food, and pushes those concerned to regard teen food choice as complex, and as part of larger identification processes through which subjects are made and re-made by intricate processes of moral boundary work in which they take up or resist socially produced discourses of health. Complicating discourses about obesogenic environments, which suggest a direct correlation between the spatial proximity of teens to fast food establishments and adolescent obesity, we demonstrate that teens' fast food consumption—or lack thereof—is the result of a dynamic negotiation with discourses of healthy eating that permeate Western culture. Our study therefore adds to critical obesity scholarship by challenging dominant perspectives on obesity and eating.

References

Backett, K. (1992). Taboos and excesses: Lay health moralities in middle class families. *Sociology of Health and Illness, 14*, 255–274.

Beaulac, J., Kristjansson, E., & Cummins, S. (2009). A systematic review of food deserts, 1966–2007. *Preventing Chronic Disease: Public Health Research, Practice, and Policy, 6*, 1–10.

Beck, L. (October 14, 2009). Where you live affects your chance of obesity. *The Globe and Mail*, L1.

Black, J. L., & Macinko, J. (2010). The changing distribution and determinants of obesity in the neighborhoods of New York City, 2003-2007. *American Journal of Epidemiology, 171*, 765-775.

Black, J. L., Macinko, J., Dixon, L. B., & Fryer, G. E. (2010). Neighborhood and obesity in New York City. *Health & Place, 16*, 489-499.

Block, J. P., Shribner, R. A., & DeSalvo, K. B. (2004). Fast food, race/ethnicity, and income: A geographic analysis. *American Journal of Preventative Medicine, 27*, 211-217.

Bourdieu, P. (1984). *Distinction: A social critique of the judgment of taste*. London: Routledge and Kegan Paul.

Bugge, A. B. (2011). Lovin' it? A study of youth and the culture of fast food. *Food, Culture & Society, 14*, 71-89.

Bugge, A. B., & Lavik, R. (2010). Eating out: A multifaceted activity in contemporary Norway. *Food, Culture & Society, 13*, 215-240.

Burrows, L. (2009). Pedagogizing families through obesity discourse. In J. Wright & V. Harwood (Eds.), *Biopolitics and the "obesity epidemic": Governing bodies* (pp. 127-140). New York: Routledge.

Campos, P. (2004). *The obesity myth: Why America's obsession with weight is hazardous to your health*. New York: Gotham Books.

Colls, R., & Evans, B. (2008). Embodying responsibility: Children's health and supermarket initiatives. *Environment and Planning A, 40*, 615-631.

Crush, J. (November 20, 2009). The "urban poor" flaw. *The Globe and Mail*, A21.

Cummins, S. C. J., McKay, L., & MacIntyre, S. (2005). McDonald's restaurants and neighborhood deprivation in Scotland and England. *American Journal of Preventative Medicine, 29*, 308-310.

Ernsberger, P. (2009). Does social class explain the connection between weight and health? In E. Rothblum, & S. Solovay (Eds.), *The fat studies reader* (pp. 25-36). New York: New York University Press.

Evans, B., & Colls, R. (2009). Measuring fatness, governing bodies: The spatialities of the body mass index (BMI) in anti-obesity policy. *Antipode, 41*, 1051-1083.

Everett, H. (2009). Vernacular health moralities and culinary tourism in Newfoundland and Labrador. *Journal of American Folklore, 122*, 28-52.

Fee, M. (2006). Racializing narratives: Obesity, diabetes and the "Aboriginal" thrifty genotype. *Social Science & Medicine, 62*, 2988-2997.

Galloway, T. (2006). Obesity rates among rural Ontario schoolchildren. *Canadian Journal of Public Health, 97*, 353-356.

Gard, M. (2011). *The end of the obesity epidemic*. London: Routledge.

Gard, M., & Wright, J. (2005). *The obesity epidemic: Science, morality and ideology*. London: Routledge.

Garriguet, D. (2004). *Nutrition: Findings from the Canadian community health survey; Overview of Canadians' eating habits*. Available at: Ottawa: Minister of Industry http://www.statcan.gc.ca/pub/82-620-m/82-620-m2006002-eng.pdf [Accessed 02.05.11].

Gilbert, D. (2008). *The American class structure in an age of growing inequality* (7th ed.). Thousand Oaks, CA: Pine Forge Press.

Gilman, S. L. (2010). *Obesity: The biography*. Oxford: Oxford University Press.

Goren, A., Harries, J. L., Schwartz, M. B., & Brownell, K. D. (2010). Predicting support for restricting food marketing to youth. *Health Affairs, 29*, 410-424.

Health Canada. (2006). *Healthy living: It's your health; Obesity*. Available at: Ottawa: Health Canada http://www.hc-sc.gc.ca/hl-vs/iyh-vsv/life-vie/obes-eng.php [accessed November, 2010].

Herndon, A. M. (2005). Collateral damage from friendly fire? Race, nation, class and the "war against obesity." *Social Semiotics, 15*, 127-141.

Herndon, A. M. (2010). Mommy made me do it: Mothering fat children in the midst of the obesity epidemic. *Food, Culture & Society, 13*, 331-350.

Jago, R., Baranowski, T., Baranowski, J. D., Cullen, K. W., & Thompson, D. (2007). Distance to food stores & adolescent male fruit and vegetable consumption: Medication effects. *International Journal of Behavioral Nutrition and Physical Activity, 4*. http://www.ijbnpa.org/content/4/1/35 [Accessed 02.05.11].

Johnston, J., & Baumann, S. (2010). *Foodies: Democracy and distinction in the gourmet foodscape*. New York: Routledge.

King, T., Kavanagh, A. M., Jolley, D., Turrell, G., & Crawford, D. (2006). Weight and place: A multilevel cross-sectional survey of area-level social disadvantage and overweight/obesity in Australia. *International Journal of Obesity, 30*, 281-287.

Koehly, L. M., & Loscalzo, A. (2009). Adolescent obesity and social networks. *Preventing Chronic Disease: Public Health Research, Practice, and Policy, 6*, 1-8. Available at: www.cdc.gov/pcd/issues/2009/jul/08_0265.htm (accessed October 25, 2010).

Lamont, M. (1992). *Money, morals, & manners: The culture of the French and American upper-middle class*. Chicago: University of Chicago Press.

Lamont, M. (2000). *The dignity of working men: Morality and the boundaries of race, class, and immigration*. Cambridge, MA: Harvard University Press.

Larson, N. I., Story, M. T., & Nelson, M. C. (2009). Neighborhood environments: Disparities in access to healthy foods in the U.S. *American Journal of Preventative Medicine, 36*, 74-81.

LeBesco, K. (2004). *Revolting bodies? The struggle to redefine fat identity.* Amherst, MA: University of Massachusetts Press.

Lupton, D. (1996). *Food, the body and the self.* London: Sage.

Moffat, T., Galloway, T., & Latham, J. (2005). Stature and adiposity among children in contrasting neighbourhoods in the city of Hamilton, Ontario, Canada. *American Journal of Human Biology, 17,* 355-367.

Monaghan, L. F. (2008). *Men and the war on obesity: A sociological study.* London: Routledge.

Moore, L. V., & Roux, V. D. (2006). Associations of neighborhood characteristics with the location and type of food stores. *American Journal of Public Health, 96,* 325-331.

Murray, S. (2009). Marked as "pathological": "Fat" bodies as virtual confessors. In J. Wright & V. Harwood (Eds.), *Biopolitics and the "obesity epidemic": Governing bodies* (pp. 78-90). New York: Routledge.

Papemy, A. (February 16, 2010). Urban food strategy unveiled. *The Globe and Mail,* A17.

Poudrier, J. (2007). The geneticization of Aboriginal diabetes and obesity: Adding another scene to the story of the thrifty gene. *CRSA/RCSA, 44,* 237-261.

Powell, L. M., Auld, M. C., Chaloupka, F. J., O'Malley, P. M., & Johnston, L. D. (2007a). Associations between access to food stores and adolescent body mass index. *American Journal of Preventative Medicine, 33,* S301-S307.

Powell, L. M., Caloupka, F. J., & Bao, Y. (2007b). The availability of fast-food and full-service restaurants in the United States: Associations with neighborhood characteristics. *American Journal of Preventative Medicine, 33,* S240-S245.

Powell, L. M., Szczypka, B. A., & Chaloupka, F. J. (2010). Trends in exposure to television food advertisements among children and adolescents in the United States. *Archives of Pediatric Adolescent Medicine, 164,* 794-802.

Rail, G. (2009). Canadian youth's discursive constructions of health in the context of obesity discourse. In J. Wright & V. Harwood (Eds.), *Biopolitics and the "obesity epidemic": Governing bodies* (pp. 141-156). New York: Routledge.

Reidpath, D. D., Burns, C., Garrard, J., Mahoney, M., & Townsend, M. (2002). An ecological study of the relationship between social and environmental determinants of obesity. *Health & Place, 8,* 141-145.

Rich, E., & Evans, J. (2009). Performative health in schools: Welfare policy, neoliberalism and social regulation? In J. Wright & V. Harwood (Eds.), *Biopolitics and the "obesity epidemic": Governing bodies* (pp. 157-171). New York: Routledge.

Riediger, N. D., Shooshtari, S., & Moghadasian, M. H. (2007). The influence of sociodemographic factors on the patterns of fruit and vegetable consumption in Canadian adolescents. *Journal of the American Dietetic Association, 107,* 1511-1518.

Said, E. W. (1979). *Orientalism*. New York: Vintage.

Schneider, D. (2000). International trends in adolescent nutrition. *Social Science & Medicine, 51*, 955-967.

Smith, D. M., & Cummins, S. (2008). Obese cities: How our environment shapes overweight. *Geography Compass, 3*, 518–535.

Spurlock, M. (2004). *Supersize me*. New York: Hart Shop Video.

Statistics Canada. (2009). *Low income cut-offs for 2008 and low income measures for 2007*. Available at: Ottawa: Minister of Industry http://www.statcan.gc.ca/pub/75f0002m/75f0002m2009002-eng.pdf [accessed October 2010].

Stead, M., McDermott, L., MacKintosh, A. M., & Adamson, A. (2011). Why healthy eating is bad for young people's health: Identity, belonging and food. *Social Science & Medicine, 72*, 1131-1139.

Subway International, n.d. Jared's journey. Available at: www.subwayfreshbuzz.com/jareds_journey/ [accessed October 2010].

Taylor, J. P., Evers, S., & McKenna, M. (2005). Determinants of health eating in children and youth. *Canadian Journal of Public Health, 96*(Suppl 3), S20–S26.

Weeks, C. (July 21, 2009). More young Canadians at risk for heart disease. *The Globe and Mail*, L1.

Wills, W., Backett-Milburn, K., Lawton, J., & Roberts, M.-L. (2009). Consuming fast food: The perceptions and practices of middle-class young teenagers. In A. James, A. T. Kjorhold, & V. Tingstad (Eds.), *Children, food and identity in everyday life* (pp. 52-68). Houndsmills, Basingstoke, Hampshire: Palgrave Macmillan.

World Health Organization. (2000). *Obesity: Preventing and managing the global epidemic*. Report of a WHO consultation. Geneva: World Health Organization.

Wright, J., O'Flynn, G., & Macdonald, D. (2006). Being fit and looking healthy: Young women's and men's constructions of health and fitness. *Sex Roles, 54*, 707–716.

CHAPTER 30

Class and Power: The Major Themes

John Porter

The Canadian Middle-Class Image

One of the most persistent images that Canadians have of their society is that it has no classes. This image becomes translated into the assertion that Canadians are all relatively equal in their possessions, in the amount of money they earn, and in the opportunities which they and their children have to get on in the world. An important element in this image of classlessness is that, with the absence of formal aristocracy and aristocratic institutions, Canada is a society in which equalitarian values have asserted themselves over authoritarian values. Canada, it is thought, shares not only a continent with the United States, but also a democratic ideology which rejects the historical class and power structures of Europe.

Social images are one thing and social realities another. Yet the two are not completely separate. Social images are not entirely fictional characters with only a coincidental likeness to a real society, living or dead. Often the images can be traced to an earlier historical period of the society, its golden age perhaps, which, thanks to the historians, is held up, long after it has been transformed into something else, as a model way of life. As well as their historical sources, images can be traced to their contemporary creators, particularly in the world of the mass media and popular culture. When a society's writers, journalists, editors, and other image-creators are a relatively small and closely linked group, and have more or less the same social background, the images they produce can, because they are consistent, appear to be much more true to life than if their group were larger, less cohesive, and more heterogeneous in composition.

The historical source of the image of a classless Canada is the equality among pioneers in the frontier environment of the last century. In the early part of the present century there was a similar equality of status among those who were settlers in the west, although, as we shall see, these settlers were by no means treated equally. A rural, agricultural, primary producing society is a much less differentiated society than one which has highly concentrated industries in large cities. Equality in the rural society may be much more apparent than real, but the rural environment has been for Canada an important source of the image of equality. Later we shall examine more closely how the historical image has become out of date with the transformation of Canadian society from the rural to the urban type.

Although the historical image of rural equality lingers it has gradually given way in the urban industrial setting to an image of a middle level classlessness in which there is a general uniformity of possessions. For families these possessions include a separate dwelling with an array of electrical equipment, a car, and perhaps a summer cottage. Family members, together or as individuals, engage in a certain amount of ritualistic behaviour in churches and service clubs. Modern advertising has done much to standardize the image of middle-class consumption levels and middle-class behaviour. Consumers' magazines are devoted to the task of constructing the ideal way of life through articles on childrearing, homemaking, sexual behaviour, health, sports, and hobbies. Often, too, corporations which do not produce family commodities directly will have large advertisements to demonstrate how general social well-being at this middle level is an outcome of their own operations.

That there is neither very rich nor very poor in Canada is an important part of the image. There are no barriers to opportunity. Education is free. Therefore, making use of it is largely a question of personal ambition. Even university education is available to all, except that it may require for some a little more summer work and thrift. There is a view widely held by many university graduates that they, and most other graduates, have worked their way through college. Consequently it is felt anyone else can do the same.

In some superficial respects the image of middle-class uniformity may appear plausible. The main values of the society are concerned with the consumption of commodities, and in the so-called affluence that has followed World War II there seem to have been commodities for everybody, except, perhaps, a small group of the permanently poor at the bottom. Credit facilities are available for large numbers of low income families, enabling them, too, to be consumers of commodities over and above the basic necessities of life. The vast array of credit facilities, some of them extraordinarily ingenious, have inequalities built into them, in that the cost of borrowing money varies with the amount already possessed. There are vast differences in the quality of goods bought by the middle income levels and the lower income levels. One commodity, for instance, which low income families can rarely purchase is privacy, particularly the privacy of a house to themselves. It is perhaps the value of privacy and the capacity to afford it which has become the dividing line between the real and the apparent middle class.

If low income families achieve high consumption levels it is usually through having more than one income earner in the household. Often this is the wife and mother, but it may be an older child who has left school, and who is expected to contribute to the family budget. Alternatively, high consumption levels may be achieved at a cost in leisure. Many low income family heads have two jobs, a possibility which has arisen with the shorter working day and the five-day week. This "moonlighting," as it is called in labour circles, tends to offset the progress which has been made in raising the level of wages and reducing the hours of work. There is no way of knowing how extensive "moonlighting" is, except that we know that trade unions denounce it as a practice which tends to take away the gains which have been obtained for workers. For large segments of the population, therefore, a high level of consumption is obtained by means which are alien to a true middle-class standard. In a later chapter where we shall examine closely the distribution of income we shall see what a small proportion of Canadian families were able to live a middle-class style of life in the middle 1950s, the high tide of post-war affluence.

At the high end of the social class spectrum, also in contrast to the middle level image, are the families of great wealth and influence. They are not perhaps as ostentatious as the very wealthy of other societies, and Canada has no "celebrity world" with which these families must compete for prestige in the way Mills has suggested is important for the very rich in American society.[1]

Almost every large Canadian city has its wealthy and prominent families of several generations. They have their own social life, their children go to private schools, they have their clubs and associations, and they take on the charitable and philanthropic roles which have so long been the "duty" of those of high status. Although this upper class is always being joined by the new rich, it still contributes, as we shall see later, far more than its proportionate share to the elite of big business. The concentration of wealth in the upper classes is indicated by the fact that in Canada in 1955 the top one per cent of income recipients received about 40 per cent of all income from dividends. [...]

Images which conflict with the one of middle-class equality rarely find expression, partly because the literate middle class is both the producer and the consumer of the image. Even at times in what purports to be serious social analysis, middle-class intellectuals project the image of their own class onto the social classes above and below them. There is scarcely any critical analysis of Canadian social life upon which a conflicting image could be based. The idea of class differences has scarcely entered into the stream of Canadian academic writing despite the fact that class differences stand in the way of implementing one of the most important values of western society, that is equality.[2] The fact, which we shall see later, that Canada draws its intellectuals either from abroad or from its own middle class, means that there is almost no one producing a view of the world which reflects the experience of the poor or the underprivileged. It was as though they did not exist. [...]

Closely related to differences in class levels are differences in the exercising of power and decision-making in the society. Often it is thought that once a society becomes an electoral democracy based on universal suffrage power becomes diffused throughout the general population so that everyone participates somehow in the selection of social goals. There is, however, a whole range of institutional resistances to the transfer of power to a democratic political system. [...]

Notes

1. C.W. Mills, *The Power Elite* (New York, 1956), chap. 4.
2. Nor does class appear as a theme in Canadian literature. See R.L. McDougall, "The Dodo and the Cruising Auk," *Canadian Literature*, no. 18 (Autumn 1963).

SECTION 4B

GENDER AND SEXUALITIES

CHAPTER 31

Our Bodies Are Not Ourselves: Tranny Guys and the Racialized Class Politics of Incoherence

Jean Bobby Noble

> That was when I realized a shocking thing. I couldn't become a man without becoming The Man. Even if I didn't want to.
>
> —Jeffrey Eugenides (2002: 518)

In my first department meeting as a professor at York University, one held during the CUPE strike on our campus in 2000, the department was attempting to address the gender imbalance among its rank of full professors. Given that many of the full professors are male, the department was taking the very important step of finding a remedy to this situation. One senior professor (but not full professor), a woman who teaches, among other things, feminist literature, made the very curious claim that given how easy it is these days to change one's gender—and this even after the Ontario government de-listed sex-reassignment surgeries—that she would volunteer to do so if it would allow her to access the pay increase that accompanied a full professorship. A round of laughter ensued in which all seemingly agreed that this was indeed an easy process and the meeting continued. I sat a little dumbfounded that—in the midst of the CUPE 3903 union labour action on the campus, a local that has been remarkably progressive in its inclusion of trans issues in its mandate, and in the face of the aggressive de-listing of sex-reassignment procedures *and* the sad reality that male full professors still outranked the females—any of these matters would be so easily the source of laughter among faculty. This work is addressed to, in part, not only the female professor in question but to those folks inside of feminism who might claim that trans is not a feminist issue.

[I]ssues around the prefix *trans*-present not only theoretical but lived opportunities to refine our intersectional reading practices. The perspective I want to explore here is one that will allow us to see trans issues as not only those of gender but also those of race and class as well. The titles of two significant feminist books on class—Dorothy Allison's *Skin* and bell hooks's *Where We Stand*—signal the precise articulation I want to explore here: that between (trans-)[1] embodiment, class, and labour. Each text argues, among other things, that materializing class within feminist theoretical paradigms is often accomplished through corporeal metaphors. Moreover, each also suggests to us that class, the one term within our intersectional frameworks that is often neglected, is itself perceived to be about a kind of hyper-embodiment and hyper-visibility, especially for those of us who are working class and racialized White. If the anti-racist field of whiteness studies is correct, as I will argue later it is, then being classed as White is whiteness racialized as visible, especially since whiteness operates through ironic codes of invisibility and, hence, epistemological and discursive power. That is, whiteness comes into visibility as whiteness when it is articulated through class. If that is true, then under what conditions can transed bodies, bodies that similarly matter when invisible and/or fetishized, emerge within the feminist analytical intersections of capitalism, class, and race? I want to play in those fields by offering my own trans body—which is White but formerly off-White,[2] formerly lesbian but now female-to-male trans-sexual—as a case study in resistance. A practice of strategically unmaking the self—that is, working the labour of self-making against the categorical imperative—is a class, trans, anti-racist, and union politic I want to cultivate in this era where "self" is the hottest and most insidious capitalist commodity.[3]

The union motto that I want to borrow—an injury to one is an injury to all—has been in my life since I was very young.[4] My maternal grandmother was a member of CUPE for her entire working life; she was a hospital worker when services, like laundry and food, were still provided in-house. She worked in a hospital laundry for almost 40 years. I spent one summer as a young teenager working in that same laundry with her and just barely lasted the first month. Conditions were horrific. Unpacking the laundry from the hospital hampers was one of the nastiest jobs I have ever witnessed. Thankfully, I suppose, the staff wouldn't let me near the job of separating soiled sheets, bloodied towels from the operating rooms, and so on. Temperatures were extremely high and dangerous. Between massive pressing machines that ironed linens and sheets, the huge dryers, and washers that laundered sheets at very high temperatures, workers were dehydrated on a regular basis. After working for 40 years in daily conditions like these, my grandmother was given a CUPE ring that I still have and wear on a chain around my neck. I remember visiting her on her lunch break when I was much younger; I would wait for her in the hospital cafeteria and when the laundry women came into the room, they certainly were quite a sight. Into that otherwise unremarkably populated cafeteria walked a group of White, working-class, big, tough-looking, often hard-drinking women dressed in white dress-uniforms that looked out of place on them. They lumbered into the cafeteria, lit cigarettes, opened their homemade lunches, and stared down all who dared to look. Those women, a formidable bunch of working-class women who were literally at the bottom of the health-services industry but upon whom it depended, made a mark on me. Much later when I walked the CUPE 3903 picket line at York University with my teaching assistants as a new faculty member, something of those early workers infused my determination to see that strike through to its conclusion. I doubt that much of CUPE 3903's current work on trans-sexual issues would have made much sense to those women with whom my grandmother worked, although I suspect a couple of them might have understood the stakes. Because of the political commitment to social justice issues, CUPE 3903 has passed a number of resolutions that include the struggles of trans-sexual peoples into their primary mandate. They also support their trans-sexual members with funding; when I had surgery, CUPE 3903's Ways and Means fund helped me pay for a procedure that has been de-listed in the Conservatives' butchery of Ontario health care.[5]

The men in my family were less union-affiliated but just as affected by the class-based issues of labour activism. My grandfather was one of the "Little Immigrants," groups of White, working-class, orphaned British children shipped to Canada from the homes of Thomas John Barnardo, a philanthropist in 19th-century London, England. Thomas Barnardo, along with others, established a series of reformatory and industrial schools known as "ragged schools" (because of the ragged clothing of the attendees) for homeless and abandoned children. In the 19th century, they struck a deal with the Canadian government whereby they would export large numbers of these children to Canada to work as "farm" help and "mother's helpers" in Canadian homes and farms (Bagnell 1980: 91). At its peak, this emigration was responsible for shipping between 80,000 and 100,000 (orphaned or abandoned) children to Canada, a ready-made, exploitable "servant" class (Bagnell 1980: 9). Most of these children, now known as the Barnardo kids, would end up working as indentured domestic servants. My grandfather was one of those who came to Canada via Montreal in 1916 as a young boy to be adopted into a farm family, or so he thought. Instead, he lived in the barn, was ill fed, beaten, and overworked until he was old enough to run away. He did, and set up a life for himself in Canada as a labourer, eventually marrying my grandmother in northern Ontario. As one of the students of a ragged school, my grandfather was still unable to read and write when he died in 1992.

About one thing I felt certain: these were the primary influences on my gender. My grandfather had an entirely ambivalent relationship with England: I suspect he had always felt abandoned and banished from it, although as a young boy from a very poor family, he had already lived the life of an exile on the streets of London. He remained vehemently class-identified and anti-British for his entire life, continuously evoking cultural traces of England and, unknowingly, its particular form of class whiteness while constantly disparaging both at the same time. I find traces of both grandparents in the words I use to describe myself ("a guy who is half lesbian") and, in finding these traces, have built a sense of self quite different from their own. The rough and yet somehow vulnerable masculinity of the butches and FtMs brings my grandmother back to me, while, in some kind of temporal and geographical displacement, I find traces of my grandfather's off-whiteness in the class-based traces of manhood I now wear as corporeal signifiers.

To be sure, my family and I are all White. When I say "off-White," I do not mean to suggest at all that somehow being poor and/or working class means that one is no longer White. What I mean is that whiteness, like gender and class, has a history of invention, construction, and utility. Embedded in those histories are the processes that manufacture whiteness in the service of modern nation building. [...]

If racialized bodies are the product of both our own labour and the work of a racial social manufacturing machine, then developing not just a tolerance, but an acquired taste, for destabilizing paradoxes within our feminist vocabularies might be one way to trouble that machinery. Female-to-male trans-sexuals embody but are also articulated by paradox: Loren Cameron's (1996) photographs in *Body Alchemy* visually represent this paradox. The guys whom Cameron photographs, especially those without clothes, really are half guy, half something else. My own body does this too: from the waist up, with or without clothes, I display a White male chest. Naked, from the waist down, my body reads closest conventionally female body even though that is not how it reads to me. Clothed, from the waist down, my body is overdetermined by signifiers of whiteness and masculinity and I am just a guy. Given that the surgical production of a penis leaves much to be desired—and the penis they can build costs so much that it is out of reach for most guys—trans men cannot leave the "trans" behind and be "men." Self-naming and, by implication, self-definition, then, these crucial axioms that feminist movements fought long and hard for become tricky: I find myself at an even greater loss when it comes to finding a language to describe myself. Just recently, I have settled upon the following paradox: "I am a guy who is half lesbian." I have a long lesbian history, which I do not deny despite tremendous pressure, but have just recently come out as a straight (albeit trans-sexual) man or "I am a lesbian man": Identifying myself through paradox as a "guy who is half lesbian" really comes closest to bringing a number of historical moments together to form *something like an identity*.

Refracting identity through simile ("something like" or "closest to") is crucial to my sense of self. While I am suggesting *something like*—that is, something comparable or similar to—I am also suggesting but *something that fails to*—that is, something that fails to cohere as a thing unto itself, hence the need for the comparison to begin with. In the case of my own sense of self, for instance, the tension between "guy" and "lesbian" does the work of articulating in language what my body is currently doing through gender signifiers. The result, of course, is that many FtMs cannot always be read as "men" (without the quotation marks) in every circumstance, presuming, of course, that any man can. Take gym locker rooms as an example. These are sites of poignant contradiction within our current capitalist discourses about bodies. Gyms and health clubs are strange sites of Marxist alienation and disembodiment even in the face of an apparent hyper-embodiedness. Fragmenting bodies into "legs," "abs," "chest," "shoulders," and "arms" (and then systems like "cardio"), the class culture of working out before or after work (not employment/work as physically demanding) requires one to become, quite literally, subject to or to step into a machine that has been designed to isolate a muscle or set of muscles and work them with the goal of having them look like they do more than get worked on at the gym. The gym body is developed not necessarily from use but from an extreme form of docility, repetition, and discipline. Capitalism requires each of these when manufacturing labouring bodies. Don't get me wrong: working out is not necessarily a terrible thing to do. After years of disembodiment, I decided to take the plunge and sign up with a fitness program. Like most gyms, it relies heavily on a gendered division of space determined by conventional understandings of the supposed self-evidence of the body. Given that I read completely as male, showering in public would compromise that reading. Being undressed in a locker room—and given the degree to which straight men furtively but quite decidedly look at each other—would, quite literally, be my undoing.

Then again, signifying as a guy, which I do more consistently now that I no longer have breasts, I do so with a success that makes me politically suspect to some lesbians while at other times interesting to gay men. Toronto's Pride 2003 was an interesting experience; two things happened that marked a shift in my identity from very masculine lesbian to guy. First, I seemed to be much more interesting to gay men as an object of desire. This is evident by the way in which I am now just more noticeable; gay men flirt with me now in a way they've not done so before. At dinner, in a queer-esque restaurant, a number of men stopped by our table to say hello, pass on a pride greeting or, in one case, to invite me upstairs to an event that was happening later that night. But let me describe myself to you: in my life as a "woman," I failed miserably. I signified as extremely butch, stone butch, macho even. I am heavy-set, continue to wear a kind of crew cut, dress in black pants and crisp shirts, and do not communicate signals that could be easily construed as gay (read: gay man) in any way at all. And yet precisely because of my gender performance (if categories are necessary, I could be considered a smallish bear), I am cruised on a regular basis by gay men.

But masculinity is not the only subject of unmaking found in No Man's Land. The other thing I felt quite compelled to do during the weekend's activities was to insist that my very out lesbian-femme girlfriend of African descent hold my hand as much as possible.[6] This irony resonates even more strongly for several reasons. In a historical moment where femmes are accused of not being lesbian enough, or where queer femininity is cast in a suspicious light, it was a bit of an oddity to realize that I passed as *less than bio-guy* when outed as *something else* through my lesbian partner. Queer femininity or, as Anna Camilleri calls it, femininity gone wrong, is equally bound by contradiction, paradox, and, in the best sense of the term, perversion. The curious difference, though, where trans-folks often need to be recognized for their gender resignifications, queer femmes often rearticulate sexual scripts and do not receive enough credit for that very political work. That is, to be very specific, as a trans guy it is extremely important to me to be seen as male whereas for my femme partner, it's far more important for her to be seen as lesbian. My partner is a woman of African descent, which means that, because of our impoverished and anti-intersectional economies, a battle of dualities plays out on her body to claim her—through identification or disidentification—either as "Black" or "queer" (but rarely both) in No Man's Land. This is not her battle but a battle over how her body is being read. The signifiers most easily read as femme and/or lesbian in our culture are those of White femininity. Lesbians of colour, including many femmes and butches, have written extensively about the whiteness of gay, lesbian, bisexual, and trans language, signifiers, histories, and so on. The semiotic deficiencies of subjectivity within White supremacy disallow signifying as Black and femme simultaneously. For my partner, visibility is frequently conditional: either she is read as her sexuality or she is read as her race. Being a racialized, gendered, and sexualized subject all at the same time is seen as unthinkable within our current paradigms of identity, which privilege—indeed, demand—singularity of identification. Models of intersectionality, which allow me, for instance, to read myself as raced (White, British), gendered (masculine), and sexualized (hetero-gendered and queerly straight) all at the same time are still sadly missing in our political lexicons. If FtMs wear masculinity as what Jay Prosser calls a second skin in order to feel visible and, strangely, invisible at the same time, femmes, on the other hand, wear a queer gendered-ness as a second skin that renders them invisible as lesbians. Femmes of colour, to risk an awkward phrase, are hailed as racialized subjects, which can render them invisible as queers *inside* queer communities. Each of these is accomplished through a triangulation, each through the other, and tells us that despite the work we have done, we have still so much more to do.

One of the most significant things I have done to unmake this supposedly femininely signified body is to have top surgery to remove my breasts. On June 9, 2003, I underwent top surgery, a euphemism for a surgical procedure properly known as bilateral mastectomy with male chest reconstruction. As I sat at my desk several days after the procedure, I wore a wide binder around my now scrawny-looking white chest. Underneath that binder, strangely similar to one I had worn when I wanted to bind my breasts, are two lateral scars where those breasts used to sit. Just above those scars are my nipples, grafted onto my newly configured chest but still healing under dressings to ensure that the grafts take. To be clear, in this procedure, the graft (the nipples) are removed completely from the skin. Once the breast tissue is removed, the nipples are then reattached as grafts. After about two weeks, the "new" nipples have attached again to the skin, only this time in a new position on the newly configured chest. But the *metaphor* of grafting is an interesting one and all too relevant to what I have just come through in this "transition."

I prefer the trope of "grafting" to "transition" because it allows me to reconfigure what I mean by trans-gender or trans-sexual. All too often, the relation between the "trans" and either "gender" or "sexual" is misread to mean that one transcends the other or that trans people, in essence, are surgically and hormonally given "new" bodies. That is, the terms "trans-gender" or "trans-sexual" are often misread to suggest a radical departure from birth bodies into squeaky clean new ones. But the terms are often misread as transcending the gender of those birth bodies into an entirely new gender. I counter that belief in my earlier book *Masculinities without Men?* but also now on and through my body; indeed, even more so now since my nipples were literally grafted back onto my chest: neither of these misreadings is as helpful as they could be.[7] My *gender* now looks different from the one I grew up with but my body is, paradoxically, almost still the same. I have the same scars, the same stretch marks, the same bumps, bruises, and birthmarks that I have always had, only it is all different now. Grafting allows me to think that relation. Not only does this trope allow me to look at the way my "new" body is grafted out of, onto, through my "old," but it is also a way of rethinking trans-gendered (read: differently gendered) bodies as effects of the sex/gender system in crisis and transition. It means my newish-looking gender is the effect of a productive failure of that manufacturing system, not its success. In those failings, trans men can become "men" in some contexts; some, but not all. But neither do trans-sexual and trans-gender folks transcend the sex/gender system; instead, trans folks are an important site where its inabilities, as Judith Butler argues, to live up to its own imperatives (that gender be the artifact of sex) are rendered obvious.

The process of grafting, as self-remaking and queer reproduction outside of a heteronormative model, spawns (certainly for FtMs) something else outside of our sexual vocabularies and grammars. But this is not androgyny, a mix, or blending of both (read: natural) genders. As Doan (1994: 153) puts it, "the notion of hybridity resonates with doing violence to nature, which results [...] in the scientific equivalent of freaks, mongrels, half-breeds and crossbreeds." This is a strategy of naturally denaturalizing biological essentialisms with a "sexual politics of heterogeneity and a vision of hybridized gender constructions outside an either/or proposition" in order to naturalize "cultural oddities, monstrosities, abnormalities, and [what appear to be] conformities" (Doan 1994: 154). The trope of grafting thus allows me to articulate the paradox signalled by "I am a lesbian man" or "I am a guy who is half lesbian." This picture of transed bodies as grafted, where one materialization is haunted by the other, as opposed to crossing or exiting, also allows me to articulate the radical dependencies that these identities (lesbian and trans guy or, to update the lexicon, female masculinity and trans-sexual masculinity) have for me but also with each other historically (the invert + the lesbian + the trans-sexual). To say "I am a lesbian man" or "I am a guy who is half lesbian" both materializes or externalizes a body that is not always immediately visible yet is still absolutely necessary for the performative paradox to work. It means to answer "yes" to "Am I that name?"[8] and to amend the question so that it reads multiply instead of singularly: "Am I this and that at the same time?" Thus, intelligibility for the female-to-male trans-sexual man means contesting the alignment of bodies, genders, and sexualities to force a crisis by grafting articulations onto each other in the same way that my nipple grafts work. I remember the day I heard a trans man say about his former breasts: "It's such a paradox to have to cut some part of myself off in order to feel whole." Those words are inscribed painfully across my chest today more than ever, but make no mistake: this is the body not as foundation but as archive; this is the same chest, the same body, the same flesh I have always known, only now its text is totally different.[9]

For all my bravado around top surgery, one of the things I have learned through the process is that these are costly choices. Certainly they are costly financially and now that many provincial governments have de-listed these services, trans folks are left to their own devices to pay for vital procedures. In addition, there's something about going to my extremely trans-friendly doctor that I find profoundly disturbing. My anxiety traces a particular distress around the medically overdetermined conditions of embodiment. This is still the medicalization of bodies, genders, and lives, and as much as the diagnosis "gender identity disorder" is a formal alibi, it still reflects the reality that trans folks are forced to make the best choices for ourselves in a field of overdetermined possibilities. Even though Toronto's Clarke Institute is no longer the sole gatekeeper of sex-reassignment procedures, the job of dispensing hormone therapies and giving referrals to surgeons, etc., still rests with usually non-transed physicians. And the means of rendering oneself intelligible, which is especially true for FtMs who do not achieve full embodiment of their chosen gender, is still the clinical alibi of "gender identity disorder."

That said, politically, the pressure to complete paperwork to change my former F to an M is tremendous. While I signify a version of White masculinity, I have chosen to keep the F. The existence of that F, though, has led me to draw some rather interesting conclusions about its limits. When I have handed that document over to various individuals, most people seem to pay little attention, if any, to the F. I am often, because of my gender presentation, disidentified with that F. Similarly, my image of myself as masculine is becoming reoriented in the process as well. Such incommensurability between self and body is the No Man's Land in which transed lives are lived. While medicalized interventions render this gap less dangerous, they do not, at least for FtMs, render the gap non-existent. Since my surgery, I am aware that I signify quite differently and that I need to transform my own consciousness to keep up. I now find myself asking what kind of *guy* am I presenting because masculinity on the perception of a male body is quite different than masculinity on the perception of a female body. But I am still a guy with an F designation. This discursive contradiction, paradox even, allows me, as Duggan and McHugh suggest (1996: 110) in the "Fem(me)inist Manifesto," to "inhabit normal abnormally." It means, as the best feminist interventions have always told us, that I need to be painfully aware of how I signify, of what kinds of power accrue to my whiteness and masculinity, and then work against both of those to challenge those power grids. It means, as a White man, outing myself whenever and wherever possible as a race traitor, not because I am partnered with a woman of colour but because of my commitment to an antiracist critical practice that includes doing the pedagogical work of challenging racism among other straight White men. Who better to occupy the space of *guy* but former lesbians who have walked the streets as women, loved as fierce and sometimes stone butches, and who have come of political age in the context of lesbian-feminism? For me, that's a proud history that does not get left behind in the operating room.

But it is precisely *because* of that same gender performance that some lesbians, on the other hand, have expressed frustration when I, a straight White man, appear in lesbian (although not lesbian/woman only) spaces. The most pernicious of these chills occurred at United Kingdom 2: International Drag King Show, a trans-friendly and literate event produced in Toronto that showcases drag king performances from across North America and, this year, Amsterdam. The irony resonates strongly: at an event that offers female and trans masculinity for consumption, I passed so well as a non-transed person—indeed, as just a straight White guy—that my presence was troubling to one young woman in particular who felt little discomfort about communicating her disapproval. That chill was repeated a number of other times during Toronto's Dyke March day (I did not go on the dyke march) so that I quite aggressively hunted down a t-shirt that would, at the very least, dis-identify my seemingly heterosexual masculinity with heteronormativity.

That said, then, if it is possible to render my masculinity anti-heteronormative, then might it also be possible to remake whiteness, not necessarily just self-conscious but similarly incoherent? That is, if I've been suggesting that trans men risk incoherence, can White masculinity also risk incoherence as a political strategy, one that refuses the hegemonic bargains offered to White trans manhood? White masculinity is, of course, an intersection of parts where a fantasy of singularity is privileged instead. [For] James Baldwin, whiteness, is secured by its violent imperative of universal, categorical singularity (that is, non-intersectionality). Trans manhood has the ability to exist on a similar frequency as biological masculinity without the coherence or clarity of meaning. Trans White masculinity is key for its failure to cohere [...] into hegemonic or visible *matter*. (Again, simile is key here.) Dionne Brand presents a similar argument about this in her work, *A Map to the Door of No Return*, when she writes of bodies as matter being socially constructed with extremely potent stakes:

> There are ways of constructing the world—that is, of putting it together each morning, what it should look like piece by piece—and I don't feel that I share that with the people of this small town. Each morning I think we wake up and open our eyes and set the particles of forms together—we make solidity with our eyes and with the matter in our brains. [...] We collect each molecule, summing them up into "flesh" or "leaf" or "water" or "air." Before that everything is liquid, ubiquitous and mute. We accumulate information over our lives which brings various things into solidity, into view. What I am afraid of is that waking up in another room, minutes away by car, the mechanic wakes up and takes my face for a target [...] He cannot see me when I come into the gas station; he sees something else [...] as if I do not exist [...] or as if something he cannot understand has arrived—as if something he despises has arrived. A thing he does not recognize. Some days when I go to the gas station [...] I drive through the possibility of losing solidity at any moment. (Brand 2002: 141–42)

Brand argues for race what Fausto-Sterling and Butler argue about sex and gender and what I want to advocate as a trans practice of masculinity:

> To be material is to speak about the process of materialization. And if viewpoints about [identity] are already embedded in our philosophical concepts of how matter forms into bodies, the matter of bodies cannot form a neutral, pre-existing ground from which to understand the origin of [...] different. Since matter already contains notions of [identity], it cannot be a neutral recourse on which to build "scientific" or "objective" theories of [the trans subject] ... the idea of the material comes to us

> already tainted, containing within it pre-existing ideas about [identity] … the body as a system […] simultaneously produces and is produced by social meanings. (Fausto-Sterling 2000: 22–23)

Entrance into these fictionalities of matter, of coherent White skin, is purchased through an ideological belief in a naturalized whiteness and naturalized masculinity. The reading of a body as gendered male and racialized White involves presenting signifiers within an economy where the signifiers accumulate toward the appearance of a coherently gendered and racialized body.

Baldwin's work on the price of the White ticket is crucial here. "White people are not white," writes James Baldwin (1985: xiv), "part of the price of the white ticket is to delude themselves into believing that they are." […] Entrance into the fictionality of whiteness is purchased through an ideological class belief in naturalized whiteness. What White is, then, is a class-based race: the higher up you go, the whiter you get. One is not born White, one buys his or her way into whiteness and *becomes* White. That price, Baldwin writes, includes, necessitates even, believing in the fiction of whiteness as signifier of the universal subject, the just plain, simple, and singular Man and Woman. But the price is afforded by what later theorists of whiteness will call its psychological and social wages: skin colour and class (upward) mobility. This is what the men and women of my ancestry purchased for me off the labour of their class-based whiteness (what I previously called off-White, White, but not middle-class White): entrance, as an educated adult, into a whitened middle class. While I grew up on welfare, we became *whiter* through the generations.

While I am no longer working class (the transition into that whitened middle class was a far harder transition for me than "changing" genders), I continue to be very aware of a rising discourse of whiteness, which, as some writers detail, is racializing class-based whiteness in what seem to me to be all the wrong ways. Five years ago I would have argued that self-consciousness for White people could be anything but wrong. But as many race theorists have taught us, White supremacy, like other colonial systems, is historical and amenable to new circumstances and critique. In the last few decades, there has been a huge proliferation of thinking and writing about whiteness. […]

The first cultural theorist whose work is seminal to whiteness scholarship is film critic Richard Dyer. In 1988, he published an extremely important essay simply called "White." In that early essay (subsequently published later as part of a full-length book of the same name), Dyer enacts a theoretical shift that enables us to ask the questions about whiteness that we are asking today. This shift shares much in common with the contradictions about sexuality detailed by Eve Sedgwick in *Epistemology of the Closet* (1990). Questions about race and sexuality have been bound by a set of epistemological contradictions: on the one hand, some questions of identity race theory have been conservatively constructed as what Sedgwick calls a *minoritizing* discourse (seeing that identity as an issue of active importance only for a small, distinct, relatively fixed group, like Caribbean-Canadians or First Nations peoples, for instance). On the other hand, what we need to do instead is to retheorize race and sexuality as what Sedgwick dubs a "universalizing discourse," an issue or discourse of active importance in the lives of subjects across the spectrum of identity categories. This particular shift in thinking allows us, like Dyer and Sedgwick in their work, to ask particular kinds of questions about whiteness and heterosexuality, questions that shift the critical gaze from the so-called racialized object (Black people, etc.) to the so-called racial subject (White folks doing the looking). In other words, instead of allowing the White critical gaze to look and taxonomize colours or cultures, a universalizing discourse allows us to turn the gaze back onto whiteness. And shifting that gaze is exactly what Dyer's essay accomplishes. Where race theory interrogates the production of racialized identities, critical whiteness studies examines the ways that whiteness *qua* whiteness has somehow been left out of those terms.

[...] One of the consequences of allowing whiteness to remain unmarked as a race, as Dyer suggests, is that whiteness becomes the norm. Whiteness, in other words, constructs itself as coterminous with the endless plenitude of human diversity, with the non-particularizable general. [...] What this means is that whiteness remains so entirely hyper-visible as everything that it also becomes, paradoxically, invisible as nothing, the norm, as an invisible backdrop against which all other races are produced. It also means that whiteness was not a found category but one that was historically invented and/or constructed.

What's at stake in a particular set of arguments [made by Frankenberg] is a denaturalization of whiteness. That is, denaturalizing whiteness means to universalize whiteness, not as the norm but as just another race among a spectrum of racial identities that could do the work of articulating both whiteness and antiracism work differently, albeit another race with systemic power. As I began to research, [...] I realized that whiteness, like many of the things I have been exploring in this work, has a history and representational currency. Thinking through representations of whiteness in popular culture and fiction allows me to argue not just the persistence of racism around us but also the ways in which identities can either challenge or be complicit with that persistence. [...]

Whiteness will always force its subjects to privilege their own unmarked invisibilities over any other marker of "difference" among its subjects (class, gender, and sexuality). But the price of becoming White is quite different than the price and, or, more accurately, the cost of knowing one is White. These two things are not exactly the same thing at all; *becoming* White means that one is no longer aware of oneself as a race and believes that one simply melts into the amorphous mass of the norm; *knowing* one is White means understanding oneself as a product of White supremacy or systemic racism that is larger than one individual and that also precedes our entry into the public domain. How can whiteness be used to dismantle that larger system? [...]

[Annalee] Newitz argues that there are some forms of whiteness that have had a particular kind of visibility. In her thesis, she argues further that one way we might understand White racial identity at the close of the 20th century is as a social construction characterized most forcefully by a growing awareness of its own internal contradictions and a growing deployment of class divisions within whiteness. These are manifested in White-on-White class conflicts that produce a White racial self-consciousness based on various forms of divisiveness and self-loathing. White consciousness, she argues, emerges as a distinct and visible racial identity when it can be identified as class or as primitive, inhuman, and, ironically, hyper-visible: poor White trash. She continues to suggest that lower-class whiteness functions as a racially marked identity (Newitz 1997: 138). Whites who are not "trash" seem innocent of racially marked whiteness. Poor Whites are, in other words, less White and guilty of a "savagery" that upper-class Whites have transcended.

At the same time this particular deflection and deferral can be converted into what Newitz calls a confession of whiteness or a racialized look or positioning of redemption, a gesture of concern that will give us the appearance of innocence or redemption as White but which takes the place of real action to eliminate social injustice (Newitz 1997: 139). It becomes, in other words, a form of self-punishment that gets played out within and among White groups, producing a White nihilism. Nihilism was a doctrine that denied purpose, hope, a larger order, and that translated quickly into the self-destructive behaviours we've seen before. In a racial context, it is the actualization of what she argues is at the core of White supremacy to begin with: fear, inferiority, and failure. "When whites," she argues, "are put in touch with that fear, a kind of self-destructive nihilism results" (Newitz 1997: 139). This then converts into a pre-emptive self-hatred. Whites, in her estimation, imagine themselves as people of colour might and then name themselves preemptively to circumvent the power of being named by others. "One might understand these narratives," she argues, "as fantasies about whites resolving their racial problems without ever having to deal with people of colour" (Newitz 1997: 139). This is, in other words, a form of psychological defence, one that is racist and "a politically reactionary form of ideological defense" (Newitz 1997: 144). No one, after all, can insult you if you insult yourself first.

[...] I have been suggesting all along that the labour of making oneself—indeed, of becoming a man—is fraught with responsibilities that go with the territory whether we know it or not. This labour is not unlike the labour of capitalized waged work, especially when, as the whiteness theorists have told us, whiteness accrues with it an additional social and psychological wage. The question then is less how much of ourselves do we sell with intention and more how much we are willing to articulate our bodies against the hegemonic bargain offered to us. For me, that is the measure of the privilege of masculinity without also being The Man.

I like to think that my grandmother and her co-workers understood something of these stakes as working-class and union women. If class and race are the subject of invention and ideological production, then theorizing trans-sexual issues as *labour* also does not seem that strange to me. In many ways, that's precisely the argument of this book. Gender identities—that is, gendered selves—are the product of, but also condition, particular kinds of labour. If the sex/gender system works, like any other ideological system, through misrecognition where we misperceive ourselves as natural human beings rather than as ideologically produced subjects, then it requires, as many theorists have pointed out, our complicit co-operation in order to accomplish that misrecognition. One of the rewards of that activity is the belief in a natural gender that is not man-made. Feminism has been arguing now for over a century that active insubordination with the imperatives of that system is one of the ways to make change happen and to refuse to allow that system to accomplish itself. A new century demands that feminism also begin to acknowledge its own complicity with the biological essentialisms at the core of the sex/gender systems. If it is true that gender identities are acts of coproduction, then the process of becoming a self, of making a self, which is so much a part of what trans-identities tell us, is also labour that can be used against the sex/gender system. A North Carolina drag king named Pat Triarch calls gender queers and trans folks "deconstruction workers," who, by quite literally putting misfitting bodies on the (dis-assembly) line, begin to resist and rebuild the *man-made* gender imperatives that pass as those of nature. These bodies are not bodies as foundation but trans-bodies as archive, witness, risking political incoherence.

Notes

1. The pedantic distinction between "trans-gender" and "trans-sexual" cannot hold, especially for female-to-male trans-sexual men for whom surgeries are always incomplete. To avoid being repetitive here, I used the prefix *trans-* to signify subjectivities where bodies are at odds with gender presentation, regardless of whether that misalignment is self-evident in conventional ways or not. The entire question of what's visible, when, how, and by whom is precisely what is at stake in this chapter, so policing or prescribing or hierarchizing kinds of political embodiment is a topical identity politic and moral panic that I eschew.
2. I am not claiming to be outside of White supremacy, nor am I claiming that somehow working-class whiteness is not White. What I am trying to explore here is the possibility within intersectionality of different kinds of whiteness, positioned at different angles to power in White supremacy, where the type of power is mitigated by overlapping and intersecting vectors of power by class, able-bodied-ness, sexuality, gender, and so forth. But the relation to racialized power is constant and I am not at all suggesting otherwise.
3. There is a curious and undertheorized history of what has come to be known as the "self-help discourse"; there was a time in early second wave feminism, due to the work of rape crisis and battered women's/shelter activists/workers, when recovering from the trauma and violence of the sex/gender system was an inherently political act of resistance. Hegemonic appropriations of these ideas rearticulated this notion of a reconfigured self in extremely conservative ways: self is what cosmetic procedures provide ("The Swan"); it's the product of an upper-class leisure-time activity (in most recent years, "Oprah"); self is what's taken up by the beauty myths and also what's used as an advertising strategy (see Subway's new campaign for lighter food consumption, which shows several people stating why they prefer Subway's new light menu, including a young, blonde, White woman from the anorexia demographic saying "I choose to actually eat"); a newly configured self is what Dr. Phil's diet campaign berates and shames folks into becoming. One of the few feminist texts to begin examining this history is Ann Cvetkovich's (2003) *An Archive of Feelings: Trauma, Sexuality and Lesbian Public Cultures.*
4. This is, of course, the primary trope and political rallying cry of Leslie Feinberg's (1991) novel, *Stone Butch Blues*, one of the most important working-class and trans narratives to call for a practice of strategic unmaking.

5. The CUPE 3903 Women's Caucus has not only counted trans-sexual women amongst its members, but in a truly unprecedented intervention in this border war, recently changed its name (it is now the "Trans Identified and Women Identified" Caucus) to create space for trans-sexual men as well. It is clear that this local is able to fold the concerns of its trans-sexual and trans-gendered members into its mandate as issues of labour, not "life-style" as the Ontario Conservative government has so deemed.
6. The work of this section owes a debt to OmiSoore H. Dryden, my partner, with whom I have spent many pleasurable hours in delightful conversation.
7. *Masculinities without Men?* (2004).
8. This is an allusion to Denise Riley's (1988) extremely important work, *"Am I That Name?": Feminism and the Category of "Women" in History.*
9. See Ann Cvetkovich, *An Archive of Feelings.* On the relation between trauma and counter-cultural resistance movements as an archive or record of trauma but also of resistance, Cvetkovich (2003: 20) writes: "I am interested [...] in the way trauma digs itself in at the level of the everyday, and in the incommensurability of large-scale events and the ongoing material details of experience ... I hope to seize authority over trauma discourses from medical and scientific discourse in order to place it back in the hands of those who make culture, as well as to forge new models for how affective life can serve as the foundation for public but counter-cultural archive as well."

References

Allison, Dorothy. 1994. *Skin: Talking about Sex, Class and Literature.* Ithaca: Firebrand Books.

Bagnell, Kenneth. 1980. *The Little Immigrants: The Orphans Who Came to Canada.* Toronto: Macmillan of Canada.

Baldwin, James. 1985. *The Price of the Ticket: Collected Nonfiction, 1948–1985.* New York: St. Martin's Press.

Brand, Dionne. 2002. *A Map to the Door of No Return.* Toronto: Coach House.

Butler, Judith. 1990. *Gender Trouble: Feminism and the Subversion of Identity.* New York and London: Routledge, Chapman & Hall, Inc.

Cameron, Loren. 1996. *Body Alchemy: Transsexual Portraits.* Pittsburgh: Cleis Press.

Camilleri, Anna. 2004. *I Am a Red Dress: Incantations on a Grandmother, a Mother, and a Daughter.* Vancouver: Arsenal Pulp Press.

Cvetkovich, Ann. 2003. *An Archive of Feelings: Trauma, Sexuality and Lesbian Public Cultures.* Durham: Duke University Press.

Doan, Laura. 1994. "Jeanette Winterson's Sexing the Postmodern." In *The Lesbian Postmodern,* edited by Laura Doan, 137–55. New York: Columbia University Press.

Duggan, Lisa, and Kathleen McHugh. 1996. "A Fem(me)inist Manifesto." *Women & Performance: A Journal of Feminist Theory* 8, no. 2: 107–10.

Dyer, Richard. 1988. "white" *Screen* 29, no. 4: 44–64.

Eugenides, Jeffrey. 2002. *Middlesex.* Toronto: Random House.

Fausto-Sterling, Anne. 2000. *Sexing the Body: Gender Politics and the Construction of Sexuality.* New York: Basic Books.

Feinberg, Leslie. 1991. *Stone Butch Blues.* Ithaca, NY: Firebrand.

Frankenberg, Ruth. 1993. *White Women, Race Matters: The Social Construction of Whiteness.* Minneapolis: University of Minnesota Press.

hooks, bell. 2000. *Where We Stand: Class Matters.* New York and London: Routledge.

Newitz, Annalee. 1997. "White Savagery and Humiliation, or a New Racial Consciousness in the Media." In *White Trash: Race and Class in America*, edited by Matt Wray and Annalee Newitz, 131–54. New York: Routledge.

Noble, Jean Bobby. 2004. *Masculinities without Men?* Vancouver: University of British Columbia Press.

Prosser, Jay. 1998. *Second Skins: The Body Narratives of Transsexuality.* New York: Columbia University Press.

Riley, Denise. 1988. *"Am I That Name?": Feminism and the Category of "Women" in History.* Houndmills: Macmillan Press.

Sedgwick, Eve Kosofsky. 1990. *Epistemology of the Closet.* Berkeley and Los Angeles: University of California Press.

CHAPTER 32

Sexual Ethics and Young Women's Accounts of Heterosexual Casual Sex

Melanie A. Beres and Panteá Farvid

Recently, Foucault's work on ethics and sexuality has been used to discuss the possibilities for exploring and cultivating an "ethical erotics" (Carmody, 2003, 2005, 2009). Such a focus not only allows space for the multiplicity and fluidity of sexual relations, but can also offer great possibilities for the primary prevention of sexual violence. Foucault's articulation of ethics has been used by Carmody (2005) to explore the sexual stories of adults of a variety of ages and sexual orientations and she found evidence that many exhibited sexual ethics within their sexual relationships, including their casual sex experiences. In addition, her latest work (Carmody, 2009) provides a number of examples where young people have successfully learnt and put into practice an ethical approach in their casual and ongoing relationships. In this article we follow and extend such a contention with our analysis of young women's casual sex experiences. We focus on what Foucault calls *rapport à soi* (the relationship one has with one's self) to explore reports of practices of casual sex as they relate to sexual ethics. Our main focus and interest is in showing how dominant gendered discourses of heterosexuality are implicated in and at times impede an ethics of casual sex.

Foucault and (Sexual) Ethics

Much of Foucault's work on ethics is part of his later works in *The History of Sexuality: An Introduction* and *The History of Sexuality: The Use of Pleasure* (Davidson, 2005). Foucault saw ethics as the component of morality that concerns a person's relationship with the self. In *The History of Sexuality: The Use of Pleasure* Foucault makes a distinction between morality—a set of rules and actions that are "permitted" in a given society, and ethics—the practice of self-formation (Foucault, 1985). He argues that "Freedom is the ontological condition of ethics. But ethics is the considered form that freedom takes when it is informed by reflection" (Rabinow, 1997: 284). Furthermore, practices of freedom (or ethics) require a degree of liberation. Foucault recognizes that power plays an important role in the possibilities of a practice of ethics because of constraints of freedom (Rabinow, 1997). Although power relations are negotiated in a dynamic way, it is particularly pertinent to consider the application of ethics to groups whose power, "freedom," or autonomy have been more constrained by unequal and gendered power relations. Some groups, more than others, are constrained in the practice of ethics, due to, but not dictated by, gender, class, and race differentials.

When explaining the practice of ethics Foucault uses the notion of *rapport à soi*, or the care of the self. He defines *rapport à soi* as being the kind of relationship one *ought* to have with oneself—that is, how individuals are "supposed" to constitute themselves as moral subjects of their own actions within any given society (Rabinow, 1997). The relationship that a person has with him or herself requires not only knowledge of the self but "self-reflection." This reflection requires that individuals reflect not only on how they feel about a particular act, their desires, and pleasures, but also reflect on how dominant cultural representations (or discourses) of sexuality have an impact on their own understanding of sexuality. Alongside such reflections, critiques of dominant constructions of sexuality also indicate a particular reflexive engagement with a person's sexuality that is not only indicative of sexual ethics, but also opens up space for the subversion of dominant heteronormative discourses of sex. So the "care for the self" implies ethical behaviour because to care for the self implies complex social relations. [...]

In this article we overlay Foucault's articulation of sexual ethics with a feminist critical analysis of heterosexual practices. [...] In our analysis, we draw on Hollway's (1989) description of heteronormative discourses of sexuality. These include the "male sexual drive" discourse (which suggests that men have a biologically insatiable desire for sex, are forever in search of sex, and once aroused are seen as *needing* sexual gratification via coitus and orgasm); the "have/hold" discourse (which positions sex within the context of a monogamous relationship, where women are the subjects of this discourse and are seeking committed relationships through sex); and the "permissive discourse" (where it becomes possible for both men and women to participate in sex outside of a committed relationship and pursue sexual pleasure, but the version of sex that is upheld is one that is imbedded within the male sex drive discourse). Through these discourses, a restrictive set of subjectivities becomes available to women (and men) with little space for female-centred sexual activity or sexual activity that does not promote phallocentric (male) sexuality (Potts, 2000).

Casual sex in particular is a contested site of gendered relations and those who participate in casual sex are often constructed as irresponsible and reckless. In particular, women's participation in casual sex has been construed as problematic and at times unacceptable. Even in this current "pro-sex" era (where programmes like *Sex and the City* have somewhat "mainstreamed" women's participation in casual sex), the prevalence of a "sexual double standard" (see Crawford and Popp, 2003) means that young women who openly engage in casual sex are often labelled as promiscuous and/or blamed for any associated negative consequences.

In the following analysis we apply Foucault's model of sexual ethics to young women's accounts of heterosexual casual sex. We explore what is represented as appropriate conduct in relation to women's casual sex and how Foucault's understanding of the "care for the self," "self-reflection," and "care for the other" were implicated in the stories we were told.

Eliciting Stories

This article presents the analysis of two data sets collected independently by the authors for two separate and unrelated projects. Both projects focused on an in-depth analysis of young adults' experiences of heterosexual casual sex. One project explored young women's and men's experiences of casual sex and focused on understanding how young adults communicated and interpreted their partners' desire to have sex and how they interpreted consent. Only the interviews with the women were used for the analysis here. This project took place in a small resort community in Canada. In-depth interviews were conducted with 11 women (aged 19–25) in 2005. All but one participant were White, one identified as Black, and all were middle-class. All but one were from English-speaking parts of Canada and one woman was from Quebec, the predominantly French province.

The second project, conducted by the second author in New Zealand, explored young heterosexual women's ideas and experiences relating to casual sex. In-depth interviews were conducted with 15 women (aged 19–25) in 2004. Interviews covered a range of topics including definitions of casual sex, the women's experiences of casual sex, and societal perceptions of casual sex. Of the 15 participants interviewed, 10 identified as Pākehā New Zealanders,[1] two as Māori, one as Pākehā/Māori, one as Pākehā/Samoan, and one as New Zealand Chinese. Although the participants came from a variety of ethnic backgrounds, most were tertiary educated and middle class.

[...] In our analysis, we approach the data from a social constructionist perspective (Burr, 2003). While "information about the social world is achievable through in depth interviews" (Miller and Glassner, 1997: 99) and through this dialogue we can explore how people create meanings around particular social practices, we understand "experience" itself as socially and culturally produced. Therefore the women's accounts are not taken as an indicator of what "really" happened, but as a socially constructed exchange within the interview setting. While we are not denying a material reality within which experiences may have occurred, we are not looking to present these stories as "truths" about such a reality (Yardley, 1997). We are more interested in how aspects of sexual ethics played out in the women's reported experiences and the broader gendered discourses of heterosexuality that shape these accounts. Although there were many similarities between the two studies, there were also some important differences in the recruitment style and interview focus. These differences did not relate to the broad analytic focus of this article (i.e., sexual ethics), thus we do not carry out a direct comparison of stories from the two countries.

In this article we have done an in-depth analysis of the ways in which sexual ethics played out in women's stories of heterosexual casual sex and the meanings ascribed to such practices. In particular we approached the data looking at how the women talked about "care for the self," how they reflected on past casual sex experiences, and accounts of "caring for the other." We also noted talk that reflected a lack of care for self or that highlighted constraints on women's abilities to care for themselves in more positive ways. While our focus is on the ways in which participants' talk about casual sex expresses elements of self-care and *rapport à soi*, it is not our intention to label any experience, behaviour, or persons as inherently ethical or unethical. Rather, we use this analysis to explore the issue of sexual ethics within this specific context to offer insight into some of the ways that women express a form of agency and self-reflection around their sexual desires, pleasures, and acts that may disrupt and/or reify traditional heteronormative discourses.

Defining Casual Sex

In both projects, we allowed the participants to describe what they understood as "casual sex," and were given similar definitions. A variety of scenarios were considered casual sex, ranging from one-time sexual experiences with someone a woman had met that day, to a long-term sexual arrangement outside of a "committed" relationship, to sex with an ex-boyfriend. In line with previous research (Oliver and Sedikides 1992; Paul et al., 2000; Weaver and Herold, 2000), the main element of casual sex was depicted as its "uncommitted" nature. Sexual practices included mainly penis–vagina intercourse, but coitus was not the only "act" that rendered a sexual encounter as "casual sex"; oral sex (for both partners), or other forms of sexual play and touching, were also usually defined as casual sex.

Sexual Ethics and Women's Account of Heterosexual Casual Sex

We begin the analysis with a discussion of the ways that women's talk reflected "care for the self." Women expressed self-care in different ways throughout different casual sex contexts. Forms of self-care included "setting limits," accounts of satisfying their own desires, accounts of knowing "what they want," and differing forms of "self-preservation." We discuss these respectively, then turn to accounts of self-reflection and care for the other.

SELF-CARE

According to Foucault, "care for the self" is the fulcrum of ethical sexual behaviour as it implies "care for the other" (Rabinow, 1997). Self-care was explicitly evident in some women's reports of "setting limits" in casual sex. This was either in reports of activities they participated in or enforced (such as condom use), or the contexts in which they were willing to participate in casual sex:

> *Agnes:* Now I like have this thing where I won't sleep with guys on the first date, just because I don't like the feeling of being used the next day and for me that's a really big thing, and so, but this guy ... we hooked up one night and then, I wouldn't sleep with him, so the next night, he ended up spending the night and I slept with him and then he never talked to me again. And so now, like even that little theory of mine, is totally like ... blown out the window. (Canada)

[...] Agnes reflects on her emotional reaction to some of her other sexual experiences, where being "ignored" after having sex with someone on a first date led to setting certain limits on the context within which she would engage in (casual) sex. Her account is also situated within a traditional heterosexual framework of women as "gatekeepers" of sex, and responsible for managing men's sexual desires (see O'Sullivan and Byers, 1992; Tolman, 2002; Gavey, 2005). Reports like Agnes' of setting limits to protect one's emotional needs in casual sex were often less successful than setting limits to protect health or physical needs. For example, while Agnes reports successfully imposing particular limits on her sexual partners (not engaging in intercourse during the first sexual encounter), this did not have the intended effect. Her account is a good example of how women negotiate competing subject positions within the permissive and have/hold discourses—both of which are embedded in heteronormative practices of sex that have limited capacity for the exercise of power and "freedom" in relation to sexual ethics.

These versions of "care for the self," where women are placing limits on sexual activity, remain embedded in dominant discourses of heterosexuality. While women's reports of imposing limits can be seen as indicative of "care for the self," and as a useful strategy considering the limited subject positions offered through heteronormative discourses, they offer limited scope for the subversions of such discourses. Some women were able to open up space for subversion by exercising other versions of self-care. This was evident in discussions with some women about pleasure and casual sex:

> *Karen:* I don't mind like, like helping myself get off when I'm having sex 'cause some guys are good at it, some guys know how to do it, and you don't have to worry about it, but some guys are totally clueless, especially maybe not so experienced guys and so I don't have an issue at all with for me it's for me and I know that I don't have a problem with [saying] I want to do this, I want to do that. (Canada)

In this account, Karen presents herself as knowledgeable about what she finds pleasurable in sex and said she will not hesitate to pleasure herself if she is not getting what she wants from a sexual encounter (although she does not elaborate on what this pleasure is). She labels some (inexperienced) men as naïve when it comes to providing this pleasure and herself as the agent in such situations where she describes herself as comfortable enough to ask for what she "wants." In a heteronormative context that privileges men's pleasure, it is perhaps not surprising to hear women talk about achieving pleasure as a deliberate act on their (and sometimes their partner's) part. By taking care of her own pleasure, Karen begins to disrupt heteronormative assumptions about sex and takes up an agentic sexual subject position.

Women's stories that reflected this type of "care for the self," where they expressed a sense of control over the casual sex situation, were often presented as mutually desired sexual experiences or experiences where the women were seeking casual sex. These women often relayed quite deliberate accounts of pursuing casual sex. Through seeking casual sex in this way the women challenged traditional versions of heterosexuality that depict women as passive recipients of men's sexual desires. However, in these accounts women still largely drew on a "drive" discourse to account for their desire for casual sex. While such accounts both disrupt and reinforce particular forms of normative heterosexuality, they still offer up disruptions and fissures to traditional constructions of (passive) female sexuality and depict a more agentic sexuality for women who engage in casual sex.

In contrast, some women depicted casual sex as sex that "just happened," with neither partner in control nor instigating the sexual exchange. Evident in such accounts was an expression of a lack of control over the women's casual sex experiences. These women reported methods of "care for the self" that included forms of "self-preservation." Self-preservation strategies, like other strategies, were often situated with gendered discourses of heterosexuality. However, in such accounts women did not necessarily challenge traditional ideals of heterosex, and their talk and management of casual sex were very much situated within such discourses. For example, a sexual double standard (where men who have many sexual partners are positively deemed as "studs," whilst women are negatively deemed as "sluts"; see Lees, 1993; Kitzinger, 1995; Jackson and Cram, 2003) was implicated unreflexively within such accounts. This type of self-care was directed at constructing the women's identity as a "good girl" and not "slutty." For example:

> *Karen:* Before I kind of, used my uncertainty of like, ahh, something to make me feel better. Oh I didn't go in looking for sex, I ... not had it forced on me but I was like, I don't know, I felt a little less of a slut if it wasn't something I really intended on doing, [if] it just happened. (Canada)

Karen's reflections resonate strongly with the "sex just happened" version of casual sex. Her account is indicative of a sexual double standard within casual sex (see Farvid, 2006), where an active and desiring female sexuality is positioned negatively. This account of "self-preservation" can be seen as strategic in the way it is used in day-to-day interactions for managing Karen's identity as a "good girl" (and not a slut) and allowing her to present a more "decent" story of casual sex. Her account is situated within more traditional discourses of "passive" feminine sexuality (see Gavey and McPhillips, 1999; Gavey, 2005).

Women who adopted a self-preservation approach to "care for the self" often spoke less positively about their casual sex experiences than women who expressed being in more control during casual sex encounters. Accounts where women talk of changing their behaviour to better care for themselves demonstrate an ethic of care and concern for the self, even if their accounts were heavily situated within and negotiated gendered discourses of heterosexuality.

SELF-REFLECTION

Some women we interviewed often implemented self-care strategies as a result of reflecting on their previous casual sex experiences. For example, it was after reflecting on the emotional cost of having sex with someone on a first "date" that Agnes decided to place limits on when she would have sex with someone for the first time. Some women went beyond a reflection on specific casual sex experiences and reflected on their desire for engaging in casual sex more broadly:

> *Anna:* I think every experience you have you sort of grow or develop or have, you know, start forming your opinions about things like now I know that I mean what is the point of having sex? Is it for physical or is it for, you know, for something else? So I start questioning my, my intentions for things (Int: yep) so I think just maturity-wise I think you sort of do grow a bit and you start just are you actually doing things for yourself? Or are you doing things for, you know, because this is what you think you should be doing? (New Zealand)

Anna talks of questioning where her "desire" for casual sex came from, and if it was physical (which is depicted as "ideal") or if she engaged in casual sex for "other" reasons. She questions whether it is something she "really" wants to do for herself, or something that she feels she *should* be doing. Here Anna demonstrates that "caring for the self" implies more than attention to immediate physical and/or emotional needs associated with casual sex. Anna's account was unique in questioning the notion that "sexually liberated" young women *should* now be engaging in (casual) sex.

While "care for the self" implies an understanding of one's intentions and desires for casual sex, including the physical and emotional consequences of sex, in order to produce an ethical sexuality, women also must reflect on how such acts are situated within a broader cultural context and informed by heteronormative discourses of sexuality (Carmody, 2005). Many participants in both countries demonstrated this type of self-reflection by questioning the sexual double standard. For example:

> *Melissa:* Guys can have sex with however many [girls] they want and they're y'know, they're perceived to be a stud or y'know like a, a great chick magnet or whatever, whereas girls can't do the same, and they just get labelled as like as slut, or y'know like a whore or anything like that so, you must've heard of Christina Aguillera's and 'Lil Kim's song um, "Can't Hold Us Down"? The lyrics they just talk about this exact thing, and it is one of my favourite songs because it is um, y'know I think it is quite disgusting how we get, um females get different labels from guys, and I think it's, I think it's very wrong! (New Zealand)

Like Melissa, many of the women problematized the sexual double standard, depicting it as inaccurate and unjust. Unlike the women who gave accounts of "sex just happened," these women positioned themselves as culturally aware of such double standards, and some unapologetically talked of pursuing casual sex and expressing desire for it, in spite of such a double standard. Such reflections on the sexual double standard represent moments of *rapport à soi*, where the women knowingly and actively problematized such cultural definitions. By questioning the sexual double standard, the women opened up discursive space for the disruption and resistance of such cultural imperatives.

Other women challenged gendered social expectations more broadly. For example, one woman reflected on the role of casual sex in her life and not only challenged gendered assumptions about sexuality, but also challenged broader cultural assumptions about women's priorities in life:

> *Cathy:* I guess it's just becoming a bit more acceptable that girls nowadays they've got different priorities. Like relationships aren't always the first priority. Like for me ... I'm more interested in the way I'm going with my career, so I sort of wanna head that way before I get into a relationship. Whereas in the old days, I think it was sort of get into a relationship then get into a career or not even have a career ... Like you can get different things from different people. You can get your emotional stuff from your closest friends, the physical stuff obviously from your casual sex. (New Zealand)

Here Cathy is actively reflecting on the life choices she's made. She portrays a romantic relationship as a potential impediment to the pursuit of her career. Her account disrupts the traditional notion of romantic relationships (with men) as the main focus of women's lives (articulated through the have/hold discourse) and rejects the cultural idea that a woman needs a relationship with a man to be complete. Cathy is deliberate in her account of how she gets a variety of perceived needs met, and describes using casual sex to meet her "physical" needs, while her relational needs are met through relationships with her friends. While other women also reported engaging in casual sex to meet their "sexual needs," this was often while they were in-between relationships. Many talked of not wanting a relationship—but still wanting to have sex. Cathy's account is fairly unique in that she was one of the few who articulated the role of casual sex in relation to other parts of her life, not limited to her sexual/relational desires.

"Self-reflection" played an important role in women's accounts of casual sex and was integral to the production of a sexual ethic within these accounts. Not all women contemplated the meaning of casual sex in relation to their broader life and career goals as did Cathy, but their contemplation at least allowed for the negotiation of casual sex experiences in ways to better "care for the self" and negotiate their needs and desires.

CARE FOR THE OTHER

The final important part of an ethics of sex is "care for the other." This was the sparsest area for demonstrations of an ethics of casual sex within our interview data. There were only a couple of women who talked quite deliberately about caring for the other. For example, Siena, a hepatitis B carrier, talked about the importance of ensuring her long-term casual sex partner wore condoms to protect himself from contracting the virus. Similarly, Julie would disclose her history of genital warts to her partners. While these women were focused on forms of "care" related to physical health, other women demonstrated "care for the other" differently. For example, Karen [...] reported concerns for [her] partner's emotional well-being and willingness to engage in casual sex.

> *Karen:* I know I wanted to have sex, like that was something that was going to happen for me. But I did ask him because I kinda felt ... just because I was so forward with it all the time, I just wanted to make sure he was along for the, like was there as well ... 'cause yeah, 'cause a lot of times I probably haven't been with the guy, and it just happened anyways, you just kind of follow along with the progression of things ... Like I asked him before we had sex, are you sure you're okay with this? And he was like, yeah! Like what the fuck, like why are you asking that question? (Canada)

In [this] account Karen [...] express[es] concern for [her] partner's willingness to engage in casual sex. After reflecting on some of her experiences of going along with casual sex, Karen reports asking her partner if he wanted to have sex to ensure that he was ready. Similarly, [a women named] Stacy talks of a concern for her partner's comfort. These unique accounts demonstrate "care for the other" in heterosexual casual sex encounters. These two women subtly disrupt the male sexual drive discourse by engaging in this type of checking. This disruption is quite evident in Karen's account of her male partner's shocked response. No other women questioned their partner's desire or readiness for casual sex in this way. Considering the prevalence of the male sexual drive discourse, it is not surprising that there were relatively few accounts of this type of "care for the other" in the women's casual sex stories. Foucault argued that caring for the self implies a care ethic for the other through a constant and dynamic process of active self-reflection. However, in our analysis "care for the self" was not necessarily reflective of "care for the other." We argue that gendered power relations and traditional discourse of heterosexuality constrained a more fluid negotiation of care for the other by the women in our studies.

Foucault has argued that certain groups (in particular people who have more limited access to dominant forms of power) are constrained in the way they enact ethical conduct. Our research demonstrates that it is crucial to analyse "care for self" and "care for the other" within broader cultural constructs of gendered power relations that make only certain forms and practices of ethics available to most women. In considering dominant heterosexual discourses that privilege male sexual needs and desires, it is not surprising that women's stories focused on caring for the self and subverting such discourses, leaving little room for effective means of "caring for the other." We argue that the lack of overt expressions of "care for the other" does not necessarily reflect a lack of ethical engagement with sexuality by the women. Instead it is most likely indicative of the constraints on ethical relations resulting from gendered discourses and power relations.

Conclusions

In this article, we analysed young women's stories of heterosexual casual sex using Foucault's notion of sexual ethics. We demonstrated some of the ways in which the young women engaged in moments of "care for the self," "self-reflection," and (to a much lesser extent) "care for the other"—all components of sexual ethics and *rapport à soi*. The main thread running through our analysis of women's negotiation of casual sex and sexual ethics is the way in which the accounts were heavily situated within, (re)produced, and at times disrupted gendered heterosexual discourses. We demonstrated how young women successfully negotiated "care for the self" within the confines of such gendered discourses. Women who expressed forms of "care for the self" that emphasized their own desires generally gave more positive accounts of casual sex than women who expressed a lack of agency and control over their casual sex experiences.

While some women were successful in negotiating sexual ethics, our main contention is that dominant heteronormative discourses of sex impede women's negotiation of more positive forms of sexual ethics (e.g., as demonstrated by accounts of the role of alcohol in women's self-care). The women were at times limited in the types of self-care they engaged in, because their accounts often remained embedded within gendered constructions of sexuality. In spite of this, we did identify many varied ways that the women cleverly negotiated gendered (and at times contradictory) discourses of heterosex to deploy strategies of self-care in casual sex. This was evident in accounts of "setting limits," agency and control, satisfying their own desires, and "self-preservation," as well as reflections on the influences of broader sociocultural expectations on their experience of casual sex.

Considering the constraints on women to develop sexual ethics within a gendered cultural system, the cultivation of sexual ethics and *rapport à soi* may offer space for radical subversion of dominant forms of heterosexuality. This can be done by promoting new forms of intimacy that encourage women and men to work outside and beyond a gendered binary of sexuality, towards mutually negotiated and pleasurable sexual encounters. The cultivation of an ethical subjectivity for both women and men has the potential to destabilize the current power systems. It is our contention that this requires that both women and men reflect on their sexual desires and practices, adopt a more diverse and ethically informed approach to sex, in order to subvert dominant heterosexual discourses.

Note

1. Pākehā refers to non-Māori New Zealanders of European descent.

References

Burr, Vivien (2003) *Social Constructionism*. London: Routledge.

Carmody, Moira (2003) "Sexual Ethics and Violence Prevention," *Social and Legal Studies* 12(2): 199–216.

Carmody, Moira (2005) "Ethical Erotics: Reconceptualizing Anti-rape Education," *Sexualities* 8(4): 465–80.

Carmody, Moira (2009) *Sex and Ethics: Young People and Ethical Sex*. South Yarra, Vic: Palgrave Macmillan.

Crawford, Mary and Popp, Danielle (2003) "Sexual Double Standards: A Review and Methodological Critique of Two Decades of Research," *The Journal of Sex Research* 40(1): 13–26.

Davidson, Arnold (2005) "Ethics as Ascetics: Foucault, the History of Ethics, and Ancient Thought," in G. Gutting (ed.) *The Cambridge Companion to Foucault*, pp. 123–48. Cambridge and New York: Cambridge University Press.

Farvid, Panteá (2006) "'The Girls [Still] Don't Want the Rep': Re-examining the 'Sexual Double Standard,'" paper presented at the *Joint Conference of the APS & NZPsS*. Auckland, New Zealand.

Foucault, Michel (1985) *The Use of Pleasure: The History of Sexuality 2*. London: Penguin Books.

Gavey, Nicola (2005) *Just Sex? The Cultural Scaffolding of Rape*. London: Routledge.

Gavey, Nicola and McPhillips, Kathryn (1999) "Subject to Romance: Heterosexual Passivity as an Obstacle to Women Initiating Condom Use," *Psychology of Women Quarterly* 23(2): 349–67.

Hollway, Wendy (1989) *Subjectivity and Method in Psychology: Gender, Meaning, and Science*. London: SAGE.

Jackson, S.M. and Cram, F. (2003) "Disrupting the Sexual Double Standard: Young Women's Talk about Heterosexuality," *British Journal of Social Psychology* 42(1): 113–27.

Kitzinger, Jenny (1995) "'I'm Sexually Attractive but I'm Powerful': Young Women Negotiating Sexual Reputation," *Women's Studies International Forum* 18(2): 187–96.

Lees, Sue (1993) *Sugar and Spice: Sexuality and Adolescent Girls*. London: Penguin.

Miller, Jody and Glassner Barry (1997) "The 'Inside' and the 'Outside': Finding Realities in Interviews," in D. Silverman (ed.) *Qualitative Research: Theory, Method, and Practice*, pp. 99–112. London: SAGE Publications.

Oliver, Mary and Sedikides, Constantine (1992) "Effects of Sexual Permissiveness on Desirability of Partner as a Function of Low and High Commitment to Relationship," *Social Psychology Quarterly* 55(3): 321–33.

O'Sullivan, Lucia and Byers, Sandra (1992) "College Students' Incorporation of Initiator and Restrictor Roles in Sexual Dating Interactions," *Journal of Sex Research* 29(3): 235–446.

Paul, E.L., McManus, B., and Hayes, A. (2000) "'Hookups': Characteristics and Correlates of College Students' Spontaneous and Anonymous Sexual Experiences," *The Journal of Sex Research* 37(1): 76–88.

Potts, Annie (2000) "'The Essence of a Hard on': Hegemonic Masculinity and the Cultural Construction of 'Erectile Dysfunction,'" *Men and Masculinities* 3(1): 85–103.

Rabinow, Paul (1997) *Michel Foucault: Ethics, Essential Works of Foucault 1954–1984*. London: Penguin Books.

Tolman, Deborah L. (2002) *Dilemmas of Desire*. Cambridge, MA: Harvard University Press.

Weaver, S.J. and Herold, E.S. (2000) "Casual Sex and Women," *Journal of Psychology and Human Sexuality* 12(3): 23–41.

Yardley, Lucy (1997) "Introducing Discursive Methods," in L. Yardley *Material Discourses of Health and Illness*, pp. 25–49. London: Routledge.

CHAPTER 33

"Real Fast and Tough": The Construction of Canadian Hockey Masculinity

Kristi A. Allain

A song by famous Canadian pop music artist Tom Cochrane and Red Rider (1988) claims that within the world of hockey there is only one way to be successful. Cochrane sings, "Real fast and tough is the only clear lane to the big league." This model of desirable hockey play has infiltrated almost all levels of men's and boy's elite-level hockey in Canada,[1] and hockey culture rewards players who demonstrate this rough-and-tough style (Vaz, 1982). Although this model of hockey is widely accepted within elite-level Canadian boys' and men's hockey, it is not universal. Outside of Canadian hockey, particularly in Europe and Russia,[2] there appears to be a privileging of various hockey skills, including stick handling, passing, and skating. This later style is known as European hockey, whereas the former is known as Canadian hockey. Neither style is intrinsically better than the other. In fact, researchers such as Stark (2001) suggest that today there are fewer measurable differences in style of play than there were in the past. What is significant about these perceived variations is the way that ideas about difference are taken up within the world of semiprofessional and professional Canadian hockey.

The Canadian Hockey League (CHL) is widely considered to be a gateway to the National Hockey League (NHL). Since the 1960s, 50% of all players drafted into the NHL have played hockey in the CHL (Young, B., personal communication, October 25, 2007). The CHL is a junior-level, semiprofessional ice hockey league that accommodates young men mostly between the ages of 16 and 20. The league has 60 teams, 51 teams in Canada and 9 teams in the U.S. The vast majority of players who compete in the league are from Canada, although American teams tend to have more U.S.-born players on their rosters.[3] For the purpose of clarity, when I speak of Canadian- and American-born players who play in the CHL, I will call them North American players. Although the league has teams in the U.S. and players who were born in the U.S., North American players in the CHL are thought to privilege a Canadian style of play.

Within Canadian hockey, expressions of gender tend to be played out in particular ways. Canadian men's elite-level hockey (and to a lesser extent the hockey played by boys) privileges particular expressions of hegemonic masculinity while simultaneously marginalizing alternative masculinities, which are considered feminine. Adams (2006) comments, "At the elite competitive levels, men's hockey—the hockey that really counts—promotes a hard, aggressive, masculinity" (p. 73). Hegemonic masculinity, as defined by Connell (1990), is "the culturally idealized form of masculine character (in a historical setting), which may not be the usual form of masculinity at all" (p. 83). According to Connell (1995), hegemonic masculinity is regulated both internally and externally by its separation from, and marginalization of, practices associated with gay men and women. Practices of hegemonic masculinity also vary across time and space.

Connell and Messerschmidt (2005) point out that expressions of hegemonic masculinity are normative but not necessarily normal. Within Canadian men's hockey today, hegemonic masculinity is expressed by the honor accorded the following traits: "respect, honour, courage, loyalty, aggressiveness, dominance, independence, occupational achievement, risk-taking, assertiveness and competitiveness ..." (Weinstein, Smith & Wiesenthal, 1995, p. 837). Interestingly, elite-level boys' and men's hockey in Canada celebrates practices associated with hegemonic masculinity (i.e., the normative features of masculinity) but also tends to be an acceptable place for this expression of masculinity to be performed in very literal ways (i.e., these features are sometimes expressed as normal). For example, players can demonstrate their courage through physical confrontations.

Meanings given to hegemonic masculinity are culturally variable. Therefore, it is likely that men's elite-level hockey as it is played in Europe and Russia privileges its own notions of hegemonic masculinity. Further, appropriate expressions of masculinity in Europe and Russia likely vary considerably by nation. I recognize that many other people are marginalized by performances of Canadian hockey hegemonic masculinity and its expression in the locker room, such as racial and ethnic minorities—specifically Francophone men, gay men, women. Further, I acknowledge that these constructions are not necessarily discrete or singular. Given that hegemonic masculinity is constructed in opposition to marginalized men and women (Connell, 1995), various gender relations will necessarily inform an examination of hockey masculinities. A specific examination of the aforementioned issues, however, is beyond the scope of this article.

The framework I use to explore hegemonic masculinity and the CHL is drawn from Messner's investigation of gender and little league soccer (2002). Messner advocates examining gender using three intersecting levels of analysis—"at the level of social interaction" (performance), "at the level of structural context" (structure), and "at the level of cultural symbol" (culture) (p. 2). The exploration of gender at the level of social interaction requires an assessment of how gender is performed in various social settings. To examine gender at this level, I will address how gender is performed within the CHL by North American players and the resulting impact on non-North American players. To examine gender at the level of structural context. I pay attention to how institutional structures variously support or challenge dominant notions of gender. I will examine this issue paying particular attention to the CHL's rules of play and how the game is constructed to maintain relations of hegemonic masculinity. Finally, when Messner addresses gender at the level of cultural symbol, he examines how dominant notions of gender are supported or challenged by popular culture. In Canadian hockey, media (i.e., print, television, and Internet) work to both construct and reinforce the common-sense ways the game should be played. These media celebrate notions of masculinity that privilege aggression; violence; playing with pain; and a rough, Canadian style of play.

This article will use scholarly literature, an analysis of Canadian hockey policy, and interviews with non-North American hockey players to examine hegemonic masculinity in the CHL. These interviews were conducted for a previous project that examined the experiences of non-North American hockey players in the CHL (see Allain, 2004). Although this research did not explicitly address masculinity, this theme emerged during the research process. To carry out the aforementioned research, I conducted 10 semistructured narrative interviews with players who were currently or had once competed in the CHL. Interviews took 1–2 hours to complete and addressed the player's experiences while competing in the league. The players interviewed were from Russia, the Czech Republic, and Slovakia, because players from these three nations were most numerous among non-North American players in the CHL. All players were at least 18 years of age at the time of the interview and had completed at least one full season in the CHL.

Social Interaction: Learning to Perform Gender

The locker room is a training ground where men are taught to loathe all that is considered feminine. Within this space, men express open derision for any displays of vulnerability or sensitivity. Robinson (1998) states, "There is no worse insult, in the world of hockey, than being told you are a girl" (p. 94). Men who express emotions that might be considered feminine, including sympathy, fear, and caring, are often singled out and labeled as effeminate—a label that has no positive attributes within hegemonic sports discourse.

The main policing mechanisms used to enforce consent with the dominant conversation are misogyny and homophobia: boys and men who reveal themselves as vulnerable are subsequently targeted symbolically as "women," "pussies," and "faggots" on athletic teams (Messner, 2002, p. 35).

It is this performance of masculinity that in part marginalizes non-North American players. Unlike their North American counterparts, these athletes have little frame of reference or understanding of the way masculinity is performed by their teammates, particularly in the locker room—one of their first encounters with Canadian hockey culture.[4] The players I interviewed expressed their surprise at the behavior of their teammates. These included overt attempts by North American hockey players to oppress and marginalize the non-North American players. One player explained, "Ah, some guys was outrageous. They 21 and they thinking that they can do anything they want.... I remember one time I wasn't even allowed to ... drink on the bus." Another complained that his teammates extorted money from him because he was a European player.[5] They charged him $15.00 a kilometer for car rides. Another player complained that he was not assigned a seat of his own on the team bus—a luxury afforded all rookie first-round draft picks, of which he was one.

Limited understanding of Canadian hockey masculinity often isolated non-North American players and impeded their ability to become "one of the boys." Robidoux (2001) explains that it is with a player's teammates that men perform masculinity. The language they use to maintain this hockey community, however, is often misogynistic and homophobic. Robidoux found that players who cannot live up to the image of hegemonic masculinity presented by the players in the locker room become the "bitch" of the group. During my player interviews, non-North American players complained that other North American hockey players called them names—these names drew on the readily available misogynistic and homophobic discourses that Robidoux describes. An interviewee commented,

> *Participant:* I mean you always get that. You know, "You're a blaw, blaw, blaw." You know?
>
> *Interviewer:* What's a "blaw, blaw, blaw"?
>
> *Participant:* [Lowers his head and blushes] Er, "You're a pussy," or stuff like that, you know?

Participants often discussed the dynamics of the hockey locker room using the word *humor*—a term that could be interpreted as a euphemism for displays of sexualized hypermasculinity. It is important to note that within the world of hockey there are rules about discussing the locker room with outsiders. Players often state publicly, "What happens in the room stays in the room." For this reason it is not surprising that the interviewed players did not express their discomfort in the North American locker room in great detail. They clearly stated, however, that this was a space of which they had little cultural understanding, and as a result, they were isolated from sharing in its experiences. One player noted,

> In the locker room, it was really quiet for me and for him [Czech teammate]. You know, it was really hard for me to get the jokes from them. I understand we got different kind of jokes in Czech, you know?[6]

[...] Another player succinctly described his relationship with his North American teammates as follows: "All of them were pretty good. We still good people, right? But there was some kind of obstruction." Given this, it is not surprising that Canadian hockey culture worked to marginalize and isolate its non-North American participants. Other factors, however, such as the structure of the game and its leagues, contributed to the creation of this environment.

Structure: The CHL and the Canadian Game

Messner (2002) stresses the importance of examining how the institutions that support sport, such as sports programs and leagues, work to maintain the gendered structure of sport. Within boys' and men's elite-level hockey in Canada, the various hockey leagues and coaches help to create a common sense notion of how the game ought to be played, and who should play it. In Canada, boys and girls often play the game separately from one another, especially at highly competitive levels. Messner argues that this segregation means boys and girls are taught from a very young age that they are "naturally" different from one another. Although there are both advantages and disadvantages to sex-segregated sports participation, this segregation allows expressions of hegemonic masculinity perpetuated in the locker room by coaching staff and within boys' hockey and the leagues to continue with little resistance.

The segregated structure of hockey not only limits girls' and women's access to the game, but it promotes a very narrow definition of how the game should be performed on the ice. Young boys are socialized into the world of competitive elite-level hockey at an early age. It is during this time that they internalize the culture of abuse and violence. [...]

Today's notion of desirable masculine hockey practice in Canada is not universally accepted, nor has it been the standard of play for Canadian hockey players throughout history. According to Stark (2001), Canadian men's hockey was once associated with a "gentlemanly" masculinity. This meant performing "crowd-pleasing offence ... [and] 'skating and stick-handling elegance'" (p. 3). Stark believes that this less aggressive style of hockey is related to the fact that international hockey was first played by amateur athletes. During this time, it was thought that amateur athletes wanted to model a certain style of refined masculinity to the international community. This gentlemanly Canadian men's hockey identity was prevalent until the late 1940s and early 1950s.

Today, although players in Europe, Russia, and North America learn a game based on similar rules, the style of game played by European and Russian hockey players is thought to differ dramatically from the hockey style played by Canadian players. European hockey, as it is known, is thought to privilege a passing and skating game, whereas the Canadian game is assumed to privilege a hard-hitting, aggressive style. Some of these differences might be accounted for by variations in ice size and rules of play. Specifically, European hockey is generally played on a larger ice surface, encouraging a game that privileges passing and skating. According to the International Ice Hockey Federation (IIHF), the governing body of non-North American hockey, regulation ice size is 60–61 m long, by 29–30 m wide. NHL ice size (to which the CHL conforms) is 60 m long by 25.5 m wide. In addition, the IIHF has imposed strict sanctions on fighting in the European game unlike the CHL, in which players are issued a 5 min fighting penalty. European and Russian hockey players who fight are often removed from the current game and suspended for one or two subsequent games.

Players who travel from Europe or Russia to play hockey in the CHL often struggle with differences in game play. Interviewees frequently commented that adjusting to the Canadian game was the most difficult hurdle they had to overcome as migrant athletes. A Russian player summed up the difference, "Ah, it is not so much a physical game in Russia hockey as here. Like, there is a physical game but not as much.... Well, different style of hockey. Like totally different."

Another commented on his first impressions of the CHL,

> I mean, you know, I just didn't want to get involved in something I'd never done [fighting]. You know, there is different techniques in the fighting on the ice and if you don't fight on the ice you can't fight, you know.... And the hitting. It was intimidating,

> obviously because I'd never even played with a half shield on.[7] [laughs] And you have guys coming with no teeth, and they like trying to run you in the corners, and I just wasn't used to that.

Differences in the way a game is played do not intrinsically make one game better. Ultimately, it is the ways these differences are interpreted and internalized that prove problematic for non-North American players. Vaz (1982) states that players who cannot or will not put their bodies at risk by fighting, hitting, and going into the corners are deemed weak and ineffective by Canadian hockey standards. As most Europeans and Russians have little experience with the Canadian game, they are automatically disadvantaged in the league. [...]

The privileging of particular hockey skills ultimately shapes their experiences within various North American hockey leagues, and non-North American players experience constant pressure to conform to these norms. Not surprisingly, the culture of hockey works in conjunction with the structure and performance of the game to support dominant practices of hegemonic masculinity.

Culture: The Canadian "Tough Guy" and the European "Chicken"

Messner (2002) claims that an examination of the way sports practices are represented in the media and other sites of popular culture is important for understanding the social context in which particular sports are situated. Many people engage in sports through the media. The media explain how spectators should view the game and come to understand it. They also give players, coaches, and other actors insight into how a player should actually play the game and the valued behaviors of the game. In Canadian sports culture, what it means to be a Canadian hockey player has been defined by national viewings of hockey moments—the most recognizable being the 1972 Canada–Russia hockey series, or Summit Series as it is commonly known, in which the Canadian team narrowly beat the Russian national team.

The series, its coverage, and Canada's win came to legitimize a Canadian style of play that focused on a rough and sometimes excessively violent[8] expression of the game, which worked conversely to construct the Russian game as balletic. Sport sociologist Adams (2005) argues that the male dancer has been associated with effeminacy in sport discourse since the 1800s. The dancer is often depicted as expressing problematic notions of masculinity. Specifically, the bodies of boys and men are not to express beauty and grace, nor are they to be examined and desired (especially by other men). When Canadian sports writers state that Russian hockey players are balletic in their movement, they are also suggesting that these hockey players are not expressing a desirable masculinity. Such discourses work to structure the debates around appropriate hockey conduct in North America, and they ultimately imply that Russian hockey (and all non-North American hockey for that matter) is problematically effeminate.

Within Canadian hockey culture, the most flagrant perpetuator of these stereotypes is hockey icon Don Cherry. Although he might be the most outspoken, he is certainly not alone in perpetuating these views. Cherry is the controversial host of *Coaches' Corner*. This program is part of CBC's flagship program, *Hockey Night in Canada.* Cherry garners much public attention and was a finalist in a Canadian media campaign to select the "Greatest Canadian" (CBC, 2006). Cherry has been both revered and reviled for his commentary on the way the game should be played and by whom. Cherry celebrates what he characterizes as old-time hockey—specifically, a time before the influx of European and Russian players and American interests in the Canadian game (Gillet, White & Young, 1996). A woman who boarded a non-North American CHL player commented:

> I remember it was one of the first weekends ______ [player's name] was with us. The team was on their northern trip.... Anyway, it was Saturday night and I was at home watching *Hockey Night in Canada.* Don Cherry came on, he was ranting about those Russians, saying that they should all be rounded up and sent home on a plane. All I could think about was ______ [player's name]. I knew that the team would be in the hotel watching. All I could think about was how humiliating it must have been for him. (Personal communication, March 4, 2003)

Cherry is openly hostile to those who want to diminish expressions of hegemonic masculinity, including fighting, within the game. In his broadcasts he characterizes the league's tough guys using words most commonly associated with combat and war. According to Cherry, these athletes, almost always Anglophone Canadians (and almost never Europeans or Russians), are "warriors" and are expected to draw upon a "warrior code" of battle. He privileges a physically aggressive and violent game, as characterized by the title of his video collection "Rock'em Sock'em." Those players who live up to his ideas of masculinity—almost always "good ol' Canadian boys"—are the center point of his hockey broadcasts. [...]

Cherry's commentary is not simply a celebration of his Canadian boys—it is centered on the degradation of those [who] choose not to or cannot be identified in this way. On a weekly basis, he purposefully mispronounces the names of French Canadian and European players, suggesting that their play is second rate, and as a result, there is no need to learn their names. His television broadcast was sanctioned for suggesting that both European and French Canadian players were not as tough as their Anglophone Canadian counterparts, given their propensity for visor wearing. Although attacks on European- and Russian-born players have been prevalent for years, it is only when Cherry's discriminatory conduct offends other Canadians (i.e., Francophones) that his actions lead to sanctioning (CBC News, 2004, February 11).

Canadian common-sense understanding of hockey is predicated on the idea that the European game is lacking appropriate masculine character. This view is so widely accepted that its problematic nature is only recognizable when it works to offend Francophone Canadians. Outspoken player Sean Avery commented that Francophone players (like their European counterparts) are characterized as sneaky and lacking in toughness. He commented, "I think it was typical of most French guys in our league with a visor on, running around and playing tough and not back[ing] anything up" (quoted by Robinson & Bradshaw, 2005, September 20). Although the media was critical of these comments, the same ideas are frequently circulated about non-North American players but receive little or no public criticism.

The Eastern European and Russian hockey players that I interviewed were well aware of Don Cherry and his comments about European and Russian hockey players. Some of these players believed that Cherry's views might even reflect a Canadian sensibility about appropriate hockey conduct. Most of the interviewed players took a defensive stance when asked about Cherry and his views on non-North American hockey talent. They often chose to highlight the importance of non-North American players in professional and semiprofessional hockey instead of spending time challenging Cherry's views.

> *Interviewer:* What do you think about Don Cherry and what he says about Eastern European hockey players?
>
> *Participant:* [pause] I don't like him. First of all how he dresses [both laugh]. Second of all, like this is an opinion and I have a different opinion, whatever. You, you have to admit in the NHL, the Europeans are basically leading the way. And without them, I'm not saying they're the best players … but without 'em the game wouldn't be the way it is. And if that's what he thinks and he can't see it, then that's probably not very smart. But it's just his opinion, you know, and ah, I disagree with it. But it doesn't … you know … I'm not going to … if that's what he thinks, good for him!
>
> *Interviewer:* Do you think he represents any part of the Canadian population or what they think?
>
> *Participant:* It could be. Probably is. But, like I said, it's so obvious in the NHL or whatever, they're really, really good, and if you don't see it, then too bad for you. There's probably some people behind him that say, "That's how it is. And the hockey's soft and shouldn't be that soft and whatever, whatever." But that's just like I said, it's their opinion. They have the right to have their opinion.

Another player commented on Don Cherry,

> I don't really like that guy [laughs loudly]…. I don't know…. If the NHL didn't have Europeans right now, it wouldn't be that good hockey because Europeans bring so much more things and more techniques, and everything is not just about the fights now.

Although the interviewed players attempted to downplay the significance of hockey critics such as Don Cherry, it is clear that the media works to generate a culture of appropriate Canadian hockey conduct, and that this conduct is premised on a rough-and-tough Canadian game. Further, the Canadian media considers non-North American players as outside of this cultural practice.

Intersection: Challenges, Resistance, and the Impact on Non-North American Players

These levels of analysis advocated by Messner (2002)—performance, structure, and culture—intersect with and affect non-North American players competing in the CHL. The players I interviewed indicated they were aware of the images and ideas about non-North American players that circulated throughout the league. Players commented that European and Russian players needed to be considerably better than their North American counterparts to overcome their image as weak, afraid, and lacking in the toughness and guts required to make it in the CHL. European and Russian players recognized that their presence on a team was often unwanted, because North American players viewed them as stealing jobs that were rightfully theirs.

> I remember … they [North American teammates] were complaining because the European players [were] taking, you know, jobs from Canadian kids and stuff like that. I mean, two spots in the roster of the team isn't that much. And if you can help, I think it is a good idea.… If you are a good player, then they like you. If you are not a good player, then they don't like you that much, you know what I mean?

The construction of Canadian hockey as hegemonically masculine (and the only legitimate form of the game), and the alternative construction of the European game as soft are reinforced in various ways. These include the dominant performance of masculinity in the hockey locker room and the support of various Canadian hockey leagues' style of play, both by the rules they advance and maintain and by the kinds of players they develop and forward through elite-level hockey (Vaz, 1982). Furthermore, popular notions about the way the game should be played are projected covertly (the constant emphasis on the big hit or the hockey fight) and overtly (through the hockey commentary of icons such as Don Cherry). Non-North American players often feel these attitudes and are affected by them. Borje Salming, a Swedish player in the 80s and 90s and one of the best defensemen to play the game, commented, "There were a lot of taunts of 'Chicken Swede.' There were threats to kill me. I heard every bad word there is" (quoted in Hockey Hall of Fame, 2006a).

Although the impact of desirable Canadian hockey masculinity on European and Russian hockey players is great, this does not suggest that these players do not resist both their treatment and the general culture of Canadian hockey. Players interviewed not only fought back against various violent and aggressive acts by others in the league (i.e., by challenging them to physical confrontations to gain respect as discussed earlier in this article), but they also took care to distance themselves from their North American teammates and generate close relationships among other non-North American players in the league. In fact, throughout the interview process, only one player referred to any of his North American teammates by name. This player had been traded with his North American teammate and the experience seemed to be a point of identification between them. More often, when non-North Americans spoke about North American players in the CHL, they said they were nice but that there was a distance between them. Interviewees spent little time discussing their relationships with non-North Americans in detail. When they did, players often said the relationships were strained. One player, when speaking of his relationships with his North American teammates, said, "We just don't know each other." Other players who were interviewed echoed this sentiment.

These players developed their own communities of practice outside of their CHL hockey teams (frequently with other non-North American players in the league). The concept of communities of practice was developed by Wenger (1998) and is based on his ethnographic work with an insurance company claims department. He noted that employees tended to interact with one another in a distinct fashion, which he named a "community of practice." These communities were contingent on three characteristics: "mutual engagement," "a joint enterprise," and "a shared repertoire" (p. 73). A community of practice requires its members to build close-knit relationships around a common purpose or goal. Interestingly, within the CHL, these communities of practice formed by non-North American players can be seen as a form of resistance to exclusion. Non-North American players, who were marginalized from their teammates and who could not share in the closeness generated in this environment, strategically generated a community of practice elsewhere.

When interviewees spoke about players from their home nations who also played in the CHL, but not necessarily on the same team, they often became quite animated. They referred to these players as friends and spoke about them in an interested and caring way.

> On our team, we actually had a guy from Slovakia, a Slovakian guy and we lived together, so. That was fun! And ah, I met a couple of guys in the Internet. You know Slovakian chat rooms and you know, I just. They even in different leagues like the WHL, you know the Quebec league, and you know (we) just talk about how they doing and stuff.

These players challenged Canadian hockey culture and the primacy of team building by generating meaningful relationships with fellow nationals who happened to play on competitive teams around the CHL.

Within Canadian hockey culture, community building and alliances are usually generated among a player's teammates, and relationships outside of this environment are generally sanctioned. Some players challenged this premise by meeting with others outside of their hockey team who happened to live in the communities where they were playing hockey. One player met with local university students who were also from Europe. He commented on the significance of this,

> You know [I have] friends, but off the ice, off the team. I think that helps a lot (with adjustment to life in the CHL). Sometimes you don't want to hang out with just the

guys, you know? You want to know some people differently than that.

This player stated that his teammates would not have understood and therefore he never spoke to them about these meetings. [...]

According to Connell and Messerschmidt (2005), men benefit in some ways from ascendant forms of masculinity in a particular historical context. Some men, however, clearly benefit more than others do. In this case, non-North American hockey players in the CHL are excluded from full participation in, and identification with, dominant expressions of Canadian hockey masculinity. Connell and Messerschmidt suggest that men positioned in this way form subordinate or marginalized masculinities. Subordinate masculinities by their very existence in some ways work to create tensions within hegemonic masculine practices. Connell and Messerschmidt state, "Research has ... documented the durability or survivability of nonhegemonic patterns of masculinity, which may represent well-crafted responses to race/ethnic marginalization, physical disability, class inequality, or stigmatized sexuality" (p. 848). The creation of communities of practice by non-North American players in the CHL speaks to this sustainability. European and Russian players who competed in the CHL appeared to show resistance to Canadian hockey culture. It was through these communities of practice that players built deep, personal, and lasting relationships and resisted the construction of appropriate Canadian hockey communities and desirable masculine hockey practice.

Conclusion

This article shows that the creation of a desirable masculine practice within Canadian hockey culture is generated in a variety of ways. These include the players' own performances of masculinity, the structure of the game, and mass cultural representations of hockey found in commentary, advertising, and print and television media. As stated by Cantelon (2006) and Stark (2001), a hegemonically desirable Canadian hockey masculinity predicated on a hard-hitting, physically aggressive game has been ascendant in Canadian hockey practice for at least 50 years. Interestingly, the development of this practice was a response to non-North American players' interest (and success) in the game. Although this notion of desirable masculinity within Canadian hockey culture is not static, it has successfully survived challenges to its hegemonic position as the one legitimate form of Canadian hockey practice. These challenges have come from alternative styles, including what is thought to be a more finesse-style, women's game; non-North American hockey players playing both inside and outside North America; and alternative styles within North American hockey itself.

Researchers such as Connell and Messerschmidt (2005) state that hegemonic masculinity is about more than the desirable practices it endorses. It is about "the policing of men as well as the exclusion or discrediting of women" (p. 844). Canadian hockey is an apt example of this sort of policing and exclusion in action. North American participants in the game have policed the alternative practices of masculinity exhibited by non-North American players. These challenges to the way the game ought to be played have been policed through various degrading discourses, physical abuse, and exclusion from full membership in the community of teammates. Although non-North American players have enacted various resistance strategies, they have made very little impact on perceptions of the way the game should be played. It is interesting to note that non-North American players who fully embrace Canadian style hockey are commonly thought of as the exception.

Over the last few years, there have been high-profile incidents of violence in the NHL. These incidents include Todd Bertuzzi's on-ice attack of Steve Moore, which left Moore with a broken neck. As a result of this incident and others, dissent over the way the game is played and marketed has been growing, in both Canada and the U.S. Critics of the game have argued that it is difficult to grow the game in the U.S. (something analysts claim to be imperative to the NHL's financial health) given the reliance in professional men's hockey on aggression and fighting. It will be both interesting and important to assess how (and if) these particular issues work to challenge and reconstruct what is today considered desirable masculine hockey practices.

Notes

1. Although the vast majority of NHL learns are located in the U.S., the majority of the players in the league are Canadian. During the 2005–2006 hockey season, 53.6% of all players in the NHL were Canadian-born (Haché, 2007). Further, many non-Canadian players, particularly U.S.-born athletes, were trained in the CHL.
2. This article will focus on the distinction between Canadian-style hockey and non-North American hockey. Although Canadian-style hockey is the most prevalent and publicized style of hockey practiced among elite-level boys and men in North America, there are other hockey leagues that challenge Canadian hegemonic hockey masculinity. An examination of alternative masculinities in North American hockey, however, is beyond the scope of this article.
3. For example, in the 2007–2008 season, the Peterborough Petes from Peterborough, ON had 20 Canadian-, 3 U.S.-, and 2 Eastern European-born players on its roster. The Plymouth Whalers from Plymouth, MI had 15 Canadian-, 9 U.S.-, and 2 Eastern European-born players.
4. This is not to say that Russian and European hockey practice is not related to the marginalization of women. Currently, there are no studies in English conducted on this phenomenon. During the 2004–2005 NHL hockey lockout, however, three NHL players from Sweden competing in a professional Swedish hockey league were accused of raping a woman (CBC Sports, 2005, June 1).
5. CHL teams generally pay non-North American players more than their North American counterparts do. This increased wage is to cover expenses that would generally be covered by a player's parents.
6. It is important to note that all player quotes are transcribed verbatim. This was done to allow the players to speak through the research, as well as to highlight their (mis)use of the English language (a significant issue for their understanding of the Canadian hockey subculture).

7. A half shield is a piece of clear plastic attached to a player's helmet to protect his or her eyes. In the CHL, half shields are mandatory. In European hockey, however, players under the age of 19 must wear full facial protection.
8. During the hockey series, Canadian player Bobby Clarke broke the leg of Russian player Valeri Kharlamov with a slash (Hockey Hall of Fame, 2006b).

References

Adams, M.L. (2005). "Death to the prancing prince": Effeminacy, sport discourse, and the salvation of men's dancing. *Body & Society, 11*(4), 63–86.

Adams, M.L. (2006). The game of whose lives? Gender, race, and entitlement in Canada's "national" game. In D. Whitson & R. Gruneau (Eds.), *Artificial ice: Hockey, commerce, and cultural identity* (pp. 71–84). Toronto: Garamond Press.

Allain, K.A. (2004). *In other words: An examination into the experiences of non-North Americans in the Canadian hockey League.* Unpublished master's thesis, Queen's University, Kingston, Ontario, Canada.

Cantelon, H. (2006). Have skates, will travel: Canada, Europe, and the hockey labour market. In D. Whitson & R. Gruneau (Eds.), *Artificial ice: Hockey, commerce, and cultural identity* (pp. 215–236). Toronto: Garamond Press.

CBC. (2006). *CBC The greatest Canadian.* Retrieved April 20, 2006 from www.cbc.ca/greatest/

CBC News. (2004, February 11). Cherry's claim on visors do add up. *CBC News.* Retrieved March 27, 2006 from www.cbc.ca/story/news/national/2004/02/11morecherry040211.html

CBC Sports. (2005, June 1). Swedish hockey bans three NHLers for one year. CBC Sports. Retrieved April 20, 2006 from www.cbc.ca/story/sports/national/2005/06/01/Sports/Swedish050601.html

Connell, R.W. (1990). An iron man: The body and some contradictions of hegemonic masculinity. In M.A. Messner & D.F. Sabo (Eds.), *Sport, men, and the gender order: Critical feminist perspectives* (pp. 83–96). Champaign, IL: Human Kinetics Books.

Connell, R.W. (1995). *Masculinities.* Los Angeles, CA: University of California Press.

Connell, R.W. & Messerschmidt, J.W. (2005). Hegemonic masculinity: Rethinking the concept. *Gender & Society, 19*(6), 829–859.

Gillet, J., White, P. & Young, K. (1996). The prime minister of Saturday night: Don Cherry, the CBC, and the cultural production of intolerance. In H. Holmes & D. Taras (Eds.), *Seeing ourselves: Media power and policy in Canada* (pp. 59–72). Toronto, ON: Harcourt Brace Jovanovich.

Gruneau, R. & Whitson, D. (1993). *Hockey night in Canada: Sport, identities, and cultural politics*. Toronto: Garamond Press.

Hache, A. (2007). Analysis of the NHL players by country of birth. *Physics of Hockey.com*. Retrieved September 24, 2007 from http://www.thephysicsofhockey.com/topics/htm.

Hockey Hall of Fame (2006a). One on one with Borje Salming. *LegendsofHockey.net*. Retrieved April 20, 2006 from http://www.legendsofhockey.net/spot_oneononep199602.htm

Hockey Hall of Fame (2006b). Valeri Kharlamor—player category: Honoured posthumously. *Legends of Hockey.net*. Retrieved April 20, 2006 from www.legendsofhockey.net/html/ind05kharlamor.

Messner, M.A. (2002). *Talking the field: Women, men, and sports*. Minneapolis, MN: University of Minnesota Press.

Robidoux, M.A. (2001). *Men at play: A working understanding of professional hockey*. Kingston, ON: McGill-Queen's University Press.

Robinson, D. & Bradshaw, J. (2005). Is the NHL euro-francophobic? [Point-counterpoint]. *Queen's Journal, 133*(10). Retrieved August 13, 2008, from www.queensjournal.ca/story/2005-09-30/sports/nhl-euro-francophobic/

Robinson, L. (1998). *Crossing the line: Violence and sexual assault in Canada's national sport*. Toronto, ON: McClelland & Stewart Inc.

Stark, T. (2001). The pioneer, the poet, and the pal: Masculinities and national identities in Canadian, Swedish, and Soviet-Russian ice hockey during the cold war. In C. Howell (Ed.), *Putting it on ice volume II: International "Canada's Game."* Halifax, Nova Scotia: Grosebrook Research Institute.

Tom Cochrane and Red Rider. (1988). *Big league* (audio recording). Mississauga, ON: EMI Music Canada.

Vaz, E.W. (1982). *The professionalization of young hockey players*. Lincoln, NE: University of Nebraska Press.

Weinstein, M.D., Smith, M.D. & Wiesenthal, D.L. (1995). Masculinity and hockey violence. *Sex Roles, 33*, 831–847.

Wenger, E. (1998). *Communities of practice: Learning, meaning, and identity*. New York, NY: Cambridge University Press.

SECTION 4C

ETHNICITY AND RACE

CHAPTER 34

"Canadian-First": Mixed Race Self-Identification and Canadian Belonging

Jillian Paragg

Introduction

> You walk into a room full of strangers, and all they see is a brown person. And then they think that you're the exotic person, so they want to know all about your race and stuff. But then it's almost anti-climactic when you're saying "well, I'm Canadian."

In this quote Ja, a research participant, explains how, in her daily interactions, people do not read her as "Canadian" because she is racialized as non-white, and that they in turn expect and demand an explanation of her difference from "mainstream" conceptions of who is "Canadian." Not being read or identified by others as "Canadian" was a common thread in semi-structured in-depth interviews I conducted with 19 young adults of mixed race in a Western Canadian urban location over the course of a year. In this paper, I address moments of (in)ability for people of mixed race to claim "Canadian." Mixed-race people have a complex relationship with identifying and narrating their identities as "Canadian" through the operation of race and ethnicity in the Canadian context and because of ambivalent and contradictory readings of their bodies. Race discourse operates in complex ways. For the purpose of this project, while recognizing the complexity of defining "mixed race," I define "mixed-race people" as people whose biological parents are from different racialized groups, meaning different "socially defined racial groups" (Streeter 1996, 316). For example, this could be a person who has one parent who is socially marked as white and one parent who is socially marked as non-white, or a person whose parents are both socially marked as non-white, but are from different racialized groups.[1]

In the past decade, significant changes have occurred in the way race discourse and mixed race are constructed, mobilized, and talked about in Canada. These range from: increased demographic diversity in the Canadian context; the centrality of multiculturalism, as both value system and official policy, in Canada's national imaginary; the increase in interracial couples in the Canadian context (Milan, Maheux, and Chui 2010); and other changes outside the Canadian context such as Obama's inauguration as President in the U.S. [...] According to this study's interviews, people of mixed race continue to be positioned outside of the nation state. In this sense, the more the Canadian context has changed, the more the positioning of mixed-race people has stayed the same: outside of the nation, excluded from belonging.

In interviews with women of mixed race in Canada, Mahtani (2002) found that her respondents experienced difficulty identifying as "Canadian" because others were interested in identifying them ethnically. However, she found that they also appropriated "Canadian" for their own uses outside of the dominant national imaginary's representation of "Canadian" as white (Mahtani 2002). Extending Mahtani's work, I found that respondents in this study do not have great difficulty *self*-identifying as "Canadian," in fact they strongly do, identifying as what I term "Canadian-first." Rather, difficulty arises when respondents are not read as "Canadian" by *others*, which impacts how they narrate their identities. In this sense, respondents have a deeply ambiguous relationship with the term "Canadian," in that in conversations with others it becomes difficult to identify themselves as "Canadian." I found that respondents deploy the term in three ways: by expressing a sense of being "Canadian-first"; by stating that there exists an understanding that "Canadian means white"; and by strategically using the term "Canadian" in their interactions with others, expressing an active appropriation of the term. However, none of these deployments is mutually exclusive: they overlap and bleed into one another, playing off and impacting one another. In addition, mixed-race people might teach us something about how white and non-white people variously claim "Canadianness," contributing to the literature on how "race" and "Canadian" map onto each other (Pendakur and Mata 1998).

This paper engages the idea that to be read as "Canadian" depends on race, redressing a gap in the literature on "Canadian identity" (Boyd 1999; Boyd and Norris 2001; Kalbach and Kalbach 1999; Lee and Edmonston 2010; Pendakur and Mata 1998; Thomas 2005) and discusses mixed-race respondents' relationship and experiences with the term "Canadian" using interview excerpts to consider their difficulties in claiming "Canadian" as an identity, adding to nascent Canadian Critical Mixed-Race studies. I begin with an overview of literature that considers who identifies as "Canadian," and then engage in a brief discussion of mixed-race literature and provide an overview of the study's theoretical framework, mainly how the white/non-white binary is set up and reinforced through multicultural policy. I then discuss the interviews and how respondents deploy "Canadian" in their identity narratives.

Literature Review: Who Identifies as "Canadian"?

In the 2006 census 32.2% or 10.1 million members of the Canadian population reported "Canadian" as some part of their ethnic origin. As Lee and Edmonston (2010) crucially note, questions on "ethnic origin" and the formatting of these questions vary from year to year, which also signal the conceptual ambiguity in the social construction of "ethnicity" itself. Prior to 1971, Statistics Canada discouraged the use of "Canadian" as an ethnic origin on census reporting because of concerns over confusion between "citizenship" and "ancestry" reporting. However from 1971 onwards self-enumeration was introduced (Lee and Edmonston 2010). The 1981 census was the first to supply a write-in box in addition to a check-off list of ethnic groups, enabling the reporting of multiple ethnicities for the first time. In 1986 three write-in boxes were supplied, in addition to the check-off list of ethnic groups, in order for respondents to answer the question "to which ethnic or cultural group(s) do you or did your ancestors belong?" (Lee and Edmonston 2010, 79). In 1991 two write-in boxes were also supplied, and "Canadian" was one of the most frequent write-in responses that year. In the 1996 census there was no longer a check-off list, and respondents were instructed to write in as many ethnic groups as were applicable to the four supplied write-in boxes. In both 1996 and 2001 "Canadian" was listed as an example response to the question on ethnic origin, because of its frequency on the previous censuses (Boyd and Norris 2001; Lee and Edmonston 2010).

Scholars have cited the "Count-me-Canadian" campaign (Boyd 1999), as well as the Molson "I Am Canadian" ad campaign (Stevens 2013), as factors in the increase in reporting of "Canadian" as an ethnic origin on the census in the 1990s and into the 2000s. Lee and Edmonston (2010) also theorize from their findings that identifying as Canadian may also be a reaction to marginalized statuses in that "younger and less educated people, non-metropolitan residents, and Francophones were more likely to report 'Canadian' ethnicity" (94).

In their in-depth study of changing census responses, Boyd and Norris (2001) found that "Canadian" was the fastest-growing ethnic group on the census between 1986 and 1996. They note that people who responded using "Canadian" had previously drawn from British and French ethnic origin groups before "Canadian" was introduced as an option on the census. Similarly, Thomas (2005) found that those reporting "Canadian" as their ethno-cultural background on the 2001 census had previously identified as French and English ethnic groups.

Statistics Canada reports that "most individuals who reported 'Canadian' in the 2001 and 2006 censuses had English or French as a mother tongue, were born in Canada, and had both parents born inside Canada" (Statistics Canada 2008, 8).[2] This group—of persons whose first language is English or French, and whose parents were born in Canada—is likely largely made up of people who are racialized as white. While Indigenous peoples would also fall within this group, it would constitute a small portion of this population, since the Indigenous population makes up 3.9% of Canada's population as counted in the 2006 census (Statistics Canada 2011). Overtly discriminatory immigration laws existed in Canada until the 1960s, and these laws prevented racialized groups such as Black, Chinese, and Japanese immigrants from coming to Canada in greater numbers (Abu-Laban and Gabriel 2002; Day 2000; Kelley and Trebilcock

2010). Therefore the percentage of populations who would have French or English as a first language and both parents born in Canada can be assumed to be largely white. However, as I argue in this paper, the lack of racialized populations claiming "Canadian" may also be affected by the difficulties and resistances to claiming "Canadian" that racialized groups experience.

Lacking in Boyd and Norris (2001) and Thomas's (2005) studies is a consideration of the term "Canadian" in relation to non-white groups. While Boyd and Norris (2001) implicitly discuss "Canadian" in relation to non-white groups, through their finding that people who responded with "Canadian" predominantly drew from British or French ethnic origin groups (implying that people of non-British or non-French origin did not respond using "Canadian"), this could have been more explicitly stated. Boyd and Norris's (2001) findings indicate how "Canadian" as an ethnic origin appeared in the census, but they do not interrogate the implications of or recognize how the ability to claim "Canadian" is racialized. Perhaps this was out of the scope of their study, but it is an important outcome from their findings, as it appears that it is predominantly whites who respond with "Canadian" to the ethnic origin question.

Pendakur and Mata (1998) found that ethnic and racialized minorities tend not to report "Canadian" as an ethnic origin on the census: "despite the fact that there is a high proportion of people reporting Canadian, this reporting does not have a visible impact on the reporting of minority ethnic groups" (Pendakur and Mata 1998, 125). While Pendakur and Mata (1998) note this racialized trend, they do not expand on why this may be. I seek to fill this gap by examining how the ability to claim "Canadian" is racialized, through the experiences of mixed-race people.

Additionally, as Kalbach and Kalbach (1999) and Lee and Edmonston (2010) point out, the census has not asked a direct question on respondents' current or self-ethnic identification. The question solely asks about ethnic origin, leading to self-identification being inferred through ethnic origin reporting. The self-identification of "Canadian" by whites and non-whites, although discussed, also remains largely unexplored in academic literature (Mackey 2002).

I argue that the ability to claim "Canadian" as an identity, and that who is recognized and accepted as Canadian is racialized, leads non-whites to narrate their identities in particular ways around the term "Canadian" (Mackey 2002; Paragg 2011). For people of mixed race, the demand to narrate their identities is compounded through their ambivalent social location, which crosses or does not fit within the anticipated binary race discourse of the Canadian context. There is a tension in how people of mixed race can claim "Canadian" and the "what are you?" question, which is asked of people of mixed race because of the ambivalence with which these questions are read. This was a prominent theme in my interviews.

Mixed-Race Literature

There is a dearth of literature on mixed-race identity in Canada. The key figure in Critical Mixed-Race studies in the Canadian context is Mahtani (2002, 2005, 2014), whose work I draw on and extend in this paper. I also draw from the work of Taylor, James, and Saul (2007), McNeil (2010) and DeRango-Adem and Thompson (2010). In contrast to the Canadian context, the body of mixed-race literature in the U.S. and the U.K. contexts has grown immensely in the past two decades. Its discussions and debates of mixed race in particular can and should be considered by Canadian mixed-race scholars, despite these countries' different engagements with race.

A developing theme in Critical Mixed-Race studies in the Canadian, the U.S. and the U.K. contexts discusses how questioning seeks to situate people of mixed race within dominant racial binaries: the questioning demand "what are you?" reflects the limited and binary racialized landscape (Bradshaw 1992; Gilbert 2005; Nakashima 1992; Song 2003). As Song (2003) states, "the politicized discourse around racial identity tends to be dual and exclusive in nature: i.e., black or white rather than black and white" (2003, 63-4). Canada's racial formation has operated differently, theorized as a white and non-white binary (Bannerji 2000; Mackey 2002), and it is through this binary that the racial gaze reads bodies. I posit that the "what are you?" question—as the unspoken question that Ja responds to in the opening quote of this paper—is a manifestation of the external racial gaze (Paragg 2011). A range of literatures theorize the external gaze as an important concept. Feminist film theory posits that power is exerted over women as they are constituted as objects "of looking" by what has been termed the "male gaze" (Mulvey 1975). Similarly, the external racial gaze imposes fixed racial categories onto people who belong to racialized groups. Reading people through "the act of looking" exerts power over the one who is "looked upon" and named. The external gaze has been positioned in a number of ways, for instance, as the "imperial gaze" (Mawani 2002) or as the "white gaze" (Perkins 2005). In addition, the literature on the racial gaze tends to emphasize how the gaze fixes (Fanon 1967). I begin with the premise that the "what are you?" question is the verbal form of the gazer's need to fix. Through questioning, the gazer attempts to situate the person of mixed race in the schema of its ordered world, which in the Canadian context operates within a binary of white/non-white (Bannerji 2000; Gilbert 2005; Mackey 2002; Song 2003).

The external gaze is enacted within race discourses' operation in the Canadian context. Two key and linked components of Canadian race discourse include first, the binary of white/non-white and second, official multiculturalism. As scholars such as Bannerji (2000) and Mackey (2002) argue, in the Canadian social landscape, race discourse operates within a set of binary oppositions. This is an oppositional way of thinking about race categories: a need to fix the self and the Other as white or non-white. In turn, multicultural policy sets up and reinforces this basic binary structure of "white Canadian" and "non-white Cultural Other." I now turn to a brief discussion of the project's theoretical framework. I consider Canadian multiculturalism in relation to the "what are you?" question, which also assists in setting up how mixed-race people come to narrate their identities, and how they see themselves as "being Canadian" (or not).

Theoretical Framework: Multiculturalism and Questioning

The "what are you?" question, and how people of mixed race respond, in turn speak to the operation of race and the politics of race in the Canadian context. Throughout the interviews, research participants described the narratives they develop and use to respond to this ongoing interrogation. As established in mixed-race literature, the self-identification of mixed-race people may not be compatible with the identity that is prescribed to them by those who read them (Rockquemore and Brunsma 2004). Respondents attested that they are regularly asked the question "what are you?" in their everyday lives, empirically confirming what has been theorized in Critical Mixed-Race studies (Bradshaw 1992; Gilbert 2005; Nakashima 1992; Song 2003). The "what are you?" question is pervasive in practically every context respondents find themselves in (work, school, social activities, and travel), and between them and any number of people in their lives (co-workers, customers, teachers, friends, and strangers).

That questioning occurs through the "what are you?" question in the Canadian context likely results from the operation of the white/non-white binary (which does not solely use "black" as its counterpoint to "white") and Canadian multicultural discourse (Bannerji 2000; Mackey 2002). In this context, the asking of someone's "background" is framed in a socially acceptable celebratory way, i.e., "I'm only asking you what your background is because I want to celebrate you and your culture with you." Respondents also expressed slippages in their narratives between race, culture, ethnicity, and nationality, also speaking to the impact of multicultural discourse in the Canadian context. White bodies in the Canadian context are also asked questions like "what is your background?" and slippages between race, culture, and ethnicity in the Canadian multicultural—yet white-dominated—nation are also evident in the questioning of white bodies, but it is outside the scope of this paper. My inference is that the intent behind such questions on white bodies differs from the questioning of non-white monoracial bodies. The question is not entwined in the same power relations of Othering and fixing (Fanon 1967).

Race, ethnicity, and culture can operate through slippages *between* them, particularly in the Canadian context. Multiculturalism in Canada is both official policy and a discourse in the Canadian national imaginary, and contemporary representations and understandings of race, ethnicity, and culture are discursively produced *through* multiculturalism (Bannerji 2000; Mahtani 2002). This in turn mediates how people come to understand their own and each other's identities. Official Canadian multiculturalism reinforces the need to "belong" to a culture, strongly emphasizing "origin," yet it places very strict boundaries on who can belong and what identities are acceptable. For example, as Mahtani states, in "the Canadian context, the concept of racialized ethnicities (as opposed to race) has figured largely regarding questions of identity for Canadians" (2002, 71). Mahtani's use of "racialized ethnicities" signals how the terms "race," "ethnicity," and "culture" are often read next to each other and used interchangeably in the Canadian context. Such slippages are part of the operation of the external gaze in the Canadian context. For people of mixed race, slippages between race, ethnicity, and culture are especially salient.

In the Canadian context, slippages are further exacerbated by multiculturalism: the gaze is not just about the white/non-white binary, but rather the imaginary of linear immigrant origins coming together, speaking back to the dominant "mosaic" metaphor that exists in the Canadian context, which emphasizes the cultural multiplicity of the context as opposed to the

U.S. "melting pot" and "one-drop" discourses, which differently operate to regulate identity (Porter 1968). In other words, while the gaze in Canada is racialized, it is articulated through a "narrative of origins" that enables a slippage where the racialized operation of the gaze is filtered out and shows how it is at work.

Bannerji (2000) posits that a white/non-white binary exists within the multicultural Canadian context. She theorizes that a hegemonic understanding and assumption of Canada as "organically white" gives whites an automatic pass as Canadian. Non-whites are in turn racialized as the Other, and are positioned as the "multicultural element" that enriches Canada culturally. Non-whites are reduced to solely having a cultural status. They are positioned as "static cultural beings." Overall, Bannerji (2000) sees official multicultural policy as equating "Canadianness" with whiteness, setting up the basic binary structure of "white Canadian" and "non-white Other."

The white/non-white binary in turn enables questioning that seeks to fix people in the binary. The racialized aspect of who can claim Canadian and who is accepted as Canadian leads to non-white bodies being questioned regarding "where they are from." The myth of "origin" and the story of the Canadian nation play off each other in the imaginary of the multicultural nation (Gagnon 2000). Questioning seeks to fix non-white monoracial bodies relative to the nation through a singular origin, allowing a kind of linear narrative of subject position: "you were there, then you came here."

While the theoretical framework of this study stems from a consideration of the operation of the white/non-white binary in the multicultural Canadian context, it should also be noted that while Canada deploys an official policy of multiculturalism, the province of Quebec does not employ official multiculturalism. Rather than claiming an official multicultural stance, Quebec takes up an intercultural project. In this context, interculturalism and multiculturalism compete as pluralist frameworks for social policy. While it is out of the scope of this paper to address these issues in depth, it should be noted that multiculturalism and whiteness may operate differently in the Quebec context. Additionally, the historical identification of "Canadien" in the Quebec context may impact reporting of "Canadian" among Francophones on the census (Lee and Edmonston 2010). Therefore, it is necessary to identify this study as an account of mixed race English Canadians' narratives around "Canadian."

In contrast to the "non-Canadian" reading of non-whites in English Canada, and the ambivalence with which mixed-race people are identified, Mackey (2002) found in her ethnographic study that whites construct themselves as "ordinary people" or "ordinary Canadians." Whites can easily position themselves as "Canadian," and can claim "Canadian" without added questioning. While there are non-white racialized groups in the Canadian nation who may claim hyphenated Canadian identities (i.e., Indo-Canadian or Chinese-Canadian), the designation of ordinary or generic "*Canadian*-Canadian" is not available to them.

Unlike non-white monoracial and white bodies, mixed-race bodies are not only questioned due to the racialized aspect of who can claim "Canadian" and who is accepted as "Canadian," but they are questioned because they are not easily placed within the white/non-white binary at work in the Canadian context. Additionally they multiply and thus confound the linear narrative of origin. The questioning of people of mixed race does not necessarily seek to place the person of mixed race on the edge of the nation (like non-white monoracial bodies), but rather works as a kind of suspended puzzle over where and how to place them within the multicultural nation. It seems to be asking "through what transgression of racial/ ethnic/ national boundaries did you come to be, so that I might place you within the framework I know?"

In the following section, I turn to the interview findings to highlight the ambiguous relationships respondents had with the identification of "Canadian"; however, I first provide a brief discussion of the study's method.

"Being Canadian": Mixed-Race Narratives

METHOD

I conducted semi-structured in-depth interviews with 19 young adult women and men of mixed race in Edmonton, Alberta, between the fall of 2009 and the fall of 2010. I recruited the research participants through word of mouth and snowball sampling, as well as through various university departments, student associations, and student organization listservs at the University of Alberta. Because the majority of the respondents were recruited through the University of Alberta, the range of participants were likely limited to individuals able to access post-secondary education (i.e., those of higher socio-economic status). In turn, post-secondary education provides access to knowledge(s), discourses, language(s) or vocabulary, and ways of thinking about race and identity that other contexts may not provide. Mahtani (2005) also found post-secondary education affected how mixed-race women "read their race" (80). I do not want to downplay how mixed-race respondents' everyday lived experiences and negotiations impact how they think and talk about race and identity, regardless of their post-secondary education. However, post-secondary education may also teach students ways of being "politically correct" in their language, which also came out in the participant narratives, particularly through many of them expressing an aversion to the term "race."

The respondents ranged in age from 21 to 32. I also sought out only Canadian-born research participants. This helped to manage the range of the study because the respondents are from a particular historical cohort who grew up in an officially multicultural and increasingly culturally and racially diverse Canada. All of the respondents were also English speaking. As previously noted, if the interviews took place in Quebec and in the specific intercultural approach to pluralism of that context—or with French speakers outside of Quebec—the discussions between the interview participants and myself would likely have been different, particularly with regard to issues of language, identity, and claiming "Canadian." In addition, two of the respondents identified with Indigenous identities. The term "Métis" is associated with people of Indigenous backgrounds who are "mixed," and tends to be positioned as separate and distinct from "mixed-race" discourse or other racialized discourses in the Canadian context in that it has formed within its own specific historical context (Lawrence 2004; Mawani 2002, 2009). I was not expecting people with Indigenous identities to respond to the recruitment ad. I used the term "mixed race" to recruit participants, and I admittedly, naively, assumed that Indigenous peoples might identify as Métis, but not necessarily as "mixed race." While it is out of the scope of this paper, the division between Indigenous "mixed identities" and non-Indigenous "mixed identities" in mixed-race literature and scholarship needs to be further interrogated (Mahtani 2014).

The location of the study, the city of Edmonton, Alberta, is becoming an increasingly racially diverse city; however, it is not as racially diverse as Canada's largest cities.[3] Overall the experiences and narratives of the respondents reflect the racialized context of the city of Edmonton. Furthermore, the other contexts experienced in the respondents' lives also largely impacted their experiences. For example, a divide between urban and rural contexts (in particular, differences in the racial diversity of these contexts) was predominant in respondents' narratives and impacted their experiences. Many respondents talked about growing up in smaller towns whose populations tended to be predominantly white, and contrasted these experiences with the racial diversity of Edmonton, or other cities where they have resided. As such, these contexts have and continue to greatly impact how respondents narrate their identities.

STUDY FINDINGS

In the interviews the mixed-race respondents expressed an ambiguous relationship with the term "Canadian" throughout their narratives, in that it was used in multiple and overlapping ways. I found that "Canadian" was deployed by respondents through their self-identification as "Canadian-first." However, while the respondents self-identified as Canadian in their narratives, they did not use the term when asked about their racial backgrounds, unless the parent they were describing was white. This signals a recognition that there exists an understanding that "Canadian means white." Through this understanding respondents expressed that they strategically use the term "Canadian" in their interactions with others, demonstrating an active appropriation of the term. I will now turn to a further exploration of these three deployments.

1. "CANADIAN-FIRST"

When I asked respondents in the interview "how do you self-identify?" the majority of them responded stating "Canadian." However, when I asked them to describe their "racial background," respondents tended to express a separate identity narrative. Participants' narratives in response to me asking them "what is your racial background?" are closely tied to their need to have narratives ready for when they are asked the "what are you?" question (Paragg 2015). In other words, while respondents strongly *self*-identified as "Canadian-first," they expressed a separate sub-identity narrative when asked their "racial background," usually having to do with their parents' "origins."

In contrast, in the interviews none of the respondents defined their "racial background" as Canadian, unless the parent they were describing was white, and this only occurred in two cases. For example, when I asked Erin "what is your racial background?" in the interview, she stated, "my father was from Pakistan and my mother was second-generation Canadian, she was British." When I asked Michael the same question, he responded stating, "my mother is Hispanic from Peru, my father is from Canada." When I asked Michael to expand on what he meant by "from Canada," he stated "white."

When I asked respondents "what is your racial background?" in the interview, it became evident that how they think about and narrate their "racial background" is formed in a specific way. This was reflected in many of the respondents' use of their parents' "countries of origin" when asked to describe their racial backgrounds. Through this response participants position race as an "inheritance by blood" through their parents' nations, which signals the "haunting of blood" legacy that exists within racial discourse, resulting from a historical intertwining of race and biology (Alcoff 2006; Morris 2007; Winant 2007). This may also signal the influence of official multicultural discourse in the Canadian context, which tends to emphasize "origin" or "background" (Compton 2002; Mahtani 2002). In addition, throughout respondents' narratives there were slippages between race and ethnicity, which occurs within Canadian multicultural discourse as previously discussed (Taylor, James, and Saul 2007).

Ali's self-identification and the narrative she used to describe her racial background differ, but are connected in important ways. She stated of her self-identification, "I identify as Canadian first and foremost," but when I asked her to describe her "racial background" she stated, "my mom's side of the family is of a Japanese ancestry, my dad's side of the family is Polish and Norwegian, and so … mixed between Caucasian and Asian I would say." Here, she expresses the notion of a unique individual mix of race/blood/culture alongside being Canadian—a broad identity claim that serves to encompass, claim, or overarch any such specificity. Similarly, when I asked Jolanda what her "racial background" was she stated, "I am half Jamaican and half Dutch." However, of her self-identification, she said:

> I identify more as a Canadian. I think. I don't have any strong ties to my extended family either way. I don't know barely anybody on my dad's side, and … I don't know, we're just not that close with my mom's side either. So, it was sort of just like, my immediate family were just, that was just my little world growing up. So … my identity only kind of really revolved around them.

Neil responded to my question of "what is your racial background?" by stating, "my father is from Holland, he's Dutch … he's a pure Hollander, or … Pure Dutch, and my mom is from China. I think it's Beijing, and she's pure—pure Chinese." When I asked him "how do you self-identify?" he stated, "I identify myself as Canadian, but I do know that I didn't come from Canada, I came—like my parents came from those cultures." Neil's response signals the power of origins in the respondents' racial background narratives. The language of "purity" is also of note here, denoting how also central to the legacy of race are notions of "inheritance of blood" (Alcoff 2006; Morris 2007; Winant 2007). Overall, in Ali, Jolanda, and Neil's narratives the notion of "race" being the nation which your parents are from, inherited by blood, is evident, further demonstrating the slippages between race, ethnicity, and nationality in the Canadian context (Mahtani 2002; Taylor, James, and Saul 2007).

When I asked Veronica "how do you self-identify?" she responded stating, "I guess I consider myself Canadian." However, she expressed a separate narrative regarding her racial background, stating, "I'm half-Chinese, and half-Caribbean. So, my mom was from Trinidad and Tobago; San Fernando, Trinidad and Tobago. And then my dad was from Shanghai, China." She went on to state, "when people ask me what my heritage is, yeah, I definitely do say—I don't say Canadian actually, I say 'half-Chinese, half-Caribbean.'" Veronica's racial background narrative is explicitly tied to a need to have narratives ready for when she is asked the "what are you?" question.

My reading of "Canadian-first" is that it is primarily a narrative that falls in line with multicultural discourse. It is a narrative of belonging. That respondents express being "Canadian-first" is both a product of multicultural discourse and yet is a strategic deployment to undermine those same discourses, which I will return to later. It may also signal how respondents grew up in an increasingly multicultural Canada, and subscribe to the official discourses around "we are all Canadian" (Ali 2008). However, at the same time, their expression of "Canadian-first" is a private narrative, one that describes their "self-identification" rather than the narratives they offer to people in their everyday lives. "Canadian-first" in respondents' narratives can also be read as a way to opt out of categorization and a way to make a claim on belonging, outside of dominant conceptions of who is and is not Canadian, working to complicate the "*Canadian*-Canadian" narrative (Mackey 2002), which I expand on later in this paper.

Some respondents, like Ja, expressed a sub-identity narrative within their self-identification as "Canadian," usually having to do with their parents' "origins." For instance, Ja described her "racial background," stating, "I am Trinidadian and Dutch-Canadian." Of her "self-identification" she stated:

> Well *when normally I'm asked that question* I just say "Canadian." Just because it's really who I am. If anything, like, I have a Trinidadian cultural experience, but it's very Canadian.... But, when people ask the breakdown, I just say "well half Trinidadian, half Dutch-Canadian," so. That's it (laughter). (emphasis added)

Needing to have the "breakdown" ready for her questioners, Ja also signals that her response of "Canadian" to the "what are you?" question is not enough. If she responds in this way she will be asked to "break it down further," demonstrating how she has to narrate her racial identification because she is marked by race, and how "Canadian" as an origin category is not available to non-whites in the Canadian context (Boyd and Norris 2001; Mackey 2002).

In her self-identification narrative, Anne also self-identified as "Canadian." Through her use of the term, Anne's claim to being "Canadian" might be seen as a kind of "third space" (Bhabha 1990), an "in-between" identification that does not subscribe to binaries:

> I've definitely started identifying with "Canadian" ... in the last couple years. Because ... when we were younger [we were] always just "half Chinese half German," but I think because my dad started saying that, he's like "no, we're Canadian" ... "we're a Canadian family," that really hit me. Yeah, it's not like I'm taking on Chinese traditions and I'm not ... taking on any German traditions, really either, that I am more Canadian than I am either of the other.

Here, Anne's framing of Canadian as a "third" space expresses a type of exhaustion of constantly having to narrate her family's "origin story." I theorize that through Anne's self-identification she is opting out of the binary, while simultaneously responding to its power reinforced by multiculturalism. Here, "Canadian-first" does defy "other" categorizations and re-claims or even particularizes "Canadian." Anne uses "Canadian" as its own set of cultural and identificatory practices, potentially speaking to something emancipatory or subversive in mixed-race people claiming "Canadian-first."

In addition, Anne was the only one of my respondents who claimed "Canadian" when I asked her what her "racial background" was:

> Very Canadian I would say. Because a lot of—like my dad grew up—was born and raised in Hong Kong, and he moved here when he was about 17, and he went to school, he worked, and he met my mom in Manitoba. And then they got married. So, there was never like a time where we were raised in Chinese culture really, or really strong Chinese culture. Like we picked up some things from him, and we picked up some German things from my mom. But, yeah. *I would definitely say Canadian.* Just like any other Canadian family I would—I feel like. Yeah. (my emphasis)

However, implicit in Anne's narrative is the notion that since her family lacks Chinese and German cultural traditions, her family is "Canadian." They are not "cultural Others" and are therefore "Canadian" (Bannerji 2000).

In her study, Mackey (2002) found that white participants use liberal discourse to make intolerance logical and rational, setting up an exclusionary national identity, epitomized through the logic of "*Canadian*-Canadian" in their narratives. Whites position themselves as "real Canadians," and "Canadian" is the only identity narrative that they need. In contrast, while non-whites can and do claim "Canadian," they tend to have a narrative that follows this in order to justify "what they are." Throughout the interviews, while the majority of respondents strongly *self*-identified only as "Canadian," none of the respondents defined their "racial background" as only Canadian. In their narratives respondents expressed a narrative of being "Canadian" but it was framed through their self-identifying as "Canadian-first," followed by a sub-identity narrative usually having to do with their parents' "origins."

The narratives people offered me for their "racial backgrounds" aligned with the sub-story that they tell following their "Canadian-first" narrative when they are questioned in their everyday lives. This narrative is a type of addendum that they have. In contrast, as Mackey (2002) found, whites can claim "*Canadian*-Canadian" without the need of an addendum.

I argue that "*Canadian*-Canadian" and "Canadian-first" narratives both follow from multicultural discourse and overlap. Whites are set up through multicultural policy as comprising the "core Culture." In this frame, while there are many cultures in Canada, they should operate under one set of rules, as the "core Culture" manages and tolerates difference (Bannerji 2000). In turn, non-whites need to explain their identity because of this dominant discourse. For non-whites, while there is the possibility of claiming "Canadian," that claim is policed through this set of core rules, which work to manage difference. In contrast, whites do not have or need the "Canadian-first" narrative, because they are already always read as "*Canadian*-Canadian." I now turn to how the respondents understand the term "Canadian."

2. "CANADIAN AS WHITE"

With the exception of Anne, while respondents strongly identify as "Canadian" in their self-identification narratives, they do not identify as Canadian in their discussions of their racial background, unless, in the case of Erin and Michel, their parents are white. Respondents expressed an understanding that others do not see them as Canadian, and have an understanding that "Canadian means white," which importantly reflects the dominant discourse.

Throughout her interviews, Mackey's (2002) white respondents insisted that non-whites need to identify as "Canadian." My respondents self-identify as "Canadian," but they do so knowing that others may not perceive them as "Canadian." Extending Mackey (2002), I position that this assertion on the part of her white respondents sets up a catch-22: they argue that non-whites need to identify as Canadian, but non-whites, regardless if they do, are not identified by *others* as Canadian. Overall, respondents expressed feeling simultaneously included and excluded by the term "Canadian," in that they strongly self-identify as "Canadian-first," but recognize that "Canadian refers to white." However, they also had a difficult time articulating what "Canadian culture" is or refers to, like Mackey's (2002) respondents.

Many respondents expressed that "Canadian refers to white," and that they are not read as Canadian. Discussing how she responds when she is asked the "what are you?" question, Jess stated, "if I just say 'oh, I'm Canadian'—because I am Canadian—but if I say that ... they're just going to be a little bit more confused." Here, Jess expressed how she is not read as "Canadian" despite her self-identification as Canadian. Ja, speaking of her experience of growing up in a predominantly white context, recognized that others do not perceive her as Canadian because of her "darker" skin. She stated, "but being obviously darker than everyone else ... everyone else identifies me as someone more 'exotic.' Like, the first thing they see, they don't see a, you know, a 'Canadian' when they first talk to me." Ja's "dark" or "non-white" skin marks her outside of the context of Canada—positioning her as exotic—and leads her to not be perceived as Canadian.

Anne also spoke of her experiences growing up in a predominantly white context. Because of her non-white appearance growing up in a small town, others in that context found it impossible to read her and her siblings as Canadian. She stated:

> I don't feel different, but I think because we look different that we're automatically assumed that we're different. And especially in our small town, like people *always* associate us with Chinese, so it's like that's how people saw us all the time. We would never be kind of Canadian. They had all of these assumptions about us. Yeah. And all of these jokes, kind of like that we were all Asian, that was our identity, I guess.

Growing up in this context, Anne and her siblings were solely read as Chinese, speaking to the mutually exclusive white/non-white binary at work in the Canadian context (Bannerji 2000; Mackey 2002), which identifies whites as "Canadian" and non-whites are the multicultural element that enriches Canada, but who are themselves not "Canadian."

Despite the recognition and problematization on the part of respondents that "Canadian means white," some of the respondents expressed the notion that there exist "*Canadian*-Canadians" (Mackey 2002). Others conveyed the notion that "*Canadian*-Canadian" culture is cultureless, and expressed particular ideas of what "being multicultural" entails, articulating what has been referred to as "song and dance" multiculturalism (George 2006; Mahtani 2002). Signaling this type of multiculturalism, Melissa stated that Canada's culture is hard to pinpoint, and "weak" compared to other countries. She asserted that Canada lacks a "strong" culture, stating, "the culture of Canada is what—la poutine? Like, maple syrup? It's hard to identify with that, whereas if your 'other half' is [for example] West Indian—Trinidad and Tobago—you can identify with carnival, with the types of food—roti, etc." Melissa's ideas about what constitutes culture seem to have been impacted by official multicultural policy and its increasing commodification of minority cultures' performances and food (Abu-Laban and Gabriel 2002).

Further to Melissa's statement, other respondents talked about how Canada's culture is not just hard to pinpoint, but is actually non-existent, framing Canada as "cultureless." This raises the question about Canadian identity centering on the notion that "we are multicultural." However, the narratives and experiences of the mixed race respondents demonstrate how that very claim depends on race (and the binary external gaze), including how whiteness feeds on racial others, and yet is specified because of how belonging is policed (hooks 1992). Similarly, Mackey (2002) found that there exists the perception that Canada lacks an identity, and that there is a lack of "cultural status" for "*Canadian*-Canadians." Veronica implicitly expressed this in her narrative, while also struggling where to position her family within the Canadian nation, coming up against the idea that "Canada is white." She stated of her parents, "they didn't bring many cultural type experiences to our family … we are probably as *Canadian* as we get (laughing) … which is unfortunate, but, like, that I couldn't share some of the same ways—you know like they were brought up … *we are Chinese and Caribbean, and, but other than that it's like we're Canadian*, you know, so …" (my emphasis). Here Veronica expressed a tension in how to position her family. They are a Canadian family, yet because of their Chinese and Caribbean origins there is a hesitancy and tension in identifying her family as "Canadian."

Michael also had particular ideas about who has culture and who does not, and links it to race in relation to the Canadian nation, signaling how he is implicated in a context that sets up non-whites as "cultural Others" (Bannerji 2000), a binary between whiteness and multicultural authenticity. Of his mother's non-white background he stated, "I don't feel like I can lay claim to that heritage as much as I would like to. I feel like that would be in a way an insult to people who are *authentically* all the way there, and I'm more attuned to this environment than theirs, and so I identify as Caucasian more.... *But I'm more cultured than other white people*" (my emphasis). Here Michael seems to be proud, in that he wants to claim that his identity is more "interesting." He points to the normalized dominance of "Canadian equals white" while also using his own "mixedness" to push back at the blandness of that "Canadian culture." Michael expressed that non-whites have more culture than whites, insinuating a lack of culture on the part of whites. As the presumed centre, whiteness depends on not being "specific." This speaks back to the double-bind of whiteness. "Whiteness" is the norm, and as such is unmarked, blank, yet it also "feeds" off racial others in order to position itself as the norm (Frankenberg 1993; hooks 1992). The claim of a "white centre" *itself* depends on race. Whiteness needs the "cultural difference of otherness" to retain its normalcy and dominance.

In her narrative, Rachel expressed an understanding that Canada is not viewed as having culture through its perceived inherent whiteness. She stated, "I don't know if there is a Canadian culture, but I think the predominant thought is that there's not because there's just white people." Later in the interview she stated that there exists the idea of "how can I participate in this multicultural world when I'm just white? You know, that kind of thing. Like, I'm not sure that people consider 'Canadian' to be a culture." Overall, Rachel noted how ideas about culture are linked to race and projected onto ideas about the Canadian multicultural nation.

In her narrative, Erin worked to disrupt the idea that Canada is "cultureless," that there is "no Canadian culture," exposing how the binary of whites as "Canadian" and non-whites as "cultural Others" is implicated in a relationship of privilege. She put it this way:

> People always assume ... "oh I don't have a culture, I'm just Canadian" [but I'm] like, "oh, you have *such* a culture" ... that's why immigrant people have such a hard time with you is because you have this culture and you don't recognize it. So ... that's like part of the privilege too I guess, is like saying "oh, I have no culture" ... because mine is so dominant and so omnipresent that I don't even need to recognize that I have one. That's like people who say they don't have an accent. Well definitely to someone else in the world you do have an accent.

Here, Erin challenges the narrative that only non-whites "hold culture," and exposes the relation of privilege and power at work in the Canadian context in which this notion is embedded. There is a dominant Canadian culture, but its dominance renders it invisible. As the presumed "center" whiteness depends on not being "specific"; but this is a double edged-sword, in that it is then in search of "being something" but then to name it as something is to specify it, potentially undermining its privileged dominance.

While respondents recognize that others do not identify them as "Canadian," respondents continue to deploy the term for their self-identification. In addition, they also deploy the term in a strategic way when they are questioned as to "what they are." This speaks to a strategic use of the term "Canadian" on the part of the respondents, and one that seeks to actively challenge others' assumptions about who is Canadian, as well as their assumptions about people of mixed race.

3. "CANADIAN" AS STRATEGIC IDENTIFICATION

Through their recognition that others do not identify them as "Canadian," respondents discussed how they engage in a strategic use of the term "Canadian" in their narratives. They use the term "Canadian" to actively complicate and confuse others' assumptions of them. It is a way of saying "I'm not going to help you navigate." Additionally, they work to appropriate the idea that "white means Canadian." In this sense, while the respondents may have a "Canadian-first" narrative, they may also use this narrative in a "strategic" way, demonstrating how these various deployments of "Canadian" overlap and work with and through one another. For example, let us reconsider one of Ja's statements as strategic, which I previously positioned as "Canadian-first." In this narrative, it is also evident that Ja works to challenge the assumption that she is not Canadian in that it is "who she really is":

> Well *when normally I'm asked that question,* I just say "Canadian." Just because it's really who I am. If anything, like, I have a Trinidadian cultural experience, but it's very Canadian.... But, when people ask the breakdown, I just say "well half Trinidadian, half Dutch-Canadian," so. That's it (laughter). (my emphasis)

The respondents are aware that others do not perceive them as "Canadian," which is itself evidenced in the interaction of the "what are you?" question. Yet respondents will at times strategically use the term "Canadian" in response to that question. They do so for a number of reasons, including to "mess with people" and to complicate their assumptions. For instance, Jolanda stated of responding with "Canadian": "I might have at some point just to like mess with somebody, because I knew obviously what they were trying to ask." James also stated he responds with "Canadian" to the "what are you?" question when he wants to "be a smart ass."

Melissa had experiences of not being read as "Canadian." She posited that this is because she does not "look Canadian"—she does not look white. In the interview, she talked about the experience of being questioned, and described the usual interaction that she finds herself in when being questioned: "'where are you from?' 'well I'm Canadian.' 'Oh, okay, but *where* are you from?'... and people ... are hinting at the fact that *you don't look Canadian.*" Melissa went on to discuss her experiences living abroad and how the idea that "Canadian" is considered white is also at work outside of the Canadian context. Her experiences of not being read as "Canadian" have also occurred outside of Canada while living abroad. She stated "living in China as a Canadian ... I identified more as 'Canadian' [but] Canada is considered white." Here, Melissa also emphasized that she strongly identified as Canadian outside of the Canadian context, positioning it as a type of "traveler's identity."

Like Melissa, Monica also described how she strongly identifies as "Canadian" while traveling, but that she does so because she enjoys complicating the assumption that "Canadian refers to white." However, Monica also notes that it is easier for her in some ways to identify as "Canadian" outside of the Canadian context. She stated:

> When I'm in Canada, I don't ever refer to myself as "Canadian," actually. When I'm outside of Canada, I always refer to myself as Canadian. And I like to do that particularly because it confuses people. It depends where I am, but if I'm in … when somebody's thinking that I'm something else, for example, when they think I'm from India or I'm from Spain or something, and I say "Canadian," and then I get the kind of sideways turn, I just leave it at that. And it's easier to do that when I'm not in Canada, when I'm in Canada, I mean as soon as I open my mouth and stuff I think there's … it's when I open my mouth and start speaking people know that I'm Canadian, like *Canadian*, I guess … but then the questions follow. Like, "how did you get brown?" basically, right (laughter).

In her experience in the Canadian context, Monica finds that people are taken aback to find that someone who has brown skin has a "Canadian accent" as non-whites are not perceived as Canadian. Mable summed it up this way: "a lot of people still, I think, view Canada especially as being a Caucasian country. And so—and I think even Canadians … for some reason." From respondents' experiences traveling abroad, they have encountered the discourse that "Canada is multicultural" as well as the discourse that "Canada is white," demonstrating how race operates differently within and beyond the nation. Here, Monica states that in some ways it is easier for her to claim "Canadian" while abroad, perhaps gesturing to the discourse that "Canada is multicultural." At the same time, the discourse that "Canada is white" or the *Canadian*-Canadian discourse operates alongside Canada's "multicultural image" in that people from Canada who are non-white (who are not *Canadian*-Canadian) are asked questions around "how they are brown."

Mable purposefully responds to the "what are you?" question with "Canadian," even when she knows the questioner wants to know what her "race" is. Through responding with "Canadian" in this way, Mable also works to expose and disrupt the white/non-white binary in the Canadian context, which equates "Canadian" with "white" (Bannerji 2000):

> I guess I view myself more as just being *a Canadian*. And so, when I tell people … like people who I kind of get a hint that they're wanting to know what my racial background is … if I just tell them that I'm Canadian, I think it kind of suggests to them that I don't either know what I am (laughing) or that my parents must be Caucasian.

I argue that responding to the questioning with "Canadian" is strategic, and it also works to expose the questioner's slippages between national and racial identity inherent in the question "what are you?" To ask "what are you?" masks the racialized question in the "innocence" of national/ethnic origin, particularly in the multicultural Canadian context. The asking of questions around "origin" is, in some sense, encouraged and justified through multicultural discourse, in that the "celebration" of people's origins and origin stories is emphasized.

The person of mixed race knows that "Canadian" is not the response the questioner is looking for. By responding to the "what are you?" question with "Canadian," Mable is not only challenging the questioner's notion that she cannot be *Canadian*-Canadian because she is non-white (Mackey 2002), she is also interested in forcing the questioner to a consciousness of the slippages of racial and national identity, or at least a consciousness of the need to differentiate and fix.

Conclusion

Returning to my earlier discussion of previous analyses of the Canadian census (Boyd and Norris 2001; Lee and Edmonston 2010; Pendakur and Mata 1998; Thomas 2005), my research demonstrates that the identification of "Canadian" remains inaccessible to those who identify as mixed race. Despite the frenzy to prove we are a multicultural, "raceless," equitable society, research shows that mixed-race people are still positioned outside of Canadianness, even ten years past Mahtani's (2002) study. The interviewees' narratives point to the difficulty of claiming "Canadian." Mixed-race respondents express an ambiguous and often complex relationship with the term "Canadian." They use "Canadian" for their self-identification, yet when it comes to describing their racial backgrounds they do not. Because "white" is equated with "Canadian," they are forced to narrate their identities in particular ways around that term, and they express recognition of how "white" and "Canadian" are linked. The most obvious context in which they are asked to narrate their identities is in the interaction of being asked "what are you?" For people of mixed race, questioning is further compounded through their transgression of the white/non-white binary. Questioning also seeks to fix them in the white/non-white binary that they cross. However, despite an awareness that "Canadian means white," mixed-race respondents actively appropriate the term in the questioning interaction, using it in a strategic way to confound others' assumptions about them. In addition, these findings do not just tell us how mixed-race people identify, but also contribute to understanding how whiteness, Canadianness, and multiculturalism are mutually constitutive—interrelated in complex ways. [...]

Notes

1. It could be argued that by using the term "non-white" one privileges the term "white," making it the norm against which all other groups are measured (James 2001). However, by using "white" it is not my intention to privilege the term. The term "white" has been used in mixed-race scholarship as a point of reference, in that research on mixed-race identity has been largely focused on individuals with white and black parentage. It is my

intention to disrupt this and capture a more diverse range of experiences. Furthermore, other scholars have argued that using the term "white" is useful in that it denotes the existence of power relations at work in our society. For instance, Mukherjee states: "I use the term 'non-white' in order to talk about the binary relationship of power in which 'white' is the dominant term" (2001, 214).

2. The data have not yet been released from the 2011 census. However, with the shift to a voluntary household survey from the mandatory long-form census, there will be an inability to compare the 2011 census data to all previous data sets (Dillon 2010; Green and Milligan 2010).
3. For instance, according to the 2006 Federal Census, what Statistics Canada refers to as the "visible minority" population, meaning individuals belonging to non-white racialized groups, included 22.9% of the total population in the Edmonton census metropolis area (CMA) (Statistics Canada 2006a), which is an increase of 3.2% from the 2001 Federal census (Statistics Canada 2001). This is in contrast to a "visible minority" population of 42.9% of the total population in the Toronto CMA in 2006 (Statistics Canada 2006b).

References

Abu-Laban, Yasmeen, and Christina Gabriel. 2002. *Selling Diversity.* Peterborough: Broadview Press.

Alcoff, Linda Martin. 2006. *Visible Identities: Race, Gender, and the Self.* New York, NY: Oxford University Press.

Ali, Mehrunnisa Ahmad. 2008. Second Generation Youth's Belief in the Myth of Canadian Multiculturalism. *Canadian Ethnic Studies/ Études ethniques au Canada* 40.2: 89-107.

Bannerji, Himani. 2000. *The Dark Side of the Nation: Essays on Multiculturalism, Nationalism and Gender.* Toronto: Canadian Scholars' Press.

Bhabha, Homi. 1990. Interview with Homi Bhabha: The Third Space. In *Identity Community, Culture and Difference*, ed. Jonathan Rutherford, 207-221. London, UK: Lawrence and Wishart.

Boyd, Monica. 1999. Canadian, Eh? Ethnic Origin Shifts in the Canadian Census. *Canadian Ethnic Studies* 31.3: 1-19.

Boyd, Monica, and Doug Norris. 2001. Who Are the "Canadians"?: Changing Census Responses, 1986-1996. *Canadian Ethnic Studies/ Études ethniques au Canada* 33.1: 1-24.

Bradshaw, Carla K. 1992. Beauty and the Beast: On Racial Ambiguity. In *Racially Mixed People in America,* ed. Maria P. P. Root, 77-88. London, UK: Sage.

Compton, Wade. 2002. The Epic Moment: An Interview with Wayde Compton. *West Coast Line* 36.2: 131-145.

Day, Richard J. F. 2000. *Multiculturalism and the History of Canadian Diversity.* Toronto: University of Toronto Press.

DeRango-Adem, Adebe, and Andrea Thompson, eds. 2010. *Other Tongues: Mixed-Race Women Speak Out.* Toronto: INANNA.

Dillon, Lisa. 2010. The Value of the Long Form Canadian Census for Long Term National and International Research. *Canadian Public Policy* 36.3: 389-393.

Fanon, Franz. 1967. *Black Skin White Masks.* New York, NY: Grove Press.

Frankenberg, Ruth. 1993. *White Women, Race Matters: The Social Construction of Whiteness.* New York, NY: Routledge.

Gagnon, Monika Kin. 2000. *Other Conundrums: Race, Culture, and Canadian Art.* Vancouver: Arsenal.

George, Usha. 2006. Multiculturalism Issues in Canada. *Canadian Diversity* 5.2: 60-61.

Gilbert, David. 2005. Interrogating Mixed-Race: A Crisis of Ambiguity? *Social Identities* 11.1: 55-74.

Green, David A., and Kevin Milligan. 2010. The Importance of the Long Form Census to Canada. *Canadian Public Policy* 36.3: 383-388.

hooks, bell. 1992. *Black Looks: Race and Representation.* Toronto: Between the Lines.

James, Carl E. 2001. Introduction: Encounters in Race, Ethnicity, and Language. In *Talking About Identity: Encounters in Race, Ethnicity, and Language,* eds. Carl E. James and Adrienne Shadd, 1-8. Toronto: Between the Lines.

Kalbach, Madeline A., and Warren E. Kalbach. 1999. Becoming Canadian: Problems of an Emerging Identity. *Canadian Ethnic Studies* 3.2: 1-19.

Kelley, Ninette, and M. J. Trebilcock. 2010. *The Making of the Mosaic: A History of Canadian Immigration Policy.* Toronto: University of Toronto Press.

Lawrence, Bonita. 2004. *"Real" Indians and Others: Mixed-Blood Urban Native People and Indigenous Nationhood.* Vancouver: University of British Columbia Press.

Lee, Sharon M., and Barry Edmonston. 2010. "Canadian" as National Ethnic Origin: Trends and Implications. *Canadian Ethnic Studies* 41/42.3-1: 77-108.

Mackey, Eva. 2002. *The House of Difference: Cultural Politics and National Identity in Canada.* 2nd ed. Toronto: University of Toronto Press.

Mahtani, Minelle. 2002. Interrogating the Hyphen-Nation: Canadian Multicultural Policy and "Mixed Race" Identities. *Social Identities* 8.1: 67-90.

———. 2005. Mixed Metaphors: Positioning "Mixed Race" Identity. In *Situating "Race" and Racisms in Space, Time, and Theory: Critical Essays for Activists and Scholars,* eds. Jo-Anne Lee and John Sutton Lutz, 77-93. Montreal and Kingston: McGill-Queen's University Press.

———. 2014. *Mixed Race Amnesia: Resisting the Romanticization of Multiraciality.* Seattle: University of Washington Press.

Mawani, Renisa. 2002. In Between and Out of Place: Mixed-Race Identity, Liquor, and the Law in British Columbia, 1850-1914. In *Race, Space and the Law: Unmapping a White Settler Society*, ed. Sherene Razack, 47-69. Toronto: Between the Lines.

———. 2009. *Colonial Proximities: Crossracial Encounters and Juridical Truths in British Columbia, 1871-1921.* Vancouver: University of British Columbia Press.

McNeil, Daniel. 2010. *Sex and Race in the Black Atlantic: Mulatto Devils and Multiracial Messiahs.* Toronto: Routledge.

Milan, Anne, Hélène Maheux, and Tina Chui. 2010. A Portrait of Couples in Mixed Unions. *Statistics Canada*, April 20. http://www.statcan.gc.ca/pub/11-008-x/2010001/article/11143-eng.htm.

Morris, Aldon D. 2007. Sociology of Race and W. E. B. Du Bois: The Path Not Taken. In *Sociology in America: A History*, ed. Craig Calhoun, 503-534. Chicago, IL: University of Chicago Press.

Mukherjee, Arun. 2001. The "Race Consciousness" of a South Asian (Canadian, of Course) Female Academic. In *Talking About Identity: Encounters in Race, Ethnicity, and Language*, eds. Carl E. James, and Adrienne Shadd, 212-218. Toronto: Between the Lines.

Mulvey, Laura. 1975. Visual Pleasure and Narrative Cinema. *Screen* 16.3: 6-18.

Nakashima, Cynthia L. 1992. An Invisible Monster: The Creation and Denial of Mixed-Race People in America. In *Racially Mixed People in America*, ed. Maria P. P. Root, 162-178. London, UK: Sage.

Paragg, Jillian. 2011. Ambivalence, The External Gaze and Negotiation: Exploring Mixed Race Identity. Master's thesis, University of Alberta.

———. 2015. What Are You?: Mixed Race Responses to the Racial Gaze. Unpublished paper.

Pendakur, Ravi, and Fernando Mata. 1998. Patterns of Ethnic Identification and the "Canadian" Response. *Canadian Ethnic Studies/Études ethniques au Canada* 30.2: 125-137.

Perkins, Maureen. 2005. Thoroughly Modern Mulatta: Rethinking "Old World" Stereotypes in a "New World" Setting. *Biography* 28.1: 104-116.

Porter, John. 1968. *The Vertical Mosaic: An Analysis of Social Class and Power in Canada.* Toronto: University of Toronto Press.

Rockquemore, Kerry Ann, and David L. Brunsma. 2004. Negotiating Racial Identity: Biracial Women and Interactional Validation. *Women and Therapy* 27.1-2: 85-102.

Song, Miri. 2003. *Choosing Ethnic Identity.* Cambridge, UK: Polity Press.

Statistics Canada. 2001. Community Profiles: Edmonton. http://www12.statcan.ca/english/Profil01/ CP01/Index.cfm?Lang=E.

———. 2006a. Community Profiles: Edmonton. http://www12.statcan.ca/census-recensement/2006/dp-pd/prof/92-591/index.cfm.

———. 2006b. Community Profiles: Toronto. http://www12.statcan.ca/census-recensement/2006/dp- pd/prof/92-591/index.cfm.

———. 2008. *Canada's Ethnocultural Mosaic, 2006 Census.*

———. 2011. Population Projections by Aboriginal Identity in Canada. http://www.statcan.gc.ca/daily-quotidien/111207/dq111207a-eng.htm.

Stevens, Gillian. 2013. "I am Canadian": The Rise of Canadian Identity in Canada's Censuses, 1981-1996. 23rd Annual Warren E. Kalbach Population Conference: "Applying Demographic Techniques to Contemporary Issues." University of Alberta. March 8.

Streeter, Caroline A. 1996. Ambiguous Bodies: Locating Black/White Women in Cultural Representations. In *The Multiracial Experience: Racial Borders as the New Frontier*, ed. Maria P. P. Root, 305-320. Thousand Oaks, CA: Sage.

Taylor, Leanne, Carl E. James, and Roger Saul. 2007. Who Belongs? Exploring Race and Racialization in Canada. In *Race, Racialization, and Antiracism in Canada and Beyond*, eds. Genevieve Fuji Johnson and Randy Enomoto, 151-178. Toronto: University of Toronto Press.

Thomas, Derrick. 2005. I am Canadian. *Canadian Social Trends* 76 (Spring): 24-32.

Winant, Howard. 2007. The Dark Side of the Force: One Hundred Years of the Sociology of Race. In *Sociology in America: A History*, ed. Craig Calhoun, 535-571. Chicago, IL: University of Chicago Press.

CHAPTER 35

African-Centred Education: Situating the Tradition

George Dei and Arlo Kempf

Introduction

In North American and European contexts, the push by African men and women to maintain and develop learning and knowledge that recognize and sustain the history, capacity, and interests of African peoples begins with the forced immigration of Africans to these areas under various systems of capture, enslavement, and indenture. The collapse of the European trade in enslaved peoples—as many African-American and Caribbean scholars, activists, and popular intellectuals have argued—did very little to quell the persistent and extreme discrimination faced by African-descended people throughout the African Diaspora. Indeed, many activists, scholars, and groups have long understood the importance of building awareness among African peoples of the ways that racism, Eurocentricity, and race power work in order to resist the White supremacy facing Africans in the Diaspora.

African-American scholar, poet, and activist W. E. B. Du Bois (1868–1963) was the first African-American to earn and receive a doctorate from Harvard University. He was also one of the first Americans to formally theorize the race problem in the United States. To this day, he remains one of the central inspirations for Afrocentricity (Du Bois 1996). Du Bois co-founded the National Association for the Advancement of Colored People (NAACP) and was the editor-in-chief of the NAACP's groundbreaking journal, *The Crisis: A Record of the Darker Races*. Du Bois argued that Africans needed to understand race differently in order to resist and overcome racism. Du Bois was among the first to point to the impact of race on the ways in which African-Americans understood the world around them. He coined the term "double-consciousness" to refer to the ways in which African-Americans developed a sense of self through both self-perception and the process of being perceived and defined by non-African Americans. He writes: "It is a peculiar sensation, this double-consciousness, this sense of always looking at one's self through the eyes of others, of measuring one's soul by the tape of a world that looks on in amused contempt and pity. One ever feels his two-ness,—an American, a Negro; two souls, two thoughts, two unreconciled strivings; two warring ideals in one dark body, whose dogged strength alone keeps it from being torn asunder" (1996, p. xxxiv). Du Bois's understandings of race stimulated countless forms of resistance, and he is widely remembered as the founder of the modern civil rights movement in the US.

Although he had a profoundly different understanding of, and approach to, challenging the racism and oppression facing Africans in Africa and the Diaspora, Marcus Mosiah Garvey (1887–1940) was another key inspiration for Afrocentricity. Garvey founded the global organization known as the Universal Negro Improvement Association and African Communities League (UNIL-ACL). Garvey and the UNIL-ACL campaigned for the Back-to-Africa movement, arguing that Africans in the Diaspora needed to return to Africa to escape the daily race-based struggle in the Diaspora—indeed, to remove themselves from the race dialogue in the Americas and Europe and return to a homeland not governed by colonial White supremacy. By 1920, the UNIL-UC had over four million members. Garvey taught a love of Africa and a love of the African self (Garvey 1986). This was a substantial departure from the educational offerings available to African-Americans through mainstream schooling and curriculum, which preached White cultural supremacy, and certainly devoted little time to the agency of African-Americans. Although Garvey and Du Bois were unrivalled innovators, Africans have always and everywhere they've found themselves resisted oppression, both in action and in theory. Indeed, the contemporary discussion and practice of Afrocentricity stands on the shoulders of those who have come before. African-centred education builds on the work and struggles of the radicals, the activists, the poets, the scholars, and the regular people in Africa and the Diaspora who have fought in their own ways against oppression. These figures include Frederick Douglas, Harriet Tubman, Booker T. Washington, Langston Hughes, Franz Fanon, Aimé Césaire, Amílcar Cabral, Rosa Parks, Viola Desmond, Martin Luther King Junior, James Baldwin, Malcolm X, Nelson Mandela, and countless others.

Having recognized the rich intellectual soil in which Afrocentricity has grown, this chapter conducts a brief review of relevant literature on African-centred schooling and offers a scholarly context for the debate concerning African-centred education. It is significant to stress that, while intellectual thought about African-centred education has a long history, the pedagogy of Afrocentricity does not automatically translate into African-centred schooling. The most widely recognized ideas regarding the operationalization of African-centred schooling have been coloured by the scholarly work of Molefi Kete Asante, Maulana Karenga, Kofi Lomotey, Akwasi Akoto, Marianna Ani, Carol D. Lee, Peter C. Murrell, and Mwalimu J. Shujaa, to name a few. These authors have articulated similar conceptualizations of what African-centred schooling should do in order to combat the pervasive mis-education and under-education of African youth in Euro-American contexts. "Euro-America" refers here to both Europe and the Americas, of which Canada is a part. These scholars rightly contend that, in racialized spaces where African youth have been subjected to Eurocentrism's ontological and epistemological abasement for centuries, African-centred schooling seems to be the only recourse to stemming this critical lack in African youth education. Summing up the goal and purpose of African-centred schools, Lee (1992) noted:

> [T]he independent African-centred school movement has taken a proactive stance, defining within a community context the possibilities and gift that Black children offer the world, and creating institutions to manifest its ideals. [These] institu-

> tions validate knowledge, help to shape visions, inculcate values, and provide the foundation for community stability ... [they] strive to educate and socialize African children to assume their future roles as political, intellectual, spiritual and economic leaders in their communities. Its vision is one in which Black people are firmly rooted in family and community ... (161)

Like Lee (1992), most proponents of African-centred educational options view African-centred schooling as an avenue for ensuring the holistic education of African children and nurturing their successful social, spiritual, and academic development.

In order to understand such paradigmatic thinking, it is important for us to provide an overview of some of the works at the heart of this philosophy, honing in on some central ideas and arguments as they relate to African-centred education, schooling, and pedagogy. We begin with a very brief survey of the literature dealing with the historical development of African-centred schooling in the United States and the United Kingdom. Next, we discuss works that specifically deal with the theory and praxis of African-centred schooling and education. Here, the goal is to elucidate the visions and goals of Afrocentricity and African-centred education as envisioned by Molefi Kete Asante, the founder of the school of thought. Finally, we examine some of the debates in the literature concerning the key challenges and issues of bringing African-centred schooling, education, pedagogy, and theory to praxis. This is of importance to educationalists, policy makers, and curriculum planners aspiring to charter their own African-centred school in terms of both broadening their understanding of the challenges they may face and providing a sense of existing conversations on African-centred education.

African-Centred Schools: Early Development and Historical Trajectory

As noted above, the movement toward African-centred education has a long history. The literature on the development of Independent Black Institutions, Charter Schools, and Black Supplementary Schools (so-called in Britain) provides valuable insight into the early educational activism of Africans in the Diaspora. In particular, Anderson (1988), Butchart (1980), Ratteray (1992), and Watkins (2001) attend to the details of these movements, while Ratteray and Shujaa (1987) trace this history to the 1790s during the European system of trade in enslaved people. During this time, free and enslaved African peoples were engaged (albeit primarily on the individual and small-group levels) in silent resistances in order to secure their basic rights to education. These authors remind us of the many historical accounts of enslaved Africans hiding books and struggling to read in the dark despite harsh legal sanctions and possible punishment by death for those discovered to be in defiance of colonial law (Ratteray and Shujaa 1987).

Equally worthy of note are works by Lee (1992) and Mirza and Reay (Reay and Mirza 1997; Mirza and Reay 2000), which detail the collective struggles for self-education not only during the period of slavery but also during the post-Reconstruction/post-slavery period (1865–1900). Mirza and Reay trace the growth of Sabbath schools and reading clubs in the Southern United States and Britain. In this category of literature, we also find Lawson Bush's (2004) writings examining the evolution of Independent Black Institutions (IBIs) in the American context dating as far back as the signing of the Emancipation Proclamation in 1863. These writings reveal African communities' zeal for educational self-determination amidst seemingly insurmountable financial, legal, and social constraints. Bush writes: "White northern missionaries were … surprised by the will of the formerly enslaved Africans to educate themselves. Books or fragments of books were seen in the hands of African-American men, women and children everywhere they traveled in the South" (2004: 387). Importantly, Bush's work locates the Back-to-Africa movement, the Pan-African movement, and the Black Consciousness Movement (and their leaders) as having tremendously impacted many of the early African-centred institutions. Tracing the history of the Sister Clara Muhammad school (one of the earliest Islamic schools focused on teaching history that placed Black people at the centre of civilization), Rashid and Muhammad (1992) discuss the impact that Marcus Garvey's Universal Negro Improvement Association and its motto of Black self-determination and racial pride had on the institution's pedagogy of liberation based on knowing the self, loving the self, and doing for self. The literature also reveals the challenges of developing these institutions. Indeed, African-centred institutions have historically been marred by periodic declines (most notably during the period between 1890 and 1935 in the United States).

Notwithstanding these setbacks, unfair and restrictive state laws coupled with lack of government funding and support propelled the African community to form IBIs funded, built, staffed, and maintained by their own communities. This is noteworthy, as it demonstrates that people of African descent in the Americas (and, to a lesser extent, in Europe) have always held education in high regard that empowers them to move toward self-determination and charter an independent ontological path outside of Eurocentric teaching, learning, and schooling (Bush 1997; Bush 2004; Reay and Mirza 1997). The same holds true throughout the African Diaspora, where Africans have either taken advantage of—or fought to create—schooling opportunities for their communities. Indeed, this human thirst for learning (and it would be incorrect to understand such an impulse as being culturally or geographically specific or unique to Africa or Africans) explains the epistemological focus of the colonial project—from literacy laws in the US, to forced segregation in schooling in Canada, to the forcible exclusion of African peoples from formal education in the Caribbean during the early European colonial era (beginning in the early 1600s).

In 2013, there are more than 100 African-centred schools in the US, some private, some public, and some charter at the elementary and secondary levels. On the whole, African-centred schooling in the US has been a site for academic enrichment for African and African-American children and has yielded above-average grades and test results on a number of national and regional standardized tests. (This empirical data is discussed in greater detail in Chapter 7.) Putting aside for a moment the politics of charter schools and the privatization of education, the African-centred curricular focus has proven consistently central to the academic success of children attending African-centred schools or programs across the US. As described in the introduction, Canada has a shorter and less developed history of African-centred learning than the US; however, the latest student test scores from the Toronto District School Board's Africentric Alternative School indicate that students in the Canadian context, like their peers in the US, stand to benefit from African-centred approaches as well. This school is the result of a 30-plus year community struggle and has been supported by the academic work of George Sefa Dei (1993; 1995; 1996a; 1997; 2000; 2008a), Dei et al. (1995), Dei and Kempf (2007), Brathwaite and James (1996), and—more recently—Allen (2011). Professors George Sefa Dei, Carl James, and Erica Lawson have each contributed countless hours as academic advisors to groups and committees at the community, government, and academic levels. Along with Arlo Kempf, these three have also been active in media circles and have defended African-centred schooling on television, radio, and in various print media across Canada. In addition to pulling from a broader and primarily US-based literature, the fight for African-centred schooling in Canada draws on a small but growing body of work, which has largely emerged from the initial community-based push for African-centred schooling.

Despite ongoing controversy (e.g., the media outcry following the establishment of an African-centred school by US President Barack Obama's church, and the Canadian media circus surrounding the establishment of a second Africentric school in Toronto), the movement for African-centred teaching and learning continues, with steady growth in the US and discussions of African-centred schools in Montreal and Halifax, Canada.

Conceptualizing African-Centred Schooling and Education: Philosophical and Ideological Underpinnings

The existing literature points to three types of African-centred models of schooling: Independent Black Institutions (IBIs), charter schools, and Black supplementary schools. Lawson (2004) defines an Independent Black Institution as a private, self-governing institution not dependent upon a larger public or sectarian organization. The author extends this definition to include schools supported and governed by Black religious organizations. IBIs primarily serve the African-American community and most often have a governing board comprised for the most part of African-Americans. In contrast, charter schools enter into a contract with a state school board or local county board of education, which may delineate the goals, purpose, and management structure of the charter school. In this model, the state, county, or district guides the process so as to ensure that the school executes its plans to meet the needs of its target population. They differ from traditional public schools in that they are given more autonomy in exchange for a promise to achieve improved educational outcomes (Bush 2004: 393). This autonomy challenges the labour and wage protections of teachers, as most charters are non-unionized and can operate for profit. Black Supplementary Schools (as they are called in Britain) are similar to IBIs in that they are operated privately outside of the scope of traditional schools. Similar to IBIs, they are operated, organized, and controlled by and for African-Diasporic communities. Unlike IBIs, however, they are supplementary schools and are officially regarded as an addition or supplement to mainstream schooling (Reay and Mirza 1997: 477). Despite these divergences, all three models were developed or used out of African peoples' desire to seek redress for the exclusion and educational shortcomings of mainstream schools.

In the US context, the principles and guiding philosophies of African-centred education and pedagogy have been laid out by scholars like Molefi Kete Asante, Kofi Lomotey, Maulana Karenga, and Mwalimu Shujaa. Carol D. Lee's "Profile of an Independent Black Institution: African-Centred Education at Work" (1992), provides an excellent and detailed synopsis of the goals and objectives of African-centred education. In delineating the contours of African-centred education, Lee (1992: 165–166) points out that African-centred education aims to accomplish the following:

1. Legitimize African stores of knowledge.
2. Positively exploit and scaffold productive community and cultural practices,
3. Extend and build upon indigenous African languages.
4. Reinforce community ties and idealize [the concept of] service to one's family, community, nation, race, and world.
5. Promote positive social relationships.
6. Impart a worldview that idealizes a positive, self-sufficient future for one's people without denying the self-worth and right to self-determination of others.
7. Support cultural continuity while promoting critical consciousness.
8. Promote the vision of individuals and communities as producers rather than as simply consumers.

The fusion of morality, ethics, and knowledge acquisition is of pedagogical significance in an African-centred educational setting. This is in keeping with the Kemetic proposition that moral social practice is necessary for the development of humanity.[1] According to the proponents of Afrocentricity, an African-centred pedagogy/curriculum aims to unite academic excellence and positive character, and to foster an environment where interdependence, community, and reciprocity are part and parcel of the learning process. African-centred education is guided by *Nguzo Saba*, Karenga's (1988) principles of Kwanzaa: unity, self-determination, collective work and responsibility, cooperative economics, creativity, purpose, and faith. While the application of these foundational principles is key to the successful realization of an African educational institution, African-centred pedagogy requires willing teachers who are not only knowledgeable about Black history but whose realities and personal/subject locations are also grounded in "the social ethics of African culture." As Shujaa (1994) states:

> When discussing African-centered education ... more emphasis should be placed on pedagogy than on curriculum. My reasoning for this is that pedagogy conveys the importance of the teacher to the education process while curriculum is too often reduced to documentation.... It is the African centeredness of the teacher's thinking that determines the African-centeredness of the teaching. (256–265)

Put differently, it is clear that—for an African-centred model of education to work effectively—teachers and educators must live, breathe, and be constantly engaged in the social philosophy and praxis of *Maat* (Karenga 2004). Reflecting on Karenga, Kempf (2011) provides the following overview of *Maatian* ethics:

> Etymologically Maat is traced to notions of straightness and evenness. Drawing from a substantial literature on Maat, Karenga reveals its meaning as one signifying a guiding force, a cosmic order, truth, ideal wisdom, a metaphysical ideal and an epistemological ideal. As a wide-ranging concept, it expresses itself in four domains: 1) the universal—the totality of ordered existence; 2) the political domain—regulating justice and injustice; 3) the social domain—relationships and duty in the context of community; and, 4) the personal domain in which—following the rules and principles of Maat—is to realize concretely the universal order in oneself. (102)

Other scholarly writings have added to the conception of African-centred pedagogy. Among these are Akoto (1994), Hilliard (1997), Lee (1994), Murrell (2002), and Shujaa (1994). Other works provide useful examples of pedagogical methods that can be employed in instructing African youth in an African-centred educational setting. Hoover's "The Nairobi Day School: An African-American Independent School, 1966–1984" (1992) outlines some of the strategies used by educators at the Nairobi Day School to achieve an African-centred model of education. The school's pedagogy and philosophy were based on the concept of community-based dialogical learning developed by Brazilian popular educator Paulo Freire (1921–1997). In keeping with Freire's pedagogical approach, teaching emphasized the development of students' motor and cognitive skills while emphasizing the teachings of their own cultures from a material and problem-posing perspective. In this approach, students are understood as knowers and as legitimate producers of knowledge. Students are also encouraged to consider problems facing society, and to view themselves as capable, change-making agents. This strongly parallels an African-centred approach, in which the cultural knowledge of African-descended students is constructively interrogated, legitimized, and celebrated. To this end, the study of Black history, culture, and languages were an integral part of the schools' pedagogy. Teachers at the school would centre and celebrate Black culture and history in the form of politically oriented music, rhymes, and short stories. Students were taught to recognize syllable patterns through rhymes, raps, and stories, which simultaneously increased their spelling, literacy skills, and political pride.

Another useful example is found in the New Concept Development Centre (NCDC) of Milwaukee, where students were taught numeracy skills using the Egyptian (Kemetic), Yoruba, and Arabic system of numeracy in conjunction with western approaches. In the aforementioned examples, games from West Africa were employed as part of the curriculum and pedagogy. This approach emphasized a pedagogy that linked cultural knowledge to traditional school subject matters. For instance, playing games such as Oware[2] tied the abstract to the concrete and supported the acquisition of logical inference and decision-making skills, which would become useful for navigating real world experiences (Lee 1992; Hoover 1992). For his part, Harris (1992) illustrates the pedagogical, instructional, and communicative effectiveness of Yoruba traditional education (such as proverbs and folktales) in achieving educational reforms that are in keeping with the ideas of visionary Afrocentrists like Asante.

Although some general principles are instructive, African-centred schooling requires recognition of specific social, historical, geographical, and cultural contexts, since every school exists to support a specific community in a specific time and place. To go one step further, inasmuch as each African-centred school is different, each exists for a different reason. In addition to promoting the holistic development of school as community and community as education, the importance of context also draws upon the diversity of offerings implicit and explicit in African-centred teaching and learning. The African continent cannot be understood through culturally reductionist paradigms. Similarly, the African Diaspora refers to a plurality of people, cultures, knowledges, histories, relations, and experiences. With this in mind, African-centred learning draws from a dynamic and fluid understanding of *Africa* and *African*, which is constituted by the African peoples of today as well as those who have come before.

It is evident from the literature that, in making this vision a reality, African-centred educators have to anticipate and prepare for the particular challenges, issues, and setbacks that can emerge in the process of African-centred teaching, learning, and schooling. The following section examines some of the scholarship that is instructive in this regard.

The Challenges, Issues, and Prospects of Actualizing African-Centred Schooling

An examination of the literature on African-centred schooling and education reveals the realities, issues, and continuing challenges that teachers, administrators, parents, and members of the African community have encountered in actualizing an African-centred model of education. African-centred schools have grappled with problems like structural maintenance (e.g., obtaining and sustaining safe and healthy physical facilities) and with ensuring that the ideological goals of African-centred curriculum and pedagogy are implemented. As Shujaa (1992) points out, African-centred schools are constantly caught in a peculiar conundrum when they struggle to fulfill their African-centred mission, philosophy, and pedagogy. Schools often encounter challenges in coalescing the African-centred ideology while staying true to parental and student expectations. Shujaa notes that most parents who decide to enrol their children in these types of institutions act in accordance with a pre-existing African-centred orientation. In other words, parents who advocate for this type of schooling for their children do so to ensure that their children are educated in an environment that is in keeping with the values, attitudes, and beliefs espoused in the home. When African-centred schools fail to actualize the parents' ideological and philosophical ideas, expectations go unsatisfied. Considering that the number of parents choosing African-centred independent schools due to their ideological orientation is growing (Shujaa 1992: 157), this question is particularly relevant.

Another challenge often present at these institutions is noted in Murrell's 1999 and 2002 reports from his five-year case study of the George Washington Carver Charter School. In that work, he charts the clash of ideology between different state-funded African-centred schools, which are often subject to state institutional controls. Murrell (2002) notes that one of the challenges the school faced was trying to unite the state's public-school board regulations regarding student grade-level achievement with the unique approaches of an African-centred curriculum. According to Murrell (1999; 2002), many African-centred schools still struggled with residual ties to traditional schools because state boards and—surprisingly—some parents called for assessment methods like standardized tests, which are traditionally associated and practiced in Eurocentric schooling contexts. These tests were often viewed as a necessary pedagogical tool even though such methods may contradict the alternative methods of assessment preferred by some proponents of African-centred schooling. External demands can thus retard innovation and impede the local development of African-centred pedagogy (Murrell 1999: 579–580). To be clear, we recognize the potential of good testing to support racially, socially, and economically marginalized youth so that they might compete with more advantaged students on relatively objective terrain; however, measurement as such has been elusive to date.

A final issue of note concerns the persistent underfunding—and regular de-funding—of African-centred schools. In the most extreme cases, this can lead to school closure. The impact of poor or inadequate funding for professional learning and development, for curricular resources for teachers and students, and on infrastructure maintenance can dramatically impact the chances of school-wide success. This raises the issue of whether publicly funded African-centred schools are ever set up to fail. As far as curricular content is concerned, Lee points out that inadequate in-service staff training and "narrow ideological foci with little grounding and support from the communities being served" are persistent issues (1992: 174). The realization of an African-centred pedagogy against the backdrop of state expectations and external controls presents unique challenges that need to be understood and overcome in order to make successful African-centred schooling a reality.

Hoover (1992) reminds us that those who question Afrocentricity's educational offerings would do well to look at the successes and challenges of the Nairobi Day school project. As we detail in Chapter 7, this and a number of other African-centred models (such as the NCDC) have supported tremendous student success and have managed to find a balance of the dual need for academic excellence and corrective Black/African history (Hoover 1992). We might add that any reading that posits African-centred schooling and academic excellence as being mutually exclusive is, at best, short-sighted. Indeed, the African-centred curricular focus on skills, caring, and community-orientated philosophy is as relevant today as it ever has been. However, while recognizing the possibilities, one must also be cognizant of the many challenges of implementing and maintaining such schools in settings like Ontario, where institutionalized racism at various levels makes this task all the more difficult.

Notes

1. For more on Kemetic philosophy, Asante's *The Egyptian Philosophers: Ancient African Voices from Imhotep to Akhenaten* (2000), and Maulana Karenga's *Maat: The Moral Ideal in Ancient Egypt—A Study in Classical African Ethics* (2004) are particularly instructive.
2. Oware, a centuries-old game hugely popular in West Africa today, involves a wooden board usually containing eight to 12 depressions in and out of which marble-sized objects are strategically moved. Two people usually play, taking alternating turns, with the object of obtaining all of the marbles.

References

Akoto, A. (1994). "Notes on an African-Centered Pedagogy." In M. Shujaa (ed.), *Too Much Schooling Too Little Education: A Paradox of Black Life in White Societies* (319–337). Trenton: Africa World Press.

Allen, A. (2011). "Improving the Education and Life Chances of African-Canadians: A Vision for Preparing Students for the World of the 21st Century." In V. D'Oyley (ed.), *Re/visioning: Canadian Perspectives of the Education of Africans in the 21st Century* (77–88). Toronto: Captus Press Inc.

Anderson, J. D. (1988). *The Education of Blacks in the South, 1860–1935*. Chapel Hill: University of North Carolina Press.

Asante, M. K. (2000). *The Egyptian Philosophers: Ancient African Voices from Imhotep to Akhenaten*. Chicago: African-American Images.

Brathwaite, K., and James, C. (eds.). (1996). *Educating African-Canadians*. Toronto: James Lorimer & Company Ltd.

Bush, L. (1997). "Independent Black Institutions in America: A Rejection of Schooling, an Opportunity for Education." *Urban Education*, 22(1): 96–116.

———. (2004). "Access, School Choice and Independent Black Institutions: A Historical Perspective." *Journal of Black Studies*, 34(3): 386–401.

Butchart, R. (1980). *Northern Schools, Southern Blacks, and Reconstruction: Freedmen's Education, 1862–1875*. Westport, CT: Greenwood.

Dei, G. J. S. (1993). "Narrative Discourses of Black Parents and the Canadian Public School System." *Canadian Ethnic Studies*, 25(3): 45–65.

———. (1995). "Examining the Case for African-Centered Schools in Ontario." *McGill Journal of Education*, 30(2): 179–198.

———. (1996a). "Listening to Voices: Developing a Pedagogy of Change from Narratives of African-Canadian Students and Parents." In K. Brathwaite and C. James (eds.), *Educating African-Canadians* (32–57). Toronto: James Lorimer & Company Ltd.

———. (1997). "Beware of False Dichotomies: Revisiting the Idea of 'Black-focused' Schools in Canadian Contexts." *Journal of Canadian Studies*, 31(4): 58–79.

———. (2000). "Rethinking the Role of Indigenous Knowledges in the Academy." *International Journal of Inclusive Education*, 4(2): 111–132.

———. (2008a). "Schooling as Community: Race, Schooling, and the Education of African Youth." *Journal of Black Studies*, 38(3): 346–366.

Dei, G. J. S., Holmes, L., Mazzuca, J., McIsaac, E., and Campbell, R. (1995). *Drop Out or Push Out?* Report submitted to the Ontario Ministry of Education, Toronto.

Dei, G. J. S., and Kempf, A. (2007, November 16). "Debunking Myths about African-Centered Schools." *Toronto Star*, AA8.

Du Bois, W. E. B. (1996). *The Souls of Black Folk*. New York: New American Library.

Garvey, J. G. (ed.). (1986). *The Philosophy and Opinions of Marcus Garvey*. New York: Majority Press.

Harris, D. W. (1992). "Africentrism and Curriculum: Concepts, Issues and Prospects." *Journal of Negro Education*, 61(3): 301–316.

Hilliard, A. G. (1997). "Teacher Education from an African-American Perspective." In J. J. Irvine (ed.), *Critical Knowledge for Diverse Teachers and Learners* (125–148). Washington, DC: American Association for Colleges of Teacher Education.

Hoover, M. (1992). "The Nairobi Day School: An African-American Independent School, 1966–1984." *Journal of Negro Education*, 61(2): 201–210.

Karenga, M. (1988). "Black Studies and the Problematics of Paradigm: The Philosophical Dimension." *Journal of Black Studies*, 18(4): 395–414.

———. (2004). *Maat: The Moral Ideal in Ancient Egypt: A Study in Classical African Ethics*. New York: Routledge.

Kempf, A. (2011). "North African Knowledges and the Western Classroom: Situating Selected Literature." In W. Wane, A. Kempf, and M. Simmons (eds.), *The Politics of Cultural Knowledge* (111–128). Rotterdam: Sense.

Lee, C. D. (1992). "Profile of an Independent Black Institution: African-Centered Education at Work." *Journal of Negro Education*, 61(2): 161–177.

———. (1994). "African-Centered Pedagogy: Complexities and Possibilities." In M Shujaa (ed.), *Too Much Schooling, Too Little Education: A Paradox of Black Life in White Societies* (295–318). Trenton: African World Press.

Mirza, H. S., and Reay, D. (2000). "Spaces and Places of Black Educational Desire: Rethinking Black Supplementary Schools as a New Social Movement." *Sociology: The Journal of the British Sociological Association*, 34(3): 521–544.

Murrell, P. C. (1999). "Chartering the Village: The Making of an African-Centered Charter School." *Urban Education*, 33(5): 565–583.

———. (2002). *African-Centered Pedagogy: Developing Schools of Achievement for African-American Children*. Albany: State University of New York Press.

Ratteray, J. (1992). "Independent Neighbourhood Schools: A Framework for the Education of African-Americans." *Journal of Negro Education*, 61(4): 139–147.

Ratteray, J., and Shujaa, M. J. (1987). *Dare to Choose: Parental Choice at Independent Neighborhood Schools*. Washington, DC: Institute of Independent Education.

Reay, D., and Mirza, H. S. (1997). "Uncovering Genealogies of the Margins: Black Supplementary Schooling." *British Journal of Sociology of Education*, 18(4): 477–499.

Rashid, H., and Muhammad, Z. (1992). "The Sister Clara Muhammad Schools: Pioneers in the Development of Islamic Education in America." *Journal of Negro Education*, 61(4): 178–185.

Shujaa, M. J. (1992). Afrocentric Transformation and Parental Choice in African America Independent Schools. *Journal of Negro Education*, 61(2), 148-159.

———. (1994). "Afrocentric Transformation and Parental Choice in African-American Independent Shools." In M. J. Shujaa (ed.), *Too Much Schooling, Too Little Education: A Paradox of Black Life in White Societies* (361–376). Trenton: Africa World Press.

Watkins, W. H. (2001). *The White Architects of Black Education: Ideology and Power in America, 1865–1954*. New York: Teachers College Press.

CHAPTER 36

"Born" Freaks, "Made" Freaks, and Media Circuses: Systemic Management of Race and Gender in the Reena Virk Case

Nicole Pietsch

Introduction

When news of the murder of Reena Virk became known to the Canadian public in November of 1997, it could not be written, described, or reported without accompanying debate: the public at once agreed that there was something fantastic or unusual—"something intolerable"—about Reena's death (Grosz 1996, 61).

Victoria, British Columbia, had certainly seen other murders—some even more appalling or forensically complex—yet the Virk case incited both domestic and international responses that were indignant and repetitive in theme: *horrifying*, *chilling*, and an indicator of some endemic "*moral blind spot*" (Wood 1999, 18). The details of note in this case were not the *what* but the *whom*: the victim, Reena Virk, was a 14-year-old girl of South Asian descent. Those guilty of assaulting Virk were eight predominantly white, middle-class youth, seven of whom were female. Eventually the charge of murder was placed upon two of the eight—the lone male attacker, 16-year-old Warren Glowatski, and Kelly Ellard, a white, middle-class girl of 15.

What is the relevance of social categories such as "white," "young," "middle class," and "female," both within a criminal justice case and to the public gaze? The Virk murder was replete with confident assertions about the irrelevance of social location. Yet, while racism as a factor in the violence committed against Reena Virk has been "mostly absent from the media, and certainly not part of the legal arguments," both these systems proved to be largely obsessed with the analogous—though certainly less politically laden—notions of "fitting in," "deviance," and the new "phenomenon of girl violence" (Batacharya 2006, 184). On the one hand, commentators relegated Reena and her difference to mere "individual characteristics" (181) with no political or social significance. But the same commentators watched the girls who met "the requirements of hegemonic femininity—i.e., white, middle-class, heterosexual, able-bodied"—and waited for them to indeed prove themselves "the 'fairer sex'" (183). In addition, commentators waited for those who did *not* meet these requirements to garner blame for the crime. Reena's murder was, at once, a case fixated upon white girlhood, yet openly dissociated from the significance of race and gender and their implications for violence.

This chapter uses a feminist post-structuralist analysis in order to critically examine popular representations of Reena Virk's murder. This framework recognizes that socially constructed and pre-existing discourses assign specific qualities and judgments to subjects. I will address discourses surrounding those diversely located individuals involved in the case and ask whether these subjects fit socially constructed ideals of gender and race, and, if not, how we should understand them. A post-structuralist framework will also identify historical values that have contributed to race-specific (including white) conceptualizations of normality, abnormality, and normative femininity; in other words, according to social hierarchies, who is deemed normal, and who is deemed a "born freak." Last, I will address how resistance to socially conscribed categories complicates (and is managed within) this hierarchical system, introducing the notion of "made freaks": individuals who call social hierarchies and attendant privilege into question simply by accepting and enacting behaviour outside their gender designation.

Using a textual analysis, I will scrutinize journalistic interpretations of the Virk case, Rebecca Godfrey's 2005 true crime book *Under the Bridge*, and portrayals of both victim and perpetrators throughout the actual Virk legal cases. I will illustrate how constructs of white femininity inform our expectations of "girlhood"—including who may claim membership to this girlhood and who cannot. Sequentially, I will show how the law, despite being "framed in an ideology that emphasizes objectivity and universalism" (Marchetti 2008, 155), proves laden with these very same prejudices. My concern is to suggest that our understanding of, and response to, acts of gender-based violence are not universally applied. Instead, these understandings and responses are more dependent upon the victim's—and in the Virk case, perpetrator's—ability to meet the requirements of hegemonic femininity.

Invisibility/Ignorance

> There were stories in the newspaper of the "awkward misfit" ... stories told to detectives of "some Indian chick," of "Rhea," or "Trina."[1]
>
> —REBECCA GODFREY, *UNDER THE BRIDGE: THE TRUE STORY OF THE MURDER OF REENA VIRK*

Reena Virk's existence in View Royal, a suburb in Victoria, British Columbia, must be understood specifically in terms of her gendered and racialized *relationality*. In the book *Under the Bridge: The True Story of the Murder of Reena Virk*, author Rebecca Godfrey characterizes Reena as "dark skinned and heavy in a town and time that valued the thin and the blonde" (Godfrey 2005, 29). Phrased in this way, the remark appears to lean toward a critique of such values, but the book goes on, unwittingly, to reproduce the same partiality. It is difficult to find a passage about Reena in *Under the Bridge*. Its pages are largely concerned with the emotions, interests, and histories of "the thin and the blonde"—that is, predominantly, her assailants. For the sake of interest, I entered the victims' name as well as those convicted of her murder into my Internet search engine: *Kelly Ellard* garners 86,000 web pages; *Reena Virk*, 23,600—less than a third of the former. While I expected some variation, this considerable disparity seems astounding. Over and over again in the story of Reena Virk, Reena herself remains the minor female character—only significant by her association to the central character(s).

But who, then, is the central character? If Reena is, by definition, relationally different, somebody else—some*thing* categorically else—represents the socially average. In Elizabeth R. Cole and Alyssa N. Zucker's *Black and White Women's Perspectives on Femininity*, the authors describe a socially constructed "prescriptive set of normative feminine behaviours" and attributes; these include, among others, "beauty, demeanour ... sexuality, and (White) race" (Cole and Zucker 2007, 1). Dominant femininity, the authors argue—as well as "the typically White upper-middle class women who can achieve it"—is "conspicuously valued within mainstream [North] American culture" (1). Inevitably, these standards create "a normative yardstick for all femininities in which [non-white] women are relegated to the bottom of the gender hierarchy" (1). Indeed, non-white women have, historically, been treated as though they exist outside femininity's boundaries. For example, racist depictions of black women as unattractive, aggressive, sexually promiscuous, and bad mothers stand in direct contrast to hegemonic representations of femininity that award white women a naturalized, higher social and political status. Black feminist Patricia Hill Collins affirms that black women's daily experiences with both racial and gender oppression result in needs and problems distinct from white women and black men, including a need for "replacing denigrated images of Black women with self-defined images" (Collins 1997, 13). Similarly, social constructions of Aboriginal women are created relative to white womanhood: throughout colonial history in countries such as Australia and Canada, Aboriginal women were seen as markedly sexual, in contrast to the passive, prudish Victorian woman (Pinnuck and Dowling 2002, 54). This comparison is so often repeated in contemporary racial stereotypes that the descriptions are naturalized and appear to be real and therefore invisible to those in hegemonic social locations.

Likewise, media depictions of Reena Virk describe her in terms of what she was *not*. Although she is the central figure within this story, she is also the lone female of South Asian descent. And so, both aesthetically and socially, Reena is depicted only as a contrast to other, usually white, girls. Reena is relegated to "the incidental, the inessential as opposed to the essential" (De Beauvoir 1997, 13). Thus, it is her perpetrators who remain the comparable centre of the media and legal case. In her life and her death, like most marginalized subjects, Reena was/is the Other, "deprive[d] ... of its absolute sense and [made] manifest its relativity" (14) to those in positions of normalized privilege around her. Without the stated feminine benchmarks of thinness, whiteness, and class, Virk remains virtually indescribable. "Reena Virk had a hard time fitting in," a reporter notes. "It didn't help that she was slightly overweight and the dark-skinned child of immigrants who were not well-to-do" (Batacharya 2006, 181). Commentators, as above, found no language beyond the normative feminine to depict her. And so, over and over again, the media fails to locate Reena as a legitimate or valuable female.

Like other non-white females, Reena's racialized version of femininity was also unequally valued in her social circle (Cole and Zucker 2007). In both journalistic accounts and Godfrey's true crime narrative *Under the Bridge*, this bias is simply regurgitated. Godfrey's narrative maintains a bias that casts Reena's social location as entirely incidental, despite ample evidence of how she was socially rejected. Godfrey does not link the two phenomena together; instead, Reena's comparatively explicit *difference* from white females in her midst is simply characterized as social ineptness. Throughout the book, Godfrey conveys Reena as the perpetual fifth wheel and *wannabe*. In fact, there is an underlying theme in both *Under the Bridge* and newspaper articles about Virk's death of Reena's repeated attempts at participation, which were always coming up short:

> [Josephine] remembered Reena trying to tag along with her and Dusty, and trying to impress them both. (Godfrey 2005, 50)

> [Reena had] shown them.... She could be just like them. She could kiss the same boys. She could be a troublemaker. (50)

> Reena's size and physical maturity made her different. (Tafler 1998, 16)

> Tall and heavy, she towered over other girls her age. She was considered unattractive. (16)

In the above excerpts, there is no acknowledgement that systemically and politically, within an inner circle where popularity hinges on criteria associated with whiteness and thinness, Reena was the automatic, permanent Other. Nonetheless, it is fascinating that Reena continued to operate as if she was an equal in this circle; at the very least, she continued to anticipate the eventual possibility of this equality. In this regard, she existed in a conceptual no man's land: as a racialized female body, she did not fit into socially constructed standards of femininity (white, thin, pretty); yet as a keen participant in View Royal's youth culture, she did not match the expected behaviours dictated by her skin colour either. In reviewing the gender- and racially based verbal abuse that Reena endured from her peers, Tess Chakkalakal remarks with interest:

> These names did not procure their intended effect. That is, Reena Virk appears not to have listened to these names—she acted as if she was not an "ugly," "East Indian," "a bearded lady," "a freak." She acted as if she had power, as if she could do things that a girl of her size, colour and ethnicity was clearly prohibited from doing. (2000, 163)

Indeed, according to media reported anecdotes, Reena consistently pressed herself as a peer among her group: for example, she dated a boy in her circle, spent time at localities frequented by area youth, and continually sought the company and approval of teens in this community (Tafler 1998, 16). Her resistance shows both resilience and self-respect, yet, like others who fail to "successfully perform" normative gender (and raced) behaviours, Reena faced resultant social censure, social intangibility, and exclusion from multiple social categories (Cole and Zucker 2007).

Media representations of Reena Virk ally themselves with this rebuke. Godfrey normatively describes Reena as a young woman who positioned herself in an improbable, bad, or incorrect place. Godfrey's language depicts Reena as tipping dangerously out of bounds of family expectations, stating that "[Reena] wanted to celebrate and JWs [Jehovah's Witnesses] believed celebrations should be subdued," and in consequence, "there'd been some talk of [her] excommunication" (Godfrey 2005, 32). Godfrey additionally depicts Reena as behaving in ways outside her expected behavioural element: "How could a girl like Reena be accepted? She could try to be like the others, paint her nails blue, listen to the same songs" (33). Finally, Godfrey characterizes Reena as, consequently, falling into enemy territory: "[A youth counsellor] would write in her notes that Reena was 'affiliating herself with the Crips [a youth gang] because they were people who had respect'" (64). Godfrey's remarks characterize Reena as repeatedly and permanently out of place. As a female, Reena fails, and as a youth of colour resisting racialized hierarchies, she regains no footing. Under the gaze of racial oppression, Reena simply remains an *insubstantial* feminine.

Resistance

She didn't know her place in the world.[2]

—Sid Tafler, "Who Was Reena Virk?" *Saturday Night*

In *Gender Treachery: Homophobia, Masculinity, and Threatened Identities*, Patrick Hopkins notes that social identity is a dynamic of achieving the appropriate gender performance, as well as avoiding oppositional others. One's performance means enacting a socially constructed gendered essence, wherein maleness and femaleness are opposite, inevitable, and binary:

> Girls are weak, boys are strong, girls play stupid games, boys play real games, girls that want to play football are weird, boys that do not want to play football are faggots.... What it means to have a particular identity depends on what it means not to have some other identity. (Hopkins 1996, 103, 97–98)

But Reena Virk toppled the very notion of gender categorization. In popular media such as news journalism and Godfrey's *Under the Bridge*, Reena remains a not-quite or less-than-real woman—viable (and describable) only in terms of her inadequacy. As a young woman marginalized by (and seen to be struggling against) the social categories ascribed to her, Reena Virk appeared to the mainstream as permanently anomalous—not quite this, yet not quite that either. What is society's view of this particular type of gender traitor? Politically and socially marginalized, yet always resistant to this reality, the media found Reena Virk acutely contradictory: a paradox, lacking categorization.

Reena's difference, indeed, total ambiguity—*not this, not that, not quite what anybody else was*—is cited everywhere as a contributing factor to her death. In her rejection of the social categories ascribed to her, their attendant behavioural tenets, and the implicit social hierarchy ascribed to categorization itself, Reena represented a creature outside, or in opposition to, *the very idea* of social categorization. Reena appeared not to be a rightful member of *any* social category. The popular media rhetoric tells us that she simply did not *fit*, and this "not fitting" led to a slow but inevitable process of social erasure: rejection, acts of violence perpetrated against her and, ultimately, her death. Comments by Reena's mother's cousin corroborates this dominant understanding: "They [the youth who attacked Reena] knew they could pick on her," Beena Kashyap remarked. "They knew her history—not being accepted.... They knew they could kill her that night" (Tafler 1998, 18). Similarly, according to journalist Sid Tafler, "the disturbing truth is that Reena Virk wasn't just in the wrong place at the wrong time. She arrived at the centre of the tragedy [of her murder] after a long and ultimately futile attempt to find a comfortable place for herself within her family and her community" (16).

The media appeared preoccupied with, if not fixated upon, what Reena was *not*. Yet in the same moment, commentators on the case routinely failed to recognize what she *was*. Reena's most salient divergence from her peers—that she was not white—is barely articulated or evaluated as relevant in the Virk case. A preference for not recognizing Reena Virk as a racialized woman permeated the legal trials concerning her victimization. Inside the courtroom and in the media, Reena was more often described in terms of *sameness*—a youth, a girl, a participant in a particular social circle—interrupted by a smattering of individual incompetence. To quote Godfrey, "Reena was a young girl who appears to have had a certain social awkwardness about her" (2005, 248).

In the courtroom, Reena was understood as a girl, and a girl *only*, notwithstanding that "social hierarchy is inevitably at play" in multiracial and multi-classed groups (Batacharya 2006, 185). In the legal case concerning Reena's victimization, her girlhood was conveniently homogenized; according to Sheila Batacharya, the "only point at which the jury [had] to acknowledge the fact that Reena Virk was a young South Asian woman was in viewing the autopsy photos of her body"—and even this "raising [of] issues of difference" via submission of evidence was nearly blocked by the defence (2006, 186–87). All of a sudden, race became invisible, irrelevant or, at the very least, unspoken.

Where non-white girls and women are *not* portrayed as negative or deficient compared to white girls and women, it often means that they—or their "race"—are simply not represented at all. This is not always apparent or relevant to those in positions of racial privilege, who have the luxury to *always* be included or prioritized. In her work on media representations of the feminine ideal and girls' resistance, author Lisa Duke argues that, usually, "white dominance is ... an accepted and unspoken truth" in media and public life (2002, 219). For example, in magazines marketed to teenaged females, black girls recognize at once that "the mainstream teen magazine ignores and overlooks the most fundamental concerns and interests of African Americans ... [but] white girls ... [are] unaware that the world created in teen magazines [is] ... a White one" (219). Whiteness, to the benefit of its members, is at once highly conspicuous, yet totally invisible.

Despite policy recognition for explicit acts of hate crime, Canadian law, in practice, remains blithely colour-blind: ineffective at recognizing the systemic presentations of racial supremacy operating in daily life. Reena's invisible brownness, as well as the subsequent estimation of her white assailant, Kelly Ellard, in court, highlights this. According to Jiwani:

> In her decision, Judge Morrison's portrayal of Ellard as a person who loved animals, had positive and caring relationships with her family and friends, and posed a low risk to society in general, combined with her denial of racism in the murder. By implication, the judge seemed to be suggesting that racists do not love animals, have no positive relations with others, and pose a high risk in terms of displaying overtly criminal behaviour. (2006, 77).

Here, racism is conceptualized as an unambiguous, atypical, and overall anti-social activity. Yet in truth, most everyday acts of racism—for example, the stereotyping of ethnic groups, the erasure of minority experience from histories, or the under-representation of non-whites in workplaces or politics—are systemic, naturalized, and rewarded by larger society.

In a case that was outwardly, even frantically, obsessed with girlhood, Reena's status as a brown-skinned girl—as opposed to a *white*-skinned girl—remained totally invisible. Being female, in this case, was considered *primary*, while race was constructed as *immaterial*. This, in effect, implied that the girls involved in the assault and murder had something inherently in common (and, in addition, had no salient differences among them): equal membership in a homogenous category determined through gender. Yet historically, femaleness has not necessarily created grounds for any natural solidarity. To assume sameness or intrinsic camaraderie misses the de facto hierarchies that exist *among* women. As Ringrose points out:

> Sisterhood evokes motifs of sameness, nurturing, caring and feminine bonding that don't seem to grapple with feminism's own difficult history of eliding differences between women, differences that are in part this problem of who meets the ... ideal of femininity and who is cast out from its bounds. (2006, 413).

Women's experiences and daily realities can vary greatly when class, race, sexual identity, and ability differences are factored in. Still, in court, Reena was presented as really not much different from her perpetrators; in other words, *a girl is a girl is a girl*. The legal dissemination of the crime against her (and this dissemination's resistance to recognizing non-whiteness) was satisfied to interrupt political marginalization with surface notions of social popularity, as though to suggest that any other girl might have been treated in this (violent) way. As a result, the crime against Reena is never truly unpacked. An act of violence becomes decontextualized, willy-nilly, and victimization appears to be happenstance. But this evaluation is a comfortable oversimplification, a fallacy of "universal girlhood, and all of the race and gender constructions it hinges [up]on," wherein the roles of victim and perpetrator appear indiscriminate and even interchangeable (Batacharya 2006, 187).

However, we know that many acts of interpersonal violence are *not* simply happenstance. For girls and women from marginalized communities, the threat of violence is rooted in historical dynamics of unbalanced social power. Gender, race, and other social determinants influence the targets of violence, as well as the frequency and severity of that violence. Risk of victimization increases if one is very young, a woman of colour, non-heterosexual, or poor. For example, 50 percent of all Canadian women will survive at least one incident of sexual or physical violence, yet for Aboriginal women in Ontario, this number climbs to an astounding eight in ten (80 percent).[3] So while the habit of ignoring race is generally "understood [by white people] to be a graceful, even generous, liberal gesture" (Sullivan 2006, 127), for marginalized groups it represents a tactical act of omission. Indeed, being a person of colour is as significant a part of Reena's story as her being female and being young—or being the strategic victim of this crime.

Repression/Identifying Subversives

> Don't not-be what you are. Perform like a [wo]man.
>
> —Patrick Hopkins, *Gender Treachery: Homophobia, Masculinity, and Threatened Identities*[4]

For a girl to behave contrary to normative tenets of girlhood suggests a breakdown of convention—an illicit broadening of what it means to practise femininity. It also means a blurring of allowable feminine conduct with non-feminine conduct—which, by extension, threatens definitions of allowable *masculinity* as well. The (white) girl who does not behave like a girl is a hazard—not just to herself, but to the behavioural underpinnings of a society.

Femininity is defined not only by what it is (i.e., passive, emotional, pretty, thin) but also what it *is not* (i.e., attributes opposite [to] the former—aggressive, intellectual, athletic) (Hopkins 1996, 98). To perform as an appropriate male or female, one necessarily participates in certain predictable behaviours, and avoids others. As Hopkins notes:

> What it means to have a particular identity depends on what it means not to have some other identity, and by the kinds of relationships one has to other possible and actual identities. (97–98)

Identity is described as what one *is*, as well as what is Other in relation to it. Not only are identities differentiated along a binary plane, but so are the attendant levels of social privilege associated with each differentiated identity. To allow a coalescing of these categories creates a socio-political crisis wherein identity is *fluid*—and normalized hierarchies are, therein, systematically flouted.

Dissidents within the system represent the possibility that hierarchies can be turned on their heads or, at the very least, flattened out. For this reason, acts (and agents) of gender, race, or class *treachery* are usually strongly resisted. Acts of gender or race subversion are, therefore, met with public alarm, anger, or punishment. Resistance is also an unpopular position; just as marginalized groups are relegated to low positions inside the socio-political hierarchy, so are those who *willingly defy* the hierarchy and its bounded categories.

In *Intolerable Ambiguity: Freaks as/at the Limit*, author Elizabeth Grosz unpacks the general history of North American sideshows and criteria for "freak" membership. Until the Second World War, sideshows presented a gamut of human oddities for display and public amusement (Grosz 1996). These oddities, or "freak" exhibits, traditionally exhibited bodies that were exotic (i.e., racialized) or physically anomalous (differently abled or with congenital deformity). Sideshows successfully exhibited those who were socially located Others, as well as those whose physical presentation resisted binary categories of social location altogether: for example, the Bearded Lady, the Fat Lady, or the Tiniest Man Alive.

Such a freak is "an object of simultaneous horror and fascination," Grosz notes, because he or she "is an ambiguous being whose existence imperils categories and oppositions dominant in social life" (Grosz 1996, 57). These sideshow employees blurred conventional frontiers, exhibiting the very embodiment of *crossing-over* foundational cultural limits:

> [Sideshow freaks] occupy the impossible middle ground between the oppositions dividing human from animal: (Jo-Jo, the dog-faced boy...; the "wild man" or "geek", nature from culture (feral children, the "wild men of Borneo") ... [and] one sex from the other (the bearded lady, hermaphrodites, Joseph-Josephines). (Grosz 1996, 57)

The "freak," at once illicit and amazing, characterized a socially unallowable position. The sideshow member was both censured (i.e., socially marginalized) and labelled (i.e., a freak) for occupying this position. Reena Virk, too, occupied this social definition: as local anecdotes and the media tell it, she was *different*, ambiguous, or unfitting to any one social category. One journalist recounts from various interviews: "[Reena] was a twelve-year-old girl trapped in an eighteen-year-old body.... And, perhaps the ultimate curse for a teenage girl, she developed facial hair, which invited cruel nicknames: 'Daddy' and 'the Bearded Lady'" (Tafler 1998, 16). Like others identified as categorically ambiguous, Reena was labelled a freak. In her peer circle, she did not fit and, as such, living a life of exploitation and abuse was considered par for the course.

But Reena's "not fitting" was more innovative than this. Reena may have been defined by others as not fitting in, but she also actively *defied* definition—an act of resistance.

The "What is it?" sideshow represented dual privilege and social inferiority, encapsulated inside one ambiguous body. Reena Virk embodied this position well. She tested racialized rules by envisioning herself as a level participant within her youth circle, and resisted public expectations of racialized feminine behaviour. Reena physically presented as the racialized Other; yet socially—and even after repeated rejections and namings of her differences by peers—she behaved as though she was their undisputed equal: "She [Reena] was victimized a number of different times by her peer group," Jane Naydiuk, an officer with the Saanich police child-abuse team, affirms. Reena was "treated shabbily. [But] she kept going back" (Tafler 1998, 17).

Like historical sideshow freaks, Reena presented an inherent "alien otherness" (Grosz 1996, 65) when compared to those in hegemonic positions, and a drifting nondescript ("What is it?") when she dared to try to join them. In this way, Reena embodied an ambiguity that reminded the hegemony of the thin divide between normal and Other.

The freak confirms the viewer as bounded, belonging to a "proper" (hegemonic) social category. The viewer's horror lies in the recognition that this monstrous being is at the heart of his or her own identity, for it is all that must be ejected or abjected from self-image to make the bounded, category-obeying self possible (64–65). Reena at once represented despicable difference to be (personally) avoided and "intolerable ambiguity" (55) to be (socially) eliminated. She was not simply a socially located Other, but an *audacious* Other that openly coaxed the possibility of a sharing of social privilege—"the immersion or loss of [marginalized] identity with another" (64–65) (privileged) identity. For her ambiguity (and unwitting promotion of it), Reena Virk was punished in life, and both literally and philosophically erased in death.

And what of the girls in this case who occupied the *normative position*—yet proceeded to cross over into ambiguity? Kelly Ellard, for example, was white, middle-class, popular, and fit the hegemonic physical description exemplifying feminine girlhood. Yet, in assaulting and killing Reena Virk, Kelly exhibited something else. Kelly, notwithstanding her physical membership in the category, "betray[ed] that which [she was] naturally" (Hopkins 1996, 103)—a white girl—and all the tenets and behaviours associated with it. Kelly Ellard thus represents an unnatural, self-prescribed Other: a woman from a privileged demographic—that is, typically young, white, able-bodied, heterosexual, and middle-class—who failed to maintain the appropriate presentation of femininity. As she entered the criminal justice system, Kelly went from conceptual "lady" (Batacharya 2006, 185) to "bad girl" (185) to "fallen woman" (Pietsch 2002, 92). Under the gaze of the media, Kelly, too, became an exhibit, a "human being who exist[ed] outside and in defiance of the structure of binary oppositions that govern our basic concepts and modes of self-definition" (Grosz 1996, 57). As a white girl who wilfully contravened expectations of femininity, Kelly fell out of her social category; yet as an embodied, white, young woman, she *still* appears to be intrinsically incapable of committing such a crime.

The legal case against Kelly appears to be as much about proving her a veritable good (that is, performatively successful/proper) girl or bad (unsuccessful/subversive) girl as it does about proving innocence or guilt. During the trials, Kelly Ellard is routinely conceptualized by the defence as "a good girl with middle class values who has fallen victim to the influence of delinquent youth," and by investigating detectives and the Crown as a wholly "failed wom-[an] or social deviant" (Batacharya 2006, 183). A total of three trials have been held in the attempt to resolve the murder charge against Kelly, nonetheless resulting in an ambivalent outcome: a guilty verdict (March 2000), a mistrial (June 2004), another guilty verdict (2005), and an appeal calling for a fourth trial (filed in August 2005) (187). Indeed, even today Kelly remains indeterminate. She is not male, yet she exhibits aggressive and unapologetically criminal activity. She is white and female, yet her performance is at a distance from conventional constructs of feminine passivity. Kelly—a girl who originated from a privileged social position, then regressed away from it and toward gender subversion—is nondescript, a conceptual "What is it?" in reverse.

Like the sideshow oddity, a woman who enters the criminal justice system is "incongruous"—by definition "out of place" or astray from her gendered designation, and beyond the perimeter of cultural limits (49). Women in the criminal justice system and prisons are routinely identified as aberrant—falling far outside the expected boundaries of femininity, conceptually ousted from the category "female," yet not quite reaching the masculine standard either.

How is this stretching of cultural limits defined by media and other social commentators? The notion of girls' aggression-as-victimization, for example, is increasingly used to explain acts of violence perpetrated by young white women. Analytical rhetoric around girls' aggression posits violent behaviour as a "new" trend, produced by contemporary conditions: as girls struggle to "survive the double message of being simultaneously submissive and independent," they repress their aggression, which is then redirected at themselves and other girls (Ringrose 2006, 408). Inside this theory, aggression is carefully reconceptualized so that gender is able to stick to its conventional foundations: femininity is found to be (stereotypically) vulnerable, ill, victimized, and (still) passive-aggressive, while binary masculine descriptors remain comfortably far away. The theory supports the popular notion that girls exhibit "a distinctly feminine and indirect form of aggression, entirely different from that of boys" (410), and also functions to keep "feminine" a safe distance away from "masculine." These are integral distinctions required to maintain binary categories—as well as the status quo of socio-political hierarchies.

Through her acts of violence, Kelly Ellard is deemed a noncompliant—"bad"—girl. Yet as a *white* girl, she has the privilege to *not* be held personally accountable for this badness. Instead, the aggression of white girls is regularly described as acquired and pathological—as though an illness, a contagion contracted from affected Others, or an environmental hazard of contemporary culture. And so we note that this theory—girls' aggression-as-victimization—stands in contrast to the social construction of girls and women of colour, who are more commonly stereotyped as *natural* aggressors, criminals, or bad girls (Cole and Zucker 2007, 2). Women and girls of colour are not likely to have their acts of violence or criminal records explained or forgiven via such conjectures: the criminally involved "Urban Girl is assumed to be poor, of color and out of control" *as a rule*, rather than inadvertently (Brubaker 2007, 530). A woman of colour who disobeys the rules of femininity is written off—irresolvable, an essentialized, biological recreant; the white woman who violates the rules of femininity is more often defined as simply "disobedient," victimized, or "disordered" (Pietsch 2002, 92–93). Indeed, Kelly Ellard "has become a national warning for what can happen when girls from apparently good families ... run with the wrong crowd" (Batacharya 2006, 183)—or, alternatively, become casualties of their own "return of the repressed" feelings through violent acting out (Ringrose 2006, 408).

Race, Space, and Place

She deserved it.

—Sid Tafler, "Who Was Reena Virk?" *Saturday Night* magazine[5]

Reena Virk's murder tells of racial, class, and sexual hierarchies that "profoundly shape violence against women," even in places we may consider to be safe: in social settings, in public space, and among peers (Batacharya 2006, 182). Reena did little to incite the wrath of her attackers the night of her murder. She had, on an earlier date, taken the address book of another girl: as one story goes, this was the transgression for which she was lured to her assault. Yet of the eight youth who attacked Reena under the bridge, only two or three even knew of the stolen address book; and neither of those convicted of her murder—Warren Glowatski and Kelly Ellard—had met Reena before that night. Upon the night of her death, all Reena did—just like all the other kids—was show up at Shoreline Junior Community Secondary School.

Reena's presence at Shoreline that night was, however, *different* from that of the other youth for, as Sullivan notes, space is not a neutral, empty arena in which people of various racialized identities are located. Instead, in a North American context, space "constitutes and is constituted by white privilege" (Sullivan 2006, 143). Although space and place might seem, at face value, free from ownership by *any* social category, the idea of space as racially neutral often is complicit with notions of privilege and exclusivity (143). In truth, historically and today, "the space one inhabit[s] help[s] determine what sort of person one [is]" (151). Even today, physical spaces designated for socializing, shopping, and living are also marked by race and class consciousness. The bodies residing within each physical space are, therein, correspondingly marked as well.

Social identity and "personhood often correlate with the way that one is forced or allowed to live in relationship to space and place" (Sullivan 2006, 143), as well as with the way that one is *not allowed* to relate to a particular space. For example, when Reena arrived "to party" with other youth the night of November 14, 1997, she came by invitation. This invitation was actually intended to lure her into the presence of a specific social circle, as well as into a specific space (the vicinity of Shoreline). Therefore, the evening of Reena's assault began with her entering a social circle from which she was conventionally excluded (and one that intended to betrayed her). As well, the school was a physical space that was not familiarly hers: Reena attended a number of different schools that year, and was currently with Colquitz Junior Secondary—but never Shoreline (Tafler 1998, 16). Within this dynamic, we see Reena tentatively extend herself into places and spaces where she—both socially and racially—"constitutes its other" (Batacharya 2006, 185). It is inside this social and spatial context that she was strategically victimized.

The first act of physical violence was delivered by a young white woman, identified in court as N.C:

> When N.C. is described as the leader of an inner circle, social hierarchy is inevitably at play.... The cigarette burn to [Reena's] forehead [the first action in an eventual, escalating series of attacks] delivered by N.C. can be interpreted as a racial act, symbolic branding as well as punishment for transgressing the boundaries of the inner circle. (Batacharya 2006, 185)

Prior to the above act, Reena was relegated to a subordinate place on the racial and gender hierarchy, and this was communicated to her through repeated social exclusion and bullying. Reena resisted this categorization. For her attempts to enter into a social circle that was both exclusive and racially hierarchical, she was disciplined even further—exemplifying what Hopkins notes is the response, when faced with category traitors, of those in hegemonic positions of power who feel that they "must take a stand against th[e] insurgent group" (Hopkins 1996, 106). The logistical complaints discussed among the youths against Reena "were minor and possibly trumped up: she was accused of spreading rumours about one of the girls, of taking up with another girl's boyfriend, of rifling through one girl's address book and calling the girl's friends on the phone" (Tafler 1998, 18). Really, Reena was demonized for her attempts to enter into an elite realm. Again, as Grosz conveys in her discussion of the sideshow, freaks are offensive because they "imperil the very definitions we rely on to classify humans, identities ... and boundaries dividing self from otherness" (Grosz 1996, 57). Reena Virk's attempts at equal participation in the peer circle—as well as equal presence in hegemonic space—imperilled the boundaries of racial privilege. And so a vicious backlash festered: "the story spread over phone lines and at teen hangouts, they [the area youth] were going to teach Reena a lesson" (Tafler 1998, 19). One of the best tactics for resisting the insurgents or traitors is terror, Hopkins tells us, and "on individual levels [this is achieved] with violence" (Hopkins 1996, 106). The recompense for category subversion, in Reena's case, was physical victimization and death.

Conclusion

Popular opinion today still claims that upon the night of Reena's death, there were simply "a bunch of flammable kids and somebody lit a match" (Batacharya 2006, 187). Yet this account fails to confront what creates or feeds flammability within a multiracial and multi-classed society. What "match" (i.e., social prompt or trigger) is it exactly that elicits, encourages, or condones certain acts of violence? And violence against whom? As Tess Chakkalakal pointedly asks: "Why Reena Virk?" (2000, 163).

Reena Virk's life was disproportionately affected by violence. Among her peers, "she was harassed, called names, treated shabbily" repeatedly and continuously (Tafler 1998, 19). As this chapter has attested, race and gender hierarchies indeed informed Reena's Otherness: her social exclusion, her ongoing victimization, and, ultimately, her death.

Yet still the Canadian media and legal systems remain confounded by her murder. Reena's murder case revealed that our media and legal system's understanding of gender-based violence is deeply dependent upon the victim's—and, as we have seen, the perpetrator's—ability to meet the requirements of hegemonic white femininity. While the law and journalists quickly rejected the social category of race as a motive (or even an element of any significance) in Reena's victimization, it was the very social locations of those involved that held the public's gaze, and came to inform the legal wrangling. The victim, the crime, and the assailants all defied our cultural limits—they "cross[ed] the borders" of gender, age, and racial performance, thereby trouncing "our most fundamental categories of self-definition" (Grosz 1996, 57).

As rhetoric about girl deviance continues to dominate explanations for the crime against Reena, these cultural limits and classifications remain totally invisible. Media and legal analyses of Reena Virk's victimization tend to make little reference to the social location of any of the subjects involved, and no reference at all to the function of sexism or racism operant in this case. I argue, instead, that it is our dogged refusal to address social hierarchies and their implications for violence that constructs this crime as senseless or chaotic—and, therein, sustains such violence as comfortably and politically benign.

Notes

1. Godfrey (2005, 242).
2. Tafler (1998, 16).
3. Metropolitan Action Committee on Violence against Women and Children. 2009, April 3. Violence against Women Partners [Sheet] Retrieved from www.metrac.org/programs/info/prevent/stat_sex.htm. Date accessed: April 30, 2010.
4. Hopkins (1996, 103).
5. Tafler (1998, 18).

References

Batacharya, Sheila. 2006. A fair trial: Race and the retrial of Kelly Ellard. *Canadian Woman Studies* 25, 1/2: 181–189.

Brubaker, Sarah Jane. 2007. Denied, embracing, and resisting medicalization: African American teen mothers' perceptions of formal pregnancy and childbirth care. *Gender & Society* 21, 4: 528–552.

Chakkalakal, Tess. 2000. Reckless eyeballing: Being Reena in Canada. In *Rude: Contemporary black Canadian cultural criticism*, ed. Rinaldo Walcott, 161–167. Toronto: Insomniac Press.

Cole, Elizabeth R., and Alyssa N. Zucker. 2007. Black and white women's perspectives on femininity. *Cultural Diversity and Ethnic Minority Psychology* 13, 1: 1–9.

Collins, Patricia Hill. 1997. Defining black feminist thought. In *The second wave*, ed. Linda Nicholson, 241–257. New York: Routledge.

De Beauvoir, Simone. 1997. Introduction to *The second sex*. In *The second wave*, ed. Linda Nicholson, 11–18. New York: Routledge.

Duke, Lisa. 2002. Get real! Cultural relevance and resistance to the mediated feminine ideal. *Psychology and Marketing* 19, 2: 211–233.

Godfrey, Rebecca. 2005. *Under the bridge: The true story of the murder of Reena Virk*. Toronto: HarperCollins Publishers Ltd.

Grosz, Elizabeth. 1996. Intolerable ambiguity: Freaks as/at the limit. In *Freakery: Cultural spectacles of the extraordinary body*, ed. Rosemarie Garland Thomas, 55–66. New York: New York University Press.

Hopkins, Patrick. 1996. Gender treachery: Homophobia, masculinity, and threatened identities. In *Rethinking masculinities: Philosophical explorations in light of feminism* (2nd ed.), eds. Larry May and Patrick Hopkins, 95–115. Maryland: Rowman & Littlefield Publishers, Inc.

Jiwani, Yasmin. 2006. *Discourses of denial: Mediations of race, gender, and violence*. Vancouver: UBC Press.

Lester, Toni. 2002. Race, sexuality, and the question of multiple, marginalized identities in U.S. and European discrimination law. In *Gender nonconformity, race, and sexuality: Charting the connections*, ed. Toni Lester, 84–99. Madison, WI: The University of Wisconsin Press.

Marchetti, Elena. 2008. Intersectional race and gender analyses: Why legal processes just don't get it. *Social and Legal Studies* 17, 2: 155–174.

Pietsch, Nicole. 2002. Un/titled: Constructions of illegitimate motherhood as gender insurrection. *Journal of the Association for Research on Mothering: Mothering, Sex & Sexuality* 4, 1: 88–100.

Pinnuck, Francine, and Shannon Dowling. 2002. The gendered and racialized space within Australian prisons. In *Gender nonconformity, race, and sexuality: Charting the connections*, ed. Toni Lester, 44–60. Madison, WI: The University of Wisconsin Press.

Ringrose, Jessica. 2006. A new universal mean girl: Examining the discursive construction and social regulation of a new feminine pathology. *Feminism and Psychology* 16, 4: 405–424.

Sullivan, Shannon. 2006. *Revealing whiteness: The unconscious habits of racial privilege*. Bloomington, IN: Indiana University Press.

Tafler, Sid. 1998, April. Who was Reena Virk? *Saturday Night* 113, 3: 15–22.

Wood, Chris. 1999, May 3. A moral blind spot. *MacLean's* 112, 18: 26.

Wright, Bradford W. 2001. *Comic book nation: The transformation of youth culture in America*. Baltimore, MD: The Johns Hopkins University Press.

RETHINKING SECTION 4

Discussion Questions

Chapter 28

1. Why are historical accounts necessary before embarking on contemporary studies?
2. What are the implications of a "race-absent" historical narrative in Canada?

Chapter 29

1. Food choices are not only about individual health but also often involve moral judgments. What types of ethical judgments are associated with obesity and high rates of fast food consumption in public discourse?
2. What relationship does the study find between social class and fast food consumption among teens?
3. The author describes participants as identifying a "hierarchy of fast food." How does this hierarchy influence the ways in which individuals negotiate their food consumption choices?

Chapter 30

1. What factors account for the image that Canada is a class-less, or a primarily middle-class society?
2. What is the relationship between class, power, and decision-making authority in Canadian society?

Chapter 31

1. Noble describes the female-to-male trans experience as both embodying and being articulated as a paradox. How does this relate to the individual construct of identity?
2. To what does Noble attribute the "invisibility" of FtMs and femmes within the queer community?
3. What benefits to viewing trans-sexual issues as labour does Noble describe?

Chapter 32

1. What role does self-reflection play in an articulation of sexual ethics for the young women presented here?

2. Foucault makes a distinction between ethics and morality. How do the girls' portrayals of their casual sexual encounters demonstrate this distinction?
3. Outline the ways in which the interviewees' accounts were situated within, (re)produced, and at times disrupted gendered heterosexual discourses.

Chapter 33

1. What is meant by Connell and Messerschmidt's (2005) assertion that expressions of hegemonic masculinity are normative but not necessarily normal? How does this apply to the conduct of masculinity in Canadian hockey?
2. What role do the media play in the perpetuation of the desirable masculine hockey player?
3. How do the three levels of analysis—performance, structure, and culture—intersect?

Chapter 34

1. Racial identity is influenced not only by self-identification but also by "external gaze." In what ways does the external gaze influence the ways in which a person of mixed race self-identifies?
2. Why is it important to distinguish citizenship from ancestry when examining the question of racial identity?
3. How does viewing racial identity on a white/non-white binary contribute to Othering and challenge the traditional discourse of multiculturalism in Canada?

Chapter 35

1. How do the philosophical and ideological approaches of African-centred schools differ from those of traditional public schools?
2. What are some examples of the ways Afrocentric teachings link cultural knowledge with traditional school subject matters?
3. There are conflicting views as to the role of standardized testing in Afrocentric schooling. What are the arguments for and against including standardized testing in Afrocentric schools?

Chapter 36

1. How is the law implicated with prejudice, according to Pietsch?
2. What does the Reena Virk case tell us about "girlhood"?
3. How are race, space, and place implicated in the Virk case?

SECTION 5

SOCIAL MOVEMENTS, SOCIAL CHANGE, AND EMERGING FIELDS

The Readings

This section considers social movements, social change, and emerging fields within sociology. All of the chapters engage with social movements and social change. The Nibert chapter arguing for the development of animal studies within sociology presages the now emerging field of critical animal studies.

The first chapter by David Nibert makes the case for extending Sociology's critical lens to human-animal relations. It delineates the ties between racism, sexism, and what he terms speciesism, and forwards an analysis of oppression, power, and ideology that support the subordination of non-human animals. It foregrounds the role of the state in fostering and supporting exploitative power relationships. It concludes by calling on Sociology to answer the question "sociology for whom?" with "sociology for all humans and other animals."

The second chapter considers a case study of an initiative to bring a social justice project into being in Hamilton, Ontario. Outlining the difficulties and pitfalls in dealing with municipal governments, community organizations, and other stakeholders, it finds that social movement projects such as community gardens face significant pitfalls and may end up not serving the people they aim to assist.

Finally, Barker provides a critical examination of the emergence and development of the Idle No More movement. Framing the collection of protests within a particular political moment, he explores the ways in which online activism disrupted place-based political action and challenged Canadian sovereignty and settler identity in important ways. This chapter illustrates how networks of solidarity and movement building were formed beginning in 2012, but also speaks to the limitations and difficulties faced by Canadian Indigenous social movements.

CHAPTER 37

Humans and Other Animals: Sociology's Moral and Intellectual Challenge

David Nibert

Introduction

Anthropology is profoundly anthropocentric, as Barbara Noske has observed.

> [A]nimals tend to be portrayed as passive objects that are dealt with and thought and felt about. Far from being considered agents or subjects in their own right, the animals themselves are virtually overlooked by anthropologists. They and their relations with humans tend to be considered unworthy of anthropological interest. Most anthropologists would think it perfectly natural to pay little or no attention to the way things look, smell, feel, taste or sound to the animals involved. Consequently, questions pertaining to animal welfare in the West or in the Third World rarely figure in anthropological thought. (1993: 185)

The same can be said of sociology. While many sociologists bring the power of sociological analysis to a range of social issues and to different forms of oppression, challenging tradition, convention, and existing political-economic arrangements, as a rule most sociologists accept human treatment of other animals[1] as normal and natural. The reluctance of most sociologists to recognize the elite-driven arrangements that oppress other animals and to bring them into scholarly and public focus highlights the question asked by Alfred McClung Lee: "Sociology for Whom?" (Lee 1978). Sociological acquiescence in the socially constructed perception and treatment of other animals only perpetuates the grotesque consequences for countless numbers of both humans and other animals and does little to challenge an unjust and unsustainable global political economy—one that is decidedly dysfunctional. This paper will suggest a theoretical device to further the development of a more inclusive sociology—one that advances the study of society, not just human society—and will use this device to make a case for including other animals as subjects in the realm of sociological inquiry.

Linkages of Racism, Sexism, and Speciesism

Most social scientists [...] promote the idea that the oppression of various groups is deeply grounded in the institutional arrangements and belief systems of human societies. This is to say that oppressive treatment of groups of humans is not natural or inevitable; rather, it is part of the cultural practices that are deeply established in social arrangements. Daniel Rossides summarizes the findings and perspectives of such scholars and activists when he writes that discrimination against devalued groups is "socially induced and maintained" (1997: 19).

Many sociologists now accept the idea that the oppression of various devalued groups in human societies is not independent and unrelated; rather, the arrangements that lead to various forms of oppression are intricately woven together in such a way that the exploitation of one group frequently augments and compounds the mistreatment of others. [A] rapidly growing number of sociologists regard race, class, and gender as "interlocking" and "interactive systems" that should be analyzed in the context of "social institutions and belief systems" (Anderson and Hill-Collins 1992: xii). [...]

Over the past three decades a number of scholars and activists have denounced "speciesism" and compared it explicitly to racism and sexism (Singer 1990; Regan 1982; Spiegel 1996). The application of sociological ideas furthers an examination of the legitimacy of such comparisons. First, though, a challenge to the customary definition of two important terms is necessary. The appropriateness of the term minority group must be reconsidered; a more accurate and inclusive term is recommended in its place. Then, the term speciesism will be interpreted from a sociological vantage point.

The term minority group was coined early in the 20th century to refer to groups that differed from the one that controlled society. Initially used to refer to ethnic minorities, sociologists now commonly use the term to refer to any group in human society whose members differ from the controlling group (Sagarin 1971). Unfortunately, for many years most sociologists portrayed controlling group members as normative or typical members of society, while minority group members have been viewed as "alien" or "special" (Nibert 1996). What is more, traditional academic definitions of minority group have largely soft-pedaled the causes, consequences, and realities of the frequently oppressive social arrangements imposed on minority groups, often making them appear to be both natural and inevitable. As a result, the term minority group has been used extensively because it does not imply a critique of basic social arrangements.

Not surprisingly, due in part to the widespread use of the euphemistic term minority group, most who benefit from the privilege that stems from the exploitation of such groups seldom are motivated or encouraged to become aware of and reflect on their material and psychological stake in oppressive social arrangements. Consequently, the ostensibly objective term minority groups should be replaced with one that is more accurate and straightforward—"oppressed groups."

The following definition of "oppressed group" is derived in large part from an analysis of oppression developed by Iris Young (1990). An oppressed group shares physical, cultural, or economic characteristics and is subjected, for the economic, political, and social gain of a privileged group, to a social system that institutionalizes its exploitation, marginalization, powerlessness, deprivation, or vulnerability to violence. This term is more forthright than "minority group," and is inclusive of humans of color, humans living in poverty, women, humans who are older, humans with disabilities, and humans with different sexual orientations, and also can include other animals. The term "oppressed group" not only is more appropriate and honest but also avoids the human-centered concept of minority groups and helps examine the prevailing view that human use and mistreatment of other animals lies in the realm of the "natural affairs."

The second theoretical adjustment needed for examination of the comparison of racism, sexism, and speciesism is a clear conceptualization of the term speciesism. The view that speciesism is prejudice or discrimination, a view promoted by many advocates and defenders of other animals, impedes an examination of the social structural causes of oppression of other animals. Sociologists tend to use the suffix "ism" in a more specific way than what is generally meant by those talking about speciesism. Most sociologists consider racism, as well as sexism, classism, and other "isms," to be ideologies. That is, they are neither prejudice nor mistreatment. Rather, an ideology is a set of socially shared beliefs that legitimates an existing or desired social order. Treatment of the term speciesism as ideology will thus assist in furthering an understanding of the causes of human mistreatment of other animals and in comparing their treatment with that of other devalued groups.

The application of the sociological perspective in general, then, and selected minority group theory in particular, to the oppression of other animals holds a great deal of promise for expanding the understanding of the causes of speciesism and its relationship to, and entanglement with, the oppression of devalued groups of humans.

In exploring the parallels and entanglements of racism, sexism, and speciesism it is helpful to turn to Donald Noel's 1968 theoretical framework to explain the origin of ethnic stratification (Noel 1968). Noel maintained that ethnic stratification was the product of three interactive forces: (1) competition for resources, or some form of exploitation of one group by another, (2) unequal power, and (3) ethnocentrism—"the view of things in which one's own group is the center of everything, and all others are scaled and rated with reference to it" (Sumner 1906: 13). While his theory made room for social-psychological considerations, they were placed in the context of structural forces. The value of Noel's theory is not just its close linking of material motivation with issues of power and belief systems but also its distillation of complex and interdependent social forces into a compact and readily understood model.

Noel's model will be revised somewhat in this analysis of the comparison of the oppression of humans and other animals into a three-pronged theoretical device that accentuates the economic context of most episodes of competition and exploitation. Moreover, the consideration of unequal power will be focused largely on the use of the various powers that are vested in those who control the state. Finally, the concept of ethnocentrism will be regarded here as a process primarily fueled by a larger system of ideological control.

This modified version of Noel's theory of ethnic stratification [...] has substantial application to an analysis of the oppression of other animals. The motivating factor—the pursuit of economic self-interest—is easily applied to humans' displacement, exploitation, and extermination of other animals as human society expands. First, humans compete with other animals for economic resources, including the use of land. Second, exploitation of other animals serves numerous economic ends for human animals, providing sources of food, power, clothing, furniture, entertainment, and research tools.

This theory also points to the importance of power. One important aspect of power is the ability of one group to exert its will over another, regardless of resistance. Abuses of power are seen throughout history as various human groups have devised weapons and techniques to dominate other animals and to displace, control, capture, exploit, or exterminate them. The most concentrated form of power for most of the past 10,000 years has been the state.

Finally, ideological conditioning is the third essential requirement for oppressive social arrangements. Oppression requires rationalization and legitimation; it must appear as the right thing to do, both to the oppressing group and in the eyes of others. A set of ideas that devalues an entire group—an ideology such as racism, sexism, or speciesism—thus is socially constructed. That ideology explains and supports the development and perpetuation of social institutions that foster the elimination or exploitation of the oppressed group. Moreover, the ideology justifying that action is promulgated throughout the social system in order to garner public acceptance and reduce dissent. Over time, these socially constructed ideas will come to be accepted as real and true, and the "lower" or "special" position of the oppressed group will be viewed as the natural order of things, promoting ethnocentrism and anthropocentrism.

Generally speaking, then, humans tend to disperse, eliminate, or exploit a group they perceive to be unlike themselves (an outgroup or the "other"), particularly when it is in their economic interests to do so. Next, the oppressing group must have the power to subordinate members of the at-risk group. While physical force is the key to this subordination, such force is usually vested in part in political control. Those who exercise political control wield the power of the state, with the ability to make and oversee the implementation of law. Finally, ideological manipulation fuels prejudiced attitudes and discriminatory acts, which help protect and maintain oppressive economic and social arrangements by making them appear natural and, thus, acceptable.

This model is based on the supposition that oppressive treatment of entire groups, including other animals, is a systemic phenomenon and cannot be explained by biological reductionism. Significantly, while this model depicts systemic oppression as occurring in a linear fashion, in reality the various aspects of the system are largely interdependent and operate more or less simultaneously. The reciprocal influences are not entirely symmetrical, due to the primary influence of material and economic considerations.

Historical Roots of Oppression

The economic factors that primarily cause the oppression of humans and other animals can be traced to the latter stages of hunting and gathering society. Systematic stalking and killing of other animals contributed to other inequalities, such as the devaluation of women.

Hunting shaped relations between female and male humans largely because the bodies of other animals became a prized asset and killing them enhanced male prestige and privilege. Men achieved elevated prestige through the acquisition and distribution of resources derived from the bodies of other animals, even though women generally provided more reliable, if more mundane, forms of nourishment and resources through foraging. What is more, the decrease that hunting caused in men's participation in foraging and in caring for children and others needing assistance no doubt required women to devote more of their time to these tasks—resulting in less time for rest and leisure. Concomitantly, the increased labor and caretaking exacted from women freed males to increase the time they could devote to hunting. The developing mistreatment and exploitation of women and of other animals each was based upon and compounded by the other—a constant historical pattern.

The advent of early agricultural society brought with it opportunities for individual privilege and power—primarily for elite males—by increasing the possibilities for systematic oppression. Countless humans were assigned to hegemonically created social positions of "slave" and "serf" that devalued them, collectively and personally. So it was with other animals, who were relegated to such social positions as "livestock" and "game" and whose exploitation greatly facilitated the development of highly stratified and oppressive agricultural societies. Untold numbers of "others" were yoked to pestles, plows, wagons, and chariots for their entire lives, while countless other individuals were used as currency or devoured as victuals—primarily by the privileged. Humans and other animals were forced to fight each other to the death to amuse elites and to distract the masses from their daily experiences and from consideration of the sources of their deprivation. Similar entertainment and diversionary uses of devalued others occurred during the Middle Ages, when manorial lords and high-placed Church officials continued mass exploitation. Under such conditions, devalued others were also scapegoated for system ills, as in the case of women and cats who were scapegoated for individual or collective misfortunes and executed as witches and witches' accomplices.

Capitalism largely continued the 10,000-year-old tradition of exploiting humans and other animals to create wealth and privilege for the few, exploitation that continued to bind the fate of devalued humans and other animals. For instance, the enclosure movements in Europe forced exploited humans out of the countryside, where the land they used was taken to raise captive sheep. The hair of sheep was taken and sent to developing urban areas where those displaced from the land, transformed into an urban proletariat, suffered in textile mills. The Irish, subjugated by the British military, were forced off their land; much of it then was used to raise cows, whose bodies were sent back to feed the elite in England. In the Western hemisphere, humans such as John Jacob Astor killed innumerable other animals—whose skin and hair were worn largely by elites to advertise their elevated social status—while exploiting indigenous humans. Meanwhile, countless other animals were massacred or "cleared" from the land so that humans of color could be forced to produce profitable cash crops there. Cattle barons accrued great wealth raising cows for slaughter while the "meat producers" exploited workers who had the task of killing and dismembering other animals; contaminated and tainted "meat" was sold to the public and the U.S. military at inflated prices.

The 20th century brought corporate dominance of the economy, and millions of farmers were forced from the countryside as the capitalist imperative for growth and expansion fueled large-scale factory farming. Food, especially "meat," is very abundant in affluent nations today, an availability supplemented by nonstop, widespread, and manipulative advertisements.

Few are aware of the terrible costs associated with the food abundance in advanced capitalist nations, and of the inherent unsustainability of the affluent's culinary opulence, particularly their consumption of "meat." Numerous agencies and organizations, including the Office of the U.S. Surgeon General, the National Academy of Sciences, the National Cancer Society, and the American Heart Association, have linked high levels of "meat" consumption to such conditions as diabetes, high blood pressure, arteriosclerosis, stroke, and certain forms of cancer (U.S. Department of Health and Human Services 1988). The increasing consumption of "meat" and "dairy" products is also linked to the growing problem of obesity in the United States. A 1999 study conducted by the Centers for Disease Control found that the number of citizens considered obese—defined as being more than 30 percent over ideal body weight—was one in five, up from one in eight in 1991 (Crossette 2000). [...]

Due to corporate machinations in an economic system characterized by greed and an incessant drive to maximize profits, the Worldwatch Institute's 2000 report estimated that 1.2 billion humans, the largest number it ever reported, are "underfed and undernourished," while another 1.2 billion are "eating too much or too much of the wrong food." The United States has become the most overfed, under-nourished, and overweight society in the world. [...]

In a nation that is supposed to be the epitome of capitalist progress, nearly half of Americans suffer at least one chronic disease, and that number is expected to grow by 30 million within the next 20 years (Associated Press 2000). Preventive care and less refined, plant-based diets are inconsistent with the production of food under modern capitalism and with the profitable "treatment" of the diseases linked to its consumption. Meanwhile, the vast majority of the oppressed individuals defined as "food" are faceless, nameless, and largely invisible.

Humans, Other Animals, and the Environment

When natural scientists report on the costs of concentrated agricultural production and predict the further effects of agribusiness practices, they usually voice their warnings using such terms as "further reductions in biodiversity," "further destruction of ecosystems," and "Third World population migrations." Such abstract and arcane expressions do not make real or visible to the public the pain, suffering, and death of countless humans and other animals that both underlie and result from what Vandana Shiva calls the "rotten food culture" (Shiva 1997). Powerful transnational corporations use ubiquitous advertisements to exhort everyone to consume "hamburgers" and "fried chicken," while Third World elites create poverty in their nations by taking over the land to send feed and other animals raised to be food to countries like the United States.

Feeding a privileged portion of the human population, especially under contemporary agribusiness with its emphasis on "meat" production, necessitates high levels of deforestation and desertification (the destruction of soil, rendering it infertile and desert-like), adds to air pollution (caused in no small part by the vast amounts of methane gas generated by huge populations of other animals, particularly hundreds of millions of cows), exhausts fresh water supplies, and compounds already critical levels of water pollution. Few life-sustaining resources will remain for future generations of humans and other animals as long as agricultural production under capitalism exists to make profits rather than to feed the world.

A report by a panel of scientists whose work appeared in a 2001 article in the journal *Science* projects an increase in the human population from 6 billion in 2000 to 9 billion by 2050 (Tilman et al. 2001). This increase will double the world's food demands by mid-century, partly because people in wealthy countries will want diets rich in "meat," which takes more resources to produce. The report suggests that, if contemporary forms of agriculture persist, by 2050 the global agricultural land base will have to increase by at least 109 hectares of land, resulting in the worldwide loss of forests and natural ecosystems in a total area larger than the United States. The displacement, destruction, and death brought on by appropriation of so much of the remaining homeland of devalued humans and other animals would be cataclysmic. The panel writes:

> Because of regional availabilities of suitable land, this expansion of agricultural land is expected to occur predominantly in Latin America and sub-Saharan Africa. This could lead to the loss of about a third of remaining tropical and temperate forests, savannas, and grasslands and of the services, including carbon storage, provided by these ecosystems. (Tilman et al. 2001: 283)

The State as a Primary Tool of Oppression

These economic arrangements—which are largely created by elites and which certainly facilitate their interests—have been sanctioned and protected by the various powers of the state. Military force and chauvinistic political systems have created and solidified oppression for thousands of years. From legal sanctioning of slavery to the creation of "humane" slaughter policy, the power of the state usually has been controlled by the beneficiaries of oppression. The fairly recent rise of capitalist-based globalization seeks to further reduce impediments to profit-taking as the governments of the most powerful nations package and promote trade agreements that weaken or eliminate protections for workers, consumers, other animals, and the environment. They purport to "aid" less powerful and affluent nations through such international financial institutions as the International Monetary Fund and the World Bank, which in many instances require desperation-inducing austerity plans and support the development of such land-intensive and oppressive enterprises as "cattle" ranching and "animal feed" production. In the event that indigenous peoples and displaced populations in the oppressed nations of the world resist expropriation of the land they call home and rely on for their survival, military forces of dictatorial leaders violently repress such dissent—frequently with assistance from the United States (Blum 1995).

Less obvious forms of structural violence in the economic arena result from U.S. government policies that protect agribusiness and other corporate interests through agricultural subsidies. Agribusiness in the United States receives public funds to produce "major commodities like sugar, corn, and wheat below cost" (Oxfam 2002: 3). The prices of these crops are so low that small farmers in Third World countries cannot compete or make a living and these nations become unable to be self-sufficient food providers—facilitating hunger and famine and the many diseases that follow malnutrition. Many oppressed nations have become dependent upon exports of cash crops to pay increasing debts to banking institutions in powerful capitalist nations and to purchase food.

At another level, minimalist government regulations in the United States that purport to oversee the welfare of other animals subjected to the practices of agribusiness, pharmaceutical, entertainment, and other industries are underfunded, underenforced, and serve primarily as ideological subterfuge to quiet public concern.

The Social Construction of Speciesism

Oppression usually is naturalized—that is, it is made to appear as a normal and innate part of worldly existence. The metaphysical and theological ideologies that for thousands of years explained the "natural" place of the enslaved, women, children, other animals, and other devalued and oppressed groups today largely have been replaced with "scientific" ideologies that justify and naturalize the contemporary socio-economic order. The benefits and success of capitalism, the desirability of wealth, and the "inferior" qualities of women, humans of color, those with disabilities, those of advanced age, and other animals are deeply woven into contemporary reality. Powerful messages coming from such diverse sources as church, school, family, state, peers, and the mass media create widespread and deep acceptance—and internalization—of this socially constructed reality.

Over the past 100 years many oppressed groups have been disparaged for their alleged "low mental caliber" and consequently scaled low in a hierarchy of worth. The measurement of an individual's or group's value was based on the purported level of intelligence, measured or attributed in ethnocentric, anthropocentric ways. In addition, ecofeminists have observed that ideas about the hierarchy of worth are deeply entwined with patriarchy, a system of social organization in which masculinity is valued over femininity (both being social constructions). Ecofeminist Janis Birkeland put it this way:

> In the dominant Patriarchal cultures, reality is divided according to gender, and a higher value is placed on those attributes associated with masculinity, a construction that is called "hierarchical dualism." In these cultures, women have historically been seen as closer to the earth or nature.... Also, women and nature have been juxtaposed against mind and spirit, which have been associated in Western cosmology with the "masculine" and elevated to a higher plane of being.... [I]t is clear that a complex morality based on dominance and exploitation has developed in conjunction with the devaluing of nature and "feminine" values. (1993: 18-19)

General acceptance of the existence and naturalness of such a hierarchy continues to legitimate oppression of other animals, women, humans of color, humans with disabilities, and other devalued groups. The denigration of some groups, generated to a large degree by cupidity, is increased by high levels of socially cultivated egocentrism and is woven into both the culture and individual psyches in a way that shapes personal identities. Those who perceive themselves to be superior to others sometimes display their socially induced prejudice by acts of discrimination, frequently by creating physical, social, and emotional distance between themselves and the devalued. At times, discriminatory acts are perpetrated only for the amusement value of denigrating and harming the "lowly other" and to display the perpetrator's power. The prevailing beliefs and values required to legitimize widespread institutionalized oppression, such as that practiced by agribusiness and the pharmaceutical and chemical industries, shape the reality and cultivate the general personality types of human members of society. In an often predatory system, where the prevailing ideology glorifies wealth and power, more humans will be inclined to accept or tolerate, if not practice, violence against those "others" who are perceived as poor, weak, or powerless. The widespread acceptance of the general concept of the hierarchy of worth of living beings both rationalizes oppressive acts and arrangements and thoroughly entangles the various beliefs that arise from a hierarchical worldview. Only the rejection of the entire notion of such hierarchy can remove the ideological support for oppression of any group and begin to make all groups secure.

The important point to take from this analysis, particularly for those interested in challenging and reducing oppression, are that the principal causal factor underlying the oppression of humans and other animals is material in nature and that oppression primarily serves the interests of elites—particularly male elites. Oppression is supported by the state, and an ideological support system is manufactured to legitimate the tyrannical treatment of others.

The Future of Sociology

The social construction of speciesism is deeply entangled with the oppression of devalued humans, and such oppression has only intensified with the rapid advance of modern global capitalism. However, the unethical and chauvinistic treatment of other animals, the entanglement of oppressions, and the unsustainability of the current prevailing arrangements based on this oppression all have been largely overlooked by the sociological community. Reflecting on the nature of capitalist society, R. H. Tawney observed, "The appeal of ... [capitalist] ... society must be powerful, for it has laid the whole modern world under its spell" (Tawney 1948: 29–30). Sociologists, particularly in the United States, certainly are not entirely immune from this spell. Members of the discipline, who like most other humans in society partake in the privileges derived from entangled oppressions—such as eating and drinking substances derived from the bodies of "others," wearing their skin and hair, and enjoying the entertainment value their exploitation provides—can do so only by accepting the self-interested realities crafted by powerful agribusiness, pharmaceutical, and other industries that rely on public acquiescence in oppressive social arrangements. Privilege is not easy to give up. Silence, denial, and substantial intellectual acrobatics are necessary for oppression of all forms to continue. [...]

This 21st-century variation of "the new sociology" (Horowitz 1964) should begin by treating other animals as subjects who have personalities, wills, desires, and social relations and who are capable of experiencing both pleasure and suffering. Their lives should be studied both in relation to human animals and—to the extent that they can be—in the absence of human imposition. While the lives of other animals can be studied in the context of their own communities and societies, it is also necessary to include them in the broader use of the term society. The tremendous power that humans, particularly the elite, exert over the other inhabitants of the earth and the social positions assigned to groups of other animals—"livestock," "game," "zoo animal," "lab animal," and so forth—require their substantive inclusion in the concept of society that has hitherto referred only to human society.

A major paradigm shift is necessary to set the discipline on a new course. To further the creation of a sustainable and just world, and for the advancement of science, the question posed by Alfred McClung Lee, "sociology for whom?" should be answered: *sociology for all humans and other animals.*

Note

1. One of the ways in which oppression masquerades as somehow right and natural, particularly in more affluent nations, is through the use of language. The very words we use exert considerable control over our consciousness and our views of the world. I have struggled with the English language in my attempt to use words and phrases that do not automatically reflect hierarchical rankings of living beings. For example, I largely refrain from using the terms "people," "nonhuman" and "animals," choosing instead to use the phrase "humans and other animals." This wording emphasizes human commonality with other inhabitants of the planet, rather than fostering a perception of separate-ness and "other-ness" that helps to rationalize disregard and mistreatment of other animals.

References

Andersen, M. L. and Hill Collins, P. (1992). *Race, Class, and Gender: An Anthology.* Belmont, CA: Wadsworth.

Associated Press. (2000). "Chronic Ills Hit Nearly 1 of 2 in U.S." *Dayton Daily News*, December 1, 4A.

Birkeland, J. (1993). "Ecofeminism: Linking Theory and Practice," in *Ecofeminism: Women, Animals, Nature*, ed. Greta Gaard. Philadelphia: Temple University Press, 18-19.

Blum, W. (1995). *Killing Hope: U.S. Military and CIA Intervention since World War II.* Monroe, ME: Common Courage Press.

Crossette, B. (2000). "In Numbers, the Heavy Now Match the Starved." *New York Times*, January 18, A10.

Horowitz, I. L. (1964). *The New Sociology: Essays in Social Science and Social Theory in Honor of C. Wright Mills.* New York: Oxford University Press.

Lee, A. M. (1978). *Sociology for Whom?* New York: Oxford University Press.

Nibert, D. (1996). "Minority Group as Sociological Euphemism." *Race, Gender & Class*, 3, 129–136.

Noel, D. (1968). "The Theory of Ethnic Stratification." *Social Problems*, 16, 157–172.

Noske, B. (1993). "The Animal Question in Anthropology." *Society & Animals: Social Scientific Studies of the Human Experience of Other Animals*, 1, 185–187.

Oxfam America. (2002). "Oxfam Dumps Sugar at WSSD." *Oxfam Exchange*, Washington, DC, 2, 3.

Regan, T. (1982). *All That Dwell There: Animal Rights and Environmental Ethics.* Berkeley: University of California Press.

Rossides, D. W. (1997). *Social Stratification: The Interplay of Class, Race, and Gender* (Third Edition). Upper Saddle River, NJ: Prentice Hall.

Sagarin, E. (1971). *The Other Minorities.* Toronto: Ginn and Company.

Shiva, V. (1997). "Vandana Shiva on McDonald's, Exploitation and the Global Economy." http://www.mcspotlight.org/people/interviews.

Singer, P. (1990). *Animal Liberation*, rev. ed. New York: Avon.

Spiegel, M. (1996). *The Dreaded Comparison: Human and Animal Slavery.* New York: Mirror Books.

Sumner, W. (1906). *Folkways.* Boston: Ginn and Company.

Tawney, R. H. (1948 [1920]). *The Acquisitive Society.* New York: Harcourt Brace Jovanovich.

Tilman, D. et. al. (2001). "Forecasting Agriculturally Driven Global Environmental Change." *Science*, 292, 281–284.

U.S. Department of Health and Human Services. (1988). *Surgeon General's Report on Nutrition and Health.* Pub. no. 88-50210. Washington, DC.

Young, I. (1990). *Justice and the Politics of Difference.* Princeton, NJ: Princeton University Press.

CHAPTER 38

Growing a Just Garden: Environmental Justice and the Development of a Community Garden Policy for Hamilton, Ontario

Erika S. Jermé and Sarah Wakefield

1. Introduction

There is something compelling about seeing urban gardeners in action, cultivating their plot of land under the watchful gaze of skyscrapers, local businesses, or row houses. As local food movements proliferate across North America, this scene is becoming increasingly common, to the extent that many municipalities now explicitly codify how community gardens should develop and operate within their boundaries.

In developing community garden policies, municipalities have an opportunity to enhance environmental justice. Using the process of drafting a community garden policy in the city of Hamilton, Ontario, as a case study, this paper has two aims. First, it illustrates how an environmental justice lens could inform the creation of an effective, inclusive community gardening policy. Second, it demonstrates how particular aspects of the policy development process can generate and naturalize spaces of inequality and injustice, even when the intentions of the policy actors are progressive. The lessons learned in this case study have implications not only for understanding policy development, but also for enhancing our understanding of how environmental injustice is produced.

The paper begins by introducing the concept of environmental justice. The emerging literature on community gardens is also discussed, focusing on their expanding role as a community amenity and possible vehicle for social and environmental justice. Next, the paper elaborates on the particular case study—community garden policy in Hamilton, Canada—and describes the methods used to explore the case. The paper then provides examples of community garden policies that, in one way or another, promote environmental justice. Finally, the process of developing a community garden policy in the case study community is documented, highlighting both the successes and failures of this policy initiative and identifying issues that compromised the potential of the new policy to promote environmental justice. The paper concludes with suggestions for improving the policy process to enhance its ability to incorporate environmental justice concerns.

2. Planning for Justice: Environmental Justice as a Food Planning Framework

2.1. ENVIRONMENTAL JUSTICE IN THE LITERATURE

Social and economic inequalities find expression in the built environment (e.g., spatially concentrated poverty and/or racial segregation), and these social inequalities overlap with—and, many argue, lead to—environmental disamenities (e.g., the presence of polluting facilities (United Church of Christ, 1987, 2007), environmental contamination (Cutter & Solecki, 1996; Morley, 2006), or the absence of green spaces (Heynen, Perkins, & Roy, 2006; Wolch, Wilson, & Fehrenbach, 2005). These disamenities are in turn linked in various ways to poor health outcomes among the segments of the population exposed to them (Corburn, 2004; Gee & Payne-Sturges, 2004; Vlahov, Gibble, Freudenberg, & Galea, 2004; Wakefield & Baxter, 2010).

An environmental justice framework draws attention to questions of how environmental amenities and hazards are allocated, to whom, and why. Inherent in this framework is a belief that all communities and people have the right to live in a safe, healthy environment (Bullard, 2005). Therefore, environmental justice draws attention to distributional relationships—for example, the disproportionate presence of polluting industries in low-income and racialized communities—and advocates for equity in these relationships (see, for example, Rees & Westra, 2003).

Much of the early environmental justice literature focused on extreme or extraordinary cases of contamination (e.g., the siting of toxic facilities) and the overt political struggles to oppose these injustices (see Bullard, 1990). More recently attention has been focused on the everyday: the mundane and ordinary spaces in which we live, work, and play, and the micro-political practices that create and reinforce these spaces (Hobson, 2006; Milbourne, 2012; Whitehead, 2009). This is an important extension of the environmental justice concept, as it recognizes that justice is grounded in the factors that shape individual (and community) access to life-enhancing opportunities, and allows investigation of a greater range of spaces of injustice and contestation (see also Nussbaum, 2006; Whitehead, 2009).

As such, environmental justice theorists and activists focus attention on planning processes as well as their outcomes (Brulle & Pellow, 2006; Corburn, 2003, 2004; Faber & McCarthy, 2003; Gibson-Wood & Wakefield, 2012; Pulido, 2000; Schlosberg, 2004). Procedural justice—fairness in decision-making processes—has become a key aspect of environmental justice theorizing, leading scholars to more thoroughly explore "the forces that generate, stabilize, or even naturalize spaces of inequality and injustice" (Holifield, Porter, & Walker, 2009, p. 599). Related work has emphasized the importance of recognizing the experience and knowledge of individuals and communities whose contributions have often been marginalized in environmental decision-making (Gosine & Teelucksingh, 2008; Haluza-Delay, O'Riley, Cole, & Agyeman, 2009; Holifield, 2012; Schlosberg, 2004, 2007; Urkidi & Walter, 2011). At the same time, the emphasis on "participation" in some (particularly state-led) environmental justice venues has been criticized as reinforcing the idea that community participation in—and responsibility for—governance can fill the gaps left by state withdrawal from various regulatory fields (Holifield, 2004). Overall, our understanding of how the state structures the expression of environmental (in)justices, and shapes actors' ability to address those injustices, remains limited (Kurtz, 2009).

Walker and Bulkeley (2006, p. 658) have argued that environmental justice offers "a new framing for research and policy attention in which equity is brought to the foreground." This paper interrogates this assertion by attempting to apply an environmental justice lens to community gardening policy, and then exploring how—in relation to community gardens—environmental injustices can be re-inscribed as a result of a neo-liberalized and justice-insensitive policy context. The following section describes how community gardens can be related to environmental justice concerns.

2.2. ENVIRONMENTAL JUSTICE AND COMMUNITY GARDENS

A community garden is a plot of land cultivated by multiple people, either collectively or in individual plots (Teig et al., 2009). These gardens are often characterized by a degree of public ownership and democratic control (Ferris, Norman, & Sempik, 2001; Schukoske, 2000). The relationship between community gardens and city governments is complex, reflective of development pressures on the land, political will, and the degree of organization of gardeners. According to Hess (2009, p. 142), "many present day arrangements [between municipal governments and gardening groups] are the result of intense political struggles over a city government's right to sell its land and the citizens' right to use city-owned land" (see also Smith & Kurtz, 2003).

Community gardens are credited with a variety of benefits to individuals and communities, from better nutrition and a greater sense of well-being (Alaimo, Packnett, Miles, & Kruger, 2008; Corrigan, 2011; Twiss et al., 2003; Wakefield, Yeudall, Taron, Reynolds, & Skinner, 2007) to enhanced local ecology (Clavin, 2011; Matteson, Ascher, & Langellotto, 2008; Mougeot, 2006; Schmelzkopf, 2002). Research suggests that the development of gardens on vacant lots abates blight, reduces crime, and prevents illegal dumping of trash or hazardous materials (Gorham, Waliczek, Snelgrove, & Zajicek, 2009; Schukoske, 2000), increasing local property values (Voicu & Been, 2008) while greening inner cities (Ferris et al., 2001). Given that low-income and minority neighbourhoods tend to be areas with limited access to healthy, affordable food (Beaulac, Kristjansson, & Cummings, 2009; Latham & Moffat, 2007; Morland, Wing, Diez Roux, & Poole, 2002), and that these same communities are also less likely to have access to green space (see Wolch et al., 2005) or uncontaminated soil (see Morley, 2006) in which to grow their own food, community gardens in marginalized communities are seen as tangible ways to reduce environmental inequities.

In addition, some evidence suggests that community gardens can help build cohesion and connection in a community (Firth, Maye, & Pearson, 2011; Kingsley & Townsend, 2006). The "participatory landscapes" (Saldivar-Tanaka & Krasny, 2004) of the garden spaces, as well as the complex networks of individuals and organizations who act collectively on garden projects (Baker, 2004) are thought to facilitate broader democratic engagement and activism (Glover, Parry, & Shinew, 2005; Holland, 2004; Saldivar-Tanaka & Krasny, 2004). Milbourne (2012, pp. 953–954) suggests that community garden projects "are producing new socioecological spaces within these places, with horticultural and environmental practices being translated into new forms of sociality, public participation, sustainability and justice.... The site of the community garden has thus come to represent the spatial manifestation of transitions from injustice to justice as well as the empowerment of local community."

Not all commentators have been so sanguine about the progressive potential of community gardens: for example, Pudup (2008, p. 1228) asserts that, rather than being positive agents of change, community gardens often serve as:

> organized projects specifically designed as spaces of neoliberal governmentality, that is, spaces in which gardening puts individuals in charge of their own adjustment(s) to economic restructuring and social dislocation through self-help technologies centered on personal contact with nature.

Thus, governments may promote gardens with the intention of controlling populations or instilling desirable behaviours (Gottlieb, 2001; Lawson, 2004; Pollan, 1991; Pudup, 2008), without taking the wishes and desires of those populations into account.

In a similar vein, Kurtz (2001) and Rosol (2010) both highlight how community gardens—which function as semi- or pseudo-public spaces, but are autonomously organized, managed, and regulated—can serve to embed neo-liberal rationalities (see also Eizenberg, 2012; Staeheli, Mitchell, & Gibson, 2002). By restricting the use of spaces within existing public land to certain individuals (e.g., to allotment gardeners in a new community garden within a park), or by encouraging the development of "community" gardens on private land (such as churchyards or apartment building verges), individuals and communities could be inadvertently facilitating the withdrawal of the state from the provision of public amenities.

The incommensurability of these two facets of community gardens—on the one hand, widely lauded vehicles for positive community transformation, and on the other, mechanisms of neo-liberal identity formation—is noted by Emmett (2011). He suggests that this reflects an undercurrent in our understandings of environmental justice:

> Unevenness marks the languages of environmental justice.... In one cultural domain, justice emphasizes property rights couched in a language of housing; in another domain, justice means access to land and a right to grow food for current residents. Such unevenness is compounded by the undeniable geographical unevenness of risk and amenity in American cities. (Emmett, 2011, p. 83)

However, a complete interrogation of how particular community garden practices support or challenge neo-liberal governance is not the purpose of this paper. Instead, it focuses on how the development of community garden policy in one municipality in Canada can be used to illustrate the forces that produce and naturalize spaces of injustice. The section following explores how community gardens have been integrated into planning and policy decisions, and how environmental justice is implicated in this process.

2.3. PLANNING AND PLANTING: UNDERSTANDING THE CONTEXT OF COMMUNITY GARDEN POLICY DECISIONS

Planning has a clear role to play in the (re)allocation of amenities and disamenities (both the extraordinary and mundane), particularly in urban environments. Planning involves decision-making related to the distribution of resources and the shaping of communities and regions (American Planning Association, 2011). Planners act as intermediaries between experts, politicians, and the public, and are responsible for making policy recommendations that take into account technical as well as community-based knowledge (Corburn, 2003; Forester, 1989). Thus, planning is an inherently subjective and political process: "planning practice involves choices regarding which information is deemed relevant, what decision-making processes will be used, and when, or if, various publics will be involved in making the plan" (Corburn, 2004, p. 543; see also Forester, 1989; Sandercock, 2003). Too often planning decisions reinforce rather than rectify existing inequalities based on social status, race, gender, etc. (Krumholz, 1982; Sandercock, 2003). Concerns about procedural and representational justice are therefore relevant in the planning context.

Traditionally, planners (particularly urban planners) have had little engagement with food issues; however, planning for food has gained increased prominence in the field in recent years (Soma & Wakefield, 2011), with community gardens as one component of that emerging portfolio. Based on a review of community garden programmes over the last 120 years, Lawson (2004) suggests that planners have an ambivalent relationship with community gardens. Gardens are often commended for their ability to meet a variety of social and environmental goals. At the same time, their ambiguous nature in relation to prevailing norms of property and permanence has meant that they are rarely considered in planning decisions. Lawson asserts that "community gardens illustrate unresolved tensions between planning as a profession and as a civic concern, and between comprehensive planning and interim, local interventions" (Lawson, 2004, p. 151).

By supporting community gardens, local governments seek to provide access to a sustainable source of healthy food and opportunities for physical activity and social interaction (Public Health Law & Policy, 2009). A recent review by Zoellner, Zanko, Price, Bonner, and Hill (2012) suggests a number of ways that planners and policy-makers can support community gardens. Among other recommendations, they suggest that policy-makers "should consider and promote land-use policies that allow dedicated community space to develop, implement, and maintain community gardens" (p. 118). They also suggest that while community gardens may lead to a variety of benefits in a community, involvement of community residents to initiate, support, and maintain the gardens is central to their success, as key barriers include lack (or loss) of leadership and resources.

Others have noted the importance of sufficient resources (both human and financial) to the development and maintenance of community gardens. For example, Saldivar-Tanaka and Krasny (2004) discuss the importance of organizations and agencies that support community gardens, providing assistance with issues as diverse as securing land tenure, garden organization, and horticultural practices. Glover et al. (2005, p. 451) note that the ability of community gardens to achieve their goals is often dependent on a garden group's "ability to leverage a variety of resources situated within itself, that is, among its membership and outsiders whom it can convince to support its cause." Three points are worth noting here: first, that the complexity of garden management requires some sort of social infrastructure (whether formal or informal); second, that garden development and maintenance requires a range of skills; and finally, that more organized gardens (and gardeners) may be better positioned to work within the policy context to achieve their goals. This could lead to certain better-resourced communities being better provided with community gardens, a result inconsistent with environmental justice. The following case study explores the challenges to incorporating justice into community garden policy.

3. Environmental Justice through Community Gardens? A Case Study

This paper uses the development of a community garden policy in Hamilton, Ontario, Canada, as a case study. Hamilton is an industrial city situated on the western tip of Lake Ontario, 60 km southwest of Toronto. As a result of declining employment opportunities in this former steel industry centre, the city has one of the highest poverty rates in Ontario, with 18% of its over 500,000 inhabitants living in poverty. Poverty rates are significantly higher in certain areas, with more than half the population living in poverty in some neighbourhoods (Social Planning and Research Council of Hamilton, 2009; Figure 38.1). These neighbourhoods are clustered in the downtown core, in close proximity to heavy industry.

FIGURE 38.1 COMMUNITY GARDEN LOCATIONS AND POVERTY RATES, HAMILTON, ONTARIO, 2008

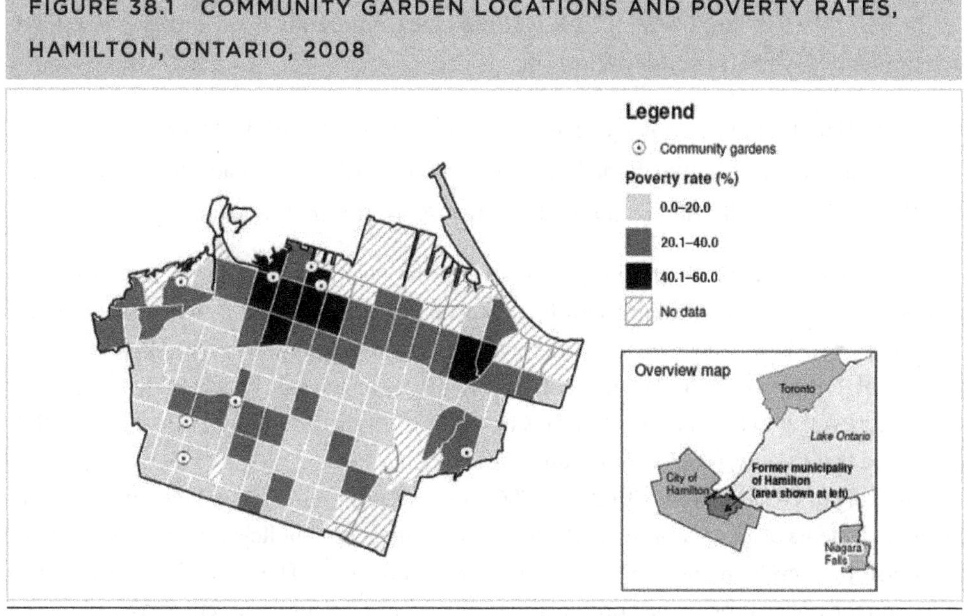

Source: Social Planning and Research Council of Hamilton, 2009, used with permission.

Food insecurity is one result of the high poverty rates in the city. A 2009 study by Hamilton Public Health Services found that low-income families in the city could not afford to purchase nutritious food while simultaneously covering other basic needs such as child care, clothing, transportation, and school supplies (City of Hamilton, 2009d). As a result, many turn to emergency food: in 2009, 7,685 households (19,602 individuals) sought supplemental food from food banks (Hamilton Food Share, 2009). Moreover, a study of food availability found that Hamilton's downtown core has fewer supermarkets per capita than the more affluent uptown neighbourhoods, and that variety stores—characterized by higher prices and less fresh produce than supermarkets—are the more prevalent food outlets in the downtown (Latham & Moffat, 2007).

In 2009 the City of Hamilton operated two allotment-style gardens, with a third under development. Despite the relatively high price of the garden spaces, plots in the two city council-run gardens sold out each year, and plots in the new garden sold out in two weeks (personal communication, city council staff, 2009). Less than a dozen other community gardens operated independently, often through religious institutions or community health centres; only a small number of these gardens were located in areas with concentrated poverty (Figure 38.1). These gardens were linked loosely together through the Hamilton Community Garden Network (HCGN), a fledgling volunteer organization attempting to provide support for garden coordination, education, and resource-sharing. However, lacking resources and infrastructure, the HCGN's efforts were ad hoc and limited in continuity and outreach. At the same time, enquiries to the city council about community gardening opportunities (e.g., about the process for starting a new garden) were being forwarded to the HCGN due to inadequate capacity within the city bureaucracy to deal with such questions. Thus, despite resident interest, little was being done to support community gardens in the city.

In 2007 the Hamilton Board of Health created the Community Food Security Stakeholders' Committee (CFSSC) mandated to:

> move Hamilton towards being a place where all community residents obtain a safe, culturally acceptable, nutritionally adequate diet through a sustainable food system that maximizes self-reliance and social justice. (City of Hamilton, 2007, p. 4)

The CFSSC included volunteer representatives from a variety of sectors, including agriculture, social services, environment, and food processing, as well as three city councillors and city staff from relevant departments (e.g., Public Health Services, Planning and Economic Development, Public Works, and Community Services). As one means of achieving community food security, and to help address the gaps in existing efforts to support gardens, the CFSSC advocated that the city adopt a community garden policy.

Working in collaboration with the CFSSC, the research project described here sought to identify elements of an environmentally just community garden policy and use these insights to inform the development of a community garden policy for Hamilton. It also sought to reflect on the policy process as it unfolded, seeking lessons for future practice. As such, it can be considered a participatory action research (PAR) project, aiming "to contribute both to the practical concerns of people in an immediate problematic situation and to further the goals of social science simultaneously" (Gilmore, Krantz, & Ramirez, 1986, p. 161).

This project had three main components: (1) an environmental scan of existing community garden policies and related literature to identify best practices (using an environmental justice lens), (2) interviews and focus groups in the study community to assess local needs, and facilitators and barriers to garden development, and (3) participant observation of the policy process as it unfolded in the study community. Community garden policies in a variety of North American cities were evaluated for elements likely to contribute to environmental justice and therefore desirable for inclusion in Hamilton's policy. Next, semi-structured key informant interviews were conducted with eight policy-makers and activists, including experts in urban agriculture, representatives of the City of Hamilton, and representatives of community development organizations. A focus group was also held with ten community gardeners and garden supporters in Hamilton. Further insights into the policy-making process were gained through observation at CFSSC, HCGN, and Hamilton Board of Health meetings, and through ongoing conversations with key actors in the policy-making process (the primary author led the interviews and focus group and observed meetings, while the co-author chaired meetings of the CFSSC and engaged in ongoing conversations about the policy direction with key actors).

4. Growing Community: Garden Policies through an Environmental Justice Lens

This research reviewed existing community garden policies to illustrate elements of an environmentally just policy. Using Schlosberg (2004) as a starting point, the authors decided that to be just, a policy must *recognize* different levels of power and socio-economic status within the city, must allow these different groups to *participate* both in the policy process and in the act of gardening itself, and must ultimately provide for a fair *distribution* of community gardens across the city. Below, the key elements of an environmentally just policy identified through this research are outlined, namely: equitable distribution of gardens; stability and security of land tenure; support for the affordability of gardening; provision of gardening support and education to enhance equity of access; and the need for some degree of garden autonomy and self-management. While each of these elements emerged in the literature review, many of them also emerged in interviews with community members, with the need for secure land tenure flagged as local gardeners' greatest challenge, followed closely by the need for gardening support and education and for garden self-management. Each element is described in more detail below.

4.1. EQUITABLE DISTRIBUTION OF GARDENS

Historically, green space and leisure areas have been under-provided for lower-income neighbourhoods in Hamilton (Cruikshank & Bouchier, 2004). Food security and lack of access to green space are both problems in the city's low-income neighbourhoods; an environmentally just community garden policy would therefore prioritize the development of gardens in these areas. In addition, lower income households are less likely to have private yards to garden in; a just garden policy would take this inequity into account. For example, Cambridge, Massachusetts, gives priority for participation in community gardens to families who lack access to land (City of Cambridge, No Date).

Interviews with community members in Hamilton emphasized that gardens should be located throughout the city, easily accessible by transit, and clustered with other community assets such as libraries or community centres. This view reflects a common belief among respondents that community gardens are an important amenity to which *all* residents should have access. It is important to note, however, that an *equal* distribution of community gardens across the city may not be a *fair* one. In cases where existing community amenities are few, and food security is a larger issue, an argument can be made for working to rectify these existing distributional inequalities by directing resources towards areas with the greatest need. This means that a policy that emphasizes the development of a garden in every ward (e.g., City of Toronto, 2003) could be considered less consistent with an environmental justice approach than one that prioritizes underserved areas for the development of new gardens.

4.2. SECURING LAND TENURE

In-depth interviews and focus groups suggested that stability of land tenure is the greatest challenge faced by gardeners in Hamilton. This problem is common throughout North America (Public Health Law & Policy, 2009). In many cities the local government reserves the right to terminate a lease agreement granting use of publicly owned land, sometimes on very short notice (Schukoske, 2000). Some municipalities have acted to make tenure at least marginally more secure. The City of Vancouver council issues five-year leases, but garden groups can apply for longer-term leases if the garden is part of a community outreach programme or if they provide a long-term plan for the space (City of Vancouver, 2005).

4.3. MAKING GARDENING ACCESSIBLE TO LOW-INCOME COMMUNITIES

Most city council-operated community gardens rely on user fees to help recover some of the costs of land, water, equipment, and education. One concern with charging user fees to finance community gardens is that even a small fee may exclude those who stand to benefit the most (Tarasuk, 2001). Some cities have tried to reduce these barriers: in Montreal, for example, the city council waives user fees for people receiving social assistance (Ville de Montréal, 2005).

Often gardeners work with non-profit organizations to help cover some of the costs of beginning and maintaining a community garden. In Chicago, for example, the non-profit NeighborSpace protects community-managed open spaces, including community gardens, by acquiring the land on behalf of the community and providing liability insurance coverage (NeighborSpace, 2010). In Hamilton, many of the independent community gardens—and virtually all of those in low-income communities—have partnered with a community organization to meet their infrastructure needs. However, these social service organizations may not always share the same goals as local residents, or work equitably in partnership with them. Creating an environment where local residents maintain control over their local green space should be an important goal.

4.4. PROVISION OF GARDENING EDUCATION AND SUPPORT

In the focus group and interviews, informants stressed that access to information and advice is an essential service to support community gardens, and clearly desired some type of paid resource person to help gardeners. Some cities provide this support by having staff time devoted to community gardens. In Montreal, each arrondissement has a neighbourhood development worker and a "garden animator" who work together to provide information and services to community gardens (Ville de Montréal, 2005). The City of Toronto council funds a full-time community garden coordinator and two part-time facilitators (City of Toronto, 2009). Focus group respondents—all local gardeners—repeatedly stated the importance of having a person in charge of disseminating information, organizing workshops, and facilitating relationships between gardeners and the city council. This facilitating role is particularly important in terms of equity, as the garden coordinator could actively support community members from all backgrounds in approaching the city council for access to a garden. In addition, several interviewees stressed the need to strengthen the network of gardeners to advocate and fundraise more effectively for community gardens and to provide needed support to new and existing gardens. The HCGN was also seen as badly in need of funding, as it is currently the primary source of information about community gardens in Hamilton.

4.5. AUTONOMY OF GARDENS

Different interests use community gardens to serve different purposes, and may seek to meet the needs and fulfil the interests of those outside the community. In particular, state actors may use gardens as mechanisms for spatial and social regulation. However, recognizing the importance of community initiation and control in a garden does not necessarily imply that the state should have no role in facilitating the garden development. Indeed, interviews revealed a tension in the need for a policy providing government support to gardens, but in a manner that does not control or overly constrain gardeners. Respondents agreed that the municipality should recognize the importance of community gardening and provide resources to enable the development of gardens citywide. In particular, help acquiring land, establishing water connections, and providing information were the services most desired by local gardeners.

Overall, when using an environmental justice lens it is important to locate community gardens in the context of the historical and present-day social, political, economic, and environmental processes that have conspired to create inequities in the distribution of food and other resources (Alkon & Norgaard, 2009). By taking existing inequities into account, new policies can work to "level the playing field" in ways that contribute to environmental justice.

In practice, however, policy and planning decisions have tended to reinforce rather than challenge existing inequities. The next section details the process of developing and implementing a community garden policy in Hamilton, highlighting both the successes and limitations of this policy initiative.

5. Developing Hamilton's Community Garden Policy: The Policy Process

The initial research described in this paper identified the desires of Hamilton's gardeners and enumerated key elements of an environmentally just policy, with the aim of influencing the policy outcome. The paper now moves on to an analysis of the policy process in this particular instance, and the implications for environmental justice.

5.1. THE BEGINNINGS OF A POLICY: INITIATIVE AND JURISDICTION

As noted earlier, the CFSSC identified the need for a community garden policy as part of the city council's overarching commitment to community food security (City of Hamilton, 2009a). The research and policy analysis described above was initially undertaken to further their advocacy in this area. However, the CFSSC, as an advisory sub-committee of the Board of Health, does not have the power to draft policy, or to compel staff to do so. Like many similar committees (e.g., the Toronto Food Policy Council), the CFSSC acts to raise awareness of issues with council and staff, and works collaboratively with actors (both internal and external to the city council) to achieve its goals.

One of the city councillors on the CFSSC tabled a motion at city council requesting the development of a policy (City of Hamilton, 2009b). It was subsequently determined that the Public Works department should take responsibility for drafting the policy, given their responsibility for managing the existing community gardens and maintaining the City's land inventory (City of Hamilton, 2009c). The initial background research conducted by the CFSSC was provided to Public Works to support their work. Public Works staff consulted with staff in other city council departments (particularly Public Health) and with the HCGN early in the process; however, few specifics of the policy were available prior to the unveiling of a complete draft in March 2010, which was presented orally to both the CFSSC and the HCGN.

5.2. THE FIRST DRAFT

The first draft of the community garden policy introduced several helpful measures. First, under the draft policy, Public Works committed to developing an inventory of City-owned land suitable for gardening. Criteria for identifying these lands included proximity to a water source, no conflicting adjacent land uses, no concerning past land uses (e.g., historical contamination), and no plans for the land to be developed for other purposes. Second, Public Works committed to facilitating the licence agreement process between the City and any interested community garden group; these licences would grant the group access to the land through a three-year lease. The Public Works department would cede control of their existing gardens to the gardeners, and any new gardens would be established using a self-governance model. Finally, Public Works asked for an annual budget allocation of C$20,000 to create five new 25 × 50 m gardens each year. The money would be spent on the initial setup of the gardens, primarily preparing the land with a rototiller. Despite the inclusion of this aid as a new budget line item, the community garden policy was seen as revenue neutral, since city council costs associated with managing their existing gardens were thought to exceed this cost.

In general, response to the draft policy was favourable, for several reasons. First, it was seen as a significant and positive shift to have the City actively encouraging community gardens through any kind of policy; second, the provision of resources to increase the number of gardens was promising, particularly in an era of cost-cutting; and third, most gardeners saw the opportunity for greater self-management within the existing City gardens as a positive shift.

Despite these promising features in the first draft, the document's provisions with respect to equity and environmental justice were somewhat limited when compared with the possibilities identified in the background research. For example, the policy did not explicitly prioritize certain areas for garden development. Indeed, the land inventory criteria—if applied without an eye towards environmental justice—would likely mean that the most impoverished areas of the city would be deemed unsuitable for community gardens, given their greater density and historical and contemporary industrial activity (and therefore greater likelihood of land contamination, existence of pressures on land for alternative uses, and possibility for conflicting adjacent land uses).

The draft policy also did not include the cost of a staff person to help would-be gardeners navigate the process of applying for land from the city council, or to provide other support. This omission illustrates the underlying expectation that residents would be equally able to organize themselves to participate in the public realm, overlooking the power differentials that could prevent marginalized groups from accessing community gardening. Thus, existing unequal distributions of healthy food and green space could be reproduced rather than alleviated by the draft policy.

Similarly, the transfer of control of the gardens to the gardeners seems at first glance to be a win-win situation, as it gives gardeners greater autonomy and allows Public Works staff to focus their resources on preparing rather than managing the gardens. However, as a consequence of assuming control of the land, the community gardens would be required to purchase their own liability insurance, an estimated annual cost of C$800. This cost presents a significant financial barrier, and would disproportionately affect the lowest income gardeners. This requirement also reflects an underlying assumption that all people have equal confidence and skills not only to approach the city council to ask for a garden but to negotiate an insurance policy, develop relationships with neighbours, and resolve conflicts—activities that the City had previously undertaken on behalf of gardeners in its role as garden manager.

5.3. FROM DRAFTING TO DIGGING: FINALIZING THE COMMUNITY GARDEN POLICY

The HCGN and the CFFSC provided comments to Public Works department staff on the draft policy, which raised the concerns mentioned above. However, during the next few weeks it became clear, based on follow-up conversations with city staff, that Public Works senior managers had already approved the draft policy; alterations would have required this "sign-off" process to be repeated, potentially jeopardizing the policy.

A few alterations to the draft were made prior to its being brought forward to the Public Works Committee (the committee of elected councillors that provides direction to the Public Works department). For example, the initial list of services provided by Public Works to new gardens was rigid (primarily rototilling); this wording was changed slightly to allow Public Works to offer a variety of services that could be chosen based on the garden's needs (up to C$4,000 per garden). However, the body of the document remained fundamentally unchanged (City of Hamilton, 2010a).

Members of the CFSSC and the HCGN deputed at the 19 April 2010 meeting of the Public Works Committee to show their support for a community garden policy and to express their views on what the policy should provide. These deputations lauded the idea of the policy and congratulated staff for their hard work; however, they also lamented the lack of "soft" resources—particularly for support staff—available for community garden development, and the failure to prioritize inner-city neighbourhoods for garden development (City of Hamilton, 2010b).

Questions from the Public Works Committee members for deputants, and later for Public Works staff, focused on concerns about garden aesthetics (particularly "messiness" and the possibility of site abandonment), and on costs to city council coffers (City of Hamilton, 2010b). It was very clear that several councillors saw city council investment in community gardens as an unwarranted frill, and it was only the fact that this policy would in the end be revenue neutral (and perhaps over the long term revenue saving) that allowed it to be voted through. One downtown councillor raised a concern about environmental contamination on garden sites adjacent to the city's industrial areas; however, no follow-up questions were asked about the equity issues raised in the deputations. The Community Gardening Policy was then approved by the Public Works committee and ultimately by council (City of Hamilton, 2010a).

Disappointed by the lack of a community garden coordinator to facilitate garden development and maintenance, the HCGN applied for charitable funding to support the coordinator position. This funding application was successful, but provided support for the facilitator for only one year. At the time of writing, this coordinator had provided significant support to the existing community gardens in the city, particularly those transitioning from city council management. At around the same time, City Housing Hamilton (the local public housing provider) quietly hired a community garden coordinator for its own properties, who has supported the development of a large number of new gardens on City Housing land. In addition, a number of local social service organizations (including at least two emergency food providers) have constructed new community gardens on their own properties. These developments have significantly enhanced the equity of the distribution of community gardens in Hamilton (Figure 38.2).

Thus, since 2009, a number of new community gardens have been developed or are in the planning stages in Hamilton. Many of these gardens have received some support from the city council (primarily compost donations), but few are on city-owned land and so have not received the full range of subsidized services. The community garden budget allocation was ultimately not approved as a new budget line item, but the Public Works department has committed to continuing to fund community garden development through its existing budget.

Overall, the policy initiative described here could be seen as a partial success. Without detracting from the very important successes achieved by the policy, the next section of the paper explores the structural and other barriers that limited procedural and distributional equity in this context.

FIGURE 38.2 COMMUNITY GARDEN LOCATIONS AND POVERTY RATES, HAMILTON, ONTARIO, 2011

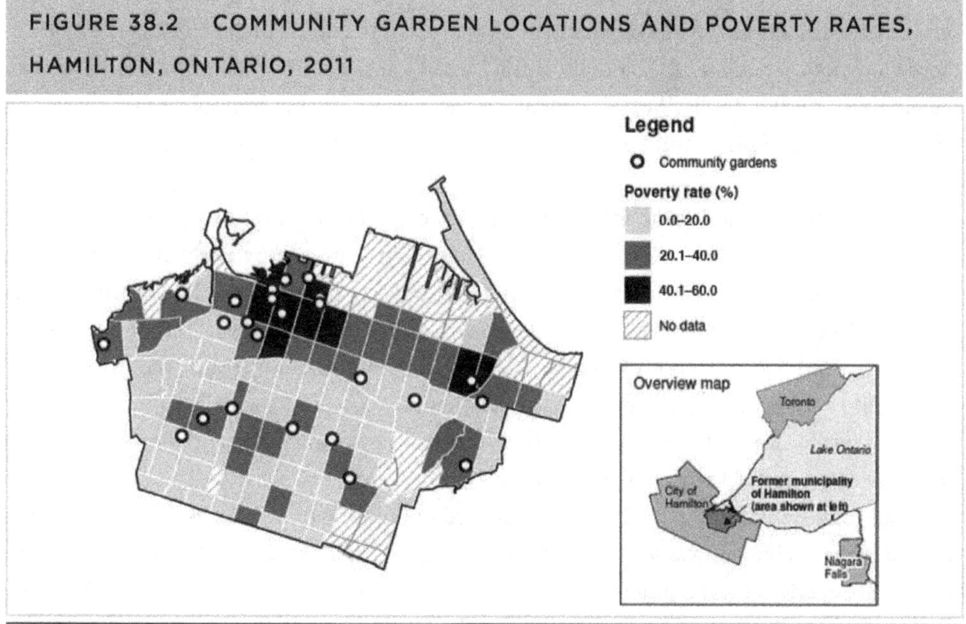

Source: Social Planning and Research Council of Hamilton, 2009, used with permission.

6. Barriers to Environmentally Just Policy-Making

By examining the process through which the community garden policy was drafted and eventually enacted, it is possible to identify structural, procedural, and attitudinal constraints that shaped the policy and limited its potential to facilitate environmental justice. Namely, the departmental division of labour and expertise, the procedural constraints placed on actors by a relatively hierarchical organizational structure, and the primacy of cost containment as a goal of—or at least a necessary limitation on—policy development, all served to shape Hamilton's community garden policy. Importantly, this process was also shaped by the relative inattention given to issues of environmental and social justice in policy development, particularly outside of the departments of Public Health Services and Community Services. It should be noted that the purpose of this section is not to suggest that "bad actors" limited the achievement of environmental justice goals. In fact, the goal is exactly the opposite—to expose how, even when acting with the best interests of the community in mind, particular institutional structures and conceptual frames (neither of which is unique to Hamilton) can inadvertently limit the efficacy of policy initiatives in relation to environmental justice.

6.1. DEPARTMENTAL DIVISION OF LABOUR

The community garden policy described here was developed by the Public Works department; it follows that this department's expertise and values are reflected in the document. The services that the Public Works department offer are tied to land, which is unsurprising given the department's mandate to maintain infrastructure and public land in the city. However, the emphasis on the Public Works' mandate in the community garden policy meant that the "softer" side of planning, and particularly questions of equity and knowledge transfer, were not prioritized.

The fact that Public Works was given sole responsibility for drafting the policy is illustrative of a central constraint on the policy process. While managing parkland is within the scope of the department's work, food security and poverty do not typically fall within their purview. Other city council departments, such as Community Services or Public Health Services, have expertise in these areas; however, because Public Works operated the city council's community gardens using money from the horticulture general fund, it became the department responsible for drafting the policy. Thus, budget lines—rather than mission, skill sets, or interests—determined the policy direction.

Once "ownership" of the policy was transferred to Public Works, the ability of other actors to impact the policy process was severely constrained. Other city council departments were no longer directly involved in its writing. The involvement of the CFSSC in the development of the policy was limited by their advisory role. The HCGN could lobby for a certain outcome, but their influence on the policy process was even less direct than that of the CFSSC. Finally, city councillors could express their desire for the policy to contain certain elements, but again were not directly involved in actually writing the policy. Thus, although these various actors had clear interests in the policy and sought to influence it, they were not involved in the actual decision-making around how the policy was written.

6.2. CONSTRAINED ACTORS, CONSTRAINED PROCEDURES

Public Works staff operated under a number of constraints that affected how the policy was developed. They were understandably concerned that any additional support given to community gardens would add to their already full workloads: while very committed in principle to community garden development, it was impossible for them to provide facilitation support to community gardens (which in any case was not well correlated with their skill sets) without overburdening themselves. However, the lack of involvement of other departments and actors—who might have been able to offer additional support through their own mandates (e.g., Public Health supporting community gardening education as a component of healthy living)—meant that this additional support simply went unmentioned in the policy.

In addition, a set of constraints related to the internal reporting structures of the city council also impacted the policy outcome. While there was outreach to the gardening community early on in the process, and Public Works met on an ongoing basis with staff from other departments, these stakeholders were not involved in the *writing* of the policy. Indeed, Public Works staff were unable to share the draft policy publicly (including with the HCGN or even the CFSSC) prior to its approval by higher-ranking staff in the department. Once this approval was given, subsequent substantive changes to the draft became difficult, as they would require that the internal departmental approval process should begin again.

Public Works gave presentations to both the CFSSC and HCGN, describing the draft policy orally and in PowerPoint slides. But while the presenters described the draft policy in detail and answered the groups' questions, they could not share the document itself. Therefore, these groups could not comment on the actual wording of the document until it was placed on the Public Works Committee agenda (as an item for approval). Incorporating even the limited input from meetings with stakeholders was challenging, as the document had already been passed further up the chain of command for approval to move forward.

The need for the City to ensure that any document meets a certain standard before it is made public is understandable. At the same time, the degree of secrecy within the policy writing process precludes public—and even interdepartmental—input and may result in a policy that does not accurately reflect the needs or desires of the public. Similarly, a lack of transparency in consultations may lead to misunderstandings, particularly if people have the impression that their input will be used to change the language of a policy when in reality it is quite unlikely to.

6.3. PRIMACY OF COST CONTAINMENT

A significant barrier to addressing the community's needs in the development of the community garden policy was the lack of resources available within the city council. The Public Works department, with an existing budget line in this area, was able to reallocate existing resources and use them in a new and creative way; however, at no time in the process was there a sense that new or additional funding would be available to supplement the existing funding. Instead, it was clear any resources would need to be reallocated from within existing programmes.

In particular, creating a new staff position to support community gardens was seen as next to impossible. New staff positions are a significant commitment for departments—not only are they costly additions to (always stressed) budgets, but they are very difficult to eliminate once they have been developed, making a "trial run" difficult. Discussion at the Public Works Committee meeting where the community garden policy was approved made it clear that a new staff position would not have been considered.

In an ideal world, municipalities would have sufficient coffers from which to fund the programmes and provide the services needed by the public. In reality, funding for Canadian municipalities comes from limited sources, primarily from the province, property taxes, and fees and charges (Tindal & Tindal, 2009). These revenue streams have come under increasing pressure, particularly from downloading and/or cutbacks at the provincial level, making new investment difficult, even when the likely benefits to community health of the investment are substantial. Within this neo-liberal environment, charities and individuals, rather than the state, are expected to provide services needed by the community, as exemplified by the HCGN seeking charitable funding to provide a community garden coordinator.

6.4. FAILURE TO USE A JUSTICE LENS

Overall, environmental justice was not a central consideration in the development of the community garden policy. While some city council staff in the Public Health Services and Community Services departments routinely adopt a social justice (if not an environmental justice) perspective, this is not the norm in the Public Works, Planning and Economic Development, or other departments. Similarly, most city councillors did not seem to appreciate the salience of an equity approach to policy development when the policy was not explicitly related to poverty. This attitude is not terribly surprising, given the different educational backgrounds, training, and work experience of staff. At the same time, it limits the extent to which social and environmental justice issues are considered across City activities.

7. Conclusion

This paper has used an environmental justice framework to both inform and interrogate the development of a community garden policy for the City of Hamilton. The community garden policy described here reflects what were clearly "rational" decisions when made within the constraints of City bureaucracy. The outcome of these decisions, though, is a policy that does not make gardening accessible to all: indeed, a closer look reveals that this policy could in fact *reduce* rather than enhance environmental justice in the city. By placing most of the onus of garden development and operation on community groups, the policy does not recognize the differentials in power and resources of different groups in the city.

Based on the research described above, it is possible to suggest some improvements to the policy process, in order to improve both procedural and distributional justice. First, the "silo" approach to governance, in which a single department has responsibility for policy development, needs to give way to a more collaborative approach, wherein various departments and organizations with relevant knowledge and interests pool ideas and resources. It is important to reiterate that Hamilton's CFSSC has representatives from a variety of City departments, and significant collaboration occurred between departments in the early stages of policy development. However, as the policy worked its way through the administrative structure of the lead department, opportunities for meaningful engagement of those outside the department were limited, despite the best intentions of the key actors in the process. Other studies have noted that interdepartmental collaboration, and an institutional culture that supports such collaboration, is crucial for effective action on contemporary social and environmental problems (Boonekamp, Colomer, Tomas, & Nuñez, 1999; Burch, 2010). Policy development in Hamilton, and no doubt other municipalities as well, would benefit from an approach that allows collaboration to occur at all stages in the policy development process.

Similarly, the public consultation process used in policy development needs to be more substantive. The academic planning literature is, of course, replete with suggestions of how public engagement can be improved. However, many of these suggestions fail to account for the structures of governance that rigorously control the flow of information and centralize decision-making. In order to provide meaningful opportunities for citizen inclusion in decision-making, a rethinking of existing norms of policy development is required. In particular, the expectation that all "draft" documents and policies be vetted by senior management before they can be shared with interested stakeholders severely limits the extent to which members of the public can participate meaningfully in policy development.[1]

An overarching constraint on policy development is the limited availability of resources for new programmes. Under neo-liberalism, federal and provincial governments have downloaded increasing responsibilities on municipalities, while simultaneously reducing transfer payments to cities (Peck & Tickell, 2002; Tindal & Tindal, 2009). At the same time, contemporary (neo-liberal) political discourse emphasizes cutting taxes as a primary societal goal. While this problem is well recognized, it is important to reiterate how it limits the development of policies that support (environmental) justice and the responsiveness of government to changing contexts and priorities. Policy innovation and experimentation require resources; without a funding stream to draw upon, many policy and planning initiatives will not get beyond the early stages, even when they could enhance sustainability, quality of life, and local resilience—particularly among vulnerable populations—at a relatively low cost.

In response to the fiscal constraints of the city council, the HCGN and others have attempted to "fill the gaps" by working with charitable donors and local agencies, and drawing on their own resources. Some would argue that this is an example of successful civil society organizing (and possibly evidence that government support is not really necessary). However, relying on non-profits for funding is not ideal. Unlike local government, non-profit agencies are not accountable to the public, and may seek to further a particular interest in exchange for the services or funding they provide (INCITE!, 2007; Marwell, 2004). Funding is often short-term, leading to financial instability, and the entire process relies heavily on volunteers—e.g., for administration, accounting, and fundraising—whose skills in these areas may be limited and whose time could arguably be spent better elsewhere (e.g., actually gardening). Indeed, the shift to community-based initiatives in the absence of government support is likely to hinder the equitable development of community gardens.

In this context, is the development of community gardens even a good thing? The literature is ambivalent as to the overall benefit of gardens: on the one hand, a variety of benefits are attributed to them (e.g., Corrigan, 2011; Firth et al., 2011; Milbourne, 2012), while on the other, they are seen as a Trojan horse to make communities take responsibility for replacing services previously provided by the state (e.g., Pudup, 2008; Rosol, 2010). These critiques point to the importance of community initiation and control of gardens to ensure that gardeners' aims—rather than the government's—are met. Further, it is key that community gardens should not become stand-ins for government action on income equality, affordable housing, and other root causes of hunger (Tarasuk, 2001).

Given the explosion of community gardens across North America, the question of whether gardens are "good" may be moot; however, as planners increasingly act within the food policy realm, the intentions and implications of community garden policies merit reflection. This study lends some credence to the view that community gardens can serve to entrench neo-liberalism. Similarly, it illustrates how commonplace bureaucratic practices can restrict procedural justice and, by extension, distributional justice. At the same time, it points to more hopeful possibilities. Although Hamilton's policy-makers did not embrace environmental justice, garden supporters clearly saw these mundane spaces of production as a legitimate realm of environmental justice and have since worked for at least an equitable distribution of gardens. Similarly, City Housing Hamilton's adoption of a community garden coordinator illustrates that creative forces can work from within the bureaucracy to provide services that otherwise would have been downloaded to the community.

Environmental justice cannot, however, be realized by individuals acting on their own, no matter how creative their negotiation of the bureaucracy. Overall, this research suggests that the explicit adoption of an environmental justice lens in policy development and planning would allow issues of environmental and social justice to be brought into the policy process. In the case study described above, justice concerns were not part of policy discussions outside of the departments of Public Health and Community Services. However, residents' lives are impacted by all city departments; without greater recognition of the relevance of distributional and procedural justice in planning and policy decisions, opportunities to reduce environmental injustice are lost. Planners—and not just social planners—need to take issues of distributional and procedural justice more seriously. More specifically, policies that support positive outcomes in the community as a whole are often seen as inherently just, without taking into account differential access to resources within the community. Increasing sensitivity to these distinctions—and their practical implications for the equity of planning initiatives—is central to progressive policy development.

Note

1. Changing this norm does not necessarily mean that institutions can no longer control their messages—by creating multi-stakeholder teams that work together on policy documents (e.g., policy drafting subcommittees) in secure, confidential environments (whether

through password-protected websites or confidential meetings), control over information could be maintained, while the ability of key stakeholders to participate in policy development would be dramatically increased.

References

Alaimo, K., Packnett, E., Miles, R. A., & Kruger, D. J. (2008). Fruit and vegetable intake among urban community gardeners. *Journal of Nutrition Education and Behavior*, 40(2), 94–101.

Alkon, A. H., & Norgaard, K. M. (2009). Breaking the food chains: An investigation of food justice activism. *Sociological Inquiry*, 79(3), 289–305.

American Planning Association. (2011). What is planning? Retrieved from http://planning.org/aboutplanning/whatisplanning.htm

Baker, L. E. (2004). Tending cultural landscapes and food citizenship in Toronto's community gardens. *Geographical Review*, 94(3), 305–325.

Beaulac, J., Kristjansson, E., & Cummings, S. (2009). A systematic review of food deserts, 1966–2007. *Preventing Chronic Disease*, 6(3), A105. Retrieved from http://www.cdc.gov/pcd/issues/2009/jul/08_0163.htm

Boonekamp, G. M. M., Colomer, C., Tomas, A., & Nuñez, A. (1999). Healthy cities evaluation: The coordinators perspective. *Health Promotion International*, 14(2), 103–110.

Brulle, R. J., & Pellow, D. N. (2006). Environmental justice: Human health and environmental inequalities. *Annual Review of Public Health*, 27(1), 103–124.

Bullard, R. D. (1990). *Dumping in Dixie: Race, class, and environmental quality*. Boulder: Westview Press.

Bullard, R. D. (2005). *The quest for environmental justice: Human rights and the politics of pollution*. San Francisco: Sierra Club Books.

Burch, S. (2010). Transforming barriers into enablers of action on climate change: Insights from three municipal case studies in British Columbia, Canada. *Global Environmental Change*, 20(2), 287–297.

City of Cambridge. (No Date). Cambridge community garden program policy for city-owned land. Retrieved from http://www.cambridgema.gov/ccc/communitygardenprogram1.aspx

City of Hamilton. (2007). Terms of reference for the Community Food Security Stakeholders Committee, Public Health Services, Healthy Living Division. Retrieved from http://www.hamilton.ca/NR/rdonlyres/ DE441F90-D161-4C86-832C-E1598CAB8315/0/Nov26BOH07031aFoodSecurityCommitteeTerms ofReference.pdf

City of Hamilton. (2009a). Community Food Security Stakeholder Committee BOH07031(b) (City Wide), Public Health Services, Healthy Living Division. Retrieved from http://www.hamilton.ca/NR/rdonlyres/096AEEE5-2210-4D39-9123-7AF871961473/0/Feb23BOH07031bCommunityFoodSecurity.pdf

City of Hamilton. (2009b). Notice of motion, Board of Health. Retrieved from http://www.hamilton.ca/NR/rdonlyres/3F371004-3EAB-4CFE-996C-96C7E07B3044/0/Nov23Item101McHattieNoticeofMotion.pdf

City of Hamilton. (2009c). City council minutes. Retrieved from http://www.hamilton.ca/NR/rdonlyres/ E25C7F82-699E-4847-B149-9F324D934691/0/Dec09Minutes.pdf

City of Hamilton. (2009d). Nutritious food basket – BOH09024, Board of Health.

City of Hamilton. (2010a). Community garden policy (PW 10044)—(city wide). Retrieved from http://www.hamilton.ca/CityDepartments/PublicWorks/Parks/Horticulture/CommunityGardens.htm

City of Hamilton. (2010b). Public Works committee minutes. Retrieved from http://www.hamilton.ca/CityDepartments/CorporateServices/Clerks/AgendaMinutes/PublicWorks/2010/April19PublicWorksCommitteeAgenda.htm

City of Toronto. (2003). *Tending the garden*. Toronto: Food and Hunger Action Committee.

City of Toronto. (2009). Community gardens in the city of Toronto. Retrieved from http://www.toronto.ca/parks/programs/community.htm

City of Vancouver. (2005). Operational guidelines for community gardens on city owned land other than parks. http://vancouver.ca/commsvcs/socialplanning/initiatives/foodpolicy/projects/pdf/commgardensguide.pdf

Clavin, A. A. (2011). Realising ecological sustainability in community gardens: A capability approach. *Local Environment*, 16(10), 945–962.

Corburn, J. (2003). Bringing local knowledge into environmental decision making: Improving urban planning for communities at risk. *Journal of Planning Education and Research*, 22(4), 420–433.

Corburn, J. (2004). Confronting the challenges in reconnecting urban planning and public health. *American Journal of Public Health*, 94(4), 541–546.

Corrigan, M. P. (2011). Growing what you eat: Developing community gardens in Baltimore, Maryland. *Maryland, Applied Geography*, 31(4), 1232–1241.

Cruikshank, K., & Bouchier, N. B. (2004). Blighted areas and obnoxious industries: Constructing environmental inequality on an industrial waterfront, Hamilton, Ontario, 1890–1960. *Environmental History*, 9(3), 464–496.

Cutter, S. L., & Solecki, W. D. (1996). Setting environmental justice in space and place: Acute and chronic airborne toxic releases in the Southeastern United States. *Urban Geography*, 17(5), 380–399.

Eizenberg, E. (2012). The changing meaning of community space: Two models of NGO management of community gardens in New York City. *International Journal of Urban and Regional Research*, 36(1), 106–120.

Emmett, R. (2011). Community gardens, ghetto pastoral, and environmental justice. *Interdisciplinary Studies in Literature and Environment*, 18(1), 67–86.

Faber, D. R., & McCarthy, D. (2003). Neo-liberalism, globalization and the struggle for ecological democracy: Linking sustainability and environmental justice. In J. Agyeman, R. D. Bullard, & B. Evans (Eds.), *Just sustainabilities: Development in an unequal world* (pp. 38–63). Cambridge, MA: MIT Press.

Ferris, J., Norman, C., & Sempik, J. (2001). People, land and sustainability: Community gardens and the social dimension of sustainable development. *Social Policy & Administration*, 35(5), 559–568.

Firth, C., Maye, D., & Pearson, D. (2011). Developing "community" in community gardens. *Local Environment*, 16(6), 555–568.

Forester, J. (1989). *Planning in the face of power*. Berkeley: University of California Press.

Gee, G. C., & Payne-Sturges, D. C. (2004). Environmental health disparities: A framework integrating psychosocial and environmental concepts. *Environmental Health Perspectives*, 112(17), 1645–1653.

Gibson-Wood, H., & Wakefield, S. (2012). "Participation," white privilege and environmental justice: Understanding environmentalism among Hispanics in Toronto. *Antipode*. (Online first: DOI: 10.1111/j.1467-8330.2012.01019.x).

Gilmore, T., Krantz, J., & Ramirez, R. (1986). Action based modes of inquiry and the host-researcher relationship. *Consultation*, 5(3), 161.

Glover, T. D., Parry, D. C., & Shinew, K. J. (2005). Building relationships, accessing resources: Mobilizing social capital in community garden contexts. *Journal of Leisure Research*, 37(4), 450–474.

Gorham, M. R., Waliczek, T. M., Snelgrove, A., & Zajicek, J. M. (2009). The impact of community gardens on numbers of property crimes in urban Houston. *HortTechnology*, 19(2), 291–296.

Gosine, A., & Teelucksingh, C. (2008). *Environmental justice and racism in Canada: An introduction*. Toronto: Edmond Montgomery Publications.

Gottlieb, R. (2001). *Environmentalism unbound: Exploring new pathways for change*. Cambridge, MA: MIT Press.

Haluza-Delay, R., O'Riley, P., Cole, P., & Agyeman, J. (2009). Introduction. In J. Agyeman et al. (Eds.), *Speaking for ourselves: Environmental justice in Canada*. Vancouver: UBC Press.

Hamilton Food Share. (2009). Hamilton hunger count 2009. Retrieved from http://www.hamiltonfoodshare.org/hunger-in-our-backyard/index.htm

Hess, D. J. (2009). *Localist movements in a global economy: Sustainability, justice, and urban development in the United States.* Cambridge, MA: MIT Press.

Heynen, N., Perkins, H. A., & Roy, P. (2006). The political ecology of uneven urban green space: The impact of political economy on race and ethnicity in producing environmental inequality in Milwaukee. *Urban Affairs Review*, 42(1), 3–25.

Hobson, K. (2006). Enacting environmental justice in Singapore: Performative justice and the Green Volunteer network. *Geoforum*, 37(5), 671–681.

Holifield, R. (2004). Neoliberalism and environmental justice in the United States environmental protection agency: Translating policy into managerial practice in hazardous waste remediation. *Geoforum*, 35(3), 285–297.

Holifield, R. (2012). Environmental justice as recognition and participation in risk assessment: Negotiating and translating health risk at a superfund site in Indian country. *Annals of the Association of American Geographers*, 102(3), 591–613.

Holifield, R., Porter, M., & Walker, G. (2009). Introduction spaces of environmental justice: Frameworks for critical engagement. *Antipode*, 41(4), 591–612.

Holland, L. (2004). Diversity and connections in community gardens: A contribution to local sustainability. *Local Environment*, 9(3), 285–305.

INCITE! Women of Color Against Violence. (2007). *The revolution will not be funded: Beyond the non-profit industrial complex.* Cambridge, MA: South End Press.

Kingsley, J., & Townsend, M. (2006). "Dig in" to social capital: Community gardens as mechanisms for growing urban social connectedness. *Urban Policy and Research*, 24(4), 525–537.

Krumholz, N. (1982). A retrospective view of equity planning: Cleveland 1969–1979. *Journal of the American Planning Association*, 48(2), 163–174.

Kurtz, H. (2001). Differentiating multiple meanings of garden and community. *Urban Geography*, 22(7), 656–670.

Kurtz, H. E. (2009). Acknowledging the racial state: An agenda for environmental justice research. *Antipode*, 41(4), 684–704.

Latham, J., & Moffat, T. (2007). Determinants of variation in food cost and availability in two socioeconomically contrasting neighbourhoods of Hamilton, Ontario, Canada. *Health and Place*, 13(1), 273–287.

Lawson, L. (2004). The planner in the garden: A historical view into the relationship between planning and community gardens. *Journal of Planning History*, 3(2), 151–176.

Marwell, N. P. (2004). Privatizing the welfare state: Non-profit community-based organizations as political actors. *American Sociological Review*, 69(2), 265–291.

Matteson, K. C., Ascher, J. S., & Langellotto, G. A. (2008). Bee richness and abundance in New York City urban gardens. *Annals of the Entomological Society of America*, 101(1), 140–150.

Milbourne, P. (2012). Everyday (in)justices and ordinary environmentalisms: Community gardening in disadvantaged urban neighbourhoods. *Local Environment*, 17(9), 943–957.

Morland, K., Wing, S., Diez Roux, A., & Poole, C. (2002). Neighborhood characteristics associated with the location of food stores and food service places. *American Journal of Preventive Medicine*, 22(1), 23–29.

Morley, R. (2006). The cost of being poor: Poverty, lead poisoning, and policy implementation. *JAMA: The Journal of the American Medical Association*, 295(14), 1711–1712.

Mougeot, L. J. A. (2006). *Growing better cities: Urban agriculture for sustainable development.* Ottawa: IDRC.

NeighborSpace. (2010). Retrieved from http://neighbor-space.org/main.htm

Nussbaum, M. (2006). *Frontiers of justice: Disability, nationality, species membership*. Cambridge, MA: Belknap Press.

Peck, J., & Tickell, A. (2002). Neoliberalizing space. *Antipode*, 34(3), 380–404.

Pollan, M. (1991). *Second nature: A gardener's education*. New York, NY: Grove Press.

Public Health Law & Policy. (2009). Establishing land use protections for community gardens. Retrieved from www.healthyplanning.org

Pudup, M. B. (2008). It takes a garden: Cultivating citizen-subjects in organized garden projects. *Geoforum*, 39(3), 1228–1240.

Pulido, L. (2000). Rethinking environmental racism: White privilege and urban development in Southern California. *Annals of the Association of American Geographers*, 90(1), 12–40.

Rees, W. E., & Westra, L. (2003). When consumption does violence: Can there be sustainability and justice in a resource constrained world? In J. Agyeman, R. D. Bullard, & B. Evans (Eds.), *Just sustainabilities: Development in an unequal world* (pp. 99–124). Cambridge, MA: MIT Press.

Rosol, M. (2010). Public participation in post-Fordist urban green space governance: The case of community gardens in Berlin. *International Journal of Urban and Regional Research*, 34(3), 548–563.

Saldivar-Tanaka, L., & Krasny, M. E. (2004). Culturing community development, neighborhood open space, and civic agriculture: The case of Latino Community gardens in New York City. *Agriculture and Human Values*, 21(4), 399–412.

Sandercock, L. (2003). *Cosmopolis II: Mongrel cities in the 21st century.* London: Continuum.

Schlosberg, D. (2004). Reconceiving environmental justice: Global movements and political theories. *Environmental Politics*, 13(3), 517–540.

Schlosberg, D. (2007). *Defining environmental justice: Theories, movements, and nature*. New York, NY: Oxford University Press.

Schmelzkopf, K. (2002). Incommensurability, land use, and the right to space: Community gardens in New York City. *Urban Geography*, 23(4), 323–343.

Schukoske, J. E. (2000). Community development through gardening: State and local policies transforming urban open space. *New York University Journal of Legislation and Public Policy*, 3(2), 351–392.

Smith, C. M., & Kurtz, H. E. (2003). Community gardens and politics of scale in New York City. *Geographical Review*, 93(2), 193–212.

Social Planning and Research Council of Hamilton. (2009). Incomes and poverty in Hamilton. Retrieved from http://www.sprc.hamilton.on.ca/Reports/pdf/Incomes-and-Poverty-Report-final-May-2009.pdf

Soma, T., & Wakefield, S. (2011). The emerging role of a food system planner: Integrating food considerations into planning. *Journal of Agriculture, Food Systems, and Community Development*, 2(1), 53–64.

Staeheli, L. A., Mitchell, D., & Gibson, K. (2002). Conflicting rights to the city in New York's community gardens. *GeoJournal*, 58(2/3), 197–205.

Tarasuk, V. (2001). A critical examination of community-based responses to household food insecurity in Canada. *Health Education Behavior*, 28(4), 487–499.

Teig, E., Amulya, J., Bardwell, L., Buchenau, M., Marshall, J. A., & Litt, J. S. (2009). Collective efficacy in Denver, Colorado: Strengthening neighborhoods and health through community gardens. *Health and Place*, 15(4), 1115–1122.

Tindal, C. R., & Tindal, S. N. (2009). *Local government in Canada* (7th ed.). Toronto: Nelson Education Ltd.

Twiss, J., Dickinson, J., Duma, S., Kleinman, T., Paulsen, H., & Rilveria, L. (2003). Community gardens: Lessons learned from California healthy cities and communities. *American Journal of Public Health*, 93(9), 1435–1438.

United Church of Christ Commission for Racial Justice. (1987). *Toxic waste and race in the United States: A national report on the racial and socioeconomic characteristics of communities with hazardous wastes sites*. New York, NY: United Church of Christ.

United Church of Christ Commission for Racial Justice. (2007). *Toxic waste and race at twenty*: 1987–2007. New York, NY: United Church of Christ.

Urkidi, L., & Walter, M. (2011). Dimensions of environmental justice in anti-gold mining movements in Latin America. *Geoforum*, 42(6), 683–695.

Ville de Montréal. (2005). Le Cahier de Gestion du Programme des Jardins Communautaires [Community garden guide]. Retrieved from http://ville.montreal.qc.ca/pls/portal/docs/page/prt_vdm_fr/media/docum ents/Cahier_de_gestion.pdf

Vlahov, D., Gibble, E., Freudenberg, N., & Galea, S. (2004). Cities and health: History, approaches, and key questions. *Academic Medicine*, 79(12), 1133–1138.

Voicu, I., & Been, V. (2008). The effect of community gardens on neighboring property values. *Real Estate Economics*, 36(2), 241–283.

Wakefield, S., Yeudall, F., Taron, C., Reynolds, J., & Skinner, A. (2007). Growing urban health: Community gardening in south-east Toronto. *Health Promotion International*, 22(2), 92–101.

Wakefield, S. E., & Baxter, J. (2010). Linking health inequality and environmental justice: Articulating a precautionary framework for research and action. *Environmental Justice*, 3(3), 95–102.

Walker, G., & Bulkeley, H. (2006). Geographies of environmental justice. *Geoforum*, 37(5), 655–659.

Whitehead, M. (2009). The wood for the trees: Ordinary environmental injustice and the everyday right to urban nature. *International Journal of Urban and Regional Research*, 33(3), 662–681.

Wolch, J., Wilson, J. P., & Fehrenbach, J. (2005). Parks and park funding in Los Angeles: An equity-mapping analysis. *Urban Geography*, 26(1), 4–35.

Zoellner, J., Zanko, A., Price, B., Bonner, J., & Hill, J. L. (2012). Exploring community gardens in a health disparate population: Findings from a mixed methods pilot study. *Progress in Community Health Partnerships: Research, Education, and Action*, 6(2), 117–118.

CHAPTER 39

"A Direct Act of Resurgence, a Direct Act of Sovereignty": Reflections on Idle No More, Indigenous Activism, and Canadian Settler Colonialism

Adam J. Barker

Introduction

In the freezing Canadian winter of 2012, as the holiday period loomed large in mainstream consciousness, a massive grassroots political protest movement emerged that challenged the very basis of Canadian sovereignty and political identity. Idle No More, an iteration of Indigenous resistance to Settler colonization that extends back through five centuries, began as social media rumblings, spread into community meetings and teach-ins, and then rapidly expanded into direct-action flash mobs, significant protest rallies, and a media presence that was impossible to ignore. Indigenous peoples across Canada—and later in other countries around the world—joined together to push back against both specific policies of the Canadian government and the disempowering social discourses of Settler Canadians more generally.[1] The impact of Idle No More has been powerful, but also contested; this paper seeks to contribute to the debates around the meaning of this important protest movement by contextualizing it through the lens of contemporary Canadian Settler colonialism and ongoing Indigenous resurgence. [...]

Indigenous Resistance to Settler Colonialism: An Overview

I begin by acknowledging that Canada is a Settler colonial state, whose sovereignty and political economy is premised on the dispossession of Indigenous peoples and exploitation of their land base. This point, while not uncontested, is gaining purchase. [...] Moreover, the terms "Settler" and "colonial" have been increasingly employed by activists and community members, especially in conjunction with Idle No More,[2] a trend that I assert speaks to the resonance these analyses have with peoples' lived experiences in Canada. As both state and imagined community, Canada stands as a Settler colonial "structure of invasion" (Wolfe, 1999), and in this state, Indigenous peoples face constant threats to their existence, as both formal powers invested in the state and informal socio-cultural discourses of the Canadian nation seek to erase Indigenous peoples' claims to the land in order to transfer legitimate possession to colonial authorities (Barker, 2013, pp. 224–246; Veracini, 2010, pp. 33–52). However, the fact that Settler colonization is still ongoing in Canada is telling: despite centuries of concerted and evolving efforts, the Settler colonial project has never succeeded, evidence of powerful, multifaceted, and enduring Indigenous resistances.

I believe that in order to understand the significance of Idle No More, one must first understand the tradition of Indigenous resistance that has constantly stood opposed to Settler colonial processes. Generally, I follow the lead of Taiaiake Alfred (Mohawk) and Jeff Corntassel (Cherokee), employing "Indigenous" as a situated identity. In their key 2005 article, "Being Indigenous," they state:

> Indigenous peoples are just that: *Indigenous to the lands they inhabit*, in contrast to and in contention with the colonial societies and states that have spread out from Europe and other centres of empire. It is this *oppositional, place-based existence*, along with the *consciousness of being in struggle* against the dispossessing and demeaning fact of colonization by foreign peoples, that fundamentally distinguishes Indigenous peoples from other peoples of the world. (Alfred & Corntassel, 2005, p. 597; emphasis added)

It is to a brief discussion of this oppositional, place-based existence in relation to Idle No More that I now turn.

During much of the twentieth century, Indigenous activists fought for their collective survival and recognition of their basic existence, often by (re-)claiming a particular place or site. As Kilibarda (2012) has pointed out, occupying contentious sites is one of the most powerful and long-standing tactics of Indigenous resistance in Canada and the USA. Though it is impossible to single out any particular occupation or standoff as exemplary, some are more well known than others. In the USA, the occupation of the town of Wounded Knee by members of the Oglala Sioux nation and the American Indian Movement from February to May of 1973 is likely the most widely discussed (Weyler, 1992, pp. 58–96). An analogous event in the Canadian context in terms of its impact on social discourses and general awareness is the 78-day standoff between Mohawk Warriors and Canadian police and military in 1990, known as the "Oka Crisis" (York & Pindera, 1991). Many other examples could be found of Indigenous peoples occupying particular places; none of these incidents are isolated. Neither are Indigenous occupations limited to rural or wilderness areas; while the longest-running Indigenous occupation site is that of Grassy Narrows, an Anishinaabe resistance action against logging in their traditional territory (Willow, 2011), other sites are common. The Ipperwash Standoff, which led to the death of Anishinaabe activist Dudley George at the hands of the Ontario Provincial Police in 1995, occurred in a public park (Edwards, 2003); the Musqueam have recently been protesting against the destruction of a burial site inside the bounds of greater Vancouver (Musqueam Indian Band, n.d.); the 2006 reclamation of land near Caledonia, Ontario, by activists from Six Nations Reserve, is the site of a suburban housing development (Keefer, 2007); and the Gitxsan and Wet'suwet'en people, who last year withdrew support from their treaty negotiators for cutting deals relating to the Enbridge pipeline project, occupied a space already nominally "theirs" by physically blockading their treaty office (Stueck & Bailey, 2012). [...]

It is crucial to understand the variety of sites that have been key to Indigenous occupations, in part to understand how protests and occupations of urban and suburban spaces relate to struggles over "the land," often equated with rural—especially reserve—space. Anishinaabe scholar Leanne Simpson, in an interview with noted Canadian activist and journalist Naomi Klein, drew connections between Idle No More and the transfer of land through the metaphor of extraction as a key colonial process that affects both land and people:

> Extraction and assimilation go together. Colonialism and capitalism are based on extracting and assimilating. My land is seen as a resource. My relatives in the plant and animal worlds are seen as resources. My culture and knowledge is a resource. My body is a resource and my children are a resource because they are the potential to grow, maintain, and uphold the extraction-assimilation system. The act of extraction removes all of the relationships that give whatever is being extracted meaning. (Simpson, 2013)

Against the extractive current of Settler colonial transfer, I situate Indigenous peoples' traditions and strategies of resistance in Canada and the USA as a parallel affective process. Affective resistance is premised on the understanding that social relationships—the foundations of the spaces that people build and occupy (Massey, 2009, pp. 16–17)—are a crucial site of struggle. Larsen and Johnson (2012) have posited that attachments to place can form the basis of affinity politics, as attachments to place can bring people together into spontaneous, creative action and contention. [...] The affective attachments to place need not be attachments to the place of protest, or to place as "natural" or "unreconstructed." [...] An Indigenous space can exist anywhere; it requires only Indigenous peoples, in place, enacting their indigeneity. [...]

It is important to understand the radical challenge that the assertion of Indigenous political autonomy poses to Settler colonial political structures, and also to Settler Canadian identity and culture. Canada, as state and nation, is built on the premise that Indigenous peoples are either absent or that Indigenous political challenges are "settled" (Regan, 2010). While the colonial state—with the grudging support of some Canadians—can accommodate "aboriginal" political claims as a demand for minority rights within the multicultural structure of Canadian law and policy (Alfred, 2005), Indigenous movements that reject the politics of recognition in favour of asserting Indigenous place-relationships and social spaces challenge the core of both Canadian political economy and Settler identity (Coulthard, 2014a). Just as Settler colonialism is created by Settler collectives spreading through places, building spatially stretched relationships, Indigenous resistance simultaneously disrupts Settler colonial space while reasserting Indigenous spaces, altering the spatialities of both (Barker, 2013). [...]

While often happy to claim a relationship to "aboriginal" peoples through a narrative of Canada as a peaceful, liberal, multicultural polity defined by "peacemaking"—but dominated by whiteness, capitalist property ownership, and individual rights—Canadians have often reacted with hostility to assertions of Indigenous sovereignty that challenge this narrative (Regan, 2010). It is no surprise, then, that Idle No More—as one of the most visible, multi-vocal, and politically challenging Indigenous protest movements seen in Canada—should inspire passionate reactions from many quarters. I turn now to an overview of the events of Idle No More in order to more accurately interrogate how these protests relate to longer trends of Settler colonization and Indigenous resistance.

Winter of Discontent: The Events and Contexts of Idle No More

Idle No More is a contested label for a loosely organized but intense and powerful series of public and political engagements, community discourses, and direct action protests beginning in November 2012, increasing in size and frequency through January 2013, and decreasing in visible action and engagement thereafter, though retaining a powerful political presence in Canada.[3] This movement, primarily directed against the Canadian federal government (King, 2013 February), has been largely driven by Indigenous communities, especially as a largely grassroots, non-hierarchical effort. Although it is popularly regarded that there are "four founders" of Idle No More, the movement's moniker developed organically as a signifier and began spreading through a number of teach-ins in Indigenous communities in the Canadian provinces of Saskatchewan and Alberta; the associated hashtag—#IdleNoMore[4]—grew out of its use in these contexts and was taken up as a rallying cry for mass political engagement.[5] The catalyst was a series of legislation bills pushed through Parliament in mid- to late 2012, that directly threatened Indigenous peoples' interests, especially Bill C-45, an omnibus budget bill that contained changes to the Indian Act and to environmental protections, both of which drew the ire of Indigenous leaders and communities.

Even prior to the introduction of Bill C-45 into the House of Commons on 18 October 2012, community organizers in Indigenous communities—urban and reserve—were increasingly involved in community education and dialogue, raising awareness over the actions of the government and their implications for Indigenous communities. After C-45 was introduced, these community education sessions increased in frequency and intensity. On 10 November, an educational conference in Saskatoon, Saskatchewan, was organized by four women: Sylvia McAdam (Cree), Jessica Gordon (Cree/Anishinaabe), Nina Wilson (Nakota/Cree), and Sheelah McLean. This conference is often identified as the genesis point of the phrase "Idle No More," and the organizers of the conference have become colloquially known as "the four founders" of the movement. The phrase spread quickly through the social media hashtag #IdleNoMore, which gained widespread recognition and traction.

Alongside the growing use of #IdleNoMore as a rallying cry, a prominent Indigenous leader was preparing for her own form of protest, one that would ultimately prove to have a great deal of resonance with Idle No More. Chief Theresa Spence is the elected Chief of the Attawapiskat First Nation, an isolated reserve community in northern Ontario, which has been sparring with the Canadian government for years.[6] There has been a long-standing housing shortage on the reserve, a boil-water advisory, pollution from nearby mining activity, and extreme economic depression. After several years of bureaucratic and legal frustration, on 11 December 2012, Chief Spence and a small group of supporters set up a tent and fire on an island behind the House of Commons in Ottawa, and began a hunger strike. Subsisting on only medicinal tea and fish broth, Spence demanded to speak directly with the prime minister, Stephen Harper, and the governor general, David Johnston, the titular head of state and representative of the Crown in Canada. This protest immediately captured a great deal of media attention and polarized political commentary (Simpson, 2014).

Chief Spence's hunger strike, though not officially under the banner of Idle No More, was clearly coordinated to enhance the growing protest movement (Kino-nda-niimi Collective, 2014, p. 25). As Idle No More gained momentum, several days of action were called for. The first of these was on 10 December, and it was during the day-long set of protests, occupations, demonstrations, and rallies that Spence's hunger strike was announced. Between the Day of Action and Spence's protest, Idle No More and Indigenous peoples' concerns began to capture the attention of many Canadians. However, the mainstream media was still slow to cover these events until 17 December, when a new form of protest rally took Canadians by surprise. On that day in Regina, Saskatchewan, a flash mob organized inside a shopping mall filled with Christmas traffic, and began performing a round dance. Round dances are a public dance involving as many or as few drummers and dancers as are available; the drummers play and sing a relatively simple social song, while the dancers move in a shuffling circle around the drummers. This tactic quickly spread—dubbed the "Round Dance Revolution"—due to its ease of organizing and effect at generating attention and dialogue and was successfully deployed in shopping malls and busy public spaces such as urban intersections, an unexpected physical and conceptual transgression in spaces of capitalist consumption at a time when consumerism reached its yearly fever pitch.

On 21 December, a second Day of Action was called and a massive rally was held outside the House of Commons in Ottawa, the Canadian capital, with supporting protests being held around Canada and the world. Some—such as a one-person protest outside of the Canadian embassy in Cairo (APTN National News, 2012)—received more media attention than they may have warranted; others—including protests in remote places like Yellowknife in -40°C temperatures (Allooloo, 2014, p. 197)—likely received far less. However, the most enduring image from these protests is likely the round dance held in the midst of the busiest intersection in Canada's largest city, Toronto, Ontario: just prior to the rally on Parliament Hill, Idle No More protesters turned Dundas Square, the intersection of Yonge Street and Dundas Street East and West, into a massive protest space with a huge round dance.[7] Various Indigenous-led protests continued, some under the banner of Idle No More, others not, at irregular intervals through the rest of December and into January. On 30 December 2012, for example, the first of a series of blockades of rail lines between Montreal and Toronto was conducted; at the same time, round dances and other flash mob-type actions were continuing across Canada and the USA, some involving violent encounters with Settler people,[8] or arrests.[9]

In January 2013, amidst the backdrops of ongoing flash mobs, blockades, and local rallies and teach-ins, Prime Minister Harper announced that he would meet with representatives of the Assembly of First Nations (AFN), the government-sanctioned and funded representative body for recognized First Nation bands made up of elected chiefs and council members. Chief Spence, a continuing lightning rod for criticism of the government, stated that although her fast would continue, she would attend the meeting. This changed when Harper made clear that the governor general would not be participating, as Spence had demanded at the outset of her hunger strike; Spence immediately responded that she would boycott the meeting and that her hunger strike would continue. The day of the meeting between Harper and the AFN under Grand Chief Shawn A-in-chut Atleo (Nuu-chah-nulth), on 11 January, marked the single most concentrated day of protest and involvement in Idle No More, as rallies were held around the country organized under the hashtag #J11; the hashtag #idlenomore was used a record 55,334 times that day.[10] Despite this energy, with the outcome of the meeting between the AFN and Harper left ambiguous, and with legislation such as C-45 already passed, the discourse around Idle No More began to fragment. Further, a series of scandals not directly related to Indigenous issues rocked the federal government, distracting from the protests. After being hospitalized on 24 January and at the request of her family and community, Spence made the decision to end her hunger strike without having gained a hearing with either the prime minister or governor general.

A number of important events happened after the end of January, perhaps most notably the public shaming of long-time Harper advisor and political scientist, Tom Flannigan. Idle No More members, protesting his speaking event at the University of Lethbridge, captured Flannigan on video making dubious statements regarding the legality of viewing child pornography (Bolen, 2013), which was later posted online and ultimately resulted in Flannigan losing both his political and academic positions. But the flash mobs and public protests flagged, as did the online use of #IdleNoMore. Some members of Idle No More also began publicly questioning the tactics of organizers and protestors in other locations, especially the use of blockades at Canada–US border crossings, which had a cooling effect on community activism. Anniversary rallies planned around the country in December 2013 drew limited numbers and were unable to replicate the energy and excitement of the initial outburst in December 2012 and January 2013. However, Idle No More's impact and relationship to broader currents of Indigenous activism and resistance continue to be both felt and debated.

Modes of Engagement: Continuity and Change in Indigenous Resistance

Idle No More has been critiqued as a moniker by some precisely because Indigenous peoples have never been "idle" with respect to colonization. As Simpson, a leading voice in Idle No More and Indigenous resurgence generally, states:

> Over the past 400 years, there has never been a time when indigenous peoples were not resisting colonialism. Idle No More is the latest—visible to the mainstream—resistance and it is part of an ongoing historical and contemporary push to protect our lands, our cultures, our nationhoods, and our languages. (2013)

In this vein, I argue Idle No More should not be dismissed as a name or as a movement but rather should be discussed as one particularly effective set of efforts to innovate and revitalize Indigenous traditions of resistance in Canada, while staying true to core precepts of place-based politics.

#IdleNoMore, Social Media, and Online Organizing

Any analysis of Idle No More must begin with the relationship between the protest movement and the online hashtag. Recently, many social movements have developed in part through new and social media; the Arab Spring, for example, has been discussed as an example of how social media can aid and enhance social movements (see, e.g., Khondker, 2011). There is a resonance here with Idle No More: social media played a major role in both the development of Idle No More as a focal point for action, and of specific action tactics and strategies. The first tweet under the #idlenomore hashtag was made on 23 November 2012; two weeks later, on 7 December, there were 864 tweets with that hashtag. By 11 December, the first Day of Action, #idlenomore was tweeted 11,885 times, and the numbers continued to climb. Why did social media play such a large role in Idle No More?

First, it is important to recognize that mainstream media in Canada has traditionally been silent on issues of concern to Indigenous peoples, engaging with Indigenous peoples and communities only when they can be portrayed as threatening to the interests of corporations or framed as destablizing Settler Canadian society (Johnson, 2011; Mickler, 2010; Palacios, 2014). As Idle No More coalesced, it became apparent that this scenario would be repeated, but with the difference that

> the movement often went around mainstream media, emerging in online and independent publications as articles, essays, and interviews. This was the first time we [Indigenous activists] had the capacity and technological tools to represent ourselves … and broadcast those voices throughout Canada. (Kino-nda-niimi Collective, 2014, p. 25)

This prevented common media discourses of "savagism" from taking root, while also generating new spaces for Indigenous activists and communities to speak to each other. While the ubiquity of the hashtag can overshadow the richness of the online engagement around Idle No More, longer-form articles on blogs[11] and online magazines, as well as video and audio interviews, and livestreamed teach-ins facilitated vibrant and thoughtful discourse. This is in addition to the massive use of electronic communication that was not publicly visible, including reaching out to "coders, hackers, web developers … sharing Google Docs and various ways of building out collaborative informating sharing" (Martineau, 2014, p. 116). So while #IdleNoMore and the associated Facebook groups are the most publicly visible aspect of Idle No More's online presence, they are in truth only a small part of a much larger marshalling of electronic communication to counter Canadian corporate media bias, much of which is still ongoing.

In addition to media bias, the colonial geography of Canada has often played a role in fragmenting Indigenous resistance. Against this, the speed and accessibility of social media helped to spread word through often spatially dispersed Indigenous communities, and it became common to read on Facebook or Twitter accounts of people driving through snowstorms or from isolated locations to attend community meetings that they had heard about online. The problems of distance were especially apparent in the North, where both dispersed population and the distance from major media and populations in southern Canada made the speed and accessibility of social media organizing a valuable tool. As Dene activist Siku Allooloo relates:

> Social media … facilitated the movement, and it was hugely important in the North because it connected our actions with what was happening in the rest of the country and the world. Because of our distance, isolation and low population the North is often overlooked by Canadian society, even amongst Native populations in the South. But Northerners are very active and are sure to stay informed, so when Idle No More blew up on the scene we were quick to take action and represent in our communities.… We connected ourselves with active Natives in other parts of the country and supported one another, as everyone else was doing as well. (2014, pp. 198–199)

The extended reach of Idle No More was not just limited to rural Canada. Personally, though I watched much of Idle No More unfold from the UK, I was able to stay up-to-date without relying on mainstream media coverage, as well as contributing in my own way through making and sharing two short "talking head"-style videos,[12] alongside "signal boosting" information through social media.

Social media was also used for more than sharing information and engaging in dialogue; it was used as an effective organizational tool to coordinate protests and direct action on short timelines, in multiple locations, and with limited resources. The tactic of the Round Dance Revolution is certainly one of the prominent features of Idle No More that spread quickly online. On 17 December, the day of the first flash mob in Regina, there were only 8,072 uses of #idlenomore; this rose drastically each day afterwards for several consecutive days, as the flash mob tactic spread: 11,445 uses on 18 December; 19,594 on 19 December; 19,777 on 20 December; and the highest single-day total until mid-January, 39,648 on 21 December, coinciding with the Day of Action rallies, including the massive round dance at Dundas Square. Further, the Day of Action called for 11 January, which set the single-day record for uses of the #idlenomore hashtag, was itself organized under the #J11 hashtag; the proliferation of related hashtags became a common tactic for developing diverse actions under the broader banner of

Idle No More. The teach-ins that were the first (and probably most enduring) feature of Idle No More also relied on social and new media to bring people into direct contact and conversation, and to continue dialogues on important issues after meetings had finished. Several of these, such as those organized at the University of Victoria by the Indigenous Governance Program, were broadcast and archived online (see, e.g., Martineau, 2013 January). This is significant because there is clear evidence that these forums were an important site of discussion and debate relating to movement tactics, including the efficacy of public critique of political leadership (King, 2013 March). However, while these online social movement dynamics remain an important feature of analysis in their own right, it is important to understand how these tactics of transgression—by eliding mainstream media and by creatively co-opting technological resources—correspond to the wider land-based movement in the tradition of centuries of Indigenous activism and resistance.

Transgressing Boundaries: From Cyberspace to Contending for Place

While social media activism may be dismissed by some as banal or problematic, it played a key role in the way that Idle No More's impact was felt simultaneously in cyberspace and in physical spaces. Activists and communities organized online, but danced and marched in public, crossing multiple boundaries in the process. One of the common threads through the effective actions taken under the Idle No More banner is that they are transgressive; they provoke a response from Settler society when they assert an Indigenous presence where and when it is least expected in the Settler colonial geographical imaginary (Veracini, 2010). This is, in fact, a long-standing feature of assertions of Indigenous sovereignty. Simpson has discussed how her attempts to live according to her Anishinaabe traditions and culture are perceived by Settler people as "an aggressive act" (2012), underscoring the affective response of Settler people to Indigenous resistance and assertions of belonging on the land. Given the long history of Indigenous place-based resistance, the transgressive acts of Idle No More should not be considered apart from other forms of Indigenous anti-colonial politics, but rather as complementary to them. Idle No More, in bringing indigeneity into electronic forums, as well as physically into shopping malls and urban intersections, disrupted the Settler colonial relationships by which those spaces are integrated into Settler colonial geographical imaginaries. [...] The publicly visible aspect of Idle No More protests asserted indigeneity into Settler social space, but articulated indigeneity in ways that defied easy categorization by Settler colonial narratives. [...]

Chief Spence's protest was especially confounding for Settler Canadians, in that her demand to speak with both the prime minister (the functional head of the federal government) and the governor general (the ceremonial representative of the Crown) positioned the Canadian federal government as a necessary interlocutor in Attawapiskat, but not the ultimate (sovereign) authority. Chief Spence's demand inherently asserted that Canadian sovereignty could only be functionally practiced through a partnership between Chief and Crown, and that such a partnership would take precedence over the federal or provincial authorities in this territory. Canadian sovereignty was tacitly and subtly positioned a posteriori to a relationship between equals at the intergovernmental level.[13] This itself is a reflection of the demand for the recognition of the "true intent" of various treaties, which are demands that long predate the existence of Idle No More.

This nation-to-nation and treaty-based understanding of Canadian sovereignty was perfectly demonstrated by an Idle No More re-reading of the Royal Commission on Aboriginal Peoples, or RCAP (Canada, 1996).[14] A pamphlet generated for the 21 December Day of Action by Alfred and Tobold Rollo (see figures 39.1 and 39.2) explicitly referenced the recommendations of RCAP, including those that called for a revitalization of nation-to-nation relationships through the use of treaties:

> The Government of Canada must remove formal and informal restrictions placed on treaty negotiations with Indigenous governments over rights to land and culture. A refusal to negotiate in good faith amounts to a bare assertion of colonial sovereignty, which stands as an affront to international law and to the Constitution of Canada itself. (2012)

This and four other recommendations were condensed from those in the RCAP Final Report, but this one, in particular, is striking in part because of what it would mean if fully followed. It is important to consider what kind of treaty might be implied here, and as it was both a major symbol throughout the Idle No More protests, and is also the longest operational treaty in Canada, I look now to the Guswenta or Two-Row Treaty.

The Guswenta is a type of agreement made between the Haudenosaunee Confederacy and a number of nations—including other Indigenous nations—and has been recognized as an international treaty with clear and definite political and legal import. The Two-Row Treaty has been a major symbol at many sites of Indigenous–Settler conflict for many years—including those not in Haudenosaunee territory—because it is often considered the barest framework of mutual respect and non-interference that would be necessary for any just and decolonized relationship to function (Turner, 2006, p. 48). As Alfred and Rollo point out, by Canada's own Constitution and international law conventions, an international treaty is as fundamental to state lawmaking and policy as is a domestic constitution or Charter of Rights, and as such the Two-Row Treaty should have binding force upon the state. A state may not simply abrogate a treaty without consequence. Among the primary (ignored) recommendations of the RCAP is that the Crown should honour its treaty obligations to Indigenous nations, that treaties should be interpreted broadly and towards the "original intent," and that restitution should be made for historic and contemporary treaty violations.

FIGURE 39.1 EXTERIOR OF PAMPHLET PRODUCED IN SUPPORT OF IDLE NO MORE ACTIONS, DECEMBER 2012, REFERENCING THE RCAP RECOMMENDATIONS

About the authors of this pamphlet:

Taiaiake Alfred is a Professor in Indigenous Governance and in the Department of Political Science at the University of Victoria. He is author of Heeding the voices of our Ancestors (1995), Wasáse: Indigenous Pathways of Action and Freedom (2005), and Peace, Power, and Righteousness: An Indigenous Manifesto (2009). He worked as a researcher and advisor to the Royal Commission on Aboriginal Peoples from 1992 to 1996 in the areas of governance and youth issues.

Tobold Rollo is a PhD candidate at the University of Toronto. He specializes in Canadian politics and democratic theory. He is author of Embodied Recognition: Toward a Phenomenology of Political Affirmation (2008).

Idle No More info:

www.idlenomore.com — *on Facebook:* **"Idle No More"**
on Twitter: **@IdleNoMore4** *and* **#IdleNoMore**

www.rabble.ca/issues/indigenous
www.aptn.ca/pages/news/tag/idlenomore
www.ammsa.com/content/idlenomore-campaign

Resetting and Restoring the Relationship between Indigenous Peoples and Canada

by Taiaiake Alfred and Tobold Rollo
Coast Salish Territory, Victoria, BC, Canada
http://taiaiake.posterous.com

We bear witness today to an inspiring resurgence of Indigenous consciousness directed at injustices within the Canadian state. History demonstrates that such events constitute the necessary preconditions of social and political change. Two decades ago, Indigenous resistance to colonialism moved Canada to establish the Royal Commission on Aboriginal Peoples (RCAP). The goal of the commission was to establish the steps necessary for restoring a just relationship between Canada and Indigenous peoples. RCAP was comprehensive and inclusive, with its recommendations reflecting an extraordinary consensus between Indigenous and non-Indigenous peoples, an agreement arrived at through processes characterized by mutual respect, friendship, and peace.

Twenty years later, Indigenous peoples and settler Canadians find ourselves in a new, profound moment of resistance and resurgence. The sense of urgency and of possibility may be unprecedented. Perhaps there is no better time, then, to press forward with a restoration of the relationship delineated in RCAP. In the spirit of mutual respect, friendship, and peace, we have provided concise accounts of what we feel to be the most crucial and immanently needed recommendations:

(see inside)

Source: Alfred & Rollo, 2012.

While the appeal to this sort of treaty relationship may be made from within the system—referencing Canadian traditions of constitutional and international law, and the RCAP itself—it also challenges the state system as a whole, situating this as a definitive assertion of thirdspace sovereignty. The Two-Row Treaty, in that it is a true "living document" immersed in oral history and requiring continuous community participation, does not fit neatly into contemporary understandings of the role of the state and the extent of sovereignty over territory, thus transgressing the boundaries of Settler Canadian politics. To follow the RCAP recommendation and respect the principles of the Two-Row (or other treaties) as prior to the articulation and practice of Canadian state sovereignty would require a massive alteration to the political economy of the entire Canadian state. Obviously, this cannot be done simply by the fiat of the federal or provincial governments; it is in fact a social project of incredible scope. In this, the "thirdspace" occupied by Indigenous resistance does not simply make a demand upon the Settler government—falling into the familiar trap of the politics of recognition (Coulthard, 2007, 2014a)—but rather declares a position with respect to the entirety of Settler society, and demands that Settlers dialogue and struggle among themselves in order to respond appropriately to this Indigenous positionality. While Idle No More remained a movement with a multiplicity of demands, the assertion of a nation-to-nation relationship and the demand to honour treaties underpinned many of these, drawing protests against particular bills and policies into far more complicated discourses about the nature of Canadian political sovereignty.

FIGURE 39.2 INTERIOR OF PAMPHLET, CALLING FOR AN "UNRESTRICTED" APPROACH TO TREATIES

1. Declaration of Responsibility.

To restore this relationship, the Government of Canada must acknowledge the systematic nature of Canada's colonial past and present. Recent governments have issued apologies for specific colonial programs, such as the Residential School System, but have yet to acknowledge responsibility for the full range of colonial institutions, including legislation currently enforced under the Indian Act.

2. Legislated Recognition of Political Authority.

The Government of Canada must enact legislation that recognizes the inherent rights of Indigenous Nations to designate political authority according to their own laws, governing principles, and customs. The law will provide guidance and give expression to the already existing recognition of the right of self-determination found in Section 35 of the Canadian Constitution and the nation-to-nation relationship established by previous treaties and agreements. In addition, it will allow systems of political authority and accountability to take root in Indigenous communities that will correct the democratically defective and dysfunctional Indian Act system.

3. Legislated Devolution of Governance.

The Government of Canada must devolve control over social, cultural, economic, housing, health, and educational services to Indigenous governments, in accordance with Section 35 of the Constitution of Canada. The current 'duty to consult' must be replaced with federally structured shared-jurisdiction over lands consider for urban and economic development. Indigenous jurisdiction will provide a stop-gap measure against the erosion of environmental protections under external pressures.

4. Legislation of Crown Fiduciary Duty.

The Government of Canada must provide funding, training, and resources sufficient to assist Indigenous nations while they re-establish their capacities and autonomy as Indigenous Nations. As these capacities are realized, the cost to Canada will diminish sharply until it is no longer needed.

5. Unrestricted Modern Treaty Process.

The Government of Canada must remove formal and informal restrictions placed on treaty negotiations with Indigenous governments over rights to land and culture. A refusal to negotiate in good faith amounts to a bare assertion of colonial sovereignty, which stands as an affront to international law and to the Constitution of Canada itself.

Source: Alfred & Rollo, 2012.

Settler Canadian Politics and Idle No More

Given the challenges that Idle No More posed to fundamental premises of the Canadian nation state, the responses by Settler people have been predictably complicated. In order to understand how Settler Canadians have interpreted and reacted to Idle No More, it is necessary both to clarify some of the specific contexts of Canadian political dynamics at that time, as well as more long-standing Canadian investments in Settler colonial political systems.

Throughout the winter of 2012–2013, Idle No More, like many Indigenous movements, actively sought to engage with Settler communities to educate and seek their support. The response was, compared to some past conflicts, promising; as Alfred asserted, "Idle No More has shown that there is support among Canadians for a movement that embodies principled opposition to the destruction of the land and the extension of social justice to Indigenous peoples" (2013). However, it must be remembered that transgressive acts like spatial occupations—whether in malls or at border crossings—are intended to provoke an affective response from Settler colonial ambivalence; this response may be revealing, but it is not necessarily (or even likely) positive, supportive, or decolonizing. [...]

Further, as successful as Idle No More has been in rallying support from the Settler population, the majority of Canadians have continued to disagree with and oppose Idle No More and Indigenous sovereignty more generally. Sociologist Jeff Denis has detailed some of the more overt crimes—from violent assaults with vehicles to rapes—in which Settler perpetrators either explicitly targeted Idle No More protesters or referenced Idle No More as their motive, alongside opinion polls indicating that most Canadians did not support Idle No More or Theresa Spence, and in fact blame Indigenous peoples for the social injustices that they face (Denis, in press). How does this weigh out against the support received from Idle No More by groups such as the Canadian Nurses Association, Greenpeace, and the Council of Canadians, among others (Kino-nda-niimi Collective, 2014, p. 402)? Of course, Settler Canadians are not a homogeneous group so variance is expected, but there are some important trends to consider in understanding how Idle No More's tactics and messaging have created affective responses in place of colonial ambivalence.

There must first be recognized a strong opportunistic current within Settler Canadian politics and activism. Settler people and collectives are very good at identifying diverse spaces of opportunity in the midst of Indigenous spaces (Barker, 2013, pp. 187–199), at times representing themselves as staunch allies while in fact embodying practices that further Indigenous transfer and displacement. [...] With that in mind, I turn here away from Settler opposition to Idle No More—a predictable, colonial response—towards an interrogation of some of the positions asserted by Settler Canadians seeking to act in solidarity with Idle No More, beginning with those at the intersection of Indigenous political assertions and Canadian political institutions.

The Anti-Harper Backlash

Settler people have a long history of appropriation and false affinity with respect to Indigenous peoples and symbols for the purpose of expressing anti-establishment discontent. [...] With that in mind, it must also be recognized that it is likely impossible to understand Settler Canadian responses to Idle No More without also understanding the parallel backlash against the unpopular federal government of the Conservative Party of Canada (CPC)[15] and Prime Minister Stephen Harper, which has generated the false appearance of affinity between a variety of political actors and activists.

Stephen Harper has been the prime minister of Canada since 2006, forming first a minority and later a majority government, in no small part because of his own personal reputation for economic leadership and that of his party for fiscal responsibility in the midst of the global financial crisis.[16] However, throughout 2012 and 2013, Harper's popularity plummeted along with confidence in the CPC government (EKOS, 2013). This may actually have been sparked off by the events that also catalyzed Idle No More in the autumn and winter of 2012: the omnibus budget bills that undemocratically altered a number of key pieces of legislation. However, since then, Harper has seemingly been in a free-fall; a number of major scandals have dogged his government, most notably evidence of corruption and misappropriation of funds by a number of high-profile senators appointed by Harper (Weston, 2013). As a result, there is a growing body of the Canadian public who are galvanized against Harper specifically and the CPC more generally. Many Settler people and communities have gravitated towards Idle No

More in no small part because of its vocal, pointed, and long-standing opposition to Harper. Chief Spence, especially, had been legally and politically contending with the Harper government over funding and housing issues since it took power in 2006. Even relatively mainstream aboriginal organizations, like the AFN, have sparred with Harper dating back to his scrapping of the Kelowna Accord[17] upon taking office in 2006, and his subsequent speech that declared that Canada has "No history of colonialism" (Hui, 2009).

A "Paranoid Politics of Binarity"

Despite this, the extent to which the opposition to Harper and the CPC will translate into lasting solidarity with Indigenous struggles is questionable. Culp, in his analyses of the 2003 protests against the invasion of Iraq—which he calls "an exercise in failure" (2013, p. 16)—notes how the over-focus on George W. Bush on the part of protestors served to become "a mechanism for a restrictive, paranoid politics of binarity" (p. 22). This binary politics meant that Bush's persona became a stand-in for policies that he initiated, ultimately deflecting criticism away from the Iraq War and other imperialist, militant policies that remained in place throughout his tenure (and several of which continue under the Democratic presidency of Barak Obama). A similar dynamic is certainly observable around Harper, who has become a stand-in for the actual concerns articulated by Idle No More. By mid-2013, as the senate scandals spiralled, and protests under the banner of Idle No More tailed off, interest in Indigenous issues among mainstream Canadians plummeted. Actions in the trajectory of Idle No More continued—for example, the reclamation and renaming of PKOLS, a mountain in Coast Salish territory near Victoria, British Columbia, an event that I was fortunate enough to participate in directly—but these received comparatively little media attention.[18]

A further danger in sublimating Indigenous political concerns within critiques of the present government is that it reifies the established political system as the political authority of reference. Many movements and currents within what might be called the "generic" Canadian political left[19] seek political engagements with Indigenous peoples through larger social justice or anti-racism movements, usually at the national or international level, and often demanding structural reform; for example, the left-nationalist Council of Canadians was very vocal and supportive of Idle No More. These political organizations, even when they press for changes in policy, law, or political leadership—as many currently do—often reinforce other (hidden or ignored) structures of colonial power. As Choudry observes:

> many supposedly progressive political organisations—while proclaiming that there are alternatives to free markets, free trade and transnational corporate power and that "another world is possible"—reproduce dominant colonial worldviews and resist challenges by Indigenous peoples and activists to address colonial injustices. While some have asked whether the global justice and anti-globalisation movement is anti-capitalist, it is also important to ask whether it is anti-colonial. (2010, p. 99)

In this way, critiques of Harper and his government can excuse systemic Settler colonialism. As Leitner et al. discuss with respect to the Immigrant Workers' Freedom Ride (2003), solidarities that are strong in one context may disintegrate when entering "centres of corporate and political power" (Leitner, Sheppard, & Sziarto, 2008, p. 169). This indicates the degree to which "any social movement ... has to negotiate power relations within the movement, and the power geometry of the socio-spatial relations it is embedded in" (p. 168). Voting against the Conservative government and campaigning against Harper specifically becomes a "move to innocence" (Tuck & Yang, 2012) by which Settler Canadians can excuse their own complicity in ongoing colonialism.

By contrast, Idle No More certainly frustrated and directly contested the political agenda of Stephen Harper, but as the movement progressed beyond a narrow focus on Bill C-45, this was articulated more and more in terms of Indigenous autonomy than political critique. For example, Simpson clearly framed Spence's hunger strike as "not so much an act against Harper, but as a selfless act of bravery and sacrifice for our nations and our children" (2012). While it is worthwhile to investigate resonances between the backlash among Canadians against the Harper and CPC government, and Indigenous assertions of sovereignty through Idle No More, it is unlikely that lasting solidarity can be built on these grounds; the longer-term goals of the generic left and of communities asserting Indigenous nationhood are not necessarily compatible.

Conclusions: Idle No More as a "Movement Moment"

Rather than a self-contained political movement, Idle No More must be seen as a rallying cry within a long trajectory of Indigenous resistance and organizing against colonization and for the restoration of Indigenous nationhood and self-determination, a movement moment. In this, it has mobilized peoples in a number of different fields—some seen as antithetical, such as those pursuing systemic reform through the elected chief and council (AFN) system and those advocating direct action enactments of sovereignty—consistent with Indigenous political traditions and resistance generally. As a rallying call, it allowed for widespread and diverse challenges to Settler colonial space, drawing inspiration and ideas from each other, and encouraging these actions to proliferate. This is the kind of "cascade of contention" that social movement theorist Tarrow (1998) observes in successful social movements, and speaks to the ongoing power of embodied Indigenous resistance in spaces that Settlers take for granted as theirs (including online spaces). The most important of these cascades were clearly those between different Indigenous communities, both geographically and politically, as people came together electronically and at protests, rallies, and round dances. Throughout the growth of Idle No More, it was clear that participants were building networks of solidarity, organizational and leadership capacity, and strategic and tactical plans to take advantage of the widespread support for and through Idle No More, while respecting local conditions and terrains of struggle. [...]

With this perspective in mind, it remains important to bring a critical frame of analysis to bear on Idle No More. Cree scholar Jarrett Martineau believes that a major shortcoming of Idle No More was the inability to capitalize on an excited and mobilized grassroots that had shown a willingness to pursue sustained and creative direct action (2013 March).

For example, following initial rail line blockades, further proposed blockades of Canada–US border crossings were effectively shut down by the disapproval of leading figures associated with Idle No More in early January. The use of blockades and similar direct actions for economic disruption, while a common tactic in Indigenous protest movements, are very contentious. Many activists and community members disagreed with the use of blockades from the outset. Notably, Sylvia McAdams was quoted in an interview with *The National Post* as saying that blockades are "irritating the public and that's not the purpose behind Idle No More," as well as distancing Idle No More from Chief Spence and criticizing the number of issues beyond Bill C-45 that Idle No More had begun addressing (Carlson, 2013 January). Several blockades planned for the near future were immediately called off.[20]

This had the simultaneous effect of "capping" the escalation of Idle No More's spatial claims at the borders of Canada and the USA, and of disempowering grassroots organizers. [...] As much as round dances in public spaces are a creative and dynamic transgression of the social spaces of Settler society, the obvious and powerful boundaries of political structures must also be challenged or the movement becomes predictable, controllable, and reconcilable with Settler politics of recognition (Coulthard, 2007). [...]

Creative contentions against Settler colonial norms that were energized by Idle No More's trangressive actions have continued even if not under the same moniker. For example, the DJ trio "A Tribe Called Red," which in some respects provided the soundtrack to Idle No More, have continued to use art as a means of transgressing temporal boundaries by combining traditional and contemporary musical techniques to create a distinctively Indigenous but undeniably modern musical form. Several of their songs feature prominently on YouTube videos created around Idle No More, and their most recent album carries the explicitly political title "Nation II Nation." They were recently awarded a Juno (prestigious Canadian music award) for Breakthrough Group of the Year for 2014. Woven throughout their music are messages of Indigenous nationhood and reassertions of Indigenous cultures; this becomes an act of creative contention against Settler colonial cultural production, and one that clearly resonates with many Indigenous peoples (and Settler people as well).

While critiques are important, I must make clear: this paper does not seek to join the chorus of voices proclaiming Idle No More "dead" or "over." Rather, as a moment in the movement towards Indigenous resurgence and nationhood, Idle No More has added a valuable version to stories of rebellion and liberation that fuel the long-term success of social movements (Selbin, 2010). The moment when Idle No More is the core of affective Indigenous resistance and place-based assertions of sovereignty may come around again. As Tanya Kappo asserted at the close of a presentation on the history of Indigenous resistance in Canada from the 1960s to the present, "Nothing has changed" (2013), and that includes the refusal of Indigenous peoples to surrender to Settler colonial power. If Idle No More has demonstrated anything, it is that Indigenous peoples will not cease pursuing decolonization, nationhood, and social change because that is the condition and effect of their existence. Simpson's phrase explains it best: "For me, living as a Nishnaabekwe is a deliberate act—a direct act of resurgence, a direct act of sovereignty" (2012).

Notes

1. There is a great deal of debate over the terms "Indigenous" and "Settler," with some critics arguing that they set up "Manichean" categories that deny the complexities of the lived reality in contexts of colonial imposition and resistance (Faragher, 2014, p. 186; Byrd, 2011, xxix). Others, such as Wolfe, argue in favour of a strategic essentialism, acknowledging that such a binary is not perfectly accurate, but that it allows for a great deal of useful analysis (2013). Largely aligned with Wolfe, I deploy "Settler" as a situated identity and positionality, which overlaps with both Indigenous identities and with the multiple and shifting identities of "exogenous Others," migrants, refugees, and other newcomers with ambiguous relationships to Settler society. This usage has been partially developed in my doctoral project (Barker, 2013), and is the subject of sustained analysis in *We, the Settler People: Identity, Colonialism, and Canadian Society* (Barker & Battell Lowman, in press). My usage of "Indigenous" is in the tradition of Alfred and Corntassel (2005), and is articulated below. While I recognize that generalizations in this paper such as Settler Canadians" or "Indigenous resistance" may not hold absolutely true, I use these terms to identify trends and tendencies that emerge through sustained analyses of Settler colonization and resistance.
2. See, for example, the commonality of these terms throughout the anthology *The winter we danced: Voices from the past, the future, and the Idle No More movement* (Kino-nda-niimi Collective, 2014).
3. The overview in this section is necessarily partial; for more detailed discussions of the events surrounding and comprising Idle No More, see generally *The Winter We Danced*, and specifically the "Timeline of major events spanning the winter we danced" (Kino-nda-niimi Collective, 2014, pp. 389–409). For a timeline of Twitter usage related to #idlenomore, see the timeline generated through the website Makook, designed to track usage of that particular hashtag: "#IdleNoMore," Makook, online at: idlenomore.makook.ca/timeline.
4. The hashtag has become ubiquitous with the movement; it is discussed further below.
5. I am paraphrasing here from a presentation by Kappo (2013 May), Sturgeon Lake Cree, a long-time activist, writer, and community leader who was involved in many of the earliest teach-ins and has remained a strong voice throughout Idle No More's engagements. See also Hayden King's interview with Kappo in *The Winter We Danced* (2014, pp. 68–69).
6. For a thorough and stark view of the conditions in Attawapiskat relating to housing, water, employment, youth suicide, and other crucial issues, see Obomsawin's documentary, *The People of the Kattawapiskak River* (2012).
7. For a short visual of this protest, there are many videos posted on YouTube; the post by WorldTruthNow (2013) gives a good impression of the size and significance of the round dance.
8. See, for example, the incident on Queen Elizabeth II Highway near Edmonton on 16 January 2013, where one individual drove a truck through a group of protesters. At the same rally, another Settler, identified only as "Steve," attempted to provoke violence, with the

man commenting, "I'm tired of their movement ... I was kinda hoping someone would take a swing at me" (Wingrove, 2013; see also: Denis, in press; O'Brien, 2012).

9. Among others, five people were arrested at Flatirons Mall in Colorado on 2 January 2013 following a round dance explicitly in support of Idle No More (Steele, 2013).
10. Figure from Makook, online at: idlenomore.makook.ca/timeline.
11. A number of blogs maintained excellent coverage of Idle No More events, but a few stood out for particularly clear and engaging analysis of the context of colonization and resistance that remains crucial to understanding Indigenous activism in Canada. Several of these are referenced throughout this paper, but I would draw particular attention to the blogs of Hayden King (biidwewidam.com), Chelsea Vowel (apihtawikosisan.com), and the series of guest articles posted on *Decolonization: Indigeneity, Education & Society* (decolonization.wordpress.com), the blog page of the scholarly journal by the same name.
12. See, for example, *An Open Letter to my Settler People*, which was filmed and uploaded from the village of Sheepwash in rural Devonshire (Barker, 2012).
13. The counter-assertion by the federal government, by comparison, was that Chief Spence should meet with the minister of Aboriginal Affairs and Northern Development, which would position the Attawapiskat community as a sub-federal order of government that may only appeal to the minister for redress.
14. The RCAP was a major governmental research project, completed in 1995, comprising an intensive study by the Canadian state into the relationships between the state, Canadian (Settler) society, and Indigenous peoples and communities, following the violent upheaval of the Oka Standoff. The RCAP recommendations, with the exception of a brief few, were never implemented.
15. The CPC is the most right-wing of the major federal political parties. Other relevant federal parties include the centre-right Liberal Party, the centre-left New Democratic Party (NDP), and the Bloc Québécois, the separatist, Quebec nationalist party.
16. Harper's own reputation comes largely from his academic background and political experience; he holds a master's in economics from the University of Calgary, and has often campaigned on financial and economic platforms over social or cultural issues. The CPC, similar to the Republican Party in the USA, holds a reputation for economic responsibility based on austerity and corporate tax cuts to stimulate economic activity.
17. The Kelowna Accord was an agreement reached between the AFN and other Indigenous political leaders, and the Canadian federal government under Harper's predecessor, Liberal Prime Minister Paul Martin. It would have served as a new framework for the fiduciary responsibility between the Crown and First Nations, largely around issues of health care, education, and economic development on reserves. It was completed just prior to the election that brought the CPC and Harper to power, and was never ratified.
18. For more on the PKOLS reclamation, see: nationsrising.org/campaigns/.
19. The term "generic left" is Austin's (2010, p. 28); I use it in much the same spirit as he does, referring to the reformist, systemic, or otherwise non-radical tradition of leftist Canadian politics, often closely associated with the NDP and Green Party, and various mainstream NGOs.

20. McAdams later claimed that her words had been misconstrued, blaming media manipulation, and refusing further interviews with mainstream news outlets. Regardless, there were clearly deeply divided opinions over the efficacy of direct action for economic and political disruption throughout Idle No More.

References

Alfred, T. (2005). *Wasase: Indigenous pathways to action and freedom*. Peterborough, ON: Broadview Press.

Alfred, T. (2013, January 27). *Idle No More and Indigenous nationhood* [blog post]. Taiaiake.net. Retrieved from http://taiaiake.net/2013/01/27/idle-no-more-indigenous-nationhood/

Alfred, T., & Corntassel, J. (2005). Being indigenous: Resurgences against contemporary colonialism. *Government and Opposition*, 40(4), 597–614.

Alfred, T., & Rollo, T. (2012, December 19). *Resetting and restoring the relationship between Indigenous peoples and Canada* [pamphlet]. Retrieved from http://nationsrising.org/resources/reset-restore/

Allooloo, S. (2014). "I have waited 40 years for this. Keep it going and don't stop!": An interview with Siku Allooloo. Interviewed by Leanne Betasamosake Simpson. In Kino-nda-niimi (Eds.), *The winter we danced: Voices from the past, the future, and the Idle No More movement* (pp.193–199). Winnipeg: ARP Books.

APTN National News. (2012, December 19). *Idle No More day of action Friday will begin in Egypt*. Retrieved from http://aptn.ca/news/2012/12/19/idle-no-more-day-of-action-friday-will-begin-in-egypt/

Austin, D. (2010). Narratives of power: Historical mythologies in contemporary Quebec and Canada. *Race & Class*, 52(1), 19–32.

Barker, A. J. (2012, December 21). *An open letter to my Settler people* [video blog]. Retrieved from http://vimeo.com/56106760

Barker, A. J. (2013). (Re-)Ordering the new world: Settler colonialism, space, and identity (PhD thesis). Retrieved from https://www.academia.edu/3789748/_Re-_Ordering_the_New_World_Settler_colonialism_space_and_identity

Barker, A. J., & Battell Lowman, E. (in press). *We, the Settler people: Identity, colonialism and Canadian society*. Halifax: Fernwood Press.

Bolen, M. (2013, March 6). Tom Flanagan's 2009 child porn comments led to 2013 uproar. *The Huffington Post Canada*. Retrieved from http://www.huffingtonpost.ca/2013/03/06/tom-flanagan-2009-child-_n_2812103.html

Byrd, J. A. (2011). *The transit of empire: Indigenous critiques of colonialism*. Minneapolis: University of Minnesota Press.

Canada. (1996). *Report of the Royal Commission on Aboriginal Peoples*. Retrieved from http://www.collectionscanada.gc.ca/webarchives/20071115053257/http://www.ainc-inac.gc.ca/ch/rcap/sg/sgmm_e.html

Carlson, K. B. (2013, January 15). Idle No More co-founder distances movement from planned blockades, hunger-striking Chief Spence. *The National Post*. Retrieved from http://news.nationalpost.com/2013/01/15/idle-no-more-co- founder-distances-movement-from-planned-blockades-hunger-striking-chief-spence/

Choudry, A. (2010). What's left? Canada's "global justice" movement and colonial amnesia. *Race and Class*, 52(1), 97–102.

Coulthard, G. (2007). Subjects of empire: Indigenous peoples and the "politics of recognition" in Canada. *Contemporary Political Theory*, 6(4), 437–460.

Coulthard, G. (2014a). *Red skin, white masks: Rejecting the colonial politics of recognition.* Minneapolis: University of Minnesota Press.

Culp, A. (2013). Dispute or disrupt? Desire and violence in protests against the Iraq War. *Affinities: A Journal of Radical Theory, Culture, and Action*, 6(1), 16–47.

Denis, J. S. (in press). A four directions model: Understanding the rise and resonance of an Indigenous self-determination movement. In Elaine Coburn (Ed.), *More will sing their way to freedom: Indigenous resistance and resurgence*. Halifax: Fernwood Press.

Edwards, P. (2003). *One dead Indian: The premier, the police, and the Ipperwash crisis*. Toronto: McClelland & Stewart.

EKOS. (2013, October 29). *Stephen Harper plumbing record lows on trust, direction and approval* [poll report]. EKOS Politics. Retrieved from http://www.ekospolitics.com/wp-content/uploads/full_report_october_29_2013.pdf

Faragher, J. M. (2014). Commentary: Settler colonial studies and the North American frontier. *Settler Colonial Studies*, 4(2), 181–191.

Hui, S. (2009, October 2). Shawn Atleo criticizes Stephen Harper over "no history of colonialism" remark [blog post]. *The Straight*. Retrieved from http://www.straight.com/blogra/shawn-atleo-criticizes-stephen-harper-over-no-history-colonialism-remark

Johnson, D. M. (2011). From the Tomahawk Chop to the road block: Discourses of savagism in Whitestream Media. *American Indian Quarterly*, 35(1), 104–134.

Kappo, T. (2013, May). The continuation of the "modern Indian movement": From the red paper to Idle No More. Presentation at the Indigenous leadership Forum 2013, University of Victoria, Victoria, BC.

Kappo, T. (2014). "Our people were glowing": An interview with Tanya Kappo. Interviewed by Hayden King. In Kino-nda-niimi (Eds.), *The winter we danced: Voices from the past, the future, and the Idle No More movement* (pp. 67–70). Winnipeg: ARP Books.

Keefer, T. (2007). The politics of solidarity: Six nations, leadership, and the Settler left. *Upping the anti: A Journal of Theory and Action*, 4, 107–123.

Khondker, H. H. (2011). Role of the new media in the Arab Spring. *Globalizations*, 8(5), 675–679.

Kilibarda, K. (2012). Lessons from #Occupy in Canada: Contesting space, Settler consciousness and erasures within the 99%. *Journal of Critical Globalization Studies*, 5, 24–43.

King, H. (2013, February 8). *What's next for Idle No More? Why provincial governments should matter to the movement* [blog post]. Retrieved from http://biidwewidam.com/2013/02/08/whats-next-for-idle-no-more-why-provincial-governments-should-matter-to-the-movement/

King, H. (2013, March 5). *The utility of debate to Idle No More is beyond dispute* [blog post]. Retrieved from http://biidwewidam.com/2013/03/05/the-utility-of-debate-to-idle-no-more-is-beyond-dispute/

Kino-nda-niimi Collective, eds. (2014). *The winter we danced: Voices from the past, the future, and the Idle No More movement.* Winnipeg: ARP Books.

Larsen, S., & Johnson, J. T. (2012). Toward an open sense of place: Phenomenology, affinity, and the question of being. *Annals of the Association of American Geographers*, 102(3), 632–646.

Leitner, H., Sheppard, E., & Sziarto, K. M. (2008). The spatialities of contentious politics. *Transactions of the Institute of British Geographers*, 33(2), 157–172.

Martineau, J. (2013, January 15). *#J16Forum: Idle No More—where do we go from here?* [blog post]. Culturite blog. Retrieved from http://culturite.wordpress.com/2013/01/15/j16forum-idle-no-more-where-do-we-go-from-here/

Martineau, J. (2013, March). #IdleNoMore: Mobilizing decolonial consciousness and Indigenous resurgence. Paper presented at Concurrences in Colonial and Postcolonial Studies symposium, Reconsidering the Politics of Decolonization: Indigenous Resurgences and Settler States, Linnaeus University, Vaxjo, Sweden.

Martineau, J. (2014). "Give people a hub": An interview with Jarrett Martineau. Interviewed by Stephen Hui. In Kino-nda-niimi (Eds.), *The winter we danced: Voices from the past, the future, and the Idle No More movement* (pp. 115–117). Winnipeg: ARP Books.

Massey, D. (2009). Concepts of space and power in theory and in political practice. *Documents d'anàlisi geogràfica*, 55, 15–26.

Mickler, S. (2010). Illiberal and unmodern: Conservative columnists on Indigenous self-determination in Australia and Canada. *Borderlands*, 9(1), 1–26.

Musqueam Indian Band. (n.d.). c̓snaʔm [information sheet]. *Musqueam: A living culture* [website]. Retrieved from http://www.musqueam.bc.ca/c%CC%93%C9%99sna%CA%94%C9%99m

Obomsawin, A. (2012). *People of the Kattawapiskak River* [documentary]. Ottawa: National Film Board of Canada. Retrieved from http://www.nfb.ca/film/people_of_kattawapiskak_river/

O'Brien, J. (2012, December 20). Woman caught on tape attacking Native protest vehicle. *The Toronto Sun*. Retrieved from http://www.torontosun.com/2012/12/20/woman-caught-on-tape-attacking-native-protest-vehicle

Palacios, L. C. (2014). Racialized and gendered necropower in Canadian news and legal discourse. *Feminist Formations*, 26(1), 1–26.

Regan, P. (2010). *Unsettling the Settler within: Indian residential schools, truth telling, and reconciliation in Canada*. Vancouver: UBC Press.

Selbin, E. (2010). *Revolution, rebellion, resistance: The power of story*. London: Zed Books.

Simpson, L. (2012, December 21). Aambe! Maajaadaa! [What #IdleNoMore Means to Me]. *Decolonization: Indigeneity, education & society* [blog post]. Retrieved from http://decolonization.wordpress.com/2012/12/21/aambe-maajaadaa-what-idlenomore-means-to-me/

Simpson, L. (2013, March 5). Dancing the world into being: A conversation with Idle No More's Leanne Simpson. *Yes! Magazine*. Interviewed by Naomi Klein. Retrieved from http://www.yesmagazine.org/peace-justice/dancing-the- world-into-being-a-conversation-with-idle-no-more-leanne-simpson

Simpson, L. (2014). Fish broth and fasting. In Kino-nda-niimi (Eds.), *The winter we danced: Voices from the past, the future, and the Idle No More movement* (pp. 154–157). Winnipeg: ARP Books.

Steele, C. T. (2013, January 3). Idle No More supporters arrested at Flatirons Mall. *The Denver Progressive Examiner*. Retrieved from http://www.examiner.com/article/idle-no-more-supporters-arrested-at-flatirons-mall

Stueck, W., & Bailey, I. (2012, June 10). Gitxsan blockade coming to an end as forensic audit begins. *The Globe and Mail*. Retrieved from http://www.theglobeandmail.com/news/british-columbia/gitxsan-blockade-coming-to-an-end- as-forensic-audit-begins/article4246337/

Tarrow, S. (1998). *Power in movement: Social movements and contentious politics*. Cambridge: Cambridge University Press.

Tuck, E., & Yang, K. W. (2012). Decolonization is not a metaphor. *Decolonization: Indigeneity, Education & Society, 1*(1), 1–40.

Turner, D. (2006). *This is not a peace pipe: Towards a critical Indigenous philosophy*. Toronto: University of Toronto Press.

Veracini, L. (2010). The imagined geographies of Settler colonialism. In T. Banivanua Mar & P. Edmonds (Eds.), *Making Settler colonial space: Perspectives on race, place and identity* (pp. 179–197). Hampshire: Palgrave Macmillan.

Weston, G. (2013, January 2). Is "a walk in the snow" in Stephen Harper's future? *CBC News.* Retrieved from http://www.cbc.ca/news/politics/is-a-walk-in-the-snow-in-stephen-harper-s-future-1.2480564

Weyler, R. (1992). *Blood of the land: The government and corporate war against First Nations.* Philadelphia: New Society Publishers.

Willow, A. J. (2011). Conceiving Kakipitatapitmok: The political landscape of Anishinaabe anticlearcutting activism. *American Anthropologist*, 113(2), 262–276.

Wingrove, J. (2013, January 16). Edmonton Idle No More protest meets resistance as truck pushes crowd. *The Globe and Mail.* Retrieved from http://www.theglobeandmail.com/news/national/edmonton-idlenomore-protest-meets- resistance-as-truck-pushes-crowd/article7446747/

Wolfe, P. (1999). *Settler colonialism and the transformation of anthropology: The politics and poetics of an ethnographic event.* London: Cassell.

Wolfe, P. (2013). Recuperating binarism: A heretical introduction. *Settler Colonial Studies,* 3(3–4), 257–279.

WorldTruthNow. (2013). *Idle No More Toronto Flash Mob Shuts Down Dundas Square* [YouTube video]. Retrieved from http://www.youtube.com/watch?v=mG4bBu234ko

York, G., & Pindera, L. (1991). *People of the pines: The WARRIORS and the legacy of Oka.* Toronto: Little Brown.

RETHINKING SECTION 5

Discussion Questions

Chapter 37

1. What limitations does Nibert see when using the term "minority group" that are addressed by referring instead to "oppressed groups"?
2. What parallels does Nibert draw between racism and speciesism in offering a sociological analysis of oppression?
3. Nibert begins and ends with the question "Sociology for whom?" What advantages does Nibert highlight in including animals as part of the general framework of sociology?

Chapter 38

1. According to the authors, what are some of the social and economic inequalities that are evident when looking at the built environment?
2. Why do Jermé and Wakefield place so much importance on involvement in the planning stages of urban environments?
3. What conclusions are drawn from this study about the policy shifts needed to ensure environmental justice is factored into Public Works, Planning, and Economic Development going forward?

Chapter 39

1. How does the metaphor of "extraction" help explain the reason why a variety of urban, suburban, and rural sites were occupied as part of Idle No More activism?
2. In what ways did social media empower Idle No More activists to more effectively challenge Settler colonial spaces and relationships?
3. The article notes a risk to Idle No More of becoming "predictable, controllable, and reconcilable with Settler politics of recognition." What creative strategies were employed during the Idle No More groundswell to counter the danger of predictability?

COPYRIGHT ACKNOWLEDGEMENTS

Chapter 1: C. Wright Mills, excerpted from "The Promise" from *The Sociological Imagination* by C. Wright Mills. Copyright © Oxford, 1959, 2000.

Chapter 2: Anthony Giddens, excerpted from "Chapter 1: In Defence of Sociology," from *In Defence of Sociology*. Copyright © Polity Press, 1996.

Chapter 3: Emile Durkheim, "What is a Social Fact?" from *The Rules of Sociological Method* by Emile Durkheim, edited with an introduction by Steven Lukes. Translated by W.D. Halls. Copyright © 1982 by Steven Lukes. Translation copyright © 1982 by Macmillan Press Ltd.

Chapter 4: Karl Marx and Friedrich Engels, excerpted from "Manifesto of the Communist Party," from *The Communist Manifesto* by Karl Marx and Friedrich Engels. Edited and introduced by Jack Wayne. Copyright © Canadian Scholars' Press Inc., 1986. Introduction and original notes copyright © Jack Wayne.

Chapter 5: Max Weber, excerpted from *The Protestant Ethic and the Spirit of Capitalism*. Translated by Talcott Parsons. Republication by Dover (2003) of the edition published by Copyright © Scribner's Sons, 1958.

Chapter 6: Dorothy E. Smith, excerpted from "Women's Perspective as a Radical Critique of Sociology" from *Sociological Inquiry 44*, no. 1 (1974): 7–13. Copyright © Blackwell Publishing.

Chapter 7: Michel Foucault, excerpted from "Two Lectures," from *Power/Knowledge* by Michel Foucault. Edited by Colin Gordon. Translated by Colin Gordon, Leo Marshall, John Mepham, and Kate Soper. Copyright © 1972, 1975, 1976, 1977 Michel Foucault. Copyright © Pantheon Books, a division of Random House, Inc., 1980.

Chapter 8: Diana Coben, excerpted from "Revisiting Gramsci" from *Studies in the Education of Adults 27*, no. 1 (1995): 36–51. Copyright © the National Institute of Adult Continuing Education.

Chapter 9: Michael Omni and Howard Winant, excerpted from "Racial Formations," from *Racial Formations in the United States: From the 1960s to the 1990s*. Copyright © Taylor & Francis Group, 1986.

Chapter 10: Alan Bryman, James Teevan, and Edward Bell, excerpted from "General Research Orientations," from *Social Research Methods* by Alan Bryman, Second Edition. Copyright © Oxford, 2004.

Chapter 11: Karen L. Potts and Leslie Brown, excerpted from "Becoming an Anti-Oppressive Researcher" in *Research as Resistance: Critical, Indigenous and Anti-Oppressive Approaches*, Second Edition. Edited by Leslie Brown and Susan Strega. Copyright © Canadian Scholars' Press Inc., 2015.

Chapter 12: Jacqueline Lewis, excerpted from "Learning to Strip: The Socialization Experiences of Exotic Dancers" in *The Canadian Journal of Human Sexuality 7*, no. 1 (1998): 51–66. Copyright © SIECCAN.

Chapter 13: Erving Goffman, excerpted from the introduction to *The Presentation of Self in Everyday Life*. Copyright © Anchor Books, 1959.

Chapter 14: Kevin Walby and Jeffrey Monaghan, excerpted from "Private Eyes and Public Order: Policing and the Surveillance in the Suppression of Animal Rights Activists in Canada," in *Social Movement Studies 10*, no. 1. (2011): 21–37. Copyright © Taylor and Francis Group.

Chapter 15: Walter S. DeKeseredy and Molly Dragiewicz, excerpted from "Woman Abuse in Canada: Sociological Reflections on the Past, Suggestions for the Future," in *Violence Against Women 20*, no. 2 (2014): 228–244. Copyright © SAGE Publications.

Chapter 16: Stephanie Coontz, excerpted from "The Way We Weren't: The Myth and Reality of the 'Traditional' Family." Copyright © Stephanie Coontz, 2005. Originally appeared in the *National Forum 75*, no. 3 (1995): 11–14.

Chapter 17: Kate Bezanson, excerpted from "Neo-liberalism, Families and Work-Life Balance" in *The Shifting Landscapes of Work*. Edited by A.N. Duffy and D. Glenda. Copyright © Nelson, 2010.

Chapter 18: Anika Stafford, excerpted from "Beyond Normalization: An Analysis of Heteronormativity in Children's Picture Books," from *Who's Your Daddy? And Other Writings on Queer Parenting*. Edited by Rachel Epstein. Copyright © Sumach Press, 2009.

Chapter 19: Margaret Hillyard Little, excerpted from "Just Another Neo-liberal Worker: Tracing the State's Treatment of Low-Income Mothers," in *International Journal of Sociology of the Family 38*, No. 1 (2012): 1–18. Copyright © International Journals, Inc.

Chapter 20: Kerry Preibisch and Gerardo Otero, excerpted from "Does Citizenship Status Matter in Canadian Agriculture? Workplace Health and Safety for Migrant and Immigrant Laborers," in *Rural Sociology 79* (2014): 174–199. Copyright © Wiley & Sons.

Chapter 21: Rebecca Raby and Shauna Pomerantz, excerpted from "Playing It Down/Playing It Up: Girls' Strategic Negotiations of Academic Success," in *British Journal of Sociology of Education 36*, 4 (2015): 507–525. Copyright © Taylor and Francis Group.

Chapter 22: Carol Schick, excerpted from "Keeping the Ivory Tower White: Discourse of Racial Domination," in *Race, Space and the Law: Unmapping a White Settler Society*. Edited by Sherne H. Razack. Copyright © Between the Lines, 2002.

Chapter 23: Darren Blakeborough, excerpted from "'Old People are Useless': Representations of Aging on the Simpsons," in the *Canadian Journal on Aging/La Revue Canadienne du Viellissement 27*, no. 1 (2008): 57–67. Copyright © Canadian Association on Gerontology.

Chapter 24: Ann Pederson, Dennis Raphael, and Ellisa Johnson, excerpted from "Gender, Race, and Health Inequalities," in *Staying Alive*, Second Edition. Edited by Toba Bryant, Dennis Raphael, and Marcia Rioux. Copyright © Canadian Scholars' Press, Inc., 2010.

Chapter 25: Nick J. Mulé and Miriam Smith, excerpted from "Invisible Populations: LGBTQ People and Federal Health Policy in Canada," in *Canadian Public Administration 57*, 2 (2014): 234–255. Copyright © John Wiley & Sons.

Chapter 26: Jade Boyd, excerpted from "'You Bring Great Masculinity and Truth': Sexuality, Whiteness, and the Regulation of the Male Body in Motion," in *Feminist Media Studies 15*, 4 (2015): 675–690. Copyright © Taylor and Francis Group.

Chapter 27: Alice Marwick and danah boyd, excerpted from "'It's Just Drama': Teen Perspectives on Conflict and Aggression in a Net-worked Era," in *Journal of Youth Studies 17*, 9 (2014): 1187–1204. Copyright © Taylor and Francis Group.

Chapter 28: Anne O'Connell, excerpted from "Building Their Readiness for Economic 'Freedom': The New Poor Law and Emancipation" in the *Journal of Sociology and Social Welfare 36*, no. 2 (2009): 85–103. Copyright © Western Michigan University, School of Social Work.

Chapter 29: Deborah McPhail, Gwen E. Chapman, and Brenda L. Beagan, excerpted from "'Too Much of That Stuff Can't Be Good': Canadian Teens, Morality, and Fast Food Consumption," in *Social Science & Medicine 73*, 2 (2011): 301–307. Copyright © Elsevier.

Chapter 30: John Porter, excerpted from "Class and Power: Major Themes" from *The Vertical Mosaic: An Analysis of Social Class and Power in Canada*. Copyright © University of Toronto Press, 1965.

Chapter 31: Jean Bobby Noble, excerpted from "Our Bodies are Not Ourselves: Tranny Guys and the Racialized Class Politics of Incoherence," in *Queerly Canadian: An Introductory Reader in Sexuality Studies*. Edited by Maureen FitzGerald and Scott Rayter. Copyright © Canadian Scholars' Press, Inc., 2012.

Chapter 32: Melanie A. Beres and Panteá Farvid, excerpted from "Sexual Ethics and Young Women's Accounts of Heterosexual Casual Sex," in *Sexualities 13*, no. 3 (2010): 377–393. Copyright © SAGE Publications.

Chapter 33: Kristi A. Allain, excerpted from "'Real Fast and Tough': The Construction of Canadian Hockey Masculinity," in *Sociology of Sport Journal 25* (2008): 462–481. Copyright © Human Kinetics Publishers, Inc.

Chapter 34: Jillian Paragg, excerpted from "Canadian-First": Mized Race Self-Identification and Canadian Belonging," in *Canadian Ethnic Studies 47*, no. 2 (2015): 21–44. Copyright © Canadian Ethnic Studies Association.

Chapter 35: George Dei and Arlo Kempf, excerpted from "African-Centred Education: Situating the Tradition," in *New Perspectives on African-Centred Education in Canada*. Copyright © Canadian Scholars' Press, Inc., 2013.

Chapter 36: Nicole Pietsch, excerpted from "'Born' Freaks, 'Made' Freaks, and Media Circuses: Systemic Management of Race and Gender in the Reena Virk Case" from *Reena Virk: Critical Perspectives on a Canadian Murder.* Edited by M. Rajiva and S. Batacharya. Copyright © Canadian Scholars' Press Inc., 2010.

Chapter 37: David Nibert, excerpted from "Humans and Other Animals: Sociology's Moral and Intellectual Challenge," in *International Journal of Sociology and Social Policy 23*, 3 (2003): 4–25. Copyright © Emerald Group Publishing Limited.

Chapter 38: Erika S. Jermé and Sarah Wakefield, excerpted from "Growing a Just Garden: Environmental Justice and the Development of a Community Garden Policy for Hamilton, Ontario," in *Planning Theory & Practice 14*, 3, (2013): 295–314. Copyright © Taylor & Francis Group.

Chapter 39: Adam J. Barker, excerpted from "'A Direct Act of Resurgence, a Direct Act of Sovereignty': Reflections on Idle No More, Indigenous Activism, and Canadian Settler Colonialism," in *Globalizations 12*, 1 (2015): 43–65. Copyright © Taylor & Francis Group.